ALBERTA

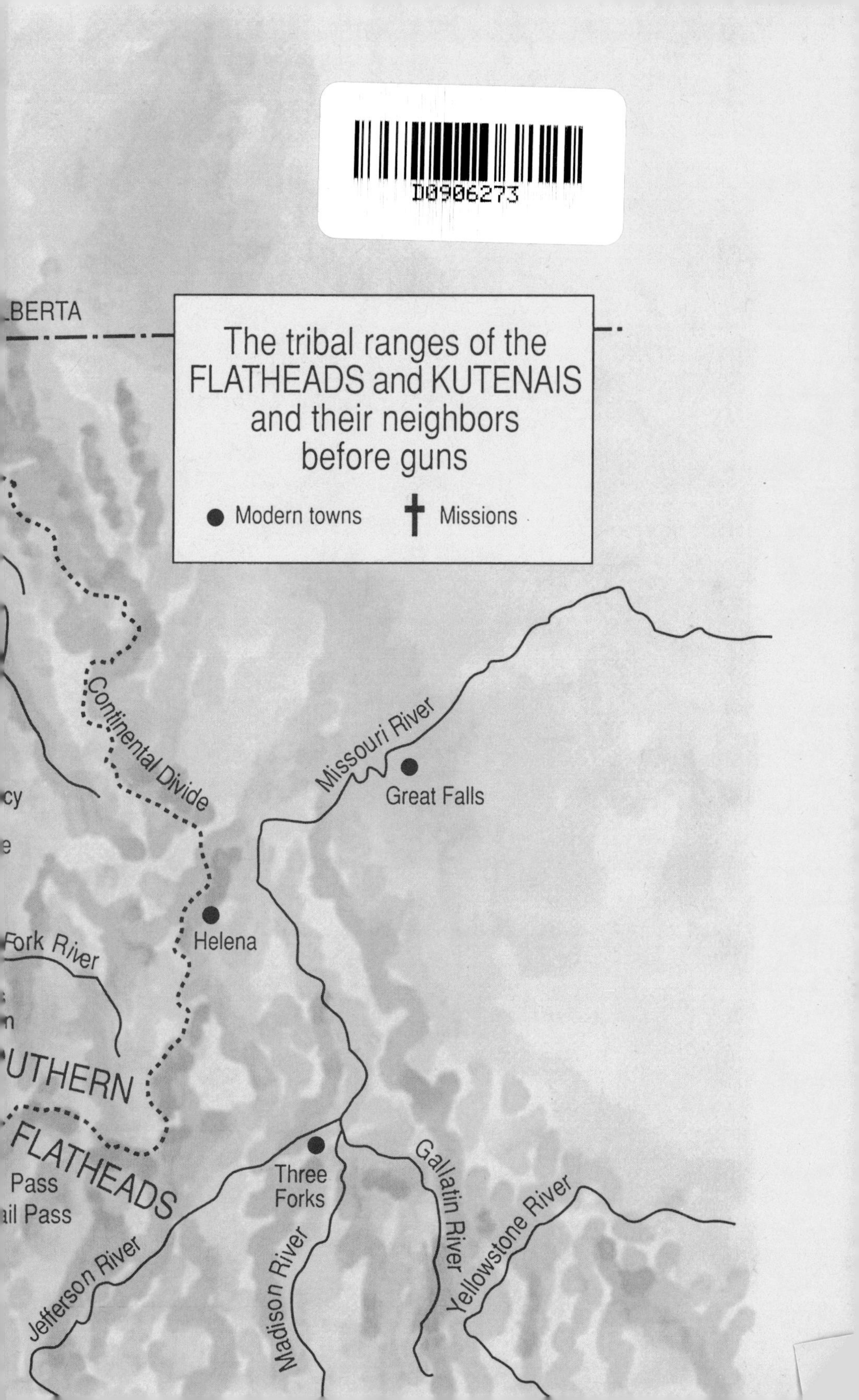

The tribal ranges of the
FLATHEADS and KUTENAIS
and their neighbors
before guns

● Modern towns   ✝ Missions

Continental Divide

Missouri River

● Great Falls

cy

e

Fork River

s

n

● Helena

SOUTHERN

FLATHEADS

Pass

ail Pass

Jefferson River

Three
Forks

Madison River

Gallatin River

Yellowstone River

Little Coyote

By Charles J. Keim

Aghvook, White Eskimo
Fair Chase With Alaskan Guides (Co-author)
The Gallant Try
Alaska Game Trails With a Master Guide
CHANGE and Other Short Stories About Contemporary Alaska
So My Sons Will Remember
Five Minutes of Silence
Little Coyote

Little Coyote

An epic novel about the
Flathead Indians
1805-1891

Charles J. Keim

A SHINING MOUNTAINS BOOK
from
PICTORIAL HISTORIES PUBLISHING CO.
Missoula, Montana

LIBRARY OF CONGRESS
CATALOG CARD NUMBER 96-70273

ISBN 1-57510-022-3

First Printing: November 1996

A SHINING MOUNTAINS BOOK
from
PICTORIAL HISTORIES PUBLISHING COMPANY
713 South Third Street, Missoula, Montana 59801

In memory of the late Clarence Woodcock, prayer warrior and friend, who served as chairman of the Flathead Culture Committee, and the late Christine Woodcock, his mother and a Flathead tribal elder.

Acknowledgments

Few achievements are the work of one person. I am deeply indebted to all who helped make *Little Coyote* a reality, beginning with the nuns at Cathedral High School in Helena, Montana. They encouraged study for "great things to do by and by," and outside research, including projects such as reading Reuben G. Thwaite's eight volumes of *Original Journals of the Lewis and Clark Expedition*. That started the dream.

My appreciation, too, to the late Dr. Harold McCracken and Dr. Walter Prescott Webb for encouraging me to write about our first Americans.

Some individuals deserve special recognition, including the late Christine Woodcock, Flathead tribal elder, who suggested the title; her late son, Clarence Woodcock, director of the Flathead Culture Committee, who patiently provided answers and materials for more than a decade; Margaret Gray Waggoner, for suggesting highly productive sources of information; Prof. Robert C. Carriker, Department of History, Gonzaga University; Rev. Fr. Clifford Carroll, S.J., Oregon Province Archives of the Society of Jesus, Crosby Library, Gonzaga University; Dr. Lucylle Hartz Evans, author and noted authority on the Flathead people; my late uncle, L. Custer Keim, authority on Montana history, together with my aunt, Florence Keim, for making accessible to me his superb Montana/ Western Americana library and for giving me permanent access to their early-1930s log cabin in Montana's Bitter Root Valley, where I wrote most of the manuscript; and writer Steve Smith, who, while teaching with me at the University of Alaska, and, later in Montana, discussed early ideas about the project. He also edited the manuscript and handled other tasks connected with publication. Thanks, too, to Verna G. Brown, Missoula, Montana, who typed the manuscript onto computer disks; Steven Cramer, Missoula, who designed the book; illustrator Kathleen Harestad, Missoula, who handled all artwork chores, including the dust jacket; publisher Stan Cohen, whose advice was helpful, and, finally, my wife, Bettyjoyce Keim, for enduring encouragement.

Charles J. Keim
Fox Island, WA

The land was there, beckoning a young, vigorous, diverse America, an America ever filling with new arrivals, a nation of descendants of migrants from every country on the globe—a land-hungry people looking toward the west.

They moved.

For more than two centuries they moved ever westward through the forested land, subduing its aboriginal owners as they bowed their own backs to the tasks that made the land flower. As they stood erect and shaded their eyes with toil-roughened hands, they looked ever westward. As the setting sun beckoned, the people moved and still the land flowered. Now they stood on the very rim of the Great Plains, an area roughly one-fifth the size of the United States, extending east and west from the Mississippi Valley to the Rocky Mountains, north and south from Canada to Texas.

Here the westward movement stopped.

"The Great American Desert" and "almost unfit for cultivation," Major Stephen H. Long had labeled this land with much truth after his expedition of 1819. The old methods simply wouldn't work here because these grasslands had less rain, fewer navigable streams to transport the crops, and insufficient trees for fences.

The 225,000 aboriginal owners there and in the contiguous Rocky Mountain region, while formidable, were scarcely a consideration. These first Americans could live off their land, but no more could resist the Colt revolver, the Winchester repeating rifle and white man's diseases and liquors than could the buffalo—their food, clothing and shelter—stand against the Springfield, Sharps, Winchester or Remington-Rider.

So the people stopped, but only for a time. The technology that had produced these weapons and the old and heretofore successful techniques for land development soon provided the windmill, dry farming methods and irrigation. The railroads pushed across the land. The barbed wire encircled it and muted the jingle of the cowboys' spurs. The reservations snapped closed on aboriginal remnants, body and spirit.

And then once again the people could move, ever westward—to where the sun sets in the western sea.

From Five Minutes of Silence, *a novel*

Part 1

The Gun-Seekers

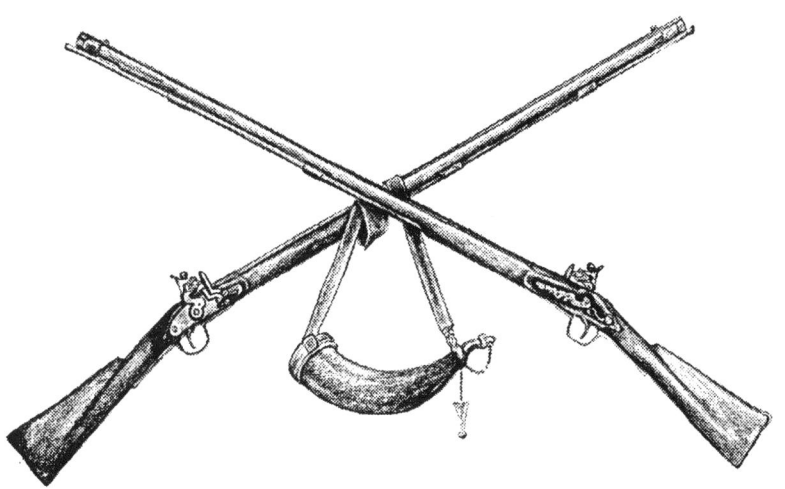

Prologue

The man was instantly awake, as though someone had shaken him or the great bell in the nearby church had tolled to mark this important October day before it had begun. But he had had this wakefulness for as many of his sixty years as he could remember. Though weighted with great cares, his mind could tell his body when to sleep and when to awaken, and the body would obey. Now he lay there for a time quietly rubbing the old hurt under his lower right rib. Then, more quietly still, he left the bed so he would not awaken Isabel. He picked up his clothing and walked outside the cabin to dress.

The three horses he had corralled in his small farmyard the day before looked up as he approached. The white pack horse docilely accepted her load, but the larger sorrel with the long, flowing mane and tail reared despite the man's soothing words. At length the animal accepted the bridle and ancient pillow saddle of grass-filled elk hide. The man mounted the smaller pinto. Holding the lead rope of the pack animal in one hand and the reins of the sorrel in the other, he slowly guided their way through the small settlement and down a dirt road back from, but paralleling, the river. Low-lying patches of fog covered sections of the road as though part of the previous day's scattered clouds had fallen from the sky and formed broken grayish drifts. A buck white-tail deer paused uncertainly at the trail's edge, swiveling his antlered head up and down the path before he bounded across it, the fog quietly parting then closing.

Several times the pinto tried to snatch at clumps of drying grass revealed when the light breeze broke through fringing trees and brushed away the fog. The man instantly would bring up her head and, with gentle kicks of his heels, keep her moving toward the faint line of cottonwoods. Soon he set a new direction with the pressure of his legs. The mare entered a narrow branch trail where the rider smelled the smoke at the same instant the three horses raised their heads. They wanted to pause in their steady clopping over the now-gravelly soil. Soon a fire began lighting up a small patch of the valley blackness.

In a few moments the man could see the tall lodge and its contents burning fiercely. Figures of warriors, buffalo, horses, men of other colors, and a family of coyotes, growing in size from a pup to an adult, all painted in bright colors on the ancient and brownish-white hide covering, were dancing energetically from the ballooning force of the flames and heat as though desperately trying to tell for the last time the stories they represented. Then the paintings began shriveling, reddening and winking out one by one. The coyote pup painting was the last to disappear as the poles burned through and collapsed in a final shower of sparks that trailed off to nothingness in the darkness.

"Little Grizzly Bear Claw. You are here." The voice of an old man rose softly above the crackling flames.

"I am here, Little Coyote." The rider's quiet response was in the old language, too, formed, seemingly, deep in the throat and harmonizing with the varying sounds of birds awakening now as the smoke filtered through their cottonwood perches. The horseman dismounted and tied the animals to a small tree. Then he sat down next to the old man, whose deeply set eyes glowed like sparks in the reflected light from the waning fire.

The old man spoke: "You brought me your best horse. Put

me on the pinto. I will use that." He grasped a long, obsidian-tipped lance from the small pile of gear near his feet. The sturdy shaft of the ancient weapon was wrapped in thin rawhide. Using the lance as a prop he arose and painfully straightened his naked body, which seemed as old, withered and weathered as the aged trees that survive years and storms while clinging tenaciously to life on cliff edge at highest timber line. A small, leather pouch began to swing pendulum-like from his neck. Attached to this *sumesh*, or power bag, was the badly worn tail-tip of a small coyote pup.

"You are *i-sts-sókoi*. The sorrel is your horse, too," Little Grizzly Bear Claw said. The younger man approached his older war-friend dearer than a brother. "The night air of *s'tcut ánalka*, the half-summer month, is cold. We will put on our clothing now."

Little Coyote raised his bony right leg and Little Grizzly Bear Claw helped pull on a long and supple buckskin legging heavy with decorative beading. The matched left legging followed with some difficulty because Little Coyote could not raise that frightfully scarred limb as high as he had the other. Little Coyote laid the lance back on the ground and Little Grizzly Bear Claw helped pull a soft, highly beaded, long-sleeved, buckskin shirt over the old man's head, then over his heavily scarred right shoulder and left arm. Next, the younger man put a pair of plain moccasins on his companion's feet and a simple leather thong around his head to hold the long, white hair close to it. A wide belt of buckskin with the figure of a coyote pup in white beads outlined with brown completed his attire.

Little Grizzly Bear Claw rummaged in a large sack on his pack horse and placed a rabbit-skin blanket around the old man's shoulders. Very quickly he removed his badly tattered, woolen, army trousers and equally worn shirt and coat and replaced them in the pack bag for his own set of buckskin clothing. The outfit resembled that of his companion except all of it was heavily fringed and the sleeves of the shirt from shoulder to elbow were adorned with weasel tails. He wore no head band to restrict his long, dark hair tinged with silver. Instead, his hair was braided into two long plaits, one on each side of his head. Sewed to his wide belt was the small claw of a grizzly bear, around which were concentric circles of multi-colored beads.

"Are you all Flathead again, Little Grizzly Bear Claw?" the old man asked. He held himself more erect now as he leaned on the lance. He smiled. His fine, white teeth, like his eyes, reflected the light of the near-dead fire.

"All Flathead, except for this." Little Grizzly Bear Claw reached under his shirt and held out a small crucifix that hung by a thong from his neck. He smiled, too, the strong lips lifting with some effort from their perpetual downward shape seemingly denoting prolonged great sadness.

"That crucifix I will allow," Little Coyote said. "It was my gift to you, and the gift of the Black Robe Mengarini to me after I helped him learn our Flathead tongue and he helped to teach me the more precise use of the white man's English." The old man paused. "So long ago . . . yes, *siistc*, winter, the winter, perhaps, of white man's 1845." His sigh was like the soft wind over dried prairie grass. "More than half of my years ago. Yes, the crucifix is allowed, my *i-sts-sókoi*. You carry that and I carry the knowledge of white man's language better than you, for we no more could rid ourselves of those than could we the white man. We will go now?"

The great sorrel turned nervously for several moments until his ancient rider's voice and firm tugs quieted him. Little Coyote accepted his lance, then asked his friend to tie the white-tanned and rolled-up elk hide and paint bag onto the pack horse. That done, Little Grizzly Bear Claw almost reverently stooped to pick up the equally ancient pipe case of rounded and highly decorated birch bark. He carefully tucked that away, then grasped the lead rope of the pack horse and mounted the pinto. The little group headed west, Little Coyote taking the lead as the quickening morning breeze dissipated the fog. The water shallowed out into broad ripples over gravelly bottom around a sweeping bend where they approached the river. They forded the river after allowing the horses to drink, then for a time followed a man-made trail. Moving ever westward, they soon branched off to a deeply worn game trail that began slanting upward toward the great peak whose crown of recent snow now was shining in the first rays of the new day's Sun. The men stopped on a grassy bench. The horses browsed while Little Coyote sat against a rectangular boulder that ages before had tumbled from the eastern face of the great peak. The old man closed his eyes as he looked toward the brightening sky. His lips began moving, but he made no sound. The younger warrior again rummaged in the bag atop the horse. From it he withdrew his army reject clothing, then a crumpled felt hat with an eagle feather, which he removed from the band. He rolled up the clothing and placed it and the hat under a rocky shelf to await his return. He jabbed the eagle feather firmly into the base of one braid of his hair, then as the warming fingers of Sun moved downward from the peak to touch them, he slowly began eating a few strips of dried meat and some cold mush of cracked wheat. He had left most of this food with Isabel. There was only enough to take him up and down the mountain, none for Little Coyote. The younger man knew the older had begun his final fast before he had fired his lodge, and, like all the tribe, his involuntary partial fast long before that. Little Grizzly Bear Claw reflectively chewed the last bite of the poor jerky. He shifted his gaze to Little Coyote when the old man softly spoke several prayer words aloud, though his eyes remained closed.

He is so thin, Little Grizzly Bear Claw thought. So frail, yet that resolute jaw had remained firm despite the wrinkles, between which now thin lines of shadow alternated with light as Sun strengthened even more. And those heavily veined, thin hands, how they contrasted with the strong, sinewy hands and arms of this man with whom more than forty-five years earlier he had formed the *i-sts-sókoi* bond when the Blackfeet . . .

Little Grizzly Bear Claw swallowed the remaining fibers of the jerky. He would like to sit here longer and ponder the past, as well as the grim choices that lay ahead for him in the long days to come. But the day was young, the weather good, and they yet must climb the peak the Black Robes had named "St. Mary's."

Though Little Grizzly Bear Claw had not moved, Little Coyote opened his eyes, which were duller now. Grasping the

7

rock, the old man struggled to his feet. The men resumed the trek, Little Coyote moving ahead on a trail until it would run out, then, goading the powerful sorrel upward through some smaller trees and brush, finding another trail wending ever upward for them to follow. Almost imperceptibly, Little Coyote began drooping forward, his body no longer cooperating with the powerful lunges of the sorrel.

"We will rest here," he said, though they were well below the summit. They made camp in the shelter of a rock outcrop. That evening the younger warrior moved a short distance away from his friend and ate his jerky and mush. As he put aside his own troubles and fell asleep, he could hear the old man's songs, the words of which sometimes included Little Coyote's Flathead name—*Sin-sch-ch-leh*. As the night became black, Little Grizzly Bear Claw also could hear the more distant yelps of the coyote, from whom the people in earlier times—and some even now—believed they had descended.

The men and horses camped next mid-morning on a small bench just below the summit of the peak. Most of the early snow on the bench had melted. Before dismounting, Little Coyote pointed his lance at a small cairn of rocks. Then he removed his power bag with the attached tail from around his neck. This time Little Grizzly Bear Claw helped him dismount, after which the old warrior used the sorrel to help him hobble to the cairn.

"Part of my medicine is here, surrounded by the stones. Now it also is on the stones," Little Coyote said. He placed the power bag and tail on the cairn and weighted them down with another stone, which he lifted with difficulty. "I would rest here, where my body will remain. And my ghost will remain near you, *i-sts-sókoi*, or wherever you and our people will be. My soul, as you and the Black Robes call it, well . . . we will hunt together again. That I know. That I knew before the arrival of white man and, much later, the Black Robes. Yes. Now I am tired. I would smoke."

Little Coyote painfully placed the rabbit-skin blanket on the ground in front of the cairn and sat in its center. Little Grizzly

Bear Claw brought him his sacred medicine pipe, given to him by Shining Shirt at the time of his death. Little Coyote tamped tobacco into the pipe's elaborately carved bowl with his bony fingers. He waited patiently for Little Grizzly Bear Claw to start a small fire with flint, steel and tinder, then ignite the tobacco with a small twist of grass. The old warrior sucked hard, his thin cheeks pulling inward and his lips resembling the puckered top of the tobacco bag. He did not lift the pipe to the four directions, but, instead, this time held it aloft only to Sun then down to the earth on which he now sat and soon would lie. He nodded and Little Grizzly Bear Claw carried the pipe to the cairn.

"Now, much loved *i-sts-sókoi*, I would have you paint the sorrel as I direct," Little Coyote said to his friend.

While Sun climbed to its zenith and then began descending, its warmth dried the many figures and symbols Little Grizzly Bear Claw painted on the shiny coat of the nervous sorrel. The figures comprised almost a duplicate of the figures/symbols story account of Little Coyote's lifetime exploits that had decorated the old man's lodge before its fiery destruction. At length, Little Coyote said, "It is enough. Now let me blacken my face before you place the paint bag in the cairn. Bring me my other bundle." He leaned against the cairn, wearily motioned for his friend to sit beside him, then spoke.

"As you know, when Black Robe Mengarini learned our tongue, and I greatly improved my knowledge of the white man's English until I could write it down, Black Robe told me he would write a list of our words so people could use them for a greater exchange of words and thought and friendship. I am sure *he* spoke with a straight tongue. But I had seen the first white men arrive, and I did not much like what I began to see and what my rare visions of the future rightly told me I would see—the warring Blackfeet, Bannacks and others we largely could keep out of our valley. But white man, though we never fought him, succeeded where our enemies could not."

Little Coyote paused, then raised his thin arms chest high and moved them outward from his body as though brushing away what was unimportant in the past so he could concentrate on what lay ahead. Taking a deep breath, he lowered his arms and continued.

"I, too, began putting together a long story in which there is truth for our people and others to know. The Black Robes and John Owen quietly helped me with the earlier parts of the task, though while they did so they not always agreed with all of what they saw."

He unrolled the heavy elk hide across his and his companion's legs, rested for a moment, then completed his task after setting aside a smaller tied bundle inside the roll. Painted on the elk hide in small figures and symbols was Little Coyote's life story. The markings began in the center and moved in almost-concentric circles outward until little space remained on the hide for more. But then, Little Coyote was of great age.

Now Little Coyote began to unwrap the bundle. When his weakened fingers fumbled at the knots of the buckskin ties, he wearily pushed the bundle toward his friend. Now the sentences became shorter and Little Coyote wanly conveyed some thoughts with the sign language: *Keep the story hide and think sometimes of your friend. Give the manuscript to someone you can trust. If Flathead, he must promise by Sun and the Good Spirit, if white, by the Holy Book, that it will become a book. Not now. When people are ready to understand. The way the story is told may change. But not the story.* Now the old man slumped against the cairn and spoke: "My vision told me that when this becomes a book, it will help all people to understand. Then, perhaps, they will be ready to give the help, the fairness, that so long has been denied."

Little Grizzly Bear Claw had many questions, but he replaced the manuscript in the pack sack as his friend whispered, "I can do no more." For a time Little Coyote seemed to be listening, then, eyes closed, he again began his death songs. They grew more quiet as the valley below darkened. Once he weakly beckoned and Little Grizzly Bear Claw drew close. With great effort, the old man whispered, "Long ago I interpreted your vision when you and Little Bear Claw, your father, were at the hot springs. You would leave our Bitter Root Valley with the people.

Now on this mountain, where my vision and my story began and my life ends, I, too, have been told you will take our people from our valley." He swallowed with great effort, then seemed to strengthen more than on the long trip up the mountain. "Yes, in four days you will go to *Sniel-eman*, the meeting-place valley, to live. Only after you join Little Bear Claw and me at the sand hills will our people begin to receive white man's justice in a vastly changed world."

Little Coyote opened his eyes. For a moment they burned fiercely from his blackened visage. "For the journey you will need meat. After you lance the sorrel, take the meat." Falteringly, he smiled. Some of the dried, black paint flaked from his cheeks and below his lips. "Do not worry. You will place the hide over me and leave the sorrel's bones and guts for the coyotes. And there will be a bit of meat for them, too." His grip on Little Grizzly Bear Claw's wrist became very strong.

Now darkness enveloped the peak as the death song became a broken whisper and Little Coyote's grip on his friend's wrist slowly relaxed. At length, Little Grizzly Bear Claw could hear only the coyote on a nearby ridge. At intervals the creature yipped three times—the animal's ancient and well-known warning of an approaching stranger. Then that creature, too, was silent.

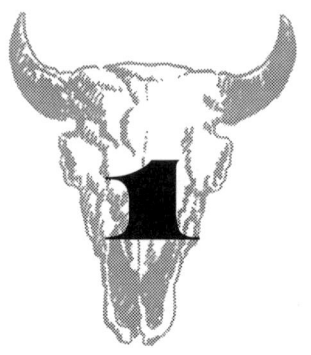

The northwesterly breeze that had been buffeting the youth as he climbed ever higher began to wane; the misty clouds that had brought a skiff of wet snow the night before were swirling past him now—thinner, lifting, not dense enough to win their battle with Sun. These were only the late days of *kólog*, the moon of the Onions, and just nearing the first days of *spakéin kspiakami*, moon of the Harvest of Ripe Things. All around him on this bench of land below the great peak and high above the river were the ripened berries that he had eaten plentifully at this season for as many of his thirteen summers as he could remember.

He reached for a handful, paused, then brought them close to his dark and keen eyes. He could see their juice under the ripened skins. Passing the berries under his nose, which detected the pleasing aroma of the bruised ones, he then brought them to his mouth. He yearned for their taste and nourishment more than ever before because he had had neither food nor drink since his purification sweat bath two suns ago. Finally, he raised the berries toward strengthening Sun and cast them upward as an offering. The vehemence of his action startled the bluejay that had been watching him from its perch on the broken limb of a towering fir. With a protesting "jeeah" the bird flew higher into the tree but, mindful of a nearby hawk, did not break from its shelter. His senses more finely honed for important signs such as this good-medicine bluejay, the youth watched the hawk gracefully circle above him, spiral after silent spiral, until it suddenly dove toward a small meadow in the great valley and then disappeared behind a heavy fringe of red willow after which the people had named their river.

The hawk had sent him no personal vision, but had directed his gaze toward the far river bank. There, he could see a thin file of what he was certain were his people and a band of horses threading toward the south end of the valley and upriver. They would join the large encampment already set up and prepare for a trek to the three forks that formed the great river. They and their friends, the Shoshonis, would hunt the buffalo for winter food.

At the sight of his people, the youth's spirit began rising like the steam from the nearby hillsides and patches of meadow far below. Parts of the river were shining now, almost as though the rays of sunlight that earlier had slanted downward through the ragged clouds had fallen to earth in sinuous, disjointed bands. Another hawk effortlessly rose ever higher into the clearing sky. A flock of small birds fluttered in the nearby bushes and trees, singing their joy and excitement at their freedom to fly great distances southward before heavy snows covered most of their food. The thought of food set the youth's belly to growling again; he felt his growing weakness. As best he could, he put that thought from his mind as he lay back and rested in warming Sun.

At length he yawned, stretched and lifted his bare and flexed legs into the air. The muscles in his calves were bunched and hard. He felt his biceps. They were hard, as were his belly muscles. He felt pride that he had come this far alone seeking a vision, as suggested by his uncle, Races His Horse. His uncle had taught him much before falling to the Blackfeet only a short time ago. There had been misgivings about the vision quest on the part of the youth's father, Running Buffalo Bull, though that warrior had learned in a vision before his son's birth that his mother should forego giving him even a temporary name immediately after his birth. Instead, he should be named after his return from the quest. He had come early on this search because he disliked being nameless.

At that recurring thought, the youth sat upright. The peak loomed above. Now he wanted to climb, to work hard. There lurked in his mind the certainty that unless he got busy, the growing encampment of his people would commence their trek to the south, then east, and he might lose an opportunity this time to accompany them on the hunt. Instead, he might be told yet again that he must remain in the valley with many of the women, the younger children and, mostly, only the very old warriors.

He reached for his bow and the quiver of bird and small-game arrows. In doing so he turned slightly to the south—and saw the coyote.

Like himself, the creature was half-grown, but the youth knew there was more to their kinship than size and age. Running Buffalo Bull had taught his son that in the interim between birth in spring and the fall leave-taking of parents, little coyotes learned much. The lessons came first from their mother in the den, then outside the den for many more days, after which the father would return to the den so both adults could teach the pups to hunt. In the ways of the coyote, this animal now had left its parents' territory to strike out for itself.

The animal still wore its coat that blended with summer surroundings, though there were signs of lighter-colored fur that would blend with the terrain in the coming winter. The coyote was within easy range of his bow had the youth cared to try one of his small arrows. A moment later it stepped from around a jumble of broken stone into full view. This puzzled the youth. Surely the breeze was carrying his scent to the coyote. It had hunted in the valley and it and its wary parents had encountered the people who, tradition said, had descended from coyote. Paradoxically, though revered and hunted by the people, coyote, in the beginning, had given them fire—even this bow and arrows the youth was tempted to use. But he was on a different hunt now, and his thoughts about his people and the buffalo hunt reminded him once more that the mountain peak lay ahead. Much earlier, his inner voice had told him he must seek his vision atop the peak. Now, as he and the little coyote stared at each other, a stronger voice began to caution: *"Wait! There was the good-medicine bluejay. Wait and watch."*

So he sat there, and after a time the young coyote sat, too, turning as it did so to look directly at the youth. As the breeze died and Sun warmed the almost-naked youth even more, the coyote continued to sit there—staring, until soon the boy-man saw only the head, the face, the ears, eyes, long muzzle and nose and, at times, even the panting tongue. Now, as the youth closed his eyes, the after-image of that mask remained, hovering there, staring, even as it diminished, and when he reopened his eyes the reality was there—staring, unmoving. Ever so cautiously, the youth relaxed his grip on his bow and the thin quiver of arrows. As he continued to stare, he straightened his cramped leg and more cautiously yet turned his entire body to face the little coyote.

The sounds of the birds nearby died away in the youth's ears, though once he heard the repetitive "jeeah, jeeah, jeeah" of a bluejay. Perhaps it was saying, "Stay, stay, stay."

So the youth and the coyote sat there until *s'ciitakéin*, the time when the sun nears the western hills. Now, when the youth closed his eyes, the after-image mask of the coyote changed quickly from red to white to dark. This pattern continued through *tcsoóskan*, when the sun is just over the hills, and into *slléikal*, the evening. After more time, the coyote slid its front paws and haunches forward and rested its body on the ground. As the youth reclined on the ground, their stares remained locked until darkness fell. Now the youth put his head on one outstretched arm, with the after-image of the little coyote turning quickly from red to white to dark, but no longer fading into nothingness.

Somewhere from far in the distance of another world, a chorus of coyote barks floated up the mountain and into the youth's only half-hearing ears. He no longer felt the hunger, the growing cold nor the hard stones under his body. Now he saw himself sitting atop the peak while a procession comprised of a few red masks of people floated into his view. Then a growing number of white masks appeared until they were as numerous, surely, as the stars he somehow knew were winking overhead. A great dark mask ended the procession and, floating above them all, spoke: "Such faces you will see again. Though you will be a great warrior, you will counsel the people not to war with them, no matter the provocations, for these white faces are as numerous as the berries in this valley, and your people are few. Thus you will counsel the people. Thus you will counsel the people. Thus you will . . . "

The youth heard himself muttering, "Thus you will counsel the people," and he sat stiffly erect, his senses re-connecting to tell him *sgalgált*, the daylight hours, had arrived and with them was a possible danger.

The coyote had crept toward him until it stood just below, scarcely twice the youth's length away. Now he saw only the animal's teeth, the wrinkled muzzle drawn back into a puzzling half-snarl. The youth launched an arrow into the animal's throat, and when the writhing, bleeding and yipping body struck his, he reached for the throat and grasped it. They thrashed about and the coyote's blood splashed onto the youth's chest and mixed with his own as the sharp arrowhead, which protruded from the back of the animal's neck, cut his own chest and arms. Then the animal lay still. The youth continued to squeeze, feeling the thumping of the heart, hearing the gasps for breath. Strangely, the strength of the coyote seemed to flow from its body through the youth's arms and into his own body.

He stood and whirled the carcass away from him. It fell, bloody muzzle pointing uphill, and that's where the youth carried the carcass. With an edge of his sharpest arrow he carefully cut through the hide and broke off the animal's tail. Then, almost spent, he erected, just below the summit of the peak, a cairn of heavy rocks over the tailless coyote. Gasping, he climbed atop the cairn, faced *spakaní*, Sun, and raised the little coyote's tail with both bloody hands and arms. He closed his eyes. Only the after-image of Sun remained, reddish then white, and there it hovered, though the youth opened and closed his eyes several times. At length, the image darkened and disappeared. Then his prayer of thanksgiving to Sun was fervent. Equally fervent was his prayer to the coyote for letting itself be killed. Nimbly, the youth half-ran, half-jumped downward to the nearest berry patch. Soon the huckleberries' juices flowed over his bloody hands and dyed the lower half of his face bluish-black. A grouse fell to his second arrow. He plucked and cleaned the bird, then climbed atop a large boulder overlooking the valley to eat it.

As he sat down, the youth looked around and saw a bluejay answering scold for scold a squirrel he could hear but not see. The sight of the bluejay began to shift his thinking to the vision of the night before, but interpretation of the vision lay in the mind of ancient *Piel'xalks*, Shining Shirt, the *sgumoiga*, the seer shaman, whom he soon would see.

So while strength returned to his legs, the youth's attention focused first on the world closest to him. A wary crow landed on the top branch of a pine and silently watched this human who seemed to make no unfriendly move. Opening its wings, the bird dropped into the widespread pattern of the grouse feathers at the gutting place. It looked upward, turning its head inquisitively this way and that. It hopped into the bushes and grass, rustled around, then lumbered into the sky, trailing the long string of entrails. The youth watched the bird until it disappeared from view. Pursuing it were two more of the dark birds, their raucous cries reaching his ears even after they, too, no longer were visible.

To the east across the wide part of the valley the higher peaks of a wall of mountains carried new snow, too, in some places reaching down into the blackish-green fringes of trees. Portions of the river not hidden by trees and brush still shimmered in the sunlight. Dark clouds to the far south where the valley arced out of sight promised more new snow in the high peaks there, perhaps on the very mountain pass the people must climb to start for the buffalo country. There were clouds to the north, and where the valley also arced out of sight they were moving faster than the others.

Here, from where he sat, the youth acknowledged that he could travel in two hard days to the southern end of his valley world, and in another two days to the northern end. In less than one day he could reach the base of the eastern wall of protective mountains. Several times he had been taken on the well-armed treks outside the valley. Surely now he was strong enough to go to the buffalo country.

Picking up his weapons, he began hurrying down the mountain peak, angling south in the direction of the trail that ran along this side of the river. He had high expectations, about two days of travel ahead of him, and much to tell.

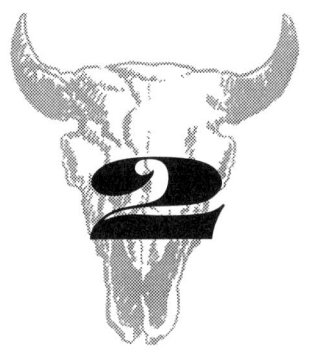

As the youth angled downward toward the path on his side of the river, he was tempted to follow the trail southward despite warnings he had heard for years: "When many of our people are in our valley and are traveling in large groups, use the trail. When there are few, avoid it, lest you walk into a Blackfeet trap, as does the almost mindless rabbit into the snare." Running Buffalo Bull and the youth's uncles had taught him well: "From the days of your first steps, learn to walk as a warrior, ride as a warrior, think as a warrior, act as a warrior."

Still, the youth knew traveling was easiest nearest the river, so he angled more directly toward the path to cross it and walk between it and the river. Perhaps by walking fast he could even overtake the people he had seen moving to the encampment before his vision. As he left the more rocky slope of the mountain, taking care not to strike bushes and set them to waving, the sounds of his movement were more quiet, absorbed by the grasses. When he neared a stand of willow, four, then five, white-tail deer broke from the brush; two with tails erect, three with tails down, they began quietly bouncing uphill. They ran until the lead doe, evidently catching a vagrant wisp of the youth's scent, turned and led the others, all tails up now, toward the path, perhaps to race ahead and again cut uphill into the more protective stands of great trees and heavy brush. The youth almost reflexively had fitted an arrow onto the bow, but he relaxed as he watched the deer angle downward and out of sight. Perhaps the new snows higher up had brought them down, for the people had seen few deer of late, and were hungry. Deer meat would be welcome, though he would have far to haul it, but he had not yet killed a deer and there was slight chance that his small arrows would do so, except at very short distances. Now, however, he held both his bow and the arrow that had killed the little coyote in his left hand as he again began walking toward the trail. Suddenly, the same five deer began bounding almost directly toward him. They paused uncertainly, partially turned, and began racing straight up the long, sloping hillside.

The youth sat down in a clump of tall grass and remained motionless. Dry, broken stems gouged his back, thighs and rump. What had caused the deer to choose a lesser danger and return? He plucked a bunch of long-stemmed, dying grass and, holding it before his face and head, cautiously looked ahead, trying hard to hear any new sound. At first there was only the rustling of the light breeze in the grass, the occasional "bzzzz" of a bee seeking food from some of the shorter flowers that had escaped first frosts, and the melodious "tyeep, tyeep, tyeep" of a robin seemingly from near the trail and ahead. As he strained his eyes and ears, the youth heard the excited chattering of a squirrel near the trail and somewhat behind him. "Chickaree, chickaree," it scolded defiantly. Then, more frantically, it was telling the youth that something had invaded its small home range. Simultaneously, the robin's call changed to a more agitated "tut-tut-tut" and the youth saw the bird rise high above the trees near the trail and wing southward.

Perhaps some of the people have taken this trail and, being late, are hurrying to get to the encampment, he thought. *Yes, that might be the answer. Must be it.* Relieved, he continued to sit for a while, wondering. Then slowly, almost unnoticed at first, the sounds near or on the trail rose above the squirrel's scolding and into his consciousness—the voices of children, a woman's laugh.

Yes, they are heading toward the encampment, he thought, but as quickly—*what had startled the deer and the robin from the direction the people must yet go?*

Suppressing his first impulse to race toward the sounds of the people, the youth again picked up the bunch of grass and behind its cover peered ahead to determine the distance from which the deer had veered away from him and up the hillside.

Most likely they broke uphill about the same distance from me as from whatever frightened them, he reasoned. So, again picking up his bow and arrow, he crawled toward that point at which they had raced directly uphill. Here the grass was short, so he wriggled forward on his belly for a time; then he ran in a crouching position to where the grass merged with willow. He was almost upright when he reached the heavy stand of trees. Now he soundlessly moved forward, using the stalwart trunks of the pines as cover.

The pinto was well hidden from both approaches on the trail. The youth saw the horse's rump as it moved twice, probably to dislodge a fly. As he crept closer he could see that the tail had been tied down to prevent it from swishing into the air and revealing the animal's presence. Again he wanted to race toward the friendly sounds, but an inner voice, much like that of his dead uncle and of his father, said, *"Wait!"* Then, *"There on the mountain, by waiting, you saw first the bluejay and next the coyote,"* and, *"Here there were the deer and the squirrel and the robin. Wait and watch."*

The youth slowly removed the quiver from his back and withdrew his next sharpest and straightest arrow, the one with which he had killed the grouse. Now he had two for quick loosing. The coyote tail he earlier had pushed into the quiver for easy carrying now became a pad to prevent the remaining arrows from rattling. Again slinging the quiver, he crawled forward. Now there were new noises—the clop, clop of several horses and, again, the excited calls of children, seemingly close enough to see had he been on the trail.

As suddenly as a grouse flushes almost between a walker's legs, a tall, muscular warrior stood erect and loosed an arrow down the trail. He ran forward as he did so, his war club raised. His shrill cry and the suddenness of his movements terrified the youth. He dropped down, the bow half-drawn, and remained there until the frightened cries of children and the shout of a woman, accompanied by grunts, created an urgency in him that demanded action. He sprang to the trail. Again the woman shouted, but he focused only on two men locked together and rolling on the ground. The stub end of a war arrow protruded from the lower right shoulder of the smaller figure and hampered his movements.

The youth drew his arrow back to its head, ready to loose, but he feared he might hit the wrong man. Should he run forward and try a hazardous shot or stab the Blackfeet with an arrow? No, arrows were too fragile for that. He ran toward the fighters, clenching his teeth then uttering a loud shout. The sound alternated between the shrill voice of a frightened boy and the deeper tones of a would-be man. Viciously, he slashed the Blackfeet across the eyes with the bow, then stepped back. The Blackfeet leaped to his feet and faced uncertainly for a sliver of time this boy-man painted helter-skelter with coyote and human blood, lower face darkened from a feast of berries and aiming a bird point at his neck. Confidently, the warrior ran forward to eradicate this menace with his uplifted war club. But the long, sharp obsidian blade of a lance caught him in the back and protruded from the front of his chest. The lance pointed at the youth, who had loosed his arrow into the warrior's throat. The warrior toppled forward, the impact of his body raising a tiny storm of dust and fir needles. Through the dust the youth could see the woman reaching for her husband's bow and arrows should the lance she had launched fail in its task.

Stupefied, the youth abruptly sat down, his second arrow still ready to fly. There he sat until the woman shook him hard. "We must remove the arrow from my husband's shoulder!" she shouted. "Come! You help!"

The youth relaxed his bow, laid it aside and stumbled toward the wounded man, who was trying ineffectually to feel the depth and movement of the arrow. Together the woman and the youth experimentally pushed the arrow farther into the man's body. The broken-off shaft moved. The point was not embedded in bone. While the man sat there, they pushed and guided and pushed until the war head emerged from the man's back. They severed the thin strands of sinew binding the arrowhead to the shaft and removed it. The woman pulled back, once, twice, then hard, and the now-headless shaft slid from the flesh amid a gush of blood. Throughout the operation the man remained silent. The woman examined the blood and let it continue to flow freely while she removed some herbs from a pack atop one of the six horses. She forced a small twist of them into each partially closed hole and bound more atop that while two small, wide-eyed, dark faces of a boy and girl peered from this bush and that until the children were only a few steps away from their parents. Now the wounded man spoke.

"You are the son of Running Buffalo Bull. You have proved worthy of him. Eagle Claw owes you his life. Young Willow was too far down the trail to reach the lance before the club would strike."

The man stood, then leaned weakly against a tree, his face ashen from his experience. Again Young Willow rummaged in the pack. She gave more herbs to her husband, brought him water, then stripped thin, red, willow bark from a nearby bush. He chewed much of that for a time, all the while looking about and listening as though he expected to hear other people. Soon, he began walking about. He looked briefly at the dead Blackfeet man.

"Now," he asked the youth, "where are you injured? Where is the source of the much blood I see on you?"

Even as the youth hastily explained, all of them prepared to move off the trail and toward the river. Eagle Claw retrieved his dead foe's weapons and calmly began scalping him. The youth heard the slight sucking sound of the procedure as he moved toward the pinto. She was a beautiful animal, laden with an elk-skin bag and adorned with a painted red hand on one flank and a black hand on the other. He untied her tail, mounted the animal and joined the cavalcade of six others as it slanted downward and edged closer to the river. They forded at a shallows, the youth taking time to scrub off the coyote blood while the injured warrior, as best he could, helped his wife tighten the packs of their animals. Also on their horses were the carcasses of two deer. The man explained why he and his family had been alone on the trail.

"We were to have joined the last large group moving south," he said, "but we had no meat. There is little in the valley now. I began to hunt and got these deer. The plan we were told was that the people would move south down that same trail."

"From the mountain," the youth replied, "I saw them on this side of the trail we have just moved to." Out of respect, he did not ask the question he was wondering so much about. Eagle Claw seemed to read his thoughts.

"As we moved down the trail we've just left, we could see there were no tracks of a recent large movement. But, of course, we did not know which ford our people had planned to use to get onto this trail. And even with the loaded horses, we should have stayed off the trail. But my medicine did work well, though I had to exchange this arrow hole in me for the scalp." With his left hand, the man clasped the eagle claw dangling from his neck. "But I must not often test it so sorely as this time. We must move quickly now to try to catch up with the others. It is unlikely the skulking Blackfeet was alone in our valley."

They ate deer liver, and as he filled his belly for the first time in several days the youth pondered why a warrior like Eagle Claw would explain at such length to a stripling who lacked even a name. He stopped chewing for a moment and lowered his head in total concentration on that fact. The answer flowed as readily as the nearby river: Eagle Claw regarded him as more than a no-name. There was both wonder and satisfaction in that. Eagle Claw also recognized that an informed ally is the most effective ally. The youth resumed chewing, once more aware of the delicious and strengthening food and the peril of their situation. Just for an instant he almost could hear the half-jesting, half-chiding voice of his mother, Little Yellow Bird: "My son, if you are going to nap briefly with your chin on your chest, would you not be more comfortable lying on the furs?"

The little band moved quickly up the river bank and onto the other deeply worn trail. Both Eagle Claw and his wife placed a child behind them and pushed their horses to a trot. The youth trailed behind the last of the pack animals, exulting in the movement of the pinto, her easy stride and maneuverability. Experimentally, he slackened the reins and slowly pressured the animal with his left leg and thigh. Obediently, the pinto began veering right and off the trail, selecting the most open gaps between the trees and brush. He pressured with his right leg and once again the animal swung back to the trail. Now the youth wanted to reach back and examine what the pack sack held; he restrained himself, for there yet was the matter of ownership. Unless Eagle Claw would speak, the youth would return to his family with the coyote tail and his account of the vision. That would be ample, he told himself, yet . . .

After a long ride, Eagle Claw signaled a halt atop a high rise in the trail. He dismounted and hung both arms over his horse and rested against its barrel for a moment. Then he led the band into a circular excavation with heavy logs and rocks placed around its rim. A tiny water seep threaded through one side. They ate the remainder of the liver and small cakes made from flour ground from the roots of the bitterroot plant, whence the people's beloved valley derived its name—*Spetleman*, place of the bitterroot. Eagle Claw urged haste.

"We will not cook more meat," he said. "Our medicine has been much overused today. You see, the breezes flow against us. We must guard against the smoke telling our enemies how close we are. Now we must leave this stronghold. I am certain we are being followed, for the foe we killed should be missed by now. But perhaps his friends are moving more slowly than we because their scout did not return to report. Perhaps they fear ambush, and do not know there are but . . ." He looked briefly at his wife and longer at the youth. ". . . three warriors on the horses."

As they moved out of the fortification, Eagle Claw again looked closely at the youth. "I must know. When you whipped the Blackfeet with the bow, did you do so to count a warrior's strike?"

To have answered "Yes" would have given the youth great importance, both now and at the encampment.

"I counted no coup," the youth replied. "I wanted him to stand to take my arrow, lest I hit you."

Eagle Claw stiffly walked over to his wife, who was lifting the youngest child to her horse's back. As they talked, the youth pondered his response. He could only be truthful, though even that admission held elements of bravery he was not certain he possessed. He remembered his fear after the Blackfeet had fallen. In his more circumscribed little world before he had set out on his vision quest, he had been trying to conquer within himself a tendency—a weakness as he viewed it—to want the plaudits of others. Yet, all his years he had learned that within the people there was a need to point out one's accomplishments, which, when corroborated by others, brought the honors of recognition, riches in worldly goods sometimes, and the mantle of leadership, helping, perhaps, the very survival of the people. Yes, while it was necessary generally to encourage this boastfulness, the youth was glad that the people frowned with equal, if not greater force, upon the lie. Well, he would have to more deeply ponder all these perplexities one encountered as he entered this world of older people. But not now. Eagle Claw was slowly walking toward him.

"The Blackfeet was dead when your arrow struck," Eagle Claw said. "He had not yet fallen, but he was dead, and my woman killed him. Rightly, the scalp is hers. The horse is yours, and the pack, for you could have taken them and left at once before coming to help us. Thus the Blackfeet repays you for your efforts. But I would have been dead before the lance had killed the Blackfeet had you not struck him. This lance of my father and my father's father is yours, son of Running Buffalo Bull, to repay you for my life. This lance I have taken from the Blackfeet will serve me well."

Eagle Claw placed his obsidian-tipped weapon in the astonished youth's hands, mounted his horse with great dignity and obvious pain and started down the hill at the fastest pace of the day. The youth's mind reeled from the impact of this fast succession of important events, but centered again and again on Eagle Claw's reference to him as "warrior."

It was well they continued to move fast, for as they gave the horses a brief rest atop the next rise, all of them could see Blackfeet horsemen carefully picking their way down from the fort they had left only a short time ago.

Eagle Claw stiffly bent over to examine the tracks of the people they were trying to overtake. Again he conferred briefly with his wife. Lifting both children from the horses, she had one cling to her neck in front of her body and put the other on her back. Then, she carefully walked uphill off the trail over broken rocks that absorbed no tracks. When she returned, alone, she carefully re-set several rocks she had displaced while going uphill. Like the deer fawn, the children silently would remain where she had hidden them until told to emerge.

"With this shoulder, I am useless with the bow, son of Running Buffalo Bull," Eagle Claw said. "My wife is very good with it. At shorter range, your bow is effective, too. I will race ahead and bring back some of the people. If there must be a fight, make it from the fort at that next hill. I will leave the Blackfeet's bow and arrows with you. I will try very hard to be back before you have to use them."

Then, laying his quirt to his horse with his good arm, Eagle Claw raced southward.

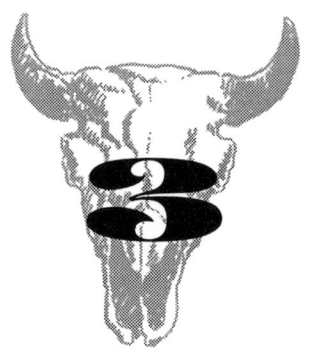

His mind whirling with events of the past three days, the youth had taken little time to form any strong opinions of Eagle Claw, except that the warrior was fair-minded and had stood up bravely to his wound. Young Willow was comely, clean in her buckskin gown and younger than his mother, Little Yellow Bird. Judging from her work with the lance and her shaking him into movement after the death of the Blackfeet, she also was determined and brave—and most likely wondering how much she could depend on a no-name! Her silence at Eagle Claw's rapid departure gave added assurance her husband had made a wise decision in going for help. With the Blackfeet cautiously moving toward them from the north, there was no time for further speculation about the woman. Eagle Claw had referred to the youth as a warrior, no lightly given compliment, and while the youth did not feel he had earned that coveted status, he must try to act as one. First, they must gain more time.

As they raced to the smaller fort ahead, the youth moved his pinto as close to Young Willow's horse as the width of the path and the other trailing animals would allow. "We yet have six horses!" he shouted to her. "We have four lives, those of your two children and our own. We must delay the Blackfeet. Would you think about putting four of the horses in this fort, risking their loss against the loss of your children and our lives?" They stopped. "We could push some sharpened branches into the earth inside this fort and pull some of your family's clothing over them to look like our people from a distance. If we act quickly we can race ahead to the next fort atop that lower hill and defend from that. We would be closer to our warriors when they come."

Before he had fully explained his plan, Young Willow began breaking off branches from nearby trees. She hacked at the ends of the branches with her flint knife, scrambled through some of the packs and pulled buckskin shirts over the branches. She pushed the roughly pointed ends into the ground and inner embankment of the fort so the upper portions would be visible from a distance, whether from the trail or, more likely, off the trail, for that would be the way the Blackfeet would attack. This would consume more time.

The youth removed the two deer carcasses from the pack horses and pulled the remaining shirt over the head and the small forked antlers of one. Then he placed the carcass so it resembled a person peering through a wide gap between stones and logs at the fort's rim. This was the most realistic effigy of all, but there was no shirt for the second carcass unless . . . He opened the Blackfeet's pack on the pinto. Inside, among other paraphernalia, was the resplendent garb of surely an important warrior. The youth replaced the great war bonnet in the round, birch bark case lest, by his using the bonnet, the ruse be recognized from a distance. Then he pulled the long buckskin shirt over the second carcass. Now, as he and Young Willow raced down the next lap of the trail, he looked back. Yes, the fort looked well-defended, with the rumps and heads and swishing tails of the four horses rising above the rim and the clothing-clad branches moving in the breeze.

Sun had fallen only a short distance more toward the western wall of mountains by the time the youth and Young Willow had laid out the arrows, three bows and two lances for easy reach inside the smaller fort. Soon they heard a distant and frightening shout of anger, rage and grief, followed by like voices of others from the direction of the fort they had left.

From the south there was the muffled sound of hurrying hoofbeats. Leading a band of eleven Flathead warriors was Thunder Voice, a sub-chief and close friend of Three Eagles, the Flatheads' most powerful chief next to head chief Tjolzhitsay. Raising his hand, Thunder Voice slowed his great black horse and approached the fort.

"The Blackfeet?" he asked. The horse pranced and tried to turn as the sub-chief looked down on the youth.

"They are leaving the fort just beyond us," the youth replied. Very quickly he related what he and Young Willow had done to delay the attackers. The chief's piercing, dark eyes bored into the youth until he faltered with his message. He shifted the long obsidian-bladed lance from hand to hand as though the haft suddenly had become too hot for his grasp. Young Willow stepped forward and completed the explanation. "The dead Blackfeet was a sub-chief, at least," she concluded, and extracted the war bonnet from its case.

Now the smallest hint of a smile broke Thunder Voice's craggily handsome face. The pursuing Blackfeet were closer now; the impatiently milling Flathead party could hear their raging cries.

Thunder Voice seized the war bonnet from Young Willow's hands. "When they rage, the bad medicine of anger shadows the good medicine of cleverness and care," he told his warriors in a low voice. "You," with a quick gesture at the woman, "take the horses back into the trees below us. And you, no-name, rub this headdress well into those horse droppings and put other droppings into it. Walk off the trail toward the Blackfeet. At the start of the slope of this hill, very carefully toss the war bonnet onto the trail. Yes, your *sumesh* is good, but do not overwork your power. Withdraw into the screening trees and walk back toward this place until you find our warriors hiding off the trail, then hold the horses with the woman. Yes, the Blackfeet will heat their rage even more when they see the despoiled war bonnet, and they will hurry up the trail thinking this fort is defended with a small force that had to flee. While rage turns their minds into that of a grouse, and as they pass us, we will knock them down." The braves faded into the brush. "Hold!" Thunder Voice shouted at the youth, who prepared to carry the war bonnet to the trail. "Why would you sacrifice Eagle Claw's four horses by leaving them in the fort?"

"There was no sacrifice intended," the youth replied. "My thought was that our warriors would return and get those horses back, and a few more from the Blackfeet if we could delay them."

A stronger hint of a smile relaxed the sub-chief's stern features. Now he sent the youth hurrying on his way with a slight inclination of his head. This time the youth's task seemed far less onerous. When he hastened to rejoin Young Willow with the horses, he pondered deeply Thunder Voice's repeated assertion that anger shadows wisdom.

The terrifying war cries of the pursuing Blackfeet drowned out the hoofbeats of their horses. The youth, watching Young Willow, saw her look fearfully in the enemies' direction, perhaps thinking about her children. Her movement caused a restlessness among the horses, which had pricked up their ears at the approaching sounds. The horses strained at the ropes as though they, too, wished to join the impending fight. The youth tried to analyze his own emotions. He conceded he was very afraid, too, and wondered how he and Young Willow could have stood up to their foes. Most of them would have been inside the fort before he and the woman could have let fly enough arrows to halt them. He more fully understood Eagle Claw's desperate ride for help.

Now, closer, the challenging cries carried a new note, more savage still, of outrage, grief and deathly threat as the Blackfeet evidently found the headdress. The war ponies strained even harder at the ropes as the noise intensified with the loud, familiar—and comforting, the youth conceded—war cries of his Flathead people, raggedly first, then in full chorus. The youth's pinto began struggling hardest of all to pull away until her owner tied the reins to a tree and snubbed the creature closer yet with a leather rope from a more docile pack horse. Soon the cries began diminishing, climaxed by tremendous, exultant whoops.

"It is over; soon our men will be here," Young Willow said. Her smile warmed the youth and reassured him. "I will go for my children." Then she was gone up the trail, from which a warrior soon shouted for the youth to bring the horses.

Some of the Blackfeet bodies lay sprawled on the trail, most felled by more than one arrow. Two lay in a small clearing leading into the trees off the trail. Farther downhill near where the youth had tossed the war bonnet were two more, transfixed by Flathead lances. He wondered how that could be until he discovered, amid the exultant shouting and the recounting of strikes made before the loosing of arrows, that Thunder Voice had thought of a final master stroke. The sub-chief had suggested to a warrior that, once the enemy band had galloped past him, he carry across the trail a leather rope already fastened to a stout tree, then tie the loose end at mounted body height to another tree. Thus, if any Blackfeet should retreat amid the fray, they likely would not see the rope in time to avoid it.

"This ruse spared the horses but felled the foe and I lanced them!" one warrior said with a whoop. Others added their chants of victory, prayer and boasts. The gawking youth scarcely knew what to do, where to turn amid the turmoil and the apportionment of the Blackfeet horses, personal equipment and weapons. So he stood there with the horses until the owners, some with hands bloodied from the scalping, came to reclaim them. With relief, he saw Young Willow riding up the hill with four horses tied one to the other. Soon he could see her son's arms around her waist and the little girl seated protectively ahead of her mother.

"Ho, no-name!" she called. "We lost nothing." She looked more closely around her now as she neared the carnage. "And we seem to have gained much."

Thunder Voice strode toward the youth and the woman, then spoke: "Eagle Claw approaches slowly. He will receive yet another horse. He very much has a warrior woman, and it will be said in the councils. You have served well, far beyond your years," the sub-chief said to the youth. "That will be said in the councils. Will you trade that pinto of the Blackfeet sub-chief for these two fine animals I own because my arrows found their owners?"

The youth gripped the reins of the pinto so hard he could feel the rough edges digging into his palms. "No, Thunder Voice. Per—" His voice faltered. "Perhaps my *sumesh* flows from this horse, for more of importance to me has occurred since I owned her than ever before." *Have I said things right?* he wondered. *Have I said what will make certain I will keep the pinto, yet do not risk Thunder Voice's wrath?*

The sub-chief's stern features gave way to a full grin.

"The son of Running Buffalo Bull has some of the wisdom of his father," Thunder Voice said. "He also has a strong heart and a strong spirit." He grunted and turned away. There was much to do before these warriors could catch up with the people they had left such a short time ago.

The youth sighed with relief as he looked at the southwestern sky. It was filled with dark, foreboding clouds. Heavy snows from these could delay the departure of much of the encampment, now located in the valley of sweet roots, for the three forks of the great river. The plan had been set out for the first day of the ninth moon of *spakéin kspiakami*, "Harvest of Ripe Things."

That day, quite auspiciously, had just almost ended.

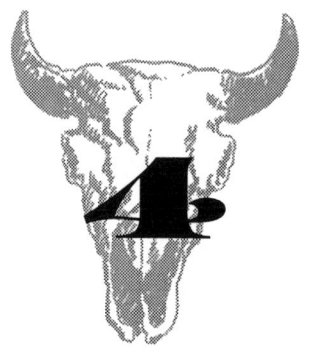

Young Willow and Eagle Claw could keep up more easily with the exultant rescue party when the no-name youth asked the woman to transfer her son to his pinto. The boy clung tightly to him, looking this way and that, his bright eyes eagerly absorbing the activities surrounding him. At times the movement of the pinto rocked him to near sleep and at others jarred him to further wakefulness and adventure while the mountains narrowed ever closer on both sides. As the valley darkened, the warriors slowed their movement and began eying the deer carcasses on Eagle Claw's pack horses.

"We have much to eat," Eagle Claw told Thunder Voice, and moments later the sub-chief called a halt near a small side stream fringed with red willow fingering down to a heavy stand of it along the Ootlashoots River. Soon, three large fires were sending sparks toward the winking stars. The men donned their buckskin shirts and began using their sharpest blades to hack slices of tallow and meat from the deer carcasses. They impaled the venison on willow wands and thrust it into the flames to sizzle as fat flowed over the meat and dropped into the fire. The air was filled with aromas that again reminded the youth he had eaten sparingly since he had begun his vision quest. Soon his belly seemingly could hold no more, but when the roasting rib cages that had been adding their aroma to the chill night air were ready for eating, he rejoiced that there were enough to include him in the division. Young Willow offered the largest leg bones to her husband, son and daughter. They cracked them with a rock and sucked out the delicious marrow with much gusto. None of the party had eaten like this for many days though the various encampments had moved from place to place quite often. "Yes," all agreed during their lively eating and recounting of their victory, "it is time for Shining Shirt's vision to tell us, finally, when we should leave for the buffalo hunts."

One by one, except for guards, the warriors threw more wood on the fires, and boughs on the space between them, and lay down to sleep. That night a deeper cold crept down from the mountains and froze little instruments of ice along the margin of the creek. The water played joyous tunes on them before Sun rose.

The last guards to seek sleep had piled large logs on the fires. Long before the easterly sky began to show gray light, all in camp awakened and huddled around the flames to take their turns at roasting the last of the venison. As the cavalcade began wending upward through the ever narrowing valley, Thunder Voice posted two warriors on fleet horses to follow in the rear as lookouts for any possible pursuing Blackfeet, although all had agreed that they had wiped out that particular band of marauders. None had escaped to tell others.

Hoof and foot marks amid droppings of many horses indicated their own people now were almost a day's journey ahead of them.

"They will have erected their lodges with those of the others at the encampment ahead," Eagle Claw remarked to the youth at mid-morning as they all stopped to drink from a small creek racing joyously and musically down a sharp ravine. "The lodge of Running Buffalo Bull will rejoice at the sight of their son, for surely there will be fear that the Blackfeet found him." The youth agreed; his thoughts dwelt on Little Yellow Bird and Running Buffalo Bull until Sun rose to the mid-day height of *sntogkéini* and the war party stood on a high hill sloping on one side into a large, bowl-like valley of high elevation at the encampment of the people.

Now each warrior painted his marks on his horse and his own body. Those with fresh scalps tied them so they would hang from the horse's mane or, if so armed, by the head of his long lance. Each warrior trailed behind him at least one Blackfeet horse, with booty attached to its saddle pad.

Shrilling victory, they raced down to the valley floor and toward the thirty-two lodges the youth had counted as he looked for the shelter with the distinctive black buffalo bull painted above the entrance. Soon a larger party of mounted warriors, led by their head chief, Tjolzhitsay, began streaming out of the encampment and toward the victors. The war party slowed and strung out for all to see that everyone had returned; the warriors maintained that formation to communicate this welcome information to the expectant encampment.

The returning Flatheads had pushed Eagle Claw's family and horses to the forefront to communicate that the rescue effort was successful. Eagle Claw held out to Young Willow the Blackfeet sub-chief's lance, to which was affixed his scalp with the long, dark locks. This gesture told the youth, who was toward the rear, that this woman already held warrior status for having killed an enemy and taken one or more scalps. His mind was a whirling mixture of conflicting emotions and he sought as much time as possible to sort them out. Running Buffalo Bull would treat him with the same fatherly warmness as before, he knew that, but would stifle pride, astonishment and curiosity when he saw this stripling son of his riding into camp astride a valuable, superbly trained horse carrying a pack of a sub-chief's belongings, as well as Eagle Claw's ancient lance. There would be added wonderment about that young coyote's tail now hanging by a leather thong from his lean neck and down to his tightly muscled belly.

And what about Little Yellow Bird? After her only son's departure for his vision quest, there had been silent tears she had tried to brush away as quickly as they had formed. She had re-entered the lodge where she had given him a great, seemingly final, hug before he had left that early morning now a childhood away.

Both parents had detached themselves from the victory display once they learned the outcome of the rescue venture. They were standing near the lodge when the youth approached and wrapped the reins of the pinto around a large peg. The youth faltered for a moment as he pondered whether he should place the lance alongside his father's, which was leaning against a willow tripod near the entrance. Very carefully, he placed it on the ground with the heavy obsidian blade almost touching the haft of his father's weapon, but well away from the stamping hooves of his impatient pinto. Then the youth stood erect, the little coyote tail dropping softly against his breast.

"We have worried since the report of the Blackfeet raiding party," his father said. Running Buffalo Bull placed his right hand on his son's shoulder, then stood back and eyed his perplexing offspring. Little Yellow Bird placed her hand over her mouth and backed into the lodge, which her son entered amid his father's comments about the high quality of the pinto. Running Buffalo Bull removed the leather pack bag and examined the lance while the youth and Little Yellow Bird, locked in a warm, welcoming hug, heard him declare, "It surely is that of Eagle Claw and his forefathers."

Mother and son were talking imperturbably as Running Buffalo Bull entered the lodge. Again, father and son eyed each other; the youth almost could feel his father's arms around him, too, but he understood how the father-child relationship had to shift, in appearances at least, after the vision quest. The youth presented his father with the Blackfeet's long and sharp obsidian blade with the buckskin wrapped around the upper part for a handle. Inside an elaborately made buckskin pouch and wrapped in a buckskin was a long-stemmed pipe of great age, highly decorated in the red of war. Surely over much time it had been chipped from black stone, then painfully hollowed out and smoothed into the shape of a buffalo. There was a pouch of the smoking tobacco. Little Yellow Bird received a smaller, but even sharper, obsidian knife and two fine fire flints. Both parents appreciatively touched, then closely examined, the highly decorated leggings and war shirt of the Blackfeet.

"If my father deems it appropriate," the youth said, "this would be a gift for Shining Shirt when he comes to your lodge to interpret my vision and help you to select my name. I am certain, Father, that there is much in my vision to select from."

Running Buffalo Bull looked up from his examination of the war shirt, but before he could reply there was a great clamor of youthful voices outside.

"Ho, no-name!" someone called. "There is much to tell."

The family stepped outside, the youth noticing that his father had placed the ancient lance in the rack alongside his own. Several young men who had been in battles were standing there, eager to see this youth they had heard of through Eagle Claw and Young Willow. In the group was the youth's friend, the horse guard leader, *Slem-cry-cre*, Little Bear Claw. Because of his own early, brave exploits, Little Bear Claw had been made the horse guard leader much sooner than usual.

Running Buffalo Bull addressed by name two of the older leaders with warrior status and nodded in a friendly fashion to each of the others.

"Yes, New Blade of Grass and Hawk, there is much to tell, and you will hear, but first Shining Shirt must know. I have sent for him, for much must be done in little time if we are to hunt the buffalo."

The other braves, wavering between youth and full warrior status, clearly were disappointed. They were tired of the heavy constraints that already were beginning to govern the earliest preparations for the buffalo hunt. Any new activity, even vicarious participation in the battle with the Blackfeet, would help to restrain them for a time.

Running Buffalo Bull would follow the vision quest procedures, but he would not risk his son's future, perhaps early acceptance into this group. He stepped into the lodge and quickly re-emerged to stand almost as though protectively shielding his son from their gaze as he handed out two gifts.

"This bow with which my son lashed the Blackfeet sub-chief is for your even younger son, New Blade of Grass. This arrow that pierced his throat is for yours, Hawk. There is good power attached to them. May it reach your sons." Running Buffalo Bull pointed behind the group. "See, Shining Shirt approaches. Soon after our meeting in our lodge, you will learn what my son has done, and its significance, for I shall summon you here after the telling and the interpretation of the vision."

Others had helped to place Shining Shirt astride the horse Running Buffalo Bull had sent for him to ride. The horse was Running Buffalo Bull's second favorite animal, next to his highly trained war and buffalo pony. The ancient *sgumóiga*, seer shaman, had ridden from his modest lodge set at the edge of the encampment nearest the mountains. He was clad in the simplest buckskin clothing. His long, white hair hung shoulder length, except where it had been shorn across his seamed forehead to frame the thin, equally lined face. Two bright eyes surmounted a noble nose. Viewed separately within this frame, these three features resembled the keen face of the great bald eagle, but the similarity ended there as one viewed the strong lips and the deeply cleft chin. One seldom stared at Shining Shirt long enough to form any further comparisons. He perpetually bore his head slightly back, not haughtily, but mystically upward and away from two crossed pieces of shiny metal of about hand length and finger width that hung by a thong from his thin neck and outside the buckskin shirt.

People said Shining Shirt looked to the lower heavens for guidance and, having received it, bestowed it almost always without question on others, if the auguries were right. Had he wished, Shining Shirt could have owned, easily, almost five-hundred horses, surely as many as were in this encampment. But as he received gifts he dispensed them, for he was as generous as he was mystical. Most of his gifts went to those most greatly in need. He was old beyond remembrance, revered almost beyond description by all of the perhaps six-hundred people in the valley, approximately four-hundred of whom were here. All knew from stories of the people, stories Shining Shirt never had to report, that he, largely, had induced them to move from the buffalo land to the protective valley. This was after bitter and successive onslaughts of the dreaded smallpox and after overpowering numbers of the Blackfeet had decimated the Flathead population. Only the isolated, productive and defensible valley and the exercise of great wisdom, flexibility and fierceness in war had prolonged the Flatheads' existence.

Running Buffalo Bull and New Blade of Grass stepped forward to hold the horse and help the ancient seer to dismount with much difficulty. The attention of all the others focused on this venerable man, but as quickly moved to Running Buffalo Bull's son as Shining Shirt's keen eyes shifted to the young brave who now stood fully revealed to him. The coyote tail dangled from the string around the youth's neck and waved in the slight breeze that was coming down from the peaks and into the mountain bowl.

"Aa—i-eee!" The thin cry from Shining Shirt expressed surprise, exultation and, perhaps, a tinge of fear, or was it relief— vindication? Shining Shirt pointed his long medicine crook at the startled youth. "It is as my visions have told me," he said. "It is *Sin-sch-ch-leh*. Yes, it is Little Coyote."

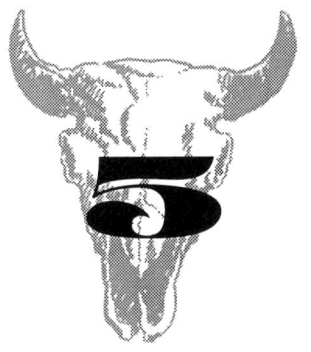

Shining Shirt reclined against a padded willow backrest facing head chief Tjolzhitsay. Tjolzhitsay had summoned the council of headmen from their warm beds to his large lodge that cold, early morning while most of the encampment still slept. All had worked hard to prepare for the long, dangerous trek to the buffalo grounds. The celebration of victory over the Blackfeet would have to wait. Shining Shirt had recommended they leave as soon as possible. Death, too, was moving quickly, touching the people's beloved seer; already, Shining Shirt was chanting the first part of his death song.

Running Buffalo Bull and his equally mystified son sat far back near the entrance of Tjolzhitsay's lodge. The youth was inwardly shaking that he had been summoned to attend a meeting of such notables. Yet there was comfort in knowing that these valley-dwellers, making up in strategy, cooperation and bravery what they lacked in numbers, were decorous, even gentle, in most of their dealings with one another.

So it was that Running Buffalo Bull, while silently wondering, too, could greet as equals most of these leaders. The warrior had served as sub-chief in many important activities; his bullhide shield and other trappings carried symbols attesting to his numerous brave strikes on the enemy.

Tjolzhitsay motioned that the council would begin. Two sub-chiefs helped Shining Shirt withdraw his long and elaborately decorated medicine pipe from the buckskin case wrapped in a beaver pelt. They helped him pack and light the pipe, after which he drew deeply on it, his thin, grayish cheeks sucking inwardly as he did so. This time he did not puff and blow smoke and point the pipe in the four directions, then toward earth, then to *spakani*— Sun. Instead, he blew a cloud of smoke upward; there was total silence as it slowly separated and thinned, threatening momentarily to move toward the direction of Sun and dissipate in the lodge. Then the strands of smoke seemed to re-collect even as they diminished; after moving in the direction of Sun, they suddenly ceased their eastward drift, rose and quickly were whisked from the smoke hole and out of sight.

"My smoke has blessed you all," Shining Shirt said. "It is as I knew. *Snagpéus*, the spirit with which I am lined and which long has dwelt among you, very soon will be gone." The seer's voice, though weak, held no tinge of regret as it carried as thinly as had the smoke through the silence. He held the pipe up to Tjolzhitsay. "Now, if you will let Running Buffalo Bull bring us his son." Shining Shirt lay wanly against the backrest once again, then continued to speak.

"Hear me carefully, Running Buffalo Bull. Yours is the right to name your son, but your vision told you to wait. There is much to be said, and the time to do so is no more than that which passes from first run at the buffalo herd and the ending of the chase. Yet, what Shining Shirt finally must say is as important as is the buffalo to our people."

He began chanting that which they already knew, his now high and reed-like voice breaking at times. He told how, as an old man, he had lost his beloved wife, Quiet Antelope, and had gone up the highest mountain to seek the land of the spirits so in some way they would be together again. On that mountain the greatest vision of his long life had told him to dedicate himself even more to the people, to counsel them that another and different race of men with white skins would enter this valley to which their diminishing numbers had retreated. There were stories in the minds of the oldest people of rare encounters with such white skins in all the earth's directions. His vision next had told him that here, in this valley, his people were to await the arrival of some of these white men dressed in black robes. The white men would teach them the ways of a single Great Spirit. They also would teach the people how, after death, they would be reunited with those they loved.

There were occasional grunts of affirmation as those in the council heard again what they already knew. There was total silence as Shining Shirt began relating the heretofore untold part of his earlier vision—how he had been directed to journey far to the land of much cactus and sun and sand and almost never-ending summer. There, amid visions in a crumbled stone shelter, he had found the bones and sun-dried flesh of men who once were. One had been clad in strange metal clothing that he could not remove—clothing that resisted the pounding of a stone. The bones inside rattled like the dry gourd with seeds. Shining Shirt would have liked to have broken off pieces of this strange shell, for he was certain he could have fashioned spear and arrow points from it—even a knife. The material was much like that he had seen, during his wide travels, in the form of knife blades. Rich warriors had given many horses to traders for the blades; those traders also had given great prices for them to other traders in even more distant tribes.

A second mummy was garbed in remnants of a long, black robe. A much-shriveled leather cord from around the neck held a symbol fashioned from the same material as the strange shell covering the first skeleton. Shining Shirt had worn this symbol, a cross, around his own neck until it now glistened like the ice in winter sun from years of swinging against his buckskin shirt. A third body was clad least of all. Near it were two large, rotted sacks of the almost-useless soft and yellow stones one sometimes found in the distant river of another strange people, reportedly with white skins. The people had given the name *Roche Jaune* to the grayish-yellow rocks on the hills above the river banks. Shining Shirt had pounded these yellow stones from one decaying bag with a harder rock; when he had learned that they would flatten out and could be pierced to wear as ornaments, he had placed part of the contents of one sack onto his pack horse. These were somewhere in his possessions he had considered too poor to give away as gifts.

Greatly agitated now, trembling and shaking on his thin legs, Shining Shirt tried without success to stand erect in the lodge. Two sub-chiefs immediately helped him up.

"The Black Robes will wear this symbol," the seer said as he touched the cross. "I have been told this in a vision. Now hear the vision of no-name here, to whom I leave my medicine crook, for as I sought but three suns ago the vision for our buffalo hunt, a greater one told me to hear the vision related by a no-name who would wear the coyote tail. Hear him well, for while exactly what he will say was hidden from me, my vision told me that the no-name, who will be Little Coyote, will tell you of the coming of the strange race. And my power will continue through him as the people decide how they will live when the new race arrives. But these eyes will not see them. Do not place me in the usual way under the earth, but above it, where my spirit sometimes will be able to give counsel."

Once more Shining Shirt was helped to the backrest. Feebly, he signaled for the pipe. He puffed hard on it and handed it to the youth, who held it to his chest and found himself wishing he once again were facing the Blackfeet with the bird-point arrow. Self-consciously, the youth related his vision of the coyote face and the masks; as he did so, tiny wisps of smoke curled upward from the pipe and enveloped the heads of all who listened.

As the youth ended his account, the listeners in the early dawn of that day could hear the distant three yips of a coyote signaling the approach of a stranger. The youth paused and looked about the council lodge. All faces were staring impassively upward at him. He looked at the pipe. The fire in it was dead, as was the spark in Shining Shirt, who had given it to him.

As the valley bowl flooded with sunlight piercing the many clouds, the leading sub-chiefs wrapped their beloved *Piél'xal'ks*,

Shining Shirt, their hero, in his best fur blanket and placed him on a scaffold between two high trees. His long, bony fingers were locked tightly around the cross. As for the vision of the stripling, Little Coyote—well, many of the people had visions. With the encampment now awake, it was time to strike the lodges and begin the journey to the buffalo grounds, an activity even more important than a war dance, which usually preceded the trek.

Slem-cry-cre, Little Bear Claw, shivered as the cold wind tore at his thin hunting shirt and pelted him with rain and sleet swirling down from the yet hidden high peaks. He wanted to remove his rolled-up skin blanket from his horse, somewhat concealed in a depression, and retreat to the niche in a small cliff above him where he yet would be able to look for the band of horses that had strayed from the encampment far below. But such a shelter would deprive him of the advantages his high lookout provided. Here he could see the bands of horses that other youths had begun moving to the meadows near camp; he could see the general locations of the other youths who, under his direction, were to watch these horses, and, like all the herders, keep a sharp lookout for the Blackfeet or other enemies who constantly invaded the valley in search of horses, women, scalps or other booty. The horse-watchers were to look toward Little Bear Claw, who, like themselves, would wave his blanket twice to signal approaching danger sufficient for them to bring the almost five-hundred horses right into the encampment.

Before the cold had come, Little Bear Claw unsuccessfully had searched distant hills, meadows and tree stands for the missing horses. Perhaps they had been found by Chief Three Eagles. Three Eagles had decided to scour for the horses at an even greater distance and assure himself that none of the Blackfeet raiding party had survived to skulk about. Shining Shirt's death would delay at least one more day the trek to the buffalo grounds.

After watching Three Eagles set off in the direction of the mountain pass, Little Bear Claw had climbed the high hill where he would be able to detect most movements below him, whether of horses, game or enemies. For a while he had watched a solemn procession carry a blanket-wrapped body to the trees on the hill below him—and then lance two fine horses.

Later, newly named Little Coyote had ridden his pinto to Little Bear Claw's lookout to ask where he should post himself to carry out the duties assigned him by New Blade of Grass and Hawk. Little Coyote was carrying his Blackfeet bow and arrows in a case and quiver closed against the moisture. He also was holding his ancient lance. Little Bear Claw learned from his friend what had occurred in the council lodge much earlier and that the burial had, indeed, been of Shining Shirt. The burial group had lanced the fine horse presented to Shining Shirt by Running Buffalo Bull; the other was for the spirit of long-dead Quiet Antelope, who surely merited another horse as the wife of such a great seer.

Little Bear Claw posted his friend closest to the encampment because Little Coyote had not yet proved that he possessed the experience to move and guard the more distant horse bands.

"You must let the rest of us be in the better positions for adventure, Little Coyote." Little Bear Claw's wide grin wrinkled the lean jaws above his square, determined chin. "Surely, you need no immediate adventure. We will continue to exchange information about our deeds. I think our group will accept you as a warrior after we fully learn about the events that brought you this fine horse." He reached out to stroke the pinto's neck; the horse nervously moved away and closer to Little Coyote.

Little Bear Claw removed his shirt, shook off the melting sleet plastered to it and again pulled it over his head. The deerhide stuck to him and hampered his efforts to adjust it over his chest and shoulders. He danced for a moment to warm himself, then once more squatted down to scan the valley and surrounding hills.

Slowly, the darker clouds lifted, revealing more of the lowest hills, close and distant. New clouds moved in, then they, too, lifted, until most of the mountains surrounding the bowl were visible. New snow on the higher peaks warned that while this ninth moon of the Harvest of Ripe Things scarcely had begun, the tenth moon of Half-Autumn and eleventh of Autumn might have more *siistc*, or winter, than this great region had experienced for many years.

Once again Little Bear Claw stood and danced, grateful that Sun was subduing even the higher clouds and melting most of the heavy frost and sleet on the lower hillsides and valley floor. Soon a tiny cloud of steam began rising from the drying hide of his hidden horse. Little Bear Claw remained motionless near a large boulder and endlessly studied the land until his eyes began to water. He sat down, wiped away the tears and momentarily lowered his eyes to rest them. A large and numbed beetle slowly crawled up his soaked legging, dispiritedly trailing its long feelers on the buckskin. The insect stopped and lifted one feeler with a leg; slowly another leg helped to elevate the other feeler, which soon was waving in a lively, inquiring fashion. The beetle began moving, stopped, then turned its body so that head and feelers pointed toward the nearest pass over the mountains. Was this a message? Little Bear Claw watched a small, gray bird hopping about in the sodden grass. It fluttered to the boulder, inquisitively cocked its head and eyed the beetle. The bird suddenly hopped onto Little Bear Claw's leg and gulped down the insect, uttering an unmelodic chirp of triumph. The bird darted high into the air, flying toward the very pass the beetle had faced. Little Bear Claw shifted his gaze from sky to land. To his delight, the white stallion he had been seeking—along with a band of four other horses—raced from the fringe of trees below. Long tails flying behind them, the horses headed toward the larger bands nearer the encampment. As they disappeared from his view behind a shelf of rocks below him, Little Bear Claw's first impulse was to seek release from his long immobility by throwing himself astride his own mount and racing in their pursuit. His growing caution, though, told him to remain even more immobile than when he had watched the beetle and the bird. Why had the stray horses suddenly appeared?

Soon a strange head appeared above the shelf of rocks below him, then another. Little Bear Claw heard the movement of leather and other trappings. The upward then downward motion of the heads, coupled with the sounds, said these were horsemen. Still, the curious headdresses atop the heads and white faces of the first two figures hinted strongly that they were *seme*, or threatening phantoms; the black head and face of a third person walking near them appeared painted for the *syúl*, or scalp dance. Now, more and more of the strange white creatures walked below him, a seeming procession of heads until those in the lead came into full sight. They were carrying strange sticks or war clubs, broad at the base and tapering upward. Some were leading some heavily loaded, jaded horses. Now an old warrior, then a young one, appeared on horses. They caught up with the three *seme* in the lead and pointed to the encampment below. The braves' garb suggested they were friendly Shoshonis, perhaps held prisoner by these *seme*. But, even more bewildering to Little Bear Claw, the Shoshonis were mounted on better horses; both carried their bow and arrows, the younger one even a lance.

When Little Bear Claw had counted more of these creatures than he had fingers and toes, he released himself from his almost rock-like rigidity, rolled upward toward the depression in which he had tethered his horse, then dropped downward into it. He quickly removed his blanket, nudged the horse above the depression, stood on its back and waved his blanket twice, then twice again. When his sharp eyes caught an answering wave, he re-rolled the blanket, secured it and arced upward and away from the strange procession that now included a woman with a baby on her back. Well above the *seme* now and somewhat ahead of them, he raced first toward, then downward, to the encampment.

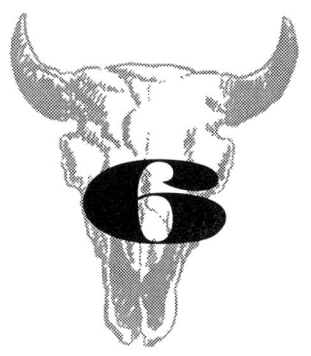

The effectiveness of Little Bear Claw's warning system immediately began manifesting itself as he urged his horse down into the bowl. The white stallion and other horses he had been looking for were caught up in the band next farthest from the encampment as the herder, after relaying Little Bear Claw's signal, began pushing his charges forward at a gallop. So it worked with them all, each band growing and converging with the next until fully five-hundred of the animals were thundering toward the area pre-designated by New Blade of Grass and Hawk. Where there might have been confusion, there was order. As the great herd began turning back on itself and quieting down in the untouched and lush fall forage, Little Bear Claw carried his report to a highly skeptical New Blade of Grass and to Hawk. Shaking their unadorned heads and setting their lips in grim, almost straight, lines, they told him to accompany them to the ever growing band of mounted warriors who, lances waving, sought the cause of the mighty disturbance.

"White-faced *seme*? One painted black for the scalp dance? In the company of our friends, the Shoshonis?" The eyes of the incredulous Tjolzhitsay seemed to bore right through Little Bear Claw as the head chief restrained his prancing, rearing war horse.

The animal was caught up in the growing excitement that had moved outward from the now-quieting herd. "And a woman with a child?"

Now Tjolzhitsay turned his elongated face so his eyes could lance Little Coyote, who had arrived with several well-marked horses for the warriors who had sent for them. Soon the approximately eighty warriors in the encampment were mounted, including Three Eagles, who spoke so all could hear.

"Little Bear Claw speaks truth, for I, too, saw these creatures from a greater distance. This strange sight has just now brought me back here. They seem to possess the guns which a few of us know, to our sorrow, some of our enemies possess, too. It would be well if New Blade of Grass would take Little Coyote toward these *seme*. Then, Little Coyote, come back quickly and tell us your thoughts." Tjolzhitsay nodded agreement with this chief who was his *i-sts-sókoi*, war friend dearer than a brother.

There was no time for Little Coyote to ponder why he was being sent. His pinto easily kept up with the horse of New Blade of Grass as both raced toward the hillside Little Bear Claw had pointed out. Soon Little Coyote discreetly had to restrain his eager mount lest it move ahead of the other. Near a fringe of trees fingering downward like the tip of a lancehead into the bowl, and out of effective arrow range and the guns Three Eagles had warned about, New Blade of Grass pulled up his horse. After quieting it, the warrior began closely observing the single file of mounted horsemen trailed by the pack animals and two-legged creatures walking behind them. All carried the strange, long war clubs Little Bear Claw had described. One of the pack animals had ears of a length never seen before. In the lead were two mounted figures who appeared to be the Shoshonis. Two more mounted figures were behind them. The leading Shoshone, long, gray hair held to his head by a wide, whitened, deer hide band, raised his arm and hand upward in the peace sign. Then he turned to wave his arm to encompass all who followed.

New Blade of Grass remained unresponsive, except to press one hand to each side of his head. He was expressing that his people were those called "Flatheads" because, unlike some of the people to the west, they did not get their heads misshaped at infancy, but kept their hair cut flat on top. When New Blade of Grass and Little Coyote saw the old Shoshone convey this information to the strangers by the same sign language, their attention shifted to the black face. This man was among the three directly behind the Shoshonis; he now had taken off his strange headpiece and was waving it in a friendly fashion.

"He wears the black paint for the scalp dance, but waves in a friendly way," New Blade of Grass muttered. "There is much I do not understand."

Before Little Coyote could reply, ponder or compare this situation with his vision on the peak, New Blade of Grass whirled his horse and began racing back to the encampment.

Tjolzhitsay and the assembled warriors became silent as the two scouts returned. New Blade of Grass reported quickly, quietly and completely.

The chief withdrew two pipes from cases handed up to him by an ancient and unmounted warrior. One pipe trailed the red feathers of war, the other the white feathers of peace.

"Which do you suggest I offer?" Tjolzhitsay's keen eyes again bored into Little Coyote.

Head bowed forward, chin almost on his chest, Little Coyote had been trying to sort out all the events connected with his vision. He hardly had been able to do so while racing forward with New Blade of Grass. As the head chief's gaze brought the young brave back to the now, he swallowed hard, hesitated, caught the unmoving face of his father, Running Buffalo Bull, then sat erect and spoke: "My poor vision is but a shadow with that of the great Shining Shirt, Chief Tjolzhitsay, but, like his, it told me, 'You will counsel the people not to war with them.'" Little Coyote swallowed hard, but the lump remained in his throat. Again, he stole a glance at his father. A quick hint of a smile flickered across Running Buffalo Bull's face and was gone as the lightning that brightens up the sky during the storm. Again, the son swallowed. This time the lump was gone, but he could feel his heart pounding. He lowered his hands and the reins of the pinto to rest on his thigh so the trembling he was certain was there would not be carried upward and accentuated for all to see at the tip of the ancient lance. Even so, the lance quivered, perhaps from the movement of the pinto.

"We will go." Tjolzhitsay nodded to three of the leading sub-chiefs. They would accompany him while all the others remained there to await his signal to come forward in peace, or to fight.

"There are three white robes, my chief, which would honor the three *seme*, or whatever."

Grunts of disapproval rose from the three sub-chiefs near Tjolzhitsay when Little Coyote spoke out. They subsided when Tjolzhitsay added, "And perhaps these *seme* will show no less honor to all my chiefs." There were a few moments of delay while the ancient pipe-carrier pulled the robes of honor from their bags.

"You will hold the horses." The head chief nodded at Little Coyote. "We will hurry. I do not like their closeness to the encampment, though New Blade of Grass says their horses are jaded."

The Flathead leaders rode to near the head of the long procession of strangers, whereupon the single long-eared animal bellowed in a voice that surely could match that of the most unearthly demon. So Little Coyote thought as he caught up from the respectful distance he had trailed behind the chiefs.

Tjolzhitsay signaled: *We are the Flatheads, the people who speak Salishan.*

"Lower all firearms!"

Little Coyote would remember these shouted words of one of the two men in the lead, who were followed by the two Shoshonis and the black man. That is what the unknowns were, men—two white, one black, and garbed in leather and other clothing.

Again the loud, commanding voice: "Lower all firearms!" The words were passed backward, repeated clearly again and yet again, until all the weapons were lowered. Some of the silent men leaned on them and began to spit much brown saliva, perhaps in respect.

The aged Shoshone stepped forward. He identified the younger Shoshone as his son, the woman as Sacagawea—Bird Woman. "We are glad we are here, Tjolzhitsay," the elder Shoshone said. "We chased the buffalo together when the Blackfeet contributed their winter meat after we drove them like the buffalo over the cliff."

"I remember well," Tjolzhitsay replied. "You are Big Hand from our friends the Shoshonis. We are pleased you have brought these strangers in peace."

"Yes. I speak for these white chiefs from land far away. They have called me Toby. They are called Clark and Lewis. Their chief of chiefs of the great and distant white nation has sent them to see your land and all that between where the sun rises and sets. He sends you gifts to pledge friendship and peace for as long as Sun will rise and set."

Big Hand spoke quietly to the younger Shoshone. He reached down into the bag and handed an object to his father. Big Hand picked up a broken piece of a tree, withdrew a metal knife from a sheath and quickly and easily cut large shavings from the stick. Carefully replacing the knife in the sheath, he handed it to Tjolzhitsay. The chief remained motionless, looking at the long file of men and horses. The woman called Sacagawea wandered from the group and sat down on the autumn grass to nurse her child. A man with much black hair on his face and wearing heavily beaded buckskin clothing sat near her, his gun across his lap. Big Hand accepted three more of the knives from his son for the three sub-chiefs.

Little Coyote nudged his pinto forward and accepted the knives. He wondered if the black mask he had seen in his vision represented this strange black man. Or, appearing as it had in the long procession of masks, did it represent this and future events as somber for his people as a scalp dance? The strangers had promised friendship and peace forever. Little Coyote turned his pinto to place himself behind the chiefs again. Only the future or other visions could tell.

Any illusions the chiefs and Little Coyote might have had

concerning the importance of the white leaders Clark and Lewis vanished when the black man declined to have one of the white robes placed over his shoulders. Instead, surprisingly, he spread it over the grass for the two white chiefs to sit on. They motioned for Tjolzhitsay and his sub-chiefs to be seated, too, and there soon was much passing back and forth of the pipe, filled at first with the white man's mixture, which proved far too strong. The chiefs mixed their bark and leaves with this tobacco the white men seemed to possess in good supply and that was of a quality far exceeding that of their own. Now Little Coyote saw several of the whites, who had moved near him to observe the ceremonies, bite off and chew great pieces of the twisted tobacco they carried in their clothing.

At length, the chief called Lewis placed a round and heavy object attached to a string over Tjolzhitsay's head. Big Hand haltingly explained that the clasped hands, the pipe and axe shown on it represented the peace the whites' chief of chiefs wished to endure forever. After much more talk, Tjolzhitsay welcomed the strangers to the encampment, explaining, as he noted the hungry look on all faces, there were but berries and the food made from roots in plentiful supply. The people, he added, soon would be leaving for the buffalo hunt that once again would assure food aplenty.

When the strangers had erected a few small lodges near the Flathead encampment and unloaded and set their pack horses to grazing, they walked into the village together. Two men were posted near their horses. They carried the guns. The others' guns were placed under strange blankets, which surely could not have come from an animal.

"These strangers resemble in some ways the Mandans, who live east beyond our buffalo grounds," Running Buffalo Bull told Little Yellow Bird and their son as the whites mingled with the Flatheads. All flocked around the visitors, noting particularly their white faces and mixed clothing. The Flathead women took special note of the tiny, high-quality beads of many colors that adorned the visitors' garments. The leaders tried to communicate, but only the sign language worked amid the noise: *Some of the*

Mandans have the white and red hair and blue eyes of some of these strangers. Running Buffalo Bull continued as his family also shook the hands in the strange way of the white men. *Perhaps at an earlier time the Mandans had such visitors, too.*

At length the chief named Lewis beckoned to the black stranger and a white one. "York," Lewis said, pointing to the black man, then "Colter," pointing to the white. Grinning, York and Colter removed their shirts. Amid the exclamations of most of the village, they walked a short distance away, followed by most of the people as young grouse follow the hen. While the less timorous Flatheads touched both the black and the white man to see if their colors were painted on, and both men chanted music to the delight of all, the white chiefs saw that their men were fed. Then with the help of Big Hand, his son, Bird Woman and a man called Drouillard, who proved to be very skilled with the language of signs, the visitors began trading for eleven horses. Drouillard explained they had lost some while working their way through the mountains.

That day and the next the whites also exchanged seven of their poorest horses, with added gifts, for fresh ones of the Flatheads. Soon the encampment was engaged in showing off mirrors, bells, paints, scissors, needles, rings, pins and other marvels for the women, especially, and a few small axes, knives and some pieces of the substance the strangers called "iron," from which had been fashioned Shining Shirt's cross. Most greatly prized were five long, iron lanceheads, one going to Tjolzhitsay, the others to the four warriors acknowledged by all to be the best buffalo-lancers. Each cost one fine horse. The chief called Clark evidently had noted Little Coyote's pinto when he had ridden out with the chiefs, because almost at once he held out a lancehead and pointed to the pinto. Little Coyote squeezed the pinto with his knees and she backed away.

Clearly, Little Coyote concluded, Clark and Lewis regarded each other as *slagt*, very good friends. Both seemed to share command in an easy way, directing their men at their tasks with a pointed arm, an easy clap on the back, a nod of the head. And there was much loud laughter among them all. Clark, he with hair the red color of the leaves after early frosts, smiled more often than Lewis. Clark once laughed with great delight when a small child squeezed between the legs of the many onlookers and, holding out his toy bow and arrow, indicated by gestures no one could mistake that he gladly would exchange it for the knife the white chief wore on his belt. Lewis reached into his garments and handed the child a short and bright piece of material, whereupon the child dropped his tiny weapons and, on uncertain, chubby legs, tottered to show the marvel to his mother.

Lewis, he with the more sober and thin face, conferred briefly with Clark, after which York, the black man, at their direction, brought the long-eared, horse-like creature into the gathering. Lewis led the animal before an impossibly high pile of firewood. He threw the lead rope over the pile and walked around it to grasp the rope. Now he could pull the creature to the very edge of the wood, as though trying to force the animal into the tangle. The creature reared back in protest and at length sat down. Again Lewis pulled hard, whereupon the animal wriggled its long ears back, raised its brown muzzle skyward, bared its grass-stained teeth and started to utter a protest that began like the sound of two big tree trunks slightly rasping together in the wind. Now the sound rose as though trees great and small, a whole forest of them, were scraping together, louder and louder, until the echoes of this unearthly sound resounded back and forth—truly a wonder that such a modest-sized animal could create sounds of such great measure and diversity. This sound set Lewis' great black dog to howling until the long-eared, braying creature ended its performance by rearing suddenly backward to wrench the rope from Lewis' grasp. The animal stood on all fours, then, with one defiant kick of both hind legs, rejoined its horse companions quietly feeding a short distance away. A laugh began in the sudden silence, then engulfed all the encampment.

Amid much good feeling and more bartering, the pipe-smoking and speeches began. As they progressed, Little Coyote noticed that both white chiefs marked down symbols on small leaves of material held together with elk hide.

Late that memorable evening of the arrival of the white men

in the valley and in the moon of the Harvest of Ripe Things, Little Coyote, while helping to guard the horses, observed the chief called Clark walking away from the dying light of the great campfires with one of the comeliest of the unmarried Flathead women. She wore a great length of new beads that glistened in the firelight.

Nine months later, in the moon of the Bitter Root, she would shorten the strand to provide a small necklace for their little son.

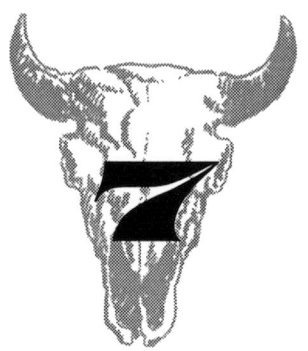

"D rouillard!"

As Little Coyote returned from his watch over the horses, he heard this sound from the chief, Lewis, become almost an echo as it passed from one white visitor to another. "Drewyer. Drewyer. Drewyer." A few of the visitors reluctantly were crawling from their blankets, hurriedly stretching, urinating, scratching their ribs and yawning in the early-morning cold before donning the rest of their clothing. Most were busily loading their old and the recently acquired horses in preparation for their trip along the north-flowing Ootlashoots River, then toward setting Sun.

"Drewyer! Drewyer! Drewyer!" Now even some of the Flathead children took up the cry as they darted in and out of the preparations, their bright eyes and merry voices examining and commenting over each new marvel they observed.

Soon they and their mothers also would be pulling down and packing their lodges if warming Sun would dry the heavy night dew from them. All would remember Drouillard's name long after that day.

As the entire encampment began bustling, there emerged from the nearest line of trees a horse laden with a fine large deer.

The dismounted rider was wearily walking alongside with one hand on the bridle, the other carrying a gun. Little Coyote raced his pinto toward the horse and man. Grinning, he offered his mount, signing he would walk the deer-laden animal into camp. Drouillard's dark face broke into a grin, too, dispelling the lines of fatigue. He gratefully straddled the pinto and hastened toward a white stranger who had hallooed "Drouillard!" and pointed toward the chiefs Clark and Lewis. A small band of children followed, chattering like the magpies in the neighboring trees. Soon they began observing the movements of the black man whom the entire encampment quickly had learned was a slave of Clark. York had stopped his busy packing of the white chiefs' equipment and was tying two small mirrors to a sharpened pole, one above the other. He tied the whitened skull of a big horn sheep to another pole. "Is he leaving a medicine offering?" the gathering crowd wondered aloud as he carried the poles away from the lodges and pounded them upright into the earth with a stone.

Drouillard, who had helped with the sign language during the long meetings the day before, rode over to Clark and Lewis. Part of the people followed him, too, for there was growing wonder among most of the encampment how he had killed the deer. By now Little Coyote had brought the horse and deer to Drouillard, who very quickly and skillfully cut the carcass in half. York carried the hind quarters to Tjolzhitsay.

Big Hand mounted his horse and communicated to the hushed encampment: "Drouillard comes from afar and has the blood of the Shawnee tribe. He is as skilled with the gun as with the language of signs. Thus he killed the deer which has been too far for your arrows."

York strode out to the poles and twisted the one with the mirrors until they caught morning Sun for all to see. Next, he opened a case and took from it one of the guns. The weapon differed from the others in that it had a round object firmly attached to its underside like the burl on a tree limb. Big Hand asked the people to stand, kneel or sit so all could see Drouillard and the two poles.

Drouillard carefully pointed the gun toward the poles. Those people nearest him heard a brief "ssst" like that of the first warning hiss of a snake. One of the mirrors broke into many pieces. Drouillard pushed something into the gun. Again, he pointed the weapon. Again the "ssst" and the second mirror shattered. When the great shout and puzzled voices stilled, he handed the marvel back to York and this time pointed the gun he had brought back from the deer hunt.

This time a great clap of noise and much smoke emerged from the gun. The pole supporting the ram's skull teetered and almost fell to the ground. York rushed forward to retrieve the skull, which he passed to Three Eagles. The skull had a new small hole midway between the gaping, hollow, eye sockets. The chief examined both the entry and exit holes of the bullet, then handed the skull to others to pass among the assemblage. Tjolzhitsay began talking earnestly with Big Hand. Drouillard, meanwhile, poured something down the throat of his gun from a polished horn he carried over his shoulder. Then he placed a small piece of buckskin and something else down the throat and pushed with the long stick carried under the gun.

The chief, Lewis, mounted his horse. With help from the woman Sacagawea, Drouillard and Big Hand, his words reached all the people; while at that time they could comprehend only part of what he said, they long would remember these words: "You have a Great Father called Jefferson. He is the chief of all the chiefs and of the people. He has made a great trade with a very distant people called 'French.' Now this land where you and the other peoples live is the great chief's land. He cares for his children, all the people here and there." Lewis pointed in all directions. "He has sent us to know you, to find ways to help you, even if he must use the thunder sticks called 'guns' for your protection. Traders will follow us to bring goods to exchange for furs. We wish for all to dwell in peace. And now we depart in peace to the Lolo trail and the great salt water."

Lewis removed his fur cap from his slightly balding head, pushed his knife more deeply into its beaded sheath and slung his powder horn over his neck and shoulder. He pointed toward the Ootlashoots River and the tiny cavalcade began stringing out in that direction in company with several experienced warriors Tjolzhitsay had named as a token of honor. They would accompany the white men downriver to the fork, then rejoin the buffalo hunters. As the explorers' party began moving more quickly, Little Coyote, still marveling over Drouillard's performance, watched Big Hand conversing animatedly with Tjolzhitsay. At length the Shoshone pointed north and west and signed that with enemies about, a journey there and back would take more than a moon. Both men dismounted and Big Hand traced what appeared to be a crude map in the moist soil. Then he both said and signed "Farewell" and sped away on his horse to the head of the column of visitors, now entering the trees.

The head chief's face was grave, indeed, when he mounted his horse. He rode to Thunder Voice, spoke briefly with him, then the two warriors each spoke to another sub-chief. In a short time they had summoned all the warriors to the same flat ground where Drouillard had performed his wonders with the air gun and his rifle.

"The people will leave for the buffalo grounds while Sun is in the sky," Tjolzhitsay said. "We cannot delay, for our friends the Shoshonis soon will meet us over the path through the mountains. We must share our strength with theirs should we meet the Blackfeet near the rivers of the three forks, or even beyond to the waters of the yellow stone."

A low murmur arose from the warriors. A few of the younger braves who had participated in their first buffalo war dance only a few moons earlier shook their lances above their heads. Little Coyote stood at the outer edge of the gathering close to his friend Little Bear Claw and continued to nurture his strong hope that he would go on the hunt, not be kept in the valley yet again with the forces that must remain.

Tjolzhitsay looked for special warriors.

"We have agreed who will remain in the valley," the head chief said. "The others will go, except for New Blade of Grass and the three warriors he has spoken to, and . . ." The head chief's keen eyes swept the assemblage. ". . . Little Bear Claw, who has much success handling horses, and . . ." Here the chief's eyes caught Little Coyote, who was almost overwhelmed with a mixture of apprehension, bewilderment and disappointment. " . . . Little Coyote, whose medicine is strong, which it must be for what lies ahead. I will speak to them while Thunder Voice, who you elected as war chief for the hunt, starts the others to the buffalo grounds." The chief urged his war pony to the north side of the warriors, who now began hurrying toward the women, children, horses and baggage. New Blade of Grass and the five others mounted their horses and followed their chief until they were some distance away from the excited hub-bub of the encampment. Tjolzhitsay dismounted near some packed earth and the others did likewise, seating themselves in a small circle to hear their chief.

"These white men," Tjolzhitsay began. "The stories of our people have told us there are others like them in the greater world around us. Shining Shirt told the council they exist, though he had never seen them while alive. Their names are in our stories about the white men who came among the people in our smaller world long ago, and not as long ago: Verendrye, Larocque, Courtin. And Torn Moccasin, now dead, told us of the white man, Thompson, who had guns and spoke to him when he visited our allies, the Kutenais, farther north. Torn Moccasin talked of the guns. So have our Iroquois brothers who have fought the Blackfeet with us and said we should seek guns and the white men in black robes, who have much power with the Good Spirit. Before Big Hand's departure, I asked him if this Clark and Lewis had traded good guns to the Blackfeet, for that would be even harder for us. He said they had seen no Blackfeet as they came through the land where the Blackfeet live. These white men had no guns to trade, else Big Hand would have obtained one. He said that four of our friends, the Shoshonis, have guns. We know to our sorrow that some of the Blackfeet already have a few guns, as have some of the Crows, the Mandans and others. They are not as good guns as Drouillard used. The Iroquois said there are good and not-so-good guns, just as there are straight and crooked arrows. But they are guns. We are few in number. Now we, too, must have guns, the best guns! And the Black Robes. I was told they are close to the Good Spirit. Shining Shirt, who was close to the Good Spirit, has gone to join Him in the sand hills. I will look into this talk about the Black Robes.

"Our people's stories tell us long ago Coyote brought us the fire. Now perhaps in a somewhat different way he will bring us the guns."

For the second time that early morning, Tjolzhitsay looked hard at Little Coyote. With the fine knife Clark and Lewis had given him, the head chief drew lines on the earth showing their valley, their river, and, ever north and sometimes slightly west, other rivers and the great Lake of the Flatheads. Beyond that, the lines showed yet another series of rivers and the great lake of their Pend d'Oreille kinsmen, then other long lakes called "The Arrows" in the land of the Kutenais.

"Know this well," Tjolzhitsay told New Blade of Grass. He jabbed the knife point three times into the outline of the last lake. "If you do not find Thompson or his people here to trade for the guns, you will go ever north until you do. You must return with as many guns as three pack loads of our furs will bring, for Big Hand told me that is what the Shoshonis traded for their guns." The chief worriedly shook his head. "There are few furs left among our people."

For a short time longer the group discussed what made the guns speak and how this black sand, or "powder" as white man called it, was measured and how the round ball of "lead" was both cast and loaded. There would be need for all these in the trade, and the flints that started the deadly fire, though the group was certain they could chip these, or even use a broken arrowhead.

Tjolzhitsay looked toward the encampment. All seemed ready to depart, though a few women still scurried about the pack animals. Children and dogs ran about helter-skelter with excitement.

An old warrior led the three fur-laden horses to the small group.

"You, Little Coyote." Tjolzhitsay rubbed his elongated chin with his left thumb and index finger, finally pinching them together and pulling the lower lip outward. For the first time the strong, commanding voice became gentle with the youth. "Your medicine is strong. Perhaps you do have a measure of Shining Shirt's *sumesh*. Yours is a sacred mission, for you must go to Shining Shirt's burial place and remove the bag of yellow stones we hung with his other few possessions under the platform in the burial tree."

Little Coyote felt himself stiffen involuntarily as the great chief said he was to break a taboo even *he* would not dare break. If Tjolzhitsay saw the reaction, he gave no sign: "If you possess part of Shining Shirt's *sumesh*, you can employ it as you will to perform this important task. Some of the traders to the north favor our enemies, the Blackfeet, in the trade for guns—perhaps out of fear, perhaps because there are so many Blackfeet with the furs, many of which they take from others. Some Blackfeet feel they are so numerous and strong they need no guns. Big Hand told me that the white man prefers yellow stones over furs or most other possessions. How much he prefers them over the guns, I do not know. You will carry the yellow stones; you will make the trade. New Blade of Grass has agreed to this for we do not know if anyone else should test his medicine by handling the yellow stones or exchanging them for the guns to help the people. Do you understand your task? Coyote brought us the fire. Little Coyote will bring us the guns that work with a different kind of fire."

With great effort Little Coyote put this fearful task of taking the yellow stones from the grave as far back into his mind as time would allow. He needed to think first about how he would trade for the guns so he could ask the chief for guidance.

"I . . ." Little Coyote wiped his sweating palms on his leggings. "I do not know the value of the guns. I had thought Shining Shirt's yellow stones worthless." *Help me, Shining Shirt,* he implored silently. *Lend me your wisdom.* "Perhaps Tjolzhitsay . . ." Little Coyote faltered, then spoke quickly for he could see a hint of impatience on the harried leader's long face. "Perhaps the trade should be made first with the furs so we can obtain the most guns with those, and I could learn from New Blade of Grass as he makes these trades. Later, we can show the yellow stones. Then, if truly white man likes the stones, as Big Hand said, we can bargain for even more and perhaps better guns."

"Little Coyote is well-named," the chief answered approvingly. New Blade of Grass signed his approval, too. "Bury some of the yellow stones at the base of the tree. Then if white man asks if you have more of them, you can in truth say you have. We have learned in our trades with others of our friends that they sometimes are more generous in the exchange if they know that more of the same trade goods will follow at a later time." Tjolzhitsay looked at New Blade of Grass and said, "You will bring the guns to the buffalo camp, should you succeed soon."

The head chief mounted his war pony. The conference had ended, as had his authority until the people would return from the buffalo grounds. Thunder Voice would be in full command. New Blade of Grass took the lead rope of the pack horses from the hand of the old warrior and began moving northward. The others raced to the encampment, eager to get what gear they would need for this great adventure. Little Bear Claw would bring Little Coyote's equipment to him. All would catch up with New Blade of Grass as soon as possible and bring him two more of his better horses should there be a need for them on the long trip.

Less eagerly, Little Coyote nudged his pony into a trot toward the burial site. What would be his explanation to the spirit of Shining Shirt?

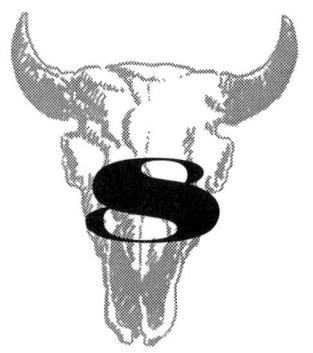

L ittle Coyote's pinto quickly carried him to where the breeze flowing down the mountainside brought the odor of the dead horses at Shining Shirt's burial place. Little Coyote followed that until a large flock of ravens rose heavily into the sky. As he dismounted and began clambering up the cliff to a stone shelf, the great black birds ponderously flapped their wings to reach the torrent of air flowing over the escarpment high above him. Then they soared in wide circles, cawing down their displeasure at the two-legged intruder who was seated now and observing the straight-trunked pine trees that held the burial platform.

Four-legged scavengers had been at work here while the excitement of the arrival of the white men had displaced the mournful thoughts of the people and their *yes-tcoótsen*, or lament for dead Shining Shirt. Skillful hands had woven protective willows resembling a bony rib cage over the wrapped figure so only time could enter there, and the spirit might come and go as it pleased. While a pallid horned lark climbed repeatedly into the sky then floated downward, filling this place of death with its sweet song, Little Coyote discerned the buckskin bag holding the yellow stones hanging motionless from one of the projecting platform poles. Next to the bag, a quiver of arrows swayed gently in the breeze, long, decorative fringes dancing this way and that.

Little Coyote raised his eyes toward Sun, which for the first time that exciting day was starting to hide in a large, fleecy cloud that had sailed in from the west.

"The people need the yellow stones, Shining Shirt. Does your generosity continue? Our chief has decreed I must obtain the stones. Do you approve? Show me a sign. Do you need them in the land of perpetual summer, where surely you now have at last found the company of your beloved wife? Our need is great and . . ." Little Coyote blurted the last words as Sun disappeared behind the cloud and the land darkened: "I must hurry."

As Little Coyote spoke thus to Shining Shirt's spirit, he heard high above him a cacophony of startled and angry caws of the overfed ravens and the challenging "kleeek-kick-ick-ick" screams of a pair of white-headed eagles. A stricken raven with one fluttering wing extended outward began spiraling toward earth, a victim of one of the eagles. Though grossly overfed, the other black birds fought back so there were no more casualties; nor did the eagle retrieve its victim in the air. Instead, the raven fell with a final jarring "caw" below the stone where Little Coyote sat. Now one of the eagles, free at last from the counter-attacking ravens well above the heavy wind currents, plummeted downward and set its talons in the bird. It beat its wings northward with its prey as Sun's strength conquered the cloud at last and the earth brightened.

"I am grateful for the sign, Shining Shirt," Little Coyote said aloud as he began scrambling downward. "I, too, will travel northward with this gift from you." Soon he was stretching on his toes and lifting the heavy buckskin bag from the projecting pole. Moments later, he, too, was leaving this place of death, holding tightly to the heavy bag and hoping he had not hidden too many of the yellow stones at the base of one of the burial trees.

He kept his pinto at an easy trot down the main trail paralleling the river. The signs showed that New Blade of Grass was setting a pace that would keep his party behind that of Clark and Lewis. Soon Little Coyote noticed that the smaller group had taken a seldom-used side-trail.

"He is a wise leader, that New Blade of Grass," the young brave murmured to the pinto. The mare pricked up her ears and daintily began high-stepping over some of the deadfall littering the trail. The larger group would be more apt to attract any roving enemies; Tjolzhitsay had cautioned against disclosing the purpose of the group's mission—indeed, had encouraged complete secrecy, if possible.

A horse whinnied ahead. Little Coyote tightened his grasp on his lance and curbed the pinto's eager stride. Soon the trail began angling downward toward a creek where a waterfall with a large pool prevented the trout from going any farther from the river. Cold Wind, youngest of the warriors selected for the northward journey, quietly stepped from behind a large tree, relaxed his bow, signaled a greeting and waved Little Coyote on. A moment more and he entered a scene of intense activity.

"You have the yellow stones?" New Blade of Grass rose from the *sinska:ye*, or drying rack, where he was smoking many large *pis*, trout, to preserve them. He held out his hand for the bag and with the other pointed to the fish and said, "Eat."

Little Coyote watched the warrior pour the yellow stones onto a large piece of bark that recently had served as a fish platter. The young warrior tentatively hefted the stones, then one by one dropped them back into the bag.

"Good," he said, and handed the bag to Little Coyote, who silently agreed both about his fish and the accomplishment thus far of his mission.

Soon he, too, had fashioned a noose from several woven horsehairs removed from his pinto's tail. He tied the noose to a short pole, then found a likely place alongside the pool. Lying on his belly, he began sliding the noose over the tail of a large trout, over its fat body and just behind the gills. With a quick upward tug he set the noose behind the gills and lifted the wriggling trout onto the bank. He gutted and split the fish and carried it to the rack. There, New Blade of Grass was feeding just the right proportion of dry and green willow into the coals to partially cook, dry and smoke what evidently were to be provisions for part of their journey. New Blade of Grass set one of the party to constructing yet another rack, so plentiful were the fish. As deep shadows crept in with a growing chill, they all ate well from the fish. They ended their meal with handsful of serviceberries and huckleberries.

Both Little Coyote and Little Bear Claw took turns at tending the fish racks as a cold breeze began moving down the mountain. New Blade of Grass had told them all that they would continue their northward trek before dawn; he warned that he expected a fast and watchful pace.

When his turn came to sleep, Little Coyote rolled gratefully into the light and warm rabbit-skin blanket Little Bear Claw had brought from the encampment with his friend's pack. Tired, his belly well-filled with the delicious fish and berries, Little Coyote lay on his back for a time and pondered his rapid change of fortune and stature within the tribe. He watched the tip of the tall pine tree under which he was lying tentatively sway like a giant finger pointing from one sparkling star to another. It was as though the tree tip were trying in the breeze to select the star to which it finally would point for the remainder of the night. Just as easily as the Good Spirit had selected him for these events, it could have selected any one of the numerous youths his own age who had sought their visions during the past few moons.

He yawned. Would sleep claim him before he had found an answer to his puzzlement? He heard the barks of coyotes that were somewhere between his party and that of the white men far below. He groped into his leather pack, past the bag of yellow stones and the other blanket. Yes, his coyote tail was there, the bony end securely sewn between a doubled piece of soft leather to which Little Yellow Bird had fastened a stout, but small, leather thong. As Little Coyote put the loop over his head and felt the hair against his chest, the coyote chorus below strengthened. One voice rose in a louder, clearer call above all the rest. For a while only that voice reached up the mountainside. Then other voices, weaker, more uncertain about the proper pitch, began once more to join in a somewhat discordant, then more harmonious, chorus. The breeze quieted and the tip of the tall pine tree pointed directly at the brightest star in Little Coyote's limited view of the sky. As a full moon rose yellow and bright above the mountain on the distant side of the great valley, Little Coyote's thoughts began flickering from his acknowledgment that among animals and man there must be leaders, to his wondering if there was an augury in the fact that he had chosen a sleeping site that put him slightly apart from the rest of his people here, and, therefore, between them and the more distant white men?

He snuggled more deeply into his blanket. His last conscious thought shifted inexplicably to the all-pervading sound of the waterfall. The waterfall provided much cold water and food for the trout, he mused, yet it trapped them from any further progression up the swift waters and made them ready prey to those who were hungry.

The single loud crack of a broken tree branch awakened Little Coyote, Cold Wind and the other two warriors—Bright Fire and Has Many Horses. Little Bear Claw evidently remained on guard. New Blade of Grass threw the two sticks into the fire below five trout sizzling on one of the now badly charred rocks. Dark clouds filled the sky, threatening rain or snow.

When the men had eaten, New Blade of Grass signaled for Little Bear Claw to bring the horses. Little Bear Claw could eat his fish as they moved over the trail. The leader grasped the lead rope of his two extra mounts, then spoke: "We will follow this trail until it bends back toward the river. Then we will follow the mountain ridges ever northward, remaining always in the high country but skirting the trees for easier traveling and for constant watch for any enemies. Has Many Horses will move far ahead on one side and Bright Fire on the other."

Has Many Horses rose from his squatting position near the fire. He threw his fish bones into the dying flame and stripped dry leaves from a nearby bush to wipe off the oil. A tall man of perhaps twenty-six summers, he was known for his quiet manner, shrewdness and bravery. His ways had made him one of the richest horse-owners in the valley. A single-handed raid several summers earlier at this north end of the valley had earned him many horses and a new name. It also had earned him the eternal hatred of the Blackfeet raiding party, which he had left with two less warriors and the inconvenient and humiliating task of traveling on foot back to their country in the buffalo grounds. Now he tested his bow string, pulled a heavier elkskin shirt from his bag and exchanged it for the lighter deerskin he was wearing.

"We will travel without stop until we see where the two rivers meet," New Blade of Grass told them. "Perhaps Has Many Horses will be waiting there with a fat deer so we can save the fish and roots for harder days ahead." Has Many Horses urged his horse up the creek bank and soon was out of sight.

Bright Fire, he of perhaps thirty-four summers, an ever-ready smile and with great attention to detail, tested his bow string. Then he carefully closed, but did not tie, the quiver flap against the threatening weather. He dug his moccasin heels into his horse's ribs to set the animal climbing upward at an angle. New Blade of Grass and his horses set off on the dimming trail and Cold Wind brought up the rear. Little Bear Claw grasped the lead rope of the pack animals; at times he turned around partway to slap them sharply on the rump with the haft of his lance when they sought to escape their duty by wandering in different directions from that set by the more hard-working lead mare.

"I will take the lead rope when your arm tires," Little Coyote told his friend. Later, he did so, and he, too, had to tap the more obstreperous trailing pack horse. It had begun pawing the gravel of a shallow creek they were crossing as though in preparation for taking a quick roll in the water.

Thus the long day passed from rising Sun till late afternoon, each member of the party caught up in his own thoughts and duties as he absorbed the information provided by the sounds of the wind and the movements of the birds, squirrels and other small creatures of the land. As a diversion, Little Coyote began learning the important language of signs. Though none of his companions was expert, each had something to contribute as the varying duties of the trail brought them in contact with him. He had much time to himself to practice that day and long after.

The threatening rain held off until just before darkness. Try as he might, Little Coyote could not see the confluence of the two rivers. He knew the rivers lay ahead because New Blade of Grass stopped until the cavalcade caught up with him. Then, the growing wind tossing his long braids of hair, New Blade of Grass pointed his lance toward a grove of cottonwood trees between two small hills.

Rain was running down Little Coyote's back and chest and streaming off his pinto when he handed the lead rope back to Little Bear Claw. At the signal of New Blade of Grass, Little Coyote moved toward a small, rocky outcrop slightly above the grove.

"You will watch," New Blade of Grass told him, then trotted his horse toward the trees.

Shivering, Little Coyote tethered his pinto to feed in a small swale and crawled under an overhanging rock. He wanted to change into his dry set of buckskins and huddle there. Instead, he picked up his lance and moved from one side of the outcrop to the other, looking, always looking, listening, smelling in all directions. As the rain continued to fall, he could hear tiny streamlets of water running off the outcrop. An occasional small gust of wind brought the sounds of trees rustling; once he heard rodents scurrying through the grass they patiently had cut and hauled to dry for winter food at the protective base of the rocks. He could smell the mustiness of older hay abandoned when spring had brought green grasses, the droppings of the four-legged harvesters of many generations and, more pleasing, the scent of rain on the trees lining the hillside.

Soon a new smell, that of roasting venison, drifted up to him. As the young warrior continued to move and watch and shiver, he visualized his companions standing under the canopy of protective boughs in dry clothing and holding long, pointed sticks with thin slices of venison meat and tallow impaled on them. He imagined the meat sizzling and dripping grease into the hot coals. His stomach growled like a young puppy above the sounds of the rain, and yet he watched. When would he be relieved? Was he forgotten? Now the rain ceased, and he was glad. He moved more rapidly, almost soundlessly, to warm his body, yet listened and looked until once-familiar bushes and rocks he had imprinted on his mind in the dying daylight seemed to become fearsome, creeping creatures, two-legged, four-legged, moving toward him or the encampment and bent on their destruction.

At length he gratefully heard Cold Wind's signal of four short cheeps of a dispirited and lonely bird. A moment later the warrior silently walked up behind Little Coyote and handed him warm slices of roasted venison impaled on the burnt-off end of a stick and wrapped in large leaves. That he had put a delicious piece of fat on both sides of the meat showed his generosity.

Delicious as was this fat and meat, Little Coyote savored even more the friendly clap on the back administered by his companion to set him off, temporary misery forgotten, in the direction of the camp of all the warriors.

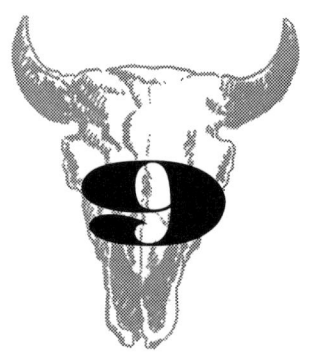

"This snow. I do not like it. It should not be falling in the moon of the Harvest of Ripe Things." New Blade of Grass had called in all the gun-seekers except Cold Wind. That warrior was scouting behind them along a high ridge from which they had viewed the southern end of the Lake of the Flatheads. They had seen the lake before the rain, which had been falling for five days, had changed to large, wet flakes.

New Blade of Grass immediately had lengthened the lead ropes on the two spare horses he was bringing. He had told Little Bear Claw to do the same with the pack horses and to have Little Coyote trail one of those.

"There will be less following in line," New Blade of Grass explained. "It will be harder to tell from tracks in the snow if we are a party of six warriors and five other horses, or of eleven warriors."

New Blade of Grass' naturally long face was longer yet, the worry lines creasing it below the lips and on the lower cheeks. He shook his head; water from the melted snow dropped to the floor of the deep gouge Nature had carved into the side of the limestone cliff. His moccasined foot nudged another piece of damp wood into the fire. Again he spoke: "There are not enough of us to ride boldly in the open, and any enemies can follow our tracks in the snow. They would look for us here, knowing that small parties would stay near the trees on the hills."

The warrior chewed contemplatively on one of the last pieces of the deer meat Has Many Horses had brought in the second day of their travels.

"We will continue to the Lake of the Flatheads to see if the trader is there," he said. "I believe because the snows threaten, he might not wish to be there so far from other traders and their fort. I also believe that we would find the guns have been traded. No . . ." New Blade of Grass took another bite of venison. ". . . I believe we would save many days of travel and be more certain of getting the guns if we would not stay and search at the Lake of the Flatheads, but go immediately west toward the Lake of the Pend d'Oreille, then follow the eastern shore northward there to reach the Lake of the Kutenais. There we would not risk so much, for they are our friends and might know about traders. Here . . ." He swallowed the meat and began to speak more forcefully. " . . .there are Blackfeet, perhaps hurrying to reach the land of the buffalo and to hunt them with their other tribesmen before the long snows come. Yes, I believe there will be more traders near the Lake of the Kutenais in the place called Canada."

New Blade of Grass was correct on two points: The gun-seekers did not find the traders at the southern end of the Lake of the Flatheads, which they reached in the early evening of the seventh day of their quest. Also, the Blackfeet found them by cutting, then following, their trail through the rapidly melting snow. Cold Wind did not die from the two musket balls fired almost simultaneously by two evidently overeager or befuddled Blackfeet braves. The shots alerted the Flathead warriors. The arrow protruding from Cold Wind's chest after penetrating his back and right lung did have what the people would come to call *snululemús'sel,* iron arrow point. The dying warrior gasped out his misadventure and more blood after racing to his people.

"There are five Blackfeet," he said. "One carries my arrow

in his thigh. I saw them find and study our tracks." Cold Wind coughed, feebly staying the hand of Bright Fire, who sought to pull the arrow through. "Two followed the tracks. The others circled back to kill me. You will see. I spat my blood inside my shirt, not on the snow. They do not know I am dead. Thus, they will think our party larger. Two had the guns." A smile creased his ashen face. "They use them foolishly."

Now he began chanting part of his death song he had prepared long ago, the words rising and falling almost to the tempo of the waves breaking on the rocky lake shore:

> *I am Cold Wind.*
> *Good Spirit, judge me.*
> *I do not fear to die.*
> *I did not cheat or lie.*
> *Good Spirit, judge me.*
> *I obeyed my chiefs.*
> *Good Spirit, judge me.*
> *I did not deal with thieves.*
> *Good Spirit, judge me . . .*

"There is more I must tell." Cold Wind interrupted his song. His voice was even weaker now, but strengthened as he tried to sort out and convey the full message. "The Blackfeet studied our tracks. They drank deeply from a strange pot. They struck at each other to hold the pot. To drink the most from it. They could not ride their horses well. I do not understand this. Yet it is significant. I am sure. They were foolish."

He resumed his death song as his companions sought to understand the import of all he had told them:

> *. . . I cared for young and old.*
> *Good Spirit, judge me.*
> *And when my deeds are told*
> *Good Spirit, help me*
> *to ever-warm lands go.*
> *Good Spirit, let me*
> *Hunt sacred buffalo.*
> *Good Spirit, let me . . .*

Soon the living Flatheads heard only the sound of the

breaking waves.

New Blade of Grass tied Cold Wind's pony near the large boulder against which the group had placed his dying friend. With his new knife he cut the animal's throat with three quick, ripping stabs.

"There will be a time to mourn," he said. For a moment he looked far, far away, almost as though he could see his friend hurrying his pony to the boundaries of the country of perpetual summer. Now he looked at Little Coyote: "Yours is the swiftest horse. You will ride slowly along the trees on the hillside toward the Blackfeet. To avoid ambush, do not enter the trees unless necessary. We must know where they are. When you learn, return to tell us. If you race from them, do so between these two large rocks. We will meet them there."

In the remaining twilight, they began preparing a more protected camp.

Little Coyote boldly followed the tracks of Cold Wind's pony uphill for a time, then, as he neared the wooded portions of the ridge, less boldly but more vigilantly began watching every tree and rock that possibly could conceal a warrior. As the darkness began claiming the trees, then the brush and the open land, he despaired making any movement at all because whatever he watched began taking on new dimensions. He halted his pinto and, head dropping somewhat, considered his situation. Perhaps more wisely, he carefully should pick his way parallel to and more than an arrow's throw away from the trees. If he would have to race away, he would know his retreat route. Yes, he would do that. He returned the arrow to the quiver and the bow to his back. The pinto moved restlessly, her ears pivoting, her muzzle pointed obliquely up the hill. Now Little Coyote also could smell the smoke. It was not that of a small, protected fire like that of his party, but a large one. As he nudged the pinto forward, he saw the reflected light on the nearest scrub pines.

A trick, or more of their foolishness Cold Wind had spoken about? Only a child would move directly toward the fire, knowing the enemy would lie in wait elsewhere. No, he would not—

The sounds of two guns roared from the direction of the fire. Little Coyote felt himself move from sudden fear; he could feel his pinto's muscles ripple, but she, too, stood fast. Another thought attached itself momentarily to others he had been having since acquiring the animal. Her name? Perhaps he could name her Not Afraid of Guns. That vagrant thought vanished as he heard yet another gun boom, then shouts, from the direction of the fire.

He turned the pinto and retraced his route for a short distance, then pointed her into the trees and up the slope far enough that he would be above the fire. As he closed the distance, the loud voices, angry at times, were broken by more sounds of gunfire. Will my friends think me dead? Little Coyote now could look down on the fire, which was throwing huge sparks into the night air.

One Blackfeet lay on the damp ground well inside the circle of light. He fumblingly and ineffectually pulled at his upper leg, then flopped over, seemingly spent, like the trout Little Coyote and his companions had caught at the waterfall. Then he seemed to gain strength and did it again. Two other Blackfeet were reloading their guns, almost falling over as they did so. Two other warriors were fighting to hold a pot. One would seize it from the other and drink greedily, only to have the pot wrenched from his unsteady grasp. Then the other would attempt to drink before the pot would be torn from his grasp, too. Now the two warriors with guns fired them into the air, the twin plumes of flame erupting from the smoke that rolled outward and upward to that of the large campfire. When a vagrant breeze brought the smell to Little Coyote, it had a bite like no smoke he could remember. Under his legs he felt the pinto's barrel expand in preparation for a mighty sneeze. The sneeze erupted before he could leap off and try to stop it. Despairingly, he looked at the Blackfeet. They ignored it! Indeed, the two warriors dropped their guns and joined in the struggle for the pot, sometimes stepping onto another who rolled close to the fire.

Clearly, all were foolish—and highly vulnerable, Little Coyote thought—if his companions were willing to strike in the darkness.

He turned the pinto and carefully walked her through the trees, then raced her downhill toward the other Flatheads.

New Blade of Grass and Bright Fire soon were looking down on the same scene with Little Coyote, except now the strange pot for which the Blackfeet had been struggling also lay on the ground.

"They act as horses that have eaten the crazy grass," Bright Fire murmured.

"And we will act like the wary wolf attracted by the fire," New Blade of Grass replied. He dismounted and removed three arrows from his quiver. Bright Fire did the same.

"You will hold the horses and be ready to race with us if there is a trap we cannot see now," New Blade of Grass instructed Little Coyote. "As on the trail in our valley only a few days ago, we must kill before making strikes, for we cannot risk even one getting away to imperil our mission." Then the two warriors were gone.

Loud, quarrelsome voices reached up to Little Coyote, screening any noises his companions might be making. Once again the young warrior had been left holding the horses. As he momentarily contemplated this fact, the certainty grew that the transition from youth to maturity, while seemingly an interminable process in younger, carefree days, did not occur in making one great step in one day from one condition to the other. Rather, he must welcome the diversity of his activities, perform them well and, if the opportunities presented themselves, even make suggestions or take reasoned actions beyond those expected of him. Well, he had been doing this, successfully mostly, even if once again he was holding the horses. He would do that well! The movements at the fire ended his contemplation. One warrior unsteadily threw more wood onto the fire; then, as sparks flew upward, he fell and moved no more. Two of his companions tried to spring to their feet. Both fell over. A fourth reached his feet and, weaving unsteadily, fumbled for one of the carelessly dropped guns. Little Coyote saw that warrior's body stiffen once, relax, then stiffen again as he fell to his side. *He has taken two arrows,* Little Coyote thought, then he continued to watch while

Bright Fire stood over the Blackfeet carrying Cold Wind's arrow.

There is little time on our journey for the torture for the loss of Cold Wind, Little Coyote thought. He was correct. In a moment the wounded Blackfeet received a more expertly placed arrow.

New Blade of Grass stood erect, faced the fire so the light would reflect on him and signaled: *Come!*

All the party was considerably enriched by the extermination of the Blackfeet. In addition to the horses and scalps, they acquired three guns, much powder, lead and flints. Though all were tired, New Blade of Grass insisted they master these new guns at once.

"There has been much firing of these guns. When Sun appears . . ." He looked at the sky. Heavy clouds scudded eastward, now and then revealing a waning moon. ". . . we will travel quietly."

So, while the night lengthened, and in the flickering light of their own enlarged fire, all the warriors, remembering as best they could Drouillard's demonstration with his gun, mastered the intricacies of measuring the powder and ramming a lead ball down the barrel over the deadly black sand, of priming the pan and adjusting or replacing the flint. In the graying light they learned the range of the musket balls and the penetration power. In both of these they were exceedingly disappointed, but "There is a lesson here," New Blade of Grass conceded. "These are not the good guns the warriors of Clark and Lewis carried and Drouillard used. So, there are good guns and some that are not so good as the arrows. Yet, their thunder will frighten the weak-hearted. We will trade only for the good guns. The Blackfeet carried no patches to put over the ball before pushing it down the barrel. Perhaps the poorer guns do not require it. We must ask about this."

New Blade of Grass listened attentively as Little Coyote explained how the strong smoke of the guns had made his pony, Not Afraid of Guns, sneeze. He agreed there was a lesson there.

There remained one more lesson to learn that long night. As the warriors had sorted out their booty, Little Coyote thoughtfully had sniffed the two strange pots over which the

Blackfeet had fought. One was empty. The other, which carelessly had been tossed onto the ground to roll near the fire, still had its plug and held perhaps a cupped handful of the liquid. It had burned the young brave's tongue when he carefully had tasted it.

"There is a craziness in the pot," he warned, "yet the Blackfeet sought it."

"And died!" New Blade of Grass added. He then motioned they would leave.

As the group set out, Little Coyote carried a Blackfeet shield that had resisted the musket ball when used as a target. The tough buffalo bull rawhide carried the Blackfeet warrior's painted symbol of a lightning flash and a buffalo head when Little Coyote picked it up. He covered the old symbols with a Blackfeet brave's blood; when that had dried, he hurriedly had used his own white paint to draw on a little coyote. Though the Flatheads' spirits were low that Cold Wind had died, they lifted somewhat when Sun rose and melted much of the remaining snow. Now they pondered their goal that lay ahead, perhaps this time at the Lake of the Pend d'Oreille.

Sun rose and set five times during the westward trip of the Flatheads to that lake, and another six times as they broke into two groups to search for the trader, Thompson, or any other, for that matter. Twice they sighted and avoided camps of the Pend d'Oreille, more to preserve the secrecy of their mission and to use the continuing good weather to advantage than to avoid the time-consuming festivities these friends would insist on.

Finally, tired and discouraged, they sat around a fire inside a crude cabin/fort the traders evidently had abandoned, at least for the winter. Bright Fire was on guard near the confluence of the two streams flowing into the lake. The fort was between the streams on the flat and cleared ground.

Has Many Horses had found the cabin in company with Little Bear Claw; he had sent the younger brave for the others.

"I found this, a strange pipe, between two trees as I scouted around this fort before approaching it," Has Many Horses said.

He arose from his sitting position and in two strides of his long legs reached his leather bag. He held aloft a stubby, white, clay pipe resembling those the Clark and Lewis party had smoked. Has Many Horses now made his longest speech of the journey: "The pipe was lost as a man on hands and knees was smoothing over, hiding, the hole between the trees where the trader cached those goods he did not trade this season. There are many marvels there, but no guns. I covered them again—carefully." He grinned, the firelight reflecting from the strong teeth. "I did not lose my pipe." He held aloft his own long-stemmed pipe, the bowl carved in the likeness of a horse. "They plan to return here."

New Blade of Grass nodded in agreement: "Else they would not have cleared the trees with much work from around this fort. The logs they piled near the fort will be used to strengthen and make it larger another time. I fear that our Pend d'Oreille friends, or the Blackfeet, traded for their guns, and there will be more guns brought here. We must hurry to obtain the best ones at their source."

So it was that once again the Flatheads began their journey, this time up the east shore of the Lake of the Pend d'Oreille, then north up the Kutenai River toward the Lake of the Kutenais in the land called Canada. They were tired now. At times this land was not fruitful and they ate of the smoked trout. Should they have to go on much longer, they would not be able to return to their people in time to participate in the buffalo hunt. And the land soon would be very cold.

Then one dismal, rainy day the Flathead party stood at the southern tip of the Lake of the Kutenais watching the waves rolling white onto the shore, their froth up to, and sometimes enveloping, the hooves of their dispirited horses.

"Which shore do we follow to find the traders, Little Coyote? Can you tell us?"

With water running down his head and face and the wind wildly tossing his two wet braids, New Blade of Grass looked directly at Little Coyote, who wanted only to seek shelter in a distant stand of trees. Instead, he gravely handed the rope of the horse he was leading to Little Bear Claw. Shivering in the wet buckskins that were plastered to his body like a wet leaf to the bark of the birch tree, he rode his horse into the lake until she was belly deep.

"Help us find the trader, Good Spirit," Little Coyote prayed aloud into the ever-strengthening wind. "Oh, Shining Shirt, be with us now to ask the Good Spirit to lead us. Show us a sign." The young brave looked for Sun hidden in the gray and stormy sky. As his eyes moved from water to distant lake shore to sky, he saw there were more trees to the west. Therefore, that shore seemed a more likely place to winter, to build a fort—even to get out of the storm now. Again his eyes sought Sun, and there it was. The brightness was only a momentary lighter area in the dark sky, true, but it was to the west. As Little Coyote raised arms and lance imploringly once again, the sodden coyote tail loosened itself from his wet buckskins and for a brief moment swung westward. It swung eastward, too, but more westward than eastward in the contrary wind.

The young warrior nudged his pinto around so now the strengthening waves were breaking over her rump. Slowly, horse and rider approached the shore and their bedraggled company. Little Coyote spoke: "To the west we will find a trader, New Blade of Grass. There, to the west among or beyond those trees. The Good Spirit, Shining Shirt and Sun have told me."

As they began moving west, Little Coyote dismissed any concern he had about their decision. Instead, he began searching deeply for the lesson in the two pots. There was an evil there, about which perhaps he soon would have to speak.

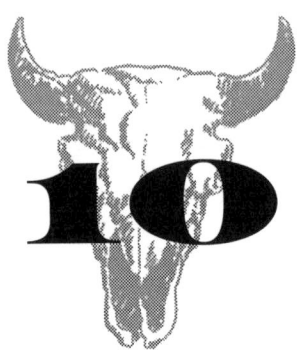

The gun-seekers found the traders after toiling through rocks, trees, brush and other obstacles northward along the western shore of the Lake of the Kutenais. Two miserable huts stood atop a small hill well away from the woods and with a high embankment dropping precipitously to the rocky lake shore. New Blade of Grass kept his warriors well hidden at the edge of the woods, from which for one more day they warily observed the tiny settlement while the weather alternated between sunshine, wind and rain.

There were seven men, all white, though three were darker-skinned than the others. Two of them cut down trees and sharpened one end of each. Another used emaciated horses to pull them to the cabins where two more men assisted him in setting the poles upright in a ditch and pounding dirt and large stones firmly around their bases with a short log. One man steadily dug more ditch in a small circular fashion around the cabins. The seventh man, wearing a strange headgear with three corners, stepped from the larger of the two structures to call from time to time to the others in a loud voice that easily reached the ears of the watching Flatheads. All workers kept their long guns near at hand.

After the second sunrise, Has Many Horses returned from his scouting trip northward.

"A white man brings two deer on a horse," he said quietly. They all watched hungrily while the man in the strange hat supervised the roasting of one carcass over a great bed of glowing coals. As Sun began touching the tips of the tallest trees behind the Flatheads and casting shadows that lengthened across the cleared space before them and this trading post, the easterly breeze brought savory smells of roasted meat.

"We should trade the small store of our smoked fish and our roots for their meat," Bright Fire joked as he swallowed his own meager fare. "Now if you will hand me a thick slice from the rear quarter. I am grateful." He smacked his lips over his next bite of fish. "No. No more hot, juicy venison."

"There will be more venison for some more of us," New Blade of Grass replied quietly, though a momentary grin played across his long face, too. "When they have eaten, we will approach them, for when a man's gut is full, he is more friendly, more inclined to talk."

Bright Fire and Little Bear Claw would remain in the woods with the five mounts they had taken from the Blackfeet.

"The traders might recognize these and be fearful of our intentions," New Blade of Grass pointed out, "and perhaps we can use the horses to better advantage when we begin to trade." He did not elaborate. He wiped the fish oil from his hands and told Bright Fire and Little Bear Claw to observe every movement made in the traders' encampment. "We do not want treachery, but the wise man who would live is ever watchful for it. We will clothe ourselves as Blackfeet to confound white man, who seems to favor our enemies in trade. If there is a power in the yellow stones, as Big Hand told us, in my mind it would not be well to tell which people we are, lest it be thought there are many of the yellow stones in our valley." He paused. "I have thought deeply. I am not so sure we would want great numbers of the white man in our valley." He began changing into the Blackfeet clothing. "Bright Fire and Little Bear Claw will keep the guns and other Blackfeet equipment. It is possible we can trade some of our own horses as well as the furs and yellow stones, because white man's horses are as worn as an old moccasin. Is there other counsel?" He looked at his companions one by one according to age, centering his gaze, finally, on Little Coyote.

"I . . ." Little Coyote began. Then, remembering that none had spoken after the wise words of New Blade of Grass, he held back the rest of his thoughts.

"Speak, Little Coyote, for this is your right in the manner of our people, perhaps your duty while your *sumesh* remains strong."

"The strange pots, New Blade of Grass. Surely they came from the traders. If their liquid turns men's minds, even of the brave and cunning Blackfeet, perhaps we should not trade for them, nor drink from them, if offered. Yet if this would be as offensive to the traders as would be refusal of our proffered food by visitors in our encampment, we can lift the pots to our mouths but not drink. In this manner perhaps we could obtain the best trades, rather than the white man, who might become careless."

There were grunts of affirmation, and this time the long face of New Blade of Grass broke into a wide grin.

"So be it. Wise words. Now we go." He rode into the open, hallooing loudly once. Then with the cavalcade of Has Many Horses, Little Coyote, the three pack horses and his own two extra mounts following behind, he began making the sign for friend. He raised his right hand in front of his neck, palm outward, with his index and second fingers extending upward. Repeatedly he raised his hand until his fingertips were as high as his head. His boldness set Little Coyote to wondering how it was that this warrior, having met white man only once before, could sally forth so confidently. Dimly, the perception began to grow that perhaps all men were much alike in certain basic ways as were the animals of the forests and the plains. Each like group had certain characteristics within its own. One should, therefore, learn those, then study the dissimilarities among individuals within the particular group. Having learned all those, he then should focus on a different group in much the same way, and on and on, meanwhile starting to compare the similarities and dissimilarities between the unlike groups in this ever unfolding process.

Yes, there was much about life to learn, but for now, perhaps, he should be concerned that as their party emerged into the open, the startled white men, as had the Flatheads in their valley at the appearance of the Clark and Lewis party, seized their weapons and spread out away from the fire.

The man in the three-cornered hat said something to his companions. They relaxed somewhat as he stepped out and made the peace sign by clasping his hands in front of his body, with the back of his left hand down. While no guns were raised, the Flatheads were, nonetheless, surrounded when they reached the fire.

We come to trade, New Blade of Grass signed.

We are traders. Welcome.

We will trade for guns. We have furs. New Blade of Grass improvised his own sign for the guns by raising both arms, leveling his lance, aiming over it and shouting, "Ooph!"

We have no guns for trade. We do not trade guns. Dismount and eat.

New Blade of Grass, most skilled among this group of Flatheads in the sign language, pretended to fumble for a moment to find the right signs for his next communication. While the white men evidently failed to read this response to the trader's lie, Has Many Horses and Little Coyote, who as yet scarcely knew the sign talk at all, quickly detected the pause as a warning for them to be on guard.

I see seven guns in the hands of white man. Do they not hold them to trade? Or do they fear us, who carry no guns?

The white leader laughed and said something to the other six. They put down their guns and resumed drinking a steaming and brown liquid and smoking their white clay pipes. The leader again signed that their visitors eat. During the few moments the Flatheads came together to dismount and tend their horses before eating, New Blade of Grass whispered warningly as he bent between two of the pack animals.

"They lie. The leader wears a new Blackfeet sheath for his knife. Its design matches that on the quiver of the Blackfeet I killed as he reached for his gun. Remain friendly. Be on guard.

If they lie as we talk by signs, I will mark it for you by turning my left foot outward. Now, Little Coyote, give me but one of the larger yellow stones."

New Blade of Grass moved his left foot outwardly several times while the three braves sat on the ground eating and he communicated with the white chief. After a time, the largest of the white men—great belly protruding from his unfastened, tight-fitting, greasy-black, buckskin shirt—waddled toward the largest log structure. He returned, wiping his black whiskers and carrying a small, brown pot that he handed to the white leader. The leader smiled, rubbed his belly to sign this was good, then threw back his head and drank deeply. He passed the pot, in turn, to the semi-circle of whites. At length it reached New Blade of Grass. He brought the pot to his lips, tilted his head and appeared to drink, even moving his throat and wiping his eyes as had the white men. Little Coyote understood why his leader had not found it hard to grimace and shudder as he had pretended to drink. The young warrior found that when his turn came to drink, the firewater, even on the tongue and lips, was strong and bit at him far more than the first gooseberries he tasted each autumn before fully ripened. The pot went around once more before the white men had emptied it.

Repeatedly, New Blade of Grass signed that he wanted to trade for guns. The white leader, his three-cornered hat now slightly askew, as often shook his head and signed negatively—until New Blade of Grass led one pack horse toward the fire and dumped its load of beaver, black bear, otter and mink fur out of the packs and onto the ground.

Once again the fat man waddled toward the largest cabin, somewhat unsteadily this time, and re-emerged carrying three muskets and trying to wipe off his whiskers with his shirt sleeve.

New Blade of Grass gravely examined the muskets before passing them to Has Many Horses and Little Coyote. The guns were identical to those the warriors had taken from the Blackfeet. New Blade of Grass could put part of his middle finger down the large smooth bore. There were patches of rust here and there, especially around the locks, strikers and pans, though he did not at once grasp the significance of this. Each gun, on the side opposite the flint lock, had a somewhat shiny, lizard-like creature cast in metal resembling the color of the yellow stone New Blade of Grass held hidden in his hand.

There was much silent haggling back and forth between the white- and red-skinned leaders. Plainly, the white at first offered only one gun for each pack horse of furs. At length there were nine such guns, nine small kegs of powder, many bars of lead and a sack of flints in the warriors' pile. In the whites' pile was a large mound of excellent furs. Two pots, one empty, the other almost so, lay on the ground where three of the white men now dozed.

New Blade of Grass stood up, stretched and looked down on his two companions. Little Coyote could see that his leader was tired. The bright eyes were less piercing, even from that superior position; care lines creased the cheeks; the voice was softer, though commanding.

"The white chief says he holds back only enough guns to assure the safety of the traders, though he has sent for more, which will take many moons to arrive." Then New Blade of Grass spoke solely to Little Coyote, and as loudly as the white men now were calling out. He did an excellent imitation of the hosts' somewhat unsteady condition. His voice lowered almost to a whisper: "I will sign that we have better goods to trade for better guns. If they exist, perhaps the power of the yellow stones will make them appear. I will mention that we have them. Then you will ride out to pretend to fetch the stones. Bright Fire and Little Bear Claw will bring various numbers of horses into open view and they will appear singly, together, then reappear in different shirts, even those of the Blackfeet, so white men in the gathering dusk really will not know how many of us remain in the woods. Leave some of the yellow stones with Bright Fire, but only you will touch them. Hasten, so the white men will see horses, Bright Fire and Little Bear Claw before darkness falls. And take them this large piece of venison. I do not think they will complain that they will not be forced to eat the fish, nor will white man complain if the yellow stones possess the magic Big Hand described."

As Little Coyote prepared to leave, he watched New Blade of Grass capture the total attention of the four men who still were awake by holding the yellow stone close to the fire to catch the stronger light on the most brightly worn side. The white leader stiffened in his seated position, then recovered and tried to appear indifferent by carefully pushing the unburned stub ends of sticks into the embers with a longer stick. But the reactions of his companions, most notably the great, fat one, destroyed his pose, for that one shouted the new word, "Gold!" He impulsively snatched the stone from the hand of New Blade of Grass. The three sleepers were instantly awake, looking about somewhat stupidly for a moment, then joining in a struggle to hold and examine the nugget.

Pretense destroyed, the white chief shrugged his shoulders and called loudly to the other men. They quieted, but only after each had looked at the nugget, tentatively hefted it, then passed it to the next until it once again gleamed a bit in the firelight, this time in the white chief's hand. The fire began consuming the stub ends of the wood, the flames reflecting alike on the faces of all the men seated there. The hollows and seams of the faces stood out more sharply, the eyes reflected the light, but there was a difference, Little Coyote noted, between the white and the red men. Now the white men resembled the hungry dogs that lurk beyond the people as they eat around the fire—wolfish, ready to snap, to growl, to fight. So! Such was the magic of a single yellow stone. Little Coyote galloped his pinto to the edge of the forest to carry out his mission.

When he returned he could see Bright Fire and Little Bear Claw moving to the edge of the trees with three of the five Blackfeet horses. They disappeared, then one of the braves reappeared dressed in a long shirt and holding all five of the horses. Little Coyote was sure all the white men saw the same, for they had watched him galloping his pinto across the open space, holding aloft the buckskin bag now containing half the yellow stones.

"Strange Hat has signed for me to call all our warriors to come in and eat more meat, and drink," New Blade of Grass informed Has Many Horses and Little Coyote when the latter had shown the sub-chief the heavy bag. "In truth, I could tell him they are eating now. We will continue to pretend that the firewater has clouded our actions. We are learning much from this experience. Now perhaps we will see better guns, more like those in the hands of the men of Clark and Lewis."

Seven guns, different among themselves as well as from the muskets for which they had traded, soon lay separately on seven of the black bear hides that had been placed fur side up on the ground near the fire. They were the white men's own guns, the ones they had held when the Flatheads first approached. Such was the dreadful power of the yellow stones. Gravely, New Blade of Grass instructed Little Coyote to place two yellow stones of nearly equal size on each fur, then signed for the powder horns to be placed there. That done, he told Little Coyote to put a smaller stone on each pelt. The sub-chief looked into the barrel end of each gun. All the holes were of different sizes, smaller than those of the muskets. He signed that he wanted the moulds to make their bullets. The white leader, his headgear now fallen to the ground and forgotten, spoke to his six other men, then joined them in their staggering movement to the cabins. They returned holding the moulds. New Blade of Grass told Little Coyote to place two small stones on each pelt. For a short time the sub-chief and the white leader communicated vigorously with their hands and arms, with the Flathead sub-chief finally shrugging and signing for Little Coyote to put one more stone on each pelt. He did the same when three kegs of gunpowder, plus more bars of lead and a sack of flints, were brought from the cabins.

"The trade is over," New Blade of Grass informed his companions, "but the wise man who might seek future help, such as for this gunpowder or gun repairs, prepares the trail." That said, he told Little Coyote to hand each white man an additional yellow stone. Only a few remained in the bag. "To avoid possible treachery which might jump from their inflamed minds, I have told the white leader that I will present him with the rest of these yellow stones they call 'gold' when Sun rises and after he instructs us in the use of these guns they have traded, for they are different from those for which we first traded. He has agreed. He also will provide us with five metal 'traps,' he calls them, and show us how to use them so we can catch more beaver for further trades. They like the beaver."

For two suns New Blade of Grass led his mounted braves and their string of ten extra horses through a maze of trees and brush and up and down streams well away from any easy route toward their valley, yet trending toward it.

"I did not trade horses to the white men," New Blade of Grass said. "They could not easily follow us on their own wretched bags of bones. They have canoes which could take them through water more swiftly than we can move on land with our pack horses." All the braves agreed that New Blade of Grass had acted wisely and had made good trades.

An added, more tangible, benefit arrived on the back of the extra mount Has Many Horses had taken with him on a hunt for meat with one of the newly acquired long rifles. It was the boned-out meat of a fat cow elk. That night at the base of a protective cliff deep in the heavy forest, the Flatheads roasted all the meat they could eat and listened carefully to Has Many Horses' account of his success with the long rifle.

"I sighted the gun for the heart," the warrior explained. "The bullet penetrated the heart. That is why I roasted and we have eaten the heart first. I believe this is good medicine. Yes, New Blade of Grass, if the people will allow it, I will keep this gun which came from their furs as well as my own, and the gold from Shining Shirt."

"After we showed the gold to Strange Hat, he signed with a straight tongue," New Blade of Grass said. "He listened well when I told him that Clark and Lewis had visited us, but I did not tell him where. He was interested in their guns as I described them. They shoot more true than the muskets because they have what they call 'rifling' in them. This rifling is in the long guns we traded away from them.

"Strange Hat, who is not the man named Thompson, said there was a great war between the America that Clark and Lewis told us about and the British, to whom Strange Hat and his men belong. America won the war, but not all the fights. Many of these long rifles made in a place called Pennsylvania were taken from prisoners, or picked up after fights. The guns were saved but not used until the traders got them. They preferred them to the muskets, but they preferred the gold to these guns from Pennsylvania. That is our good fortune."

New Blade of Grass held a rifle bullet and a musket bullet in his open palm, then spoke: "Eagle Claw told the council that Little Coyote's small-bird point caught the Blackfeet in the neck; it would have killed him, except that Young Willow already had launched the lance into the Blackfeet's back and killed him. I think Has Many Horses did well to sight the long rifle carefully where the smaller bullet, like Little Coyote's bird point, would kill. Those who learn to shoot straightest should have the Pennsylvania rifles. That is what I will tell the council." Again a half-smile lighted up the sub-chief's usually grave face. "Perhaps before we join our people in the buffalo land, those who have worked so wisely and hard to obtain these guns will have shot them enough to be the better shooters, so will get a rifle." He viewed the faces of his companions and hallooed for Little Bear Claw to come in from his guard post out in the trees.

"Yes, we now will join our people in the land of the buffalo. I did not think we would find the time to do so. If we hurry and the snow does not fall too deeply outside of the mountains, we can reach the buffalo grounds. There is an urgency. Strange Hat lied about trading guns to the Blackfeet. We do not know how many more now possess them. Our people should have these guns with them on the buffalo hunt and learn how to use them quickly."

New Blade of Grass sighed, then motioned for Little Bear Claw to return to his guard post with his steaming meat. "I think there will be a good and a bad to the arrival of Clark and Lewis," he said. "The good already is that we have learned about guns and the great value white man places on gold. The bad? Well, we shall see." Again, he sighed. "Yes, we shall see."

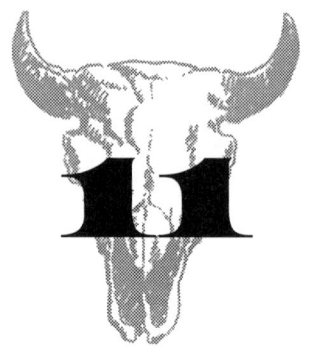

Bright Fire picked up the lead ball he had just cast for the long rifle. He dropped the hot bullet to the ground where, striking a stone, it separated into segments, the smaller of which he gingerly touched. It was cool now, so he placed both parts in the palm of his hand and thoughtfully turned them over with a finger.

"They shine more brightly than the yellow stones," he said, "yet to get those stones white man traded much of this lead, these small pots to melt it, and the moulds to form the bullets." He watched Has Many Horses tap a perfectly formed ball from his mould. "I see. To form a bullet that holds together, one must not stop pouring until the mould is full." Bright Fire dropped the two lead pieces back into the pot and continued to speculate about the Flatheads' newly acquired weapons: "Big Hand of the Shoshonis said Clark and Lewis had seen no Blackfeet, so traded no guns. I believe him. Torn Moccasin talked of guns he had seen before his death. The white traders at the Lake of the Kutenais lied when they said they did not trade guns, yet they had traded those we took from the Blackfeet after they killed Cold Wind. And they traded us their guns for the yellow stones."

Little Coyote watched while Bright Fire slowly stirred the

pot with a metal trade spoon. For a moment the surface of the molten metal glistened, then the dross rose to the top and Bright Fire carefully skimmed off this slag and dashed it to the ground before it could congeal on the spoon. He cast another lead ball and tapped it from the mould. When it had cooled he gravely picked up the shiny bullet and showed it to Little Coyote. "Yes, Little Coyote, there is much to ponder, much we must learn about white man and his marvels." He stirred the pot and again dross mottled the shimmering surface of the molten metal.

New Blade of Grass had decided that the gun-seekers must learn more about their new weapons and their use as the braves trekked toward their beloved valley, though doing so would delay even more their arrival at the buffalo grounds. Once, atop a rise from which they could see a considerable distance in all directions, he asked Bright Fire to remain while the rest moved on to another rise. Then, standing atop his horse, the sub-chief waved his fur blanket as a signal. They all saw the puff of smoke from Bright Fire's rifle and almost immediately thereafter heard the gun report. Later, and less wary because they now possessed and could use the guns, they learned that valleys and woods muffled or even hid the reports.

Soon there developed a keen competition to hit various targets. After making the best shots one day, New Blade of Grass told his companions that part of his success was due to his keeping the inside of the gun well-cleaned with the thin buckskin patches and grease, as well as placing each ball on a greased patch before ramming it over the powder. Thus the patch would remove most of the powder fouling the rifling from the previous load. Less care was needed for the larger and smoothbore muskets, which consumed much more powder and lead and, as Bright Fire said, ". . . are far less accurate—like the differences between the spear and the bow and arrows."

A herd of elk yielded four animals to five rifles as the gun-seekers forsook the ridges and re-entered their valley. During their big feast, New Blade of Grass warned each warrior to refill the small, hinged hole in the stock of the rifle with elk grease for the patches. Each of the two small encampments of Flatheads that had remained in the valley received most of the welcome meat and green hides. The people gave the hunters five pair of well-used snowshoes in return. The men moved ever southward through the intermittent, unseasonal snow flurries until they once again were in the bowl where Clark and Lewis had found them. Now there was only silence—and much snow through which they and their horses began trudging with great effort.

With dusk almost on them, the tired and hungry men searched out, unfolded and erected a dilapidated lodge in a growing breeze while Sun briefly struggled from the drab, gray clouds that had held it all the cheerless day. Little Bear Claw adjusted the smoke flaps and Has Many Horses built a fire from the wood Little Coyote had collected while thinking about the lonely vigil Shining Shirt kept at his burial place up the mountainside to the west. When there was enough wood for the night, Little Coyote, shivering in his wet clothing, stood inside the protective lodge. The lure of the buffalo hunt diminished in his misery, but he was determined not to be the first to strip. He eyed a frozen droplet of water hanging inside an irregularly shaped hole in the old shelter. The ice crystal happily caught the bright rays of disappearing Sun and sparkled brightly, lighting up its little world with all the colors until the heat from the fire reached out to touch the ice and it melted instantly. All the brightness was gone. Had Little Coyote been asked at that moment for his thoughts about the trip over the pass to the buffalo grounds, he would have replied quickly that harder days lay ahead. Puzzlingly, he might have gained some solace from conveying that sour message. He was tired, hungry and, he admitted to himself, a bit lonely for his family, particularly after greeting their people on the way up the valley. Yet, his spirit rose as the fire brightened and warmed the old lodge and the aroma of the roasting meat began to fill the air. The hard day was behind them. Though others lay ahead, he and his companions would encounter them one at a time, not all at once. This, apparently, was the attitude of his equally tired but more experienced companions. He would draw strength from them for his spirit and perhaps by remaining cheerful also would provide strength for the others—as the meat and sleep would strengthen the body.

So it was that no complaint entered the lodge, and there was a powerful lesson there.

The discussion about their impending struggle through the mountains was brief, centering mostly on the older warriors' acknowledgment that *siistc*, the winter, had come much earlier than ever in their experience, and how would the Blackfeet respond to the failure of so many of their warriors to return to their villages? Surely, this dire information quickly would spread throughout the Blackfeet world.

Mindful of how the Clark and Lewis group had arrived on jaded horses, New Blade of Grass warned that, "We must depend only on the horses we have now." The gun-seekers promptly filed out of the lodge to feed their mounts and the pack animals. Little Coyote's spirit rose even more when he was not assigned that task. On this long journey he had risen above horse-tending work; he shared it. There was much satisfaction in that, too.

Little Coyote lay awake, listening to the breathing of his four companions. The fire had died to a few small flames and many glowing embers. All were asleep, except, perhaps, Little Bear Claw, who turned on his evergreen bed, maybe pondering the morrow as was his friend.

The old shelter flapped a bit in the rising wind. Sandy snow from the lofty, agitated tree limbs struck the hide and fine particles fell through an unpatched hole onto Little Coyote's face. He carefully tucked the rabbit-skin blanket around his neck. One of the horses picketed near the lodge snorted; he could hear the movement of the other animals as they stood together in the nearby protective fringe of high brush.

I'll wear my heaviest clothing tomorrow, he thought, and was grateful yet again that Little Yellow Bird had included a light, but warm, muskrat undervest in his bag. He wanted to prop himself on an elbow and, unseen, look at the tripod erected from his lance, bow and quiver and the long rifle. How would he carry them on the morrow? Rifle on the pack horse, while he sat astride Not Afraid of Guns, bow and quiver on his back and the lance in his mittened hands? Lance and bow and arrows on the pack horse? Or the rifle . . .?

As he slept the wind died. Clouds drifted in above the mountain bowl and peaks and began dropping heavy, white snowflakes. Finally, they obliterated even the trail leading to the land of the buffalo.

The sub-chief led the way upward, scouting out and sometimes probing with a long pole to find the trail. He was guided somewhat by broken tree limbs attesting to many journeys toward the pass. He led two horses behind him, their strong legs and at times their chests helping to break trail. Bright Fire, then Has Many Horses, successively took the lead, only exchanging places when legs, lungs and aching muscles could take no more. Soon the two youngest warriors took their turns, too, as did all the horses, except for the mare that trailed the old lodge toboggan-like behind her.

As the dull sky threatened early darkness, the sub-chief signaled a halt on a snow-laden but somewhat level shelf surrounded on three sides by smaller trees and brush. The three older men scooped away much of the snow with their snowshoes. Little Coyote broke off armsful of dead twigs for the lodge fire; Little Bear Claw fed the horses a small amount of the diminishing load of hay they had bundled up from the valley.

The two young men stopped to rest briefly near the eagerly eating horses. Little Coyote handed a twist of hay to Not Afraid of Guns. She nickered softly, then snatched the grass, careful to mouth it so little fell into the soft snow.

"She will teach me much about the buffalo hunt," he told his wet and shivering friend.

"Yes, and the fat roasts will fill this belly until it resembles a pregnant mare," Little Bear Claw said with a grin. "Come. New Blade of Grass has produced a wonder with the elk meat, dried onions, camas and much good fat."

A newly acquired copper pot hanging from a stout branch suspended over the fire bubbled forth a tempting aroma. Soon wet clothing was drying from makeshift racks, each of the men protecting his naked buttocks from the cold ground by sitting on his blanket atop evergreen boughs. Each dipped a mountain sheep horn spoon into the pot, warming both belly and spirit.

On the third such day of struggle, New Blade of Grass wearily led his two horses to the base of an elongated and snow-covered rocky wall. Far below, a few rays of sunshine penetrating the gray clouds made disjointed bright patches on the valley floor between the mountain ridges on which they labored and another range to the east. New Blade of Grass rubbed a wet, mittened hand across his face, pushing the hair plastering his forehead back under the fur cap.

"The grass for the horses is almost gone," he said. "The meat, well . . . , there is far less than my belly calls for. There surely is more snow here than below. We should take the older trail into the valley?" His gaze centered on Bright Fire and Has Many Horses, then briefly on the two younger men. There was no dissent, so they began angling downward, sometimes pushing snow ahead of them and stumbling through entanglements hidden underneath. Always, the sub-chief moved the cavalcade away from any precipices that would endanger their precious cargo.

That day and the next the struggle began to ease for men and horses, yet, strangely, Little Coyote noted, a new feeling of diminishment steadily began growing as they moved out of the towering mountains that had exalted their spirits while tiring their bodies. As they began struggling over the drearily empty valley floor, all of them towered physically over the low, snow-covered bushes and grasses that closely hugged the melancholy land. Only an owl soundlessly stared at the procession tiredly moving past its white mound, around which were scattered numerous small pellets encircling the hair and bones of the tiny rodent inhabitants of this hungry region. Equally soundlessly the owl flapped ahead of them, each wing beat almost touching the ground, as though the owl's spirit, like theirs, could soar no higher.

"The owl will add to the almost-empty pots!" Little Bear Claw fitted an arrow to his bow when the creature rested at length on another mound.

"Hold!" The sub-chief stopped on his snowshoes and raised an arm high above his head. "It leads us to a larger creature." Soon all the group was together, watching the figure moving confidently toward them.

"It is *s'tcect*, my wife's brother, Broken Tooth," Bright Fire murmured. "I know that robe, and he knows my horses. He moves strongly on the snowshoes, perhaps better than any of our people. Why does a great buffalo hunter return this way alone?"

Broken Tooth answered the question even before he had dashed off the rime that the moist air from his laboring lungs had frozen around his face: "Our people and our Shoshone friends have scarcely hunted the buffalo near the three forks. Many Blackfeet fill the hills around our encampment. Already we mourn Tall Person and Badger. Bull Elk took an arrow, but he moves again. We must have the meat or soon begin eating our horses. And we need your help, perhaps that of others left behind in our valley if we are to hold off the Blackfeet while we hunt the buffalo. Ah, you brought guns!" A rare grin split his tired face, widely enough for the broken incisor to show. "We put an arrow into Racing Pony of the Blackfeet. During the torture he boasted loudly that they had many guns and soon would have more to keep us from the buffalo grounds forever."

Broken Tooth removed his pack and it fell heavily into the snow. "Perhaps this tough buffalo meat will strengthen us for the journey of four suns," he said. "The remainder of an old bull I ran down on my snowshoes lies ahead. Let us hurry."

The gun-seekers back-tracked on Broken Tooth's twin snowshoe trail. Soon they were angling northeasterly into a snow-covered, ever widening valley similar to the land they had traversed thus far. They still were unable to ride the often-floundering horses. Little Coyote had ample time to contemplate the foolishness of his earlier fantasies about riding boldly and impressively with his weapons and astride Not Afraid of Guns as he coped with this tiring reality that extended to a second day. Ravens began circling above the slow-moving procession, loudly cawing their hunger and frustration as the party entered the bed of a frozen stream feeding the headwaters of one of the rivers that formed the three forks.

Broken Tooth had followed this stream bed to help conceal both himself and his trail. His companions followed his stocky, seemingly tireless body through a tangle of willow and into a heavily braided river bend where wind had scoured away much of the snow to expose many tiny, grass-covered islands. Here the warrior had forced the old buffalo into flight and had killed him as he tried to lunge through the deep snow and up the stream bank. The hunter had skinned and boned out the carcass while it still was warm.

"We should work, then perhaps talk," New Blade of Grass grunted as he wiped his sweating face. He praised Broken Tooth for this important kill and for his skill in cutting the meat into easily handled chunks, separated by boughs so they would not become one frozen mass. They kicked and tugged up the hard-frozen, bowl-like hide Broken Tooth had shaped over and even under the meat and bones. Only the frozen, pulverized grass contents of the gut pile stained the nearby oval of packed snow. While Broken Tooth cut a series of holes into the edges of the thick hide, the other men began loading the meat onto this toboggan-shaped hide. Broken Tooth laced in the meat with a leather rope and a pack mare pulled this load almost an arrow's flight to where they had unloaded the horses before picketing them on the exposed grass of the most hidden little island. Near their supplies the men erected the old lodge, careful that even the tips of the poles were hidden by the stream bank and the fringing vegetation from any person traversing nearby in the valley.

They roasted enough small slices of meat to last the remainder of their journey, cutting the thin strips against the grain to offset the toughness. They ate this and marrow soup made from the contents of the larger buffalo bones they had cracked open. When their bellies were full they slept, one of them keeping vigil from a small, sheltered hollow scooped out of the snowbank near the river bend. Here the guard could see or hear enemy or friend moving toward them from north or northeast.

Little Coyote's turn as guard came second, when the moon seemed to be darting in and out among the fast-moving clouds blown by high winds which, strangely, scarcely brushed the earth. He tucked his rabbit-skin blanket around his legs, then carefully wrapped the rest of his body, the warmth almost immediately taking his mind off the uncomfortable cut brush on which he sat. Only the top of his head, his ears and eyes were exposed, as was the muzzle tip of his rifle.

The ravens were gone before darkness, collectively voicing satisfaction they had found bits of food where the buffalo had been uncovered, dissatisfaction that strong beaks and feet could not work the smaller bones and frozen trimmings.

Not so the coyotes. Possibly alerted earlier in the day by the noisy and high-flying ravens, the wary creatures silently moved in from several directions to clean up what man and the large birds had left. The signal to do so—a single, short howl—came from an adult that first had ventured close to the camp. Little Coyote strained his eyes to see them and occasionally was rewarded with help from the hide-and-seek moon. Though the food supply was limited, there was no fighting, no loud snarls or yips contesting ownership. Two times Little Coyote glimpsed an adult animal loping toward the lodge to look and listen, then hurriedly returning to the food, adding yet more sounds of the cracking bones to the cold night air.

Then, like the fog that quietly steals into the valley at night and as silently sneaks away at dawn, the animals were gone. Again the night was still until far out in the frozen vastness one long, drawn-out howl was followed by another and another until the chorus filled the night—then abruptly stopped. Little Coyote almost could visualize the animals communicating excitedly about their next foray, which, depending on the wisdom of the leaders, again would result in success—food—or protracted hunger. Not much luck was involved, Little Coyote concluded. This persistence, this cunning, this attention to detail ensured their survival against the great odds of cold weather, hungry country, larger predators, and even man. Former no-name would end his turn at watch with a much deeper appreciation of his new name.

"We should work, then perhaps talk," a tired New Blade of Grass had said on their arrival at this camp. The work was largely done. The talking remained. As Little Coyote sat through that cold night he easily could guess what major problems they would talk about on the morrow. The young brave's as-yet-unanswered question was what would he say about one of those problems. Most of his mind held onto that problem, while a smaller part again began pondering this visit by the coyotes. Perhaps a bit of the answer to his yet-forming question lay there. He held onto that possibility until relieved by a yawning, shivering Has Many Horses. Then, once again rolled up in his blanket inside the ancient lodge, his musings shifted from conscious to subconscious as he drifted into sleep. There, the sorting out, the evaluations began shaping a structured decision for careful voicing upon awakening.

New Blade of Grass filled his pipe. The precious tobacco he had obtained from the gun-traders was less strong than that which Clark and Lewis had proffered. Standing before the fire, he asked his companions if they wished to smoke. Two filed outside to scan the valley once more in the pre-dawn, then returned. All sat down, keenly aware that within the loosely knit, highly individualistic, political structure of their people the six of them faced a problem. Little Coyote silently approved the sub-chief's decision to call them before eating. This could help to hasten their decision and give them more time to reach and help the encampment.

Head Chief Tjolzhitsay had empowered New Blade of Grass to seek the guns. The chief had done so before he temporarily relinquished his authority so that Thunder Voice could lead the people both to and from the buffalo grounds. The gun-seekers had not yet delivered the guns, so there was an important question: Was New Blade of Grass still answerable to Tjolzhitsay? Had Tjolzhitsay resumed authority in the emergency related to the Blackfeet danger that Broken Tooth had described, or did the hunt for the buffalo continue to take precedence though it had been interrupted before it really had begun?

Could New Blade of Grass, therefore, as a duly appointed sub-chief, plan the tactic needed to get the gun-seekers through the Blackfeet and into the encampment though this might entail a fierce fight? Or, had this become the responsibility and right of Broken Tooth?

Little Coyote would learn now and remember forever afterward that councils, large or small, took time and much recounting so all would have all the information, sometimes much more, on which to base a decision.

Solemnly, the sub-chief lighted his pipe with a coal from the fire. He puffed vigorously on the pipe and signed the four directions, toward the earth and where Sun still slept. He handed the pipe to Broken Tooth first, signifying there was a question of precedence in which the experienced warrior must give counsel, perhaps carry out the decisions. The pipe order then became Bright Fire, Has Many Horses, Little Bear Claw, and, finally, Little Coyote.

The sub-chief carefully set down the pipe. The fire embers almost died and were strengthened while he recounted the adventures of the gun-seekers. Then, abruptly, he asked: "Did Tjolzhitsay or Thunder Voice send Broken Tooth to us?"

Broken Tooth recounted the travels of the people over the pass, down the mountain and across the valley floors. As he spoke, more willow wood added new flames and warmth to the lodge. Then Broken Tooth replied to the question: "Both Tjolzhitsay and Thunder Voice called and sent me to you."

This final statement left the question of authority hanging there in the lodge almost as visibly as any weapon or other piece of equipment. The answer, quite as clearly, would have to come from this council. Now the four other warriors agreed that a possible fight with some of the Blackfeet lay ahead. As to how they would reach the encampment, there was agreement they should approach as close as possible to their people at night and use any hills, valleys, brush or trees that would screen them. Yet, based on Broken Tooth's detailed description of the location of the encampment, there was the question of that last grand rush to it from the small forest nearby. All but two agreed with Broken Tooth's belief that they should rush forth boldly, prepared to fight to protect the slower pack animals. Perhaps Tjolzhitsay and Thunder Voice would lead warriors out from the camp to help.

The two dissenters were New Blade of Grass, troubled deeply by the danger of losing the guns they had worked so hard to obtain and how the guns would strengthen the Blackfeet, and Little Coyote, who had not voiced his view. No anger entered the discussion though now the sub-chief and Broken Tooth sought to persuade the others. The fire died and the lodge became cold despite the heated discussion. The sub-chief suggested they again scan the valley while a new fire warmed the lodge. When they returned from the now partially sunlit outdoors and were seated,

Little Coyote placed the coyote pup's tail around his neck and put on his lap the shield he had recovered from the dead Blackfeet when Cold Wind had died. The coyote on the shield caught the firelight.

"All my friends have counseled well," he began, "and the words of Broken Tooth are wise ones from a brave warrior. As I kept vigil last night a family of coyotes, whom Sun created and from whom we sprang, brought me a vision. They were summoned by a wise and brave coyote to the pile of buffalo bones. I shall call that wise coyote Broken Tooth, who brought word of the peril to the encampment of our people. Likewise, I shall look upon the bones of the sacred buffalo as our guns and other supplies, for they mean our life, just as the bones they could crack held life for the coyotes. They quietly ate these bones and carried them off in their bellies. When the coyotes had eaten, they all assembled and sang their satisfaction and joy that they had carried out their plan with great success. My counsel . . ." Little Coyote, astonished at his boldness and the forbearance of his listeners, spoke even more rapidly. ". . . is that once again Broken Tooth, who found his way here and has led us back, return to the encampment, tell of his success and at night bring us more warriors. Others can wait in the encampment for our signal of a fired musket to come out to join us as we hasten as best we can in this deep snow. I have only recently learned there is a time to bravely count strikes and perform other individual brave acts, for these help strong hearts to grow in each warrior, for our people to remain strong. There are other occasions when we all must work together, as we have done often enough in the past, for our smaller numbers to exist in our valley when great numbers of enemies besiege us on all sides. That is the wisdom Coyote has given us. That is the wisdom we must think about following now. How our final plan is worked out is for wiser, more experienced warriors than myself. That is all. I have spoken."

Very gently Little Coyote set down his blood-covered shield and removed and placed the coyote tail on it. The popping sound of a burning willow stick seemed almost deafening in the silence.

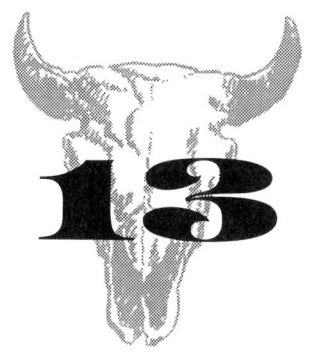

E ast of the gun-seekers towered the tallest peak of the Tobacco Root Mountains. The valley ahead began to narrow. Broken Tooth halted and waited for the straggling procession to catch up.

"Perhaps the Blackfeet have found my snowshoe tracks," he warned. "More snow has not come to hide them. We should follow this creek bed up the side of these mountains, cross the high ridge and go down." He wiped his generous nose on the badger-fur ruff of his mittens. "Such a journey will put us onto another of the frozen rivers that form the three forks. If possible, the warriors that Tjolzhitsay and Thunder Voice send to you will take you to our people there." He removed his pack from one of the two horses he had been tending, wiped his broad face and grinned good-naturedly at Little Bear Claw and Little Coyote. The broken incisor reminded the latter of the gap in the mountains ahead. "You learn the ways to the buffalo grounds in a hard manner for this first journey. That is good. Perhaps you will make many such journeys, all filled with much work and danger." He crammed two large chunks of the frozen meat into his pack. "Our people always must have the buffalo, and the young must learn so they can teach the ways to those who come after them.

Yes, we must have the buffalo to live . . ." He closed the pack and tentatively hefted it. ". . . as the Blackfeet must have them, too."

Broken Tooth grunted into the heavy pack, then strongly lurched ahead. Though his snowshoes sank deeply, he soon was out of sight.

The snow on this somewhat protected northeasterly slope presented another problem—a thin crust that often held up the snowshoes, causing the wearers to slide almost uncontrollably while trying to urge on the horses, which at times were lunging belly deep.

At dusk they camped in a small park, too weary to try to kill with the silent arrows a fat buffalo cow from the large herd they drove ahead. Little Coyote regretted there was so little light for him to view for the first time a large herd of animals. He watched the huge, shaggy creatures lumber wildly through the deep snow, then slow and begin to dig their way single file up the hillside to the west. The dark line topped the ridge. At the apex the line disjointed like the back of a great black snake to reveal, momentarily before its disappearance, each animal silhouetted against the dark sky. Soon all were gone.

Or, so Little Coyote thought. His was the last watch of the long night. Extremely tired, he went to sleep almost immediately inside the old lodge. The buffalo filled his dreams as they had the park before their flight. Once, unaccountably warm, he awoke and wrapped himself more loosely in the blanket. Again he slept, this time without dreams until Bright Fire shook him hard before crawling into his own blanket. Little Coyote donned his leggings, moccasins, vest, powder horn and bullet pouch, picked up his blanket and rifle and laboriously snowshoed up Bright Fire's trail on the highest hillside to the lookout at the base of a large boulder.

He stood for a time, listening in the darkness and hearing nothing except the faint rasp of a tuft of rabbit hair against one ear that he hadn't fully exposed. He shrugged his head and that noise ceased as another intruded, heavily, to the west. Alerted, he let his blanket drop and stood there, rifle held across his chest. Only a faint breeze moved from the west, cold against his body, probing for openings in his clothing to chill him further as he stood there unmoving as the boulder, itself. Then for an instant there was a warmth on that hill above the river of cold air below—faint, as had been that sound of the rabbit hairs against his ear. As quickly as the shrug of his head had dispelled the sound, the warmth was gone. Yet it had been there. He was certain of that. Twice more it came, seemingly from the east—intermittently, true, and soon almost forgotten at the further intrusion of the larger sound that had alerted him into near immobility and total concentration of all senses.

Now the sound from the west grew, reminding Little Coyote of that made by his horses breaking through the snow crust. He knelt near the base of the boulder, looking eastward as he did so and noting the light streaks through the thinner portions of the dark clouds. These streaks grew wider, brighter, as he continued to kneel there, shivering now despite one more warm caress darting out too briefly amid the enveloping cold from the west.

The shaggy hump, the topknot, then the tips of the bull buffalo's horns showed first as the creature climbed upward. Soon Little Coyote could smell the animal and, as he pondered that, he detected the sounds made by many more such creatures. Perhaps the herd they had driven from the park was returning. If so, what had caused their movement? He thought about that in the growing light and wished he could climb atop the boulder for a greater view. But he was held there by the rolling eyes of the bull, which also sought sound and smell to re-enforce some primordial certainty that this tiny creature almost within touching distance was something to avoid. The warrior again felt the momentary warm caress of air on his face until the bull took one more wary step forward to mutter a grunt with sour breath.

"Hunh!" The bull twirled on his forefeet with great agility and plowed strongly down the slope of the hill from whence he had come. Soon the young warrior could hear other legs breaking through the snow crust, until the sounds seemed to fill the world.

Shivering, he pulled his blanket around him, the impressions made by this encounter almost drowning out those created by the warm caresses—almost.

New Blade of Grass listened with great interest as Little Coyote told him about the encounter with the buffalo. He showed little interest in the mention of the warm breeze as he set the braves to dividing the guns, powder and lead into equal piles for the pack horses.

"Each of us will lead the same number of horses," he said. "Thus, if the Blackfeet should fight us, there will be less danger of losing all the guns."

The sub-chief shook out, twisted and rubbed his extra pair of buckskin leggings he had dried during the night. He pulled on the softened garments, took several steps, removed them and again rubbed and wrinkled the areas that would fit below the crotch. Content, he rubbed together a dry pair of heavy moccasins and put in some soft grass. Their suppleness somewhat restored, he asked Little Bear Claw to look to the horses once more, then scan the countryside between them and the second of the rivers that formed the forks. The Flatheads would move down that, hugging embankments, scrub brush and sparse timber as well as other cover until they would reach the small forest near the encampment of their people. Re-enforced by the warriors sent to them, they planned to make the final effort to enter the camp across a wide stretch of open country that Broken Tooth had described as having little cover at all, thus protecting the encampment from enemies skulking too closely. When Little Bear Claw returned, the five men ate and reluctantly hoisted the old lodge into the protective branches of a tall evergreen. While they looked to their horses, Bright Fire set out to scout the country for any sign of the Blackfeet.

"It is likely the sharp-eyed Blackfeet will find this lodge," the sub-chief grunted. "What thoughts do you have about what might face us?"

Most of the brief discussion centered on that final dash to the encampment. How many Blackfeet would they encounter? Would they be able to ride horses at all? Little Coyote remained silent, lest his earlier suggestions lose some of their value. The grouse that drums too long gets an arrow. He once more examined

110

the loads of the horses in his charge and handed several twists of grass to Not Afraid of Guns while his companions talked.

"Your *sumesh* still is strong, Little Coyote," New Blade of Grass said. "What are your thoughts?"

"This talk has been wise. I have only to add that our warriors we hope will be able to join us will not yet know the advantages of the guns. They will wish to make many brave strikes and perform other notable deeds. They will not be restrained. Perhaps we should stay close together and protect our guns and powder by firing at any Blackfeet only when we are sure our bullets will strike them, as we did the four elk in our valley. Thus will we surprise the Blackfeet and help our brothers. We can reach out with the rifles. If we do not have time to reload the rifles if the Blackfeet continue to come closer, then we can use the muskets and, finally, our bows and arrows and lances."

New Blade of Grass secured his robe more tightly around his shoulders, grasped the lines to his horses and set out. After a lengthy interval, the men stopped for a rest.

"We will stay together as we try to reach the encampment from the woods." The sub-chief wrinkled his forehead in deep thought as the words struggled to come out. "I find it hard to even think about changing our way of fighting. Yet, I have remembered that Thunder Voice employed a plan that wiped out the Blackfeet on the valley trail and brought us many horses. Yes, we must change our ways of fighting as surely as the tree changes its leaves for each new season. Thus it grows. I can accept this." He shifted his gaze to Little Coyote, who once again observed and thoughtfully pondered the worry lines creasing his sub-chief's face as his voice grew softer. "Yes, I can accept this change. Can the others accept it?"

Bright Fire did not hurry back to the others that late afternoon with his information about the Blackfeet. Rather, he let his companions work their way down to him.

Already four lodges had gone up on the south slope of a hill, tapering downward and curving like *a:mt*, the end of the moon, almost to the stream bed. Even as the weary Flatheads watched, two more lodges took form.

"They place them well—against *sne'wt*, the wind, from the north," Has Many Horses, muttered. He tugged on a line, pulling his favorite horse to him. Its constant punching through the heavy snow crust was starting to wear through the hide, leaving a thin toll of blood circling each track. The sub-chief set his warriors to cutting two of the oldest buckskin shirts into strips and wrapping them loosely around the lower legs of their best mounts.

"The placement of the lodges will force any strangers like ourselves to move into the open, away from any protective cover." Bright Fire's usual cheerfulness seemed lost in his tired body. He squatted down on his snowshoes, pulling his robe more closely around him as the cold breeze quickly dried the perspiration on his heated body. "They will see and follow our tracks."

Their sub-chief nodded and looked to the west. "*Tcsoóskan*, when Sun is just over the hills, has come. We will remain here, then travel in the darkness away from their encampment but angling toward ours. They will find us, but they, too, must move on foot. Perhaps they did not bring the snowshoes, but we will prepare as though they have. Eat now. There is much hard work ahead. And perhaps another Blackfeet encampment."

The gun-seekers had planned well. So had the Blackfeet. Their distant and fierce yells alerted the weary travelers who had toiled throughout *skukuéts*, the dark. As *sgalgált*, the daylight, began, the Flatheads could see a small group of people struggling toward them from the direction of the Blackfeet camp they had bypassed. From the north came a larger group, evidently from another camp that lay ahead.

"There is no hope of reaching our people, or even the forest," New Blade of Grass told his four companions, who had closed up and were peering both north and south from between the bodies of their equally tired horses.

"The Blackfeet move on snowshoes. They come up fast." Has Many Horses removed his own snowshoes, leaped atop his favorite mount, then stood up. "Seven follow our trail from the south, maybe twice that from the north. There will be a good fight."

"Little Coyote, we will test your *sumesh* yet again." Pointing to seven of the poorest horses, New Blade of Grass had their burdens removed. The men placed the horses in a rough circle, legs tied, then methodically cut their throats. The hungry snow turned red about the animals as they struggled against their restraints, then fell. The men pulled the horses so their legs pointed outward; they feebly kicked, then quieted. The gun-seekers scooped the snow from within this red-rimmed fortress, piling it between the carcasses, and placed the buffalo meat and other gear, except the powder kegs, atop that. As they worked, the warriors clearly could hear the exultant, almost triumphant, yells from the smaller group closing more quickly from the south. The Flatheads pulled the remaining eight horses through a gap into the circle, closed that, hobbled the horses, then methodically loaded the muskets, keeping them low lest a sharp-eyed enemy see them. Now all their weapons were resting against the dead horses for ready use.

"There is an eagerness among the two groups to reach us first." New Blade of Grass placed his bow, quiver and lance atop the protective wall. "Very well. Let them get close and we will shoot first with the muskets. Then the rifles are sure to be ready to surprise those who hasten from the north."

The seven Blackfeet were close now, just out of good arrow range. They flowed together, seemed to rest and confer only for a moment, then charged forward. Their loud cries carried past the defensive circle and spurred the other band of attackers to more strenuous efforts.

The first hastily fired arrow struck a frozen chunk of meat. Two more hit the paunch of a dead animal.

"We will not shoot the muskets until we can hit a Blackfeet." New Blade of Grass spoke quietly, then stood on the arrow-struck carcass and defiantly waved his lance. His now shrill, taunting cries urged the Blackfeet to even greater effort, more com-petition—and less thought. Two of them cast off their blankets and raced forward in sudden silence, holding their bows ready to loose other arrows, the "shushing" sounds of their snowshoes racing through the crusted snow carrying easily to the waiting Flatheads.

The solid "thwack" of a musket ball striking a dead horse surprised Little Coyote more than the roar of the cut-off musket that one of the Blackfeet had pulled from under his blanket. Four more such sounds quickly followed. One of the hobbled horses began screaming, but there was no opportunity to see which in the melee, with the steady voice of New Blade of Grass reaching above all.

"The Blackfeet have their surprises, too!" the sub-chief shouted. "Now we will use the muskets. Little Coyote, you will watch the larger group and tell us when we must deal with them."

The ragged volley of shots reached outward as the young warrior faced north, remembering, oddly, how he had sat in stupefied fear, wonderment and surprise seemingly so long ago when the Blackfeet warrior had died from the well-placed lance launched by Young Willow.

Now he stifled similar impulses and others he had no time to differentiate as he counted the thirteen fearsome, howling figures racing toward the circle of death.

Two warriors were in the lead, one an exceedingly tall man armed with a long lance from which streamed several scalps and the butt end of which he used from time to time to maintain balance on his madly racing snowshoes. A tomahawk on the thong wrapped around his buckskin coat bounced up and down against his thigh. The other lead warrior, of medium stature, brandished a colorfully adorned coup stick, his axe on a leather loop around his wrist. Hanging from his neck was a bright disk from which were suspended several scalps. Now he moved ahead, almost to within good arrow range.

Little Coyote rested his rifle in his left hand atop the side of a dead horse. The front sight moved from the chest area of the tall warrior to the bright disk of the other before he pulled the trigger. The "craaack" of the long gun reached his ears as the shorter warrior faltered, recovered his balance, then fell. A warrior behind him stumbled over his dead companion and fell, too. He rose to his knees in the broken, crusty snow, got up on one snowshoe and, as he prepared to lift the other and stand erect, fell over, too, at the crack of a rifle next to Little Coyote. Bright Fire yelled his elation and reached for a musket. As Little Coyote hastily reloaded his rifle, he chanced a quick look behind him. Only one brave moved there—energetic Has Many Horses loosing an arrow into each still figure.

Two more long rifles cracked and two more warriors fell. The tall Blackfeet with the lance turned half-way around, shouted something and waved the lance northward. He and his companions courageously and laboriously began dragging their dead with them in retreat. While they were thus hampered, New Blade of Grass remorselessly ordered his warriors to load their long rifles. He looked at each gun, including that of Has Many Horses, who had vaulted back inside the circle. The warriors pushed the horses to the southern side of the fort. The sub-chief's quick eye assigned a target to each of the riflemen.

The fusillade was ragged, the aim good. As the smoke cleared, the Flatheads could see that five more Blackfeet warriors had fallen. One of these tried to get up, then fell backward on a leg that would not support him. He futilely tried to reach and remove the snowshoes and join his four companions who were rapidly moving in retreat. The tall warrior lingered until the wounded brave pushed him away. Atop a small rise almost directly west, the surviving Blackfeet stopped. The tall warrior raised his lance and shook it, his loud, vengeful cry reaching the Flatheads. Holding reloaded rifles, the gun-seekers were viewing with astonishment the carnage their weapons had produced.

Little Coyote looked toward the fallen warrior, who continued to try to undo his snowshoes. The man was canted in a depression in the deep snow. He almost would reach the snowshoes, then would fall backward, unable to overcome the mechanics of his damaged limb trying to bear the weight of his body.

New Blade of Grass solicitously examined each of his warriors, pulling on an arm, seizing a leg, examining their chests, lest one or more had taken an arrow or musket ball and was trying to hide the wound from the others. All were unhurt. There was much reason to rejoice.

"Ka-ruck ka-ruck." Already the ravens had flapped to this place of much death. As the black creatures flattened their wings and soared and wheeled, occasionally voicing their impatience, New Blade of Grass looked past his warriors and toward the four silently watching Blackfeet.

"Bring the weapons, clothing and snowshoes from the dead. There are scalps for all." He examined the wounded mare. She had fallen among the legs of the seven other nervously moving mounts. The ball from the Blackfeet musket had penetrated the side of the eye socket, carrying away a frontal portion of the skull. The sub-chief sank his knife deep into the throat and withdrew it with a ripping movement, nimbly hopping to one side to avoid the heavy spurt of blood. He wiped the blade on the side of the dying horse and this time looked long at the four Blackfeet on the hill.

When two ravens glided down to the naked bodies south of the fortress, the sub-chief shifted his view to them and to a quietly watching Little Coyote. The young warrior had entered the bloody circle with an armload of bows, arrows, snowshoes, axes, clothing and muskets. He was peering through the cumbersome load, evidently so deep in thought that he was unmindful of the burden.

Other ravens began swarming in from all parts of the sky to work faster than could the cold. Earliest to latest arrival greeted each newcomer with quarrelsome "prruk prruks" and threatening, often punishing, bills.

"What do you see, Little Coyote?" New Blade of Grass asked. Then, more loudly, "What do you hear?" When no answer came, the sub-chief sat atop the dead horse inside the fortress and watched this puzzling young warrior who seemed to see things that were not there, to listen to distant voices others could not hear.

"There is enough for all, yet they fight," Little Coyote murmured. He shifted his gaze to the Blackfeet silhouetted against the sky. He laid down his burden and prepared to get another.

"Yes, the ravens always are hungry." The sub-chief stood atop the carcass. "Ho, Bright Fire, Has Many Horses. Examine the hurt Blackfeet. If we reach our encampment safely, there will be much to take our people's minds off their hunger." He began loading the much-enlarged pile of baggage onto the greatly diminished number of horses.

The cavalcade resumed its slow trek northward, the Blackfeet captive unintelligibly jeering from his precarious perch atop the largest horse. Bright Fire unsuccessfully tried at times to silence him by roughly poking the bullet-shattered leg with the butt of his rifle. While resting atop a small rise, they watched the four Blackfeet descend to the raven-covered battle area. One warrior set out in the direction of the by-passed encampment. Two remained with the fallen warriors and insistent ravens while the fourth, tallest of all, began following the triumphant Flatheads from a carefully calculated and highly respectful distance.

14.

Little Coyote lay quietly atop the soft furs in the lodge of Running Buffalo Bull. Even his belly was content. Little Yellow Bird had made a delicious stew from dried vegetables and buffalo meat; the meat was thinly shaved from Little Coyote's share of the frozen chunks the gun-seekers had brought into camp, along with the horse meat, under the escort of numerous warriors sent by Tjolzhitsay and Thunder Voice. Both parents had greeted their son with much joy. Despite the lack of buffalo meat, there had been a wild celebration in the open space between the circle of thirty Flathead lodges and the eighteen of the Shoshonis.

The young men who had clustered around Little Coyote amid the uproar demanded an account of his adventures. He had accommodated them, but was grateful when head chief Tjolzhitsay and Thunder Voice momentarily had quieted the tumult and announced there would be a great fire the next night. Then, New Blade of Grass, Bright Fire and Has Many Horses would tell their stories to three circles of the people. Meanwhile, during the day, the council had to make many decisions; one problem was the question of leadership, what with the buffalo scattered and the snow and the Blackfeet seemingly everywhere.

"New Blade of Grass?" Tjolzhitsay's voice had become almost as loud as that of Thunder Voice.

The sub-chief, standing among the people with his family, had answered. Tjolzhitsay had asked him to come forward so all could see. With no ceremony, but with a few well-chosen words, the chief had praised him for bringing the guns to the people.

"You will be 'Gun,' if your wish is that of the people," Tjolzhitsay had said.

Little Coyote had seen the tired sub-chief raise his head in pride at this honor. Then Gun had stepped back into the crowd.

The two leaders had ordered that the Blackfeet captive be brought forth. They had pointed their lances at the defiant warrior standing crookedly on the broken leg a little apart from the people and tethered to four Flathead warriors with leather ropes. There would be the torture. They had called forth Basket, widow of Cold Wind, the gun-seeker. She would have the first blow.

Her braids raggedly severed in grief, blood yet leaking from gashes of mourning on arms, neck and breasts, Basket had approached the warrior amid almost complete silence. With her obsidian blade she carefully had made the first cut just below the man's neck, down the chest, down the flat belly past the navel, stopping just above the crotch. She would continue her work, aided by others, on the morrow; there had been sounds of approval that she had cut carefully so the life would not escape too soon in too much blood. There were voices of disappointment that while the Blackfeet's skin had opened, his mouth had remained tightly shut.

Yes, Little Coyote was content. There was the approval of the people over the success of the gun-seekers; booty; scalps; much adventure, with promise of much more yet ahead; his acceptance into the ranks of the young, even not so young, warriors; a growing conviction among the people, and, he admitted now, even within himself, that the Good Spirit was smiling especially on him and providing him with insights rare for one of his age.

The hub-bub a short distance away quieted. Once more he could hear Thunder Voice reminding the encampment there was to be no pursuit of the buffalo by individuals or small groups, and that the whip awaited those who disobeyed. More quietly, the voice of Tjolzhitsay warned of the nearness of the Blackfeet encampment only two hills away. The voices of sub-chiefs cautioned the guards yet again to keep close watch on the horses. Little Coyote began thinking of Not Afraid of Guns, how she would respond to the buffalo hunt, what she could teach him. Then as the softness of the fur bed and the warmth of the blanket began carrying the young warrior's active mind and body into sleep, he was alerted to almost full wakefulness when Running Buffalo Bull and Little Yellow Bird pushed aside the lodge flap and entered. She added a few small twigs to the hot coals; when they broke into flames, Little Coyote opened his eyes and for a time watched the shadows climb and fall on the lodge wall. His parents spoke quietly, their discussion centering on the food supply, the nearness of their son and what the council decisions would be on the morrow.

The small fire warmed the lodge. Little Coyote threw off the upper portion of the blanket, remembering as he did so the sudden warmness in the old lodge of the gun-seekers and the momentary warm caresses of the wind as he had stood guard among the buffalo herd. He yawned. He would ask his father to explain the warmth in the morning. He turned away from the tiny dancing flames and faced the lodge wall. As sleep came, somewhere deep in his mind there formed a partial linkup between those all-too-brief warm caresses of the wind and the momentary glimpse of a Shoshone maiden who, like himself, had turned away unnoticed by the others when Basket had used her blade.

Running Buffalo Bull examined his son's rifle and listened carefully as the young warrior explained its operation. The father smiled with much pride when he learned what the rifle had accomplished during the journey. As Little Yellow Bird placed more thick stew into her son's bowl, she stooped over him and prolonged the serving, smiling and receiving a smile in return amid this warriors' talk. Later, her son was sure, she would learn more about the young Shoshone maiden if he would ask her to;

he was certain he would. That settled, there still was the question about the brief touches of the warm breeze.

"The snow-eater wind comes from the east with Sun, warm and dry, to carry away the snow. This you know." Having responded to his son's question, Running Buffalo Bull pointed the rifle at the smoke hole. He squinted through the small sights as he moved them from the patch of gray sky to center the muzzle at the tip of a pole. "Yes, I understand now how one must aim." He put the rifle across his lap. "There has been no sign of such a wind here, but on the hills, perhaps there is a fight between the cold and the warm winds. We have not been on the hills because of the Blackfeet. I have felt such forces three times while they gathered on the hills, and the snow-eater won each time, though I understand it does not always win." He pulled the plug from the powder horn and carefully examined a few of the black grains; he grinned in surprise when his son placed the grains on a wood chip and pushed the chip into the flames, the "phht" clearly audible despite the tininess of the grains.

"When many of them seek to escape with fire from the rifle, they raise their voices together and drive the bullet with much power," Little Coyote explained. "Thus, perhaps, it is with the warm breaths of air. They grow into many breaths and force away the cold winds."

Running Buffalo Bull gloomily poked the fire, then said, "The heavy snow has hurt our hunt. We have not been able to hold the great drive. Indeed, we have not been able to use the horses to reach the buffalo. And all the while the Blackfeet grow in number. There will be a great fight when the snow at last goes, perhaps only in *skepts*, the spring. And there will be great hunger before we fight our way back to our valley." He pushed his poking stick into the fire. "Soon the heralds will call the council. It is the wish of both Three Eagles and Thunder Voice that you attend with me."

He picked up Little Coyote's war shield and began explaining how his son must work with the paints to keep the shield blood red, with the small white coyote in the center.

The great cry began on the westernmost fringe of the camp

among the lodges of the Shoshonis and grew in strength as it enveloped the lodges of the Flatheads. Distinguishable amid the growing uproar of people's shouts, the excited barking of dogs and cries of children was the word "Blackfeet." Running Buffalo Bull and Little Coyote seized their bows and arrows and hurriedly pushed through the lodge flap. Little Coyote placed the pup's tail around his neck as he ran. Little Yellow Bird methodically put her blanket around her shoulders and carried lighter ones to her husband and son. The two warriors ran toward the space inside the circle of lodges.

Little Coyote immediately recognized the warrior standing in the wide circle of people. He was the tall Blackfeet who almost had fallen to his rifle. Instead of the scalp-decorated long lance, the Blackfeet held aloft a long pipe from which hung a stream of white feathers. Then, as the feathers on this peace symbol streamed eastward in the western breeze, he placed the bowl end of the pipe on the end of one snowshoe and signed he came in peace to confer with the chiefs. Little Coyote noticed the man's eyes—moving, seeking, searching. Once more the Blackfeet raised the pipe and held it immobile while the feathers fluttered in the diminishing westerly breeze. Now a contrary breeze from the east, unnoticed amid the excitement, tentatively fluttered some of the smaller feathers while the sub-chiefs alerted their warriors and re-enforced the horse-watchers. While the encampment wondered, the Flathead and Shoshone leaders and certain designated warriors assembled in the great council lodge. Since this was not a head chief, Tjolzhitsay had asked his *i-sts-sókoi*, Three Eagles, to preside. Little Coyote and his father sat far back near the entrance. Only the Blackfeet remained standing; he looked down on Three Eagles and Thunder Voice haughtily, but not insultingly. Before them on a rich beaver pelt lay the two pipes—one bedecked with the red feathers of war, the other with the white feathers of peace. Which would be smoked now rested with the Blackfeet. The two leaders motioned for him to sit. He did so, then spoke.

"I am Tree, a chief among the Blackfeet." His strong, forceful voice contrasted sharply with the high pitch of old, almost-toothless Many Voices, the interpreter. "You have as prisoner, Owl, a chief among our allies, the Bloods?"

Tree's bright eyes narrowed and moved from face to face, seeking an answer to his question. Perhaps he would find it in the changing demeanors of his enemies when they learned the importance of their prisoner.

"The Flatheads and the Shoshonis have a prisoner." Three Eagles looked at Thunder Voice, who would answer the next question.

"We would have back Owl," Tree said.

Many Voices' squeaky words died almost to a whisper as the three chiefs recounted ancient and recent losses of people to Flatheads, Shoshonis and Blackfeet alike. Finally they spoke of the encounter with the gun-seekers where Owl had fallen, though there was no mention of the guns.

"The Flatheads and the Shoshonis need the buffalo," Tree said. "They gather in great numbers near our encampment." The Blackfeet sub-chief tossed a small chip into the council fire where it immediately was consumed among the larger burning embers. "Your lodges are few. The lodges of the Blackfeet soon will number the stars. I would have back Owl before my voice, which is strong now among the people here, might weaken among the newcomers. Yet, once a promise is made, all will accept it. My people agree you can hunt in peace this time and return to your valley with much food. In return, we would have Owl."

"We will talk?" Thunder Voice looked at Three Eagles. At the latter's nod of agreement, Gun signed for Tree to accompany him. He put the Blackfeet sub-chief in the lodge of an honored warrior and hurriedly returned. In the interim, Three Eagles had sought out Tjolzhitsay.

Again the talk was long in order to hide from Tree the desperation of the Flatheads' and Shoshonis' condition. If the deep snow remained, there would be little likelihood they could use the horses to hunt and transport the meat back to the encampment, much less to their valley. And Tree's words had been true: Soon the Flatheads and Shoshonis could be surrounded by their enemies, who on summer hunts often had erected lodges twice the number of the Flatheads' horses.

"We will trade Owl for the hunt?" Three Eagles received affirmation from all within the lodge—save one.

"I would be heard!"

All heads turned to learn who had spoken, their eyes centering on the broad shoulders and head of an astonished Running Buffalo Bull because much smaller Little Coyote was blocked from view by two equally large warriors.

"Who would be heard?" Thunder Voice's bellowed question carried both disapproval and challenge.

"Stand! Come forward where you can be seen!" Three Eagles' command seemed to carry a hint that whoever would dare to do so almost risked an arrow.

Little Coyote felt himself shaking as though his legs were those of a new-born foal. He slowly picked his way among the closely packed bodies. Some of those whose voices were strengthening the growing wind of disapproval deliberately impeded his movement with shoulders and, in a few instances, strong arms. One warrior pulled off his blanket, causing him to stumble.

Now he stood before the seated chiefs, a thin youth-man clad in moccasins, a breech-clout and a coyote pup's tail. Some of the assemblage laughed. They laughed, but the youth had a certain presence. The widely circulated stories of his achievements finally prompted all to heed Three Eagles' gesture for silence.

"All present, and, I suspect, Tjolzhitsay, wisely have agreed to give Owl in exchange for the hunt." Little Coyote raised one hand to silence the voices questioning that he now so readily agreed with them. Had he changed his mind during his struggle from the back of the lodge to the position before the chiefs? Again there were laughs and several knowing snickers. Little Coyote prepared to sit in accordance with custom, but Three Eagles motioned for him to continue to stand. Did the almost indiscernible, fleeing hint of a smile signify encouragement?

"The Blackfeet know we suffer, as do they, from the snow," Little Coyote said. "Without the snow we could keep Owl and hunt the buffalo on our horses or in the great drive, strong with our many warriors and now the guns Tjolzhitsay and Three Eagles so wisely sent us to seek." Little Coyote dared to lower his head ever so little and now trade Three Eagles an enigmatic smile. "Yet our strength is not that we have Owl. With our strength, which the Blackfeet do not know, we can bargain for much more if Owl is so important among the Bloods. Do you know our strength? Three Eagles and Thunder Voice have a strength which I can help to show."

Little Coyote now held his head high, arms extended outwardly to emphasize the question and heighten the suspense while he left his question unanswered. He watched the assemblage closely. When impatience threatened to overcome curiosity, he spoke again.

"There can be a snow-eater wind so we can use the horses. It could arrive before Sun is above this lodge. Demand of Tree at once that there be a safe hunt now and in the summer. By then we will know how to use the guns, even during the big drive." Little Coyote raised his arms above his head and let them drop. "The Blackfeet also will not have us surrounded while we hunt. Would we now trade one of our warriors for every buffalo we kill?" Little Coyote looked down at the chiefs and spoke again.

"I would have Three Eagles and Thunder Voice carry the sacred pipes outside the lodge." The youth removed the coyote's tail from around his neck and gravely requested the use of Three Eagles' great lance. The chief set his mouth with such force that his lips compressed into an almost-invisible line. His eyes partially closed to tight slits; as he nodded agreement his features, accented by the nose, resembled the great bird after which he was named. He motioned that all would leave the lodge.

The warriors had been seated for a long time, so were grateful to follow the chiefs and Little Coyote. Little Coyote cautiously told them he would need half the people to line up on the north side of the lodge, the others on the south side. Standing in the lane between the two lines, the youth wrapped most of the thong of the pup's tail around the lance blade. He requested Three Eagles to hold aloft the pipe of peace, then closed his eyes, raised his head to Sun and loudly prayed: "Good Spirit, knowing the greatness of these chiefs, Tjolzhitsay, Three Eagles and Thunder Voice, knowing their care for our people, knowing we need the snow-eater wind, show us your greater power now."

Now Little Coyote asked Thunder Voice to lower the pipe of war. The young seer raised the pup's tail high above his head. Almost at once the tail, and feathers on the pipes to a lesser degree, caught the breeze and gently waved east and west. Then, almost imperceptibly, the greater strength of the easterly wind began to show to the wonderment of all—not forcefully yet, but with certainty. Little Coyote thanked the Good Spirit and asked that the west wind remain the people's friend and bring them the rains and other good events, but in season.

When the warriors noisily filed back to the lodge, one burly brave shook and handed the blanket back to Little Coyote. Tree was summoned, the bargain struck and affirmed—Three Eagles and Thunder Voice of the Flatheads, Big Rock in the River of the Shoshonis, and Tree of the Blackfeet smoking the white pipe. The latter, on his snowshoes, left the lodge and encampment unsmilingly and with great dignity. Broken-legged Owl was supported, unwillingly, by two stalwart Flatheads who would accompany the Blackfeet almost to the enemy camp. But as a mark of respect and to show the honor attached to the agreements concluded, Three Eagles asked three other warriors to walk into the camp, itself.

As the snow-eater later strengthened and began its work, Thunder Voice, once more in command, relaxed the encampment discipline long enough for Broken Tooth, Running Buffalo Bull and two other great hunters to seek an isolated small band of fat cows and young bulls near camp and kill them for a great feast to precede the larger hunt.

Running Buffalo Bull had asked Little Coyote to accompany him on snowshoes toward the small forest when both succeeded in breaking away from their friends after the council. The two men walked laboriously until they reached the first low evergreens peeking from the softening snow. Father and son stopped and looked back toward the encampment. The snow-eater wind was freshening, bending to the west the smoke from the lodges. People were adjusting smoke flaps to the new conditions.

"There is something to be learned in the smoke flaps," Running Buffalo Bull said gently, his strong, earnest face straining with the intensity of his effort to explain clearly and carefully yet another lesson to his son. "We put the flaps on the tepees because the wind never blows from one direction only. After much thought, the people learned it was easier to devise the flaps than to turn the tepees to each new change of the wind. People's minds are much like the vagrant winds which blow from many directions—ever-changing, cold, warm, strong, weak, loud, quiet. Yes, ever-changing. You did very well to tell the council that all had decided wisely to give Owl in exchange for the hunt. Thus, you began to set the varying winds of their minds in your direction before suggesting that the trade also require a safe hunt in the summer."

Running Buffalo Bull placed his right hand on his son's shoulder. "You sometimes are puzzling, my son, to me and to Little Yellow Bird. I encourage you to always think of the smoke flaps when you work on people's minds." His grip tightened. "Never become impatient with those who do not have this gift of insight from the Good Spirit, sent to you at such an early age. Many will catch up with your thoughts, given patience. Others never will. The best teachers always must remain learners."

The father let his arm fall. Now he smiled. "Most of our people gamble, but I did not know that you gamble. You placed great stakes on the arrival of the snow-eater."

"A gamble? Stakes, my father?" Little Coyote said with a grin. "I was armed with your wisdom about the snow-eater." The grin faded. "And my prayer to the Good Spirit was no gamble at all."

After Little Coyote's father had helped with the small hunt, and the encampment prepared for the greater one to follow after the snow was largely gone, the young warrior carefully avoided the enticing stares of several maidens. All apparently thought that the direct paths through the slush ran past the lodge of Running Buffalo Bull. Little Yellow Bird courteously greeted them in one way or another—when she was not getting better acquainted with the Shoshonis.

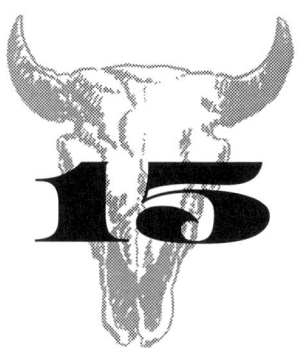

T hunder Voice halted the hunters where the stream bed
divided into two smaller branches, their banks abrim with
snow melt that had rotted away most of the thin ice cover
formed during the unseasonal cold. On the low-lying hills to the
east were small bands of grazing buffalo bulls, separated from
the larger herd of cows, calves and younger bulls to the west.
Though these were easier to kill, they also were much closer to
the Blackfeet.

"The Blackfeet will honor the word of Tree," Thunder Voice
assured the three hunting groups as he assigned their general areas
to avoid overlapping. If buffalo from one area sought escape
into another, it, too, would be covered by hunters. Also, each
group of warriors could hasten to the aid of the others should an
enemy strike. "Yes, the word of Tree, of the Blackfeet, is good,
but with many of them yet arriving, that word might not reach
them all."

Warriors skilled with the long rifles accompanied each of
the three groups as possible guardians: Little Coyote and Little
Bear Claw with Running Buffalo Bull; Bright Fire and Has Many
Horses with Broken Tooth; Gun leading his own party. Each
group had brought one musket to try against the buffalo, though

the council had decreed there would be judicious use of the powder. The leaders had parceled out the muskets, including the shortened ones obtained from the dead Blackfeet, and had arranged for instruction of the new owners.

"One does not waste these gifts the Good Spirit has sent to us as the number of our people has dwindled," Thunder Voice had proclaimed. Tjolzhitsay and Three Eagles, who carried especially long-barreled muskets, had nodded in agreement. Finally, Thunder Voice had said, "Again, seek the cows, or the bulls that are not more than two summers old. Their thick fur makes the best robes. Do I need remind you their meat is juiciest, with much good fat?"

As the three groups separated, Running Buffalo Bull led his hunters gradually upward in a northeasterly direction. "We will kill them as we charge downhill, with the added advantage they will fall closer to our encampment," he explained as he stationed the untested young brave who would race with word of the kill to the people. Thunder Voice had decreed that to save time the women would assist the men in the hard work of butchering.

As he again studied the locations of the small bands, Running Buffalo Bull nudged his mount alongside his son's. "My father and his father told me how at times the Good Spirit sent the buffalo into our valley. How much easier it would be for us to hunt them there. Yet, their fathers hunted them here and elsewhere before the people moved into our valley. Perhaps what we do now to get the meat keeps us vigilant and strong. Let us go." He began to move away to set his hunters in motion.

The hunters tried to suppress their excitement. Not so the horses. Little Coyote's voice and tugs on the reins of Not Afraid of Guns ranged from gentle to commanding as the pinto's eagerness grew after she, too, began watching the quarry.

The hunters circled around the largest band. When they were well above all the buffalo and screened by brush, Running Buffalo Bull studied the mountainside a final time.

"You will watch for this signal while we kill as many buffalo as possible," he explained to his son and the two other young hunters. "I will raise my bow above my head. Only then will you try to kill the buffalo, as you have been instructed. We will go."

Not Afraid of Guns no longer quivered with excitement. Instead, the mare almost docilely walked downward; only her head and ears remained pointed toward the quarry, much like the dog that sometimes stalks the grouse in the grass.

A buffalo cow looked toward the hunters, then continued to stare, forgetting to chew the dead grass that hung from her mouth. She snorted and her tail rose. Now Little Coyote scarcely could hold back the pinto as she gathered her muscles to run downward. Her master and the two other impatient braves now alternated between restraining their mounts and watching the other hunters. They would try to have these buffalo mill about rather than thunder downhill. The hunters' exultant cries rose above the snorts and bellows of the black bodies that began erupting in all directions. Two of the animals stumbled, then recovered as another fell and began kicking against the sodden ground. Those buffalo farthest from the hunters began racing west and downward, leading the herd with them. One smaller group broke away and moved northward. Above the turmoil the three vigilant hunters saw a bow move upward, downward, again and again, then point northward. When Little Coyote kicked the mare gently in the flanks and slackened the reins, she shot forward as though launched from a sling.

Small clods of earth kicked backward from the hooves of the young bull Little Coyote singled out. He reined his horse to the left flank of the massive creature. How would the pinto respond if he momentarily dropped the reins on her neck to use his lance? The test exceeded his hopes: She moved steadily behind the grunting bull, nimbly swerving aside as he thundered slightly uphill to try to gore and toss her with his sharp, black horns before again moving downhill. The mare followed to the right, slightly behind the hairy front foreleg, closing the gap to good lance thrust distance. Her former Blackfeet master had trained her superbly. Little Coyote grasped the lance just above balance point and aimed the blade low behind the right shoulder area. Now he grasped the lance with the left hand, too, slightly above the right, for greater steadiness and thrusting power. As the buffalo's racing front legs pumped forward, slightly separating the massive ribs, Little Coyote thrust the weapon at a downward slant. In went the sharp blade and part of the haft; as the bull flinched the pinto slowed her speed and veered slightly away, allowing Little Coyote to extract the lance head for another thrust. None was needed. The panting bull slowed, unsteadily raced uphill again then, its heart stopped by the obsidian intruder, crashed into the sodden ground near a lone tree.

His coyote-like yelps of triumph joining with the exultant cries of other successful hunters, Little Coyote dropped his lance against the inert body of his trophy and reached for his bow and arrows. A young cow a short distance downhill took three of his arrows before she stopped, her sides heaving, blood from her arrow-pierced lung bubbling from her black nostrils and mouth. Little Coyote stirred her to tottery movement and drove a fourth arrow into her heart.

As he looked for his next quarry, he saw black bodies scattered over the mountainside. Some hunters had stopped to let their horses rest; two pursued an animal over a small rise. To the south Little Coyote saw a plume of smoke and then heard the dull report of a musket followed by another puff of smoke and the sharper crack of a rifle. His father and another hunter were ending their chase by testing their guns on the buffalo. Would these new weapons prove effective against such huge creatures? Little Coyote patted his pinto's neck, then leaned forward to scratch her ears. Beyond doubt, except for his father and mother, this superbly trained pinto was his greatest treasure.

"Have you no work to do?"

Little Yellow Bird, clad in butchering clothes, placed one bloody hand on her hip and pointed the gift knife of Little Coyote toward her son and his two companions. They continued to sit there on their restless horses, staring down at the Shoshone maiden who had accompanied the woman to her son's lance-killed bull. Spattered legs, old mud-gobbed moccasins, an already blood-smeared buckskin shift and short vest seemed to emphasize the girl's beauty rather than detract from it.

"There is much work!" Little Yellow Bird continued to scold. "Did you kill a buffalo? Did others of your families do so? If that is not so, then you can help with these two of my son's. Thunder Voice said all must work quickly while there is the snow-eater and Sun that the Good Spirit sent us to help dry the meat."

Stung by these questions about their hunting prowess, Little Coyote's fellow hunters reluctantly abandoned their obvious willingness to work with the maiden and kicked their mounts in the direction of their own single kills. As they looked backward, the girl's willowy body straightened for a moment, allowing her long, dark braids to fall gently forward onto her shoulders and breasts. The braids framed a face so lovely that Little Coyote felt tuggings he did not know could exist.

How awkward he felt as he slid off his pinto's rump and wiped the bloodied lance blade across the wet stubble, then on the hair of the carcass. Leaning the lance against a tree, he rode his horse to his arrow-killed buffalo to study the location of the arrows and to position the carcass for easier butchering. He turned the head as far as he could beside the body, then with all his strength and weight drove the horns into the ground to hold the head in place. He seized the under foreleg above the hoof and, using it as a lever, pulled suddenly upward. The carcass rolled on its back and remained in place, propped by the turned head. He then opened the carcass from rib cage to tail to release some of the heat. Now he could help his mother, who quietly and effectively had arranged for the Shoshone family to work with them and share the meat.

"This is *Staán*, Antelope," Little Yellow Bird said casually. "I needed help, with my two men hunting. Your other buffalo is ready for butchering, I see. Well . . ." An uncharacteristic note of indecision colored her voice. ". . . perhaps since it is smaller, I can work on that. Then you two can join me there. I will leave three pack horses and take two, but we'll need to make more trips back to camp." As the woman led the horses away, Antelope continued to skin the buffalo, pulling the hide outward so the meat would rest on it, out of the grass and soft earth. She and

Little Yellow Bird had succeeded in propping the carcass on its belly, with the outstretched legs helping to hold it there.

Little Coyote would have been content to stand there marveling at the deftness with which the beautiful girl worked, but that was not to be. When Little Yellow Bird was out of hearing, the girl jabbed her metal knife into the exposed and bloody shoulder meat and, for the first time, spoke. Her words were in Flathead, not Shoshone, and were in a voice that seemed a blend of the music of singing birds, creeks and spring winds: "Yes, two knives can work better than one. As Thunder Voice has said, 'All must gather the meat, even the greatest hunters.'" Her emphasis of the word 'great' went almost unnoticed as the wonderful sound of her voice reached Little Coyote's ears. "Perhaps the people of Tjolzhitsay need little meat. Not so the Shoshonis. Our meat bags were empty when we began this hunt. Will you continue to stare at your great kill, or will you help?"

A gust of the snow-eater wind set her braids to swinging and pressed the old buckskins against her body. Their eyes met and as the much-delayed import of the maiden's words reached Little Coyote's mind, he stared at the beautiful lips that had uttered them. A hint of a smile was there, partially belying the seeming sharpness of her words. The essential message at this first meeting was: "We could be friends, Little Coyote, but I need not seek only your friendship."

Drawing his own knife, Little Coyote began to work on the carcass. There was much more labor than a deer, even a large bull elk, demanded. He would much rather hunt than butcher, yet under the present circumstances there were compensations. He held one, then the other, backstrap while Antelope deftly cut them from along the spine. Their bodies touched at arms and hips as both times she severed the heavier end near the massive rump. Little Coyote hung the thick, bloody ropes of meat from a stout branch of the misshapen tree. Then the couple reduced the carcass to the customary eleven pieces, whereupon the brave borrowed Antelope's knife to sever the head. He had plans for that.

Antelope turned over a flap of the hide and wiped her bloody hands on the hair. Soon she was breaking small twigs from the tree; using dry grass tassels she struck a fire. She impaled three slick pieces of fat on three larger branches, then three slabs of the great heart and three more pieces of fat. She stuck the other ends into the soft ground. While the meat sizzled and dripped, she and Little Coyote completed their work—except for loading the horses—while eating small pieces of steaming, raw liver.

They sat on the dry ground at the base of the tree. As they ate, Little Coyote periodically gazed at the fascinating creature beside him. Her face was small, as those of women went, her nose well-formed, not overly long. Her high cheek bones and firm young jaws moved gently up and down as the strong, evenly spaced teeth worked on yet another bite of the deliciously roasted meat. Her dark eyes were framed in long lashes. *How well-named she is,* the young warrior thought. Suddenly, he remembered that there was much work to do—and that a problem remained: How could the two of them—strong, but not fully grown—place such large chunks of meat on the pack animals? He could call down to busy Little Yellow Bird to lend her help, but would a warrior do that?

Antelope gracefully stood, stretched, then removed a coil of leather rope from a pack horse. While Little Coyote prolonged his last bite of meat, she deftly secured the rope around two of the largest chunks, threw the other end of the rope over a high branch and tied it to another pack horse. She led the horse downhill while the meat dragged forward for a moment across part of the hide, then slowly rose above the bloody mess. When the chunks were dangling shoulder-high, she stood there quite impatiently waiting for this slow-eating warrior to lead another horse under the load and secure it. This he did, somewhat clumsily, but perhaps he was tired from the hunt. He recaptured some of his aplomb when, after eying the heavily loaded pack horses, he securely fastened the head of the bull onto Not Afraid of Guns. It would be offensive to turn his pinto into a pack horse, but he was certain the head would be appropriate because of the use to which he would put it. Soon Antelope and Little Coyote were taking the horses downhill to Little Yellow Bird. In the lead was Antelope.

Little Yellow Bird looked approvingly at the load, then hungrily began eating the roasted meat Antelope offered her. As all three began working on the smaller buffalo, Little Coyote noted regretfully that his mother already had removed the back straps. He brightened when he remembered there was no tree here and he would have to help Antelope lift the meat to the other two horses.

Soon the cavalcade of eight horses was wending down the steaming mountainside and toward Running Buffalo Bull's well-laden animals. Running Buffalo Bull nibbled his lower lip, stared at the trio leading the horses, then spoke: "These are good kills. The lance of Eagle Claw's forefathers served you well, Little Coyote. You used it with great skill, as you did the bow of the Blackfeet you killed." There was a slightly mischievous smile on his face, unseen by Antelope since, during his lavish praise, he turned to hand his son two small objects. "This misshapen bullet from a musket was easy to find far behind a badly splintered rib of a bull. The small one from a rifle we found only after carefully butchering a buffalo and following the bullet's passage from penetration point behind the shoulder area, between the ribs and into the stout heart. But we used the rifle only after the bull was down. We will perhaps use only the musket on the buffalo." After this important bit of man-talk, the warrior retrieved the two bullets and told his wife the women should lead the pack horses toward the encampment.

"You will guard them," he told his son. Once more there was the hidden smile before he began riding obliquely upward toward another butchering site.

Soon the trio could see widely separated lines of horses and people moving down the mountainside. The lines reminded Little Coyote of a giant, many-stringed horse quirt, the wider "handle" being that point at the mountain's base where all the hunters were assembling before heading in a triumphant mass toward the encampment. They would return to the hunting and butchering area again and again during the busy day.

A large flock of ravens circled above the mountainside, a

few settling now and again at the butchering sites. The Flatheads and Shoshonis had left little food for the disappointed, sharp-eyed, ever hungry foragers.

The very old men and women, even the toddlers among the children who had hazarded the trip to the buffalo grounds, worked hard, too. They brought long, thin poles from the patch of forest, stripped them of branches and erected rows of drying racks for the meat. Soon the women were slicing it into thin strips and hanging the strips on the racks to dry. Fearful that the snow-eater and Sun might depart again, the workers built small fires under some of the racks to hasten the drying process. The Shoshonis pounded some of the dry meat into small pieces and mixed in dried berries transported from their beloved homeland. Then they broke open the buffalo bones and melted the marrow with other fats to pour over the pounded meat and berries. Soon great bags of this pemmican were stored in the Shoshonis' lodges with the growing piles of bags of jerky. The faint smell of peppermint emanated from the bags; the aromatic leaves would repel hungry insects.

Hunters continued to bring in more meat, denying Little Coyote time to spend with the delightful girl. Antelope, her mother, a younger brother of perhaps eleven summers and a baby sister worked afield and in camp with Little Yellow Bird. All the while, Thunder Voice circled the lodges of Flathead and Shoshone alike, his features softening a bit each day until at last they brightened like the craggy peak that catches the first rays of newly risen Sun.

Soon the heralds were proclaiming, "It is enough! The thanks to the Good Spirit and the great feast will be on the morrow."

Very solemnly then, Thunder Voice, Three Eagles and two important Shoshone sub-chiefs carried four shaggy buffalo heads to the center of the space between the two encampments. Thunder Voice placed the head of a great bull to face north; Three Eagles the head of a cow to face south, and the two sub-chiefs the heads of yet another bull and a calf to face west and east. Inside the circle of heads they prepared their pipes. Then each stood, one at a time, to face the direction of the head he had put in place. Tjolzhitsay appeared, looked heavenward, and presented the pipes to the four others. Now all drew deeply on their pipes. As they blew the smoke upward they raised the pipes in both hands high above their heads, thanking the Good Spirit for sending the buffalo, Sun and the snow-eater to feed the people and asking that the next hunts prove as successful.

The two young hunters who had killed their first buffalo with Little Coyote and reluctantly had left the presence of Antelope galloped their horses toward the lodge of Running Buffalo Bull during the feasting. Soon three more rode up, then two more. Other people began walking toward the lodge.

"Ho, Little Coyote, will you race?" The challenger had reined his horse to such a sudden stop that the animal slid in the still-damp soil.

Little Coyote was reluctant to accept the challenge. Broken Pipe, Antelope's father, was telling how the Shoshonis in the distant past had come onto the plains country with their allies, the Comanche. But the Sioux had driven them back into the mountain foothills, where he raised many fine horses called "Pelouse," later "Appaloosa." The four slender-legged creatures with the distinctive spotted hindquarters and rumps that had borne his family on this hunt attested to their quality. Broken Pipe's father had started the herd from stock obtained from their friends the Users of Black Paint, or Nee Mee Poo, the Real People. They were centered in the Wallowa Valley, the Land of the Winding Waters, far to the west. A few Flatheads already had traded for some of Broken Pipe's animals—at very high prices.

"They are great horsemen, these Users of Black Paint," the widely traveled horse-trader said. He spoke fluently in the Flathead tongue, but out of habit, perhaps, he signed the tribe's name by holding his extended left hand in front of his body, palm up, and rubbing the tips of his fingers and thumb of his right hand over the palm.

"Will you race?" Again the challenge from one of the hunters.

Broken Pipe stood up, facing the naked young men astride their restless, bare-backed mounts: "Will you race with the Shoshonis?" he asked.

The challenger's gaze swept the two-family group, centering, finally, on Broken Pipe's young son. Two of the impatient horsemen tittered.

Puzzled that Broken Pipe would consider racing his young son against these older horsemen, Little Coyote entered the lodge and removed his clothing. As he strode over to unpicket his pinto and place a rope in her mouth, Antelope easily shed her garments and, clad only in the two flaps of buckskin, nimbly leapt astride her horse. As Broken Pipe untethered the magnificent Appaloosa stallion and placed a rope in his mouth, Antelope tied her two long braids behind her head. Already Broken Pipe was calling for and accepting bets that involved most of his horses in this encampment and many back home.

"Race! A race!" Word spread quickly among the encampments of eaters and talkers. More bets, some enormous, some small, as varied as the sizes of the contending horses and their riders, were made almost as quickly. As more of the younger men closely viewed the contestants, they ran back to bring their horses and enter the contest, too. Soon all the people, save the disgruntled horse guards, were lined up in the broad avenue between the two encampments.

Thunder Voice gravely agreed to ride to a small rise north of the encampments to verify that all racers would ride around him before circling back to the starting point—Tjolzhitsay, himself. The chief would fire his long musket into the air so all could hear this starting signal above the uproar.

The horsemen jostled for position, Antelope and her horse almost hidden as contenders strove to be next to her. At one point Little Coyote found she skillfully had urged her horse alongside his, but as quickly he was roughly shunted aside by others. Once more the young woman succeeded in this endeavor; in the brief time they were next to each other, she shouted, "Perhaps we will meet together in front of the racers, but I'll not wait for you to catch up! After the race . . ." She forced her steed close to Little Coyote, leaned over and said so perhaps only he could hear, ". . . I will see you at the buffalo tree—if your horse can run that far."

Three Eagles' musket roared. The racers quickly outdistanced the smoke. Before it had dissipated, seven horses, among them Antelope's and Little Coyote's, held the leads. They raced toward Thunder Voice in as direct a line as the terrain would permit, horse sometimes colliding sideways with horse in those early moments. Four animals and riders almost simultaneously rounded the rise, their flying hooves pelting impassive Thunder Voice's mount with damp earth.

Soon there were three, then two—Antelope and a rider with a superb, large black. Little Coyote watched Antelope lean far forward as she urged on her Appaloosa, her lithe body moving rhythmically with the horse's renewed efforts. Now he could see only her dusky back as the other rider applied his quirt again and again to the magnificent black.

Little Coyote felt no disappointment that his pinto never had gained the lead. *There is a lesson here,* he thought. *I always must include a very fast mount among my horses when I go on raids. Not Afraid of Guns will keep up with other horses for most tasks, and she is trained to perform them well. But she is not a race horse, which mostly must have speed.*

Yet, seemingly effortlessly, the mare continued to move ahead until she was almost neck and neck with the hunter who had issued the challenge. Long hair streaming out behind him like his horse's tail, the brave grinned at Little Coyote and urged his mount to greater effort—and came in second. The people held their places until the last horse came abreast of Tjolzhitsay so all would know how payments of bets must fall. Many keen eyes sought out horses and laid plans for possible future trades. As the post-race excitement waned, young men, even some of the older, including Running Buffalo Bull and a now even richer but not surprised Broken Pipe, sought out Antelope, the winner.

Like the graceful creature for which she was named, Antelope once more had darted away.

140

16

When the first small arc of golden Sun rose above the peak, Little Coyote ended his cross-legged vigil before the flat-topped stone cairn he had erected on this mountain that had provided the buffalo. Beside him was the heavy head of the bull which, after much reflection the evening before, the young warrior had decided to return here. He needed no headdress or other trophy. He was Little Coyote and he owed great thanks to the Good Spirit who had shared the bits of wisdom that had brought him so far so soon. Seizing the shaggy head by both horns, he helped nudge it upward with his right knee until the trophy rested atop the cairn. He turned the lusterless eyes and drying, bloody, black nose until the now half-orb of brightening Sun seemed to rest between the horns. Lifting both arms in imitation of the horns, Little Coyote thanked the Good Spirit for all his experiences since that first vision on the great mountain overlooking their valley.

Now, in louder song, he gave thanks for the wisdom he had been able to channel to the people. Finally, with great fervor, he asked that all would return safely home, very mindful from this high elevation of the ever growing number of Blackfeet lodges. Shivering from his inactivity, he slowly began picking his way down the rocks toward Not Afraid of Guns. He stopped twice to look at the buffalo. They covered the ridges, the slopes of the valleys, the more open patches of land in such numbers that in the growing light they resembled black stands of low forest. When he reached the pinto he walked beside her for a while before mounting and riding downward to the buffalo tree.

Now there was no Antelope with her light gray, dark-spotted Appaloosa waiting for him. The near-emptiness of that realization blended bitter-sweet with the near-fullness of yesterday. The exuberance over her victory, buoyed by their race afterward to the tree, had diminished in neither. Sinewy, wind-cooled skin against softer, wind-cooled skin, they had hugged tightly when Little Coyote had leaped from his horse. The snow-eater had stirred waiting Antelope's long and loosened tresses till they, too, had embraced Little Coyote. Both were almost oblivious at first to the hint of chill that snow-eater contrarily had brought as Sun had lowered. Both were very aware of greater stirrings, new awakenings, that perplexingly urged "more" yet cautioned "less" in the demanding ways of Nature. Again those contradictory perplexities: Reluctantly, yet willingly, they separated to pull on the buckskins each had brought. There had been words then, many words, tremulous at first, stronger as some stirrings had blended with a new urgency of which both were keenly aware—time. Next day both encampments would commence the trek homeward and, all too soon, the Shoshonis would continue westward while the Flatheads would turn north into their valley.

The sight of several Blackfeet, emerging one by one from behind a nearby ridge, had set both young people to racing obliquely down the mountainside and toward their own encampments. They were pursued for a short time by savage and unintelligible hoots and cries from beyond the intervening deep ravine.

Now savoring yesterday and anticipating the events of this new day, Little Coyote once again gave Not Afraid of Guns her head. He reached his father's lodge as a light feather of smoke from a rekindled fire began drifting westward from the smoke hole. He met Antelope as she carried water from the creek, her hair newly braided, her face and arms yet dripping from their washing. The tell-tale dark imprint of this water on the chest and along the back of Little Coyote's buckskins prompted four sets of lowered eyebrows, four knowing looks and, amid a few "harrumphs" from Broken Pipe, the firm message during the hasty meal that there would be much to discuss during the trek homeward.

Thunder Voice signaled a halt to the long, southward-moving procession. Scouts had reported a concentration of Blackfeet where the valley narrowed and the river that helped form the three forks had heavied up from the snow melt and now was unfordable.

"It is good that with more and more of the Blackfeet arriving we chose not to remain here, as part of our people sometimes have done in the past. The word of Tree is good," Thunder Voice insisted, "but we cannot go asking if these Blackfeet have heard it. And, our people in our valley home need the meat." Calling together the sub-chiefs and all gun-carriers, he drew some lines in the soft sands. "We will put the people and our good horses between the river and the lines of pack horses. The warriors will ride between the people and the pack horses. Before we form up, all the musket and rifle bearers will fire their guns at a log racing downriver. Thus we will warn the Blackfeet that we can reach far out without antagonizing them into attack. We must not lose the food and robes."

The people and horses moved closer together and resumed their trek. When the Blackfeet, certainly equaling the Flatheads and Shoshonis in numbers, were clearly in view, Thunder Voice rode up and down the line. His bellowing shouts reached above the growing sounds of the angry river.

Here, most of the Blackfeet were but three arrow flights away, some closer. Horses were clearly discernible, as were individual figures, long lances, shields. The Blackfeet were near a hillside sloping to the river, all watching.

A Flathead warrior lifted one end of a large log and, hand over hand, raised it upward until it teetered almost vertically above the savage river. Thunder Voice lowered his arm and the log splashed into the water; it was lost for a moment, then re-emerged amid the swirling waves and debris. Thunder Voice lowered his other arm when the log reached a calmer part of the water. The volley was ragged, but there were far fewer splashes around the log than Little Coyote had expected. Hurriedly he reloaded his rifle, certain his bullet also had gone true. Half of the more quickly moving procession had cleared the sloping hillside below the Blackfeet; as each shooter completed his reloading he hastened toward the back end of the cavalcade. Now the procession had cleared the slope. While the silent watchers remained above the river, Thunder Voice again called together the sub-chiefs and gun-carriers.

"There are lessons here," Thunder Voice said. "As has truly been spoken by Little Coyote, we must change our ways of fighting, as we did when we hurried to the aid of Eagle Claw and his family. And our friends the Shoshonis must trade for the guns and learn the best ways to use them. Very quickly. I fear that more of the Blackfeet and others who are our enemies will get them, too." Now his voice softened until he seemed to be talking almost to himself. "We are so few. Yes, there must be many changes in our ways if we are to live." His voice strengthened. "When we reach the valley where Clark and Lewis met us, Tjolzhitsay says Three Eagles once more will be the leader. I will urge that before our brothers, the Shoshonis, go their own way until the spring hunt, we hold council on this matter of the guns." His face brightened as he looked upward. For now, at least, the Blackfeet were gone.

Snow-eater had melted much of the snow from the mountainsides leading up to the pass over the range, but much remained in the higher elevations. Thunder Voice sent many of the warriors and unburdened mounts ahead of the cavalcade to break trail for the others. This technique, continuing good weather and eagerness to reach home soon brought them all to the bowl where they had met Clark and Lewis. Here, amid much rejoicing despite their fatigue, they were met by some of the people who had toiled up from the northern part of the valley.

Torn with a desire to spend as much time as possible with Antelope and the seeming need to snowshoe to the grave of Shining Shirt, Little Coyote reluctantly decided on the latter. He reasoned that perhaps by seeking the help of the seer's spirit now, he sooner would be able to spend greater time with his first love. He spoke earnestly to that end after standing near the platform in utter silence and observing that the slight mound atop the platform was covered with heavy snow.

"Help me with your wisdom, oh spirit of Shining Shirt," he concluded. "My petition might be selfish this time, true, but cannot I be happy as I try to serve my people? You know well the great unhappiness that comes from being separated from one you greatly love."

The young seer felt less anxious as he slowly snowshoed away. As he left, a breeze obliterated his trail to and from the grave site. He reached the encampment at the right time, for, as promised, Thunder Voice asked Tjolzhitsay for a council meeting concerning how to obtain more guns for themselves and the Shoshonis.

The Flatheads would lead the Shoshonis and, perhaps, their friends, the Nee Mee Poo, to the gun-traders. In the sixth moon of Camas these men and their horses could fight their way through the heavy snow in the mountains to the west. They would bring horses and furs for the trades. One of the Shoshone sub-chiefs successfully argued that they leave with their brothers, the Flatheads, as many horses as possible before their return to their own homes. Thus, the horses would be spared the grueling struggle through the snows, which would wear them down and lead to poorer trades. The council also agreed that the Shoshonis must leave soon for home. Snow-eater was losing his power. Perhaps it would last until the people could go through the mountains that lay ahead.

Broken Pipe was summoned. Yes, in return for at least one of the guns the seekers would obtain, he would leave all his good horses with the Flatheads. The gun-seekers could load furs on the poorer animals in the moon of Camas, use others to break trail, and have the good trade horses follow with no loads at all in the rear.

All agreed there must be many horses, many furs. Who would lead them? Gun stood and spoke briefly. Tjolzhitsay told Little Coyote to summon Little Bear Claw.

"You will lead the gun-seekers in the moon of Camas," the chief told the young warrior. "You will meet our brothers, the Shoshonis at—" Here one of the Shoshone sub-chiefs suggested they meet at the hot springs west of the north end of the valley. "As you know, there is a trail for us to follow from our homes and those of the Nee Mee Poo," Tjolzhitsay explained. "Perhaps it is the best of all. It would be closer to the gun-traders and all, including the horses, could rest there for a time."

The council ended with this agreement. The Shoshonis would leave next day.

Broken Pipe had had his talk about Antelope with Little Coyote. The authority of Thunder Voice had brought Broken Pipe and the young warrior together through the instructions of a sub-chief about quite a different matter. They were to remain on watch at the rear for the Blackfeet the first half of the night following the successful buffalo hunt and bloodless encounter near the raging river. Other guards were in place elsewhere. The two men had stationed themselves high enough above the river that its sound would not rob them of the use of their ears, yet close enough to observe any warriors on horses who might attempt to pass through the narrow gorge.

Their mounts hidden in the nearby brush, comfortable seats scooped out at the base of a high projecting bluff, the two men had sat at first in watchful silence, Little Coyote slightly below Broken Pipe. S'tc'tc'tcút, half-moon, first quarter, climbed ever higher until the darkened waters below reflected the faint light in varying intensities and shapes. Later, two white-tail deer nimbly moved upriver, pausing to nibble a few bites of grass before disappearing. An owl hooted somewhere above them, almost immediately reassuring the vigilant men of its reality by silently gliding downward to perch on a dead tree limb near the grass below. A black bear, evidently awakened from sleep by the snow-eater, lumbered diagonally into view from their side of the river, choosing to follow the bank downstream. Here it might find a fish, an animal carcass or other food to add further fat to help survive a renewed winter sleep. Later still, three coyotes, then two more, quietly moved onto the narrow meadow to prance slowly in the grass, jumping at times and seizing a rodent. Twice the owl hooted its displeasure at this intrusion, then wisely flew to other hunting grounds.

One of the smaller coyotes, perhaps a bitch, tentatively nosed the scent of the bear, then more closely the broad trail left by the Flathead and Shoshone cavalcade.

Little Coyote heard Broken Pipe stir above him. A moment later the warrior quietly removed a few small rocks next to the younger man; even more quietly he placed them elsewhere and sat down.

Little Coyote smiled a greeting, then resumed his vigil. Broken Pipe shifted his butt to a more comfortable position. Soon he rocked his left leg, then the right, studying the richly beaded, well-worn footwear as though seeing them for the first time. He pulled his light robe more closely about him and soon let it fall loosely from his shoulders. Finally he bent forward and asked in a whisper if he could see Little Coyote's rifle. Pointing to the flint lock and trigger and warningly shaking his head, the young brave handed the weapon to Broken Pipe. He examined it closely, running his fingers exploringly, almost lovingly, around the slender stock, the patchbox, the other brass fittings. As Broken Pipe began looking down the barrel, Little Coyote reached over and gently pushed it away from the warrior's face, whispering, "There is death at that end."

"I will trade you a fine horse for this gun. The Blackfeet and Minnetares have kept us away from the traders. We have but a few guns, none among us here."

"The gun will not be traded."

"I will trade two horses."

When the figure reached five horses, Little Coyote reached over and retrieved the weapon. He peered to the front, left and right with greater emphasis than before, conveying that there would be no trade and that the pair should concentrate on the task to which they had been entrusted.

Broken Pipe became silent and remained that way until the coyotes began collecting more closely together. "They will sing now, then move away," he said. "Which direction will they go, upriver or downriver?"

"If they hear no answering songs from upriver, they will go there," Little Coyote whispered, "for it is unlikely the bear will leave them food along the river. They have learned that man, though most are their enemies now, often provide food, willingly or unwillingly, so they can survive. Later, before this night is over, they will have entered the encampment and learned that the people carry the buffalo meat. Once again, perhaps, we will see them appear, wisely heading downriver, because they will have learned the buffalo have come."

"You have learned much about the coyote," Broken Pipe said. "It has brought you its name. Has it brought you luck, good fortune?"

"The Good Spirit has sent me much good luck through coyote."

"And good fortune?"

"Good fortune, yes, but few riches."

"Yet you seek my greatest richness. Antelope. I have learned much about you. You would make a good mate. Yet you are not rich. You have indicated this night that you do not seem to like riches. Among the Shoshonis and the Nee Mee Poo Antelope wins many races, brings me many more horses. And many people who watch the races trade for my horses. Yes, it would take much, very much, perhaps more than a man possesses, to win Antelope. I do not speak unkindly. Running Buffalo Bull is a great warrior. But he is not rich. We will not speak more about this for now. Both of you are young. Perhaps you will acquire the riches that would move my mind. What they might be, I do not know. Ah, the coyotes sing."

Little Coyote sat in miserable silence throughout their song. That silence continued long after the coyotes quietly had filed upriver, then loped in shady silence downriver past the two sentinels.

The sky lightened. As Broken Pipe stepped into the meadow and beckoned, he reached into his bag and brought forth his pipe. He struck a fire and, after lighting the pipe, handed it to Little Coyote. He signed the directions and pulled deeply. Broken Pipe's gesture was friendly; the smoke was sweet. Both removed a few more rocks beneath them, rolled into their robes and sought a short sleep. Little Coyote felt small, yet he carried a weight inside that surely was as great as the peak that towered above them.

"You do not eat? This is the last of the fresh buffalo meat. See? Part of the good rump meat."

Little Yellow Bird held out the tempting small pot of meat as Little Coyote returned from the Shoshone camp. "I know. When one is young there are demands beyond food, a gnawing heaviness that grows." She held out a metal knife and two small, highly ornate buckskin bags. "Antelope's mother forgot these in our lodge though they were here for all to see. Perhaps you will return them before the Shoshonis have gone too far."

Little Coyote reached for the articles, pausing to hold his mother's hand before accepting them. He smiled. Then, carrying out his resolve formed from his all-too-brief and open farewell to Antelope amid the striking of lodges and loading of horses, he filled another bag with jerky and some Shoshone-made pemmican. He secured his robe, extra weapons and other gear on two of his horses, then leaped astride his pinto. On his way to the Shoshonis earlier, he had seen two Flathead youths setting out on their vision quests. Perhaps it was time for him to visit the great mountain.

"Tell my father I will meet him at the great Lake of the White Moose west of our river, where we gather the camas. He said you and others will erect your lodges there when you leave here."

Broken Pipe was in the lead scouting party when Little Coyote caught up with the Shoshonis, who had not left the valley floor. Antelope's mother registered little surprise at his arrival, but not so Antelope, who dispiritedly was riding alongside the family's pack horses. Her large eyes opened wide in surprise. Then they centered questioningly on her mother, who nodded assent then called out there must be an early return because there was much to do. The young couple rode a short distance from the procession, then dismounted. The scents of sweet grass and meadow-rue enveloped them both as Little Coyote drew his robe about them.

How quickly the procession moved past them as they stood there. Two young men approximately Little Coyote's age reined their horses close; one called out that there were ample Shoshone men for Shoshone maidens until several women in the cavalcade scolded them loudly for their unwarriorlike rudeness.

When Little Coyote gently raised Antelope's face to his own, he could see the quivering lips and feel the coolness of the breeze against his chest where warm tears had fallen. There was no need for him to repeat what he had told her earlier about Broken Pipe's talk.

"I have made my resolve," he told her. "Soon or not so soon I will find the riches, whatever they might be, to soften Broken Pipe's heart. And I *will* come to the camp of the Shoshonis by the next *s'tce'éi*, fall."

Now the end of the long file of horses and people had passed them. Soon the rear guard would appear. Little Coyote gave Antelope a final, lingering embrace, which was warmly returned. He stepped away and watched while she reluctantly mounted her horse. Riding up to Little Coyote, she handed him her metal knife and kicked the horse into a fast gallop. She waved once when she reached her family's pack horses.

Little Coyote grasped the lead rope of his own animals and set out for his mountain.

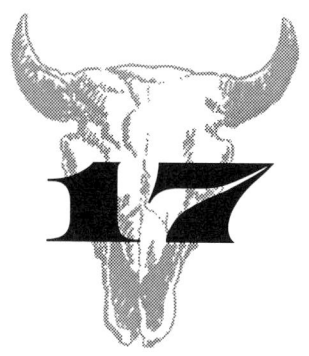

For the remainder of his life of ninety-nine summers, Little Coyote would speak fondly of "the winter of *sqleẃ*, the beaver." That long season had forced on him much careful thinking, much discovery of self, much hard work, much good luck—and had brought him to Antelope. In the inscrutable ways the Good Spirit responded to prayers for help, these successes had grown from his three unsuccessful attempts to reach the great peak where he had completed his first vision quest.

Heavy, deep snow repeatedly had thrown him back until, retreating, he had been forced to erect a small shelter of saplings and brush amid a stand of sturdy trees bordering a small meadow slightly south and east of the peak. Here his two pack horses and Not Afraid of Guns could forage while he pondered his problems, including the diminishment of his food supply during each snow-filled day. At length, hungry, woefully tired, aching inwardly from the absence of Antelope, he had sat long before his fire one night searching for answers. A handful of carefully hoarded buffalo jerky remained in his food bags. He removed the meat, hungrily eyed it, sniffed its goodness, then, raising it as an offering, cast it into the fire. Like his thoughts, the meat twisted and curled and finally was consumed in a low blue flame, before which he began nodding and, at length, dozed.

While his memories were of varying intensities afterward, three remained strongest: First was the chorus of coyote barks that had preceded his original vision quest; second, the repetition of the procession of a growing number of white masks that had ended that first vision quest; finally, totally new, the forgotten five beaver traps the gun-seekers had obtained from the eager traders who, Gun had emphasized, liked the beaver pelts best among the furs.

A chorus of coyotes brought him out of his half-sleep before the almost-dead fire. In the moonlight he watched a white-tail buck deer struggle into view and pause momentarily as he weighed the scent of the camp and the nearness of the coyotes. The first flint-tipped arrow Little Coyote loosed disappeared into belly-deep snow; the second caught the buck in the neck. One more killed him. While the coyotes yapped their frustrations, Little Coyote dragged the carcass closer to them. With Antelope's metal knife he quickly skinned the carcass, divided it into seven pieces, and left a goodly amount for the coyotes who had brought him this food.

While all were eating, Little Coyote, seated before a now-lively fire, pondered the significance of this long night. The impression of the traps offered the greatest puzzle, because long ago he had deciphered, as had Shining Shirt, the first two impressions: Little Coyote should be his name; there would be more white men to come. But the traps? Was there some deep significance linking his people, the whites and the traps they brought? Perhaps, but sated now with the good deer meat and with his young body eager for action, his mind chose the immediate solution. As he rolled the freezing deerskins for future tanning, the solution struck him almost with the impact of the arrow that had dropped the buck. Yes, he should use the traps to obtain more furs, but to what end? The deeper significance lay buried like the hidden spark in the ashes to burst into a flame at a later time, given proper fuel.

Little Coyote had much time to ponder the use of the traps during his return to the Lake of the White Moose, where his father's lodge stood with many others. Broken Pipe had emphasized his riches in horses. Fine animals that they were, other people had them, too. And more horses were available from the wild bands with the expenditure of much hard work. Or, of course, one could steal them from the enemy, admittedly a more hazardous course. Few people as yet had guns. Broken Pipe had tried very hard to exchange many horses for a gun. *Yes, I will work very hard to get some guns to place before the lodge of Broken Pipe so he will be moved to engage in a gift exchange and allow Antelope to come out and join me in mine.* Thus Little Coyote thought as he and his horses slowly worked their way homeward through the snow.

Gun gladly would let him borrow the traps. He had forgotten them. Trapping for beaver was neither interesting nor seemingly quite proper for this warrior of near sub-chief status. Yet he would be most grateful to his friend for a bit more powder and lead. They had smoked the pipe on that.

Little Bear Claw had been very eager to agree that his friend Little Coyote be a member of the second party of gun-seekers. In truth, he had planned to suggest this to Three Eagles. Little Coyote knew the way, too, in the event Nature should take Little Bear Claw. Yes, the two friends and the Shoshonis would meet at the hot springs early in the moon of Camas—with approval of Tjolzhitsay, of course. They also had smoked a pipe on that.

The head chief had set the pipe to going before talking with his welcome visitor that cold day when snow seemed to be falling throughout the valley and hiding even the nearest shore of the great lake. His face had remained grave when Little Coyote proposed he travel to the hot springs lands before the snow became too deep and trap the plentiful beaver he had been told were there.

"I would use four traps for the people, one for myself," Little Coyote had proposed. "Thus, in working hard for myself, I will work four times as hard for the people and trade those furs for guns and powder and lead." Tjolzhitsay's face had relaxed at hearing those words. "It would be fitting that the head chief of the Flatheads have this rifle while I accept the not-as-good long musket of Tjolzhitsay. I will strive even harder to obtain another rifle so I can return this musket to Tjolzhitsay. Perhaps thus he could provide another son with such a gift."

The head chief's long face had lightened into a small grin as he assented to the plan. They had smoked a pipe on that. Afterward, his mind reeling from such friendly smoking and trying to cope with his many preparations, Little Coyote had enlisted the aid of his parents. The trapping and trading expedition would last almost seven moons.

There had been no final pipe just prior to his departure downriver. Rather, he and Running Buffalo Bull had tested the iron traps.

"These are great marvels," his father had said. "It might be good to trade for a few of your own, perhaps some for me. I agree with your vision and the words of Shining Shirt and the chiefs Clark and Lewis. More white men will come here. If they bring their marvels to the lands of the people and take the furs of the animals in exchange, it would be well to have the means to excel. One does not race with a jaded horse. As a youth I lured the beaver to the dead-fall traps by placing the strong-smelling secretion from their glands leading to and near the logs. And I gathered the best trees and branches, especially of the cottonwood, to lure them to eat. Use the scent. If you use the traps in the water, even under the ice, be certain the beaver food you place is the best." Then he had shown his son how to make a dead-fall trap from a log and stretch the pelts on strong hoops of willow. Also at his father's urging, Little Coyote had left the encampment with a string of seven horses, besides his pinto. "There are small meadows in the ravines near the hot springs," Running Buffalo Bull had said. "Close the horses up in one ravine. When that grass is gone, move them to another. Thus you will have ample horses to carry the furs—five to trade and two to carry back the trade goods."

As Little Coyote had prepared to mount his pinto, his father had placed his hand on his son's shoulder in farewell: "There will be much to do. You will learn much. Perhaps of most importance will be how to deal with loneliness. You can learn much from that. Keep busy. Yes, there always is much to do.

We will miss our son, but the young coyote must run."

Little Coyote had found the sturdiest pack horse already burdened with a small, well-used lodge Little Yellow Bird had obtained for her son. As she had handed up to him two bags of dried roots and berries "to help keep the body strong, especially with the rose seed pods," he gravely had accepted them, tied their ends together and thrown them over a pack horse. The anxious look on her face, the wisp of graying hair moving across her forehead, had pried him from his pinto to give her a long, reassuring hug, then another. On his downriver trip he had stayed in the lodges of the people. There were no lodges, however, when he turned west from the valley and into the ever-deepening snow.

At length, Little Coyote set up his shelter among some trees that offered lodge poles. The shelter was in a small meadow above the hot springs, which issued from the base of a cliff. No human tracks were visible among those of animals that criss-crossed the blanket of snow. On snowshoes now, he found a nearby meadow surrounded by cliffs except for the narrow entrance. A stream of tepid water flowed from the entrance. He led the horses to the meadow and closed the entrance with dead tree trunks and branches. When he had hung a deer carcass near the lodge, he set out to reconnoiter the trapping prospects. Beaver dams abounded, the reservoirs behind them still unfrozen. Methodically, the young brave concentrated on the smaller dams. Remembering his father's advice about the beavers' need for good tree branches and bark, he often built a huge fire near a small dam. Then he removed his buckskins and, wherever possible, dragged from the water the stores of woody food hauled there by the industrious beavers to eat when the dam surfaces froze over. Shivering with cold, he would hurry to the fire, get warm, then, after much strenuous work on the snowshoes, return to the hot springs where he would soak up the heat from the water until he became almost too languid to go to his lodge. Had there not been the greater likelihood of an enemy coming to the springs before finding his lodge, he would have set up the shelter beside the hot water.

As the snow continued to deepen and close in the land, Little Coyote stacked up other tree branches with those he had removed from the dams. Again, following his father's suggestion, he worked two evenings to fashion a heavy hammer from a rock, a stout branch and some of the deer rawhide. With this he broke holes through the ever thickening ice of the dams he planned to work. Then he placed tree boughs and snow over the holes to help insulate them against heavy refreezing to great thickness. When he was ready to trap at a dam thus treated, his ice-breaking task would be much lessened. To attract beavers from their lodges to his traps, he placed small sets of the branches under the water. He arranged the traps so the beavers would drown before extricating themselves sufficiently to swim and crawl ashore, there to chew through the leather ropes attached to the trap chains and a post or tree.

At first he took few beaver; those he took he painstakingly skinned before the carcasses had frozen too hard. From these he obtained both good food and greater knowledge, so that soon, with the careful use of beaver scent, he began catching so many that he had to place their carcasses atop a platform in the trees near his lodge.

On coldest days or when the snow fell until he scarcely could see, he thawed carcasses inside the lodge and worked on those. Again and again he sharpened Antelope's knife on a flat stone and held her image in his mind. She was the stimulus he often needed during the more trying days and nights. At length, as Running Buffalo Bull had foretold, the young trapper became utterly lonesome despite the satisfying, growing stacks of pelts beginning to crowd the lodge. He brought Not Afraid of Guns to his camp, after moving the horses once more, and constructed a small corral and shelter of poles and tree boughs for her. She seemed pleased to be near her master—and better feeding.

During *skussús*, the first moon of The Wandering, when the thin crescent of *A:mt*, the End of the Moon, scarcely was visible at all, heavy snowfall, wind, deep cold and darkness came to the land. At first, Little Coyote struggled to move the horses to new foraging in a small ravine with high walls and trees to help shelter them. The ever deepening cold forced him to abandon the hard physical tasks in which he delighted—hunting, resetting the traps and snowshoeing back to the lodge with their bounty. Even gathering firewood with the aid of a small toboggan had to be postponed.

As his father had warned, Little Coyote began learning much from this loneliness as he carefully fed his lodge fire and placed the dried beaver pelts around the interior of the shelter to help keep out the cold. Cold, like the mouse, sought even the tiniest opening.

With an effort akin to the strength of those natural forces that were confining him to the lodge, he prodded his mind to plateaus above the tedious mechanics of thawing the beaver carcasses, skinning out, fleshing and drying the pelts and perfecting his knowledge of the language of signs. He contemplated his view of, and place in, the wider world outside his mind, the lodge, this place of the hot springs, and the valley where his people lived. He had both the time and lack of distractions—and the growing discipline, he was pleased to learn—to refine that view again and yet again.

The foundation on which he fashioned his philosophy at this stage of his life was that the young, through self-discipline, more easily could adapt to the new and adjust to changes that would set many older people to wondering, to fearing, then talking of and resisting the changes. Not all older people, however: "Yes, these are good traps. We should use them," his father had commented. And there was much satisfaction that the leaders, admittedly sometimes with effort, could see the advantages that lay with the employment of careful thought, not brute strength or numbers, to win over their enemies. Yes, they even could see the good in listening to one as young as himself.

He must remember that the younger people, like himself, seemed more willing to look on the world in new ways, to be more ready for the future. He must strive never to look to the past, except to draw good lessons from it. But there was a hidden trap in these thoughts: The trap was baited with the marvels one encountered during developing maturity and now, seemingly, with the wonders that were coming from white man. Was each new marvel the people accepted of truly lasting value, a means of bettering one's condition? Would ready acceptance of the marvels weaken the challenges of holding on to some old ways? Surely the struggle connected with some of the old ways helped both the individual and the tribe to remain strong. Little Coyote tentatively concluded that, while he could not stop these changes, perhaps he could help shape them. He would hold to that view, at least for now.

As the cold subsided, Little Coyote looked to the traps, then pulled two toboggan loads of good grass from near the hot springs to a hungry Not Afraid of Guns. The other seven horses also had coped with the cold. With hoar frost clinging to their coats of long hair, they crowded to the ravine entrance, unprotestingly allowing themselves to be roped in single file and led to new forage.

Little Coyote hauled all the dried pelts from the lodge to the tree platform, covering them with hides of occasional deer he had shot with the arrows. These deer hides freeze-dried. Later, he tied the heavy end of a stout pole between two closely growing trees, cleared away the snow, placed a deerskin on the ground, put a stack of pelts on that, and another deerskin on top. Then he used a series of props both to raise and lower the tied pole so its weight would press down the pelts into a manageable pile. He tied the compressed bundles, lifted the pole and raised the package onto the tree platform.

Sun began climbing ever higher into the sky. Viewing the growing number of fur bales, the trapper was grateful his father had urged that he bring more horses. When he had almost emptied the beaver lodges in the smaller dams, he began working on the larger dams until he was so tired of catching, skinning and eating beaver that he began slowing his efforts and devoting some of his energies to exploring this place of the hot springs. Deep snow still hemmed him in, though on one excursion on snowshoes he spent three nights away from his camp. At length, he reached the trail over which his friends the Shoshonis most likely would come.

Reluctantly, he resumed the tedium of trapping, thawing and skinning the beaver. One night as the dying lodge fire reflected dully in the frozen eyes of the many carcasses, he began imagining in his aloneness that these creatures were looking accusingly at him, silently asking if he would spend his entire life killing and skinning, killing and skinning lesser creatures.

Glad that snow in lower elevations was starting to melt, Little Coyote began listening eagerly each day for the sounds of people. At first he wondered whether the Shoshonis would arrive before the Flatheads.

"Little Bear Claw will arrive first because the snow conditions are better," he assured Not Afraid of Guns one day as he fed her another armful of dead grass. The mare would reach downward for a big bite, shake her head up and down to let some of the overgenerous supply fall back to the pile, then thoughtfully chew, wriggling her ears and rolling her eyes this way and that as though saying, "Little Coyote says this is so; thus it will be."

He was very mistaken.

The snow melted and the streams sang more loudly. In the third moon of the Goose Flight, Little Coyote heard and watched these heralds of *skepts*, the spring, aim their broad spear points northward while the heads of swimming beaver made their ever widening arrow points on the placid waters of their dams. Vegetation leafed out and horses eagerly began eating the new grass. Surely this is the moon of Camas, Little Coyote thought; perhaps it is even the next moon of the Serviceberries, because he had watched their bushes leaf out, blossom and begin to form the delicious food. He was tempted to strike out for the valley, but he had given his word and there was the very practical certainty that freedom from snow at the lower levels brought greater hazards of enemies, who could deprive him of his hard-earned furs, his horses, even his life.

Not Afraid of Guns alerted Little Coyote to the arrival of people early one dawn when the lowering clouds on the surrounding mountains threatened rain. Her ears moved back and forth as he led the pack horses into the now-green meadow nearest his lodge. Soon the pinto's ears stopped moving altogether; the mare pointed her head directly toward the hot springs. Low clouds hid the steam from the springs and seemed to muffle the songs of the early-rising birds. Little Coyote listened attentively. Holding his breath and remaining motionless, he concluded he heard voices, many voices. He seized his bow and quiver and carefully stole downward through the wet brush of very familiar terrain.

Amid growing clamor, he cautiously peered from the base of a large bush and beheld numerous naked bodies. All were white, save one black, and they were cavorting in the largest scooped-out hot springs, most of them thin as old horses that no longer could crop the grass. He looked about for Bird Woman. She was helping her toddler son bathe in a small, bowl-like, warm pool. Three warriors, seemingly the Users of Black Paint or Nee Mee Poo, sat nearby quietly observing the antics of the many men. The warriors leapt to their weapons when Little Coyote later rode into the encampment leading one horse loaded with fresh venison and much dried jerky.

A naked Clark, who once had offered Little Coyote a lance head for his pinto, evidently recognized the horse because he ran forward to tell Drouillard to say something to the Nee Mee Poo. Then he returned the young man's peace sign. After signing his message to the Nee Mee Poo, Drouillard bared his strong, white teeth in a friendly grin of recognition and waved to Little Coyote.

At first there was little talk as the party quickly consumed the food the Flathead had brought. The Nee Mee Poo, friendly now, explained that the Clark and Lewis party was on its way home from the great salt water to the west. The warriors recounted with some satisfaction that the deep snow in the mountains had forced Clark and Lewis to return to the land of the Nee Mee Poo where, after much persuasion by Drouillard, they had agreed to serve as guides. The cost was great—two of their fine rifles and much powder and lead. Yes, three more of the Real People, together with five of their Shoshone brothers and many horses and furs, were following far behind on the tortuous trail this party had made through the snow. These latecomers would join with the Flatheads to seek guns. Clark and Lewis again began making marks on small leaves of material held together with elk hide as they had done during the trading in the valley on their first appearance. The two white chiefs sent Drouillard and two other men to the dams to obtain beaver meat; several other men readied fishing lines. Then both leaders, chewing jerky, listened attentively during the talk between the Nee Mee Poo and the Flathead. Occasionally they glanced at the rifles they had paid the three men. They also asked for a repetition of the report concerning the Flatheads' first expedition for guns, and for information about the second expedition now forming. They carefully obtained a complete recounting of the victory over the Blackfeet in the land of the buffalo. The men conversed for a few moments, conveying immediately afterward by voice and signs that they had not meant to be impolite, but simply had agreed they were fearful about the Flatheads obtaining the guns from British traders, and what so many guns in the hands of their Indian brothers could lead to. Two of the Nee Mee Poo eagerly began concentrating their full attention on the remaining jerky Little Coyote had given to them, while the one best with the sign language communicated the white chiefs' other thoughts and the young Flathead's reply. The length and abruptness of his comments surprised even himself, but the white men were the visitors in the people's lands. And while always there lurked the memory of his vision quest—the growing procession of white masks, the warning to counsel the people not to war with the white man—there had been no warning that the white men always must agree.

"You say we are getting our guns from the people you call the Hudson's Bay Company and other British coming down from the land called Canada," Little Coyote said. "Would you have all the tribes, including the Blackfeet, get their guns and other trade goods only from you? When will you set up your trading lodges? Will you also trade guns? Or, would you have only white men carry the guns when they come here in ever increasing numbers? Will the white men gather up the guns from all tribes and never bring them again? The Flatheads have a few of the guns; we are glad that now some of our friends, the Nee Mee Poo, have guns; the Blackfeet have guns; do other near and distant tribes have guns? Perhaps to have them is to die, yet not to have them is to die."

Clark and Lewis unsmilingly looked directly at Little Coyote while his message was being sorted out. The Flathead's friendly grin had gone the way of his earlier wide smile of welcome. None of the three would smile again among themselves until they waved farewell as the long procession began moving eastward. The dark sky wept.

L ittle Coyote would have three days in which to prepare
for his departure—to end his winter of *sqleẃ*, the beaver.
He was ready by the end of the first day. In the improving
weather he dried the small lodge, folding in the rodent- and insect-
repelling grasses and twigs Little Yellow Bird had provided. He
kicked down the bales of beaver pelts and used his pinto to hoist
the lodge to the tree platform, placing overlapping dry sheets of
bark, then stones, atop the bundle.

With birds and waters singing and the air filled with heady
aromas of regeneration, Little Coyote wanted to leap astride his
pinto and dash wildly along a trail that would lead him to
Antelope. Instead, reluctantly, he chose a lookout above the
springs; there, unobserved, he could sit and wait and at night
sleep beneath an ancient tree while his horse grazed nearby.

Inevitably, the physical trails yet denied him, he once more
took to mental ones—some old and deeply worn, over which he
quickly could move, others less traveled and leading to others
that were new, unexplored. Old or new, all led to white man.

Surely by now the Clark and Lewis people had encountered
Little Bear Claw after they had disappeared from view that gloomy
day when his thoughts were so dark. He discovered that he was

somewhat regretful—surprised, too—that he, so young, had communicated his thoughts so abruptly about who should supply and who should possess the guns. He believed that Clark and Lewis were good men, kindly disposed. Perhaps he could avoid abrupt responses if he could ponder what should be his attitude toward white man now. How should he treat those who, even before Lewis' promise, "More of us will come here," his vision had told him would arrive in numbers as great as the berries in the valley? Yes, he had begun focusing his thoughts on the white men and had asked about them after his vision quest and their first appearance in the valley. He had learned that from all four directions in the wider world unfolding to him and to which the people reverently signed their pipes, there were many indications of the white men: horses; horse breeding; styles of homemade saddles; pots; knives and highly useful, yet rare, axes, and other metal trade goods that often had passed through the hands of many and distant traders. The young seer also began learning that there were the stories passed down among some of the people, too, that told of white man. The people *must* remember these.

Perhaps his most revealing discovery had been that, seemingly, no one had bothered to seek out all this disparate information and draw broad inferences from it. Had each individual acquired his bit of goods or information and lightly discussed and dismissed the source or content when crowded out by the pressing demands of life for the moment? How he wished he could have had many lengthy talks with Shining Shirt! Was his spirit helping to guide Little Coyote's thoughts now?

Were there greater numbers of people in the tribes than of white man? Little Coyote stood, yawned and rubbed his tired butt. He ate some of the trout he had caught and broiled near one of the beaver dams when the Clark and Lewis people had departed. Grasping a stout tree branch, he began pulling himself up and down until his arms became too tired to continue. Then, like the spider, he hung there, almost unmoving, trying to grasp that earlier thread about numbers, a thread he had spun out but not yet affixed and woven into the forming web of information about white men that had come from all the directions. *Were* there greater numbers of people in the tribes than of white men? There, he had it, and again failed to ponder because a horse and rider cautiously emerged from the trees near the springs. The steed was partially turned for instant retreat into the forest. They ventured farther into the clearing, as distant as possible from any cover that would conceal an enemy. No other horses followed. The man was Little Bear Claw! He looked quickly upward toward the source of the sharp, closely spaced coyote yelps. Soon the two friends were embracing.

Little Coyote stood guard above a hot springs pool while his friend prepared to soak away the aches from a hard ride. Little Bear Claw's usual grin widened into pure delight as he eased his lean body into the steaming water. But the grin vanished like the steam cloud in a sudden gust of wind when Little Coyote, eager to talk after a winter of silence, called down to him for information about the happenings among the people during his long absence.

"There is a camp of death near one of the three forks of the great river," Little Bear Claw said. "At this camp are the bodies of many of the Little Robes, our friends among the Blackfeet allies, and Thunder Voice and four of our warriors. They had gone to make trades for furs for us to take to the gun-traders. They were singing their death songs when Eagle Claw found them after a long search. They would not let him enter the camp where they were rotting from many large, red sores over their bodies. It was the dread sickness that is in the memories of the people, both our own and other friends and enemies. Eagle Claw put water close to the camp and when the songs had ended, he returned to our valley. He left all the trade goods there, including the many furs they sought, because he feared that the spotted death had touched them all and again might creep out."

Little Bear Claw lay back in the pool, unmoving. Little Coyote, saddened, thought of the lessons learned from Thunder Voice, how he thought only to help the people. The young seer was almost too fearful to ask the names of the other four warriors. Seemingly discerning his friend's apprehension, Little Bear Claw spoke their names; in the long silence that followed, the two friends could hear the soft breeze flowing down from the pristine peaks towering into the azure sky to mourn at the lower levels among the tallest trees. At last the sweet song of a meadowlark on the highest nearby tree urged happiness, an end to such dark thoughts for good men whose spirits surely could hear this music in the place of continual summer. All had been brave and honest, and had loved truth and their families.

"Running Buffalo Bull and Little Yellow Bird send you their greetings, as does my father. Were the beaver good to you, Little Coyote?"

"White man's traps gave us many beaver furs. Would that such warriors as Thunder Voice were as easily produced." Little Coyote recounted his long winter of experiences and deep thoughts to his friend. He concluded with his thoughts about white men after his last encounter with Clark and Lewis.

Little Bear Claw listened without comment. Then he reached upward for his friend's strong hand to help pull him from the pool. He stretched his dripping body on a large, sun-warmed boulder that slanted toward the water and gratefully accepted a trout and some deer jerky. While he ate, both men watched the white steam emerge from the pool: Narrowing, widening, slowing, hurrying in ever changing patterns, sometimes almost disappearing in a momentary quick breeze—but always returning.

Little Bear Claw examined the fragile symmetry of the trout skeleton before flipping it into the grasses near the pool. "I, too, have had many such thoughts." He worried off a bite of jerky and, after chewing it for a moment, tongued it to his cheek. "My meeting with the Clark and Lewis people was brief and friendly when they re-entered our valley and informed our party of gun-seekers that you still awaited the arrival of the Shoshonis and Nee Mee Poo. They did not mention the guns, though I was surprised and a bit envious when I saw that two of the Nee Mee Poo were carrying two of the fine rifles. These warriors told me that the white men had left many of their horses with them when they proceeded west to find the great salt water. Upon their return, they spent much time with the Nee Mee Poo until they could come through the snow to this place. They spoke to the Nee Mee Poo of many things they had seen. They did not want to lose the two guns, but they needed guides. When Shining Shirt died, you told me that he had told the council about men in black robes who would tell about the Good Spirit. Clark and Lewis spoke to the Nee Mee Poo about these Black Robes, too. Yes, they told The Real People many things, and they told me."

Little Coyote sat down next to his friend. This time he spoke more slowly, uncertain as yet about these thoughts: "Perhaps Clark and Lewis were aware of truths gained from their travels and experiences that they only partially voiced in their concerns about the guns coming to our people and others. Perhaps I was too sharp-tongued with them. I have thoughts about that. Perhaps the white man is not like our people and others. Perhaps they are not always warring."

Little Bear Claw swallowed his jerky. "We did not discuss these matters. I think that everywhere the bird kills the insect; the hawk kills the bird; the eagle kills the hawk when it can; the people sometimes kill an eagle and they fight among themselves, preserving their lives and staying strong. Yes, I have given this matter much thought."

Little Coyote stood and looked intently about them while his friend ate the remainder of the jerky.

"I, too, have been troubled about the numbers of the white men in this world," he said. "More surely will come here. Do we outnumber them? Are there more of us? Do they outnumber even the Blackfeet? I cannot say. I have thought much how just this small band of white strangers in such a short time, perhaps ten moons, has started many changes among the people." Little Coyote lowered his head until his chin almost touched his upper chest; the words came slowly as he sought to pull from the deep wells of his mind coherent thoughts never fully formed before. "Such changes are scarcely noticeable, true, until one begins to ponder them like the movement of a restless cow at the edge of a great buffalo herd. I have had such an opportunity. Such changes could be as the first run of that restless cow that agitates those animals closest to her and, in turn, they set into motion their neighbors until the great herd starts moving and nothing can stop it, not even the river or the steep cliff." Little Coyote paused. "Or even another great herd!"

Little Bear Claw swallowed the jerky, but he did not ask if there was more. Instead, his head and shoulders moved forward and back as though he appeared to be trying to help his friend shape his thoughts to better words.

"Sacagawea, Bird Woman of the Shoshonis, carries with her a half-white child," Little Coyote said. "Is there now in our valley encampment a half-white child fathered by Clark?" Little Bear Claw nodded affirmatively as his friend raised his head to look at him. "Clark and Lewis gave us three iron knives. They traded iron lance and arrow points for horses, also axes, the marvels they call mirrors, bells, scissors, needles, pins and rings. Has not the acceptance of these begun to change the people, as well as their desire for, or need for, better tools and other marvels? And they appear to worry about our getting guns, after they showed us their use and power and left those two fine rifles with our friends, the Nee Mee Poo."

Little Bear Claw began pulling on his buckskins. "Are you telling me, my friend of much strong *sumesh*, that we should not accept these marvels that are not evil in themselves, like the firewater that turned the brave Blackfeet into stupid grouse? And what about the wisdom of obtaining more guns for the people, your wisdom of trapping the beaver for the people . . ." He looked slyly at his friend. ". . . so you can turn the mind of Broken Pipe?"

"I thought much of this as I trapped the beaver," Little Coyote answered. "I have concluded that I do not wish to spend my life—or lose it quickly—going among the people to tell them not to accept the marvels of white man. I will, however—perhaps I am destined to do so—tell our people to use them wisely to shape the change I foresee as more white men arrive."

The two friends slowly rode toward the bales of beaver pelts, where they would await the arrival of the Shoshonis and the Nee Mee Poo. The white steam continued to emerge from the pool: Narrowing, widening, slowing, hurrying in ever changing patterns, sometimes almost disappearing in a momentary quick breeze—but always returning.

Little Bear Claw grasped a branch of the ancient fir tree under which his friend lay half-asleep. He bent it downward, more, more, until suddenly it snapped, startling the dozer to instant wakefulness. After sweeping away the small twigs, needles and other debris, Little Bear Claw seated himself to face the springs below. Grunting, he stretched forward to reach four rocks that had resisted the sweeping branch. He arranged them in the four directions.

"I am older than you and I have traveled more," he said to his mystified friend, adding quickly, "though not much." The grin he wore faded. "While you have turned lazy under the tree, I have given much thought to your question about the numbers of the people of all tribes and of the white man." He set the branch between them.

"We will name the tribes about which the people have heard or seen, and the general direction whence they came or are now." He broke a small twig off the branch.

"Piegans," he said, and placed the twig on the stone marking north. "Bloods, also of the Blackfeet," Little Coyote responded, placing another twig on the stone. And so it went: Also north— Pend d'Oreilles, Kalispels, Kutenais . . . ; east—Mandans, Hidatsas, Crows, Cheyenne, Sioux; south—Shoshonis, Bannacks, Utes, Paiutes, Apaches . . .; west—Nee Mee Poo, Palouse, Coeur d'Alenes, Spokans, Yakimas, Cayuses . . . ." Quickly the branch was bare of twigs. Little Bear Claw rose to break off another branch, so both Flatheads, with some reflection now, could add many more twigs to the four piles.

"Perhaps we will strip this great tree before we are through," he joked. "I note that already we use the names the people called 'The French Speakers' have given some of the tribes. I am not so certain this is good. Nor am I certain now that white man can boast so many tribes—of friends and enemies. Do you find comfort in this, Little Coyote?"

The seer had no opportunity to reply because his older friend was raising a cautionary hand, carefully letting the bent branch slowly resume its original position.

"Our friends, the Shoshonis and the Nee Mee Poo, or, as the French speakers say, 'Nez Percé,' come to join us." Little Bear Claw grinned. He reached down and removed two of the twigs. "From the south and the west."

As with the Clark and Lewis people, there was much eating and use of the hot springs after the party of gun-seekers trekked to the two Flatheads waiting there. They let the horses feed and rest for two more days, then set out for the Bitter Root Valley. When all were together, two young Shoshonis and one Nee Mee Poo began expressing dissatisfaction that one so young as Little Bear Claw would be in command.

"Does the buffalo calf lead the herd?" Red Paint of the Nee Mee Poo asked while the two others leaned insolently on their horses. Bad Leg of the Nee Mee Poo, a warrior of many summers, immediately called a council.

"We have reaffirmed the wisdom of Tjolzhitsay and of the chiefs of the Shoshonis and Nee Mee Poo," the older warrior announced. "You will lead with or without this whip."

Little Bear Claw, the ready grin gone, gravely accepted the whip. Then, because the party was so strong, he organized it this time so the gun-seekers could rapidly move through more open country. Red Paint and his two dissidents would scout front, left and right positions of much importance and responsibility. Soon Red Paint and Little Bear Claw had had much talk as the latter led the way. Little Bear Claw tucked the whip into the bundle of furs, but removed his shield with the three scalps from its case and hung it from his horse. There it remained for many days.

Before approaching the fort at the Lake of the Pend d'Oreille, Little Bear Claw carefully had told the story of the firewater and of the bravery of Cold Wind. To emphasize the dangers of the drink, he had led the party past the yet discernible ashes of the Blackfeet fire—and the widely scattered bones.

"We will not accept the firewater," he explained, then more grimly emphasized, "we will not endanger the success of our trades."

The small cabin/fort had been enlarged and was occupied by five eager white traders who greeted the gun-seekers with enthusiasm that continued to grow as each well-laden pack horse entered the small, newly constructed stockade. The flag gaily waving over it had red and white stripes, but differently arranged than had been those on the banner carried by the Clark and Lewis people. And there were no stars.

A large boat was moored at water's edge. As traders and gun-seekers began palavering, one of the white men continued to carry bundles from the boat to the log store and trading room, which smelled of cured tobacco and sap from the newly peeled logs. Hanging across or from pegs, leaning against the wall, stacked on boxes and barrels was such a quantity and variety of trade goods that the gun-seekers openly expressed astonishment. They desired to step across the tiny pole dividing the room to examine them. Red and white blankets, beads, scissors, awls, files, other metal objects. Focal point was a long rack of muskets of varying lengths. Hatchets, axes, arrow points and knives were on display nearby. Spirits lifted in tired bodies as the gun-seekers viewed this array. Amid the excitement one of the whites began passing out tin cups; another carried a small keg into the room, proffering some of its contents first to the oldest warrior.

"It is the firewater!" Little Bear Claw called above the hub-bub. Little Coyote jostled his way through the throng to stand at the warrior's side. "It is the firewater," he warned, and gently pushed aside the keg. The trader looked at the older man and at the much younger one and again swung the keg toward the cup. Again Little Coyote pushed it aside in the sudden silence. Now the other trader smilingly seized the warrior's cup and had his companion fill it. Then, triumphantly, he handed it to the warrior, interposing his body between the two Flatheads. The cup was empty before Little Bear Claw could force his way through the press of bodies. The warrior was holding his throat in astonishment, his eyes weeping at the unexpected impact of the spirits.

The room cleared at Little Bear Claw's command, leaving

only himself and the four traders there. The young warrior strode outside, removed the whip from the bundle of furs and returned to the building. At his call, Bad Leg, the Nee Mee Poo, and a burly Flathead brought the offending warrior into the room. Already his words were becoming foolish; when released, he stumbled about and called for more of the drink.

The first lash of the whip broke his skin. Before the fourth blow had fallen, his back was bleeding like the young mountain goat raked by the talons of a great eagle. The man fell to his knees then onto all fours, the cruel whip driving him past the startled traders and out the doorway. He lay on the ground gibbering from the effects of the drink and the lash, totally unaware of the varied looks, words and gestures aimed at this young whip-wielder.

"We will not endanger the success of our mission," Little Bear Claw repeated grimly. "Have you grumbled against the lash in the hands of such sub-chiefs as Thunder Voice when he controlled the buffalo hunts upon which the very lives of our people depended? Will you go home empty-handed while the Blackfeet do not? Would you put this creature in charge of this party?" He pointed contemptuously at the groveling warrior. "Hear me this last time! We will not endanger our trades!"

Bad Leg, Red Paint and his two friends, Little Coyote and others stepped past the now-almost-unconscious form and into the trading room, where all soon followed. The trading, thereafter, was restrained and accomplished with a minimum of both jollity and signs, except when Little Coyote refused to trade at all his impressive stack of fur bales and the horses until he could see some rifled guns. These again turned out to be the personal weapons of the white men. His one-fifth share of the furs, plus the horses, brought him three muskets for himself and two fine rifled guns and ammunition.

Bad Leg suggested that they hold back some of the finest furs and a few of the best horses to enable each of the travelers to obtain a small amount of other goods for their own families. The offending warrior, his lacerated back covered by his robe, limped from the room with a copper pot, a steel knife and red blanket.

As the man painfully made his way to tie the pot on his horse, Little Bear Claw motioned for one of the chastened traders to hand him an empty cup. The trader did so, then Little Bear Claw carried it out to the brave he had whipped.

"No, no, no!" the brave protested in mock alarm, which set everyone to laughing. Obviously, he had been lashed before for other reasons.

As the gun-seekers, with far fewer but well-laden horses, turned homeward, Little Bear Claw put this older warrior in the lead scouting position and Red Paint to his left. The first evening away from the trading post, from which they had departed richer in both goods and experience, Little Bear Claw gave each of the two men a musket and used the weapons to go through the loading, aiming, firing and cleaning procedures for the instruction of the others. Lastly, he showed them all how to carefully pour gunpowder from the small leaden kegs into the crude powder horns. He explained how, later, they could melt the empty kegs to mold the bullets. New Blade of Grass, now Gun, had taught him well.

Their great elation changed to wariness once during this journey home when they encountered a small band of Little Robes. The Little Robes had a few furs and many horses to trade; they explained that the sickness of red sores had killed all the people in one of their larger encampments. They would need guns to strengthen their smaller numbers.

Little Bear Claw shared with them the information about the firewater and told them of the traders farther north on the Lake of the Kutenais, should those on the Lake of the Pend d'Oreille be lacking in the goods they needed.

During that discussion, when the pipe made its way back to the aged sub-chief of the Little Robes, he placed two pine cones in front of him. They were separated by the distance of the length of the pipe. He placed the pipe vertically and equi-distant between the cones, then, while he spoke, repeatedly picked up the pipe and laid it down vertically at varying distances between the cones. "We are few," he said sadly, his bright eyes peering from a face as seamed as the untanned under-hide of a dried rabbit skin. "We rejoice that we have had the wisdom to remain friends of the Flatheads, Shoshonis and Nee Mee Poo, as well as with their enemies, the Blackfeet—sometimes closer with one than the other, but always we have remained friends. What you have warned us about the firewater and told us about the fort proves your hearts are good toward us."

The wise eyes slowly swept the assemblage and his voice strengthened to reach them all: "We, too, must have the guns, though I wonder if the cost might in some distant time prove too much. These eyes never have seen a white man, though my father did, many summers ago down the great river, past where the Mandans live. He, too, spoke of firewater. How fortunate that the white man seeks furs!"

The old man rose, straightened up with difficulty and, with great dignity, motioned for his horse.

"Travel with sharp eyes," he warned. "There are many Piegan about. Their anger is great toward all, except the Blackfeet and their allies. They told us that only a few suns ago, eight of them smoked and camped with some strange white men near the great falls of the great river. They said these white men told them they had been west of the mountains and had talked to their enemies, the Flatheads. These white men said soon their own traders would be following their footsteps to make trade with all tribes. This did not make the Piegans happy, for as we all know, the Blackfeet have controlled much of the trade coming from the white men to the north."

The Little Robes' sub-chief motioned his farewell. "The Piegans tried to take horses and guns of the white strangers while they slept. Two Piegans died in the argument. Chief Side Hill Calf was stabbed through his heart. The other one was shot dead by a white chief called Lewis."

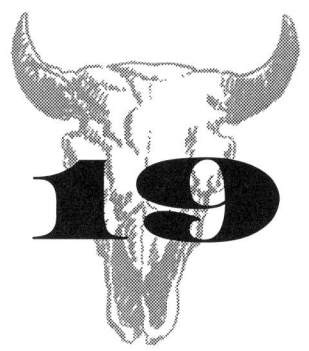

B ad Leg of the Nee Mee Poo turned in his saddle and held his flat right hand palm outward in front of his body. He moved it sharply downward, stopping it suddenly. The party halted. They would camp. The three Nee Mee Poo, five Shoshonis, Little Bear Claw and Little Coyote had come far this day after leaving the Flathead encampment near the mountain bowl where Shining Shirt slept. Tjolzhitsay had sent two notable warriors to escort Little Bear Claw and Little Coyote from the jubilant people to the council. There, the two young warriors had turned over the muskets, powder and lead and a few other carefully selected trade goods to the highly exuberant leaders. The council had conferred sub-chief status on Little Bear Claw— a very unusual honor for one so young. Some already were saying Little Bear Claw would be a worthy successor some day to Tjolzhitsay. When the head chief had begun presenting a highly prized pipe-tomahawk to each delighted council member, Little Coyote had sought Running Buffalo Bull and Little Yellow Bird to offer gifts.

"This rifled gun is for my father, as are these six traps. I have kept one such rifle for myself and four traps for my trip to the lodge of Broken Pipe. This metal pot, knife and axe are for my mother. I will seek Antelope with the traps and these three muskets, if they will prove important enough for Broken Pipe."

Reluctantly, the parents had watched their son and Little Bear Claw join the Nee Mee Poo and Shoshonis for their homeward trek, which would include the trail over which Clark and Lewis had struggled when they first had entered the valley. Little Bear Claw had been charged to visit the chiefs of their Nee Mee Poo and Shoshone allies to add his counsel to their plans for obtaining trade goods to make life easier—and safer. Their enemies also were certain to become more deeply involved in trade with white men living to the north, trade that when combined with their superior numbers would make them very successful, indeed. And more dangerous!

Little Coyote and Red Paint of the Nee Mee Poo tethered their pack horses and rode a short distance ahead of the others on the steep and dim trail. They stopped near a large boulder embedded solidly in the precipitous mountainside. The boulder afforded a small, grassy clearing for their mounts. As the men ate, watched and listened, Little Coyote closely observed Red Paint. He was perhaps seven summers older than Little Coyote, tall, with deep-set eyes, especially prominent cheek bones and a heavy growth of long, dark hair that rumpled atop his head then fell with a natural part mostly to the right side. During their trek for the guns, Little Coyote had learned there was a carefree spirit in Red Paint, a spirit so imprisoned by a strong will that first impressions of the brave hinted of a dignified, almost total, imperturbability. Yes, Little Coyote very wisely had sought Red Paint's help and friendship after that first challenge to authority before the journey for the guns. The man's sole concern had been for the success of their mission.

Their meal over, the men separated to scout well forward on foot, then returned to the boulder. The steep dropoff to the south provided them with a panoramic view of another wide valley through which a sparkling stream meandered among stands of tall trees and open, grass-filled meadows. The reflective surfaces of occasional ponds signaled various messages of waterfowl, fish and sometimes a breeze. To the distant south, east and west the men could view mountain peaks of varying heights that extended on, on and on.

Little Coyote broke the silence: "There is much beauty here, too, beyond our people's valley. I have not traveled so far in this direction. Where do your people live?"

Red Paint's features softened into a smile: "I come from a great valley still far to the west that we call 'Wallowa.' There are many bands of the Nee Mee Poo in many neighboring valleys, but I am certain our valley is of the greatest beauty. There are many fine meadows, with much game and grass, where we have many fine horses." He looked fondly at his own superb Appaloosa, which had struck up a friendly acquaintance with Not Afraid of Guns. "We trade many, but the best we keep— even as we did when the white chiefs Lewis and Clark came back from the great salt water and wanted some of our best."

Red Paint began tugging at a large, white rock perched precariously on the steep mountainside.

"When we first saw them on their way to the salt water, they had horses they had traded from your people," he said. "We never had seen white men before."

The great rock began rocking back and forth as Red Paint pushed and pulled more energetically.

"We were preparing to kill all of them as they struggled, tired and sick, through the forest without seeing us. We wondered much at the hair on their faces and how some of them used a small stick to bring fire from nowhere to light their pipes. They owe their lives to Wat-ku-ese, Stray Away, one of our women who was befriended by two strange white trappers far away and long ago when she escaped from our enemies. She told us that white men were friends and would not harm us. Perhaps you do not know that your own people helped her to reach us, though her child died and was buried near your encampment."

The rock teetered, then fell back into its small hole on the mountainside. Red Paint began digging at the downhill side with a stick, breathing heavily as he did so. "The Lewis and Clark people became great friends of one of our chiefs, Twisted Hair." The perspiring brave nimbly dodged the rock as it began rolling down the mountainside, flattening brush as it gained momentum. Little Coyote stood to watch while Red Paint continued to talk. "The whites made great canoes. Out of trees. Then they went down the river. We thought we might never see them again. They promised to return. They left their horses with us."

The crashing sounds, fairly common at these altitudes to man and animal alike, began dying away. The rock moved from sight.

Red Paint dusted off his hands. "We have profited much from their visits among us. And the black stranger we named Tse-mook-tse-mook To-to-kean, Black Indian, now has a son among our people. Perhaps some of the white men, too, for they worked very hard at this—when they had recovered from the effects of their long trek."

The sounds made by the rock were gone. Little Coyote stretched and relieved himself, noting that the pinto and Appaloosa no longer were standing head to tail to whisk away the bothersome flies with their tails. The horses were nosing some objects half-hidden in the grass and low bushes.

Soon the two warriors also were staring at a big and a very small keg, as well as a large barrel. With sight, touch and smell, the men soon agreed that the big keg had held meat, the small one firewater, and the barrel a meal ground from corn, which occasionally would find its way through trade channels from the people to the south. All containers were bound with stout metal bands that some day could be filed into arrow points.

"I saw such marvels as these among the Clark and Lewis people," Little Coyote explained. "They will not come this way again. These are of much value." Given first choice, Red Paint selected the meat keg. Little Coyote claimed the meal barrel, certain it would please Little Yellow Bird. Later, Bad Leg gratefully accepted the firewater keg from which he salvaged the metal bands.

At the Nee Mee Poo Pass, Little Coyote regretfully had watched Little Bear Claw disappear down the trail with the three Nee Mee Poo and their precious guns and other trade goods.

"We will meet here by this stream later in *kólog*, this moon of the Onion," Little Bear Claw had promised. "Thus we will return to our people in time for the trek to the buffalo grounds." His smile faded. "The Blackfeet kept their word not to fight us during the summer hunt, which you missed while catching the beaver. We will need every strong warrior on the next hunt." A hint of a smile had returned. "Will you be there as a strong warrior?" The new sub-chief put his hand on his friend's shoulder. "Or will Little Coyote and Antelope still be roaming inseparably in the secret land of *sntamtsán*, the kiss?"

Broken Pipe stepped from his lodge into morning Sun. He looked momentarily at his and Antelope's horses tethered by forelegs in front of the skin shelter, which he preferred to the grass and twig homes of most of his people. He patted both animals, then quickly circled behind the lodge to relieve himself at the pit marked by a pole. He walked to the stream, where he liberally dashed water over his face, neck, chest and arms, scooping some sand to scrub his hands. He shook them and again faced his lodge, wide-eyed from the shock of the cold water. Tethered to a small bush a short distance from the lodge, unmistakedly on his territory, was a fine pack horse. He walked around the animal, but did not touch it, as had become his habit ever since single horses, doubles, trebles, once as many as twelve, had begun appearing there as proposed engagement gifts after Antelope had become a woman. She had offered no complaints when her father had not even discussed the possibility of opening a gift exchange with the horses' owners, which could have culminated in Antelope's marriage.

This time there was a difference. A fine, long musket, two powder flasks, a bullet mould, some sheets of lead, a small iron pot and a plain bullet pouch hung enticingly from the saddle pad.

Little Coyote, standing concealed in some trees, watched Broken Pipe peer at the weapon, almost touch it, then back away. He strode to his lodge and entered it. Almost immediately, Antelope bounded outside, her lithe, eager, virtually unclothed body brushing the strings of deer hooves hanging from a wicket by the entrance to warn against possible horse thieves. As the dull music reached him, Little Coyote added several short yelps. Man and woman met almost equidistant between trees and lodge. They stood there in his blanket, muscular chest pressing hard against soft breasts, strong, eager arms striving to hold ever more closely, and both almost oblivious to warming Sun, the gladsome songs of the birds and the creek and the distant human calls within the awakening encampment.

Later, the aches of separation replaced by the even more compelling aches for greater closeness, they sat near the base of a large tree where Little Coyote had tethered Not Afraid of Guns and unloaded his personal gear. He had placed the remaining two muskets, the powder, lead and flints in the meal barrel.

When the couple could talk of more worldly matters, Little Coyote watched with great interest while Antelope, clad now in his extra shirt against the coolness of the morning, almost ignored the weapons during her careful examination of the barrel.

"This is a great marvel!" she exclaimed. "Have you brought it to turn the head of my mother, too? Already, you know, she favors Little Coyote." Once more Antelope gently reached around Little Coyote's head and brought it closer to her own; as they touched, Little Coyote pulled her body closer to him.

Abruptly, he stood, his voice husky, tremulous.

"What were Broken Pipe's words about the gun?"

"Only, 'There is a fine gun on a pack horse. Little Coyote is here.' I waited no longer, but, see, he looks more closely at the gun, as does my mother. Now he touches it!"

"I'll not wait many days for him to agree or not agree to exchange gifts," Little Coyote said. "We must join Little Bear Claw soon. Every day we wait for your father to decide becomes one day lost when we could be alone." Little Coyote resolutely picked up another gun, powder flask and bullet pouch and strode toward the lodge. He remembered how the British traders at the Lake of the Pend d'Oreille, when denied the use of the firewater to help them in their trades, had offered a few goods for many fine furs, whetted the appetite of his people by offering a bit more, then, without pauses, more until they no longer could resist. Broken Pipe is an accomplished horse-trader, Little Coyote

180

reminded himself, but he betrayed his desire for a gun when he examined mine after the buffalo hunt.

Now, before the young warrior greeted the horse-trader and his wife, he slipped the second musket through the saddle pad strap and hung the powder flask and pouch from it. He stepped back and eyed the couple.

"You have two fine guns, Little Coyote."

Broken Pipe spoke first, stepping in front of his wife to hide her wide smile and warmly murmured greeting. Then he waved his curious young son and baby girl away from the gun-laden horse. "Summon Antelope, Little Coyote, and we'll smoke." He strode importantly into his lodge.

Broken Pipe's family remained outside the shelter while the men smoked and the Shoshone trader learned of Little Coyote's success with the white man's traps.

"You used the traps well. A busy horse-trader, if he had no time to trap for himself but had traps for others to use for a share of furs, would do very well, indeed."

"There are two such traps which I should have hung with the two guns."

Little Coyote ran to his camp and back with the rattling traps before the pipe had gone out.

The shrewd eyes of Broken Pipe lighted up. "These are fine gifts which could warm my heart, but Antelope's mother has a heart that would grieve, too, should our daughter leave our lodge."

Little Coyote puffed deeply on the pipe so it would not go out, gravely handed it to the older man and again ran to the trees. Soon he had rolled the empty barrel alongside the cooking tripod outside the lodge. The baby girl promptly crawled inside it and laughed delightedly as she rocked it back and forth.

"This gift is for the mother of Antelope." Little Coyote led her to the marvel, explaining its great value for storage of food, clothing or water. She held her hand before her mouth in wonderment as the Flathead handed a sturdy file to Broken Pipe. "Rawhide can replace the iron bands about this wonder, or . . ." he grinned, "you can set someone else to making many arrow points from them with this file—for shares, of course." He filed a notch in the upper rim until the metal shone in the sunlight.

The Shoshone grinned in appreciation, then looked expectantly toward the fringe of trees from which had come such bounty. Little Coyote resolutely prepared to re-enter the lodge. The older man once more looked toward the trees, his delighted wife, and Antelope.

"Ai-ee. These women!" he exclaimed with a resigned shrug. "Antelope, fetch Star."

"Ho, Little Coyote," the trader called into the lodge. "I have a gift for you."

The magnificent light gray, dark-spotted Appaloosa was almost an exact duplicate of Antelope's horse. Little Coyote said as much when he recovered sufficiently from his own wonderment.

"Try him," Broken Pipe urged. "He is from the same sire and mare as is Antelope's horse."

The young warrior leapt astride the superb creature and raced away, the cold wind of their passage forcing him, finally, to a halt near the trees. He nudged the animal toward the two remaining traps, a powder flask, a bar of lead and a small keg of powder. In his excitement he lifted, balanced and almost tied to the new horse the smaller, double-barreled musket/shotgun. No, that would remain a gift for his new wife. Soon he was handing the other gifts, one by one, to a widely grinning Broken Pipe.

After that, events began moving almost as quickly as could Star.

Little Coyote slept fitfully that night in the lodge of Broken Pipe, distinguishing during his wakeful state between the snores of the father, the quiet breathing of the mother and two children and the restless turning on the furs where Antelope tried to sleep less than two lance lengths away. Much had happened during the day. Picketed outside the lodge near Not Afraid of Guns and his and Antelope's Appaloosas were two pack horses ready to be loaded with already-packed leather bags. Little time would elapse between the wedding ceremony and the departure of the newlyweds. Broken Pipe had decreed that the rites would incorporate parts of both the Shoshone and Flathead customs: Magic songs, a lecture by the chief, then a ring of dancers around the couple while the chief would sing the marriage song.

When Little Coyote was certain all slept, he quietly lifted the lodge wall and rolled outside into pre-dawn coolness. He loaded the pack horses and led them to a small, grass-covered meadow in the trees where he had left his own equipment. He placed the saddle pad on Not Afraid of Guns and attached to it his scalp-bedecked shield, ancient lance, bow, arrows and gun before bathing in the creek and donning his clean buckskins. As the family of Broken Pipe began greeting the earliest guests, Little Coyote led his horse to the lodge. All, especially the younger Shoshone braves, crowded about Not Afraid of Guns to eye the weapons and trophies before respectfully greeting this young Flathead who had come to take away what surely was a tribal treasure.

The wedding ceremony concluded with the Shoshone chief lifting his arms and proclaiming for all to hear: "Let the Shoshonis and Flatheads know that this joining of both people is good. It ties more strongly the bonds between us. This is my message to you, and to carry to Three Eagles."

With this admonition, Little Coyote and Antelope departed from the encampment. Mounted on their Appaloosas, their other horses strung out behind, they were followed by shouts of well-wishers who continued to feast.

"You ride unsmiling, like a great chief leading his warriors to battle." Antelope playfully bumped her horse into Little Coyote's.

He glanced briefly at his mate, smiled, then looked as far backward as he could. One person, perhaps Antelope's mother, still was waving. Little Coyote nudged Star ever so slightly with his right thigh and leg. The superbly trained horse began angling toward the trees. There, Little Coyote dismounted and picketed Not Afraid of Guns and the pack horses near grass and water. Then he removed all equipment, except bow and arrows, from Star. Nimbly he leapt atop the Appaloosa and bumped him against Antelope's. The pair rode quietly side by side along the well-worn path leading ever upward from the valley floor. On either side, deep-green-colored bushes clustered between stately trees reaching like great lances to pierce the cloudless, azure sky. Songs from myriads of birds in grass, bushes and trees rose sweetly above the steady, measured tempo of the eight clopping hooves on the soft forest floor.

The man guided his mount toward a small brook singing joyfully during its increasingly precipitous journey downward. The couple entered a small clearing filled with the heady perfume of trees, brush, grasses, flowers and soft multicolored mosses. The horses stopped.

Antelope looked wide-eyed at this strong, silently grinning man of hers, resolutely holding his blanket about his shoulders with one hand even as he reached up and lifted her downward. There would be no standing in the blanket now.

That late morning on the mountainside the pain of loneliness for Little Coyote was quickly forgotten in the ever growing sweetness accompanying the release of long-pent-up emotions—emotions that seemingly had begun so long ago during the hunt near the three forks.

Warm mid-day lengthened into even warmer early and late afternoon. When cooling evening breeze gently reminded them of waiting mounts nearby and others down the mountain, they returned to less-pressing demands and hastily erected temporary camp.

At length they slept, Antelope sleepily asking her mate why he had awakened her under the canopy of winking stars with his quiet laugh.

"As I lie here beside you, I awakened to tell the Good Spirit that, among all His gifts, I was most grateful for you."

"But the laugh?"

"I thought, too, of your chief's so-true statement as we left your father's lodge . . . 'this joining of both peoples is good.'"

Throughout that so-long night the couple found themselves agreeing energetically with the message, but in the doing completely forgetting the messenger.

Part 2

The Fur-Takers

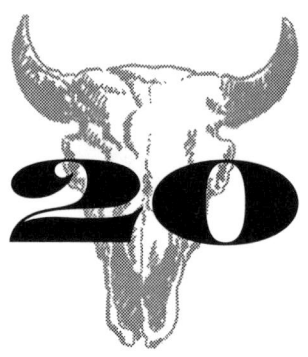

In the last days of *s'tcut ánlka*, the tenth moon, Good Spirit and Sun had been kind to the Flathead people and their allied Shoshonis and Nee Mee Poo. The Blackfeet and snow and cold wind had stayed away from this hunting encampment of more than two-hundred lodges erected in a great circle on a high embankment of the river of the yellow stones east of the three forks. True, the buffalo had taken the hunters farther than they had wished—near the wintering ground of the Crow people and of many animals from the ever bountiful Big Horn and Wind River mountains. The meat bags were full, there were many good cow and young bull hides and the encampment rejoiced and feasted. Soon the trek homeward would begin—indeed, the people already would have been on their way—had not Gun, chief of the hunt, become troubled amid all this plenty. So had Tjolzhitsay, and then the leaders of the Shoshonis and Nee Mee Poo.

The cause? John Colter, a white man of perhaps thirty or more summers.

Two suns ago Colter had sat here in the great council lodge, a pleasant smile on his lean, tanned face, his long, muscular legs stretched out until the well-worn, dark soles of his winter moccasins almost had touched the council fire. The fire had been replenished again and again as he painstakingly told interesting stories about himself and his companion, Drouillard, who two summers ago also had been with the chiefs Clark and Lewis in the valley where Shining Shirt slept. John Colter had told of others from that party who now were in the Crow country, too.

Chiefs Clark and Lewis had allowed John Colter to remain behind when two other white men had come up the great river to trap as the larger group had prepared to go down to a far-away village called St. Louis.

"Lewis and Clark met eleven small parties of trappers in twenty boats coming upriver as they went down," John Colter had said. "As the Lewis and Clark people tell others of the many beaver upriver, more and more white men will come here. I was told this by Drouillard. He went all the way to the St. Louis village. Now he, like myself, is traveling in parts of the Stinking Water, the Big Horn and the Yellowstone. We are to talk to our brothers the Crows, the Flatheads, Shoshonis, Nee Mee Poo and others. There is a party of perhaps sixty white men building a trading post and catching many beaver near where the Big Horn and Yellowstone rivers come together. Our chief is Manuel Lisa. When he sent me and Drouillard, because we know the sign and some other talk, he said to ask the people to come trade their furs."

"We brought few furs with us. We came for the buffalo," Gun had communicated.

"Manuel Lisa knows this," Colter had said, "but you come to this region with the meat bags empty. Fill them with furs before you come for the buffalo. Lisa is generous. You will carry many important things back to your valley."

The people had fed John Colter well, refilled his pack with food and told him where he would find the Crows. He had left amid much good will. Even so, the chiefs were troubled, so once more they replenished the council fire.

First, they agreed with Gun that they should gather up the furs they had brought to turn into clothing and other family uses. Two warriors known for their shrewd horse-trading would travel by night and hide by day to trade the furs for gunpowder. They were not to touch any firewater pots. They left with four horses at once.

Gun passed the pipe to Tjolzhitsay. He puffed deeply. In the quiet of the council lodge the popping of the firewood was like tiny guns, smaller even than the sound of the two-barreled rifle-shotgun Little Coyote had presented and demonstrated to Antelope. This he had done when the earliest ecstasies of the honeymoon in the land of the Shoshonis had subsided like wind-driven waves lapping the lake shore, but with the promise there of unlimited others should the tiniest breeze arise that quickly could grow into a delightfully fierce storm. Little Coyote shook his head to clear it of the delightful past as the head chief blew the tobacco smoke into the warming air.

"The chief Lewis said the man he called the Great White Father would send traders to exchange their marvels for the furs we take," Tjolzhitsay said. He tapped the hard-packed ground with his left hand. "The furs *we* take."

The Shoshone and Nee Mee Poo sub-chiefs gravely pondered these words as they passed the pipe. "He said this to the Nee Mee Poo many times when he lived with us." The sub-chief's voice carried a nuance of disappointment, impatience, concern.

"The chief Lewis said nothing about sending out the white trappers. Of course there are many beaver." Little Bear Claw's words carried those of Tjolzhitsay one slow step forward. So did Gun's.

"There are many streams with many beaver. Yet," Gun puffed once more on the pipe, ". . . there can be many buffalo in one place. If the Flatheads, the Nee Mee Poo, the Crows and, yes, even the Blackfeet and others all make their kills from that large herd, they soon are gone. Of course, the buffalo always return, but they did mostly disappear from our valley soon after we moved there."

"Yes! There are many streams, many beaver," Has Many Horses ventured, "yet there is a value in trapping them ourselves. We would wish to do so in our valley and the better places nearby." He looked at Little Coyote, who sat far back with Running Buffalo

Bull. "The place of the hot springs, and near the Lake of the White Moose, and others."

Bad Leg of the Nee Mee Poo vigorously nodded assent: "We will trap the beaver where we live." He looked at Red Paint. Red Paint's action was more expressive than the word. He signed "Yes" by almost closing all but his index fingers, resting the thumb on the side of the second finger and moving the hand slightly left and a little downwards, at the same time closing the index over the thumb. There was no delay; the practiced motion was performed but once. Vehemently.

A warrior put dry cottonwood on the fire. An errant, strong gust of wind poured through the smoke flap vent and momentarily scattered the rising column of smoke throughout the silent lodge. Its sweetish odor touched them all.

"These white men." Tjolzhitsay shook his head. "We owe them much already. Our too few guns especially. Not to have traded would have been foolish. Yet, if they trap for the furs, too, perhaps there will come a time when they will not need us—only the furs."

"We will trap the beavers. The white man will trade." Bad Leg grunted and straightened his scarred limb.

"We can accept or we can resist." Three Eagles' voice was strong. "Yes. There are many streams, many beaver. And the Canada people seem more content to trade than trap. Perhaps we should trade only with them. There will be trouble. The always-angry Blackfeet will be even more angry when they learn the Lisa fort is in the land of their enemies, the Crows."

Gun waved away a warrior who sought to put more wood on the fire.

"Little Coyote." Gun's words jarred the young warrior from his near reverie. He had been listening attentively, yet from somewhere inside, deep inside, other thoughts had seemed to be pressing through—the black soles of John Colter's well-worn moccasins, and Three Eagles' strongly voiced certainty the Blackfeet nation would resist Lisa's post.

His deep thoughts could wait. Little Coyote momentarily stood, then sat again.

"Your *sumesh* remains strong," Gun said. "We must know more about these white men. You said on your vision quest you were told to counsel the people that the white man is as numerous as the berries in our valley. We should not war with them. As they come into the land, our people and our friends must know more about them than do our enemies, just as we worked hard to obtain the guns. We are not numerous enough to make great mistakes." He looked momentarily at Bad Leg and Red Paint, then continued. "Tell me, Little Coyote, does Antelope carry your child in her belly?"

Little Coyote motioned negatively, whereupon, for the first time, Gun, with his great responsibility, relaxed his face into a half-smile. "You do not work hard enough, perhaps." The smile grew as others laughed. "Take Antelope with you then, also your horses and lodge, to this fort of Lisa's. If you hasten, you can join with the warriors we sent for the gunpowder. Learn about white men. Little Bear Claw will learn about the people from Canada. When you can provide wise counsel, return. There will be much to hear." Gun sighed. "And much to plan." Out of respect, he handed the pipe to Tjolzhitsay, who put it down. The lodge emptied.

Little Bear Claw and Little Coyote met briefly in the lodge of Running Buffalo Bull. Antelope, helped by Little Yellow Bird, hastily packed. Both young warriors were keenly aware that growing responsibilities accompanying each accomplishment within the small tribe were moving Little Bear Claw toward higher leadership positions and Little Coyote toward a more widely accepted role as warrior/seer. Neither consciously strove for such tribal recognition.

Alone, they momentarily could set aside the reserve their positions among the much older warriors seemed to demand.

"Perhaps I will not see you for two or three summers," Little Bear Claw said. "When we return from our journeys, you no longer will have time for Little Bear Claw, but will be spending your days with two or three sons."

Little Coyote grinned at his friend. "And you, will you bring back a wife from the Kutenai, or the Spokan, the Coeur d'Alene, the Pend d'Oreille? How will you learn about the people who come down from Canada if you spend all your time chasing the young women of our friends?"

Outside the lodge they could hear Little Yellow Bird suggesting that Antelope leave behind the lodge poles for faster traveling. She could select new ones when she and her husband reached the Lisa fort. The two young men looked silently at each other as they heard other voices—those of Running Buffalo Bull and of Antelope's family. The warriors gave each other a strong, affectionate hug. Then, once again assuming the demeanor expected by those whose years the two did not possess, they emerged from the lodge to face responsibilities that would test even the strongest and most mature.

Not Afraid of Guns twitched her ears forward and left to right. They remained to the right. She slowed her walk as almost instantly the Appaloosa, Star, and Antelope's horse began to listen, as did the four pack horses.

For a time Little Coyote and Antelope easily had followed the tracks the two warriors sent after the gunpowder had left in the dry bunch grass. Later to guide them slightly below the crest of a long ridge, the couple sought an occasional hoof-smashed, drying, violet-leaf sunflower, blue lupines and wild geraniums.

Apparently the Blackfeet had done the same. Little Coyote nudged his mount and tugged the lead pack horse's rope toward the nearest small, brush-filled ravine. There he and Antelope, helped by the horses' ears, listened and watched, too. The sounds were coming from the ridge, itself, louder now—the pounding of two horses. Little Coyote, bow and arrows on his back, the long rifle in his hand, ran upward along the outer edge of the ravine. In the distance he could hear more horses, along with shrill and exultant whoops. He yelped twice as two Flatheads raced into view. He raised his right hand and swiftly brought the index finger toward his face. *Come!* The two men possessed no weapons in their desperate race. When they reached the ravine, Little Coyote handed his bow and arrows to one; as Antelope did the same for the other, Little Coyote told one warrior to join Antelope on one side of the ravine. He and the other man would cover the opposite side.

"There are seven!" the warrior panted. "We had no chance. They, too, entered a small stand of trees below us here as we waited for the night so we could travel farther."

"Put your two horses near the edge of the ravine where they will be seen."

They waited.

Four Blackfeet bounded off their mounts near those of the two fugitives and raced for the ravine. Three others did the same on the other side.

Antelope fired first. The small report of the over/under weapon was followed by a shrill cry. The lead Blackfeet entering the brush from Little Coyote's side died from a carefully centered bullet in his forehead. Surprised warning shouts rose on both sides of the ravine. Two musket balls sang their song of death through the brush. An arrow thwacked against a stone. While Little Coyote reloaded, his companion drew back on the bowstring, relaxed it, then drew again and loosed the arrow. He flashed a triumphant grin at Little Coyote and signed, *Two there, two here.*

Antelope's shotgun barrel popped. If she had followed her husband's instructions, she had waited until her target was close to receive the small charge of closely bunched and lethal shot.

"They will return to their horses." Little Coyote replaced the ramrod under the rifle barrel. As they waited on their bellies for the three Blackfeet to race down the ridge edge toward their horses, he yelped once for Antelope. She and the other warrior joined them.

"None must get away!" Little Coyote warned. "We will remain silent. Only the arrows and guns will speak."

Thus it was that the two warriors sent for the gunpowder returned to the buffalo camp with seven horses, three muskets, three horns of powder, three bags of bullets, bows and arrows and clothing. There also were three scalps, much honor and stories to tell. They would give two horses to Running Buffalo Bull to await his son's and Antelope's return. Little Coyote and Antelope would take the two re-possessed pack horses and furs to Lisa; they would return with the gunpowder to share among all who had sent the furs—but only when they knew much about white man, as Gun had commanded.

"These look to be the scalps of Crows—a warrior, a woman and perhaps their children," Little Coyote told a quite calm Antelope as the two Flathead warriors departed. "We must show them honor." Antelope blackened a small, highly decorated buckskin bag with her paint powder and braided its straps into Star's long mane. The horse would carry nothing else.

Leaving this place of death to the omnipresent and noisily circling crows, the couple followed the opposite rocky side of the ridge until they reached yet another brush-filled ravine. They crept under their blankets to await the night for travel, and they slept at once. Theirs had been a hard day.

Crows, this time many Crow warriors, silently and afoot had encircled the small stand of trees in which the pair had chosen to hide the next day. Antelope, fresh from washing in a cold streamlet that swiftly flowed through ice-encrusted banks, rushed to warn Little Coyote. The ever tightening circle of thirty-three warriors displayed little friendliness and much interest in the two fresh scalps hanging from Little Coyote's shield and the two tied into the mane on either side of Antelope's Appaloosa.

Before they were examined closely, several warriors, evidently heeding an earlier command of strict silence, flexed their bows. A few others pointed their old trade muskets with filed-off barrels at the startled pair. All looked toward a large warrior, the only one astride a horse. He wore two streaks of black, oily soot on each cheek; his face was set in a cruel, triumphant smile that told Little Coyote that unless matters were set aright at once, the couple would never die quickly from arrows and lead.

"It is he who mourns," Little Coyote told Antelope as he pointed to the man on horseback. "Stand where you are." A low, angry hum swept the tight circle of warriors as Little Coyote strode resolutely toward Star. He untethered the horse and led it toward the Crow chieftain, pausing once to point both index fingers toward his eyes, then motioning that, in addition to crying, he was cutting his hair in sorrow. Little Coyote untied the buckskin pouch and handed it to the immobile chief, whose eyes glittered like those of a carefully watching rattlesnake. The chief shifted his gaze only to withdraw the four scalps from the bag. Grief displaced hate in his eyes as rapidly as the arrow flies from the bow. The man bent forward in pain and sorrow almost as though an arrow had struck him in his muscular belly.

"We took but four Blackfeet scalps; our two Flathead companions go to the camp of Tjolzhitsay and Gun with the other three," Little Coyote said. "We give you these to help your grief." In the great silence, the Flathead procured the Blackfeet scalps and threw them onto the ground in front of the grieving man.

The man straightened on his horse and slowly pushed the Crow scalps back into the pouch.

"I am Drum, chief of the Crows on the Tongue River." His words were Flathead. "I have hunted with Tjolzhitsay for Blackfeet and buffalo. We have been seeking the Blackfeet who killed my brother, his woman and children as they came to join us for the buffalo hunt. You will keep the Blackfeet scalps. These I will keep for a time. You treated them with honor. We can treat you no less. Drum is grateful, so much so I cannot now say."

Had Little Coyote and Antelope approached Lisa's fort alone, they would have received only small notice despite their furs. But small groups of other people were trickling in, evidently alerted by John Colter's and Drouillard's visits to their encampments.

Drum had placed his new friends in the lead of the thirty-five-person procession. "Many hunger for and have hastened to get the white man's marvels," he explained to the young couple as a few small groups hurried to view the newcomers. "Some are from more distant villages than John Colter and Drouillard have traveled. Here are Crows from the Powder, Tongue and Big Horn. Yes, and Shoshonis." Antelope looked closely, but did not recognize any of them. "More Crows from the Wind River, a few others from as far as the Popo Agie and Siskadee, with whom we have smoked the pipe."

Words and people were coming too fast for Little Coyote to ask questions. These would come later, at a more leisurely time. Now the procession neared the fort, which, though unfinished, was far larger than any shelter Little Coyote had seen on his trading trips north. The fort seemed almost mountain-sized to gaping Antelope. Several huge wooden boats were securely tethered to large trees.

Drum halted. He raised his hand in greeting to a man approximately the height of Little Coyote, but heavier. The man stepped from the great gate of the post. "Ho, Lisa!" Drum shouted. He quickly began signing, his messages easily interpreted as were Lisa's replies by Drouillard, the white man-part Shawnee.

Surrounded as he and Antelope were by these strange faces— and overwhelmed by the recent succession of events—Little Coyote found deep solace in Drouillard's brief, friendly wave of recognition. And there was more comfort yet as the young Flathead caught part of the basic message Drouillard both spoke and signed to Lisa and those surrounding him. "These are from the Flathead nation. It would be well to treat them as the friends they are."

harp-eyed Antelope's trader father had taught her well.
While Little Coyote picketed their nine horses and removed
the packs from six in a small stand of trees surrounded by
ample dry grass, Antelope mounted her Appaloosa and began
visiting the numerous lodges that had sprung up near the
incomplete fort like mushrooms around a tree. Soon she returned
and began rummaging through their own furs. She rolled together
one of the three beaver pelts, two foxes and one marten and again
departed, this time leading the largest pack horse in the direction
of the river. She returned soon afterward with an older, broadly
smiling Crow woman, a large dilapidated lodge and a seeming
overabundance of lodge poles.

Soon the two women had erected the smaller Flathead lodge
and the ancient one nearby. Grinning more broadly still, the Crow
woman helped Antelope carry the packs into the smaller structure.
Then she eagerly seized the furs and hastened toward the trading
room at the fort. Antelope closed the smoke flap on the old lodge
and adjusted the closure on the smaller to the chill, northern breeze
that was scudding clouds southward.

"If we are to remain here to learn the white man's ways, we
will be warm," Antelope said firmly as the young couple entered

the lodge. "On the coldest days we will put our best horses in the old lodge."

Drouillard rode over that evening, four sodden, freezing beaver jouncing unrhythmically against the shoulder of his horse. Little Coyote brought the fingers of his right hand together, curved them slightly and moved them past his mouth several times. Drouillard smiled at the invitation to eat, despite the obvious discomfort of his wet buckskins and footgear. Deftly, he severed the tails from two of the carcasses and handed them to Antelope. She incorporated one into the stew already bubbling over the lodge fire and placed the other near the flames to roast. She motioned for their guest to remove his breeches and seat himself on the buffalo robe. This he did, after pulling forward a small bundle of furs to lean against. Little Coyote removed the beaver carcasses from the horse, wiped the animal down with dry grass and picketed it to feed. He carried into the lodge his guest's blanket roll and a curious, very short gun inserted in a leather holder attached to the saddle pad. Soon Drouillard's clay pipe was sending up tiny, fragrant tendrils of smoke while his small, strong hands conversed easily with his newly found, though less-practiced, sign-talking friends.

Little Coyote skinned the beavers, interspersing his knife work with an explanation of the task Gun had assigned him. Drouillard nodded in agreement.

"Gun is wise," he said. "You and your people will do well to learn white man's ways quickly before dealing with him. My father, a French-Canadian, and my Shawnee mother became interpreters for the British in a far-away place called Detroit. Like Gun, they gave me much the same counsel. It has served me well. The whites call all the people like yourself 'Indians,' just as many Indians who met whites earlier called them 'Bostons.' You will learn that many, not all, whites regard the Indians much as you do the lowest creatures. As for half-Indians like myself, many whites, not all, regard us as, well . . . almost as nothings, as a handful of prairie grass upon which we have wiped ourselves. Away from white man's settlements, we are better accepted. Often we must try harder than the full-blood Indians to make our way in white man's world. Did you not see that the black man called York was a slave, though treated well, by the chief called Clark?"

Drouillard was aware that slaves were not new to the Flatheads. Still, he appeared surprised that his hosts were holding left hands over their mouths to express astonishment. Simultaneously, they were raising their right hands to denote deep disappointment over the other revelations. Drouillard hurriedly added: "Be on guard, always. I repeat, there are good whites. Lisa is such a man, as are the two traders he works with in St. Louis. They are fair men. They give some of their men a goods called 'money' for working for them. They call these men '*engagés.*' Others are called 'free trappers.' They can trap where they wish. Leaders such as Lisa usually give them the money or trade goods for their furs. The traders in St. Louis named me their sub-chief to work with Lisa. As I say, we half-Indians," he grinned more widely, "or half-whites, must work harder. Thus, I trapped the beaver today while the others work a bit more on the fort. I must acquit myself well in the eyes of those who named me a sub-chief."

As Drouillard gratefully accepted the stew and a hot piece of the delicious beaver tail from which Antelope had peeled the outer skin, he looked up to observe her great beauty. Then he offered a warning: "In the valley where your seer Shining Shirt sleeps, we learned the Flatheads do not approve of fornication. This, too, I will tell you: White men, like many Indians, especially when away from their women, indulge in rape, though here there are some compliant women and avaricious, even hospitable, husbands who share or trade their wives' charms. Guard your woman well. But now to finish eating!"

All ate well, after which Drouillard gave two beaver carcasses to Antelope when she handed him a fur to wipe the grease from his hands. He donned his almost-dry buckskins: "I have perhaps told you too much all at once. But I will tell you again—as you wish. You will trade these?" Drouillard was pointing to the small bundles, into one of which Antelope was re-inserting the wiping fur. Little Coyote explained their purpose. Drouillard examined them all.

"We have good gunpowder," he said, "and these furs will bring much of it in trade. And there are other marvels you seek?"

Little Coyote pointed questioningly toward the curiously short gun he had carried into the lodge and hung on the tripod alongside Drouillard's hatchet and knife, powder horn, bullet pouch and rifle.

"We call these 'pistols,'" Drouillard said. "They are most conveniently carried on the horse. And though they are even less accurate at longer range than the short-barreled trade muskets, they are most useful at short range." He handed the uncocked flintlock pistol to Little Coyote.

"You have others?" the warrior asked. He was mindful of the close encounter Gun's party had had with the Blackfeet as they hastened to bring their newly traded guns to the buffalo camp near the three forks.

Drouillard signed *yes* and somewhat painstakingly explained there was an as-yet-unopened chest of them at the fort. He found the communication surprisingly easy as he began explaining that the pistols had come from the British when they lost a great war with America.

"I will open the pistol chest for you," Drouillard said. "And I will ask Lisa to hold the others, if you want them. He quite likely will do so because he wants to get the Flathead trade. I thank you for caring for my horse. We need horses here. You could get even more of the pistols for perhaps four of your six pack horses. You then would not have to feed them when the deep snows come. I will go now. I will bring the pistol chest when the sun rises if you will let me take one of your pack horses now to carry it."

As he left, he signed *farewell*. Then, curiously, he raised his right hand and moved it upward, downward, then left and right in the form of the cross-shaped metal symbol Shining Shirt had worn throughout much of his life.

"This has been a good day," Little Coyote said as the young couple re-entered the cozy lodge. Antelope looked up from arranging the sleeping furs.

"Let us make it a good night, too," she said, smiling.

Little Coyote thus far had not argued with his bride. Nor did he now.

Drouillard was late returning next day with the couple's horse and another in tow. The trader explained the delay after Little Coyote helped him carry the chest into the lodge.

"I would like to remain here and trap the beaver," he said, "but Lisa will send me upon a second journey to tell the Indians we are here and to look for more beaver. On my first trip I went to the west and south. We have agreed that this time I should go up the Big Horn River, then the Little Big Horn, east to the Rosebud and the Tongue. I hope to find more beaver there than here." A slight frown flitted across his cheerful countenance. "Perhaps I will find Colter. I worry about him, although he said he might not return until the new grass arrives. Lisa also sent Edward Rose among the Crows. He carried many trade goods. He should return soon."

Little Coyote and Antelope told Drouillard in more detail about Colter's visit to the buffalo camp. Again Little Coyote pondered what significance, if any, lay in his almost reverie-like focus on Colter's black-soled moccasins as Colter had told the Flatheads about Lisa's fort.

Drouillard opened the chest and placed three small kegs of powder on the ground well away from the fire. Next he laid out long straps of soft lead, seven powder flasks, seven moulds, all alike, as were the seven brass-barreled pistols fully two hand-lengths long.

These are the best of the lot, Drouillard signed, *so they cost you more from the furs and the horses. They carry the marks of the British.*

As he explained how to load, Drouillard pointed to symbols that, later, Little Coyote would come to know read, "D. Egg" and "G.R.," as well as the British crown.

"And now, my friends, I will depart," Drouillard said. He looked at the sky, his grin lowering as were the clouds southward over the Big Horn, the Rosebud and what, after this journey, he would call the Wolf Teeth Mountains. "The snow will come, and I wish to reach a Crow village up the Big Horn before it arrives."

Drouillard solemnly bowed toward Antelope, who helped to load the horses, then gave Little Coyote a brief, friendly hug before wheeling the animals toward the fort. When they were well strung out, Drouillard shifted the lead rope to his left hand and, looking backward, again made the sign of the cross for the puzzled Flathead and his mate.

The chill breeze seemed to flee southward with Drouillard, carrying with it heavy, grayish-black clouds until the sky filled from the more open northern area to the southerly mountains. Then, in the all-pervasive gray, the wind died and snow began to fall, small flakes first, then larger and larger ones, more and more, until Little Coyote and Antelope no longer could see the fort and connected living quarters erected on the spearpoint of land between the Big Horn and Yellowstone. Soon, even trees in the closer stand disappeared one by one like tall people walking from sight.

Agreeing that perhaps a blizzard would follow, man and woman divided their duties. Antelope used a pack horse to haul firewood, which she stored along the inner rim of the old lodge. Little Coyote rolled several large rocks to the north of the two shelters. Then, drawing on the patient tutelage of Little Yellow Bird, he expertly cast two nooses over the tops of the lodge poles, pulled them tight, then tied the ends to the rocks. Antelope carried an armload of wood into the smaller lodge. She quickly re-emerged, wiping wet snow from her face and smiling as her mate pushed a wet strand of hair toward the back of her neck. "You take the two pack horses to the trees and grass," she said as she drew her knife and cut a vertical slit above the entrance to the older lodge. "I will bring the other three horses to this one, then tie together the entrance."

The blizzard announced its arrival in a great cloud of driven snow and ever-intensifying, roaring blasts that quickly drove the couple, shivering and wet, inside. Warm broth and dry clothing quickly revived them; in the bright firelight, while their shelter trembled and shook, and smoke at times refused to go upward, they re-acquainted themselves with the newly acquired pistols. A small, buckskin bag held two extra locks.

"The powder must go to all the people," Little Coyote said as he examined each of the seven weapons and tested springs and locks. "We will keep two. The others should go to Running Buffalo Bull, Three Eagles, Gun, Little Bear Claw and your father."

Antelope looked up delightedly from her discovery that a rough piece of buffalo hide rubbed hard and long on the brass barrel made it shine like the gold from Shining Shirt's pouch. She hugged her mate softly, harder, closer until, soon, they forgot the weapons altogether.

Much later they looked into the old lodge. The three horses whinnied their welcome and seeming gratitude that they were out of the blizzard. Once again the young couple crept between the sleeping furs as the intensifying storm pounded the shelters with angry blows. At length, thoughts drifted lazily to other less-compelling adventures: After Sun came up, Little Coyote and Antelope would visit the fort.

The blizzard persisted for two days and helped matters in two ways: Most important, the now-waning wind had swept much of the snow from the grass in the small forest, which again was visible. When the couple led the three horses there, the two pack horses looked up momentarily and then resumed foraging. Also, the wind had sculpted a long, densely packed drift that tapered downward from great height near the trees almost to the fort entrance. Bundled warmly against the biting cold, Little Coyote and Antelope walked atop the drift. They saw that only four lodges remained near the fort; no smoke issued from their flaps.

"The—what did Drouillard call us? 'Indians'—still sleep," Antelope said. She pointed toward the two-room fort's living quarters, from which projected a crude fireplace chimney. A single wisp of smoke rose straight into the sky; resembling a slightly quivering eagle feather, the quill end scarcely touched the chimney. As Little Coyote and Antelope continued to crunch over the drift, they also commented that no smoke at all rose from the chimney projecting from the large trading room. Two curious ravens seemed to appear from nowhere. They swooped low over these two small figures, then strongly beat their wings upward in tiny cracking sounds as they sought altitude from which to scan the silent and hungry world.

"Perhaps the white men are not awake, are not ready to trade," Antelope said as they neared the log gate at the fort entrance. The blizzard evidently had worked on the gate and packed snow had anchored it partially open. As the couple squeezed through, the black iron hinges squeaked a protest. There was no protest at all as they opened a newly made door and entered a small space leading to the trading room. Antelope lingered behind Little Coyote, then came alongside him as her bright eyes glanced here and there at the wonders. She stopped while he explored two of the small storage cubicles within the cold room. Then he heard movement in a larger third cubicle. A man, wearing a short buffalo robe jacket and a colorful cap that flopped almost to his shoulder, worked on. He was unaware of the Indian who had entered on fur-clad feet.

Humming a strange tune, the worker skipped up and down, then he began tipping a barrel resembling the one Little Coyote and Red Paint of the Nee Mee Poo had found on the mountain trail. A clear streamlet of firewater, which Little Coyote now could smell, flowed into a cup. The man examined it, took a deep draught, then shook himself until his big belly jounced up and down. He shudderingly said, "Aagh!" and poured the remainder into the barrel. Reaching into a container nearby, the man removed two large twists of tobacco, partially separated the leaves and forced them into the whiskey barrel. Now he vigorously rocked it back and forth, after which he poured another streamlet into the cup. The whiskey had become as light golden as the remaining dry leaves the blizzard had scattered from the birch trees. The man took a tentative taste, grimaced and spat it back into the cup. Once again he poured the whiskey back into the barrel. His hand hovered uncertainly over the tobacco container. Then, with a shrug, he extracted one more twist. He pushed it into the barrel, poured in two pots of water, replaced the stopper and rolled the barrel on its rim from a row of apparently untreated barrels to a shorter one. The man had been at his task sufficiently long to have become tipsy. As he turned toward the longer row, he saw Little Coyote standing in the crude doorway. The man's jaw dropped in surprise, then his mouth lifted into a wide smile that displayed broken and discolored teeth.

"Ah, Étienne Brandt." He pounded his chest. "You wann' brandee?" He pointed toward the shorter row of barrels.

The warrior caught the import of the man's words, but a more compelling sound sent him running into the trading room proper.

Antelope was standing in a corner, her body pressed against the newly peeled log wall and almost blocked from sight by the wide-shouldered and tall body of a man. Again she cried out, unaware of her husband's presence, keenly aware of this dark-faced, bewhiskered hulk who was trying to seize her arm as though to drag her away.

"You come with Jean Baptiste Bouché," the man rumbled. Antelope's arm now was in his firm grip.

Little Coyote seized the handiest weapon, an axe handle, from the trading room and struck the man a heavy blow on his back. The man turned, facing his attacker and roaring with rage and pain. He charged like a wounded buffalo bull. Nimbly, Little Coyote avoided him. The man ended his charge in the trading room, from which he emerged with his own uplifted axe handle.

"Bouché!" Étienne Brandt's shrill, whiskey-slurred shout momentarily diverted the enraged man. Then he turned again with uplifted club—this time to stare into a steadily held, nine-sixteenth-inch bore, cocked pistol, behind which were two steely eyes and a grim, determined mouth. The pistol centered unwaveringly on Bouché's face. The weapon remained there until a half-dressed Manuel Lisa—his high forehead, elongated face, even his long ears red with anger—persuaded the young Flathead to lower it. Bouché, arguing mightily, hand on his knife, darkly strode outside. Then the irate Lisa turned his anger on half-drunk Brandt for betraying his trust in the storeroom.

204

Drouillard explained the full import of the confrontation when he returned in fourteen suns from his second journey. When he entered Little Coyote's lodge, he removed a heavy pack and dumped its contents into a pile near the firewood.

"Coal," he explained. Then he led the bewildered Little Coyote and Antelope from the lodge and pointed toward an uneven rimrock a short distance upward. Several laden pack horses were being led away from the thick, black layer, which contrasted sharply with the snow. "If you get low on wood on very cold days, burn it, but only when there is little wind so all the smoke will go out the smoke flap. Do not sleep when it burns."

Drouillard placed the largest black lump on the brightest embers of the fire. The coal continued to burn long after the wood was reduced to gray, powdery ashes.

"This Bouché," Drouillard began directly. "The chief, Lisa, brought him to trap and to help construct the fort. He likes the firewater and women. He will not help." Drouillard stretched full-length on the robe near the fire. "I am tired, yet I must hunt for meat again because Bouché refused to bring in the meat we cached below the fort. The bears and wolves ate well. And Étienne Brandt. He is a thief. He, too, likes the firewater and women. He entices them by playing beautiful music on his violin." Drouillard pretended to play a violin. "He also remains popular with some of the men for this reason. You have heard him play?" Little Coyote nodded affirmatively. "Lisa no longer lets him work with the trade goods. Beware. Trust the grizzly before you trust those two."

Then, as the cold outside deepened, Drouillard began telling wondrous stories of strange sights he had beheld in his first exploratory journey—stories of hot springs that boiled his meat he held on a stick; of pools of boiling water that erupted into the air above the height of tall trees; of huge holes filled with bubbling mud that smelled like the smoke from a fired gun. "And," he added, "I saw beaver lodges almost everywhere I traveled."

Remembering his experiences at the hot springs where he had trapped the beaver, Little Coyote listened politely and believed completely.

As Drouillard reluctantly prepared to return to the fort, he said that Lisa wanted them to come there for a feast and important talk.

Lisa had prepared well for the feast. Elk and buffalo meat, boiled separately with much fat, was served in metal bowls and eaten with Indian-made bighorn sheep spoons. The delicious meat called "bacon" had been fried. There was a sweet food a very curious Antelope learned was called "jam" spread atop "biscuits," much thicker than those of the Indians made from the ground-up camas lily bulbs. Drouillard and two other white sub-chiefs also ate; only Drouillard and Lisa bowed their heads and made the sign of the cross and mumbled a few words prior to starting.

There was little talk during the eating, though Lisa did say he had held back the remainder of the pistols. There were thirty of them. Later there was much discussion, with skillful Drouillard conveying Lisa's desire to establish a fort at the three forks and sounding out Little Coyote's views about possible Flathead, Shoshone and Nez Percé trade. Little Coyote had trouble understanding Drouillard's sign for the latter: Right index finger slightly under and to the right of his nose, then that index pushed to the left.

"Nee Mee Poo, Nee Mee Poo," Drouillard repeated. Then he good-naturedly laughed aloud, as did the others, when the Flathead resignedly accepted the name Nez Percé. As Drouillard explained, "The French Canadians call them 'Nez Percé' because they wear ornaments in their noses. The name means 'Pierced Nose.'" So Nez Percé they would be! Little Coyote would ponder these name changes later. For now there were more important matters to communicate.

There was no laughter when Little Coyote solemnly warned that Lisa's party should be much larger if he wished to trade in the land the Blackfeet claimed. It was known that these fierce, skillful and brave warriors were becoming deeply concerned that white men were arming their mortal enemies.

"No," Lisa told the Flathead through Drouillard. "We had a council with some of the Blackfeet. We gave them many presents to show our good will and asked them to tell others. While not pleased we were building this fort near the Crows, they were pleased we would build a fort at Three Forks and—" He paused, puzzled that Little Coyote was rolling his extended index and middle fingers back and forth over his heart.

"He strongly doubts they were Blackfeet, perhaps Gros Ventre or other allies," Drouillard told Lisa.

The Flathead politely listened to Lisa's repeated insistence that he had parleyed with Blackfeet. Then, at the conclusion, he once more signed his doubts.

There was no more laughter at all when Little Coyote suggested that white men, as Clark and Lewis had promised, should trade for, rather than catch, the fur. Once again Lisa's forehead, chin and ears turned as red as they had during Little Coyote's quarrel with Bouché.

In the silence, Lisa served highly sweetened tea and, as the redness faded, presented a delighted Antelope with a packet of tea and sugar. Little Coyote received three long, metal arrow points. Their departure was on a friendly basis, with Drouillard accompanying them outside the fort. Brandt and Bouché, their appearance too well-timed for coincidence, crossed the young couple's path and malevolently glared at them after Drouillard's farewell. Little Coyote openly removed his mitten and placed his hand under his heavy outer garment. Perhaps the bluff worked, but he resolved never again to venture among the white men without at least one weapon.

In the remaining three months of winter, when not trapping beaver, Little Coyote and Antelope practiced until they became quite accurate with three weapons—Mr. Egg's brass pistols and the thrown hatchet and knife.

Colter returned to the fort as the new grass began to arrive in what Drouillard called 1808, a year in a system of dates the latter spent an early spring evening explaining to his Flathead friends. There was a momentary complexity when Drouillard had to explain the 1808 winters from *what?* "From the arrival on earth of a great seer called 'Christ,'" he said, and moved on.

He was pleased that by now Little Coyote and Antelope were beginning to use English words, too, a tribute to his spending so much time with these cheerful, vibrant people who contrasted sharply with most of those at the fort. Only an occasional lodge went up nearby; the people of the various tribes preferred to remain near the mountains, which offered better hunting as well as shelter for their horses.

One night when the frost perhaps would stay away yet again and Antelope had arranged the fire for more light than heat, Drouillard and Colter hallooed their approach. They bore tea, sugar, tobacco, clay pipes and three carefully selected, tiny, brass bells that Drouillard had fashioned into a necklace for Antelope. Two sets of three large red, white and blue trade beads separated the bells. Antelope expressed her delight by extending both hands together, backs up, in a sweeping curve outward and downward and following this with a surprising "Tha-ank you-oo," much to the delight of both guests.

Colter wanted information.

"When we are certain the frosts no longer will come at night and people become restless to move, Lisa will again send me to tell other Indians about the trading post here. I have trapped the Three Forks region before, in 1806, with Dixon and Hancock, when I left the Lewis and Clark party." He puffed thoughtfully on his pipe and looked at Little Coyote. "Lisa wishes to build a post at Three Forks. He told me that you, like myself, disagree about the strength a party needs to build the post and hold it against the Blackfeet. I understand that the Flathead people and their allies leave their homes to hunt in the summer and late fall/early winter near Three Forks, as well as, of course, in the region of the great falls. What are your thoughts?"

"Little Coyote! John Colter speaks. He asks questions!" The bells of Antelope's new necklace jingled musically as she shook her mate. Head down, he had been hearing Colter, yet in another part of his mind thinking, too, about his earlier fascination with Colter's black-soled moccasins during his council with Gun, Three Eagles and others of the people.

Startled by Antelope's shaking, the young warrior brought together thoughts from that meeting as well as other thoughts. From deep inside him they emerged to blend with his surprising answer to Colter's question. Inexplicably, even to himself, he stood and removed Shining Shirt's medicine crook from against the tripod. Leaning lightly on it, he looked down at these two white men he had come to count as friends.

"You, John Colter, can meet the large party of our people who will come to hunt near the three forks for buffalo in the spring." He made the signs for moccasin and black. "There will be fights with the strong and wily Blackfeet. Once you will stay and fight. Later, you will run, then run again." He replaced the crook against the tripod. "You *must* run!" He sat down.

"Little Coyote speaks with much certainty and wisdom from somewhere. Heed him," Drouillard said quietly.

There was more sweetened tea, then the talk shifted to the routes the Flatheads and their allies most often took to the hunting grounds in great enough numbers to fight off their enemies. And there was the white man's handshake when they said farewell. "You will return here," Little Coyote told Colter. As the brave thanked Drouillard for the gifts, he held his hand longer than was the practice. Despite his friend's happy face and strong spirit, Little Coyote felt a moment of ineffable sadness, as though he should make his friend's sign of the cross over his body to protect it. The moment passed, then Colter and Drouillard raced to reach the fort first. A distant, final halloo into the dark night signaled that Colter had won.

Antelope chopped up another double handful of elk suet and carried it outside the lodge. Inside the dwelling, Little Coyote still slept. Antelope looked first at the sky. All clouds were gone. Soon Sun would flood the land with light, and welcome warmth, too. She placed the food in the aspen bark bird-feeders she had hung against the shelter. Yellow-bellied sap-suckers, white-breasted nuthatches and grosbeaks competed at the larger feeder. Juncos and various sparrows fed at the smaller, while chickadees constantly darted in to seize a bit of tallow and hurry away to consume it. Antelope noted that now the chickadees' voices were changing from the "chick-a-dee-dee-dee" to the whistled and higher-noted "fee-bee" of spring, a season the young woman would welcome. She had experienced stirrings, longings, throughout the winter—emotions her mate gladly, eagerly and, she was certain now, fulfillingly had reciprocated. Yet there remained one emptiness unfilled: She was lonesome now for her family, for the Shoshone people.

She re-entered the lodge, selected clean and lighter clothing for herself from the stiff hide case, then laid out spring clothing for Little Coyote. He stirred, turned on his side and closed his eyes against the light that flooded in through the lodge entrance. He was content for the moment to lie there listening to the birds quarreling over the feeders, their wings sometimes scraping the shelter in their eagerness to claim a tiny prize or triumphantly carry one away. As he began to contemplate this competition and acknowledge that it was not limited to the tiniest creatures, he heard from the top of some nearby high tree the welcome, more prolonged song of the meadowlark rising above the melodic chorus flooding this part of the great valley. The usually raucous call of the omnipresent ravens had acquired a musical gurgle as the birds inquisitively flapped over new objects and arrivals in this vast land that was losing its coat of white. Near the trees a grouse insistently drummed its mating sound.

The brave turned on his back, hands clasped behind his head to lift it above the discordant sounds the fur guard hairs made as they pricked his ears. Nearer the lodge, amid the dead grasses and small plants from last year's long summer, the tinier creatures rustled, mated and multiplied—the eternal cycle. Larger ones chirped as they ran, dug and ate. Little Coyote remembered that yesterday, among the broken rocks on the lower ridges, he had found signs of the rare wolverine. The animal evidently had decided to work harder for food among the rocks rather than venture downward among these many two-legged creatures that had invaded its land.

Now Little Coyote heard a heavier, though somewhat muted, sound—a horse's hooves moving quickly at first, then slowing, as the animal began angling toward the rocks where the wolverine worked. Antelope was urging her Appaloosa upward, perhaps to view more panoramically this regenerating world, perhaps out of a restlessness born of the long winter, maybe just to enjoy the riding—so much a part of her life. Little Coyote sat up now. They had agreed she would only leave the camp in his company or in that of Colter or Drouillard. Perhaps she would not go far and he soon would hear the returning hoofbeats. Yet . . .

Snow on the craggy hillsides began melting as Sun and breezeless morning kept most of the cold near the distant peaks. Soon the first tiny streamlets of water began running down the smooth sides of the rocks. They dripped, dripped, dripped to the larger, flatter boulders nearer the valley floor. Soon these rocks also lost their snow cover, which swelled the runoff. As at her distant Shoshone home, Antelope had found an early-morning bathing spot. There, the water warmed as it fanned across a large table rock squarely in the sunlight, collected again in a fissure and, screened by the rocks from intrusive breezes, sprayed downward onto the creek's frozen surface.

Antelope tethered her horse to a sturdy bush near the spray. She placed her clean clothing on a dry rock, then removed her buckskin gown and placed it on a patch of dry grass where she, too, could feel the morning sun.

For a time she lay there, looking at her belly and hips, slightly rounder now, feeling the breasts, slightly firmer, learning about her changing body that was sheltering new life as she was sheltered by the furs, the lodge and family. She smiled as she remembered how Little Coyote only two mornings ago had looked wonderingly at her. They had thrown off the too-warm furs and lain there adding their own sounds to those of the regenerating world outside the shelter. Though her mate had not inquired, she felt he had guessed, or almost guessed, there was a change—a change she could see, could feel, deep inside. Slightly, yes, but the life was there as in the hidden eggs of the ravens, crows, red-winged blackbirds, a growing in harmony with almost everything about her. There were more stirrings, too, in tune with those of the courting birds that climbed, dipped, challenged, voiced their yearnings and satisfactions in continued flight and endless song.

As Antelope was riding her Appaloosa, Étienne Brandt was crawling from his now-too-warm blankets in the small tent he and Bouché had erected near the eastern wall of the fort. Brandt, too, had been listening to the spring songs and faint whirrings and rustlings, glad he had awakened so early while the others slept. Occasional discordant snores came from Bouché's blankets. Then, thrashing and grumbling, the *engagé* turned over and slept more deeply as a result of the stolen whiskey he and Brandt had drank the previous night. As they had pulled at the jug, Brandt had disclosed plans to ride away to the Indians next day, trailing a pack horse well-laden with other stolen goods.

Clad in his winter-filthy underwear, Brandt puffingly emerged tousled head first like a great defecation from the round tent entrance, which resembled the opening of a pucker-stringed possibles bag. The man dragged out his blankets and clothing, then re-tied the entryway. For a moment he lay grayish-black and unmoving on the blankets, grateful for the rest and the diminishing pain in his whiskey-sodden brain. He lay on his side. Being on his bulging belly was too uncomfortable; the pressure on his fat gut upset his stomach.

Several early-spring insects settled on his face and hands. He grunted as he pulled on his clothing and moccasins and stood; his paunch flattened slightly as he stretched, yawned and scratched his crotch and head. Now he set about carrying out the plan he had begun formulating after Lisa had caught him pilfering the trade goods. Lisa was not aware that the thief had cached many such goods in the rocks above the fort; there, two precious horses stolen before last night's drinking also were tethered.

Brandt looked about, then tossed the blanket roll over the palisade. He picked up the rifled gun and ammunition he also had stolen and sauntered up to the great gate. As he slid back the bar and pushed the gate open, the hinges squealed once, stopped, then squealed again as he closed the gate. He could not lock and bar it from the outside. In a few moments he had retrieved his blankets and reached the frozen creekbed and protective brush.

As he started walking upward, a tiny thread of water—slushy, almost frozen at the head—wriggled downward and across the ice like a luminous worm. The head softened as a new minute surge of water warmed it. The worm wriggled farther downstream. Brandt touched his toe into the tiny rivulet and scraped it back and forth. The worm died, scrambled into disjointed drops and segments. Almost magically, they articulated, larger now, and wriggled farther.

Breakup was starting. It would end with these waters flowing the full length of the creek, down the Yellowstone into the Missouri, past St. Louis, into the mighty Mississippi and the Gulf of Mexico. What matter? Brandt again broke the tiny rivulet. Ducking under some of the sprouting willow branches extending over the creek bed, he began climbing upward toward the stolen horses and cache of stolen goods. He would be well on his way, following the spine of the virtually snow-free ridge, before the animals were missed.

Antelope could not hear Brandt's approach. The water splashing, the questioning calls of the ravens flapping lower to eye the featherless creature standing near the spray, muffled the padding of his moccasins and the sound of his heavy breathing. Nor could Antelope see the man, though he now was a scant fifty feet away. He stood behind a jumble of rocks shaken from their foundations centuries ago and sent rolling down the hill.

She was facing away from him when he first trudged from behind the rocks. Startled, almost gasping for breath, he stood for a moment while the ravens climbed higher and scolded at the intrusion. Brandt's eyes moved quickly from Antelope's horse; for an instant he had thought that perhaps he could take three horses into an Indian camp. But now he eyed the woman's slim buttocks, which rounded down to beautifully formed long legs and small ankles, up to a well-formed back and smooth shoulders cloaked in a cascade of dark hair. She was the Indian Little Coyote's woman, sure enough, and . . . well now. He remembered Bouché's vivid and frustrated descriptions of her face. Again, Brandt looked at the horse. An Appaloosa. A prize, indeed. Could he take the horse without the woman knowing?

Now she was laughing, holding her cupped hand above her head. The water splashed into her hand and ricocheted out as she laughed again and danced when the drops raced down her back. The tiny bells around her neck tinkled; as she heard this music her dance became even more rhythmic, expressing her joy, her utter joy of living, of wonderment and awe and joy again at what she would tell Little Coyote today!

Now she turned, long hair spilling over her eyes, her hand groping to find the stream by touch and direct the spray. Brandt parked his buttocks against a rock and ogled as Antelope splashed water on her head, her hair, her neck, breasts and belly. Again she giggled and danced, less rhythmically, as a larger, colder surge of water cascaded over her. She moved gracefully to a smaller and warmer veil. Brandt inched nearer as she bent forward and shook her hair, the drops catching the sunlight and falling like a shower of rock crystals. He was grateful for the noise of the ravens. Again he looked at the horse. Now, though, he only wanted to reach out and touch the woman.

He put down the bundle of blankets and the rifle and watched the breasts, the thighs and, momentarily, the lovely face as she threw her head back, shaking aside the hair to let the water pour over her. Again she turned her back and began rubbing her long legs.

Desire for her rather than the Appaloosa crowded Brandt's mind—tiny at first like that warming thread of water crawling across the frozen surface of the creek. He shook his head and thought about the pack of trade goods and the two horses only a short distance above, and the Appaloosa here. For an instant his desire lessened, but he continued to watch Antelope. He already had the goods. They were secure; the morning was yet very young. She was there. The wanting grew into an urgency; again he tried to shake it, break the train of thought now beginning to govern his body. But this was no growing stream he could disjoint with the toe of his moccasin. How well he knew that! The wanting became a demanding, compelling thing. As he moved toward her, Brandt thought of Bouché's words as Bouché had coached him when and where to shoot his first buffalo. The words returned with great clarity and new meaning: "Stiddy now. Keerful. Closter. All right. Now! Take it!"

She was dark, amazingly like that girl in New Orleans so long ago. That memory was almost gone, interred by Brandt and chalked up to the idiocies of growing manhood. His first two wives had been the blondest and fairest women he could find. Number three had been different. Dark. Darker than this girl. He had thought perhaps number three could arouse in him the intensity of the rape in the poorest section of New Orleans. She couldn't. Brandt stalked forward, taking cover behind one rock then another. He could hear small rubbing, splashing noises— her song, the bells adding their music as she apparently jumped from one leg to the other. The rest of the people, faceless now, on that long-ago, almost-forgotten, dimly lighted New Orleans street splashed ahead in the rain, peeling off in ones and twos into drab, uninviting doorways. He remained in the rear, only barely close enough to the girl to discern her dim figure. He had seen it very closely when she had looked wistfully into a shop window on a well-lighted street. Then at last he had rushed into the hovel he had reconnoitered after her entry there. The threat of the knife had opened the soft eyes even more widely. Pressed against her throat it had kept her mouth shut and, when he was through, closed the eyes and quieted her forever.

Brandt withdrew the filthy kerchief from his pocket. The perfect gag. Never know about these Indian women, though. Maybe she'd like it.

Antelope had no opportunity to speak. One meaty hand slapped over her mouth while the other seized her waist and dragged her from the water. The surprise, the sight of the large body, her inability to raise her eyes to see his face, the certainty that he would use the knife he was drawing from his belt, were too much.

She shrieked. Almost at the same instant her attacker crumpled, releasing her as he fell on her. Then he rolled off as Little Coyote struck another swinging blow with the butt end of his ancient lance.

Little Coyote tenderly removed the rocks from under Antelope's body. He savagely stripped off Brandt's jacket and pants and put them under her. She was in the sun. She would be warm. She would recover. He put her clean clothing on her yet motionless body.

Little Coyote raised the lance, his agitation transferring to the quivering, glass-like point above Brandt's heart. One quick thrust, almost the weight of the released weapon, itself, and Brandt would be dead. But he heard "Stay! Stay!" The inner voices from his vision quest, from Shining Shirt, rose above his anger.

Trembling, he put down the lance and reached for Antelope's almost razor-sharp knife. Steadied by his cold purpose, he used the tip and only part of the blade to slit Brandt's scrotum and lift out the testicles. Two swift cuts and there they were, resembling those he had slashed roughly from buck deer so many times. But these were for the ravens.

Antelope was in the lodge before Brandt roused. He did not see his attacker. He saw only the thin line of blood threading down his massive leg, trickling through the heavy hair and into the tiny rivulet of melting snow.

Brandt painfully waddled and splashed down the small stream like a gut-shot goose, honking his pain and terror until he neared the silent fort. Bouché poured stiff shots of whiskey for them both.

"You shoulda stayed here if'n you wanted that kinda huntin'," Bouché said. He smirked, then stuck his head out of the tent. "I'll help you up to where the horses are. You're gonna hafta get the hell outta here." He looked at Brandt, who was holding his whiskey-soaked kerchief between his legs. Brandt's face contorted in a silent scream. "You hafta get outta here now," Bouché repeated, "but you're gonna be walkin'!"

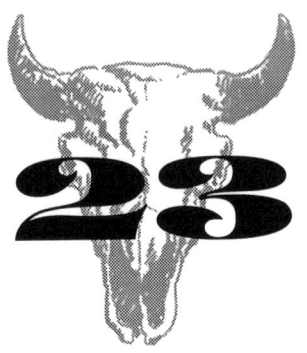

23

Antelope received a visitor one late afternoon—a Crow woman Manuel Lisa had sent. Her message, conveyed after several attempts, including pantomime with one of the guns, was that John Colter had been shot. When Little Coyote approached the lodge with two beaver suspended on either side of Not Afraid of Guns, he wondered at first if his mate's agitation over the Brandt affair had returned.

He heard Antelope's message about Colter, gave her the beavers and raced to the fort. He returned before Antelope had removed the pelts and spoke excitedly: "John Colter has a great wound in the leg! He has much fever. He rode his horse from near the three forks. He was bringing our people to Lisa's fort to trade before the buffalo hunt. Blackfeet lost a great battle. Our people come here soon. More I could not learn."

"Drouillard?" Antelope asked.

"He is trapping beaver. He does not know this."

"Come, let us watch for our people!" Antelope hurriedly tugged off her husband's wet buckskin jacket, put it on the drying rack and brought him dry clothing.

"At sunup we will look, but we will not venture far," Little Coyote said. "Lisa warns that the Blackfeet are very angry. He knows little more."

Next day, amid the early-morning songs of larks, Little Coyote and Antelope rode up the north-south trending ridge near the fort. They picketed their horses and ascended the highest knob. There they leaned against a rock as they ate from the food bag and observed the land.

Almost directly below them a small group of people, evidently two families of Crows, toiled through the low brush, seeking open ground and skirting the deeper patches of snow. More distant, to the west, a few buffalo leisurely ate their way upward on a wide, slanting hillside like the one the couple had ascended. Suddenly, the animals turned and bolted downhill like large, black boulders loosened by some unseen force.

Antelope spied the cause of the flight. A large cavalcade of horses with riders was moving toward the couple from the west. More and more came into view; Antelope detected a few Appaloosa far back, their coats similar to the larger dark and light patches of earth and snow over which they traveled.

"They are our people!" she shouted joyfully. In an instant she scooped up the food bag, descended the knob and was urging Little Coyote to mount up and join her in a careful lope downward.

Crows, perhaps three-hundred of them, led the vanguard, with Chief Drum, the black mourning stripes gone now, proudly setting the direction toward Lisa's fort. He gravely lifted a familiar looking rifle in acknowledgment of Little Coyote's greeting.

"There has been a great victory over the Blackfeet!" he shouted. Then he spoke no more as four younger warriors who evidently had been serving as flankers to the irregularly spread-out party raced in and shrilled their victory claims. Little Coyote and Antelope moved through the warriors, wondering at the minimal baggage and lack of women and children.

They received their answer when they rode into the perhaps five-hundred lagging, baggage-laden Flatheads. Though weary, the Flatheads' welcoming shouts when they sighted Little Coyote's shield and Antelope's Appaloosa were tumultuous. With many people talking at once, there was no opportunity to hear a cohesive account of the battle.

Running Buffalo Bull was there, as was Little Yellow Bird. She hugged her son, then asked Antelope for a full account of the young couple's activities during the winter. The Flatheads erected their lodges near the fort, set guards about their horses and, after eating, slept. The Crows paused a short time, then continued eastward toward Tongue River. Hard-working Gun and several noted warriors accompanied them a short distance as a mark of respect and much appreciation. How much the Flatheads owed the Crows Little Coyote and Antelope would learn next day.

Little Yellow Bird ceased her quiet chatter with Antelope when Running Buffalo Bull filled the pipe. Little Coyote had given his father some tobacco almost immediately after his parents' lodge had gone up next to his. All four now sat on the furs, westering Sun dully outlining for those inside the black buffalo bull painted on the lodge's exterior.

Running Buffalo Bull made the signs with the pipe and drew deeply, clearly pleased to be with his son and Antelope. He blew out the smoke.

"You saw John Colter?" he asked.

Little Coyote explained why he knew so little.

His father handed over the pipe. "John Colter met our people in the Beaverhead River country. We had waited for the Nee Mee Poo and," he looked at Antelope, "our friends the Shoshonis to join us for the trek to the buffalo grounds. There we would trap in force while waiting for the buffalo to bear their calves. Then we would hold a great meat hunt. Our allies did not come. Tjolzhitsay and the council considered the yet-heavy snows in the mountains. Gun said that perhaps some other grave problem held them back. He urged care lest, if we should go alone, the Blackfeet gathered in such great numbers they could defeat us. So, we waited even longer."

Once more Running Buffalo Bull accepted the pipe.

"We left very few of our people in our valley, well hidden, and set out. Gun cautioned that should we encounter the Blackfeet, the warriors with the rifles should face them together and fire first, then the muskets, and while all reloaded, the best warriors with bows and arrows would protect them. It is well we planned so. The Blackfeet attacked when we were a day's journey from the three forks after John Colter had persuaded us to trade our many furs first at Lisa's fort, then hunt the buffalo.

"We became surrounded by many hundreds of Blackfeet. It is well we were in brushy ground and that we had such a battle plan. Even so, we lost women and children and several warriors from the northern end of our valley—Smoke, Snowshoe Maker, Walks Many Trails, others. When the Blackfeet saw John Colter and heard him shout encouragement, they sought to reach him. Those who tried to count coup on him lost their lives, for he fired with his rifle, then a very strange and short gun, then threw the hatchet. Oh, he can fight, that one! The Blackfeet were very angry. It was a good fight, but there was grave danger we would lose. We did not have enough warriors. We did not have enough guns."

Even Little Yellow Bird sat tensely as her husband told this story she knew so well.

"Then there was a great shout," Running Buffalo Bull continued. "Drum and his Crow warriors, who had been seeking revenge on the Blackfeet for killing his brother and family, rode down on the Blackfeet in two groups. Then we, too, charged on them with loaded guns. The Blackfeet fled. We owe Drum much. Three Eagles gave him his long rifle."

"But my people?" Antelope's anxious voice broke the silence that followed the story.

"Two Shoshonis trailed us through the mountains after we left our valley." Little Yellow Bird's soothing assurance quieted Antelope. The older woman anticipated other questions: "Yes, our people caught many furs with the traps, as did Running Buffalo Bull." She pointed to the large bale. "We will trade them at the fort and with the Crows for horses. There will be a great buffalo hunt and there will be much meat to give to your people and the Nee Mee Poo."

Running Buffalo Bull grinned over the pipe at his son. He shook his head wonderingly, though good-naturedly, that warriors could defer so to these women! He spoke: "Tjolzhitsay has called a council as soon as Gun returns from his short journey with the Crows."

They ate. Then, while the others slept, Little Coyote put his furs and half of his father's on one of the pack horses his family had brought with them. He returned from the fort afoot, with Not Afraid of Guns carrying twenty pistols, all complete with moulds and powder flasks.

That night a very tired Gun talked at length with Little Coyote. When Gun emerged from the lodge he walked more erectly. He was grateful, he told the seer, that he could leave many burdens with this hard-to-comprehend young warrior who, once again, seemed to prove he had acquired much of Shining Shirt's wisdom—and generosity!

Tjolzhitsay pointedly held his whip in his crossed arms as the council members entered the lodge. Eagle-like visage unmoving, lips drawn slightly downward, the chief's keen eyes atop his long face seemed to pierce each warrior as he took his place on the robes. There was no fire, only an ember for the pipe ceremonies. The head chief acknowledged the presence of Gun, who sat next to a strange wooden chest. The chief's message was brief:

"These are my thoughts. I ask for yours now, for you have chosen Gun to again lead the hunt near the three forks. We cannot demand more favors from our friends the Crows, nor should we hunt here again. You worked hard, suffered much in the cold to catch your furs. Now you would exchange the hardship for marvels that would make you joyful and save much labor. Some of the younger men already have sought to do so. I told Little Coyote to inform Lisa we do not wish for him to trade until we plan how we must trade. He will not bring out the firewater pots. Increasingly, the fierce Blackfeet, many of whom once disdained to seek guns, now are doing so. They try to take the furs from others. You saw this near the three forks. They outnumbered us even with the Crows helping us. We out-fought them, and they are fierce fighters. I have spoken to all our sub-chiefs."

Tjolzhitsay swept his arm to encompass the lodge. "We out-fought them because, with our smaller tribe, we could agree to out-think them. I ask for your thoughts about this." He looked at Gun. Little Coyote caught the fleeting, enigmatic grin on the wily leader's lips. Again Tjolzhitsay spoke: "Before we left the three forks we learned of the brave deeds of our sub-chiefs and warriors. They stood fast and led and fought as a group. Gun has obtained the means to reward them."

The two men opened the chest and each held aloft a pistol.

"These are much like the one John Colter carried upon his horse to give himself another shot to defend himself," Gun explained. Then he demonstrated the loading procedures. He handed the loaded weapon to Big Eagle, who pointed it toward the smoke hole and fired.

One by one Tjolzhitsay passed out the twenty pistols to the delighted warriors who, by consensus, were the most deserving. Included was Young Willow, wife of Eagle Claw. Tjolzhitsay reminded the council that she had raced forward with a lance and transfixed an attacking Blackfeet. "As a warrior woman," Tjolzhitsay said, "you now will be called 'Willow Woman'— strong, flexible in all seasons, for all uses." Almost unobserved, Tjolzhitsay put the whip into the empty chest as a score of pistols clicked and flashed sparks in the council lodge.

"Lisa would set up a trading post at the three forks," Tjolzhitsay said. "I do not think the Blackfeet will let him. I ask you now: Will you agree that while we yet can do so, we trade one of every three of our furs for muskets and powder and lead? We now can make our own gun flints."

"Two of every four!" a pistol owner shouted. His suggestion was immediately backed by most of those present. Everyone favored a suggestion whereby each family would provide Gun with half its furs so he could supervise the trading. Families could do as they wished with their remaining furs, a provision that newly named Willow Woman supported.

"We will begin the trading then," Tjolzhitsay said as he prepared to put down the pipe. He added, "I must repeat here what has been said before. We must not seek enemies to fight.

223

We must fight enemies who seek us. Gun says we will leave almost as soon as the trading ends. Our meat bags in which we brought the furs are empty. There must be much meat when the buffalo hunt ends."

"Will we fight our way home?" a younger voice asked.

"Perhaps, but with help." This time the chief grinned for all to see. "With Gun, I asked the two Shoshonis who trailed us through the snow of the mountains to return to their people and ask them and the Nee Mee Poo to send only warriors to remain in hiding until our arrival at the killing grounds. We will provide them with the horses to carry the meat to their villages. We have learned much. We cannot risk only our people against the many Blackfeet."

Tjolzhitsay put down the pipe.

Gun was at Little Coyote's lodge as Antelope prepared the cooking fire. They were joined by the seer's parents.

"We have asked much of you already, Little Coyote," Gun said. "Now we ask more. Will you remain near Lisa's fort to study and work with the white men until they attempt to build the fort at the three forks? Our chief is pleased that you learn their talk. You can trap and, under their protection, accumulate the most important trade goods to serve the people when Lisa first brings them up the river. We will leave some furs to help you."

Antelope's tiny bells jingled her startled reaction to this request as she bent over to fan the fire with a grouse wing. While the stew was reheating, she seated herself near the pot and Little Yellow Bird, whose tense body demonstrated that she, too, thought little of this plan the men were devising.

"First tell me about Little Bear Claw!" Little Coyote had wondered much about his friend, but had received only fragments of information.

"He, too, is part of our planning." Gun leaned over and carefully brushed several tiny pieces of charcoal back into the fire with his index finger as though concentration on this task would enable him to express better what he now had to say. "Little Bear Claw is with the man from Canada. This is David Thompson.

We have learned that David Thompson was a sub-chief with the great trading party in Canada called Hudson's Bay Company. Now he is a greater sub-chief with a trading party called North West Company. Little Bear Claw says he is a good man with a part-Chippewa wife. Already he has put up a post on the upper Columbia River, as white man calls it, which flows from many rivers to the great salt water. The post is called Kootenay House. It is far to travel from our valley, as you know." The tiny charcoal pieces Gun had pushed into the fire caught the heat and glowed. "Little Bear Claw learned that the post on the Lake of the Kutenais, where we got our guns, is gone. Burned down. So is the post at the Lake of the Pend d'Oreille. Perhaps the Blackfeet did this out of anger. David Thompson plans to build a greater post there. He will call it Kullyspell House. And nearer to our valley, by what white man now calls Clark's Fork River, David Thompson will build yet another post. He will call it Saleesh House. Thus by names he seeks to honor our people and our allies." Now Gun frowned. "Little Bear Claw told us that perhaps this North West Company will send out great numbers of trappers called brigades to catch the furs and bring them to those houses. He will remain there until he is certain. We do not like this. Already there are many men trapping here. Must we catch the furs faster than the whites? We must decide who will be most fair to our people. Stay, Little Coyote, and help us to decide. I think, I do not know yet, that things will go better with us if we trade mostly with David Thompson people, where there are fewer Blackfeet." Gun stared moodily into the fire, fatigue lines creasing his face. The charcoal he had pushed into the fire had slumped into barely visible heaps of ash.

So the carefully planned trading began, with the Flathead families selecting many animal traps after the firearms and ammunition. Even so, there were furs enough for pots and hatchets and knives to ease the women's work, beads and other ornaments to please them personally. The pistols remained hidden so the increasing numbers of people from other tribes who were coming to trade would remain content and friendly.

Little Coyote and Antelope conversed briefly with Drouillard and John Colter in the trading room. Colter sat atop a tall, crudely built stool, his wounded leg resting on a lower rung. He would help Little Coyote communicate the wishes of the various Indian people and the prices outlined by Lisa and his sub-chief, Benito Vasquez. Both men stood behind a rough counter in the adjoining supply cubicle.

During a lull in the trading, Colter looked somewhat obliquely at Little Coyote and began to squirm and clear his throat as though reluctant to bring up another subject with his Flathead friend. Drouillard, evidently sensing that it might be about the Flathead's warning concerning the battle with the Blackfeet, beckoned the two Indians to examine some finely prepared beaver pelts. They just now had been left behind by a delighted Crow warrior, his smiling wife and three children, all of whom carried out their treasure of trading goods.

"The best furs prepared the best way bring the best trades," Drouillard explained while Antelope appreciatively brushed the dense hair back and forth and noted how well the plew had been fleshed and stretched.

"The Crows are very skilled," Little Coyote agreed. He thought of his first crude attempts, then improving skills, during that long, memorable winter of the beaver.

His honest face perspiring and red from his busy movements, Lisa looked at the growing bundles of fur behind him, then at the rapidly depleting trade goods. "Tell them they would do well to teach the Flatheads this good lesson." This information conveyed, Drouillard added wryly for Little Coyote's and Antelope's ears only, "How fortunate for us that the British North West Company sent their man, Antoine Larocque, this way some winters ago to trade and teach the Crows their fine skinning and preparation methods."

They watched Lisa half-run to the open door. Through it they could see that the rivers still carried great chunks of ice, logs, trees, branches, brush, even occasional badly bloated buffalo carcasses in the millennia-old grand release of spring breakup. Lisa sat down and lit his pipe, seemingly content to rest for a moment. He was up again in an instant, conversing in a strange tongue with Vasquez and pointing to the piles of unbaled furs. His forehead creased worriedly.

"We will leave for St. Louis as soon as we dare put the keelboats back on the water," he said. "Drouillard, what about Rose?"

Drouillard shrugged, held his right-hand index and middle fingers together and moved them over his heart: "I don't know. I share some of your responsibilities, so I worry, too."

In three more days the debris-choked rivers had cleared enough to risk travel downstream in the keelboats. As they were loaded, Colter hopped about with a crutch showing the boatmen how to doubly secure the valuable bales; Colter's method called for running stout ropes through the bales' restraining leather thongs, then through holes in the mid-ships cargo box, then tying the ends to the thwarts. If the boats should overturn, even break up, the furs would remain tied together and, therefore, be more retrievable. Lisa looked on approvingly, but cast anxious eyes in several directions as he worried about the still-missing Rose, who had been dispatched to trade with the Crows.

The Flatheads, hoping they could watch the flotilla leave, delayed their own departure for the three forks area yet another day. In this interim they noted that approximately forty of Lisa's men would remain behind under Vasquez to improve the fort and begin trapping as quickly as the fur would become prime that coming fall.

The Flatheads scarcely had begun discussing any far-reaching implications of that fact when Rose returned from the Crow country and gave them something to remember and discuss with mixed emotions for several winters to come. They also gained some memorable insights: Fur-traders, too, were filled with governable and ungovernable passions, which they could turn on themselves.

All except Lisa's boat were off shore, at Drouillard's order holding against the current until Lisa joined them. A small, noisy band of Crows accompanied Rose to the fort. Their shrill cries from atop their wildly galloping horses told one and all that Rose was their good friend, that they had protected his return and that their hearts were heavy that, having delivered this near-kinsman, they now must leave—bearing and wearing, the startled Lisa noted aloud, many of the trade goods with which he had entrusted Rose.

Rose blew out a great puff of smoke from his short-stemmed pipe as though to bless his departing escort with the fragrance. He sent a hearty farewell wave after that. Then he seized the bridle of the horse on which sat a comely, shy-to-the-point-of-giggling, young Crow woman. She wore so many trinkets that a wondering Colter, leaning now on his crutch, exclaimed to his friend and fellow trapper, John Potts: "Perhaps she is his display case for trade. 'Put down a fox fur for the beaded necklace, a marten for the brass gorget, six ermine for the mirrors dangling fore and aft, a beaver plew for the high Spanish combs . . .'"

Lisa was equally as sharp-eyed, but expressed no humor.

"Rose!" he shouted. "Are they running off with your pack horses of furs?"

"No, no!" Rose airily waved away the notion that these people who held him in such high regard would rob him. "We, uh, had a fracas with Blackfeet, we did! Runned off with the goods, they did, but nary a scalp was tooken from us!"

"And your Crow friends took back the goods after scalping the Blackfeet, I wager!" Lisa's suffused face worked with indignation. "You liar and cheat!" He seized Rose's horse by the bridle, tore free the reins of the horse ridden by Rose's paramour and gave the animal a smart slap on the rump. The slap sent the horse galloping away, the woman's bells, mirrors and beads jangling dissonantly as the enraged Rose leapt off his horse and onto Lisa. Rose pushed Lisa into the mud while reaching behind his back for his knife.

"You'll not kill 'im!" Potts exclaimed, and kicked the knife from Rose's hand. Immediately they were locked in a bitter, noisy, wrestling match while Lisa, trailing mud, headed for his waiting boat.

Rose swung his mighty right arm and laid Potts in the mud. Then he shouted after Lisa: "Damn, you'll not run away from this!" Rose picked up his pipe, whipped off the mud, stuck the stem into his mouth and puffed furiously as he ran to a swivel gun mounted on a log and pointing riverward. He swung the gun's menacing muzzle toward Lisa's boat and clapped the bowl of his smoking pipe over the small cannon's touchhole. The resulting fire-back from the touchhole shattered the pipe. The loud explosion from the lethal muzzle produced a four-fold effect:

The hapless, long-shanked and astounded trapper under whose legs the yet-compacted canister of bullets harmlessly sped fell into the mud and roared, "I been kilt!"

Spread out now, the shot whizzed over the boatmen, who, fortunately, were seated low on their benches. The shot thwacked into the cargo box.

The fearful crew, as Drouillard would put it when he returned from St. Louis, "worked as though the very devil from hell was on their tails."

In a sense he was, for as the astounded Flatheads moved back from the riverbank, the enraged Rose attempted to reload and fire the swivel. He reached into the nearby tin box and, tilting the weapon's muzzle skyward, shoved in powder and a canister of shot. With his pipe gone, he strove to fire the touchhole with the long-handled flint lock from the box. The first three clicks were ineffectual because, in his rage, he misdirected the sparks to either side of the touchhole. There was no fourth attempt. Colter whacked him soundly on the head with his crutch. Potts and two other men threw the staggering Rose into the mud and sat on him while Lisa's boat moved out of range toward the others. The Crow woman, having regained control of her horse, reversed its direction and set out to rejoin her much-tamer fellow Crows.

A fter the Flatheads departed, Antelope again employed a
visiting Crow woman, this time to move the two lodges
closer to the much-improved fort. An affront to her trader
instincts gave her much to talk about after her helper left.

"Is Vasquez dumb like the grouse?" she asked Little Coyote.
"The Crow woman said he gave Rose more goods and two horses
to again go among the Crows to trade after roaring, threatening
and almost pawing the earth like a buffalo bull."

"Let us forget Rose, but remember the lesson." Little Coyote
looked up from daubing warm glue on a sinew he had wrapped
around a steel arrowhead he was securing to a thin shaft.
Gathering up his five new arrows and two bows, he persuaded
Antelope to walk a short distance away to test them. Three arrows
flew very true, so he marked them with a blue dot near the nock.
The couple then walked toward the fringe of trees from which
Antelope had moved the lodges. Soon they heard the familiar
"bup . . . bup . . . bup" that told them there were grouse nearby for
the pot and durable feathers for arrows. With two shots from her
little over/under gun, Antelope dropped four birds; she fed one
to an appreciative Colter when he visited them as Sun disappeared.
Colter laughed delightedly when Antelope, in her increasingly

improving English and language of signs, again expressed her doubts about Vasquez' wisdom.

"Vasquez is wise," Colter said. "When Rose is not angry, he is a good trader." Colter hefted his crutch. "He has forgiven me for the lump I raised on his head, and is helping Potts and me make a canoe."

Reaching inside his shirt he withdrew a small buckskin bag. He emptied into the dented crown of his hat an awl with an assortment of various-sized needles. Each needle could be fastened one at a time into the hardwood handle by means of a small thumbscrew passing through a small, iron collar. The tool was a vast improvement over the usual trade awl, which had but a single needle.

As Antelope quickly mastered the intricacies of the tool, Colter removed his breeches and again sat down. He explained that while his leg wound had healed over, there remained a problem. He pressed his fingers around the long, irregularly torn scar.

"Bullet hit at an angle, not head on, and I had to do some rough cutting at the time," he said. "The bones are sound, but the muscles, well, they need care like those of the old trapper who has waded too long in ice-filled water. Like this." He rolled, massaged and pinched the leg, grimacing at times when the pain came through. "If I had some of those hot springs or mud I found on the upper Stinking Water, I think I soon would get this back to working like it should." He flexed and unflexed his legs, showing how one worked fine and the other, well . . . only so far. "Tell you what, Little Coyote, let Antelope work this leg over until I say 'whoa,' and the awl is hers. And I'll help you with our language some more."

Under Antelope's solicitous and increasingly skillful ministrations, Colter's sinews, muscles and other unseen parts moved into place and coordinated in tempo with the longer days of spring and summer. Soon her patient, unwilling to engage in the licentious activities of most of his fellow trappers, did join in their more open and boisterous physical contests. He prevailed in many such contests, but, finally, lost a heavily wagered foot race—with a horse.

That day, perspiring heavily, though breathing easily, Colter strode good-naturedly through the laughing, taunting plotters who merely had bet they had a racer he couldn't "whup."

"It's 'whoa,' Antelope," Colter said one day. "You've done a good job on my leg; any better and I reckon I could have outrun that horse they hid out on me." He hugged her, then shook Little Coyote's hand. "John Potts and I are heading for Three Forks to trap some of those beaver. It's likely we'll be back before the big freezeup with a pack or two in the canoe, then set out again on horses." He ran to the river for a quick swim.

"But two men . . . the Blackfeet!" Antelope expressed the couple's common worry as they later made their own plans for a trapping camp that fall. They settled at last for a small lake on the northern end of the Big Horn mountains Drouillard had told them about before his departure for St. Louis.

"It is but a four-day journey from here," Drouillard had explained. "One large stream feeds the lake from the south, three small streams empty it. There are beaver dams on all streams, and many a beaver. I saw no one, not even a Crow, when I passed through."

Little Coyote awakened suddenly one night and sat upright on the fur-covered mat. Gone was his dream of John Colter both reaching and shouting out for help. There was no smooth reassembling of the broken dream when once more the warrior slept; there was little memory of it at all when Antelope's early-morning stirrings about the fire awakened him again. But the mental seed planted in a rich furrow somewhere between the conscious and subconscious continued to grow, seemingly unnoticed, while the couple eagerly prepared for their own trek for beaver.

Late one morning Little Coyote walked to Lisa's fort to offer Vasquez three beaver plews in exchange for storing equipment that would not be needed for the trapping expedition. Early that afternoon he and Vasquez trudged back to the lodge carrying a naked, horribly sunburned, emaciated and badly lacerated patient for Antelope. He was John Colter. He had been gone twenty-one days.

Antelope sent Little Coyote racing to the three lodges near the fort. Before he returned with a packet of bear grease, she and Vasquez had fed the almost-incoherent man a small amount of meat stew, followed by an unmeasured drink of whiskey and a carefully measured dose of laudanum.

"Thees man!" Vasquez raised his hands in a gesture of horror, sorrow and curiosity. "He tells us he ran away from the Blackfeet. They keel John Potts. Then he talks leetle more. You take care of him, hah? You store your gear *gratia*, you unnerstan', free, no plews." He again showed Antelope and Little Coyote how to measure the laudanum then, promising to return, hurried to the fort.

Antelope gently applied the bear grease over their friend's entire body. Noting that his belly was less burned than his back, she rolled him belly down onto a large, cotton cloth she earlier had obtained from the fort for her baby. Then she and Little Coyote started working on his feet. The ankles were badly lacerated. The soles were raw, sappurating masses of swollen flesh embedded with broken and unbroken prickly pear spines. Here Antelope's new awl and smallest needle received their first use. Colter's accounts of his misadventure emerged like the cactus thorns, sometimes broken, others cleanly, during the three days Antelope and Little Coyote spent digging out the badly festering thorns. Vasquez came often and carried back to the fort the story to the few men he was keeping there to operate the swivel guns while the others trapped.

"Potts and I were looking at our traps in a good-sized creek about six miles from the Jefferson River," Colter told his friends. "Going upstream in the canoe, I thought I heard a sound as loud as a herd of buffalo running.

"'Potts,' I said, 'it's Indians! I don't hear any bellowing or grunting.' We couldn't see because there were high cliffs above us. I told Potts, 'Let's skeedaddle downstream as fast as we can.'

"'Don't be a damn coward, Colter,' Potts said. 'They are buffalo, sure as hell.'

"Well, they were Blackfeet, I reckon about five-hundred of them. Now it was too late to skeedaddle! They motioned for us to come ashore. Soon as we got there a warrior grabbed Potts' gun. I jumped out, took it back and handed it to Potts. He used the butt end to push off the canoe into the water. A warrior put an arrow into his shoulder.

"'Colter, I am wounded!' he shouted.

"'Get back here! You can't get away,' I shouted back. Poor Potts. He raised his gun and shot one warrior dead. Guess Potts figured he was a goner and might as well get it fast. He did. In an instant he had more bullets and arrows in him than I have cactus thorns.

"Four-hundred and ninety-nine of those cussed Blackfeet made me ready for a target to shoot at, luckily taking off my buckskins so they wouldn't ruin them. The chief delayed his warriors' fun. He looked me up and down and I know his eyeballs stopped for an instant when he saw this scarred-up leg. That's when I started moving about much as they'd let me, like I felt it was unmanly to be seen naked by so many men. And I made sure to limp. That was after the chief asked, 'Can you run like the antelope?' I know some of their sports, so I told him I was a better horse rider than a runner. He'd have none of that. I'd have to run against all of them. When the kinfolk and friends of the Blackfeet that poor Potts shot learned they might not get an equal shot or chop of revenge on me, they chopped up Potts then and there and threw parts of him at me.

"I guess that the warrior who got the first shot into Potts with the arrow got his scalp. But who would get mine if they all got a lick at me?

"That chief was pretty wise about some things. He led me out on the cactus-covered prairie about . . . well, maybe seven times the length of the fort, and said, 'Save yourself.' The one who killed me would get my scalp. The war whoop those divils raised started me off fast enough to surprise even myself. They were screaming their anger while I figured to run to the Jefferson, maybe six miles away. After I'd run three of those miles without getting a lance or an arrow in the back, I looked behind me. The

Blackfeet were scattered about, most of them naked, too, except they had moccasins with untanned hide soles.

"One of them carrying a short lance was closer than the rest. I ran harder, so much so the blood started running out of my nose and onto my chest to mix with poor Potts' blood. When I was about a mile from the Jefferson, I looked around again. That one brave was maybe sixty feet behind me. I figured this is it. I slowed a bit, then swiveled around sudden-like. I reckon that and the bloody sight of me startled the warrior, who was mighty tired, too. He tried to stop, stumbled and fell as he tried to throw the lance. The point broke off in the ground. I pounced on that and drove it into him. Then I started running again. When the closest Blackfeet showed up by the dead one, they milled around and waited for the others to catch up.

"I was plumb tuckered out, but I'd reached the Jefferson and jumped in. The current carried me near a great pile of driftwood and such on the point of a small island. I dived under it and found a place where I could stick up my head to breathe and still have a lot of wood on top. All day long those screeching divils searched along the river, in the cottonwood stands, even on the jumble of logs I was hiding under. God must have heard my prayers. I was afraid they were going to set that on fire, but they didn't.

"The screeching quieted down and finally stopped that night. I waited a long time, then I crawled out from under and swam down the river a long ways. I walked on these feet all the rest of the night, then at daylight hid and tried to pull out the thorns. I got a few, but I'd run them in too far. With the sun and all, and no way to kill game, I dug up roots to eat and walked for, by my reckoning, more than seven days."

Colter looked closely at Little Coyote. "God heard me, I guess, but all the time I kept thinking about your telling me, 'You will run.' How you knew, I'll never know. Drouillard said to leave it alone. What will I do now, Little Coyote?"

"You will have some more of this meat, and rest," Antelope told him. She leaned her child-heavy body over the pot and served more deer stew.

Colter sighed. "I'll make it right with you, Antelope, for fixing me up again. Got to. Why, there are so many beaver at Three Forks a man could become rich in one season. I'm heading back, but there's got to be more than two of us when we go."

Vasquez' expressive eyes widened, but his hands almost as quickly helped emphasize his inner turmoil. "I dunno', I dunno' We wait for Lisa."

Little Coyote and Antelope silently looked at each other.

"Grouse," Antelope said.

Little Coyote understood.

Colter was able to repay Antelope for her care when Little Coyote left for a short meat hunt and the baby decided to enter the world with few preliminaries.

"The Crow woman! She will help me! The baby comes!" Antelope's face twisted in momentary pain; she held both arms under her distended belly as though to restrain the birth.

Colter seized Little Coyote's obsidian lance and gingerly began hobbling toward the fort. He returned soon.

"She's gone somewhere. I can look . . ."

"There is no time. Hold the lance so I can grasp it and half-sit. You must hurry."

The infant soon emerged, squalling loudly when spanked. He was sleeping when his father returned.

"He will be Lance," Antelope said. Then, smiling as her husband lifted the baby and examined him, she fell into exhausted, contented sleep.

25

Benito Vasquez fully intended to wait for Lisa's return before trying to establish a post at Three Forks. Discounting the horror of Potts' death and Colter's run for life, the free trappers, who were not bound by contract to Lisa's company, focused, instead, on Colter's report of a region teeming with beaver. Soon, small groups of these trappers insisted Vasquez sell them supplies so they could head for Three Forks.

"We trap here," Vasquez insisted at first, but the trappers would have none of that argument. They pointed out that even the Crows had quit bringing in furs. Vasquez, viewing the few plews and cow buffalo robes in the empty storehouse, lost the argument.

"The buffalo. Who wants the buffalo when they can have beaver?" Vasquez shrugged and reluctantly began doling out his precious supplies of horses, traps, powder and lead to the free trappers, as well as to some of the trappers under contract to the company. He also assigned a few of the company's *engagés* to the groups, hoping that these more general workers would help guarantee successful outcomes with the seemingly ever present Blackfeet. All to no avail: One after another, the small parties, regardless of size or composition, would return empty-handed

237

with stories of fierce Blackfeet attacks, clever stealing and narrow escapes.

Once again Colter was healed. Those at Lisa's fort soon learned that during his convalescence he had pondered his harrowing escapes and almost had concluded he had had his fill of Blackfeet. He was weighing whether to try once more for a big take of beaver or head downriver for home.

"I have traded for a canoe and will go down the Yellowstone and Missouri rivers, trapping where I can," he told Little Coyote and Antelope. "Lisa will be coming upriver. If I have many furs, I will return to St. Louis with the party that goes there for the 1810 supplies. If I do not get many furs, well . . . perhaps you'll see me here to go back to the Three Forks. I must have many furs or money before I go home. Perhaps I should go home anyway, let the many others who are sure to come to this land subdue the Blackfeet, then return and trap." He shrugged. "That's the way it's going to be, my friends. But when I'd come back, there'd be no beaver, most likely. I've seen it happen already downriver. I love the country, the freedom, the beauty, the bounty. If white man would stay out, it always would remain that way. Strange." Again he shrugged. "We come for much of all these things, but in focusing mostly on the bounty, we seem to be losing the rest."

Colter embraced them both, chucked Lance under his chubby chin and was gone, leaving them with much to contemplate. Above all, Antelope was thinking of home.

"I, too, wish to return to our valley," Little Coyote agreed. "I have learned much about the white man, perhaps most important—his language. If men will go to Three Forks in strength, we will go. If not, we will seek the fewer furs here, since few others do so."

A day came when Little Coyote and Antelope faced another choice—head for Three Forks with the final small group of trappers or make the long journey down the Yellowstone River with Vasquez and a few men to the Mandan village on the Missouri River. There, they would await the upriver return of Lisa, Drouillard and others. Lisa's fort would be closed. Vasquez feared he no longer had enough men to defend it.

"I will not risk traveling into Blackfeet country with so few men," Little Coyote repeated. Then, noting again the disappointed look on his wife's face, he embraced her and said the visit with the Mandans would be interesting. Antelope's frown remained. "When Lisa returns," Little Coyote said, "we will go to Three Forks. Today Vasquez said there will be a fort at Three Forks. He has said this before. He says it now. He wavers because of the Blackfeet. I do not want to promise what I cannot fulfill, but Vasquez said many men coming upriver with Lisa will build it."

So the couple cached their old lodge, their furs and many other belongings in a small cave from which they had dug the coal. Vasquez chose a great pit on a small bluff well above seepage from the river.

The journey to the Mandans was both interesting and tiring. Their arrival at the large village drew little attention until Vasquez gave the Mandans presents, which they seemed to expect. Little Coyote's and Antelope's interests differed. Remembering these people had met white man many winters ago, Little Coyote noticed there were blue eyes, red hair and almost white hair among a few. They did not fight the white man; they lived in large and stout mound-shaped homes of wood and earth, sometimes several families in each, with space for the most prized horses. They were good hunters and fighters. They possessed good weapons, including a number of muskets, and knew how to use them.

Antelope remarked on their many pots, pans, tools and other marvels from the white man that seemed to make life easier. They made beautiful clothing from skins and skillfully adorned it with bead and quill work. They had many songs, dances and stories. They grew food in the earth; Vasquez prized one item particularly. He called it "corn," remarking that, given time, white man could make his whiskey here instead of laboriously boating it upriver from so many miles away. Seemingly, the Mandans had prospered here at their river crossroads.

Seemingly.

White man had left other, less obvious, evidence of his contacts, too.

That certainty came to light one afternoon when four Mandans visited Little Coyote's and Antelope's lodge, which was erected on a hillock near the large Mandan house Vasquez had obtained for his men. The visitors were a very old man of much dignity who carried a medicine staff and was skilled in the language of signs, an obviously ill woman and her two small children—a girl and a boy. The old medicine man explained that the woman was his daughter. The Blackfeet had killed her man. Invited into the lodge, the old man, almost as soon as the quartet had entered, began explaining the reason for his visit.

"I am told you have the medicine staff, too. What are your skills?"

Little Coyote was modest almost to the point of being non-committal. The old man understood. He then asked if he might bring into the lodge two warriors who had waited out of sight below the hillock. When the men listlessly entered, Little Coyote could see they were feverish-eyed and in obvious discomfort. The old man bade his three patients to strip.

"As you have seen," he said, "the white man brings us many marvels. Sometimes he leaves us with problems which do not readily show. My son's woman here, she needs the white man's medicine, as do these warriors. There are others in this village and elsewhere who have such sicknesses. My songs and medicines do not work with what white man calls 'clap' and 'the pox.' You see."

The medicine man had his patients provide as explicit an examination as a hunter would make of a dead snowshoe hare during the high cycle of their numbers lest he become ill with the rabbit fever. There were probings, touchings and strokings.

Little Coyote and Antelope were curious, enlightened and appalled.

"These sicknesses come up the river with the white man and his breeding, and stay when he leaves," the old man explained. "You ask Vasquez if he has the medicine that works."

Vasquez had the mercury medicine and specific, though hurried, advice that Little Coyote tucked away. A scout from Lisa's party had brought word the flotilla of keelboats and other craft was perhaps only a half-day downriver. The party had been delayed building a trading outpost a few miles above the Gros Ventre village to serve that group, which was somewhat friendly, and the Mandans.

"They weel only catch deh clap again, for a spoon, a bell, som odder trinket, a bit of ribbon. We have leetle medicine to spare." Vasquez threw up his hands and a look of resignation crossed his honest, open face. "I see many Indians, downriver and here. You Flatheads are chaste." He worked hard to communicate the word. "Best medicine you can give deh Flatheads is tell them to keep deh women away from deh white man." He looked hard, knowingly, at Little Coyote. "There are many Brandts."

The old Mandan was grateful for the young Flathead's aid and cast about for objects with which to show his gratitude.

"I am grateful to *you* for the lessons *I* have learned," Little Coyote said. "They will help the Flathead people. Vasquez says the woman should stay away from men for many suns." Like Vasquez, he threw up his hands. "As for the two warriors with the pox . . ."

Even before the swivel gun in the leading keelboat boomed, the Mandans had begun swarming from their domed houses like stirred-up ants in numerous ant piles. Those in bullboats, resembling inverted and smaller versions of their homes, paddled and poled ashore. Many people climbed atop the houses, all of them raising their voices louder and louder until there was a single ululating crescendo of human sound. The word had spread: Their chief was returning.

"It is John Colter!" Antelope shook her mate's elbow. Their friend stood with Drouillard on the cargo box of one of the keelboats anchored temporarily in the current while the craft bearing Chief Shahaka moved into a small space the swarming people had left open on the riverbank.

"We must wait to greet them," Little Coyote responded. They sought a higher spot from which to observe.

"Shahaka! Shahaka! Shahaka!" This single word emerged

and grew louder yet as the Mandans' old chief stepped ashore with the family members who also had gone downriver with Clark and Lewis to meet President Jefferson. The chief was clad in an ancient, ill-fitting and faded army officer's uniform, some brass buttons on the double rows missing. A few tarnished golden tassels still clung like stubborn autumn aspen leaves to the large epaulets. The belt was missing. In its stead was a piece of rope, attached to which was an old and rusty cutlass that the chief now withdrew with difficulty from its metal scabbard. That task accomplished, he raised the weapon aloft in a joyous salute. Simultaneously, he doffed a tall, partially stove-in, badly scuffed, beaver-skin hat, the moth-eaten covering scarcely recognizable.

Four Mandans raised him high on their shoulders, a notable feat apparently accomplished by their enthusiasm, for Shahaka was quite obese as well as tall. Two other muscular warriors rushed to help transport him up a hillock where all could see and hear this magnificence. Set on his own legs, he dropped the cutlass, the hat teetered from his head and he stumbled about until he fell. Shahaka was very drunk. No matter. He was home.

Amid continuing celebration, Lisa and his associates in the newly formed Missouri Fur Company held a serious meeting in the Mandan house. Afterward, they called together their large party on a hillside away from most of the noise.

Little Coyote and Antelope joyously met Drouillard and Colter and saw that among the many white men were other Indians whom their friends identified as Delaware and Shawnee hunters. Also in the party was a tall, heavily muscled Onondaga Iroquois who Drouillard said had been with the fur-traders from Canada.

"I was trapping with little luck up the Knife River near here when I heard Lisa was on his way," Colter explained. "So here I am. He wants me to guide a large party to Three Forks to set up a post. I reckon I'll go. I still need a big stake to take home." His grin had lost much of its spontaneity.

Lisa told the assemblage of Vasquez' disappointing report of few furs taken, many trading goods lost and the unsuccessful attempts to trap the rich Three Forks region.

"Pierre Choteau and I will return to St. Louis to assemble

an outfit for the spring of 1810," he declared stoutly. "Andrew Henry here, another of our company's partners, will take forty men and horses overland to Lisa's fort. Pierre Menard, yet another partner, will take the boats and the rest of you men up the Yellowstone. You'll all winter at Lisa's fort, then a large party will head for Three Forks in the spring and show those Blackfeet— and trap a cargo of beaver. Colter here will act as guide."

"That hoss shore knows how to get there allrighty, and skeedaddle back fast!" one bearded trapper shouted. He guffawed and spat a great wad of used-up tobacco while the others laughed. Lisa held up both hands.

"Menard and Henry have set up duty watches for the boats," he said. "Mind you, keep them well. We will get under way in two days. No whiskey will be issued here."

After the meeting, both Colter and Drouillard again sought out Little Coyote and Antelope.

"With your horses and gear, you'll probably want to travel with Andrew Henry and us," Drouillard suggested. When Antelope began smiling, he added, "And you'll smile some more because you're welcome to go with us to Three Forks in the spring. We'll most likely go there about the time your people start thinking of a buffalo meat hunt."

Delighted Antelope and Little Coyote wandered through the lively town, stopping once at the river bank to examine a light-weight bullboat made from buffalo skins stretched over light saplings and capable of transporting a tremendous load. Shahaka had disappeared from view. When the couple encountered the old medicine man, he informed them the chief had drunk too much firewater. But the chief's family had promised that later he would tell the village about the many wonders he had seen in white man's world. The Mandans had much to look forward to.

As Little Coyote and Antelope returned to their lodge to begin preparing for the trek to Lisa's fort, they saw four other people toiling up a small embankment to a neglected-looking house. They were the medicine man's daughter, wearing a string of beads around her sallow neck, a newly arrived boatman not on watch, and the two small children. The children sat outside the home, shivering in the cold wind coming upriver.

Lisa's fort was not totally abandoned when the Andrew Henry party reached there. Numerous lodges of friendly tribes, predominantly Crow, were set up near the river. The single Shoshone lodge occupied by Wolf That Howls, his two wives and a young son was inside the palisade with their horses. The Shoshonis patiently were waiting to trade their furs. They had been the first to arrive. Others who had been in their party had tired of waiting. Antelope eagerly sought someone she knew, but they were from a band that lived far from her own. Wolf That Howls did acknowledge he had heard of her father and his fine horses.

Before the arrival of the Pierre Menard contingent in the boats, the four Shoshonis had settled outside the fort. They would wait for the trade goods to arrive. Their faces had brightened when Antelope explained that after the coming winter, the white men would travel to Three Forks. Perhaps they would accompany them there and join with the buffalo-hunting Shoshonis, Nez Percé, Flatheads and others who quite likely would be there.

The presence of the Shoshonis and the cares and joys of motherhood did much to shorten the winter for Antelope. Little Coyote accompanied Drouillard to the lake at the northern end of the Bighorn Mountains; they brought back many plews to trade—and thoughts about white man's religion for the young seer to ponder.

In the third moon of the Goose Flight, Antelope excitedly pushed Broken Whistle ahead of her into the lodge. The boy shyly looked at Little Coyote, who was wrapping new babische around the head of his old lance. Despite the boy's many visits, he seldom spoke, preferring to listen with a big smile on his face as Antelope, mindful of her own young brother, chattered about this and that, frequently pulling her husband into the discussion. Today there was much importance to her talk.

"At sunup, Wolf That Howls, his wives and Broken Whistle will leave Fort Lisa," she said. As Little Coyote waited for more information, he carefully split the end of the babische strip and had Antelope hold down the tightened half knot so he could push the remaining ends under the last wrap. There, they would be secure after he set the lance head near the low fire to dry and tighten up.

"And," Antelope almost danced as she exploded with the news, "Menard and Henry will set out for Three Forks in three days!"

This was important, indeed. Wolf That Howls would be one of the three hunters who, during a two-day journey, would shoot animals for the large party of seventy men to follow. Broken Whistle's mother and the other woman would prepare the meat. As Antelope returned the boy to his mother, Little Coyote carefully bundled together eleven of the largest and most prime plews. When Antelope returned, the couple traded the other furs for much ammunition, some tools and such other articles Antelope thought she needed. Now Little Coyote placed the eleven plews on the rough counter. Energetic Vasquez at first refused the Flathead's request, but when the young man began stacking and retying the plews, the trader relented, possibly thinking that, in addition to these furs, there might be a greater future loss should the Flatheads look elsewhere.

Little Coyote triumphantly carried from the post a small box filled with an assortment of white man's medicines. He and his wife carried in their minds Vasquez' explanations of the uses to which they should be put.

Skepts, spring, seemed almost ready to burst forth overnight like the dormant crocuses as the trapping party set forth. True, there yet was snow on the ground and ice on the Yellowstone and many feeder creeks, but the breeze was warmer now. It carried the odor of melting snow, decaying ice and of the fruitful earth, itself. As the members of the party followed the westerly trail the meat hunters had taken along the river, their watchful eyes saw grass, small plants and bushes greening out in the sheltered places. Early spring birds sang their delight in Sun; high above, the ravens in flights of six, eight, twelve, even more, circled and dove then spiraled higher, croaking their pleasure as they seemed to reach Sun, itself. Everywhere were the smells, sights and sounds of regeneration, of release from the prolonged cold of winter. Even the most heavily laden horses seemed to move more willingly—to smell and look and hear. Out of sheer exuberance, the watchful scouts riding in front and on both sides of the straggly column kicked their mounts into fast movement whenever possible.

One such scout was Drouillard. His companion was the Iroquois, who wore around his neck a tiny cross with the figure of a man hanging on it. They rode in from their position near the river and briefly joined Little Coyote and Antelope. The two were managing to keep themselves and their horses near the head of the column. Drouillard pointed to the huge, rocky mass towering high above the almost-flat Yellowstone Valley and the other cliffs across the river.

"Pompey's Tower," he explained. "The chief Clark stopped our canoes there when we were going downriver to St. Louis in '06. Climbed there and put his name on it with his knife." Drouillard stretched and yawned. "What a day! Makes me want to climb, too." He grinned. "Feel like I could climb up that tower, flap my arms and join the ravens up there." He put his rifle across the saddle pad and flapped his arms until Antelope laughed aloud in delight. The Iroquois grinned. Spiced with the thought of adventure ahead, this was a day to thank the Good Spirit for their being alive!

"Does white man give names to mountains? Why would he use the Shoshone word 'Pomp'?" Antelope asked.

Drouillard nodded understandingly. "Yes, 'First Born.' That's what Clark called Sacagawea's baby."

The Iroquois muttered something and pointed.

"What's this?" Drouillard stopped his horse and sat very erect, looking at the blue sky, then the land ahead.

The circling ravens were dropping one by one from the sky, their melodic croaks changing to a more excited tone, an urgency.

The two men raced ahead toward a slight rise, then rode up on it. They were back quickly enough, stopping to converse briefly with Menard, who promptly waved for the column to close up. Now Menard and Henry rode up the rise with the Iroquois. Drouillard spoke briefly with Little Coyote before racing in the direction of the other scouts.

Little Coyote rode directly to Antelope.

"The sky should weep; Sun should descend behind Pompey's Tower," he said. "There is sadness ahead." He touched his mate. "Broken Whistle is dead. His mother is dead. Some enemy has killed them."

They lay there on the mound, heads broken by the tomahawk, and scalped. Drouillard and the Iroquois rode up, dismounted, straightened the bodies and placed them side by side. Little Coyote, who had ridden alongside Antelope, touched her hand as she bent far forward on her horse and wept silently, almost uncontrollably.

Drouillard and the Iroquois stood alongside the bodies, heads far forward, and made the sign of the cross. Together they said something Little Coyote did not understand. They again made the sign of the cross; as others started to place stones around and over the bodies, the two men began looking for sign around and away from what obviously had been a camp.

"'Twas Atsina, Gros Ventre of the Prairies, 'twas. Seven. We seen 'em comin'. Wolf That Howls and his t'other woman, they was out askinnin' the meat. One hyar and the boy was tendin' camp."

The white hunter who spoke English differently from Drouillard pointed to his partner, who spoke: "We wuz picketin' the hosses. We had our guns and woulda' fit 'em, but they minded us none at all. We mighta' got two, three, afore they got us. We watched 'em. They watched us as they killed the woman and young 'un. They knew they was 'nother woman and Wolf That Howls. They got away. Gros Ventres used that 'un afore they killed her."

The two men, who had ridden in soon after the discovery of the bodies, bit off big chews of tobacco, spat, leaned on their guns and awaited the verdict. They had done what seemed best, and the party agreed. No cowards these. They had volunteered for the hunting job, knowing Blackfeet or their allies such as the Gros Ventres might be about.

The meat? Well, there was some up in those bushes. Enough for one meal, maybe. The hunters spoke briefly with Menard, who again set their direction.

"Ain't no ways likely we'll see those 'uns ag'in. Went off t'other way. If'n we'd a' had more shots steada' jes two, wull, maybe we taken some Gros Ventre har." The other hunter, an older man, shook his head in disagreement, but again remained silent.

The hunters rode off, but not before each had borrowed a back-up trade musket from the supplies.

"Drouillard." Little Coyote looked up from the blanket on which Antelope sat mourning.

The trapper stopped chewing the hastily cooked meat.

"The Gros Ventre know the direction we are going," Little Coyote said. "They will follow in perhaps greater numbers."

Drouillard swallowed and nodded in agreement: "Best we not say too much about that, Little Coyote, but remain on guard. We're determined to go there anyway." He prepared to take another bite, flashing the strong, white teeth in his ready smile. "As I said, we half-Indians have to work harder. There's a balance of sorts working here. The same Indian in me will keep the Indians from catching me." He bit deeply into the meat and chewed with much relish.

Little Coyote, after insisting that Antelope eat, bit into his meat, too, and chewed it slowly, thoughtfully and with little relish.

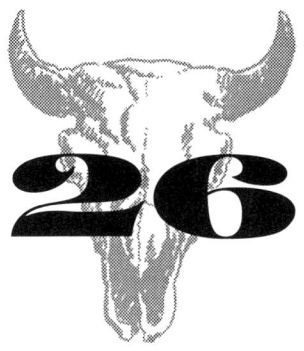

26

Nature also seemed to react against the slaying of Broken Whistle and his mother. As the trapping party left the death camp, Little Coyote leading the pack horses, Antelope quietly sobbing in her blanket, heavy clouds began piling up. They were driven from the north by a growing wind.

"No more straggling!" Menard ordered as Colter set a faster westward and upward pace that allowed little sleep and demanded much travel. With clouds now obscuring the high, snow-clad, twisted peaks of the Crazy Mountains north and the towering Absaroka range south, birds and other wild creatures sought shelter from ever strengthening wind and wet snow.

Menard stopped the head of the party. While the laboring, snow-plastered others began to catch up, Colter forced his horse along the column, his words rising and falling in the keening blizzard: "We must try to reach the pass! It leads downward to Three Forks! We cannot hunt here! Stay close together!"

So they tried, until in the pass, itself, man and beast no longer could lunge through the drifts. The people erected shelters as best they could; Little Coyote and Antelope unpacked the old horse lodge so Menard and Henry could rotate it among the more poorly sheltered. They put up their smaller lodge next to the larger and shared it with Colter, Drouillard and the Delawares, the Shawnees and the lone Iroquois. The couple's five horses willingly allowed themselves to be picketed in the lee of the two lodges.

The wind stopped.

Snow continued to fall, daylight discernible from dark only as an all-enveloping grayness. Soon all food had been shared. As the gray days passed, the marooned trappers ate the dogs first, then a horse, then another—and more until Little Coyote and Antelope contributed a pack horse. The old lodge, which had served and was serving so many so well, would have to remain forever in the pass.

The snowfall ceased.

Sun, so long hidden, came out warm to melt the snow, bright to gladden the travelers at first, soon to torture eyes and heads with its intensity. The Iroquois dug into his paint bag and shared his greasy black with the other Indians, Colter and Drouillard, the wide slashes of paint under and above the eyes protecting them somewhat against the blinding glare. Too late, others in the party relented and fumblingly began rubbing horse grease and soot from the cooking pots around their eyes. They were snowblind. Now the Indians became butchers, cooks—and protectors.

The eagle's high note shrilled downward, causing all heads and eyes, snowblind and sound, to move skyward then up and down the pass. Hands moved to weapons; Drouillard and Colter waited expectantly before instructing the snowblind to face east or west. A fired volley, however blindly pointed, would have some effect if the eagle's whistle from the alert Iroquois scout high above signaled "enemy." Two more notes. The strangers approached from the west.

So the trappers waited while the snow silently melted, adding more strength to the muffled stream song issuing from under the white blanket. The approaching Indians were aware of the trappers' presence. The smell from the fires would have conveyed that. The first two warriors approached on crude snowshoes constructed from evergreen boughs. They dodged behind the larger, snow-covered rocks. Behind them, well out of effective weapon range, came two mounted warriors single-file, rising and falling with their plunging mounts. Each trailed three horses.

"They are . . . Shoshonis!" Antelope's voice, hesitant at first, strengthened with certainty. "Their clothing, their marks on their horses are Shoshone." She set her over/under flintlock against a pack, then stood atop the pack. "Yes, they are Shoshonis!" Her voice rose exultingly. She called out and waved.

Suspicion melted like the snow. Here were thirty Shoshonis, some of whom Antelope vaguely knew. But these proud warriors were trying to travel fast, each man riding, then leading, a horse in an effort to buck through the snow. Little Coyote listened, head down, after he had studied their tired, anxious, black-streaked faces. The sub-chief's message was brief: "The Blackfeet and their allies seem everywhere. The Flatheads and Nee Mee Poo, some Shoshonis—men, women and children—are heading for the buffalo grounds near the great falls of the great river. The Flatheads sent messages to their Salishan-speaking brothers to the north to trek with them up the Blackfoot River, over the great pass and down the river of the Sun. This force cannot be stopped. They will have their buffalo meat.

"We fear for the other Shoshonis who earlier had been informed to join the Flatheads, Nee Mee Poo and the rest of us near Three Forks. There was a battle. We found signs before the great snow. We are sure that these of our people now are trekking northward up the ancient trail between the Big and Little Girdle mountains to join the others near the great falls. They need our strength."

Colter told the Shawnees and Delawares to put more precious wood on the fires. Then he and Drouillard cut off large pieces of horsemeat to roast for the Shoshonis and the Iroquois, who had come down from his eyrie. Gratefully, they ate. Then the Shoshonis mounted fresh horses and began breaking trail eastward, the sub-chief taking his turn first.

"Damn Injuns would come acrost us hyar," a trapper, whose eyesight was returning, muttered sourly. "An ya', Colter, shore was mightly keerful to feed 'em more'n we ben allowed."

Andrew Henry, the other partner in the company who generally had deferred to the older Menard, strode over to the trapper. Henry's haggard, bewhiskered and sunburned face was working angrily.

"Damn fool!" he shouted. "They probably saved the lives of several of our horses. Shut up and help pack up. We're following the trail their sixty horses broke right down to the Gallatin River."

Little Coyote looked back as his party headed westward. His eyes centered on the fresh trail the Shoshonis were breaking while moving from sight. His mind focused on the regret he felt that he and his family could not accompany them. Now, perhaps more than ever, his people needed the munitions and other articles the couple would have been forced to give to the trapping party or abandon. And, he had to admit, he did not wish to risk his family traveling with a smaller party. Ruefully, he acknowledged, there remained the problems of possible Blackfeet near Three Forks and no Flatheads to accompany him and his family back to their own valley.

As the cavalcade angled downhill, Little Coyote once more looked backward. As though waving good-bye, the door flap of the old lodge, relieved of the weight of the large rock that had held it down in the storm, opened and closed in the errant breeze that funneled through the pass. Drouillard, bringing up the rear, saw the warrior's face and signaled encouragingly. Yes, Drouillard . . . Now Little Coyote, even in the exuberance of being on the move again, could focus for a moment on the forebodings he increasingly was sensing about his part-Shawnee friend. The young Flathead looked backward a third and final time. Drouillard's horse, following the well-broken trail, had carried him into the shadow of an overhanging cliff. Little Coyote no longer could see his face.

The snow depth lessened and spirits rose as the trappers moved down the Gallatin River bank. Hunters and scouts warily forged ahead, leaving four elk, two deer and a black bear carcass near the edge of a grassy meadow. After a great feast, their bones, too, lay scattered with the bones and skulls of many humans, which Colter explained were from the battle with the Blackfeet in which the Crows had "saved our hides."

Fearfully, *engagés* and trappers looked around as though expecting to see a Blackfeet near every bush. Some claimed they did. They fired their guns, the reports often causing the most fearful to bunch together despite cooler heads warning them to spread out a bit to avoid becoming a target any skulking Blackfeet scarcely could miss. In this fearful atmosphere the party next day gratefully reached the site where Menard would have them erect the post—between and approximately two miles from the junction of the Madison and Jefferson rivers.

"Weer clost ta tuckered out, an' he sets us ta choppin' an' haulin' trees at onct," the complainer who had objected to feeding the Shoshonis whined as Menard put everyone to work. Mindful of the field of bones only a day's journey away, no one heeded the complaint. Two courses of logs were up before the day of arrival ended, sufficient for the men to fort behind should there be a surprise attack. Little Coyote and Antelope erected their lodge nearby and built a crude pole corral to hold their horses. Until the scouts and hunters returned, they would picket the horses each day, guard them while they ate, then return them to the corral at night.

At the end of the second day, Menard asked the men to build their evening meat-roasting fires near the five courses of logs that had gone up.

"Buffler! That shines!" Even the chronic complainer was exultant when the workmen quit for the day and, except for the guards, wearily straggled toward the meat poles near the abuilding fort. Buffalo, yes, a young bull, and two more elk and a deer, all skinned—livers, kidneys, brains, stripped-out sections of gut piled alongside on the green hides—all waiting for knives, roasting sticks and hungry bellies.

Such feasts, along with faster work on the fort and the surrounding stockade, were the central activities near Three Forks. Then the hunters, supported by careful scouting reports, claimed they were finding no recent Indian sign, but beaver in almost unbelievable numbers. Tension relaxed, but the work, amid a prevailing fear, continued until Sun rose for the eighth time in *s'tcyalmín*, the fourth, or courtship, moon. Then Menard, dirty buckskins hanging on his gaunt frame, work-roughened hands twisting the axe handle as he spoke, told the workers he was sending out a few trappers for a short distance. Each would be accompanied by an *engagé* to keep guard as the other worked the traps.

"Will you trap with the others?" Antelope asked Little Coyote.

She put a few dry twigs on the fire. Soon the light flickered inside the lodge. She peered carefully under the rabbit skins covering Lance. Little Coyote watched as the firelight danced across her face—anxious lest he be awake, smiling now to tell him his son slept. How he loved her, loved them both! She slid between the furs with him. The twigs quit crackling now as the fire more rapidly consumed them. From outside, the couple could hear the men talking around their own small fires. Once they heard a voice louder than the others shout: "Whyn't yuh tell 'em agin, Colter, 'bout that hell of boilin' water springs 'n' geezers 'n' mud springs yuh 'n' Drouillard seen up in t' Yallerstone 'n' Shoshone River land?" The voice ended with a derisive, cackling laugh. "Colter's Hell. Fire 'n' brimstone!" Again the laugh.

The couple heard Colter's voice, calm but indistinct, answer briefly, followed by others rising in argument. Some English words were distinguishable; other voices, which Drouillard had explained were French and Spanish, were indistinguishable. Yet, there was a detectable, unifying nuance in them all. Fear, a fear that intensified with growing darkness, a fear that had not dissipated despite forced gladness as the few trappers returned with good pelts and more tales of seemingly countless beaver waiting for the traps.

"Will you trap with the others?" Antelope repeated her question.

Little Coyote reached across the furs, the aromatic yarrow odor strengthening as he gently pulled Antelope over to him. She nibbled his ear as he wrestled her closer. She would play, but now the question again: "Will you trap with the others?"

"No."

He could feel the tension leave her body.

The question demanded a broader answer beyond that single "*Ta*," which could as easily apply to any simple question, such as, "Do you want a drink of water from the well in our fort?"

"The beaver work on white man like *stela*, the hand game of our people, but white man gambles his life." Little Coyote sat up. He put more twigs on the fire, as though the light would dispel his gloomy thoughts. "The Blackfeet are here. I cannot see them, but I feel them. They wait, where I know not. Near or afar, like the raven, they will appear, but quietly."

He disconsolately stirred the fire, then angrily threw the stick into the flames. "Drouillard! His greedy white blood has conquered his Shawnee blood. Yet there is something around him, lurking, unseen, too, so I cannot become angry with him. When Sun rises he and John Colter, with sixteen other men, will work up the Jefferson River to trap." Now Little Coyote could see the rigidity re-enter the body of Antelope, the tautened lines in that endearing face, the tightened arm. She, too, had come to view those two men as brothers.

"They choose their party well," Little Coyote said. "Good fighters—Hull, Cheek, Ayres, Freeharty, Rucker, others. As they work, they must stay together, then perhaps the Blackfeet will not overcome them. But the sight and the feel of the beaver! I fear. I am mindful of the silliness that lurks in the whiskey pots; a drink leads to others. Yes, the hand game, the whiskey and the beaver. They do much the same." He returned to the furs and held Antelope in his arms. They listened to Lance's slight rustling in the rabbit skins, the nearby voices in the darkness. There was little sleep, no joy in the camp that night.

The hardest work on the fort's heavy crossbeams proceeded with little complaint for the next few days. Other factors tended to lift the spirits as surely as did each sharpened log added to the ever closing gap in the circle of the palisade: The hunters enabled the workers to eat well; the trappers brought in many furs from nearby streams; they reported no hostile signs; the warm weather persisted; even a few crocuses emerged in the sunnier spots.

Work began on the palisade gate, but was interrupted before the gate could be hinged. Segments surviving a disaster galloped through the opening.

"Hosses comin'! Hell bent. Riders shoutin' 'bout Injuns!"

Men dropped from their work on the fort roof as the lookout, a worker who had injured an arm, shouted excitedly and began scrabbling down from a seat atop a palisade plank. Others quit work elsewhere and raced for their weapons. When Little Coyote brought horses and family into the enclosure, riflemen already had thrust their weapons through the fort's loopholes and excitedly were calling for more information.

If the horses truly were coming hell-bent, the lookout scarcely knew the creatures. They were lathered, heaving, almost tottering when they came into sight, so much so that Vallé and the two riders with him jumped off and abandoned the animals at the edge of the clearing, choosing to run the intervening distance themselves. All the while they shook their weapons above their heads, looked fearfully backward at times and shouted that the Blackfeet were behind them. Antelope hurried with Lance into the fort building. Little Coyote led the horses to the space between the fort and the palisade opposite the open gate. A swivel gun projecting from a firing port on that side seemed as though it would be least likely to be fired at, making the place safest for all the animals.

"Dead! All dead! All who went up the Jefferson! Dead! They're comin' here!" Vallé babbled the words almost incoherently as he staggered across the space between the palisade and the building. Dozens of questions greeted him and the two equally shaken *engagés* as they entered the structure. Menard angrily fired his pistol to silence them.

"Dougherty! Brown!" Menard jabbed his finger at two men who calmly were leaning against the fort wall, chewing mightily on their tobacco, spitting out the loopholes, then peering across the clearing. "Go get Ware and James. They're most likely trapping near the big pond downriver where you left them. Tell them they are needed here. Damn fast!"

Menard reloaded his pistol. The garrison could hear the ramrod tamping against the seated bullet, followed by the pounding hooves of Dougherty's and Brown's horses.

Menard stuck the reloaded pistol in his belt as Andrew Henry posted two men next to the other swivel, which was aimed directly at the palisade gateway. Henry's words to the men reached all the rest: "Look sharp and be damned careful you don't fire at our own people who might be coming in!"

Menard handed a cup of coffee to Vallé. The man took a deep drink. "Now take hold of yourself, man, and tell us what happened!" Menard ordered.

"We went up the Jefferson. 'Bout forty miles. Beaver everwhere. No Injun sign. Even on the river banks. Six of us stayed to set up camp. T'others split up and started trappin'." Little Coyote nudged Antelope and shook his head.

"They *what?*" Henry's outraged question snapped out almost as startlingly as had Menard's pistol shot. Lance squirmed restlessly on Antelope's back. Vallé splashed coffee onto his shirt front.

"Split up and started trappin'. They wasn't no Injun sign."

Henry threw his hands upward, then motioned for Vallé to continue.

"The three of us here was gettin' a pile of firewood. First thing we know'd, here comes the Injuns, some on feets, all yellin' and screechin' and behind 'em we could hear hosses. We run to where we'd put the supplies—camp." Vallé swallowed the rest of the coffee, hastily bit off a large chew of tobacco and tongued it against his cheek. He shivered. "Ayres, Hull and Cheek was layin' out gear and puttin' up a shelter. I told 'em the Injuns was comin'. They could hear 'em. I told 'em to get on their hosses and skeedaddle out of thar. We'd done all we could do so we lit out on our horses. Cheek and Hull was looking to their guns and staying put, last we saw. They and Ayres got it sure. We heard lots of shots. That delayed the Injuns some. That's how we made it out."

"I'm glad you did, but then do you know all the others were killed?" Henry's voice had softened into a mix of anger, disgust, yet hope.

Vallé spat in the direction of the palisade gateway. "We was—"

"Hosses comin'! Clost togither! Them's white man yells!" One of the men at the swivel turned to face the others. He cocked the flint lock mounted on a long stock, but held it well away from the touchhole.

Four times that day the man cocked, then uncocked, the flint lock as more small groups of survivors came pounding into the fort on spent horses. Finally, only five of the eighteen were missing. All the men were exhausted, all fearful. Two men were contradictory exceptions—Drouillard and Colter.

Drouillard and two Delawares hallooed the fort soon after Henry dissuaded Menard from having the men hinge up the massive gate.

"Seems to me, Pierre, if the Indians come charging in on horses or even afoot, they just might, in their excitement, head naturally through the opening. One swivel might wipe out most of the immediate trouble with one shot."

"They were Gros Ventres of the Prairie," Drouillard explained. "Not too many. Most likely they included the ones who killed the woman and her boy. The three of us were laying traps in a brushy creek when we heard the firing. We got back to the camp as soon as we could. Cheek and Ayres, I'm fairly certain it was them, are dead. Maybe more. All the camp gear is gone, plus horses, guns, traps—everything. We figured we could serve the living better than the dead, so hustled back here. We might be able to get back some of the gear if we head out fast. The Gros Ventres are careless. We could tell from tracks they weren't moving out fast."

The two Delawares and the Iroquois brave had sat back against the fort wall eating while Drouillard was talking. Now they stood, grasped their muskets and looked expectantly at Drouillard, then Menard and Henry. Thus the four men raised the spirits of the garrison. When Menard began naming other men of the party for the pursuit, there was no grumbling, though some shifted uncomfortably when their names were called. That attitude changed to some open dissent when Colter entered the stockade with one more trapper. Both were tired but unexcited. They explained how they had eluded six Gros Ventres who had picked up their trail. Then Colter began talking with Drouillard, his angry voice beginning to rise as he did so.

"I swore to God I would leave this damned country and never return if those five-hundred Flatheads could whip fifteen-hundred Blackfeet. And maybe He sent along those three-hundred Crows so we could." Colter grabbed his hat and flung it away in his anger at himself. "So things settled down and I started thinking beaver again. Then all the while I was running away from those divils that chopped up Potts, I kept saying, 'Lord, let me win here and I'll leave the beaver to the Indians and head home.' And the Blackfeet that was ready to kill me stumbled and fell and I killed him with his own lance head. I've pushed the Lord's patience too far. If he will forgive me for my greediness, for breaking my promises, I'll leave this place in two days and truly be damned if I ever return!"

Was Colter expressing momentary fear, merely compounded by anger? No. He clapped his hat back on his head, then started wiping off his horse and putting his few belongings and some beaver pelts into a bag. Little Coyote and Antelope hastened to provide what help and equipment they could.

If John Colter had offered, then broken, promises to the Good Spirit, he needed all the help he could muster. Yes, he should make this run.

M enard ordered all horses be brought to a pole corral inside the palisade and well back from the entrance. Half the company began cutting hay to be fed sparingly; Menard's large party set out to look for Freeharty, Rucker, Hull, Cheek and Ayres, and to try to regain horses and equipment from the Gros Ventres.

Busy as they were, Andrew Henry and Drouillard hurried over to where Little Coyote and Antelope were erecting their lodge inside the palisade.

"Little Coyote, you and your woman are handy with your guns," Henry said. "Will you stay here to guard the fort?" Henry smiled as Antelope swung Lance to her back. "Start to thinking on a plan Menard and I have been talking about so our company won't fall apart. Could we get the Flatheads or the Shoshonis to capture a Blackfeet? We'd give him many presents, send him back to his people with word that if they'd quit fighting us, we'd set up a post for them on the Marias River below the great falls."

Henry returned to the fort, where he moved the second swivel gun to help cover the open gateway. Drouillard mounted his horse, signed farewell and joined the departing rescue party.

Tired, dejected and fearful, the group returned in four days.

The men had pursued a small band of Gros Ventres without ever seeing them, though forcing the Indians to abandon many traps and three ruined horses.

"Cheek and Ayres were the dead ones, all right," Menard wearily began explaining to the silent garrison.

"Chopped up like Colter tolden 'bout Potts!" one of the returnees shouted.

Menard held up his hand to try to silence the agitated reaction to this revelation. "No sign of the others!" he shouted. "Dead, most likely." He shifted uncomfortably as the men talked among themselves about the deaths, then he pointed to the pole an *engagé* had set atop the palisade. "That's the scalp of the Gros Ventre we found dead near Cheek." He forced a triumphant note into this statement. Few heard him.

Tied to the pole by many strands of the long hair, the scalp fluttered in the breeze like a weather vane for several days. It disappeared one night just before the hunters set out for game. They immediately insisted that other armed guards accompany them in their ever widening search for scarce animals. Menard called a council, requesting the use of Little Coyote's lodge for a bit of privacy.

"Beaver everywhere—and Gros Ventre." Menard wasted no time. "So what should we do, Little Coyote? If we wait for your people to show up, maybe this fall, we'll lose valuable trapping time. Would they help us capture a Blackfeet?"

Little Coyote was not surprised when Menard's worried frown deepened. "It would be hard to reach our people to counsel with them about the plan," he said. "To help the Blackfeet is to weaken the Flatheads and their allies. It is not a good plan."

"We can't sit here," Henry said. "The men scarcely will leave the fort; they set out to hunt at night! We've—"

Shouts, then a quarrel outside the lodge interrupted him. Menard left to investigate. Those inside could hear him demanding silence, then speaking in lower tones. He returned soon, his lean face flushed, its lines seemingly deepened in the light of Antelope's fire.

"The hunters went out twenty miles. Not even a shot at

game. They saw two small bands of Gros Ventres, but they stayed out of range. Just dogged the hunters in front and behind, and deliberately scared off any game around."

"Leave most of the *engagés* here with a few good men," Drouillard interjected. "Send enough trappers and shooters with guts back up the Jefferson to trap." His voice had tones of sarcasm, determination and certainty. "Before the weather gets too hot, they'd catch plenty of beaver to make this a season yet. We've got to get some plews back to St. Louis. Any better ideas?"

"The fox waits near the game," Little Coyote said. "When the bear makes his kill, eats, then sleeps or wanders away from the meat for a time, the fox sneaks in and eats." The Flathead felt compelled to speak. The white men listened, but with impatient looks on their faces. "The Gros Ventre know where the beaver are. He knows these will bring the trappers. The Gros Ventre will wait by the beaver—and strike when the white men sleep or wander away to work the traps."

"He's right," Drouillard said. "We need to send a strong force." Drouillard looked at Menard.

"And they need to stay *together*!" Menard emphasized. "Let's pick the men. Two Delawares, two Shawnees and the Iroquois will go. Will you, a Flathead, go, Little Coyote?"

The baited question brought Antelope to her mate's side.

"Who will remain as chief at the fort?" Little Coyote asked, countering Menard's challenge.

"Henry and myself."

"I will go . . ." Antelope's bells jangled discordantly. ". . . but not to trap. I will hunt and guard." Again the bells.

Drouillard led the thirty men from the fort. The Iroquois warrior ranged ahead; the two Delawares and two Shawnees served as flankers left and right. Little Coyote and a bent and bow-legged trapper, perhaps oldest in the company, followed behind. The Flathead recognized the man as one of the two from Lisa's fort who had been sent ahead of the party to hunt and who had been present when Broken Whistle and his mother were killed. He had said nothing at all when his fellow hunter explained the killings. He finally spoke this day when he rode over to see with whom he was sharing the responsibility of rear guard:

"Tull. That's me. Yore Coyote, I ben told." He combined chewing with talking, but both keen eyes were looking at all sides—always. "Wal, ain't diskivered Injuns 'bout yit, hostiles, that is." His eyes centered appreciatively for a moment on his companion's rifle, pistol and horse. Then he turned and looked backward. "I cotton th' prairy kentry muhself. Chaw?" He held out the twist, then tucked the tobacco back into a pocket when the Flathead declined. "Glad ta see them up front're tryin' ta keep us outta' pluggin' distance f'm th' trees 'n bushes. Wull, reckon I'll jest sit a spell over thar . . ." He spat a long stream of brown juice in the direction of a large boulder. ". . . 'n wait ta see if'n any varlets is comin' arter us f'm th' ass end so ta speak." He nodded his mop of hair, then halted his horse while the others forged ahead.

On the third day of the trek, the party halted at the edge of a wide, willow-covered series of brakes near the Jefferson.

"We might as well camp here, look over the land and plan our trapping," Drouillard said. "Tull, how about you and the Delawares trying for some meat?"

"Fine idee. Thar'll be deer in th' brakes." Tull withdrew a bow and several arrows from a case on a pack horse. "Reckon we'll stick ta these tools, but ya' heeran' ary gunshot f'm us, come arunnin'."

Long after the men had eaten their fill of venison and, except for the guards, had rolled themselves in blankets and canvas, solemn Little Coyote, full-blood Flathead of almost nineteen summers, and half-blood Shawnee Drouillard, almost twice that age, sat near the base of a giant cottonwood. For a long time they discussed Colter's precipitous departure, agreeing in low tones that while they missed him and could well use his fighting spirit now, he had done what he had to do.

The drawn-out "sssptt" before Tull spoke was their first intimation he was there at all. Drouillard dropped his hand from his knife handle.

"Colter reck'nd his string'd run out, simple as that," Tull

said. "Yuh goes whar yore stick floats. Damn fool if'n yuh don't."

Relieved from his guard duties after his hunting, Tull sat down with a grateful sigh. He unlaced his wet moccasins, carefully hung them from a projection on the rough tree bark, slipped on a dry pair and stretched out his bowed legs. The two men could see his bright eyes below bushy brows, a stub of a wide nose protruding from his long whiskers, little else in the gloom.

"Don't like it hyar muhself. If'n we c'n stick arrers in three deer, reckon them Gros Ventre c'd put 'em, er a ball, in us sleepin' 'r trappin' 'r walkin'. Aller same, no diff'rence."

They sat there as the last light began winking out from the lowest to the highest eastern peaks. The movements near the sleeping men were from restless horses. The coyote howl in the distance was genuine, as were the owl hoot and an answer from another in the direction of the river; the whirring of a night hawk; the scurrying of smaller four-legged creatures in the grass. A sleeping trapper rolled over in his blanket, mumbling in his dream.

Tull spat again. "Kinda' purty hyar. Like the prairy kentry best. Hardern t' sneak up'n a body. No farms 'n plows yit either. Spect they's comin'. Seen 'em up t' Mississip 'n lower Missoury. Ever' time I move north, east er west, they cotch up. Likely hyar, too, but . . ." He stood, his knee joints cracking loudly in the silence of the night. ". . . reckon not afore this hoss goes under. Yuh, Coyote, wull, not so shore." Tull spat a final time and was gone, so silently the young Flathead almost wondered if the man had been there at all. But his words stayed, long after Little Coyote sought sleep, too.

Tull had delivered his views to the leader ahead of the others, prompted, likely, by their growing dissent. He said no more. Others spoke loudly, again and again, particularly two nights later when Drouillard ordered, "No fires at night, even to dry out our britches."

"How'n hell kin we dry out after wadin' in the water all day?" The young trapper was complaining loudly so all could hear.

"Stan' 'round nekkid while yuh're cookin' yore meat 'n dryin' yore britches th' same time."

"Jus'be shore ya use a long stick, er ya'll be fryin' parts ya wanta' keep. Orja wear 'em out in th' Mandan camp?"

The laugh brought on by the two older men went full circle, but as they began rolling up in their blankets, one of the jokesters raised a common complaint: "Drouillard, it's hell tryin' t' use nine men t' guard two trappers 'n their hosses, when jes' two trappers 'ud do."

The young voice again: "I ain't doin' any trappin' 'cept that way."

"Er leavin' camp, even." The voice was that of an older man just relieved from his guard post farthest from the others.

Like the mushroom, the last statement grew in the minds of most of the men as they finally slept. Around the cooking fires next morning the men tussled with the thought, which had grown to full size now while they chewed the more palatable beaver and diminishing portion of venison. As Drouillard began assigning duties for the day's trapping, most of the men reluctantly complied, though two refused to leave camp at all.

"I'll work aroun' camp," one stated, "fleshin', hoopin' 'n dryin' the pelts. Jus' don't want the Blackfeet doin' the same to my har."

"Er gettin' chopped up like carrots for a stew," the other grunted. "I stays here."

And they did. Four more of the whites did the same next day after the trappers found horse prints that clearly were quite old.

Finally, only Tull, another white man, the Indians and Drouillard would go out at all, unless as a group.

"Damn cowards!" Several men stood up to protest Drouillard's slur. He met this action by stalking toward them and repeating his words. "See some old hoofprints and you scare like rabbits." He signaled the two Delawares. They put some traps in a skin bag and were off. "We'll bring back the beaver carcasses so you can eat. Or do you want grass?"

Little Coyote, hunting the brakes afoot, dropped a small deer toward evening. He gutted her and slung the carcass over his shoulder, careful to leave both hands free for the bow and arrows. He heard the Drouillard party approaching camp from the opposite direction. Two more of the hunters had brought in one deer.

The men ate in silence. Drouillard and the Delawares left before camp awakened next day. They returned with six beaver, and four the next evening. Drouillard sought out Little Coyote as the cooking fires died. They watched some of the men dragging in logs they could sleep between for protection. One man dug a shallow, grave-size pit.

"Ten beaver when we could have caught more than fifty." Drouillard leaned back wearily as he tugged off his wet footgear and breeches. "Beaver everywhere."

"And Blackfeet somewhere," Little Coyote replied. "They wait like the crafty fox, my friend. If they were strong enough to kill five, they are strong enough to kill three." He laid his hand on his older friend's forearm as though to restrain him. In the distance a coyote yipped three times, its voice trailing away as the tiny breeze rustled greening willows.

Drouillard managed a tired grin. "As I told you, friend . . ." Now he placed his hand on the Flathead's shoulder. ". . . when we buried the Shoshone woman and her boy, we half-Indians have to work harder. The same Indian in me will keep the Indians from catching me. Besides, we're only about two miles from camp."

Drouillard dug into his bag for dry clothing after hanging the wet under the cottonwood: "Sure would help if you, the Shawnees, the Iroquois, the other white or Tull could get some more deer tomorrow. I'd like to keep Tull's old bones out of the cold creeks if I can. All of us have to eat. Wish we could hazard going out on the open land to get a buffalo or two. We need to feed the men better and show them what three trappers can do."

Next morning while Sun turned the highest, snow-topped western peaks into gigantic pink, then red and white mirrors, those three trappers and the six hunters left camp simultaneously while all but the guards slept. When the trappers began heading upward from the brakes to skirt the more open country for easier traveling,

Drouillard waved a farewell, followed by the familiar sign of the cross. Each hunter began weaving his careful way afoot through the willows like diverging fingers of a widely splayed hand as Sun began flooding cloudless sky and awakening land with light and warmth. It rose higher. Soon the Flathead could see heat waves shimmering from the hillsides as he broke through the densest growth. Deer tracks, new and old, began appearing in the wet sand where, earlier, streamlets from melting snow had threaded their ways through thickets and around tiny rises, but ever downward to the river. Now cold streamlets of air began coursing down from the mountains, growing with the rising heat into larger breezes that finally coalesced into a great wind. The wind created a new dimension of sound in its accelerating passage in the direction of the river.

Little Coyote bent to examine three sets of fresh prints—two does and a fawn—all sunk deeply into the sand. The deer were heading upwind from the hunter and toward the wide patch of grass where he had dropped the doe three days earlier. He found the fresh tracks again, this time the more numerous and smallest prints ahead, behind and in circles around the larger ones. The fawn had gamboled fearlessly and joyously as the more sedate does had moved purposefully toward the better grass. Good. The wind was favorable; he was nearing the small meadow.

The fawn was nudging the doe for milk when the hunter sank quietly onto his knees. He was screened by the stand of short, young willow. With patience and care he would kill them all. Soundlessly, he pressed the tips of two arrows into the soft earth until they remained erect for easy reaching. He fitted a third to the string, looking into the wind for the other animal. There she was, feeding for a moment then raising her head, the long ears turning to hear any unusual sound, the eyes darting here and there as do those of a wary trapper before he bends to set the trap. The hunter flexed his bow and centered the arrow point behind the doe's shoulder. Feeling safe for that moment, her head was moving downward to feed again.

Why, since he merely needed to release the arrow toward its mark, were his eyes growing teary, as though weeping? Was it the wind distorting the target until he no longer could see clearly? Why was elation over certainty of meat changing in this instant to a deeper emotion of sadness, a familiar, ineffable sadness? Was the wind helping other hunters? Soundlessly, he unflexed the bow and lowered his head. He wiped his eyes with his index finger. The tears were gone but the sadness remained, deepened as the physical target there in front of him sensed his presence and bounded away, taking the second doe and fawn with her toward the river. The young seer tried to concentrate the disjointed tendrils of his keen intuitive power to perceive a far more important mental target. He should run toward danger. Here? There? Where?

Drouillard!

Like a bow released at maximum tension, the certainty struck him as he whirled and swiftly began retracing the steps he so slowly, carefully, had taken in his hunt. He veered slightly to where he might intercept the Iroquois, who was hunting the closest to the river. Though it was difficult to stem his crouching run, the Flathead stopped and whistled shrilly like the eagle. Silence. He ran and tried again, waiting a seeming eternity, straining to see the Iroquois, perhaps hear shots. There it was! The answering whistle rose shrilly above and through the keening wind. Soon the two warriors were racing into camp where both white hunters had returned earlier with a small deer.

Only four men there questioned Little Coyote's certainty that Drouillard and the two Delawares were in great danger. Tull, with the wind wildly blowing his hair, strode menacingly toward them, motioning for the others to mount up: "Dumb, yaller-striped skunks!" he shouted. "Ya' knows nothin' 'bout some Injuns! Three of ya' stays hyar 'n guards camp—an' yore wuthless hides!" Tull jabbed his rifle at the fourth. "Git back t' th' fort 'n tell Menard 'n Henry ta git hyar!"

He led the other horsemen upward through the wind-driven willows to the open country where the dead grasses dipped and straightened wildly on their long stems. They found the tracks of the three horses in the wet sand near the river. Tull stopped the party and turned his head.

"Off yore hosses, spread outn' foller me. They's death hyar. I c'n feel it now, 'n mebbe live Injuns." At intervals, he stopped two men at a time with orders to look, then retreat behind their horses toward him should there be an attack. He, the other white, the Iroquois and the Flathead covered the last short distance to the river—and the scene of slaughter.

Drouillard's horse lay dead, several arrow wounds penetrating its upward side. Sand marks told how Drouillard had circled the horse again, and yet again, to keep her between himself and his enemies, trying always to back toward the river. Four wide furrows made by dragged bodies disclosed that his now-missing rifle, tomahawk, pistol and knife had performed well before arrows and balls cut him down. They found him in parts, the scalped head at the base of a high, gravel bank, the disemboweled torso at the end of his intestines, a chopped-off arm here, another flung there, a hand, one leg, the other, perhaps, cast into the river that he had sought so desperately. The men found similar remnants of the two Delawares long before Menard, Henry and several others from the fort arrived on foam-flecked horses.

They, too, read the bloody tragedy in the sands. They talked sorrowfully, loudly, then wonderingly in the keening wind while Little Coyote, the two Shawnees, the Iroquois, Tull and Andrew Henry, when he divined the reason, knelt at the river's edge, removed their shirts and splashed water over their upper torsos so the drying blood would stick less. Tull pointed to the gravel bank; Drouillard's head lay at its base. He gathered up an armload of stiffening intestines and dragged the snaky, sand-covered ropes toward the head. Henry did the same, stopped, retched violently, then resumed his task. All other parts went there, too, and soon Tull and the Iroquois clambered atop the bank and began kicking gravel, dirt and rocks downward until tiny avalanches reached the pitiful heap of flesh. Amid swirling dust, the two men worked while the others carried back the larger rocks that had rolled outward. The men placed the rocks atop the sloping mound. This time at river's edge they scrubbed with handsful of sand. With no spoken communication they returned to the common grave, where the Iroquois knelt, followed now by Menard, Henry and most of the party. The Shawnees and Tull, alone of all the whites, stood apart, as did Little Coyote.

The Iroquois made the sign of the cross and finally said, ". . . Holy Mary, Mother of God, pray for us sinners, now and at the hour of our death. Amen."

The proud Shawnee and Tull raised both arms skyward, then submissively bent far forward as one Shawnee spoke: ". . . and Great Spirit, mount these brave warriors upon their horses to pursue the game, see Sun, smell the good air, sleep in the warm Mother Earth until Sun dies, too."

Little Coyote turned toward sky and faced Sun: ". . . so, Good Spirit, let Drouillard, my brother, and these others join brave warriors from all the tribes, where there are many beaver and buffalo . . . all enmities gone."

Others bowed their heads as Menard wearily yet again intoned the last words of his ritual: ". . . And behold, I come quickly; and my reward *is* with me, to give every man according as his work shall be. I am Alpha and Omega, the beginning and the end, the first and the last."

"Plague-taked wind, 'cept fer that, we'ud heard t' shootin'!" Tull's fingers found his nose in the long hair. He blew mightily. "Gits int' t' eyes till a body scarce c'n see."

The Iroquois said nothing at all, though his lips still were silently moving. Little Coyote wiped his eyes, too, remembering how the Iroquois had removed the tiny crucifix from around his neck and tied its string to the nerveless fingers on one severed hand of Drouillard, their friend.

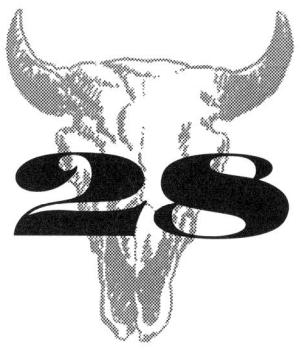

"He laughs because he is so wise. He knows he nears his home among the Shoshone and Flathead people."

Laughing, too, Antelope raised Lance high into the sunshine and listened to his delighted gurgling as the plodding, swaying motion of the horse relayed rhythmically through her body and arms and upward to him.

Little Coyote gravely tried to peer straight ahead as though this was of little interest to him. His concentration shifted briefly from the problems and joys of the present to what lay far ahead. The future concerned him as he saw several trappers nudging their horses toward mother and son and calling to the two-year-old in various friendly ways. I am the only child of Running Buffalo Bull and Little Yellow Bird, the seer reflected. Lance has no uncles to help teach him the ways of the warrior. Yes, soon I will have to choose from friends to help with that responsibility. As Three Eagles has said, "Our people must all be teachers, forever encouraged to insist on the greatest amount of individual freedom, yet practicing discipline when the good of all is threatened."

The young warrior caught himself smiling as his son again

271

laughed and reached toward Tull. The trapper, a large, red-stained cloth wrapped around his hairy head, had waved and then spat a great stream of tobacco juice while nudging his horse to keep pace alongside those of Little Coyote and Antelope.

Behind them, closely grouped, were more horsemen plus a few pack animals. The pack horses were lightly burdened, except four of the largest. Two of these carried a swivel gun each; the other two carried an ammunition box on one side and on the other side two roughly adzed, rectangular-shaped sections of log. In the center of each log a hole had been bored to fit the peg-shaped end of the iron cannon mount.

"We take these swivels even if we have to throw away other equipment," Henry had declared. "And we keep the horses carrying them in the center of our group, and together!"

The trappers tending these horses needed little supervision. None questioned that the swivel guns had saved their lives, or that the party leave the dreaded Three Forks region soon after they had buried Drouillard and the two Delawares and returned to the fort.

Menard had summed up their situation in one sentence: "We can remain here till we starve or the Blackfeet kill us all, or we can return to Lisa's fort and St. Louis."

Then he vented his frustrations in an angry outburst: "Damn the Blackfeet! Here we are in the best beaver country I know of. We could trap practically every beaver on the full length of the Jefferson and all its tributaries, leave the furs at the fort here, do the same on the Madison, then the Gallatin. Then we could float down the Missouri, portage around the falls, and float right into St. Louis. Rich as kings. Damn the Blackfeet!"

"Well, we can move to more peaceful country that has beaver, too," Henry had countered.

"Not like here, ever!"

They finally had agreed that Menard and some of the men would return to Lisa's fort with what pelts they had acquired. Henry and the remainder would travel south, as they were doing now, to make contact with the peaceful Shoshonis and Flatheads.

These were the staunchest men unenthusiastically accompanying Henry. The remainder, enthusiastic though wary, had departed with Menard. During the council at the fort Little Coyote and Antelope had been the only genuinely eager persons in the Henry party—until two-hundred Blackfeet had attacked the fort again.

Henry, as did Menard before his departure, had sent out hunters to acquire meat for their journey. "With all staying together!"

Tull, scouting in front, had headed for the river when he found fresh bear sign. He also found trouble, which he later described to his companions: "When I diskivered whar a bar had tornd up a log f'r bugs, I got down on these old knees 'n startid crawlin' t'ward th' varlet. I peered over a bush, 'n 'bang,' a Blackfeet ball giv' me a har cut moughty clost ta th' bone. Luckier 'n hell thet sarpant put th' sights at th' haid ginril-like stedda' centrin' on th' forehaid, er I'd a' gone under fer shore."

Tull "skeedaddled" back to the other hunters "most fast as thet 'ere musket ball." Staying close together in the woods and with only half the men firing during each Indian charge while the others reloaded, they slowly retreated toward the fort. They left behind a trail of twenty-two dead Blackfeet and one trapper. Appalled at such heavy losses, the Blackfeet had hesitated to make a final charge before the trappers dashed into the fort. Covering the trappers were the rifles, including those of Little Coyote and Antelope, and the handsful of balls the two swivel guns sent buzzing through the woods like angry hornets.

Tull, Little Coyote, the Shawnees and the lone Iroquois had urged the Henry party to leave the fort and the region while the Blackfeet mourned their losses. There were no objections. Henry's group carried little food, but the party began encountering numerous elk and deer as it moved upward toward the mountain pass. Everyone ate well—and became careless. Instead of picketing their horses within their camping area at night, as did the more experienced Indians and trappers, some of the tired men left them in a grassier meadow close to camp so they would not have to move them to other grazing areas. Their mounts were gone next morning. Henry, Tull and Little Coyote rode up a bald knob overlooking much of the countryside. Henry extended his brass spyglass; when he detected movement far to the north, he handed the instrument to Tull.

"They's Injuns, Crows mebbe, 'n they got more hosses t'n they c'n ride." Briefly explaining its use, Tull handed the spyglass to the Flathead. The wondrous instrument confirmed the horse thieves were Crows; Little Coyote and Tull dissuaded Henry from useless pursuit.

Reluctantly, they buried the two cannon at the southern base of the knob. Henry explained that the brass would not deteriorate under the soil.

"I plan to build a fort on this north fork of the Snake River," Henry said. He scratched a rough map on the open patch of earth to show Little Coyote. "If you come there to trade, bring some horses and come here first. If you bring one of the swivels to me, you can keep the other, though I don't know how you'd use it. Tell others we are here to trap and trade."

Henry kept the powder and lead. With much of the party afoot now, they moved more slowly down the divide and toward the northern branch of the Snake.

Game became scarce, beaver even more so, and the men were glad to eat the beaver carcasses after taking their furs. Snow atop the peaks they had just toiled through warned Henry they had better prepare now for winter. Perhaps Shoshonis and Flatheads would bring in pelts—and horses. A few Indians did begin to arrive as the men started building the small fort.

The summer days ended too soon and those of autumn waned and brought the cold. Then one day a larger group of Flatheads, Shoshonis and Nez Percé arrived—and Little Coyote, Antelope and Lance accompanied them home. They left behind three badly needed horses. Little Coyote promised to return four in their stead to the Flathead who owned them when they returned to their valley. In trade, the young seer received Henry's spyglass, which could bring objects closer and also make fire when one unscrewed the larger lens to use with ever friendly Sun!

On the journey, Little Coyote fixed deeply in his mind the river and trail systems. He also established a pattern of learning them that would help him, as well as others, throughout his long life. Equally important, he learned the value of seeking passes over the continental divide—passes over which his forebears, as well as those of his Shoshone and Nez Percé allies, had trekked from time unremembered.

After they left Henry's fort on what had come to be known as Henry's Fork of the Snake River, the Indians continued north to a lake that also bore the trader's name. Here a delighted Antelope found her Shoshone people and the lodge of her father, Broken Pipe. His usually somber face broke into a rare grin, followed by an even rarer laugh, and his lodge became the merriest in all the Shoshone camp as the family and kin viewed and exclaimed over Lance. Knowing the Nez Percé and Flatheads would be anxious to leave after food and rest, Little Coyote and Antelope agreed she and their son should remain in the Shoshone camp while the warrior carried the powder and lead to his people in their valley.

"I will return for you before the end of the eleventh moon of Autumn," he promised. "I want to bring one of the swivel guns to our people. I believe there will be little chance to get one in the future, for we have learned that white man knows the big gun can help to dominate the people of these lands. Too, if I hasten with the furs our people have now, we can return home with the few useful trade goods Henry has at his new fort before others go there in any numbers."

So, the Flatheads and Nez Percé headed west and crossed the continental divide at Red Rock Pass. They traveled along the shores of a series of lakes and then along the south bank of Red Rock River to where its water joined with the Beaverhead. The cavalcade moved ever west until it filed through Lemhi Pass northwest to the Salmon River. Here, amid regrets mixed with eagerness to reach home, the Nez Percé bade their Flathead allies farewell. The Flatheads then headed north toward Lost Trail Pass and the Bitter Root Valley.

The people of the Bitter Root encampment, preparing for their trek to the buffalo grounds, joyously greeted their seer. They were grateful, indeed, for his heavy load of ammunition, too.

Those remaining in the valley even more joyfully welcomed Little Coyote at the beginning of the twelfth moon of the Continuous Snow. On that second return he brought traps, powder and lead, his Shoshone wife and their child—and the wondrous swivel gun. Little Coyote related that he had found the Henry party in poor shape, indeed, making skin garments, catching few beaver, receiving little trade and, seemingly, more grateful for the elk carcass Little Coyote brought in than for the trade horses, even the swivel gun.

When the buffalo-hunters returned with much meat, Little Coyote presented the trade goods and swivel gun to Tjolzhitsay. The head chief seemed almost as old as Shining Shirt now, though his mind was good. He increasingly was seen in company with Little Bear Claw, who recently had returned from his stay with David Thompson of the North West Company.

Little Coyote and Little Bear Claw finally could visit one day as they tied strong poles under the old ones at Shining Shirt's burial trees.

"Tjolzhitsay has kept me near him to ask what I learned about the Black Robes while I was with Thompson," Little Bear Claw said as he separated a coil of babische lashings. "He said he wishes for our people to develop strong leaders who can deal with both the Indians and the white man. But, equally, he wishes to learn about the Black Robes, who care more for the spirit than the body. He thinks he will have our sub-chiefs deal more with the first; he will deal more with the second."

The two young Flatheads clearly were happy to be reunited.

"We will exchange stories of our adventures among the Americans and the Canadians when the snows become deep," Little Bear Claw promised as they tested the strong babische lashings. "And, my friend, it might be well if you would talk to Shining Shirt's spirit and hide the remainder of his gold at some other site."

Little Coyote removed and tossed to the ground the protective willow cage the people had placed over Shining Shirt's body so many moons earlier. Nature had done her work. As the warrior placed a stiff, untanned buffalo hide over the now-tattered one covering the ancient seer's bones, he motioned for his friend to help secure the covering with more bindings threaded through slits along the hide's edges.

"You are correct," Little Coyote said. "If I can discern after appropriate ceremonies that it is Shining Shirt's will, I will bury the gold at the base of the tree there." He pointed to a strong, healthy lodgepole pine at the nearest edge of the stand from which the people had acquired their lodge poles for as long as Running Buffalo Bull could remember. "The gold must remain here. Perhaps in my lifetime, or yours, there once more will be a great need for it."

Again the snows deepened far sooner than the people wished. Southwesterly winds often howled across the land and there was much rejoicing over the abundance of food and fuel to last through the late winter and early spring moons of white man's 1811.

Little Bear Claw, yet unmarried, was a frequent visitor to the lodge of Little Coyote and Antelope. During those short days of winter and early spring, the couple listened more to their friend than did he to them; the people already had told and retold most of what they knew about their young seer's recent travels and deeds. The two young men agreed that each had performed his duty well and had learned about the white men to help the council decide how best to deal with them.

One night while the cool, spring winds shook the stout lodge and the cheery fire defied the growing cold, Little Bear Claw handed a sleeping Lance up to Antelope. He patted the baby's bottom to indicate that the diaper pouch needed dry grass. The young sub-chief's ready grin widened when the infant awakened and fretfully sought return to the strong arms of this man who had dandled, tossed and given him so much attention.

"He will be tall," Little Bear Claw said. "Soon he must learn the ways of the horse and a warrior." The sub-chief's square jaw tightened as he watched Antelope's ministrations. She glanced upward and sideways, the bell necklace jingling as she smiled approval that the warrior had raised the subject of tutelage, himself. Little Coyote smiled, too. A worry over! But for now there was a subject that must take precedence for the sake of all the people. The council wanted their stories and recommendations concerning their assignments.

Little Bear Claw's smile faded. "How fortunate that Tjolzhitsay sent us among the white men," he said. "I can tell you with all certainty that they will be with us always. More and more of them, always. You will remember when, at the hot springs, we wondered whether the numbers of the people of all the tribes were greater than of the newcomer white men. We put twigs on piles in the four directions and began naming the tribes. Only those five short springs ago, I believed there were more of us than of the whites. I no longer think this. I believe the stories the whites have told you and you have told me, and I believe what the whites have told me. And, we have seen much."

The sub-chief stood, looked about the lodge and pointed questioningly at his hosts' knives hanging from the willow weapons rack. Little Coyote nodded, whereupon their guest removed the knives from their sheaths. He placed one knife north of the food pot in the center of the lodge, another south, and his own to the west. Finally, he placed a butchering knife to the east. All blade tips pointed toward the pot. He sat down.

Antelope, holding Lance, moved closer to her husband and their friend. Little Bear Claw would talk. The sub-chief picked up the knife north of the pot.

"As I have told you," he said, "the Canadian David Thompson of the North West Company, or his men, have built trading posts far away on the Spokane River, on the Columbia River and on the Kutenai River. Nearer, there is Kullyspell House on the eastern end of the Lake of the Pend d'Oreille, and nearer yet Saleesh House on the river now called Clark Fork. The Piegans do not like his bringing this trade for the Pend d'Oreilles, Kalispels, Kutenais, Nez Percé, Palouse, Coeur d'Alenes, Spokans, Yakimas, Cayuses and others. So, the Piegans have forced closing of some of the posts at times. They use their strength best with their brothers to keep white men out of the region east of us, as you well know." Little Bear Claw made one slash into the ground northwest of the pot to represent Spokan House, then four more toward the north to represent the others.

"And the white men are not pleased. The Hudson's Bay Company, for whom David Thompson once was a sub-chief, has erected a post they call Howes House on the north end of the Lake of the Flatheads."

He slashed one more X, then put down that knife and picked up the one east of the pot.

"You told me about Lisa's fort, and his post to serve the Gros Ventre and the Mandans." Two more slashes into the earth. "Three Forks fort." Another slash, which he scraped away.

"Lisa's people told me about many such forts beyond where we would wish to trade," Little Coyote interjected.

"As did the David Thompson people."

Antelope shifted Lance, who stirred sleepily. "If there are so many posts so soon after white man's arrival, might they not move more close by here as most of the animals elsewhere enter their traps?"

Little Coyote nodded his head in agreement as this daughter of the widely known horse-trader, Broken Pipe, voiced doubts he, himself, had. Their friend's lips tightened, and he, too, nodded worriedly, again and again as though to himself. Then he savagely slashed one X into the ground south of the pot.

"Henry's post," he said. "I know of no others—yet."

His own knife west of the pot remained untouched. For now, the two warriors had exhausted their knowledge of fur-takers' settlements. Little Coyote filled his pipe, lighted it and handed it to Little Bear Claw.

"This David Thompson," he said. "He does many things. I have told you about Lisa and my near brothers John Colter and Drouillard. Is he a man like them?"

"The people call him 'Koo-Koo-Sint,' the Star Man, for he possesses a marvel somewhat like your wondrous spyglass," Little Bear Claw replied. "With this marvel he looks at the stars. This helps him travel over strange country with the sureness with which we go to the familiar buffalo grounds. He has traveled many lands, perhaps far more than did those of the Clark and Lewis party. He has a heavy, short body much like Broken Tooth, and he moves as strongly and gets no more tired than he. He is opposed to firewater and does not trade with it. His woman is Chippewa, part at least, and works as hard as he. He is a good man. These Canadian people have good trade goods, though they lack the rifled guns and have no pistols to trade. They are fair. His sub-chiefs and many of his men are good fighters. They have proven they support our people."

That said, the sub-chief reached over and removed his quiver from the weapons rack. One by one he laid out eleven arrows; all had long, iron arrowheads. One arrow had been stained red. Little Bear Claw held up the quiver. A long, graying, black scalp ornamented its front.

"A summer ago while I was yet with the Thompson people, many of our people from the north end of our valley and our Pend d'Oreille kinsmen and others gathered at Saleesh House. There they exchanged many furs for twenty trade muskets and many iron arrowheads before starting for the buffalo grounds. Some of Thompson's men accompanied us. Many Piegans attacked us. It was a great, day-long battle for there were many of us, too. Fighting alongside me was one of Thompson's sub-chiefs. He is called Finan McDonald. He is very large with shoulders like a young buffalo bull, and, when angry, a voice to match a large bull. He has long, red hair on his face and much on his head, as you have described your friend, Tull, except for the color. He killed two of the seven Piegans who were killed and wounded another, but he fired forty-five times! My rifle was empty. An older Piegan charged Finan McDonald after he had emptied his rifle and pistol. I drove this arrow through the warrior's heart when he tried to count coup on the red-head!"

Little Bear Claw's voice had risen with the telling of this battle, but now it lowered with a note of sadness: "Five of our people were killed, and many more would have been had not white men helped us with their bravery and their weapons. Perhaps I would not be here because there were many enemy and they were well-armed, too."

"I looked for Eagle Claw when I returned," Little Coyote

said. "I learned he died there." He shook his head in sorrow.

"Yes. His mate, the warrior Willow Woman, did not let the Piegan touch him and killed one when he tried. Now she mourns, but is much honored, is much—" He stopped momentarily, then resumed as both his hosts looked closely at him. "This was a great victory because the Piegan once more proved that they are not invincible when we are well-armed and fight carefully, as did the white men. Our hearts are strong, but we need to aim better. We must anticipate which direction the enemy will jump before we fire, as we have learned with the deer. And, of course, the Piegans now are angry with the North West Company."

Tjolzhitsay spoke slowly and clearly when he called together the council. Out of courtesy, he had invited Bad Leg of the Nez Percé, who, with three other warriors, had come to trade for pack horses. When Little Bear Claw and Little Coyote had spoken for two days, the old chief's stern demeanor relaxed. He encouraged all to ask their questions and speak their views, cautioning that within ten or so suns some of them would be leaving for a buffalo hunt while others, more than ever before, must remain behind to protect the valley.

The council finally agreed that because the Blackfeet and their allies collected in greater numbers on the buffalo grounds and were more free to resist white man on the upper Missouri, it would be more prudent to trade mostly with the Canadian people so long as their goods were of high quality and readily available. This decision, it was agreed, should be explained to the Flatheads' allies.

"We will listen to Gun." At the head chief's announcement, Gun straightened up from his seated position before he spoke for the first time.

"Tjolzhitsay," he said, "sent me to our kinsmen and friends to the north and the west: The Pend d'Oreille, Kalispel, Spokan, Coeur d'Alene, Palouse, Okinogan and others. They, too, are of a mind to trade with the Canadians. Perhaps this should be with the North West Company. Much of what our friends told us about David Thompson is also what Little Bear Claw has related."

Has Many Horses spoke: "The fur companies are beginning to number the tribes of the people." Little Bear Claw glanced across the council lodge at Little Coyote, an almost undetectable grin on his face. "There is what they call Missouri Fur Company, the North West Company, the Hudson's Bay Company. I recall no names of the men who traded us the guns on our first two trips. Are there others?"

"There is another!" The strong voice of Bad Leg of the Nez Percé reached all in the lodge. When Tjolzhitsay, too, detected a hesitancy in the guest's voice, he motioned for Bad Leg to continue to speak.

"Otter is a sub-chief to Comcomly of the Chinook near where the Columbia River flows into the great salt water to the west," Bad Leg said. "Otter carried information only a moon ago to the Yakima people when he sought more horses with shells and smoked fish. The Yakima carried the information when he sought a great stud from our people. The information is that there now is a trading post at the mouth of the Columbia. The American Fur Company put it there. They bring good trade goods in great canoes with white sails."

"This, too, is of importance. We are grateful." Tjolzhitsay nodded in appreciation.

"And there is more," Bad Leg continued. "I have learned it from the Canadian Michel Bourdon, who with Finan McDonald helped you fight the Piegan. He will travel to the great salt water to the west in a few moons. David Thompson will send him there to learn more about this American Fur Company. Even now it is planning to send fur-takers among us from up the Missouri, as does Lisa. They will call themselves Pacific Fur Company. More I do not know."

Tjolzhitsay shook his head wonderingly. The council members long would remember his closing statement: "What white man calls 'Indians' fight for their buffalo. Now, perhaps, white man will fight for the Indians' furs."

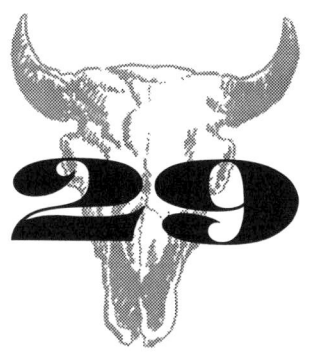

L ittle Coyote heard Lance's tiny feet scuffle across the hard-packed lodge floor and the brushing of the entry flap as the child went outside, then returned. Antelope spoke quietly and approvingly to their son, then rose from the furs. When the two went outdoors together, perhaps to the creek, Little Coyote closed his eyes and again tried to sleep. The council had met until late the previous evening listening to the Canadian Michel Bourdon and discussing what lay ahead. Much had happened since Bourdon had told Bad Leg of the Nez Percé that David Thompson would send him to the distant mouth of the Columbia River to learn about the Pacific Fur Company. Thompson, himself, had gone and had taken others, including Bourdon.

"The Americans are building a post there," Bourdon had explained to the council. "When we returned here, we traveled part-way with some of them who will build a post on the Okanogan. I think they will come closer here to trade. With many wanting the furs, Thompson wishes to try a bold move. He would have the Flatheads and their allies and the Blackfeet make peace. This would give him the trade from both, and—" Tjolzhitsay had motioned for silence when the lodge filled with angry voices at this revelation. Bourdon had hurried to complete his statement. "He would require the Blackfeet to promise access to the buffalo for the Flatheads and their friends, no warring, and also would provide the Blackfeet with weapons and other trade goods they most want and need." Again Tjolzhitsay had stemmed an eruption of dissent, insisting that only one at a time give his counsel.

Long after the night mists had appeared above the river and the moon had disappeared as a silvery crescent behind the mountains to the southwest, all had been heard. Little Coyote had spoken in favor of the view of the head chief and most of the sub-chiefs: They believed the Flathead people should try to make the peace. Despite strong hearts, brave deeds, good weapons and strategy, which wondrously had brought the people together, their numbers slowly were being reduced; this likely would continue so long as they sought the buffalo by taking perilous risks.

White Buffalo Calf long ago had lost the power to reach minds with his oratorical skills, but his thoughts had held much wisdom—most likely because he bore the name of the rare animal his parents had seen at the buffalo grounds so long ago. He had stood, small and wizened, leaning on a staff from the flexible willow tree.

"I have thought long on this," he had begun in a high, cracked voice that was even harder to understand because most of his teeth were gone. "I think of the many elk, deer, goats, other animals and fish the Good Spirit has kept in our valley most of the time. There is enough here for all because they continue to breed, and we kill no more than we can use. And it is good that we must work hard to kill them, for then, we value them more. But . . ." He paused and appeared to have forgotten where he was. ". . . as I think back, I see the faces of many of our people the Blackfeet sent to the land of perpetual summer because we sought the buffalo. Should we remain here, hunt to the south, north and west of here, but no longer go to the best buffalo grounds? We know that the beaver once were as great a people as ourselves, but displeased the Good Spirit and became what they are. And they are fewer here because we pursue them in greater numbers to trade for the white man's marvels. Do we, too, displease the Good Spirit? Do we risk His wrath by trading our lives for the buffalo? Perhaps if we stay here we will not need to deal at all with the Blackfeet or the white man."

White Buffalo Calf's arms and legs had shaken like young aspens in a strong breeze. Yet he had continued to stand there before the council for the responses that came in a storm: All insisted the people must have the buffalo. It meant their life. And how could the people obtain white man's guns, ammunition and his many marvels if the people did not deal with him while others did so?

Again the old man had straightened, though the arms and legs continued to shake: "I was not there at Lisa's fort. Yet I am told the white men obtained buffalo robes in trades with our people. I am told that in their eagerness to obtain white man's marvels, some of our people killed cows and young bulls near there for their hides, to make into robes, and left the meat for our brother coyote and other animals." The old man had raised his head and face skyward. "Our world changes. Perhaps I am too old, too tired to provide wise counsel, but the buffalo is sacred to us. It has a life. We should not take that life unless we use all of the buffalo, except for the older bulls. This has been for as long as I can remember and I have been told. What do we tell our sons? What pattern will they follow? I . . ." Again he had faltered, searching for the words. "I have strayed like the untethered horse here, but these thoughts must be a part of our thinking now and in the future. I say them now because I know that soon, even before the first leaves fall from the trees, I will be gone to join our people in the land of perpetual summer."

Out of respect, and perhaps because many of those present had had some of these thoughts, there had been no arguments with him as he was helped to sit down.

Tjolzhitsay's stern face had softened momentarily: "We have your thoughts, White Buffalo Calf. My father and his father often expressed their gratitude after you provided wise counsel. I thank you, too."

Other voices had spoken more directly to the proposed peace

conference. Finally, all had agreed there must be consultations with their allies before a group would leave for the meeting in the second month of the white man's 1812, the date Thompson had given Bourdon. But the meeting was almost eight moons away, leaving much time for such planning, much time for other activities.

Lance, no doubt encouraged by Antelope, sat atop his father's head. "Today I ride! Today I ride!" he piped joyously, meanwhile moving downward onto Little Coyote's shoulders. Little Coyote's sleepy objections scarcely could be heard, because now the tot was bouncing up and down on his parent's chest. Little Coyote reached up and seized this chubby lump of torment and wrestled him under his legs to hold him prisoner despite the boy's strenuous efforts to break off his father's great and little toes and free himself.

"Perhaps you want much more tender meat in the pot!" Little Coyote winced, loosened the hold, stood, then held the squirming, delighted child above the pot like a great crayfish. The simmering food soon enticed them all to eat and to share with their newly acquired guest, Little Bear Claw.

"Throw him in the creek if he takes your instruction poorly!" Little Coyote shouted after the departing Lance and Little Bear Claw when the meal was over. Seated proudly on Not Afraid of Guns, Lance glanced backward now and then to be certain his parents were watching.

Antelope was first to reach the small plateau overlooking part of the valley. She had tethered her Appaloosa and was sitting on a blanket, chewing a dry grass stem and feigning boredom— as though from a long wait—when her husband halted his matching light gray horse nearby. When his restless mount snorted, Antelope looked up as though startled. She shaded her eyes with one hand against warm Sun.

"I worried," she said. "Had my father's gift horse broken a leg? Perhaps you became lost." There was much concern in her voice, yet laughter in her eyes, when she lowered her hand as horse and rider shaded her. "I thought you were impatient to sit with me here while we watch our son's instruction."

"You did not follow the old trail through the trees," he responded accusingly. "Rather, you directed your horse almost straight upward after you passed the turn in the trail."

"And you were fearful lest you fall. So you chose the easier trail as would an old woman afoot gathering firewood. Come, sit beside me and rest from your ordeal." She set aside her over/under gun and patted the blanket, then held up her arms.

Little Coyote leaped down. They wrestled momentarily, both breathing hard until their dark-spotted horses nickered and swiveled their ears toward the ground.

"There are three horses." Little Coyote stood and peered downward. "Lance, Little Bear Claw and . . . yes, the warrior, Willow Woman." Antelope arose quickly, adjusting her soft buckskin dress and shaking down her braids. She pulled the blanket to the rim of the plateau. There, while holding hands, they focused their attention on their son while singing meadow larks perched atop scrub trees and the soft sighs of a slight breeze rose from the warming valley floor.

Back and forth, back and forth in the space between Little Bear Claw and Willow Woman, Lance directed Not Afraid of Guns. The horse walked, loped and, at length, galloped. Lance bounced perilously at times, but the boy, now two and one-half, clung tenaciously to the horse. Only the heads of the parents moved—back and forth, back and forth, until a field sparrow settled nearby and began piping its querulous "tsee tsee" as though to tell these two strange creatures there was much of importance to do this spring day.

Soon Lance was riding in a wide circle around his instructors. His whoops of delight and encouragement to speed up the horse reached his parents' ears. At length, Little Bear Claw held up his hand to signal the end of instruction. As Lance obediently brought his horse to the man and woman, Little Bear Claw raised his arm in recognition of the two onlookers. Soon the trio began riding upward, Little Bear Claw in the lead, then Lance and Willow Woman. The latter gripped her horse's barrel with strong legs and thighs as it dug its forelegs tentatively, then deeply, into some gravel and dirt loosened by the others. Soon they were looking downward at the still-seated parents. Willow Woman's hair, roughly cut in mourning for her dead Eagle Claw, had been trimmed evenly. Once again she was smiling—shyly, Little Coyote thought. The shyness seemed unusual for such a notable warrior mother of two children. And that face of Little Bear Claw! Little Coyote noted with satisfaction that it almost was that of a youth who was standing for the first time in a blanket with a maiden.

There was momentary silence after the greetings. Then impatient Lance dug his heels into Not Afraid of Guns. The horse trotted to the edge of the plateau, then broke into a run. The adults laughed as horse and boy performed.

Little Bear Claw spoke approvingly to the child when he returned. Lance's bright eyes darted to the faces of all four for their reactions.

"He cannot master a less-compliant horse, but rides well and is seemingly fearless—too much so," Little Bear Claw said. "But a few falls, a few bumps, will remedy that. Perhaps in another summer he will be ready to ride a horse that is not so skilled, so compliant. Then will come instruction with the bow and arrows, the lance, riding to the side of the animal. There will be more bumps—and growing wisdom. Perhaps he, too, will become a horse guard at an early age."

The family watched the sub-chief and warrior woman descend the far side of the plateau and begin riding up a higher one. Then Little Coyote, Antelope and Lance descended and raced toward the encampment for a summer of much rest and an autumn and winter Running Buffalo Bull and Little Yellow Bird long would remember as the most joyous since their own son had been the age of fast-growing Lance.

Antelope unrolled the supple, tanned elk hide, bleached almost white by much effort with carefully gathered fungi and repeated consultations with Little Yellow Bird. With the awl she had earned caring for John Colter, she punched more of the evenly spaced holes along the hide's edge. She inserted a thong through these. She stretched the hide to almost drumhead tautness on a large and strong willow frame, then coated it with beaver-tail glue. During her travels she had filled her tiny, cylindrical, birch bark boxes with paint powders. Included were yellow from exposed zones of heavily mineralized earth along the river banks; black from charred wood and other mineral finds; green from lake scum and the rims of hot springs, and clay pounded when dry, then roasted, till red.

Antelope showed her handiwork to a surprised and pleased Little Coyote one cold, blustery day of the second winter after their return from Three Forks. As he inspected the hide and some drawing instruments made from splinters of porous buffalo bone and dry willow, Antelope explained her plan.

"I watched you closely when you examined the painted robes at the Mandan village and the robes of the visiting Crow story-teller at Lisa's fort," she said. "Your shield shows good work, as do the designs on our lodge. You often have marveled at the symbols you have watched white men use. Later you will learn to use those if, as you and the council say, white man always will be with us. But now you must make drawings that show your life this far."

Little Coyote did not begin at once. Rather, he gave the matter much thought, then experimented on birch bark and scrap pieces of hide. He even drew smaller figures on some of white man's paper that Benito Vasquez had wrapped around the medicines in the chest for which the seer had traded.

"No, no," Antelope scolded. She lifted the scrap of leather into the better light from the smoke hole. "Paint smaller figures. You will use up all the space on the elk hide before you tell about coming down from the mountain after your quest." She examined the stick figure of a youth. "How thin, how woefully thin! Can you not give him a belly, strong legs and arms? Other parts?" She laughed. "Surely you were more of a man than that, even then."

Little Coyote looked up at this lovable tormenter. With much gravity he announced that the stick figure would represent himself only until Shining Shirt had given him his name. Thereafter, as on the shield, a little coyote would be his representation.

"Very well," Antelope said. "I hope that, like our most notable Shoshone seer, you will start your life story in the center of the hide, telling it in a circular fashion in ever enlarging circles."

"That would be an improvement over those I have seen," Little Coyote said. "And the figures must be small, though perhaps I shall have a short life so should use larger ones."

"A long life," Antelope corrected. "Perhaps mine shall be the short one."

Again Little Coyote looked upward. He bit his inner lip, musing at Antelope's thought. A gust of wind shook the lodge and moved the smoke flap until some of the light died.

"Enough of this for now." He stood, enfolding this greatest luck of his life in his arms. He was reluctant to let go even when Little Yellow Bird sang out her approach with Lance. The child dashed into the lodge holding up a tiny bow and a quiver of blunt arrows. Running Buffalo Bull had fashioned them during the winter days. They surely portended future howls from offended, long-suffering dogs until, at last, with sharp-tipped points, birds, grouse and perhaps even a rabbit would fall before his son's growing prowess with the ancient form of weapon.

Lance slept peacefully, his bow and arrows nearby. Antelope lay sleeping beside Little Coyote, one arm thrown across his waist. He could smell the familiar dog fennel and meadow rue aromas in her long hair. As he reviewed the day's activities, one thought above all others held Little Coyote's attention. It was prompted, undoubtedly, by the discussion of how long a life must be portrayed on the hide, and perhaps by aged White Buffalo Calf's wisdom and the certainty he soon would die.

How long is a life? What is its central aim? Little Coyote found himself marveling that, despite the dangers besetting the people on all sides, the younger, like himself, gave the subject much less thought than did the elders. The elders, while not fearing death, wished at least for a heroic one when it would come. And, surely, honorable fear must be for family rather than for self, even among the young. It seemed unnecessary even to question that only the honorable and significant should be portrayed on the hide. Did it not follow, then, that one's actions should be honorable and significant for *all* to see, for oneself to *know*? Thus he could comprehend that his people, who were not averse at all to telling of one's deeds, did insist on accuracy—truth.

Cold Wind, knowing he was dying from the Blackfeet arrow so long ago on that first trek for guns, had summarized his life in his death song. He had not cheated or lied. He obeyed his chiefs. He was no thief. He had cared for the young and the old. Indeed, in his dying breath, he acknowledged he had lived by the code the people had developed and tried to follow since, perhaps, they had sprung from Coyote.

Little Coyote nodded his head in the darkness. *Yes, there is an aloneness at death as one departs unaccompanied to the place of perpetual summer.* How could he comprehend that aloneness?

For a moment he pondered his aloneness before he had met Antelope, the greater aloneness before they had become mates. Now he tried to feel aloneness with Antelope and Lance gone. *Too much to bear!* He stirred restlessly and shifted thoughts, knowing that at this stage of his life he must ponder these matters more deeply, again and again.

Much thought must be given to Thompson's hope to make peace. Much effort, too. He fell into restless sleep while trying to think of the arguments all parties would present for or against the effort. The decision was a long way off, but the matter demanded some part of his attention in the interim. He would convey the results of his deliberations to those who would make the decision.

Little Coyote and others who had heard so much about David Thompson from an enthusiastic Little Bear Claw were disappointed at first when the Canadian met with a large group of the people just beyond the north end of their valley. The meeting followed an unsuccessful peace conference with the Blackfeet. Most of the others who had participated in the conference had continued on to the buffalo grounds. Has Many Horses would be the leader until the others returned.

Thompson had an unexpectedly short, heavy body and a small nose resembling that of the mountain man, Tull. Unlike Tull, Thompson's hair was neatly cut—straight across his forehead. The Canadian gained stature in the minds of the people when he proved he could move his body surprisingly fast. Thompson was breathing easily when, together with several Flatheads and others, he climbed a high hill and had his new acquaintances point out the features of their country. He carefully noted on paper what he saw.

"And the river's name?" he asked.

"*In-mis-sou-let-ka*, the River of Awe," Michel Bourdon replied, pointing east and west.

"Clark Fork of the Columbia now, named after the Americans' Captain Clark," Thompson commented dryly. "I meant the one flowing in from the south."

"*Oot-la-shoots*," Little Coyote said. He was proud because he understood the question and could answer, and also because his people cherished the name they had given it.

So Thompson marked it down, and the seer liked him even more. Thompson asked a few more questions about the route Clark and Lewis had taken in this region. Then, satisfied, he led the return from the hill.

That night around a large fire, Thompson explained to those who did not already know why the attempt for a truce with the Blackfeet had failed. He spoke quietly, forcefully and slowly so Bourdon could translate as accurately as possible.

"When I was a young man of seventeen summers," Thompson said, "I spent an entire winter with the Piegan. I was the only white man there. I learned much about them, including their talk and their way of doing things. I have much respect for them as fiercely independent and brave warriors." A low murmur of dissent arose from some of the listeners, causing Thompson to stand up beside his translator and hold his flat hands, backs up, out in front of his body as high as his shoulders, fingers pointing forward. As he slowly lowered his hands, people did as politely requested; they quieted down, whereupon Bourdon continued translating. "As I said, I have much respect for them as fiercely independent and brave warriors, just as I can agree with all white men who have met the Flatheads that you are the most hard-working, chaste and peaceful of the tribes until challenged. Then you prove yourselves as brave warriors with great wisdom to guide you in battle.

"Did not the Piegan agree they wanted peace so all could prosper?" Thompson asked those in the group who had attended the meeting. After their murmur of agreement, Thompson added, "The truce failed because the Piegan honorably could not promise that all the Blackfeet would abide by it, because they could not inform them all at once."

Has Many Horses was seated near Little Coyote and Little Bear Claw. His voice rose above the crackling of additional wood thrown on the fire: "The Blackfeet also said they do not want white men or others to intrude on 'their' hunting grounds or challenge their freedom."

Thompson nodded in agreement. He continued to speak quietly, forcefully and, his listeners generally conceded, sincerely: "There are advantages to living in peace. Thus, you can travel, hunt for food, enjoy your freedom untouched by mourning in the lodges for those lost in warring." Now the trader, a detectable note of sadness in his voice, spoke more slowly yet until he was certain Bourdon had worked out the translation. "I can tell you there will be another great war between the Americans and British as there was only thirty-seven summers ago. At least for a time, we British will control most of the trade in this region. It will be advantageous to continue to trade with the North West Company."

"I know this Thompson well," Little Bear Claw said softly. "I believe he sincerely wishes peace among the tribes. How strange that as the white men urge peace among the Indians, the trappers from the different companies fight among themselves to get the furs, and the different countries prepare for war."

Has Many Horses turned toward Little Bear Claw. His face remained calm. His ears had heard and he nodded his agreement. And Little Coyote, pondering these things, commented so quietly that even his two companions' ears did not hear: "Yes, and I think now they all want what the Indians have."

Thompson's next words were surprising: "Soon I will put our furs in our canoes and start down the Inmissouletka River for Canada. I will not return, but I will wish that peace efforts among white men and your peoples will continue. Not just for trade purposes. This also is the wish of the Great Spirit who is above us all."

Bourdon's, Thompson's and White Buffalo Calf's predictions came true. That caused Little Coyote to ponder further the differences between *predictions* drawn from a growing amount of knowledge and *prophesies*, which for some seemingly emerged from little knowledge—or none at all.

Wide-ranging Bourdon, himself, soon brought word that the Pacific Fur Company had built a post at the junction of the distant Spokane and Little Spokane rivers near the North West Company's Spokan House. The company also planned to establish other posts closer to the Flathead trade.

Other white men, mostly Canadians, usually in small parties and often accompanied by a few Indians from far-away tribes, drifted through the region of the Flatheads that spring and summer of 1812. One such group from the east confirmed that the Americans and the British once more were at war.

As the trees began to lose their leaves soon after White Buffalo Calf died, fourteen Pacific Fur Company men headed by sub-chiefs Russell Farnham and Ross Cox—the latter approximately Little Coyote's age—arrived at a temporary and small Flathead encampment near Saleesh House. Immediately the men began to build a tiny cabin to house their fourteen horseloads of goods. The goods were of substantial quality, and as more Flatheads arrived they eagerly traded twenty beaver pelts for a good gun and fifteen for a smaller. They considered one beaver for a foot of cloth much too dear.

The Flatheads sought the firearms for good reason. Those at Saleesh House were gone—obtained before Finan McDonald, the sub-chief then in charge of that post, had accompanied them on their buffalo hunt east of the Rocky Mountains. An attack by the Blackfeet had resulted in the loss of much of the needed meat and, more importantly, the deaths of several warriors. Gun, his long face more dejected looking than ever, had lost his wife—taken prisoner with several other women. His brief, ominous and chillingly worded, "They must and will pay," left no doubt about his future intentions.

Tjolzhitsay and the council named the grieving sub-chief to lead the next late autumn's hunt. Gun and the chief carefully prepared their plans. Tjolzhitsay suggested they leave the valley by the more northerly route. Few women and children would accompany them. They would encourage their allies to do the same, yet remain separate, hidden as well as possible, but always close by. The Flatheads would entice the Blackfeet to attack, whereupon the Blackfeet would become surrounded by three forces. Now Gun explained the hunt.

"We, too, shall take prisoners," he promised, "then hunt for meat. The prisoners will help prepare the meat and carry it back as far as Saleesh House. There are ways to encourage their help. And we shall bring back some of them so all our people will have their revenge."

Tjolzhitsay named Little Bear Claw to remain in the valley with the few warriors, older men, women and children.

"The warrior woman, Willow Woman, will help you, unless you have objections," Tjolzhitsay declared. Then, after the laughter had died, he asked, "And will Little Coyote remain, too?"

The chief's request disappointed Little Coyote, who thought he should participate in the important hunt and that he would be needed in any major battle. The seer was gratified he was achieving a special position among the people. Though he gave this much thought, he could not foresee that he would need all such recognition and support possible after the hunt. Nor could he foresee that the man named Ross Cox would become his momentary ally as they strove with some success to change one dark way of the people.

By now Little Coyote had become almost as certain as were others that the Good Spirit had, indeed, endowed him with powers—powers he did not fully understand, powers that were weak in some ways, powers that were extraordinarily strong in others. With the passing of time he had learned to contemplate these powers and use the resultant insights in ways he believed were good. Also, he no longer displayed his concentration externally, such as his earlier habit of hanging his head and becoming almost oblivious to other people or events about him. He had concluded he possessed perhaps two minds, as undoubtedly did others, but his "sleeping" one was more powerful than the "awake" one, though he and others used the latter most often. Yes, somehow through the kindness of the Good Spirit, his "sleeping" one was awakening in ways that puzzled, at times even frightened, him.

Thus it was that in *s'tcé-ei*, the eleventh moon of Autumn, as he sat astride Not Afraid of Guns on a small hill and with his spyglass looked for game, he impulsively reversed the instrument. Now objects became much smaller, more distant, his field of view more circumscribed. Strangely, then, as he pondered this discovery and lowered the glass, his view of the valley narrowed and almost disappeared; his thoughts of things now, of events past, also narrowed almost to nothingness. Yet, he clearly saw John Colter—the ready grin, the easy manner, the strong spirit, the friendly nature of his white brother—as though the seer was looking through the correct end of a far more powerful instrument. Was Colter once again waving farewell as he had done to those in the fort at Three Forks? Was he disappearing into the nearby trees, forever from Little Coyote's sight? Now John Colter became smaller, more distant, smaller still, and the view was gone. For a moment the seer saw nothing at all. He blinked his eyes. He shook his head and once more became aware of the white valley below him. It seemed to become drab and gray when he knew with certainty that John Colter was dead.

Early in the twelfth moon of the Continuous Snow, Bourdon hastened back from the killing grounds with word the Flathead people had won a great victory over the Blackfeet. With Chief Tjolzhitsay's guidance, but with Gun's continuing authority as chief of the hunt, the people had taken many prisoners and obtained much meat. Little Bear Claw carefully divided those who would remain in the valley and those who would trek with him to Saleesh House with furs and pack horses to do much trading while they awaited the arrival of the victors.

When the people under Little Bear Claw arrived at Saleesh House, the victorious warriors and their prisoners already were there. With the furs brought from the valley, the Flatheads immediately traded for all the goods a man named James McMillan possessed. McMillan had replaced McDonald as sub-chief at Saleesh House in the year since the then-defeated Flatheads last had camped nearby. The Indians became apprehensive that McMillan had so little powder and lead because they feared a reprisal raid by Blackfeet eager to free their kinsmen.

"Twelve horseloads of goods, including much powder and lead, will be here in two or three days," McMillan reassured the Flatheads.

On the twenty-fourth sun of the twelfth moon, eight men arrived. They were under the leadership of Ross Cox, who, though tired from the difficult trek through the forests and snow, appeared to revel in his role as leader. Cox somewhat pompously asked that the people be called together, at which time, with Bourdon's help, he explained that he now was a North West Company man because the war had forced the Pacific Fur Company at Astoria to sell to the Canadians or be destroyed.

"Tomorrow there will be no trading," McMillan explained while the Flatheads moved about impatiently. "Every winter on the twenty-fifth day of the twelfth moon we celebrate our most important religious event. The event was the Great Spirit sending his son to earth to help the spirits of all peoples."

So on the day of Cox's arrival, and on the next, the Flatheads, out of respect for white man's religion, curbed their impatience to trade. They found diversions while the whites began to feast and sing in the comfortable log house adjoining the trading room.

The Flatheads also feasted and told the details of their victory over the Blackfeet. They paused once in their activities to watch Gun, helped by two younger warriors, spread-eagle a naked

Blackfeet maiden on a plot of ground cleared of snow. While the encampment watched, twenty eager, unmarried braves repeatedly raped her.

The white men's hymns dealing with the arrival of the Prince of Peace drifted from the post and mixed with the maiden's agonized screams until a distraught Little Coyote and Antelope left their lodge and rode into the nearby heavily wooded hills. Their horses followed the trail of a lone horse. Where the trail ended they found Cox seated on a log, his rather heavy face twisted in sorrow, his stout body jerking as though he still could hear the captive's cries. When he became aware of the couple's presence, he pulled his fur cap from his almost-shaven head so he would hear their reply to his anguished question: "What can we do? What can we do?"

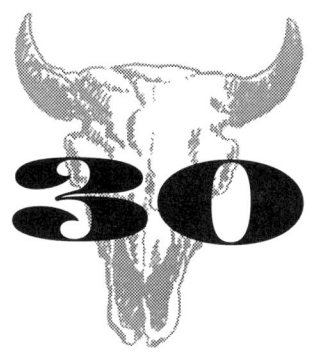

C ox's heavy jaw was set as he prepared to ride back to Saleesh House by a route different from Little Coyote's and Antelope's. Antelope, with Lance in tow, quickly walked over to talk to Little Yellow Bird; she arrived at the older woman's lodge as Running Buffalo Bull casually headed for the noisy center of encampment activities. In his own lodge, Little Coyote quickly filed off the edge of his sheath knife until it would not cut even a fawn's liver. Then he seized Shining Shirt's medicine staff and began walking toward the noise. He passed two old women muttering their displeasure at having to drag the mutilated, partially frozen corpse of the Blackfeet maiden toward the nearest woods. The girl's scalped head bumped over the snow-covered tussocks, it and her chest area bloodily marking her zig-zag passage like that of a gutted deer. The old women returned quickly since much entertainment was in progress. Little Coyote recognized them as two who long ago had lost their mates and sons and had not again found favor in other men's eyes.

Eager warriors had chopped the lower branches from a pine tree near the encampment, leaving one stout branch pointing south and another north at the same level. In a rare practice reserved only for slaves, they had tied an older Blackfeet sub-chief to this cruciform. To further humiliate and torture him, they had slashed off his genitals and suspended them from his neck to mid-chest level for a target of sorts. Lest he bleed to death from this butchery, someone, most likely with a heated hatchet head, had cauterized the wound between his spraddled legs. The Blackfeet was dead, his body transfixed by numerous arrows.

Fortunate, too, in contrast to a yet-living older warrior who was tightly tied to the base of the tree. His foot and arm tendons were severed, so only his bonds held him upright.

"We caught them like dumb grouse as they sought to defend the women and children," a warrior exulted at a nearby fire. He was heating an old musket barrel that had held a large food pot over the flames. When the upper half of the barrel glowed, the warrior lifted it with a tree bark and fur pad in his mittened hands and carried it toward the wretched prisoner. All talk ceased as the torturer pressed the metal against the man's genitals until they sizzled and popped. When there was no outcry, the torturer reheated the iron and rubbed it over other portions of the Blackfeet's body until they steamed in the cold air. The Flathead carefully avoided injuring the Blackfeet's throat and lips. The body jerked against its bonds, but the expected screams did not emerge. One by one, then, various warriors tore out the man's fingernails; when there still was no outcry, they hacked off his fingers and threw them into the fire.

At last the victim shouted. All could hear.

"You are ignorant of torture! We torture your kin far better until they cry like babies, then scream like wounded horses. You are not *men!*" The body winced as one warrior sought to stop this outcry or change its message by adding the seared genitals and most of the chopped-off toes to the fire. "You are old women who cannot fight! My arrow blinded that two-legged dog!"

One Eye leaped forward with his knife and gouged out one of the Blackfeet's eyes. He cast it into the hungry flames before chopping the blade downward. Now the victim's nose hung over his lips.

He fixed his bloody stare on one of the nearest warriors: "I know you. I scalped your father. Was it your brother I killed as he sought to protect the older dog?" The offended warrior strode to the victim, grasped his long, silver-and-black braids and carefully cut around his head at hairline level. Those closest could hear the sucking "schlooop-schlooop" as he wrenched off the scalp. He prepared to stab the sufferer, but an alert Gun stepped forward and roughly stayed his arm.

The apparition still held his head high, blood flowing down the spectral, deeply sagging and folded features. Little Coyote stepped forward to saw his dulled, useless knife blade across the creature's bloody shoulder. Powerlessly he looked into the man's grotesque face, almost forgetting for the moment his purpose as he sought a recognizable semblance of a human being. Then he caught the eye, and stared deeper, ever deeper, into this bloody orb that seemed to mirror all the suffering the seer had observed in his yet-short lifetime on earth. At that moment he thought crazily that, perhaps, at approaching death the spirit fled to the eyes for a last look at this world before it entered the air, because that is what he would remember with near certainty for the remainder of his life, that is what he saw here. And now so quickly the bloody eye began to grow dull.

Now Little Coyote remembered: "Insult sub-chief Gun. Tell how you tortured his wife, and you will die quickly, Blackfeet," he hissed into the oddly hanging ears. He stepped back and shakily wiped the knife blade and his hands through a small patch of untrammeled snow.

The human wreck was defiant still, the seemingly over-sized lips hanging loosely downward and away from the teeth.

"You, Gun." The words came slowly, blubberingly. "Your wife . . . my prisoner . . . after your defeat. She could not cry . . . no tongue. Not see . . . no eyes. Younger warriors used her . . . like a bitch dog in heat. She—"

Gun's pistol ball stilled the Blackfeet at last.

The two old women carried and kicked firebrands to the base of the tree and added more fuel. The fire burned upward and through the bonds of the two corpses. The bodies fell into the flames. The women stepped toward the now-smaller group of prisoners. Amid an ever spreading pall of stinking smoke, they scrutinized the remaining females, then jerked the most comely forward and tore off her garments. Her body of perhaps fifteen summers shivered from apprehension; her eyes stared from her tear- and dirt-streaked face. One of the four remaining Blackfeet warriors, his arms bound behind him, tried to interpose his body between the girl and the crones. The younger whipped and jabbed him repeatedly between the legs with her stout staff; the other beat him about the head until he fell almost senseless to the trampled snow.

"Are you men?" the older hag shouted to the younger braves, three of whom dragged the whimpering girl toward the stakes. Others began jostling for their places in line.

Again a pistol boomed. This time it was Cox's. He was astride his horse. He placed the pistol in his belt, then put his hands on the saddle horn. Bourdon stood beside him to translate.

"You have told McMillan and me you torture as do all the Indians!" Cox said so all could hear. "You have told me white men are womanish not to do so. You have told me you must have your revenge, as your enemies seek theirs. I tell you again, white warriors do not torture. They kill, true, in battles. You have seen this. They have helped you. I tell you white men believe it is womanish to torture people who cannot defend themselves!"

A resentful murmur swept up to the horseman. Cox blinked, but his voice remained strong and he gripped the saddle horn until his unmittened knuckles whitened.

"White men believe it offends the Great Spirit to torture helpless people. On this most important religious day we cannot permit it."

"Careful, white man!" One of the eager braves near the head of the line fumbled momentarily at his crotch, then stepped forward. He seized his knife and began walking toward Cox.

"I see only a heated-up brave, courageous, I am sure, but have you no seer to respond to this religious question? I tell you, if you continue this practice here, we will not supply you with our trade goods! We will leave with them and never return!"

Bourdon looked upward apprehensively as he interpreted this threat. His eyes rolled; shaking his head, he relayed his misgivings. There were audible mutterings, most coming from the now-broken line of braves.

Cox took his hands off the saddle horn.

"White man!"

Little Coyote stepped between the disappointed men and the beleaguered Cox and Bourdon. The other watching whites backed into the post.

"White man!" Little Coyote shouted again. "I say we must respect your view of the white man's religion. I also ask that if our chiefs tell us not to seek revenge upon these dogs, will you trade the powder and lead and guns, else perhaps the Blackfeet will be doing this." He swept his arm to encompass them all.

"No! No!" The oldest woman pointed at the Blackfeet. "All must die, and at our pleasure!" She stepped to the brave still holding his knife and facing Cox and Bourdon. She showed her contempt for the young man by thrusting her middle and index fingers toward his face. Then, overcome in her rage, she shouted, "Has your manhood shrunken to this?" She grasped at his crotch. In his surprise and pain at this grievous insult, the brave dropped his knife. The hag pounced on it and stumblingly moved toward the staked-out Blackfeet girl.

"No, old woman! The people's needs come before the individual's." Gun seized her by the hair and threw her to the ground. He looked for Cox and, not seeing him, jabbed his finger toward Bourdon. "We will talk. It is the wish of Tjolzhitsay."

Cox emerged from the trading room with a five-gallon keg of rum, one of three he had brought with the trading goods.

"No, white man! There will be no firewater." Gun's long face shook with passion as he shouted at Cox and wrestled the knife from the hag.

Seemingly crestfallen, Cox lugged the keg back toward the post, hazarding a quick look at Little Coyote in passing.

There had been a commensurate loss of face. Talks could begin on somewhat equal terms. The old women dragged the female corpse back from the woods and tumbled it atop those of the two men. Before the talks started, the shivering prisoners watched their reduction into ashes.

Tjolzhitsay impassively listened as the council members repetitiously recounted the people's long and widely known suffering at the hands of the Blackfeet. Outside the lodge the two old women repeatedly brought other people to shout their demands that the captives die. A concerted, loud, angry howl of protest caused the chief to motion for Running Buffalo Bull to determine the reason.

"McMillan feeds the Blackfeet," Running Buffalo Bull explained. "He has given them some robes. In our language he has learned among us he said, 'Tjolzhitsay has decreed the torture stop. Lack of food, drink and robes is torture. I follow your head chief's orders.'"

The chief wonderingly shook his head: "Tell McMillan we will hear him and Cox."

Cox spoke, McMillan translated after they had set down a seemingly heavy box, a small cup, a pot and a bag: "Your friend Thompson sought a truce between the Flatheads, their allies, and their enemies, the Blackfeet. This almost came about. You know why it failed. Yet, the willingness was there."

So all could see, Cox put the cup and the pot on the box. From the bag he filled both with the largest and most treasured blue trade beads.

"You see. Two Blackfeet die." He removed two beads from the pot and placed them in the bag. "Only one Flathead dies." He removed one bead from the cup. "Three Blackfeet die. One Flathead dies. Four Blackfeet die. One Flathead dies." And so he talked until the cup was empty. The pot remained almost full.

"Perhaps we can move your hearts to send the prisoners back to their people." The head chief's upraised hands stilled the outcry. "If you will provide them with poor food and your worst horses, in our gratitude we will give you trade goods for the best food, for the best horses, for we stand to gain by our continued trade with you." McMillan stopped translating, poured the pot of beads into the bag and passed it to the assemblage. He urged everyone to take an equal share.

"The words of the returning prisoners might change the

hearts of the Blackfeet now or in the future," Cox continued. "We cannot know, but if they were agreeable to a truce not long ago, do not kill that willingness by killing more Blackfeet prisoners. In battles, yes. Perhaps they will not kill prisoners in the future."

"Or not take prisoners at all," Gun grimly noted.

"Your bravery, your better battle plans have helped you till now," Cox responded. "Believing as we do that it offends the Great Spirit to torture and kill helpless prisoners, we reluctantly must say again that if you continue to do so, we must quit this place forever. If you do not torture and kill prisoners we will remain among you, and for your furs provide you with enough guns and powder and lead to hold off the Blackfeet and prevent them from taking you prisoner.

"I tell you this: You are hard workers; you are faithful to your mates; you do not lie; you are clean; you are honest; you follow your chiefs; you are wise and brave in battle. The Great Spirit will like you the better for not torturing and killing prisoners. Do you not believe this is true?"

"Little Coyote. What do you say?" Tjolzhitsay fixed his eyes on the young seer. Little Coyote stood. He had untied the scalps from the ancient lance and his shields and retied them to the full-length sleeves of his leather coat. They hung so all would see when he raised Shining Shirt's medicine staff above his head and looked to the sky as if for guidance, then lowered its butt to the floor.

"The Good Spirit told me repeatedly on my vision quest we never should fight the white man," Little Coyote said. "The Good Spirit has never given me a different message as we see more and more of the white men enter our lives. Our people have prospered since Shining Shirt's death. The Good Spirit has kept him with us. To not agree with the white men on this matter would be fighting him enough for him to leave us. We need to follow the Good Spirit's wishes."

"And we need white man's guns!" Running Buffalo Bull said loudly for all in the lodge to hear. "In every battle, we also lose guns."

Tjolzhitsay looked up, seemingly disapprovingly. He saw who spoke, then shrugged his shoulders. "Do you say more, Little Coyote?"

"I have spoken." Little Coyote was certain he detected an ever-so-slight look of relief.

"There will be no more torture. We will send the prisoners back to their lodges." Almost hastily, Tjolzhitsay put down his whip and nodded for McMillan to open the box. The trader hurriedly held up a short, brass-mounted flintlock weapon with a great muzzle flaring out from its large bore. It resembled the horn the Clark and Lewis people had carried through the valley.

"It is a blunderbuss from England," McMillan said. "It fires much powder, true, but also many bullets. We can supply both. There are five of them here, all with straps for easier holding over the shoulder. They require little aiming. Understandably, the Flatheads are reluctant to trap the many beaver by working singly or in pairs because, as you and the Lisa people learned too well, that is when the Blackfeet strike. Yet one man holding this gun has the firepower of many guns for short distances. I give four to Tjolzhitsay for all the people and one to Gun for his great loss and for knowing the people's needs come before the individual's. We would show how they fire."

Some remainders of roughly sawn boards were lined against the log wall of the trading room when the council members emerged from the lodge. The people who were clamoring outside quieted and forced the persistent old women to do the same.

Cox stood on the box and showed how to load the blunderbuss. "This much powder, a large wad of almost anything . . ." He seized a small handful of old, limp leaves that had blown against the wall before the snow had come. ". . . and now the bullets." He put in a handful. "Now more leaves to hold them in." He primed the pan and handed the weapon to the head chief. "Gun, will you load yours?" The sub-chief gravely did so.

Cox and McMillan motioned the quiet crowd to move back, particularly at both ends of the line. Tjolzhitsay placed the strap on his shoulder and cocked the flint lock. Grasping the gun by the short forestock and the stock near the butt plate, he pointed it almost at hip height toward the boards. The explosion twisted the weapon in the chief's hands. Gun's weapon did the same. When the pall of smoke cleared, all could see the devastation to the boards. Some people wonderingly stuck their fingers into the splintery holes; others picked out the misshapen bullets that had stuck in the logs behind and, at the suggestion of Three Eagles, saved them.

"They can be used again without being melted and recast," Tjolzhitsay's very observant and practical *i-sts-sókoi* pointed out.

One of McMillan's men carried out a keg of powder, another many bars of lead.

"We are grateful for your decision." McMillan and Cox shook the chief's hand. Even Gun's features broke into a reluctant grin. "Three Eagles is right. Also, if we run out of bullets when we fight the Blackfeet, and I know we will fight them, we can use rocks in necessity, or fire the guns with no bullets at all and escape in the smoke." The grin faded. "Have you traded any of these to the Blackfeet?" Now he, Three Eagles and Tjolzhitsay looked closely at both white men.

"No. We have kept but three for ourselves. We could obtain no more. They continue to be needed in England and on her great ships when they encounter dangerous men, too."

Running Buffalo Bull walked to the lodges with his son. That evening, as the two families discussed the important happenings that day, the older warrior quietly offered after a time to help his son work with the small file and stone to put a new edge on his badly dulled knife.

There was food aplenty in the valley when the people returned. Beaver pelts piled ever higher as small groups, under Three Eagles' direction, coordinated their trapping efforts. The groups moved greater distances and to more productive streams when protected by watchful guards, including those armed with one of the blunderbusses. The council agreed that with each family owning at least one gun now, most of the pelts could remain the property of the trapper.

There was yet another way to obtain trade goods. The arrival of Tull in company with five other men brought that about. He hadn't changed much. His longer hair covered the wound from the Blackfeet musket ball; his beard and mustache were more tobacco-stained. The same shrewd eyes peered from bushy brows, almost the only indication this was the face side of the mound of hair atop the leather-clad body. Tull was genuinely glad to see all members of Little Coyote's family; he stepped back after hugging them bearlike and looked them up and down.

"These be my fambly, sorta'," he proudly told his companions. "They's parts o' this kentry this hoss ain't seed, ner these t'others hyar. We figgered we'd go on our own, so ta speak. We c'd use some firepower goin' east this time 'n figgered you'd hep us out fr' some trade goods. Point is, you'uns ginerally know whar those Blackfeet sarpants *ain't*!"

So the bargain was struck, the practice started that would persist for more years than Little Coyote yet had lived. Before his departure, Tull withdrew a small roll of buckskin from his pack and carefully unrolled it.

"Henry, he sent it ta ya', Coyote. Got it he did on a trip ta St. Looey. Came from Colter. Chure bizness, but, wull, if'n they's parts ya' c'd share, wull . . ." Tull blurted it out. "I like the ol' hoss 'n I'd like ta know more'n Henry c'd tell, which war next ta nothin' seein' th' letter was giv' ta him f'm somebody else. Yep, still moughty curus ta hear what the ol' hoss is up ta. Now, Bonneau, hyar, he c'n read some." Tull pointed to the youngest of his five trappers.

That afternoon the three men and Antelope sat on a buffalo robe outside the lodge and in the wan afternoon light of the cheerless day worked out the contents of the brief message from John Colter:

Greetings to my brother, Little Coyote, and my sister, Antelope:

I miss you all and I long for your land of the shining mountains. I have come to think that our Great Spirit gave me some time there, then whisked me out alive so I would know what we call heaven is like—so I would live a better life to get there.

I have a mate now, too. A fine woman named Sally. She is carrying my child. We live north of the village of Charette at Sullens Spring near the mouth of Big Boeuf Creek close to St. Louis. Our lodge always will be open to you or yours if ever you come this way.

Now I look more Indian than you do—a yellow-colored Indian. My insides by the belly hurt, sometimes more than the musket ball that Blackfoot put in my leg.

The white medicine man here says I got the sickness from living in St. Louis and drinking water too close to a cess pool. Maybe so. I figure some cold water from one of those beaver streams, the sight of your mountains, and some fresh buffalo meat would set me right. If ever you or yours come here, we want to see you.

Your brother,

Another hand had written nine words under the signature:

He died, from jaundice. His son is Hiram.

Bonneau silently handed the letter to Tull and walked away. "Wull . . . wull, think o' that!"

The trio sat there until dim Sun had set behind the mountains near the great peak where Little Coyote had received his vision. A chill breeze came up almost immediately; as they moved inside Little Coyote peered briefly at the peak. He did not see, but he imagined Drouillard meeting John Colter to hand him a drink of cold water, show him the mountains and serve him some buffalo meat. There was a comfort there. *We have those things now,* he thought, then he entered the lodge where they would share their meat with Tull.

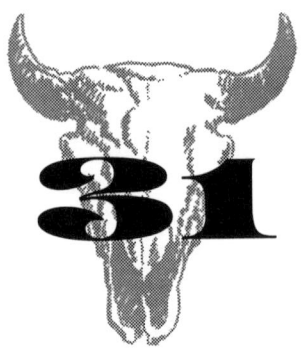

Little Coyote groped in the buffalo-hide bag until he felt the land turtle shell Lance had brought with him from the Saleesh House encampment nine summers earlier. So many changes, so long ago! The tiny symbols chronicling the time and events on his story hide encompassed one complete circle spiraling outward from the center like the mountain sheep skulls and horns now hanging from Not Afraid of Guns. Most symbols represented his own earliest and important activities starting with his vision quest, though the start of the second spiral contained representations of the equipment and activities of white man. The Blackfeet were much a part of that arc, too.

The Flathead people had performed no torture since that time at Saleesh House, though, as Gun had predicted, the battles with the Blackfeet had continued with increased ferocity. The Blackfeet no longer limited their raids into Flathead country while fiercely fighting all comers to the better buffalo grounds. Instead, their warriors were attacking wherever the white men appeared to take away the furs. Seemingly, that now was from every direction and by every means—keelboat, mackinaw, pirogue and canoe, horse and afoot. Only one summer earlier, the Hudson's Bay Company had taken over the North West Company. With greater strength it, too, was sending out many brigades of men to trade with the Indians, as well as to trap.

On this early day just before Sun had greeted the world, these matters remorselessly continued gnawing like a hungry beaver on the outer edge of the seer's "awake" mind as he studied for a final time the structure and form of the turtle shell before setting out for Shield Maker's lodge.

Not Afraid of Guns carefully picked her way through the favorite horses tethered near lodges, then watchful dogs, spare lodge poles, ropes, stones, hide and equipment racks, cooking fire sites, meat and fish drying beyond reach of dogs. All helped to remind the pinto's rider that he must talk carefully with Shield Maker. There was a matter of protocol.

He encountered but one of the people, sleepy-eyed, aging Bull Hump, whose gigantic, pendulous belly hung over his privates until they were almost as lost as wood ticks on the body of a horse. Heavy legs spread far apart, Bull Hump slowly dribbled—but he dribbled, like the start of a spring freshet at breakup. He was oblivious to Little Coyote, whom he had summoned three Suns earlier because he could not empty his bladder, had not for three Suns, until he scarcely lived. Little Coyote ever so carefully had covered a long and stout feather quill with wild sheep fat after clipping off both ends, then had inserted it with greater care yet. Bull Hump had accepted the pain as did a Blackfeet at the hands of a torturer. This treatment had brought forth a torrent that had filled a pot. Apparently, the potent brew of sage leaves and white man's coffee and tea was continuing to work. The seer could hear Bull Hump's rumbling grunts of relief as the pony passed him. Little Coyote smiled, then returned to his thoughts about protocol.

Shield Maker would not intrude on what custom had decreed was the seer's province; Little Coyote scarcely could do so with Shield Maker. Custom among their people seemed almost to equal what a few of the white men had tried to explain as "law." Yet, there were ways to set the wise and skilled old man's minds into new channels of thought. Little Coyote knew such effort would require much tact—and at least his pistol. There was regret there. The weapon had served him well while Lance, on inner-horse-guard duty this day, had lived thirteen summers. In another summer the youth would go on his vision quest. He should have a stout shield on his return. Little Coyote had some definite ideas about shields. But how to convey them to Shield Maker?

That man's ideas on the structure, size and shape of his shields were grounded on utility over the ages. The heat-treated parfleche, made from the thick skin of the bull buffalo's neck, helped his creations to resist lances, arrows and sometimes musket balls at even surprisingly short ranges. Owners also knew that Shield Maker's rituals gave both the shield and the fine buckskin carrying cover other protective powers transcending form and structure.

The artisan always had deferred to Little Coyote as seer, not servilely, but in the bounds of custom as others had deferred to him in the worldly and unworldly spheres of shield-making. The old man's opportunity to have challenged Little Coyote would have been when the warrior/seer was carrying the shield of the Blackfeet on his return from the first trek for guns. The inexperienced and so-young Little Coyote had felt it quite proper to keep the shield, to use Blackfeet blood to paint over the dead warrior's symbols of buffalo head and lightning flash, then to paint on his own white coyote. Evidently Shield Maker saw no challenge to his position there: He had recognized long ago—as did Little Coyote—that certain successful activities resulting ultimately in benefits for the people carried their own pre-eminence to which even chiefs at times deferred. And, of course, long-revered Shining Shirt had given no-name both a name and public recognition when the youth had returned from his own vision quest.

Shield Maker readily complied with Little Coyote's request that they ride their horses to a level area along the Ootlashoots River where they could observe the promised shooting demonstration. If the older man wondered at this early-morning request before fire or food, his deeply seamed face did not betray the question. What's more, his wise, old eyes widened no more than necessary to view in one sweeping glance the paraphernalia hanging from the buffalo pony. Shield Maker even agreeably carried on his horse a large, untrimmed piece of parfleche he soon would soak and shrink over a shield hoop.

At medium range, Little Coyote's pistol ball failed to penetrate the hairless rawhide, which had not yet even been heat-treated. Neither did his arrow nor the ball from Shield Maker's musket. The bullet from Little Coyote's long rifle punched a neat hole in the hide and plowed a tiny furrow in the serenely flowing river beyond.

Little Coyote looked at the top half of the turtle shell and drove three lodge stakes deeply into the ground, the center one slightly ahead of the other two. Then he bent and fitted the stiff parfleche between them so the center portion of the hide was raised outward then slanted evenly toward both sides. This time the pistol and musket balls caromed off the parfleche and into the river. So did the arrow. At longer range, the rifle bullet did the same. Little Coyote moved back toward the target, motioning for Shield Maker to do the same. The old man did so, eyes opened widely, his movements energetic now—eager—belying the weight of his many summers. He knew shields and arrows and spears, but he had not kept fully abreast of the wonders of white man's guns, particularly the rifled ones.

Again the pistol and musket balls ricocheted into the water, but the rifle bullet penetrated the parfleche.

"This is the medicine of my son, Lance," Little Coyote said. "I give it to you, for you deal in the matter of shields and their attendant rituals. My son's medicine tells me to request you to fashion for him a shield with the sloping top like that of the turtle's shield and the slightly elongated ends of the bottom half, which protected the lower neck and tail of the creature who inhabited it. Your wisdom will show you how to fashion this. Glue into the entire shield a thin layer of wide strips fashioned from these sheep horns, which Bow Maker sometimes uses to strengthen the short bows he makes for the mounted buffalo hunters."

Shield Maker accepted the turtle shell and motioned for the warrior to remove the horns and place them on the ground.

"There is the matter of additional weight." He spoke slowly, neither accepting nor rejecting the request.

"My son already is tall and strong."

"And the matter of the elongated shield. It would be harder for the horseman to handle in fights than the circular one that Coyote carried to us from Sun."

"Lance learns easily. Under Little Bear Claw he soon will master that skill as he has the bow, the lance and my pistol. Little Bear Claw says Lance soon will surpass the most skilled horseman with these weapons. He will have more skills than the sub-chief's son acquired through Willow Woman and dead Eagle Claw."

Shield Maker sat down in the rocky sand and sparse grass to contemplate what he had seen, heard and must do. He pressed his lips together with his work-hardened thumb and index finger. The river gurgled beneath an undercut section of bank. The men could hear distant cries of children and dogs from the awakening camp.

"I have pondered what the guns do," Shield Maker said. "I have known much of what you have told me, but not what the turtle shell has told you."

"Other rifles will come with white man, better than this long rifle, which was not made for killing the buffalo and grizzly bear. I can tell you that, but as to protection against them, that is a matter for Shield Maker and the Good Spirit. And you will need this pistol, as well as your musket, for testing your handiwork and shield medicine. It is my gift to you."

Shield Maker silently watched the warrior place the pistol, mould, bullet pouch and powder horn near the rams' horns, then mount a much lightened Not Afraid of Guns.

"I will fashion the shield," he said. "I will remain here to ponder these matters more deeply. I am grateful for the turtle shell."

As he rode away, Little Coyote felt gratified that he had not tripped over the matter of protocol. Nor, he conceded, had Shield Maker. Only the distant horse guards could have seen the two men leave the encampment together. Many people would see Shield Maker return to camp alone with the paraphernalia from which he would begin to shape a partial solution to the problems that lay ahead.

Antelope was gone from the lodge when Little Coyote returned. So was her Appaloosa and Lance's horse. Their son would have been relieved from horse guard at Sun's arrival when the seer and Shield Maker were shooting. Gone, too, were his parents, even Little Bear Claw and Willow Woman and their son and daughter. A horse guard settled the seer's puzzlement. The man pointed to the south and west.

"A young Shoshone brave, Pony Whip, son of the trader, Broken Pipe, rode in to tell the outer guard a party of the Shoshonis approaches. Your family and others have gone to greet them."

Little Coyote nudged the pinto up a slight rise a short gallop from the encampment. Here, distance and the forest absorbed the camp noises to the north; he also could see any openly approaching party. He dismounted and began chewing some dry meat while Sun brought warmth and more light to reflect from the snow patches atop and near the great peaks surrounding his beloved valley. While his aging pony swished her tail rhythmically, he sat against a deeply embedded boulder and reviewed what he considered a satisfactory meeting with Shield Maker. Then he fell to pondering what might be bringing the Shoshonis here. Certainly Broken Pipe's main purpose would have to do with trade and, perhaps, would be connected to what Bourdon had told the seer four summers earlier. The Canadian had joined a brigade that the man Donald Mackenzie of the then North West Company had led on an exploring expedition. The trek was through the beaver-rich Snake River Valley and some of its tributaries where many of the Shoshonis lived. Little Coyote continued to contemplate these matters after the pony's ears signaled something was approaching. When he could hear voices, he mounted the pinto and, well screened in the light and shadow of trees, watched the cavalcade approach.

Running Buffalo Bull led the nearest party of thirty-two people. Far back was another group driving a large herd of horses. Antelope rode alongside her father and mother while Lance alternately raced his horse between the family and the horse herd. Little Coyote nudged his horse into view when the lead party was almost directly below him. Lance hastened to greet him, his long hair streaming behind him, the tall, filling-out body suddenly disappearing behind the horse's barrel just before his arrival. As the horse stopped, the youth expertly used that jarring movement to help bring himself upright.

"Broken Pipe brings seventeen fine Appaloosas, Father, to trade for many of our lesser mounts and pack horses. My uncle, Pony Whip, is accompanying him!"

Little Coyote restrained an impulse to smile as his son sought to control the excitement in his voice, much as he had done when he, Young Willow and now dead Eagle Claw had fought the Blackfeet after his vision quest. Lance's face was thinner than was his own then; the youth's cheek bones were higher, more evident, with the facial structure thinning downward to a smaller nose, the strong lips and the beautifully contoured chin of Antelope. Almost irresistibly the father's gaze was drawn back to those large, penetrating eyes that seemed to view all the world at once in constant wonder. Surely they were his son's most striking feature, particularly when knowledge and, perhaps, command would grow from wonder.

Little Coyote could see his friend Red Paint and several other warriors of the Nez Percé. Soon after their various greetings, the seer met War Arrow, a tall Nez Percé sub-chief approximately the same age as Running Buffalo Bull. Broken Pipe had grown heavier during the three summers since their last meeting. He smiled broadly, proudly, as he watched Lance leap astride his pony and set it pounding back toward the horse herd that his son had helped to urge much closer during the greetings.

"Three of my finest horses are included among the seventeen I have in the herd," Broken Pipe said. "After his vision quest, Lance will learn one will be for him. The other two are for Little Coyote and Antelope. I will take in exchange the two now-old ones I gave to you before you became mates. They, too, will go into the trades with the less-demanding trappers. The Shoshonis inhabiting the Snake River country have asked me to tell our brothers, the Flatheads, about the problems there as the white trappers arrive, pursued always by the ever vengeful and wider-ranging Blackfeet."

War Arrow listened. Then, as the horse herd reached them, he shouted, "We will talk about the fort the whites have erected at the mouth of the Walla Walla River."

"I am deeply troubled, beset by problems on every side. You, my friend, are the only warrior who can help me."

Little Bear Claw's face was set in sadness; his voice broke as he tried to speak. He was accompanying Little Coyote to the council Tjolzhitsay had asked Three Eagles to call after the hubbub over the arrival of the Shoshonis and Nez Percé had died.

Little Coyote stopped in mid-stride, seizing his friend by the shoulder. "Should I help now? Does the matter take precedence over the council meeting?"

"Certainly." Little Bear Claw's voice remained mournful, the lips drooping ever downward, but his eyes could not lie. "Certainly," he repeated, "in the mind of my son, Fast Runner. He is smitten by Antelope's sister, Warm Breeze, and gladly would have our council and the Shoshonis and Nez Percés devote their full attention to this matter. Willow Woman says only you can settle this problem quickly. Tell me, will you try to do so, lest perhaps I never sleep again? My lodge is filled with a never-ending, hopeless voice saying that the maiden will leave soon and will never visit again—at least without a mate."

"I fear you will die from lack of sleep. Remain here. Perhaps I can persuade Antelope to carry the heaviness of your problem while we ponder the less weighty ones at council."

He returned almost instantly.

"Antelope says to sleep well. If a grateful Willow Woman will allow you to do so."

They stopped laughing as they neared the council lodge, but commenced again as they were forced to weave in, out and around the seventeen Appaloosas Broken Pipe had arranged with nearby lodge owners to tether strategically so all comers would be forced to see—and, most certainly, admire.

The two friends knew this would be an important meeting as soon as they viewed the seating arrangement. After the pipe ceremony, Tjolzhitsay would pass the pipe first to Broken Pipe seated to the south; War Arrow to the west; then Bright Fire, who well knew the locations of their kin and allies to the north, so would head the party that would take them the messages of the council. Then the pipe would pass to Three Eagles, Gun and Broken Tooth. They could speak in that same order.

The trader surprised his son-in-law with his skills at speech. Gone was the hinting, cajoling, often-boastful approach that had made him a rich horse-trader, indeed. His voice was strong, almost commanding, as he conveyed the worries and hopes of his people. Little Coyote almost envied how Broken Pipe had, during his trading encounters, gained a knowledge of white man's ways that surely surpassed in many respects that of such mountain men as, say, friend Tull.

"Only in your recent fifth moon of the Bitter Root, Comcomly, chief of the Chinook near where the Columbia River flows into the great salt water to the west, sent us important words. The Chinook received the words from white men who have been coming there in great ships, to the Chinooks' sorrow, for many summers. Many of them have learned to speak with white men about their ways and have been much debased by them. The important words came to us directly from Otter, the sub-chief, when he sought more of my horses. He, too, knows the white man; he says too well. The great council of the distant White Father, which they call 'Congress,' has decreed that henceforth only companies can conduct the trading. What is called 'the government' no longer can operate the posts. Our people held council on these words. We, and you—all of our allies—have seen fur companies fight among themselves to get the most furs. Indeed, as we already have learned, the British great council forced the North West Company and the Hudson's Bay Company to become one because of such bloody fighting. Otter says Comcomly has pondered these matters deeply. The American companies will continue, perhaps intensify, their fighting as more of them come into the Indian regions to take the furs. This will bring greater Blackfeet opposition—and opportunities for much loot. We ask: Are the Blackfeet fools to fight them? Are we fools not to do the same?"

A murmur rose from the council, with many wishing to answer. Restrained more by Broken Pipe's eloquence than by the head chief's upraised hand, they quieted as the Shoshone trader continued to speak: "We are learning a strange truth. White man, no matter which company he belongs to, no matter how they war among themselves, will band together almost instantly to fight when the Indians threaten any of them. We have not learned to do the same. In the past we have allied to go to the buffalo grounds in good strength. Now, with more white men moving into the as-yet little-trapped and rich areas to take away the furs, the Shoshonis say perhaps we should develop strategies among ourselves as we have done to get the buffalo."

Tjolzhitsay asked the question perhaps uppermost in the minds of all who had worked their way through Broken Pipe's Appaloosas to reach the council: "You have let it be known you wish to exchange your fine horses for great numbers of lesser horses to trade to those many white men coming into the Snake River lands. Have you not already decided you would not support resisting white man?"

"I speak for Broken Pipe," the Shoshone trader replied. "The willow prospers in almost any soil because it can bend in great winds from any direction. I prospered by trading only among the people before white man came. Some say perhaps when the beaver furs are gone, white man will return whence he came. I do not believe this. Already I see some nicely tanned cow and calf buffalo robes going to white man. Will he want all the buffalo, even the untanned hides of bulls, when the beaver are gone, then leave this land? I do not believe this. Otter told me some white men have been staying to live near the shore of the great salt water. They do not like to have the Indians about. The white man always will be with us. Our sometimes allies, the Crows, do not fight white man. Your Shining Shirt cautioned against fighting white man. I do not know much about white man. What should be our plans? My people ask this."

Broken Pipe no longer looked at the people in the crowded lodge. He had raised his head toward the smoke flap where a few hints of clouds appeared in the blue of the tiny sky. His voice remained strong, yet he seemed to be speaking only to himself:

"I have learned much about horses. When I drive a few of my horses into a corral, they miss their freedom but are reasonably compliant if well-fed, particularly those I have castrated. When I put even more horses into the same corral they become restless, particularly the stallions I have not gelded. Their restlessness affects the others. When the corral becomes overcrowded with too many horses, they fight among themselves when, to my mind, they easily could break out of the corral if given leadership the stallions or a wise mare could provide. This they do not do. I think perhaps the time will come when, with the beaver gone for pelts, perhaps the buffalo gone for hides, there will be fighting with the white man as the people find themselves crowded together by them. All will never become submissive like my gelded horses."

The lodge was silent.

"Has Broken Pipe spoken?" Tjolzhitsay's voice broke the silence.

"I have spoken."

Little Coyote, who knew this man so well, watched him closely as he sat down. For a moment the trader's shoulders slumped imperceptibly. Then he reached forward to pull up his moccasins, which were secure on his feet. For a moment longer, he remained bent forward. Then he sat erectly, looking about to see if others were watching. All, save for the seer, had immediately focused their attention on War Arrow, who spoke bluntly:

"The white man called Donald Mackenzie, a sub-chief of the North West Company, came with many Canadians and Iroquois and others to build a strong fort where the Walla Walla River flows into what they call the Columbia. Now the Hudson's Bay Company flies the British banner over this place they have called Fort Nez Percés. They trade with us, the Walla Wallas,

Cayuses and other tribes. Already they make each tribe think it is the most favored so we will not unite to drive them out. They trap the beaver and other animals. We are not always friendly with all the Shoshonis, but we share their concerns and so have talked, even with the poorer ones to the south who live in the lodges of sticks and grass. There are some beaver there, too. Bourdon, the friend of the Flatheads, who even now is leading a trapping party into the Snake River country, accompanied Mackenzie on his first journey there after the fort was built. Bourdon told us more are planned."

War Arrow paused for a moment. "These are not small parties. The first we watched closely when it formed at the fort. We counted fifty-five men, one-hundred-ninety-five horses (Broken Pipe nodded his head in confirmation), three-hundred beaver traps and much more equipment, but no food. They would shoot their food. Many among us are of a mind to unite and drive them out.

"The Iroquois' leader, Ignace Hatchiorauquasha, John Gray, the whites call him, accompanied Mackenzie and even now is preparing to trap in the land of the Shoshonis with Bourdon when the colder weather makes better furs. We have smoked many pipes with Hatchiorauquasha. He has disclosed many things that interest us very much—though they also puzzle us. He has told us about the white man's Great Spirit and his son, Jesus. He is called the Prince of Peace. Yet Hatchiorauquasha also has told us that far to the east and leading to the west, even up the Missouri River, wherever white man has come, he has taken the furs, fought the many different tribes and, mostly, insisted the surviving Indian people act like gelded horses, about which Broken Pipe has spoken most eloquently. If they do not, they kill them further, sparing neither the old nor young. And they take the land which the Good Spirit gave to all. The Nez Percé ask: 'How should we deal with white man?' I have spoken for now."

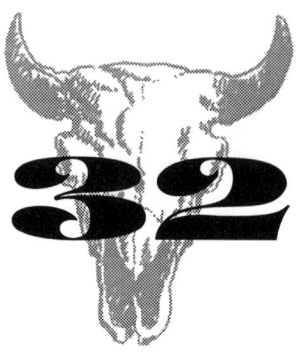

Tjolzhitsay found Little Coyote sitting on a small cliff facing east and looking at silvery segments of the Ootlashoots River winding northward across the valley floor. *S'tc'tc'tcút*, half moon, first quarter, was shining brightly, illuminating even the most distant peaks while the warm, southwest breeze carried upward a heady grassy/resinous scent. No greeting broke the tranquility as Little Coyote moved slightly to provide space for the aging chief to sit and lean against the rock, too. Their horses seemed content to stand quietly under a towering tree, the roots of which had cracked away tiny portions of the cliff as they probed into it. A night hawk made two circles over the meadow below, the whirring of each evenly spaced descent clearly audible.

"My youngest, perhaps my last son, Big Hawk, must seek his vision quest soon," Tjolzhitsay said. "He prepares himself as does your son, Lance."

"May the Good Spirit guide them both."

"All of us."

An owl hooted at the near edge of the meadow and the answer coming from the eastern rim seemed an echo. The men watched both owls silently glide low across the meadow; very soon they heard one, then another, set of despairing squeaks as the ghostly birds seized and carried off their prey.

"I did not remind the council that you, as has my *i-sts-sókoi*, have warned against fighting white man," Tjolzhitsay said. "Rather, I felt that we should talk about your thinking and, from my thoughts, yours, and the council's, form a plan to deal with white man when we again meet on this matter soon after Sun arrives."

"I have sat here asking the Good Spirit to help give us an answer," Little Coyote replied. "He has enabled me to see that our people's lives, *our* lives, are like the many rivers. We know that our river flows through the valley serenely at times, at others turbulent, even dangerous. Yet we see only parts of its flowings, day or night, because the brush and trees and distance hide some of the parts. And the river has beginnings. We have seen parts of them. The river flows into greater rivers. We have seen some of them, but have never viewed the great salt water where the waters of our river end. Others have seen what we have not, and we have seen what they have not. Their rivers, like their lives, too, have their beginnings, their serenity, their turbulence, their dangerous torrents and cataracts, and those rivers have their joinings with others also to become part of the great sea. We know that the Good Spirit sees all, orders all. We are small; we must not mindlessly ignore white man, seek only his marvels, when first his life begins to mingle with ours. We are small; we must focus on our river, see and know which parts of it are hidden by the trees and brush, and perhaps learn more about the parts and workings of the other rivers. But we cannot see all the waters. Other people elsewhere have found answers to their similar problems. Parts of our answer might come from theirs. And our answer might become part of their solutions, too. So we must not hurry like the river parts that rush tumultuously, unheedingly, through the narrow canyons, crashing into the great rocks which often lie hidden. I have pondered this matter deeply over much time, not just now. I know we should not fight white man. I cannot know for others. Perhaps there will be further lessons to be gained from those who do fight white man. I know that we who are so few must have many of his goods, most particularly good guns because others who are many are getting the guns. How much must we lose to gain the protection that comes from white man, his guns? What we are losing now does not show much. Will the losses show more in time as the river water wears away even the rocky base of this cliff?"

"I, too, have had similar thoughts." The head chief walked to his horse, tamped tobacco into two clay trade pipes, then returned with a small flintlock fire starter. With two rapid clicks of the hammer, sufficient sparks showered from the flint and steel to ignite the fine bark and splinters in the small receptacle below the steel. They lighted their pipes and smoked quietly while the moon rose higher and circled southward.

Tjolzhitsay lowered his pipe, coughing violently. He swallowed hard and wiped tears from his high cheekbones.

"If we become enemies with the Hudson's Bay Company," he said, "we will lose their trade, which they have provided since the British fought the Americans again, and even after. We know little about the Americans' trade now on the parts of the upper Missouri River mostly east of us. We face the Blackfeet more there than here or south or west. I believe we must not fight white man—from any direction."

Little Coyote puffed three last times: "There is much wisdom in what you say. I say, too, our people must perfect even more the way they fight. You saw Broken Pipe's fine horses?"

The chief chuckled and the evening brightened for the moment. "Even ancient Blind Eyes knows they are there. He stumbled twice over their tethers and had to summon help to guide him from the tangle. I have gained much respect for Broken Pipe. Perhaps we need more such traders and fewer sub-chiefs."

"Yes, we must study and plan as do the best of traders," Little Coyote said. "We must acquire and use the best of horses in battle, horses the enemy would prize almost as much as our scalps. We must become even more highly skilled at using the bodies of the finest horses to protect our own, so the enemy, even if only for a fleeting moment, will hold his fire lest he damage or kill the horse. We, unlike our enemies, must fire when we are sure of our targets, perhaps deliberately kill the horses to kill the riders. Yes, we no longer must trade our best horses, of which we have more than we are people, and we must acquire and breed and train the best we can get from others. I do not like this, but we must not share *all* these thoughts and practices even with our friends who, in the sometimes mysterious ways of the world, for small or great reasons, could become our enemies. Perhaps, only perhaps, by design and not chance, we must ally ourselves closely with white man as he becomes the largest force in the land of the furs." He handed the empty pipe back to the head chief.

Tjolzhitsay sighed: "I like what you say about the rivers. I wonder if white men have tried as hard to understand us as we have labored to comprehend them and their ways. But enough. I will talk to Three Eagles, Gun, Broken Tooth, Bright Fire and other sub-chiefs. The council will be against fighting white man if I tell them Little Bear Claw has consented to learn more about white man's ways and how much he now trades on the upper Missouri. Also, if you, Little Coyote, will go to the Snake River country for much the same purpose and once again visit our friends, the Nez Percé, near the fort that War Arrow has spoken about."

Little Coyote laughed loudly, sending the owls, which had returned to their hunt, silently flapping away with empty talons. "I avoided getting tangled like Blind Eyes in the tethers of Broken Pipe's horses, yet I become tangled because of my own words. I will go, but after my son returns from his vision quest."

In their ride to the valley floor, chief and seer stopped but once—to watch one owl return to the hunting ground from the east, followed shortly by the second from the west.

"White man is a shrewd trader for the furs, and increasingly is bringing the firewater pots to turn the tribes' minds till they often give away their catches. Even so, white man must try harder to really understand the people if he does not wish for his bones to become scattered like those of the buffalo. Strangely, when he has acquired the furs, he can become most careless. I have gained this wisdom and more."

Tjolzhitsay looked over the heads of the council to fix his eyes on Little Coyote, who nodded in agreement at Little Bear Claw's words. Next to Little Bear Claw was Pony Whip of the Shoshonis. This brother-in-law of Little Coyote had been in the party of Shoshonis who had accompanied Little Bear Claw and some of the Salish from the Bitter Root and Flathead valleys and beyond to seek trade with white man if they once again were in the Three Forks area. The party returned early in that spring of 1823 before Lance had come back from his vision quest or Little Coyote had gone to the Snake River country as Tjolzhitsay had requested.

Little Bear Claw and Pony Whip were woefully thin, their faces still drawn from much hardship. Though their voices were weak, they were eager to share their words and adventures with the council.

"Manuel Lisa is dead at St. Louis," Little Bear Claw said. "The Missouri Fur Company has built a new post at Lisa's fort at the mouth of the Big Horn River. The chief, Joshua Pilcher, has called it Fort Benton. I do not think white men will be there long." Little Bear Claw paused to ask Tjolzhitsay if he would request Pony Whip to talk, too, so together they could tell what more they had learned about white man, the treachery of the Blackfeet, and their great battle. "From this," Little Bear Claw said, "you will learn why we believe we should continue to make most of our trades west of the great divide, and why it is even more important that we learn about the trade in the Snake River country."

So the Flathead and the Shoshone told their story. Little Bear Claw spoke first: "While we were meeting here in our valley with Broken Pipe and War Arrow, almost two-hundred white men, led by sub-chiefs Robert Jones and Michael Immel, came to Fort Benton. Under the eyes of the peaceful Crows they caught many furs that winter. The Crows are glad when white man comes to them, for they gain many trade goods, some of which help them in their wars with the Sioux. Perhaps there is a lesson there. This spring Jones and Immel and thirty more men—many armed with a fine, new rifle gun—came to the Three Forks country, where they caught many furs and we traded them many more. They also traded for more horses to carry fifty-two packs of beaver back to Fort Benton."

Pony Whip joined in: "We tried very hard to get some of the rifled guns, but they would not trade. They were too afraid of the Blackfeet, though they worked hard to find and make peace with them. We warned them that though they saw no Blackfeet, they were about, much like the white goat on his lofty, snow-patched peak where little of the world below escapes his keen eyesight. We told white man the Blackfeet were letting white man collect the furs so they could take them away from them, along with their horses and scalps. We did not feel secure to be in a party of only thirty-four men, counting ourselves, despite their new weapons."

Pony Whip and Little Bear Claw spoke quietly together before Little Bear Claw asked the head chief a question. The chief signed assent. Pony Whip removed the elaborately beaded buckskin scabbard from a heavy rifle and held the weapon aloft so all could see. His voice strengthened: "Little Bear Claw and I obtained seven of these guns. We give this one to Tjolzhitsay. A man, Hawken, now makes them in St. Louis. This gun belonged to Immel before the Blackfeet killed him. The others were owned by Jones and five white men before the Blackfeet killed them, too. The scabbard is my gift of friendship with the Flatheads. I took it with my first scalp from a Piegan."

The rifle resembled those Little Coyote had seen in the hands of the Clark and Lewis people. It also was much like his own Pennsylvania rifle, but with a much-shortened, heavier barrel and a larger bore, which made the weapon far more effective on larger game—and men!

Pony Whip continued: "I will carry three to my father, Broken Pipe, and Little Bear Claw will have three, for we sent back to this valley all the trade goods, including fine muskets, with the Shoshone and Flathead trading party that helped us bring the furs and horses to the Three Forks. The two of us then accompanied the thirty-two men toward Fort Benton; during that journey we traded our own many horses and much hardship, almost our lives, for these Hawken rifles."

Tjolzhitsay gravely accepted the gifts, then allowed much time to pass while all the council examined and exclaimed over the Hawken gun. He signed that those who wished could leave the lodge to relieve themselves. Those who did so returned quickly. There was much to hear. Little Bear Claw resumed the story:

"Immel and Jones and their trappers, who were a much tougher, harder breed of men and who were good shooters, were fearful when we set out for Fort Benton. Often, one would rather see the enemy than, knowing he is lurking about, not see him." Loud voices of assent filled the lodge, but only briefly. "Early one day, some Blackfeet suddenly were there on a hilltop looking at us as we once more prepared to set out. We knew they were a large scouting force and we warned against allowing them to come too close so they could study our weapons, men and possible loot. Immel and Jones were careful, but not enough, for they had sought the Blackfeet to talk trade with them, and now, finally, they had found them.

"'Our Missouri Fur Company will build a fort below the great falls to trade only with the Blackfeet if there is peace,' Immel and Jones promised.

"The Blackfeet appeared joyous at these words, but we knew, and their eyes told us, their joy came from the prospects they could get thirty-four scalps, many fine weapons, horses and furs. Blackfeet and white sub-chiefs promised the friendship they were making over the smoke would last as long as this branch of the Yellowstone River, along which we traveled, would flow. We were eager to seek the safety of the nearby Crow camp from which the whites had trapped the last winter; we knew and we told the white men that the Blackfeet were eager to hasten away to bring more warriors to fight us."

Pony Whip continued the story: "The white men set out quickly for the Crow camp. When we were less than a day's journey from the camp, the whites took their pack horses through a defile with trees and brush on either side. We warned against this, but the whites argued this would be faster, as we had urged them to be. One should not knowingly touch the pan of a set trap. When the two of us first entered the brush, we separated from the white men under this cover and took ourselves and our horses around the defile, scouting carefully as we did so. We found many tracks leading toward the defile. As we prepared to hide the horses and set out to warn the whites, though we were yet far away, we heard the exultant screams rising from the throats of four-hundred Blackfeet when they attacked. They fired the silent arrows at first, then some guns. Jones and Immel quickly died, as did five others. Other whites were wounded. Though their sub-chiefs were dead, the whites quickly listened to others who were good leaders, and there were many of them. There is a lesson here, too. The whites cut off some of the beaver packs and fired from behind those and some dead horses. Yes, these Americans are good fighters and good shots. They do not all fire their guns at once. Rather, about half of them fire, then when they are loading, the others fire. We would have uselessly died had we attempted to fight our way through even the outer edge of the attackers to reach the whites. Soon we watched the Blackfeet riding up a hillside with the white men's horses, most of their furs and the bodies of their dead. Very carefully, then, we rejoined the whites, for we did not wish to die from their guns.

"They had wounded men, a few beaver packs and no horses. We used ours to help the whites reach the Crow camp. We traded the whites all but four of our horses for the guns of the dead men."

Tjolzhitsay raised the question surely in the minds of the rapt listeners: "But you returned with three Blackfeet scalps."

"We wished to return quickly, but carefully, to the Three Forks area while the Blackfeet celebrated their great victory," Little Bear Claw said. "Yet we knew they would send warriors to learn if they had left behind any of their own dead in the brush. We watched three Blackfeet return to the defile. We killed them and hastened on, following a stream to hide our passing."

Thus far Pony Whip and Little Bear Claw had told their story with unanimity. Now the Shoshone stepped forward and spoke: "Little Bear Claw is too modest. He set us to hiding our horses then descending into the defile, which now was beginning to stink from the dead horses. We placed ourselves near a dead horse and a rock, which any enemy could only reach from in front. Little Bear Claw said he would employ a stratagem his father used and is in the stories of your people. Little Bear Claw weakly called for help in the Blackfeet tongue while we readied our silent arrival. When three Blackfeet were near, we slew them. I killed two, Little Bear Claw one, because when the Blackfeet called the seemingly wounded one to try to show himself, your sub-chief raised his body with his arms, though holding the tomahawk in the grass. He slapped the nearest Blackfeet with his quirt, then killed him with the tomahawk as my arrows found the others."

The lodge was silent, but all eyes focused on Little Bear Claw as Pony Whip concluded his story: "We set out at night and lost the three Blackfeet horses while attempting to cross the river into which we threw the Blackfeet bodies. When we failed to make a first crossing with those, we swam back to our own mounts and, after a long search, found a shallower place which cost us yet another horse. In our haste we wore out one, then another, of our remaining horses carrying the Hawken guns. Now we had but one as we continued to travel at night, but more slowly as we neared more familiar ground. We did not pause to hunt, but ate horse flesh.

"We are here. The killing of the whites was unfortunate. Yet there is good fortune for us in their misfortune. The Blackfeet will not have their fort near the great falls. While we were completing our journey toward the Crow camp after the battle, the most fearful whites, and they were few, told us perhaps the Missouri Fur Company would die because they have few furs to exchange for the goods they must bring up the Missouri to trade. There are many things to say about what we have learned. We remember most what one of the company's sub-chiefs said at the Crow camp: 'The whites must use men who are hunters and fighters to do the trapping. Only then will he trap the furs more safely and keep them after he gets them. And there must be many more of these men.' We have spoken."

330

Pony Whip ate well and rested among his Flathead friends and kin while Lance was on his vision quest. The youth returned fully as tired and hungry as had his uncle and father from their travels.

"I walked east, climbing ever upward on the Skalkaho trail until I came to a waterfall," Lance said. "I sat above that and prayed to Sun and the Good Spirit, who answered me on the third day. In my vision I saw many warriors fighting, and sometimes I fought, too—and well. I remember well the final battle. I was helped with food and water and weapons by a woman I dimly perceived as Antelope, my mother. Hand in hand we left that battle in peace, followed at a great distance by an old man who leaned over so far from his heavy load on his back that I could not see his face. Then a lightning bolt struck the ground between us and the old man. When I again could see, he was gone. My mother and I sat down to eat with our people amid much rejoicing that we had returned. Then my vision ended."

Grave-faced Shield Maker quietly listened to Lance's story, whereupon he quickly said he would paint a red lightning bolt on one side of the slightly sloping front of the young brave's shield and fill in the remainder of that side and the other with black paint. Perhaps at some other time there would be a revelation to determine which other symbols should be painted there.

Shield Maker, knowing that eager Lance would like to examine the shield, told him he could get it in two days. That would leave another day before his father and Pony Whip would depart for the Shoshone country.

Little Coyote placed his hand on his son's shoulder: "If you will get enough food into your belly to walk on steady legs or hold you astride a horse, and pull a bow with arms that once again are strong, you will accompany us. Now go talk to your mother as a brave about a vision quest gift from your grandfather, Broken Pipe."

Elatedly, Lance raced away on his horse, proving he was certain in his own mind he already was fit. Little Coyote talked long with Shield Maker before leading Not Afraid of Guns back to his lodge. He was keenly aware that he returned as though burdened like an old man with a load far too heavy for his years.

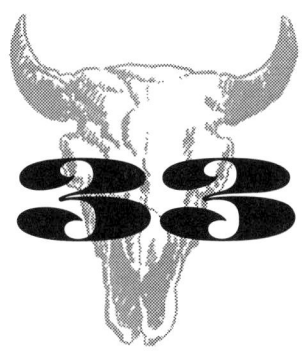

33

Michel Bourdon sat next to Finan McDonald, who was impaling even more buffalo meat on his roasting stick. Bourdon's small, expressive hands, which moved with his tongue as he talked, momentarily seemed out of place in his lap. His narrow shoulders and slender body belied the strength that had carried him successfully through many hard ventures of which Little Coyote was aware. One was that memorable battle thirteen summers earlier when both these white men had helped the one-hundred-fifty Flatheads win over a larger Blackfeet party at the buffalo grounds. Bourdon's thin, dark face and large nose resembled those of numerous *engagés* the Flatheads had come to know, but the eyes were different—sharp, piercing, darting here and there like those of a hungry raven, seeing much, missing nothing of importance. And he could lead men, white or Indian, with a common-sense mixture of hearty fellowship and flexibility. McDonald clearly was drawn to this small man, due more to shared hazardous experiences than because the large often befriend the small. Both had mastered the tongues of many tribes; also, Bourdon had learned much about the Flatheads since he had shown fear at interpreting for Cox at Saleesh House so long ago when the trader had threatened to leave the Indians if they persisted in torture.

By white man's measure McDonald was nearing six and one-half feet in his moccasins, the wide, brawny shoulders diminishing downward to a surprisingly slim waist. For now, he had jammed the roasting stick into the earth near the fire and was laughing with the sound of a buffalo bull at the rut. His merriment was infecting most of the other forty-nine white men in the party, except for watchful guards taking turns roasting meat nearby. Pony Whip and Lance were laughing, too, at Little Coyote's quiet comment that should the Blackfeet ever attempt to scalp the great man, they would have to use an axe—both to remove and chop up the hairy scalp and, perhaps, even the beard so six warriors could flaunt their trophies.

Tull, in comparison with McDonald, brought to mind a mountain goat's head and face and the shaggiest buffalo bull shedding matted, winter hair in summer. Little Coyote felt reassured in the presence of these men because, almost from the moment he, his son and *scest,* brother-in-law, had left the Bitter Root Valley for the Snake River country, they had seen Blackfeet scouting parties. The sharpened vigilance of the three, aided by the spyglass, had enabled them to see and cautiously approach the McDonald party. There they were welcomed, encouraged to go with them to Pony Whip's land of the Shoshonis. Now all were approaching the southern end of the Beaverhead Mountains, which were familiar, indeed, to the medicine man.

There was no loitering, no banter or yarn-spinning around the fires after the eating. "Ye'll put them oot after eating your meat," McDonald had ordered in the thick burr of his native Scottish Highlands. "And ye'll mind the guard duty Bourdon assigns ye, 'less ye wish to trade your scalps for just a wee moment of carelessness." None needed to be reminded that only a few days earlier, at the Big Hole, one of their number had been killed while McDonald tried to talk with the relentless Piegans. Frequently, from safe musket-ball distance, the killer had taunted the party by waving the luckless man's scalp on his coup stick. There was little grumbling. Few crossed McDonald and remained healthy. Besides, Bourdon's problems with his trapping party the year before had been discussed around less-dangerous fires and carried lessons, too. Four of his free men and ten Iroquois had deserted. In battles with the Blackfeet he had lost two men, the Blackfeet seven. The defection had forced him to cache seven-hundred of his two-thousand-two-hundred beaver pelts. Perhaps this expedition would secure these and many more from the Snake country that had attracted Bourdon and others five years earlier.

"On the morrow, in the better light, if ye'll no object, I'd like to examine your rifled guns," McDonald rumbled to the Flatheads and Shoshone as he crawled into his blanket. "I've no doot we could flatten that Blackfeet that waves the scalp aboot wi' one of them, but 'tis likely we'll need them, including their surprise value, before we're through in this country, which I dinna' like. Nor do I like the Company's ordering me to take summer fur. 'Tis such practices as this, and leaving no seed, that already ha' ruint the Flathead country for furs."

McDonald commenced snoring almost immediately, but that last comment—not this noise as though the bull had been lung shot—was what kept Little Coyote awake after most of the camp slept.

Little Bear Claw had given one Hawken rifle to Gun, kept one for himself and presented the third to Little Coyote before his departure. Little Coyote, in turn, had given his cherished long rifle to Lance, reminding the overwhelmed young brave that he should rely mostly on his bow and arrows while fighting from his horse. Pony Whip carried a Hawken and had put the other two on his pack horse for Broken Pipe.

"If ye'll kindly keep them all loaded and at hand near me as we travel, I'll be much obliged," McDonald had requested as the weapons became the brief topic around the early-morning cooking fires. "'Tis sure, the Company must come up wi' a comparable gun for the trade if they wish to outdo the Americans."

Little Coyote's familiarity with this mountainous country led him to appreciate even more McDonald's and Bourdon's vigilance as the party carefully and laboriously wound its way southward with scouts forward and at both sides. The terrain was beginning to level out when Sun was almost directly above them. The scout at point waited for McDonald to ride up, then informed him he was certain he had heard a horse whinnying in the distance.

"It shore as hell warn't an elk buglin'," the scout commented as McDonald questioned him sharply. "Come an' lissen for yoreself." McDonald clapped him on the back and asked him to return to point.

"Bourdon, if ye'll kindly put two more of the best men up front." McDonald roared the words above the clattering of hooves on the dim game trail, which angled upward over broken shale leading toward one side of a brushy ravine. As larger shale slabs loosened, puffs of dust rose and were swept northward in the rising breeze.

Though the Blackfeet had secreted their horses farther away and hidden themselves like ground sparrows, their attack was hasty, ill-organized and ineffective. Evidently they began firing on the trappers almost as quickly as the lead horses came into range. Most remained hidden in the heavy brush. A horse screamed above shrill battle cries as a musket ball penetrated its guts when the pack train began arcing back on itself to safer ground. No trappers were hit in that first volley.

Bourdon hastened to McDonald and both men looked upward as the trappers began shooting. The three lead scouts were well above the ravine. One stood in his stirrups and quickly signaled with arms: Ten, twenty, thirty, forty, fifty, sixty, seventy enemy. The man threw both arms upward and outward. Perhaps more. Who could tell?

"Dismount and hold your fire!" McDonald's roar penetrated noise, wind, dust and confusion. The men obeyed.

"Bourdon, if ye'll take fifteen men and join the scouts above." Briefly, he directed a mixed stew of curses in the direction of the howling Blackfeet—the Scottish, English, French, Flathead, Kutenai and other expletives ridding him of momentary rage. "We'll stay here, trapping them sort of, if they're not too many. We'll put an arc around the ravine, maybe flush them out to your men. They want a fight? Well . . ." Again the incomprehensible mix of expletives. " . . . we'll give it to them!"

A trapper trying to turn his excited horse dropped. He kicked up a pitiful dust on the trail, then stilled. Another, thoughtlessly still astride his mount, was punched backward as a ball took him in the face. Blood spurted down his sleeve onto the horse's rump. He fell, the terrified horse momentarily dragging him until the left foot pulled from the stirrup as the corpse struck a boulder off the path.

"Charge your muskets wi' buckshot!" McDonald yelled.

Little Coyote, Lance and Pony Whip fired slowly, carefully, at moving targets as the trappers poured charge after charge of buckshot into the brush. Once, Lance hastily tapped his father on the shoulder, pointed, then fired at a Blackfeet who had rushed a short way from the brush and exultingly waved a coup stick with a scalp attached. The Blackfeet dropped as though hit on the head with a war club when the ball from the long rifle struck him. There were fewer shouts, but more arrows, from the Blackfeet now. A small wedge of them struggled uphill toward the Bourdon group, engaged them briefly, then retreated to the buckshot-peppered brush. Another trapper fell, ineffectually plucking at an arrow in his upper gut.

"Hold your fire!" A few more shots poured from the trappers' muskets after McDonald's roared command. He snapped an order to a wiry trapper near him.

"I'm sending this man to tell Bourdon we're firing the brush. Ten of ye, get to the other side. When we get the fire going in this wind, some of us will join ye on that side as the flames either roast or drive them out. Gi' on wi' ye!"

McDonald started one fire and directed four men to thrust torches of long, dry grass into it. They spread out along the side of the ravine, protected by volleys of buckshot. In a few moments an irregular line of five fires leaped forward, raggedly joined and raced toward the ravine. One edge of flame curled into the ravine, where the wind funneled more strongly. Now the flames spread across one side and the front. For only a moment there was silence, except for the hungry crackling of the now-leaping fire. Above the McDonald grove, Bourdon's men began a steady firing.

Blackfeet, unscathed by buckshot or fire, began running from the yet-unburned brush. Fumblingly, they sought to recharge their muskets or fit arrows to bows in the heat and smoke. They died shrieking defiance, still trying to fight. The even more luckless, hair and garments aflame, ran, stumbled and crawled through the raging flames, some dying before they took a bullet or charge of buckshot. A few powder horns and flasks burst with puffs of sulphurous smoke and waves of stench. The searing, muffled explosions only added to the torture. Little Coyote moved out of the thin fringe of smoke from which he was firing, recharged his Hawken gun, then lowered it to watch the nine naked survivors scamper or painfully limp, with the assistance of others, up the least defended part of the hill. Two horribly burned laggards took bullets as the warriors approached, then veered away from, the Bourdon force.

"Let these devils go to carry word to the Blackfeet they'll attack us at their peril." As the Indians disappeared, McDonald reassembled his forces.

The Scotsman, grief masked by his hairy face but evident in his subdued voice, ordered the immediate and well-hidden burial of his friend Michel Bourdon and five other trappers. The sixty-eight Blackfeet were left where they had been shot or roasted. Their muskets and ammunition that had not been burned went into McDonald's stock of trading goods. While the party camped that night well away from this place of death, the fire moved on, then began to die for want of fodder.

Poignant memories of widely traveled John Colter's descriptive talks flooded Little Coyote's mind as he, too, appreciatively viewed the region through which McDonald's Snake Brigade passed in a southeasterly direction after the bloody victory over the Blackfeet: Bear River, Green River, long days of travel through game-filled valleys encircled by high, jagged-peaked mountains. Above all silently towered ever beckoning *Les Trois Tetons*, reassuring landmarks that in the minds of these often womanless trappers wondrously could diminish—metamorphose—from mineral to flesh. The process happened banteringly, lewdly, by day, quietly, yearningly, at night.

The trappers drew more Blackfeet blood but lost none of their own during several lesser engagements. Almost everywhere they extracted a rich harvest of furs that fall and winter. "Four-thousand-four-hundred-and-fifty-nine plews, counting Bourdon's seven-hundred," McDonald announced as the men pressed the last pack preparatory to returning to Spokan House, "but e'en so, this country I'll not be seeing again—e'en if the plews were gold."

The red-head's deep-seated loyalty to his employer remained strong despite his determination to return to Ontario to his Pend d'Oreille wife, Peggy, and their children. He divulged this aim to the two Flatheads and Shoshone one night over the fire as they neared the turnoff point where the three Indians would seek out Broken Pipe.

For a moment McDonald seemed to be talking to himself: "E'en the boar grizzly tires wi' the years, the cold water and the fighting—always the fighting—time, weather and man." His voice strengthened and he looked at Little Coyote. "Ye seek to learn for your people the effect of white man moving into the Snake country. Well, I'll tell ya, there's what we call 'politics' aworking here, too. That'll be hard for ye to fight. Our Hudson's Bay Company wants us to trap every beaver in the Snake country—get everything oot of it, make it profitless for the growing numbers of Americans to move into. And the Company'll make a fur desert so they'll stay oot of the Columbia country. There we're strong and inclined to leave some seed beaver wherever we go." He pulled reflectively, morosely, on his pipe, his words almost incomprehensible. "Get in the Snake and get them and get oot, I guess ye could say." He lowered his pipe and again fixed his gleaming eyes on Little Coyote. "That leaves little for the Indians, I'd say, and I dinna' like that, either." These words were very clear, indeed.

"Politics." That word, re-enforced by McDonald's "That'll be hard for ye to fight," demanded that Little Coyote learn as much as possible from the vigilant, harassed Scot in the short time they would be together. McDonald's explanations about politics came disjointedly, simply, very generally, but effectively as the busy brigade leader urged his horse from place to place in the heavily burdened and long pack line. McDonald's primary task, after all, was to see to the details that would help his trappers safely reach Spokan House with this rich take of furs.

Yes, Little Coyote could understand why the British and the Americans wished to keep the fur empire for themselves; how the British controlled much of the country from Astoria east to the upper Missouri during the recent great war. Yes, he could understand how, in 1818, the British and Americans—Bostons— could agree to share the "Oregon" country. McDonald, not fully comprehending Oregon himself, scarcely could convey the vastness of that region he described as "west of the Rockies between Spanish California and Russian Alaska." To help convey the immensity of the country, McDonald drew a few explanatory lines in the earth during eating times. Yes, the Flathead could understand how, as the Americans increased in numbers, the British would be reluctant to yield to them. And what about the Spanish tribe and the Russian tribe?

"Too weak; they'll have to get oot," McDonald rumbled with deep conviction. The seer pondered, then understood that. For a moment, McDonald used his loud voice instead of his horse to reach out and damn the point man, who had started the train downhill instead of holding to the high country as ordered.

"Perhaps, then, the British have the greatest number of warriors, greater than the Americans, Russians and Spanish," Little Coyote suggested.

McDonald, still angrily eying the lead horseman and guards, fixed his eyes on this persistent Flathead who was proving as bothersome as the horsefly droning near his horse's rump.

"I dinna' think that." He tapped his bushy head. "They think and hold council about these things better than others. If they need—want—to gain things, power or control, they think how they can do so, often wi' the help of others." McDonald's horse started, then whipped its tail furiously at the offending, blood-hungry fly. "I'll tell ye, Little Coyote, the Flatheads have been using politics to get to the buffalo country, to ally themselves wi' others for other gains. I've learned this, I have: Bigness, whether in a body or a tribe, dinna' always win, and I've the bruises to prove it. The widely scattered and larger tribes have less control as they break down and move in small groups from place to place. The most effective tribes can be smaller ones that talk, think together, and—" He looked disbelievingly upward. "That son-of-a-bitchin' lead man is going down the hill again!" He kicked his startled horse in the flanks and began racing upward, his roaring reaching ahead. "Damn ye to hell! Why in hell canna' ye do as ye're told?"

At the turnoff, McDonald solemnly grasped the three Indians' hands in turn and said "Farewell." He continued to hold the medicine man's hand in his big paw, looked down once, then straight into his eyes: "This is hard for me to say. But 'tis truth. A strong reason I'm leaving the Company is that I can rise no higher than I am right now—a man to fight for the furs—and maybe die. I dinna' learn to write the King's English and I canna' do it now to my advantage. Too old. Learn the language. Learn to speak it better, to write it well. Your people will be dealing wi' white man—confusing twists and turns more perilous than this trail—I guess forever." He dropped Little Coyote's hand, reached into one of his great pockets and handed the Flathead three large twists of tobacco. Then he loosed a volley of incomprehensible words and kicked his horse toward the pack string, which had passed them by. The lead man looked back but did not change direction. He was heading upward and ever northward almost as straight as an arrow's flight. Now Pony Whip proudly took the lead for the trio. He and his two Flathead kin would head almost due west to the Shoshone Ice Caves.

Broken Pipe's eyes opened wider as he appreciatively hefted the two Hawken guns Pony Whip proudly gave to him after the joyous welcome along the small stream issuing from the south end of the Smoky Mountains. Lance disappeared almost immediately in a throng of young Shoshone braves who plied him with questions about his long rifle, the turtle-shell shape of his shield and the fresh Blackfeet scalp adorning it.

The trader listened attentively to the stories Pony Whip and Little Coyote told. He pursed his lips and frowned as they talked about white man's aims to trap out the Snake River region. Almost immediately Broken Pipe could see the problems he would present to the council and that they would send to the many other roving bands of Shoshonis.

"When Hudson's Bay Company brings their own trappers, there will be little reason to trade with the Shoshonis," he said. "The Company does not have the Hawken guns. It will take long for us to get such guns, so it will be long before we are strong like others." His face brightened for a moment. "Because there are numerous beaver here, perhaps we should encourage the Americans to come here. I will trade horses to the east only—for the good guns." His voice took on a somewhat hesitant tone, and he spoke more quietly, probingly as he looked at Little Coyote. "The Iroquois tell us, very interested Tjolzhitsay and the Nez Percé about the Black Robes and their religion, which can work wonders. What would be . . ." He paused as though reluctant to say more, but Little Coyote knew this trader father-in-law of his. ". . . your thoughts about perhaps trying to bring some Black Robes into the fur country? Could they mix their powers with yours and other seers to strengthen what you call the *sumesh* of all our allies?" Broken Pipe did not wait for an answer, apparently having found that, for now, questions only created more questions. "There will be many seeking good guns," he said. "Will there be enough beaver? When they are gone, will white man want my horses?"

T hough tired from their trek of more than two-hundred of white man's miles northwestward from the Shoshone Ice Caves, Little Coyote and Lance appreciatively looked about as they rode through the Wallowa Valley. The valley was lush in the green of late spring, teeming with wild game and horses and almost surrounded by the peaks of the Wallowa and Blue mountains.

"How much like our own valley, my father!" Lance marveled.

As they looked on, some Nez Percé approached, momentarily scattering a large herd of superb horses they were guarding. Very quickly Little Coyote began to understand the many reasons these riders, and soon the entire encampment, greeted the two Flatheads with much honor. Aged, smiling Bad Leg and stolid War Arrow conducted the seer to the council lodge. Younger Red Paint warmly embraced his friend, then took Lance to his own lodge to meet other younger warriors.

Chief of this Nez Percé band was Tuekakas, a tall, powerfully built warrior of approximately forty-seven summers with a sharply chiseled face, prominent cheekbones, penetrating eyes and a high, combed-back pile of hair atop his head. The hair ended in a long braid behind each ear. After the pipe, Tuekakas raised his arms and spoke in a deep, commanding voice:

"We honor Little Coyote because he is warrior-seer of our Flathead brothers. We honor him because, in the stories of the Nee Mee Poo, Coyote slew the great monster and, whirling it, scattered its blood throughout this part of the world. From the drops of blood came our Real People. In those beginnings Coyote told the Real People there would come a new time, a time of many human beings, and in that time the Real People would face much hardship and sorrow. Owl Skin . . ." Tuekakas respectfully gestured toward an ancient man seated near the pipe. ". . . tell us we should seek your counsel, too, to help us learn if the Age of Sorrow approaches. Do the many white men bring us this sorrow? Should we seek further wisdom, perhaps the power of the white man's Black Robes, about whom we have learned much from the Iroquois and Canadian trappers? Others of the Nee Mee Poo band have counseled we should. Or, should we drive white man from our midst?"

Owl Skin stirred now and, with the help of a sub-chief, stood so all could see and hear as he leaned heavily on his medicine crook. He reminded Little Coyote of Shining Shirt of so long ago. The medicine man's blanket fell from his woefully thin shoulders and hung, arrested by an encircling thong, about his stick of a waist. His bony ribs, like those of a long-starved dog, protruded even more as he drew in a deep breath to speak in a cracked, high voice.

"I knew much of Shining Shirt," Owl Skin said. "We exchanged wisdom. We encouraged alliances to the chiefs. We seek your wisdom. I cannot talk long." He turned slightly to the right and fixed his blind eyes on Little Coyote. "Before our chiefs, I ask you to consider if the Age of Sorrow approaches. How do we deal with it? I ask you to ponder some words. The white chiefs Lewis and Clark said these words to us."

The ancient seer almost chanted them, pausing between each short statement to breathe deeply so he could continue:

"'The Great White Father has sent us here to know you—to find ways to help you.

He will protect you.
You must keep the peace.
Your Great White Father will send traders
to supply you with all your needs
in exchange for the furs
of many animals,
most particularly the beaver.'"

"Already I do not like what others have seen and what I have heard," Owl Skin said. "Sit with us again when you return from the fort of the Nez Percés."

Little Coyote looked at Tuekakas. The chief was nodding approval. Owl Skin's legs and voice strengthened. He raised his staff high above his head: "The eyes of the spirit within me see the Age of Troubles. Not now." He jabbed the air with his crook. "Not now." Again he raised the crook and took a deep breath. "Soon, but after my bones have joined those of the father of Tuekakas in the sacred soil of our Wallowa Valley."

Owl Skin, again assisted by the sub-chief, slowly sat down and pulled his robe around his skeleton-like body. He sat there, immovable as an ancient mummy, dried by Sun and wind, while the council members talked. They shook their heads in dismay on learning the Hudson's Bay Company would trap all the beaver on the tributaries of the upper Snake. Though the Nez Percé often fought with some of the Shoshone bands, they did not like to hear these words. They began to understand more fully another reason why the people at Fort Nez Percés wished to bring peace throughout the land—until the beaver houses were as empty as all the chambers of last summer's wasp nest.

Lance winced as a musket ball thunked into the back of dead Not Afraid of Guns. The noise of the musket was close, from behind a thin fringe of brush on a sand hill. Another ball plowed a small furrow of sand, but stopped short of the yet-warm carcass of the Appaloosa Broken Pipe had given him. Little Coyote had killed his beloved buffalo horse first for them to fort behind, arguing they both could ride the larger, younger Appaloosa if the surrounding Blackfeet should decide a direct charge would be too costly and leave. When some of the Blackfeet circled slightly ahead, the Appaloosa had to die, too. This could be a long siege. The two Flatheads were lying in the sand dunes a few miles south of the Centennial Mountains, from which they had planned to move west and north, then cross the pass in the Beaverhead Mountains to their valley. There was brackish water—a seep in their horseflesh fort from a tiny lake just east of larger Mud Lake. And they could eat the horses should the food in the saddlebag run out. Already, strips of meat were drying on rumps and backs of the two carcasses. But two warriors against fourteen? There was hope, though. There had been seventeen, but the other three were dead of close-range shots from Lance's bow and rifle and his father's Hawken gun. The chase had driven Little Coyote and Lance into the sand from the protective ravine they had been traveling. When the sand had slowed their race, forcing them to abandon two horses, they had stopped while water was yet available.

Lance chewed a piece of jerky for a few moments, shoulders and head against the bloating belly of the buffalo pony. "If we had but one of the swivel guns from Fort Nez Percés or the one of our people, my father, we could strive hard to insult the Blackfeet into a wild charge."

"It will come soon enough." Little Coyote tossed a pinch of sand into the air. A slight puff of dust moved southward, the direction of most of their besiegers. He accepted a piece of jerky from his son and chewed meditatively. Yes, a swivel from Fort Nez Percés would be useful, but he wanted little else from that place, which almost had cost him his son.

In sharp contrast to the welcome in the Wallowa Valley, their arrival at the fort had been almost unobserved. The place had been bustling with a mixture of Cayuses, Nez Percé and Walla Wallas outside the fort, French Canadians and other whites both outside and inside the largest structure Little Coyote had yet seen. Surrounding all was a palisade of heavy planks more than three times his height. The outside of this wall had been adzed and chiseled smooth so no one could clamber up it. Atop this wall was yet another wall, about shoulder high to Little Coyote, which provided loopholes for firing guns. An inside walkway at the base of this wall enabled guards to patrol back and forth and look downward on the surrounding area. Each corner of the palisade had a blockhouse, which the visitors learned held water barrels to fight fires. Inside the high palisade was a yard, then another wall, also with an inner walkway. The wall was more than twice the seer's height. Behind this wall were cabins and storehouses, accessible only by a heavy outer gate, re-enforced with iron. Those wishing to trade had to come into the yard and approach an opening scarcely war-shield size in the smaller wall near the trading room. The opening could be closed with an iron flap. Few Indians ever were allowed inside. This undoubtedly would have been the two Flatheads' treatment, too, had not Lance, tired from his long journey, sat down near the inside gate. He had pulled his blanket above his head and shoulders to rest. His father had decided to study this marvel the Hudson's Bay Company had built in the event the Indians did not welcome the Company's intrusion, or if others sought to raid rather than trade for the supplies within.

As he had walked across the space between the two palisades, the medicine man noted the mouth of a small cannon protruding from each of the four blockhouses, then swivel guns along the walkways, and a small mortar above the main outside gate. The weapons could well cover the area about the fort. The Columbia River was to the west, rocky cliffs to the south. North and east were treeless plains. Workmen had gone upstream almost one-hundred of white man's miles to cut and float down the logs for the structure. The work and care in constructing the huge fort indicated the traders expected to take rich harvests of fur, indeed, from the country—and not lose them, even to powerfully armed white men.

The large body looked familiar as Little Coyote had watched a man approach the heavy inside gate. The man stopped, eyed Lance dozing in his blanket against the log wall, then quietly tapped on the door for the sentry to unbar it. It creaked partially open, held there by the arm of the gateman inside.

"Damn, dirty Indian!" Brandt's voice had reached Little Coyote at a distance too far for him to run forward and prevent the trapper from jerking the gate from the restraining arm and, with both hands, smashing it into his son.

Lance, now alerted, had taken care of himself. He had rolled aside and out of his blanket as the gate slammed against the wall. Surprised, Brandt had turned to receive a heavy kick in the crotch. Lance's face had registered surprise at the white man's lack of reaction to this normally disabling kick. Instead of doubling over in pain, the man had reached inside his sash and pulled out a small pistol. He had cocked and pointed it at Lance before Little Coyote's words reached out ahead of his body.

"Brandt! I am Little Coyote, who gelded you!"

Brandt had whirled and fired at the seer, missing because his target had dropped to the ground. Lance had jabbed Brandt deep in the guts with the butt end of the ancient lance that long ago almost had cost the trapper his life.

Brandt had gone down and was gasping on the ground while the gatekeeper and two other men emerged to confront the Flatheads and a number of Cayuses, Walla Wallas and Nez Percé. Guards staring down from the inner-palisade walkway had nervously watched the commotion. A man, evidently a sub-chief, had come out of the fort and complied immediately when Little Coyote said, "We will talk. Inside!"

The white sub-chief had been apologetic, explaining that were the chief present, he surely would give them presents and order Brandt to leave forever.

"Brandt will leave," Little Coyote had said. "I told him my son would pin him to the earth like an insect should we find him again."

"I say. You cannot do that!"

"It will be done!"

The sub-chief's attitude had changed to indifference when he learned the two men were Flatheads. Was this because many of their furs already were trapped, or there was friction between the Hudson's Bay people here at Fort Nez Percés and Flathead Post? Once more the man showed interest, even some deference, when he learned these warriors had come from a visit with their ally, Tuekakas, and were kin to Broken Pipe of the Shoshonis. The Flatheads had left soon afterward. Though they had declined gifts, they had traded the few beaver they possessed for more gunpowder.

Little Coyote was exceedingly thankful for the gunpowder as, once more, a Blackfeet musket ball thunked into the back of his old friend Not Afraid of Guns. Father and son took turns sleeping the remainder of that long afternoon and longer night. Sun climbed the mountains and the northeast breeze freshened while the two prayed to the Good Spirit. Again they ate jerky and smoked fish while they watched the Blackfeet huddling around their roasting fires.

"Soon they will finish eating and gather together to attack," Little Coyote said. He examined his Hawken rifle while Lance, looking occasionally at his father for encouragement, did the same with the long rifle. They laid out their bows and arrows and the lance.

"We must encourage them to attack," Little Coyote said. "When they prepare to mount, they will expose their bodies fully. We will fire our rifles and perhaps kill or wound two warriors. They do not know that we have guns that reach far. We will hastily load and walk toward them for a short distance, insulting them, taunting them, daring them to attack."

Lance nodded his consent, though his father could see questions in his son's face and eyes.

"Perhaps your shield possesses a power or an answer from the Good Spirit," Little Coyote said. "Do not let them see you filling it with the driest and finest sand. We must encourage our enemies to charge directly toward us to count coup. Then we will scamper back to our fort. When I shout, we will throw our shields of sand high into the wind. The horses will shy and the sand surely will blind some of the enemy. Shoot only at those who are not rubbing their eyes. These will not fire as their horses carry them past us."

Two Blackfeet mounted their horses, waiting for the others.

Seemingly, each man would lead a file of seven warriors to encircle the Flatheads before the charge.

"I will shoot the warrior on the white horse; you will shoot at the other." Father and son carefully aimed over the now greatly bloated body of Not Afraid of Guns. One warrior fell from his mount when the rifles cracked; the other tottered as his horse began racing away. The Flatheads rushed forward, reloading and shouting insults at the rapidly mounting Blackfeet.

"Now we halt," Little Coyote cautioned an elated Lance. "Now, back to the fort."

Shrieking vengeance, the twelve Blackfeet charged in a group, eager to run down, count coup and destroy these enemies who had killed five of their number.

"Ready your shield." Little Coyote laid down his rifle within easy reach and, standing on his knees, lifted his shield a short distance. Lance did the same.

Holding their coup sticks well forward, the Blackfeet urged on their horses. Impeded by the sand, the animals jostled each other as their enraged riders began whipping them to greater efforts. When they were only a few horse lengths away, Little Coyote shouted, threw his shield upward and grasped the Hawken. Lance was even more careful, thorough, spraying the sand in a semi-circle and higher yet because he stood against the charge. All but one horse raced around the dead ones. The rider of that one died from a lance thrust as he reached forward with his coup stick. Only four warriors had escaped most of the sand. Two of these died from rifle shots as they turned their mounts back toward the Flatheads. The other two shouted warnings but bravely helped chase the horses of their yet-blinded companions out of arrow range.

The beleaguered Flatheads quickly reloaded as the Blackfeet washed out their eyes in the brackish water and gathered for another charge. This time they had their weapons at the ready— and were upwind.

"We will fire the rifles at two of their horses." Little Coyote laid on his belly. A Blackfeet horse screamed, ran erratically, then dropped. Another raced uncontrollably away with a ball from the long rifle in its guts. Little Coyote and Lance picked up their bows and arrows as one Blackfeet pointed southward with his trade musket as though to lead the charge. Unaccountably, he reined up his horse. The others did the same. They picked up the bodies of their dead companions nearby, slowed so the two riders from the shot horses could leap behind, then retreated northward away from the Flatheads' makeshift fort. Little Coyote and Lance looked about. Behind them, a large cavalcade of horsemen and pack animals was moving their way.

The approximately three-score men straggled to view the two recently killed Blackfeet. They halted while Little Coyote conveyed the situation to a keen-eyed, lithe, Salish-speaking Iroquois. Leader of this Hudson's Bay group, the Iroquois said, was Alexander Ross, who remained on his horse. They were returning to Hudson's Bay Company's Flathead Post with five-thousand beaver from a Snake River expedition. And they unwillingly were hosts to seven Americans! Yes, the Flatheads would be most welcome to accompany them over the Beaverhead Mountain pass and into the Bitter Root Valley.

Lance slipped away to scalp the two Blackfeet he and his father had killed before the charge. Helped by some Iroquois, he returned with the dead warriors' two horses and muskets. Mounting one horse, Lance went to recover two more guns from the sand.

When Sun was low in the sky, all camped at some hot springs west of the battle site. While many men cavorted in the hot water and ate under the eyes of watchful guards, Little Coyote and Lance learned much by listening well and, later, talking to the Iroquois warrior who first had greeted them. He was Ignace Hat-chiorauquasha, about whom War Arrow had spoken during the council. These Iroquois were under the leadership of Pierre Tevanitagon, although Ross' continued aloof demeanor indicated he was greatly displeased with Tevanitagon for leaving the main party with eleven others to trap separately. Fearful of the Shoshonis, Tevanitagon had turned over their catch of more than one-hundred beaver to the Americans for supplies and a promise that they would escort them back to Flathead Post. Adding to

Ross' anger was the easy manner in which the American leader had explained he felt bound to keep that promise, although Ross tried hard to assure him there now was no need to do so.

"I am sure he wishes to spy on the Hudson's Bay operations," Hatchiorauquasha said. He gestured toward the American leader. The man was clean shaven and seated apart from the other six who were eating and talking. He was reading a small, black book. Nearby was his pile of gear, including two pistols and a rifle.

"He is a fierce fighter, and only a summer ago had a great battle with a grizzly bear," the Iroquois said. "He carries the scars on his face and neck. He prays often to God, who saved him."

Little Coyote and Lance watched Hatchiorauquasha speak briefly to the man before returning to his roasting fire. The American closed his book, looked momentarily and prayerfully to the sky, carefully placed the book in a leather bag, picked up his rifle and stood erect. He was thin, surely more than six feet tall, and when he strode over to the Flatheads his walk was swift and sure-footed as an elk. The two braves rose to greet him. He spoke in English as though aware they spoke the language.

"I am Jedediah Smith. Hatchiorauquasha said you are Little Coyote and Lance." His smile was brief, but warm. He was perhaps eight or nine summers younger than Little Coyote's thirty-three, though his demeanor was that of an older man. "You were with Andrew Henry and Drouillard at Three Forks. I am with Ashley-Henry Company. We're here to obtain furs in the Rocky Mountains, the valley of the Snake—wherever we can get them. That's Sublette, Eddie, Black over there with the others. You'll meet them soon."

Smith shook their hands the white man's way, then sat down. He would talk. First though, he held out his rifle. It was a Hawken gun, almost exactly like Little Coyote's.

"The Ashley-Henry people arm their men well," Smith said. He pointed to where the other six Americans had placed their rifles. All appeared to be Hawkens. Smith leaned over to accept Little Coyote's proffered gun. The mountain man's hair fell away from his neck and ear, the former badly claw-marked, the latter obviously crudely sewn back onto the head. He expressed considerable interest in Little Coyote's account of how he had obtained the Hawken, shaking his head knowingly.

"After Jones and Immel were killed," Smith said, "Henry took over Fort Benton on the mouth of the Bighorn. Re-named it Big Horn Post. Some of his men are trapping near there now, and a couple hundred miles south in the Wind River country."

Smith examined Lance's Pennsylvania rifle, hefting it, sighting, and running his hands appreciatively over the ornate stock and patch box.

"Light, too light, but a beautiful and useful weapon all the same," he said. "Ashley and Henry aim to have Hawken make many guns for the company men, even to trade. Keep in mind the Ashley-Henry Company. You'll be hearing from us. I think we'll be giving Hudson's Bay a hard run in the Snake."

Smith arose, strode over to his pack and returned with a pound of finely ground powder.

"Good for priming the long rifle and good for shooting it." He handed the flask to an astonished Lance, who shook his hand gratefully then, and again in the Bitter Root Valley when Smith, his fellow Americans, the Hudson's Bay people and Hat-chiorauquasha left the Flathead encampment for Flathead Post. Accompanying them was a large trading party of Flatheads. When trading would begin, there would be almost a thousand people competing for the goods—Flatheads, Pend d'Oreille kin, Nez Percé, Spokanes and Kutenais. And after the furs would run out, they would begin trading horses, thousands of them, the pack horses that had carried many tons of dried buffalo meat—for trading, too.

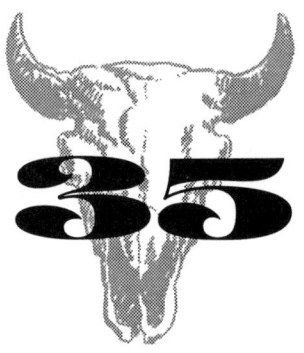

35

"Tjolzhitsay calls the council! Tjolzhitsay calls the council!" Bull Stands Apart strode through the encampment crying the announcement above the noises of children, dogs, youths and older men and women. Many of the adults were carrying in sticks they had hauled from the mountains into nearer piles when the yellowing alpine larch had begun to warm the hillsides with color and warn of approaching winter. By now Sun had risen high enough to melt the heavy frost and quicken the pace of all who had ventured from the lodges. An aromatic light pall of cottonwood and pine smoke began drifting northward from the smoke holes; disjointed fog patches climbed the peaks like great bands of mountain goats to spin out into white strands and whisk away in the greater breezes there.

Little Coyote reluctantly had pried away Antelope's warm arms and, trying to disregard her enticing murmurs of protest, had hurriedly donned his garments and walked outside. He broke the thin layer of ice in the white man's bucket and poured out some water, the glass-like shards tinkling musically as they hit the tin basin. Shivering, he carefully combed out his long hair, retied it in two braids, then re-entered the lodge. Antelope had placed the tin cup of cold, white man's coffee in the fire and was gently fanning the coals with a goose wing. She handed the cup to Little Coyote.

"These older men." She mimicked the voice of an ancient, toothless crone. "They have all day to talk, but, too early, forgetting their younger years, they tear away those who perhaps would prefer to remain abed for a while longer." Provocatively, she dropped her blanket and crept back under the furs. "Once again, as for months past, it is lonely and cold here."

Little Coyote dropped to his knees, encircled her head and shoulders with his arms and pulled her to him. "Eat well, rest well. There will be little sleep tonight." He shook her playfully and hurried outside to catch up with Running Buffalo Bull. The older warrior was limping now, his stride not so vigorous. He greeted his son warmly, looked to the far hillsides where they knew Lance was on horse guard, and told his son that Little Yellow Bird would have them all at their lodge in two more Suns. There still was much to be told. The two warriors were among the first to approach the council lodge, so they stopped briefly to observe three Iroquois and several Flatheads facing Sun, praying fervently to the Good Spirit, then concluding by raising their right hand to the forehead, chest, left then right shoulders in the form of a cross.

"They are reverent and their message is good," Running Buffalo Bull said. He looked closely at his son as though trying to detect if perhaps the seer perceived a threat to his own status with the people.

"Among the many stories I was told upon our return was that four of our people and three of the Nez Percé set out for St. Louis to find the Black Robes," Little Coyote said.

"Yes. Two of our people and two of the Nez Percé were killed in the Wyoming country. Another of our warriors died when they turned back. Only our sub-chief, Man of The Morning, returned here. He had much to say about the ordeal, but is willing to return, and I think Tjolzhitsay again will lend strong encouragement. Little Bear Claw and Willow Woman. They are on the buffalo hunt. And Tjolzhitsay, he has the white man's cough that comes and stays, then goes. I do not like this, though, as with others, sometimes it does not bring the blood."

Little Coyote nodded, regretfully, but now others were converging on the council lodge. Among them was Gun, painfully hobbling. They would wait to greet him.

"He bears many scars and has lost an eye," Running Buffalo Bull said. "One leg is not straight." Running Buffalo Bull looked at his own as though grateful that, in their growing weakness, they were stronger than his friend's. "Gun and a trapping party went afar to find many beaver, guarded by the blunderbusses. All went well until a large force of Blackfeet surrounded their camp among the trees. They would starve or burn them out. Gun and his warriors placed the heavily charged blunderbusses amid their beaver pelts. They plugged up the ends of the barrels with clay. He tied a long thong to their triggers, payed it out and hid in a tree while the others escaped at night. Gun came down from his tree to put new wood on the fires and then again hid. When the Blackfeet stole in at daybreak and reached down to exult over their great loot of furs and traps before pursuing our people, Gun pulled on the thong. Five Blackfeet died; others were hurt by the bullets and blunderbuss pieces. Gun, too, escaped, though from his tree he was vulnerable to the explosions. He, too, would have joined in the trek for the Black Robes, but he lacked the strength."

Little Coyote embraced Gun warmly and accompanied his friend to the lodge. He noted that, with his one eye, the sub-chief had to raise his head and cock it sideways to focus. When he did so, his long jaw dropped and gave his face a vacant, open-mouthed look while he stared. "There remains a bit of metal in the corner," Gun explained. "I cannot get it out."

Little Coyote faced his friend toward Sun. He peered closely into the good eye, noting the inflammation at one corner and the constantly flowing tears. The metal was in the tiny bump above the corner of the eye. Perhaps it was scraping the eyeball at times. Little Coyote thought of the small set of tweezers in the chest he had obtained at Lisa's fort.

"Tomorrow, when Sun first appears bright and strong, I will repair your eye outside our lodge," he said confidently. Then he smiled. Would he be bright and strong? Ah. There came Lance, astride his mother's Appaloosa, trailing a pack horse and proudly carrying his scalp-tasseled shield and the ancient lance. His father would sit with him near the outer circle of the lodge until their head chief called them forward after the sacred pipe ceremony.

"Thus I counseled the Nez Percé upon our return from Fort Nez Percés, thus I tell you, for you and the others to decide." Little Coyote had told the story of his and Lance's journey, which was followed by many questions. Then Tjolzhitsay's and Three Eagles' mates had handed out the rare coffee in tin cups. There was meat after the cups were empty. Now there must be decisions.

"Once again the wisdom of Shining Shirt, part of which I gained on my vision quest, must be told," Little Coyote said. "We should not fight white man." There were muted voices of dissent at this flat statement, but the dissent was as nothing compared to what the Nez Percé had voiced earlier in the Wallowa Valley. Little Coyote used the same arguments now.

"The fort is heavily armed, as is Astoria far to the west. Will there soon be others, more than now, in all directions, except among the Blackfeet, to serve as trading posts? True, some are not as strong as others, but white man carries his goods to them and protects them. He willingly would use up his goods to save his life. If we—the Shoshonis, the Nez Percé, the Cayuses, Kalispels, Kutenais and our kin the Pend d'Oreilles—all fight them as do the Blackfeet, we no longer will receive their goods."

He heard murmurs of assent now, during which Tjolzhitsay coughed loudly and long. Little Coyote waited respectfully, then continued. "And there still would be the fierce and brave Blackfeet."

He briefly told the council about the attack made on himself and Lance. "*Xe, xe*, good, good," he heard, knowing that warriors would demand longer tellings of this after the council. He told them about the small party of Iroquois trappers who had been forced to seek the protection of Jedediah Smith, how Lance and his father had prayed for the protection of the Good Spirit, and how Ross and his party had appeared.

There was much talk then about these revelations, with all

357

present voicing their views about Little Coyote's staunch belief there should be no fighting the white man. Throughout, Tjolzhitsay appeared lost in deep thought, merely designating who would speak next. When those in the council once more were given meat and water, and Sun neared the western peaks, the chief began to talk: "The greater answer to the prayers of Little Coyote and Lance came from the man Smith as he told them about the Iroquois. We are but few, even with the Pend d'Oreille and our allies. I counsel you now that, indeed, we should not fight white man, but travel with their ever growing numbers if we are to survive, just as the Iroquois sought the protection of Smith. We will remain strong in spirit, strong in our remaining numbers and among our allies. We will not throw away our pride by this action. With such wisdom we will keep our lives and remain great fighters, as the whites will see and cherish." Tjolzhitsay pointed toward Lance.

The young warrior stood hesitantly among all these warriors, then, led by Three Eagles, carried forward an armful of trade muskets and presented them to the head chief.

"Little Coyote and his son took these from the Blackfeet," Three Eagles explained. "Perhaps our people will wish to give them to our kinfolk."

Murmurs about keeping the muskets within the tribe arose. Three Eagles patiently waited for them to subside. Now he looked at his ailing *i-sts-sókoi*.

"You have viewed the Hawken guns brought back from Fort Benton," he said. "We have tested them. They will perform well, indeed, upon the buffalo—and any enemies. This Smith, he has told Little Coyote and Lance that the Ashley-Henry Company will trade such guns. I say, Tjolzhitsay, that this winter we all should work hard and travel far to catch furs. We will set the women to tanning the cow buffalo hides for trade. We will get the Hawken guns."

Three Eagles paused as Tjolzhitsay signed he was prepared to put down the whip. The head chief coughed yet again.

"This has been a long, hard day of much importance," Tjolzhitsay said. "We must know where to meet the Ashley-

Henry people before others do. We will send two men to Flathead Post to talk to this Smith, who stays there with his men despite Ross's great displeasure. But will we catch enough furs?"

There was no need to send the men. In *Skussús*, the first month of The Wandering, horse guards north of the encampment brought word of a great cavalcade coming. They were not Blackfeet; the guards also reported they had recognized Jedediah Smith and the other six Americans.

Chief of the group was Peter Skene Ogden, a man with a great head of much white and gray hair that also covered his ears. He had heavy, dark eyebrows, a fleshy face, a stern mouth and sharp eyes. He was friendly, except to the American tag-alongs, and very much in command. He would lead the Hudson Bay's Snake River Brigade. Ross would be chief of distant Spokan Post. Fortunately, the arrival of the almost four-hundred horses and perhaps eighty men, with wives and children of the trappers, coincided almost to the day with the return of the hunters from the buffalo grounds. There had been a great kill because the snow had delayed falling, making hunting and traveling easier for all. Little Coyote scarcely had time to greet a grinning Little Bear Claw before they both were summoned to Three Eagles' lodge. Soon it held Jedediah Smith, the other Americans, Gun, Little Bear Claw and Little Coyote. Three Eagles pointed to the Flatheads. "I have talked to Tjolzhitsay," he said. "He is unwell today. I will provide a feast for Ogden and his sub-chiefs. You will talk to Smith and his men about the Hawken guns?" Smith's head rose, evidently understanding the last two words.

Little Yellow Bird sent over a pot of her buffalo meat and three smoked buffalo tongues. Antelope carried some fire outside her lodge and soon the men inside prepared to eat. First, though, Gun painfully dropped to his knees, made the sign of the cross and thanked the Good Spirit. Smith said thanks in his own way; three of his men removed their caps as he did so.

Hawken guns? Yes, the company would trade them. Each would require many furs. "Will you be able to catch that many here?" Smith asked.

Gun spoke briefly to Little Bear Claw, who took a large bite of meat before signaling for Little Coyote to join him outside the lodge. Little Bear Claw soon was nodding to Gun.

"Will the Ashley-Henry traders take gold as well as furs?" As Little Coyote spoke, all the men stopped chewing. "There is a place. Perhaps we can go there to get some gold," the seer said vaguely. He repeated the statement in Flathead, which brought an affirmative nod from Smith and a hint of a grin to Gun's ravaged face. Gun had looked straight at Little Coyote as he had smiled. Loosening of the bit of brass with a knife tip, followed by the tweezers, had worked.

When the men resumed chewing, Smith bent over and studied Little Coyote's story skin on the willow frame. Antelope had pushed the frame against the lodge wall. Smith reached inside his large jacket pocket and removed his notebook, which resembled that in which Clark and Lewis had made their marks so long ago. He would draw a map.

"Ashley will try to bring trading goods to Green River, near this fork, or the Popo Agie," Smith said. "This will be in the sixth moon. His trappers will meet him there." Skillfully, quickly, Smith drew a few lines on a page, adding a new one each time Little Coyote nodded he understood. "Try the fork on Green, you call it 'Siskadee,' first, right here above the Uinta Mountains." Smith removed the sheet and handed it to his host.

The two men talked long into the night after the other Americans, followed by Gun and Little Bear Claw, departed. Clearly, Smith liked his hosts. He asked about the trails the people followed, writing in the notebook as he listened. He talked about Colter, the Lisa people, Three Forks and, finally, about Drouillard. He moved closer to the waning light of the fire. As he prepared once more to hold the book on his knee, it slipped and fell to the floor. The pages fluttered in all directions. Smith carefully tapped them together before re-inserting them between the covers. He securely tied a leather thong around the book and returned it to his pocket.

"You liked Colter and the others, that's clear," Smith said as he sipped thoughtfully at the tea he had provided for Antelope to prepare. "You'll not like all the white men you meet. Nor have I as my people traveled from New York. That's about as far east as you can go." He raised his hand and began moving it westward, raising and lowering it as he described his family's further travels. "Then my father moved us to a place called Pennsylvania, where many rifles are made, also in the Ohio country, where they moved next and stayed. I kept moving to Illinois and about three years ago got to St. Louis, then here." He dropped his hand. "The Americans are moving west, finding the easiest trails to get here. I can't say that I like all their moving, though I'm a part of it. They . . . we . . . want furs. They'll move west to get them. They want land, your land, too, most likely, as I've seen them take the land from other Indians. Kill them for it, many wondering all the time why the *Indians* want to keep it! They want to raise food on the land like, well, sort of like the Mandans you told me about. But there's something else. They just want to own the land, like you want to own a good horse or a Hawken gun. Do you understand?"

"I can understand the Blackfeet trying to keep my people from the buffalo," Little Coyote said. "But to kill just for the land? This is what I cannot understand. There is land as far as I can see, and when I go there, I can see as far again, and yet again."

Antelope echoed her husband's wonderment: "Kill for land?"

Smith put down his cup, rose and stretched. "I know. You believe the land is for all, even this bit of land in the valley—for all the Flatheads. But white man wants to say, 'This is mine. It does not belong to any other man. Keep out, or come in.' Don't fight the whites. Get to know them, but don't fight them. They are coming, as numerous as the buffalo, and as impossible to stop when they stampede. I thank you."

He bowed to Antelope and shook Little Coyote's hand.

When Smith and his men set out next day, still following the clearly disgruntled Ogden party, he carried seven gold nuggets in his possibles bag, handed him, with Tjolzhitsay's approval, by Little Coyote. The seer once again had prayed to the Good Spirit and called on Shining Shirt and the dwindling gold at his burial place. Yes, the Ashley-Henry people would hold back some Hawken guns for the Flatheads, who would attend the rendezvous on the Siskadee or thereabouts—if they brought sufficient furs. Jedediah Smith had shaken hands on that, too. And, once again, Little Coyote knew it was the Good Spirit's wish long ago that Shining Shirt and the others find the gold in the land of much cactus and sun and sand and bring it back to help his people. Again he pondered more deeply how Shining Shirt had brought back and worn the cross hanging from the neck of the skeleton clad in the remnants of a long, black robe.

The people worked hard with their much-reduced number of traps during the cold months, traveling far to get the furs, grateful that they had left seed from which the animals had multiplied in hidden places white man had not found. They packed all the buffalo robes and other furs they safely could spare. Valiant Tjolzhitsay, coughing less against the cold and on re-entering a lodge, carefully formed the party that would seek the Hawken guns. Broken Tooth would lead; Little Bear Claw would be sub-chief. Fast Runner, son of Little Bear Claw and Willow Woman, would go, eager to find the Shoshonis. With the many beaver he almost had worked himself to a shadow to trap, perhaps he could soften Broken Pipe's heart to allow Antelope's sister, Warm Breeze, to return with him. Lance eagerly accepted a place in the party, as did three older warriors and three younger braves.

As much wisdom as strength accompanied the nine men as they made final preparations to set out on the more than five-hundred-mile trek in the fifth moon of the Bitterroot. Tjolzhitsay encouraged them to follow the route toward the Lemhi defile where Finan McDonald's trappers, with buckshot and fire, had inflicted the great defeat on the Blackfeet, making it a place they might tend to avoid. Shield Maker brought them four savage dogs he said he had trained to guard against enemies. The old man also had painted on the other half of Lance's shield the figure of a man throwing sand into the air from a shield. The sand was falling as scalps at his feet. Two pack horses carried the Blackfeet muskets Little Coyote and Lance had brought back with them, plus several muskets council members had brought to support the plan for their use.

The dogs warily watched two more men approach the now-formed party. Surprisingly, Tjolzhitsay was walking fully upright again and Three Eagles was using the walking stick of his *i-sts-sókoi*. As Little Coyote had ministered to the head chief, he had noted the lessening of the deep cough. He was unaware that as Tjolzhitsay had improved, Three Eagles apparently had acquired most of the cough, which Smith had called "pneumonia" and for which he had suggested "rest, rest, rest."

Head chief and war friend dearer than a brother rested a short time before the former said, "Three Eagles carries some additional wisdom which will not further burden the horses now."

Between much coughing, Three Eagles, his strong face leaner, nose more beak-like, said, "Some of the Ashley-Henry men will accompany their fur take to St. Louis. Perhaps with this additional gold and an old musket for protection, most of them could be persuaded to trade their Hawkens. They can get others at St. Louis. The additional guns also could be of use to you on your return trip."

Three Eagles embraced Little Bear Claw and Little Coyote long and hard. The small party headed southward. Little Coyote looked back before they moved out of sight. Simultaneously, Three Eagles, assisted by Tjolzhitsay, slowly turned and waved a final farewell.

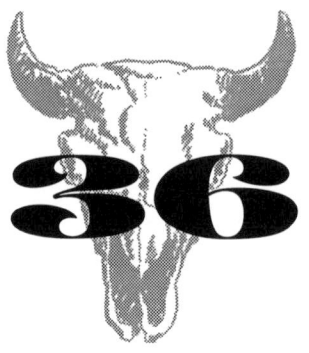

L ittle Coyote's next three sets of tiny figures on his story
hide represented the important events that affected the
people during the remainder of white man's 1825: There
was the death of Three Eagles, the successful return of the warriors
with Hawken guns and the arrival of the first of the white man's
warriors since Clark and Lewis had come into this land seemingly
such a short time ago.

Much time would pass before the medicine man would add
a figure of a white buffalo bull, which the seer believed helped
the Flatheads to achieve a short period of peace with many of the
Blackfeet.

While the hide did not note it, the Flatheads followed Little
Bear Claw's plan for sending people with groups of white men to
guide them. Safety and trading figured in Little Bear Claw's
thinking, but the more far-reaching purpose of his plan was to
know what was going on in the great area in which the Flatheads
lived and roamed. With such knowledge could come survival.

Little Bear Claw had explained his plan soon after he and
Broken Tooth had presented the Hawken guns to Tjolzhitsay and
the council. He had spoken slowly about his idea with great
solemnity and conviction, his sharp eyes searching into those of

every sub-chief and warrior in the lodge: "When we seek the buffalo, upon which depends our life, we first go with certainty to the land where we know the buffalo exist. So, with the same certainty we send prayers to the Good Spirit for help in many things and—concerning the buffalo—where *exactly* to find them. We send out scouts to learn of their movements, where we shall kill them. If we are to remain strong in spirit, strong in our remaining numbers as Chief Three Eagles planned, we must know the forces that are in motion, just as we determine the direction of the winds before we approach the buffalo. We must send our people in directions by plan to learn what others are doing and in council decide how their doing will affect us. We must do this better than other tribes. Thus, while with our bravery and better weapons we cannot halt the changes in our world, we can help to shape them."

On hearing Little Bear Claw speak, some had said, "Truly, the wisdom of Three Eagles seems to be in the spirit of Little Bear Claw."

While the council also had pondered these old and new thoughts so well expressed, Gun had explained how he had accompanied dying Three Eagles to the sacred hill above the place of Shining Shirt, where rested the bones of their people. Three Eagles, astride his favorite buffalo horse, had prayed to the Good Spirit and sung his death songs. When they had ceased, Gun had approached. Strangely, the dead chief had remained on the horse, though slumped forward on its neck. Gun said that a hawk had appeared in the eastern sky as he sorrowfully had brought the body to the encampment.

Some in council remarked that east, too, was the direction from which had come Little Bear Claw, Broken Tooth and all the others, except Fast Runner, with the fourteen Hawken guns and at least as many important adventures to relate to Tjolzhitsay and the council.

The Flatheads had met the gathering of the Ashley-Henry trappers and a few others near the fork of the Siskadee, where Ashley had brought the great pack train of goods. Few Indians were present, although there were at least twenty of Ogden's men, including Hatchiorauquasha. They had deserted and brought hundreds of beaver skins with them because, they said, the Hudson's Bay Company was paying such poor prices.

"We concluded that Ashley's idea of bringing the trade goods to the trappers was better than forcing the trappers to travel afar to bring the furs to the forts," Broken Tooth told the council. "We traded furs for seven of the guns there. The trappers were reluctant to part with their rifles when they learned that Ashley, despite the hazards of Blackfeet, was going to transport his take of more than four and one-half tons of beaver skins to the Bighorn and Yellowstone rivers, then float them down the Missouri to St. Louis."

Jedediah Smith had obtained three of the Hawkens with the gold entrusted to him. "'Do not show your gold until you reach the Yellowstone River,' Smith counseled us," Broken Tooth explained. "We followed his counsel and obtained the other four. Had we had more gold, we could have brought back more Hawken guns, so great is white man's desire for gold. But there was a greater reason some of the trappers who would accompany the furs to St. Louis felt it would be safe to part with the Hawken guns."

The smile faded from the burly Flathead's face: "I have thought much about that reason, and I tell the facts for the council to ponder. At the mouth of the Yellowstone the Ashley-Henry men met almost five-hundred of the white man's warriors. Smith told us through Hatchiorauquasha that they came up the Missouri to make peace agreements with the peoples along the way and to learn if they should build forts, including some on the upper Missouri. Ashley led some of these white warriors— 'soldiers,' Hatchiorauquasha called them—to near the great falls to find the Blackfeet or their allies, but they found none. Hatchiorauquasha said the Great White Father is angry because the Blackfeet kill his trappers, such as Immel and Jones, though other tribes down the Missouri have done the same. I wonder if more forts will be built." Broken Tooth shook his head. "I wonder, too, if a force of almost five-hundred of these soldiers, all well-armed, is the best way to carry out peace talks. Hatchiorauquasha said that much retribution swiftly has followed when tribes down the Missouri have attacked white man. I have spoken."

Seeking the Black Robes and achievement of peace with the Blackfeet now became Tjolzhitsay's major objectives. Though seeking peace took longer than it lasted, the old chief felt the effort essential. He told the council, "Though we obtain better guns and information, learn to fight even more ferociously and intelligently, we and our allies still are outnumbered. We will cease to be far sooner than the Blackfeet though we trade one life for several of theirs."

Gun seemed to grow more alive, almost younger, as he became the foremost peace emissary. He met at grave risk and with some success with the Little Robes, with the leaders of those Blackfeet returned after being spared the torture, and with Tree, to whom the Flatheads had returned Owl, sub-chief of the Bloods, after the one-sided encounter with the long rifles at the buffalo grounds. Gun also brought into the process the Pend d'Oreilles, Kalispels and other Flathead allies who had had any amicable contacts with the Blackfeet.

At length, leaders of most of the Blackfeet agreed to discuss possible peace. They would meet in *s'tcyalmín*, the fourth moon of Courtship, at the buffalo grounds close to Three Forks near the time of the hunt. Then there would be food and much rejoicing amid heavy work. During this joyous time, the word of each tribe would eliminate any seeming need for great war parties to eye one another suspiciously. Yet, there would be the usual sort of balance of forces that ensured a safer hunt. Certainly, a major stated reason for the meeting of this great council—a subject of collective concern—could be the arrival of greater numbers of fur-takers, including, now, in the very heartland of the Blackfeet. That was good beaver country, partly because the trappers largely had been kept out. Other subjects that could lead to mutual benefits would emerge as surely as the buffalo calf follows the cow.

Running Buffalo Bull and Little Coyote reined in their horses at the base of the cliff near the place of Shining Shirt. A lone raven circled this sacred hollow. Amid the bird's querulous caws, the aging warrior stiffly dismounted, sat on the blanket with his son and prayed. After a time they smoked.

"There under the poles is the cedar box kept by Shining Shirt," Running Buffalo Bull said. "You must decide if and how you will carry it away for the peace talks. Now I will repeat to you the story of the people, which my father told me, and which many know, but not well because the very mountains have changed since the events happened, and fathers or mothers sometimes become careless about telling their children. Yet, it is so. In my dream the Good Spirit told me to bring you here and tell you what you must say to Tjolzhitsay. If you fetch the box, perhaps it would be good to stop near the bones of Three Eagles for prayers. That you must decide." Running Buffalo Bull looked at his now solemn-faced son he loved so much, and smiled.

"The Good Spirit is not so often my close companion as He is that of my son. But I urge you to act. The Good Spirit sometimes has many persons carry out a small part to make a big one. Even if our peace council fails, who will know when its ripples, like those caused by the stone thrown carefully into the lake, will cease moving—perhaps on a shore too distant for us now to see."

Little Coyote turned restlessly in his sleeping robes; Antelope slept peacefully, her warm legs touching his. In the dimness of the lodge he could see her long hair covering part of her face, a few strands near her nose moving rhythmically with her breathing. Outside, a few male red-winged blackbirds called from their perches on last-year's cattails in the nearby pond. The seer's buffalo horse stirred restlessly, setting a few small, brass bells on its tether to tinkling. This was the sound that had awakened him. The large warning bell was silent, however, so the horse remained safe. For a moment the persistent thought he had pondered before and had banished again crept into his mind. No, he reaffirmed the earlier decision. No name for this horse. He must not allow himself to grow too fond of a horse. The lessons from the acquisition and loss of Not Afraid of Guns had been beneficial. He would reserve his true affections for his family, his people.

So, while the bells had brought him awake, a stronger force had sought emergence. He lay quietly again, mind cleared, and presently the force crept out like Sun over the mountains following its first tell-tale glimmers of light, promise of yet another day. He rolled from his bed, gathering up his garments as he did so, and quietly left the lodge. He led the horse away from the shelter, then mounted and ascended the hill above the pond. There, on the horse, he faced east, clearing his mind of all distractions. He thought only about the eternal mystery of the Good Spirit. That achieved, the man prayed He would look kindly on this attempt at peace. The seer sat there, scarcely aware that Sun now was showing a knife edge of brightness over the distant Crazy Mountain peaks as the horse guards set out to relieve those who had kept watch during the darkness. As the world awakened, he saw the Flatheads' entire hunting encampment just north of the confluence of the three rivers. If only the tribes could join their thoughts as peacefully as these streams formed from so many disparate creeks and springs in the vast reaches of the land! Looking up, he could see the as-yet widely dispersed and undisturbed buffalo bands. They continued to feed on the sloping and grassy hillsides, moving slowly toward the more level prairie areas beyond. With peace, all the peoples could roam the land they all loved, exulting always in the bounty of the Good Spirit!

Unseen was the larger Blackfeet encampment on the far side of a long ridge to the west. Already they were hunting, though Little Bear Claw, chief of this hunt, had not released the hunters of the Flatheads and their allies.

Last to catch Little Coyote's eye was the tree-studded ravine extending north and south between the ridge separating the two encampments. On the rim of the ravine a single tree—its massive, slanting trunk larger than the barrel of a buffalo—pointed like a great spear toward the Flathead encampment. Unaccountably, the words the seer had heard Gun and some of the Iroquois voice emerged from somewhere in his mind. He was surprised that he could remember them with clarity and that they could apply here:

". . . Thy will be done . . . ."

The time of prayer ended then, for he saw Lance racing toward their lodge. The medicine man rode down the hill, certain that Lance had learned that only some of the people would hunt. He was astride another gift Appaloosa from Broken Pipe; Fast Runner had brought the horse home with the trader's other daughter, Warm Breeze.

His long, fur-lined cape settled over Lance's muscular shoulders, chest and belly as he slowed the Appaloosa. The garment flared in the instant he leapt from his mount.

"My father, those of us who control the hunters find our task harder because we have received new word that only those armed with Hawken guns will make the first kills of the buffaloes! Neither Tjolzhitsay nor Little Bear Claw will change this. How can this be? And both have decreed there will be no display of war honors, scalps, even, throughout the hunt. They must remain in the lodges." He looked at his shield hanging from the Appaloosa. "Our chiefs demand too much!" The young warrior's eyes flashed as his lips worked in anger.

Little Coyote knew these angry currents were flowing from almost all who would hunt—even those who possessed the Hawken guns. The two men entered the lodge. Lance remained standing while Antelope, looking anxiously from calm father to angry son, hurriedly brought food.

"Little Bear Claw wisely acts as chief of this hunt, as does Tjolzhitsay, because they know of the hunters' anger," Little Coyote said. "The sight of scalps, other openly boastful symbols of success in battle, inflame the minds of people who would talk peace. That is my wisdom which all in the council accepted. Stay! Stay!"

Lance had stopped chewing and appeared ready to cast the food back into the pot. His father continued speaking: "Thus we extend one friendship hand. The other? Well, the decision to hunt at first only with the Hawken guns has many interpretations, as our chiefs readily saw. For us, we will learn better their use on the buffalo, though I agree all, especially the less experienced, need to practice the ways of the hunt, which even for the older is good for the spirit. The Blackfeet scouts surely will observe and report we possess and can use these weapons. Earlier, Broken Tooth wondered if a force of five-hundred soldiers was the best way to carry out peace talks. By our presence here, both we and the Blackfeet have agreed such an open show of force is not a good practice—if we remain calm and place our shots well."

The seer devoted his full attention to food now. After a time, so did his son. Lance chewed thoughtfully and, finally, nodded his head, swallowed his food and jumped up. As he prepared to return to his duties, he grinned: "I will come back soon, my father, with yet another plan from the younger warriors which our *elders* also will approve."

The young bull pawed at the thin patch of snow, releasing more of the flexible grass stems. He pawed again, grasped a mouthful of grass and pulled, the weight of the massive head easily breaking the stems. Now he raised his head and chewed— then dropped in his tracks. The grass stems protruded from his mouth like great quills while he furiously kicked his hind legs as though climbing a steep hill. The rifle shot echoed throughout the wide basin. The puff of smoke drifted away from the large herd of feeding cows and young bulls. The nearest animal momentarily eyed the now-motionless lump of flesh—then dropped, too, his legs scarcely kicking at all. Again the rifle shot and drifting smoke. Again and again and yet again, until now there were as many motionless bulls as cows on the open patches of ground. Then a wounded bull began racing away after the sound of a shot, agitating those animals within range of his dying run. He dropped before the sound of the second and killing shot followed. The agitated animals continued their run toward one hillside above the basin where larger and older bulls fed. Several horsemen raced downward to meet them. They closed on the remaining younger bulls and cows and fired their rifles into the heart or lung regions of the beasts. As each hunter fired, he slowed his horse, reloaded, then raced forward. Load and fire, load and fire . . . . The hunters followed the herd, passing by dead animals or those that stood and bled and walked a brief circle of death before they, too, fell.

Had an eagle flown over the basin now, it would have viewed it in much the way one studies an ant hill into which he has hastily gouged a depression with a large stick. Creatures, seemingly chaotically, were moving up and down the sides of the basin. A second sight, however, would have disclosed a discernible order: The remainder of the buffalo were lumbering almost single-file up the hillside, then fanning out on the wider prairie beyond. Over and down another slope poured the Flatheads and their allies to butcher the fallen animals. Out on the prairie now, other hunters were taking more buffalo with muskets, arrows and lances; on the west rim of the basin, Blackfeet observers, attracted by the sounds of the Hawken guns and the urgings of the ever present scouts, were moving from behind widely scattered boulders, trees and brush and coalescing. The eagle would have seen seven two-legged creatures continuing to sit together on their horses as they had prior to and throughout the time the animals had begun to fall.

Tjolzhitsay, Little Bear Claw and Gun, as well as War Arrow of the Nez Percé and three Shoshone sub-chiefs, sat beneath a protective tree and expectantly looked upward at Little Coyote. He was standing atop his horse and focusing the spyglass on the Blackfeet. They, too, appeared to be preparing for a discussion about what they had witnessed. Their conclusions could only be the same as those of the warriors on the opposite side of the basin; the Hawken guns were lethal, indeed. They could be used almost like the quiet hunting arrow to make a "stand" on a herd of buffalo, so long as the wind was right and the hunters were expert shots who could remain quiet and hidden—all of which would tend to keep the animals from agitating others into a stampede. Surely the Blackfeet would agree that the Flatheads and their friends seemed very worthy adversaries, yet were willing to talk of peace. Yes, the Flathead leaders agreed: The young warriors' suggestion to use the stand, followed by a general hunt, was praiseworthy, indeed!

Little Coyote closed his spyglass and nimbly jumped to the ground. Now the peace council could begin.

The Blackfeet provided the council lodge almost in the center of the basin. The shelter was made from more than fifty cow buffalo skins and had two wing-like additions erected against any breeze. Although there were at least seventy-five notables present, all could fit within. Others not of the council could, according to tribal tradition, stand around and even present their views. No weapons were present. In the center were two half-circles of the opposing groups. The white pipe rested on a mountain goat hide between them. Each of the leaders passed the pipe within their respective group. Tree, now a great chief among the Blackfeet, would be their spokesman. Seated next to him was Owl, whom he had rescued from the Flatheads so long ago. He was most easily recognizable by the scar from neck to crotch made by Basket's obsidian blade. Yes, Owl's scar could serve both as reproach and threat.

Gun stood. In few words he said what all present already knew—why they were here. The leaders affirmed that he would control the speakers.

Long after Sun had reached the zenith the sub-chiefs had presented heated summaries of past grievances. All then filed outside to relieve themselves and partake of the food provided by the Flatheads.

Sun seemed to move more slowly toward the Tobacco Root peaks as Gun started the sub-chiefs speaking, often grudgingly, of the small evidences of good will exhibited by all sides from time to time toward their enemies. As the evening chill appeared, the warriors filed out. They would return next day, when the chiefs would talk.

Tree stood to speak, having raised himself by a flexing of powerful leg muscles and a quick upward jump unassisted by his strong arms and hands. A thought moved into Little Coyote's mind and stayed there: *This warrior is a weapon, himself.* When he had come alone into his enemies' camp those many years ago, his entire demeanor had verged on open contempt, reined in because he was seeking to save a warrior's life. Yet, by tossing a chip into the council fire so all could see it consumed, he had reminded his enemies that their lodges were few and vulnerable. He yet carried his head slightly back in a manner that conveyed a blend of haughtiness and contempt. And those eyes, always moving, seeking, searching; now they were steely, penetrating, as were the words that came from the thin lips.

"You seek peace," Tree said. "When warriors seek peace, they seek an advantage with words they cannot win with arms. Thus they acknowledge their weakness. Your Gun said we also would talk of white man. You do not fight white man. Do you then speak for white man? We trade with Hudson's Bay Company, but we often fight them if they try to take the furs. We do not let white man find us. Only lately he sought us with his many warriors. We saw him; he did not see us. We will drive such warriors and fur-takers from the land, as we have driven others. You should join us in fighting white man. Then, perhaps, we would have much to talk about. Tell us. Why do you seek peace?"

Now Little Bear Claw looked at Tjolzhitsay, then stood—younger, less tested, a sub-chief of a small tribe. Proud, he stood there, sub-chief of great warriors within his own tribe and representative of alliances, some as tightly bound as links in a white man's chain. From all these he drew his strength. Jedediah Smith, Drouillard, Colter: All had told the seer that the Flatheads were as fierce warriors as they had found in all their travels, sometimes more so. No, he would not speak for white man, yet there was a certain strength in knowing that white man often talked about the Flatheads. If this word had reached the Flatheads, it had reached others. He would speak by stating what all seemed to know. He hoped his voice would be reasonable and strong. Tjolzhitsay, fearful he would begin prolonged coughing, readily got the council's agreement that Little Bear Claw would do as well.

"We win with arms," Little Bear Claw began. "We seek the greater advantage of peace, for then we and our enemies do not die. It is in the stories of our people that the Blackfeet drove us from our home here near the three rivers. We return here to hunt. We will continue to return here to hunt. We want to hunt, to kill the plentiful buffalo which the Good Spirit sends to all, not kill warriors *and* the buffalo. The old ways of warring are going as we fight with more of white man's guns. Too many now are dying. We find no joy in sorrowing lodges."

Little Bear Claw nodded. Little Coyote stepped forward. He was clad in new, unadorned buckskins. The little coyote tail hung from his neck. He walked to the cedar box where his chief was standing. The seer removed the cover and lifted the box, nudging aside the shield on which the box had rested. He lowered the box on its cover and leaned his coyote-decorated shield against one end of the chest. All knew who he was. He held up his arms, eyes closed, and for a brief time remained standing so still that one could begin to wonder if he had forgotten others were present. At that point, with great deliberation, he reached into the chest. Then, holding aloft a great, flat, chipped, flint axe almost half the size of his shield, he slowly walked about the council lodge. Now he leaned the massive axe against the opposite end of the box from his shield. Twice more he reached into the box to hold aloft, first, a large, chipped, flint knife almost half the size of the axe head and with saw-like edges, and second, a spear point half the size of the knife/saw, but lacking the usually carefully chipped notches for fixing it to the shaft. It was very old, indeed! Amid the silence, the seer replaced the axe in the chest, placed a beaver skin atop that, then did the same with the saw and the great spear point. Once again the medicine man placed his shield on the firmly packed ground and set the box atop it. With great dignity and total silence he resumed his seat.

Little Bear Claw lowered his head, slowly turned it left and right, then looked at the assemblage. When he spoke, his voice was so low all strained to hear. As the words, interspersed with the signs, flowed, his message became stronger, but never strident.

"Our holy men have learned from the Good Spirit that, in the time of almost-forgotten shadows, our people lived far to the west near the great salt water. Before and after perpetual cold covered the land, we became few, but we were strong. We survived.

"Sun sometimes warmed us, but more often Sun, too, seemed

to have forsaken our people. There were few buffalo then, and these were almost twice the size of the buffalo now, and harder to kill. The few beaver were the size of the black bear, the grizzly bear nearly the size of our buffalo now. Then the Good Spirit sent to the edges of the great ice blankets that covered much of the land a creature so large three warriors would have to stand on each others' shoulders to touch its back.

"In that almost-forgotten time, our people in those other places fashioned with great difficulty this great flint axe, knife and spear point as an offering to the Good Spirit to show we could make weapons to kill the huge creatures. But we were too small to use them. The Good Spirit was pleased with our willingness to try. He taught us through Coyote to use fire and the pit to trap and kill them, then use the bones, the meat, the sinews and even at times the long-haired hide of this mighty creature whose nose was as long and as strong as the trunk of a tree when used like a powerful arm. On both sides of its great mouth protruded strong, white teeth which curved like a small tree growing from a cliffside and turning upward as though trying to reach Sun, too.

"Thus the Good Spirit tested us and, yes, the ancestors of the Blackfeet and others who survived the great ice that blanketed so much of the land. He smiled on us and Sun began to warm the land even more. Small, easier-to-kill creatures filled the land, and the buffalo returned in great numbers from the land of the shadow. We prospered and living became easier—but not so easy that we turned lazy and powerless. Now other powerful tribes displaced by the ice moved in on us and we even had to leave the lands of the three forks.

"Much like the great, hairy creatures the people drove to the pit to kill, we became surrounded—the Blackfeet, the Absarokee, Cheyenne, Assinaboin, the Gros Ventre. The Good Spirit provided buffalo enough for all. The great, hairy beasts were no more. The stories of our people tell us the Good Spirit again looked kindly upon us and sent the horse, as well as wise chiefs whose bones are now in the sacred land a day's ride to the east along the Shields River, which joins the Yellowstone.

"Now the tribes began to war on one another. The Good Spirit sent the scourges of sickness among us all. When our smaller numbers dwindled even more, we trekked to our Valley of the Bitter Root where also lie the bones of our later ancestors. Our stories tell us the Good Spirit promised us that as our people carried the great axe, saw and spear point to the valley, if we would be honest—honorable—we would remain strong and wise. Now white men come. We have been told not to fight them, for they are as numerous as the berries in our valley, as many as the buffalo, as irresistible as those great blankets of ice which covered much of the land in that age of almost-forgotten shadows."

Little Bear Claw's voice strengthened. "We have found ways to remain strong. The Good Spirit continues to favor us. We voice His wishes for peace. The people prosper with peace. We do not speak for white man. We speak for ourselves. Yes, white man has taken the furs—those we have trapped, those he has trapped.

"All of us like the time of spring. We like the summer and the autumn. We do not so much like the winter. But we cannot hold back the winter, so we prepare for winter. We continue to eat and to enjoy warmth in winter because we prepare well. We cannot hold back white man any more than we can hold back winter. But we can work with white man, whose trade goods, whose numbers are here now. The Blackfeet have found advantages in some trading with white man.

"Just as we brought an end to our torture of people, we want an end to the killing among people. We would talk about this."

Again Tree stood, then spoke: "The animals fight, kill and eat each other; most often the weaker creatures die by the greater creatures, the stronger and more cunning creatures. Mostly, they do not care that even their own die. The strong survive. If they weaken, they do not survive. Should the Blackfeet care that the weak die? To stop the torture is to weaken our—"

Tree looked to the front of the lodge. There were voices, urgent, though muted, and as he stood there he and all others present saw the Flathead warrior Running Buffalo Bull approach Little Coyote. The latter caught Little Bear Claw's attention and quickly signed he did not know why he urgently must leave. Little Coyote stepped around one of the wing-like additions to the lodge and out of sight.

Lance pointed to the great tree leaning over the ravine.

"There, my father, the bull, the white bull! He is there in the brush with three more buffalo." Lance excitedly pointed to his two companions. "We found them as we carefully worked our way through the ravine, the better to look for Blackfeet scouts."

The white buffalo! Put on earth only rarely by the Good Spirit. If the people for whom it was killed showed appropriate thanks and reverence, there would be good fortune, much spiritual power.

Little Coyote knew that in the stories of the people they had had such a skin and skull before the great smallpox plague, which had decimated so many tribes. His people who had been spared had, in a secret place, returned the skin and skull with thanks to the Good Spirit. And now another? In the ravine running between the Blackfeet and Flathead encampments?

The seer's first impulse was to join his son and the other young warriors in a quick race to kill the buffalo before the Blackfeet could do so. Lance already had moved forward on his horse to provide space on it for his father. But a white bull!

"Help me, Good Spirit." Little Coyote raised his head during the fervent prayer, his vision idly catching, then strongly fixing, to that great tree inclining toward the Flathead encampment.

"Fetch me my hunting bow and my horse, and—"

"But, Father! The Blackfeet might find the bull!"

"And the ancient lance. Meanwhile, I will prepare myself." While Lance's two companions watched, the seer raised his head, holding both arms imploringly upward.

"Help me to kill the bull, Good Spirit. Thus we could show others You favor the peace efforts. Let my aim be true. If we kill the bull, let the deed serve the people well—all people well." He could hear Lance returning; he dropped his arms, but his mind remained on his prayer.

All would carry their weapons to guard against those who might forget the word their chiefs had given. Little Coyote would carry only the bow and arrows and the lance. They tethered their horses, but instead of cropping the dry grass the animals all faced north. The warriors soon watched three buffalo climb up the west side of the ravine, disappear momentarily into a patch of trees and brush, then re-emerge before reaching the rim, where they ambled from view onto the flat land beyond.

Little Coyote was sorely tempted to ask the others to remain behind, thus reducing the danger of noise or contrary breezes carrying their scent to the remaining buffalo. But the others had spotted the white bull. Perhaps their *sumesh* would be strengthened by being present for the kill. He stripped the tufts from dead grass and tossed them into the air. The breeze still favored the hunters.

Now Lance motioned they should crawl.

The large, white bull was standing next to the smaller dark one, half an arrow's throw away, when the four men reached the outer edge of the glade. The dark animal was feeding; the white one was not. He was old, extremely old. He had survived the winter, but at great cost. The rib outlines showed on the hide, which sagged below the shoulders and hump. And the startling, pinkish eyes above the sagging features! They seemed to peer at the world with infinite sadness akin to . . . yes! The spectral face of the scalped and tortured Blackfeet warrior at Saleesh House, mirroring all the suffering of the world—the sight that had ineradicably lodged in Little Coyote's mind to try to stop future torturing.

The snort of the younger bull momentarily drew the seer's view from the ancient one. The younger began to walk away, then turned and butted the older, butted him again to try to get him into motion. The old bull stood his ground, scarcely moving at all, except to turn sideways to present a full target for Little Coyote. The hunting arrow struck the bull a hand's distance above the brisket, as did the two more that quickly followed. The fourth, loosed from a standing position, struck with sufficient force to clear the body and stick in the ground beyond. The younger bull turned, then began plunging up the side of the ravine. He paused once to look back at the instant the white bull fell. The hunters raced to the kill. The seer looked into the great eye. It had widened now and, almost in the instant it fixed on its killer, began to glaze over. Before the elation of the kill flooded Little Coyote's being, a thought became a question: If good fortune could attend the too few Flatheads by this kill, in the nature of things did it now follow that the fortunes of the great buffalo herds were equally diminished? How did the Good Spirit balance this gain and this loss?

The seer would ponder that more deeply later. Now, indeed, the Flatheads and their friends had the great white bull. The four men must move quickly. For it came to Little Coyote that they now would carry the fresh hide and head to the council lodge. All would agree that the white bull represented great power— and the bull had come into the possession of the Flatheads. Little Coyote gravely handed one of the killing arrows to his three delighted companions, who quickly skinned the carcass as if their lives depended on it.

So, the peace was made in this important year in the lives of the people. When they returned to their valley there occurred one more event that they noted at the time, but gave little emphasis to because they thought it merely an extension of Little Bear Claw's statement to the council that ". . . We carefully must send our people in the various directions by plan to learn what others are doing . . . ." The event was that a small group of Flatheads and Nez Percé accompanied some fur-traders returning with the year's take to St. Louis. The people settled where the Kaw and Missouri rivers come together. They never returned.

L ittle Coyote climbed the largest boulder atop his vision quest peak. A day earlier, driven by a seemingly unassuagable restlessness in *Slá'ko*, this seventh moon of Serviceberries, he had mounted his white and sturdiest horse and set out. Trailing this good-medicine horse, he had climbed the last, most precipitous, part of the mountain on his own legs, grateful to the Good Spirit they remained strong, as did his breathing, after thirty-eight summers. Here, much like the grouse he had flushed, he could sort out his perplexities. The bird, confronted with numerous berries ranging from sweet to sour, ponders which shade of color to choose, then, having finally selected the best, feeds quickly until sated.

The seer faced Sun and asked Good Spirit to protect the lives of his people. Looking to the land, he slowly turned almost full-circle and back, seeing the dog-toothed peaks, the lower mountains, all bathed in glorious sunshine. He offered thanks for this valley haven of his people. Lowering his head, humbled, he saw the river serenely flowing through the tree-dotted land. He remembered his talk with his chief—how the river, like life, itself, flowed tranquilly, tumultuously, savagely, uncontrollably. *Help me, Good Spirit, to more closely follow your ways so I will give wise counsel to the people and provide good medicine and healing for those who hurt.* Lastly, he prayed that during the most critical periods Good Spirit would share at least a portion of His full sight into the future—a portion, however small or dark, to help others with their uncertainties. The uncertainties, again like the plentiful berries, seemed to grow in numbers during these increasing contacts with the fur-takers. He nodded his head. His mind had come full-circle to that day of his great vision when Good Spirit had told him white man was as numerous as the berries in the great valley.

For a long time the seer/medicine man/warrior sat there, almost unmoving, feeling the growing warmth of Sun while the mind more tranquilly explored the mental, the spiritual, peaks and valleys, known and unknown.

Was the horse impatient or was the grass nearby gone? Its whinny reached up to him, bringing mind back to the boulder top.

He stood, once again holding his arms outward toward westering Sun. It occurred to him that this gesture opening and closing his prayers had its counterpart now in gestures of the Iroquois and some of his own people with their reverently made sign of the cross. Soon, this matter should be one to ponder more deeply, then brought to the surface for closer examination. For now, he carefully slid off the boulder and ate some of the ripest berries from the closest bush.

When he reached his horse, it fixed its strange, glassy eyes on him. Then it looked northeastward, moving its ears, trying to match hearing with sight.

Little Coyote saw the long, at times doubling, line of the cavalcade moving south across a distant clearing. Without hurrying, he could intersect it almost where the creek forming below him and tumbling east reached the river. First, horse and man drank from the creek's deliciously cold waters; Little Coyote offered thanks from a much-cleared mind for that, too.

Little Coyote joyfully embraced both Smith and Tull. He noted that the former, clad in worn buckskins, was quiet, restrained and physically tired, but anxious to visit with his friends. There was little perceptible change in Tull. If time had carved a few lines in his features, they were well-hidden by even more hair. The hair was somewhat constrained now by a buckskin band around his forehead, "t' keep th' har outen my sightin' eye." The party camped that night in a cottonwood grove near the river; it reached the great encampment of the Flathead people early next day.

Before he left with David Jackson to talk to Tjolzhitsay, Smith explained that the two of them and Bill Sublette, three summers earlier, "in '26," had bought the Ashley-Henry outfit.

Little Coyote and Tull, briefly grunting about his "rheumatiz," hunkered down in an open, grassy patch and watched four Flathead boys energetically dig a hole in some soft earth. The mountain man had given each of the children a fish hook and a bit of string as they closely followed and observed him wherever he went.

Now Tull signaled he would talk by expertly launching a great stream of brown saliva toward a large beetle crawling next to a dog dropping. The unexpected flood upended the insect. It floated on its back, legs moving every which way, like a bull boat upside down, paddlers flailing the air. Failing to regain its footing in the deadly mixture, the bug drowned.

"That Smith. Luckier 'n hell. Ben in Californy twict most recent, lookin' fur plews, 'n 'splorin. Lotsa' his men was killed by th' Mojaves, they was, arter the sarpants 'peared friendly-like. Startid headin' back hyar with twenty men, mebbe three-hundred hosses, 'n a boy about thems' size." He gestured toward the four diggers. "Th' Injuns in th' Oregon kentry, Kelawatsets, Injuns ye' probly don' know 'bout, killed fourteen men 'n th' boy, arter th' varlets 'pear'd friendly, too, 'n some damn fool let 'em inta camp. Two whites deserted, they did. Smith 'n th' three others made it ta' Fort Vancouver. Doc McLoughlin o' th' Bay Compny he'p'd 'em rekiver a few plews 'n hosses. Couldn' let th' sarpants get th' idee they c'd do thet ta white man 'n get away. Sides, Doc is a purty decent critter."

This time the dog dropping was target of the saliva.

"Smith 'n one a' his men, Black, com'd up th' Columbia ta Fort Colville in a boat, 'n walked ta Flathead Post, then jined up with Jackson 'n com'd hyar. I ben with Jackson some time. Guidin', I am, 'n some trappin'."

Tull bit off another chew, picked up the dead beetle and crooked a gnarled finger at one of the boys: "Thisn'll fetch th' biggest fish, I reckon."

The boys began beating the grass in a circular fashion with three boughs while walking toward the hole. Grasshoppers leaped before them, some sailing away to safety. Soon the hole was alive with the insects, which the boys caught one at a time and popped into a dried bladder. Grinning, they set off toward the river.

Tull fingered out his chew and set it on a rock when Antelope brought the two men food. He spat, bowed his thanks to Antelope and fell to eating. He was wiping off his whiskers on a worn and blackened buckskin sleeve when Smith and Jackson returned. There was much talk around the fire that night. The Flathead couple rose before Sun so Antelope could prepare food for Tull, Jackson and Smith. When the latter did not arrive with the pair, Little Coyote walked out to the trees where Tull had pointed. Smith was seated on a log, reading his black book. Finally, he knelt and, hearing his friend's approach, quietly stood. He looked once again skyward, placed a bit of ribbon in the book, then closed it.

The men ate rapidly and with much satisfaction. "Dave," Smith said looking at Jackson, "if you and Tull will go on and see that the men are ready to leave, I'll talk to Little Coyote here for a spell." Tull hitched up his britches and gave the seer a friendly pat on the back. "See ya, hoss," he said. He bowed again to Antelope and tried to catch up with Jackson. With little knee action, Tull jerkily rocked his body right and left.

"Cold water is starting to catch up with his joints," Smith commented as they watched Jackson pause, then wait for the trapper. "He's been a good guide for Jackson." Now they watched Antelope, who had said something in Flathead to Little Coyote, running to catch up with Tull. "As I was saying," Smith continued, "we're trying to make it to the rendezvous where the Popo Agie and Wind rivers come together, but it's unlikely we'll get there in time." He sat down. "Your chiefs explained your people are pretty well spread out, trying to learn things and get the best trades, especially since Hudson's Bay had begun to meet our prices. We'll treat you fair, and I hope you'll come to each rendezvous—early, to get the best, and stay away from the liquor. I understand that with the beaver mostly gone here, you're heading in force into more distant places to get them. As I said, stay away from the liquor. All the companies are bringing it in now. You remember Captain Clark?"

Little Coyote nodded.

"Well, he's a big chief now. Called Superintendent of Indian Affairs at St. Louis. Remember at least a part of that. Tjolzhitsay said he sent some of you to St. Louis to get some priests . . . uh, Black Robes to come here. Clark would help out. He's a good friend of the Indians. Told me he likes you Flatheads—honest and moral . . . uh God-fearing . . . clean-living, I guess is better. He's doing his best to keep out the liquor."

"And Lewis?"

"Poor man was either murdered or killed himself back in '09. But to get back to the point. You're good people, hard workers, even did us a service by quieting down the Blackfeet a couple years back. Bill Sublette took some of our outfit into the Blackfeet country a couple of years back to trade. They did part with almost forty packs of beaver and some horses. American Fur Company is starting to talk about really concentrating on that region." Smith shook his head almost wonderingly. "Without the Blackfeet to contend with, a party could make a sweep through that area that would, in one or two seasons, make themselves rich for the rest of their lives."

Little Coyote shook his head understandingly. "Yes, Hatchiorauquasha told us about Sublette. But there also was a fight with some of your company on their way here, and the Blackfeet killed Pierre Tevanitagon. This we regret. He had told us much about the Black Robes, too." Smith nodded approvingly as the Flathead continued. "We want peace with the Blackfeet, and we rejoice that they treat the whites in a friendly manner. Despite our peace, we are wary with some of the younger Blackfeet, who have determined to keep out white man and their friends at any cost. They, too, can act like the Mojaves and Kelawatsets."

"That Tull! Talks too much."

"Now some of our people begin to question the good of the peace, too. Our younger men are restless. They argue that when the Blackfeet consent to trade with the whites, they get more guns, too."

Smith stretched over and grasped his rifle, which was leaning against his pack.

"Bill traded them a few old fusees, some trifles, too. I agree, however, that they will try to get the best guns. If American Fur gets in there, they'll supply them with good guns, you can bet on that. Others are making rifles like Hawkens now. This, my friend, is what I really wanted to show you." He handed the rifle to Little Coyote. The lock was different from those on the Flatheads' Hawkens.

"The flintlock system is gone, as you can see." Smith cocked the weapon. "Under the hammer is this tiny and hollow metal cone. Its hole leads to the powder charge in the barrel." The mountain man smiled. "I think we've all found the flintlock system gets wet at times—even when we need it the most! Now look at this."

He fitted a tiny, metal cone, closed at one end, over the metal cone on the gun. Clearly, this quite effectively would help keep water from getting into the powder charge.

"Now, friend, fire the rifle."

Little Coyote swung the rifle well away from Antelope, who was returning with a small bundle. Sighting briefly at a small tree, he pulled the trigger. There was the usual explosion, but no usual small puff of powder smoke from near the lock. The bullet thwacked into the tree. Now Smith brought the hammer halfway back and pulled off the somewhat flattened metal cap. He placed another on the nipple, brought the hammer back to full cock and pulled the trigger. There was a tiny explosion.

"The caps have fire in them, which drives into the powder charge in the barrel. But you've always got to have caps to make the rifle fire—and keep those dry!"

"Such guns and caps! Can our people get them?"

"Jackson brought me this one. There are but few as yet, but Hawken is changing over his rifles, and those of others, into caplocks, as fast as he can. Our company has arranged to get much of what he makes, paid him some even before we get them—like you gave me the gold. I will try to get them to the Flatheads first because you are strong-hearted friends and do not fight us. To be totally honest, if the American Fur Company makes peace with the Blackfeet, they are going to get a lot of guns because they have a lot of beaver for the company's trappers, as well as their own. That does make a problem for the Flatheads and their allies—and us! For some reason many of the Indians aren't keen about rifled guns. That's to your advantage. Remember this—*always* get the best guns.

"Some say I trust the Indians too much. Tull says my 'string's gettin' short.' They'll 'strike like sarpants' if they want something. Well, not all of them. I trust in the Good Spirit of us all."

Smith pulled his pack toward his lap. "You and your friends deal a lot with Hudson's Bay. You're going to need the best weapons to go into far areas to get furs to get more good guns—even buffalo." He continued rummaging into his pack. His Bible and notebook fell from the top and opened up. Once again some of the leaves from the notebook fell out and began to scatter in the slight breeze that had sprung up as the mountainsides warmed to Sun. Antelope ran after them and returned them to Smith. He put down the pistol he had been rummaging for and replaced the pages in their covers. This time, though, he neglected to put them in order as he had done when they had scattered four years earlier on the floor of Little Coyote's lodge.

"This is for you, Little Coyote. Show your people how it works. When I offered it to Tjolzhitsay, he declined and said Shield Maker has your pistol. This, too, is a caplock. See, Powell made the lock, Hawken the barrel."

Smith handed the pistol, three boxes of caps and a bullet mould to his friend, then stood up.

Greatly pleased, the seer nodded to Antelope. She handed the bundle she had brought to Smith. It was a new set of buckskins obtained from Basket, now mated to Long Spear. The buckskins would fit Smith.

"You will wear them before you leave." Antelope was insistent.

Smith removed his long-tailed shirt and pulled on the new one. It draped comfortably midway between groin and knees. He undid his belt, to which were tied his leggings. The new ones also reached from heel to hip. Uncharacteristically, he plopped his leather hat on his head and strutted back and forth until Antelope laughed delightedly.

"I am most grateful. One other thing. Fur companies are forming and breaking up. Everybody wants the furs. Pilcher's company is gone. Jackson saw him near the Lake of the Flatheads, just before I showed up. Pilcher tried to work for the Bay Company. They turned him down, though they would have been able to take furs on American territory that way. When I saw Pilcher, he told me he has sent a paper to the Great White Father's chiefs. The paper says that the valley of the Flatheads by the lake and elsewhere would make rich and good farming land. Good land, no buffalo to speak of to destroy the crops.

"Trade with our company as you can, even if I no longer am in it." Smith embraced Little Coyote, bowed to Antelope and, while in that position, picked up his pack and his rifle.

"Believe in the Good Spirit, depend on . . ." He raised his rifle and pointed to the two pistols in his sash. ". . . and hope for some luck. See you at the rendezvous."

Several days later Antelope found one more page from the notebook. There were seven lines written on it:

Tomorrow we will meet with our good friends, the Flatheads, then head for the Popo Agie. I've taken a lot of furs and made much money. If trappers keep moving in, especially powerful American Fur Company, perhaps it will be time to move on. Maybe I'll try the Santa Fe trade. With prayer, perhaps the Good Lord will tell me, as Tull says, which way my 'stick floats.'

Little Coyote folded the paper and carefully put it in a safe place with the letter from John Colter and his wife. Perhaps he would be able to return it to Smith when he and Antelope attended a rendezvous. Yes, and perhaps his people should try to intercept the pack trains of trading goods even before they reached the rendezvous sites.

There was much to decide in the council after the buffalo hunt. Little Coyote fired almost a full tin of the percussion caps in demonstrations of the caplock system on his pistol. Yes, they would trap afar and send a strong party to the 1830 rendezvous, also to be held where the Popo Agie and Wind rivers meet. If they could not yet get the caplock Hawkens, they would try for more of the others.

"We will send young warriors with the older. The younger will then learn how to deal with white man." There was an approving murmur at Tjolzhitsay's words. The murmur rose again when the chief stated that he had sent a message to Bone, a strong chief of the Pend d'Oreilles, urging they send a like force. With the peace agreement breaking down, perhaps their allies, the Kutenais to the north, should do the same. Tjolzhitsay overrode some objections that followed this latter suggestion by asking Antoine Godin, the Iroquois, to tell how the Blackfeet had killed his father while they trapped. Next, fiery Howling Wolf, a Flathead, sorrowfully and angrily described how a small Blackfeet band had killed his father, mother, wife and two sons as they camped one evening during their trek north to visit her kin, the Kutenais, and hunt the elk and trap the marshes near the Lake of the Flatheads. Only he had lived after the first attack. He had escaped in the darkness.

"Yes, the peace is cracking like the river ice in spring," Tjolzhitsay said. "Soon it will fall apart and be swept away. This saddens me, but we must plan. We must travel in larger, well-armed bands."

Broken Tooth, assisted by his stalwart son, Has Sharp Eyes, would lead the rendezvous group. Falls in Fire, a son of Has Many Horses, along with Pony Whip and Lance would be included in the others.

There was a feast in the valley when the Kutenais and Pend d'Oreilles arrived, some trepidation when all departed, and much excitement when they returned safely with many stories three moons later in ample time for the buffalo hunt.

Broken Tooth leaned back in the council lodge, grinning his pleasure that Has Sharp Eyes would tell about the rendezvous.

"The chief, Sublette, brought many trade goods to the rendezvous," Has Sharp Eyes said. "We cut his trail before he reached the waiting trappers. He had pack horses, but carried much of the goods in ten large and two small horse-pulled boxes called 'wagons.' They were mounted on what they called 'wheels,' such as we have put on the children's small playthings. They journeyed along the Blue and the Platte rivers from St. Louis. One wagon overturned into a ravine. Sublette sent on the others. We remained to help lift it up and collect the goods." Has Sharp Eyes laughed; he was echoed by his father. "That Sublette. He wrung his hands as the Flatheads, Kutenais and Pend d'Oreilles went into the ravine, then he threw his hands despairingly into the air. He thought we would take his goods!" Now everyone in the lodge laughed. "After his goods were restored, Sublette offered us firewater pots, but we wisely declined, as you shall learn."

The young warrior stopped talking and one by one handed five flintlock Hawkens to Big Hawk and the sub-chiefs. Then Broken Tooth carried two caplocks to them.

"There were no Hawkens for trade." Has Sharp Eyes laughed again. "But there were many foolish white men to drink from the firewater pots. Falls in Fire has learned much from Has Many Horses. Again, we would drink no firewater. When the encampment was lively from much drinking and cavorting and coupling with dissolute Indian women, we approached the trappers with the best guns. They wanted more 'whiskey,' but they had no pelts. We traded what we had held back. Thus, we obtained the guns. We departed while their heads were still turned. They will have to borrow the old trade muskets and have to give next year's pelts for them. Yes, we learned much about many of the white men."

Broken Tooth reached into a leather bag. He withdrew a small, buckskin bag. Almost reverently, he withdrew from that a tiny roll of buckskin, inside of which were two pages from a note book. He brought them to Little Coyote. One page was blank; on the other Jedediah Smith had sent a message. Little Coyote painstakingly read a line at a time, then translated it for all, until, at length, he was finished. The silence throughout his work was total, broken only at the end by Big Hawk's decisive, "The council must meet again when Sun first appears."

Little Coyote and Antelope. Greetings. We talked about Drouillard and Colter. You said 'John Colter once sent to me a letter.' You read it to me. So now I send you a letter.

Sublette, Jackson and I sold out to five good men. They are Gervais, Fraeb, M. Sublette, Fitzpatrick, Bridger. You can trust them. They will be called Rocky Mountain Fur Company. I have told them about the Flatheads. That you want good guns. Attend the rendezvous. You will get them. Stay away from the whiskey. Because I travel much, I learn much. American Fur Company built Fort Union among the Assiniboins on the Missouri where the Yellowstone enters. They will put another on the Yellowstone, below the mouth of the Bighorn. That company plans to put other forts on the Missouri among the Blackfeet. One at the mouth of the Marias River. One above the mouth of the Marias. One at the mouth of Poplar River.

I am sending you a page. Try writing. You can do it with white man's words. Just as you use your pictures on your story skin. White man's writing will become easier each time you try. Give your letter to M. Sublette. He will give it to Bill. He will give it to me. I have a house in St. Louis.

If God wills it, I will start on a new trail. It will be to Santa Fe for more trading. May He be with you and with me.

Jedediah Smith

Little Coyote scaled the small cliff. He looked downward at thumb-shaped Lake of the White Moose glistening in the mid-morning sun of his people's sixth moon of Camas in white man's 1830. A light breeze was marking its passage by turning parts of the lake's surface into uncountable tiny mirrors. He unslung his rifle, bullet pouch, horn and a leather bag, then pounded a heavy rock on a slate outcropping. When some of the flat sheets snapped, he worked out a large one and dusted it off. Before sitting, he briefly prayed that the Good Spirit would guide him in his work for his people in the encampment below. Except for the horse guards and a few hunters, most of the valley's inhabitants were busily digging bitterroot, onions and camas.

And Little Coyote? This day he was certain he would work harder than all his people. He would write his first letter on the notebook page Jedediah Smith had sent. He would ask Smith to help the Nez Percé and Flatheads who Tjolzhitsay soon would send again to St. Louis. The emissaries would be urging the Black Robes to visit their people. Lucien Fontenelle, hearing of their intent, had sent word that the Indians could accompany his American Fur Company party to St. Louis. The returning fur-takers could use their strength. He did not mention that his offer would engender good will as the company sought to extend operations wherever possible.

Removing the raven feather he had carried in his hair, the seer cut the quill into a pen as he had watched Benito Vasquez do in the trading room at Lisa's fort. As Little Coyote mixed an ink from some materials he used for his story skin, his mind painfully began to draw on the methods he had learned from John Colter while the trapper had healed in his lodge.

Next, he removed from the bag the blank sheet along with

John Colter's and Smith's letters. He anchored them near his hips with a small rock and lifted the slate across his lap. With care, he could use some of the words from the two letters. First, he would scratch them onto the slate with his knife point to get them as correct as possible; then he would write them on the precious paper. One certainty already had emerged: The labor would be long, the message short!

At the top of the slate he laboriously scratched the signature Jedediah Smith had put at the end of his letter. Then, painstakingly, "Greetings." Pleased, he absent-mindedly blew away the slate dust and, pondering which word he should work with next, idly began scratching a tall, unmounted, stick figure into the center of the slate. Was this habit from his extended work on the story skin? Was he almost consciously rejecting this unfamiliar word form of communication? Was yet another part of the mind saying "write the white man's words" as dis-tinguishable habit and determination conflicted on a hitherto almost-unknown mental plane? Or, was some other compelling force beginning to work here, too, like the almost-unnoticed breeze grows into a great wind?

Now the mind, with insistent force, decreed he scratch the stick figure pointing a rifle upward from hip height as he held the reins of his horse. Three quick scratches near the gun muzzle indicated it was firing.

At what? At a warrior seated on a horse and beginning to level a musket at Smith!

The figure was easy to draw. The seer raced with the knife point to portray the pictures that were forming faster than hands and blade could move. The pictures were bunching up, crowding, like buffalo seeking, too late, to evade the cliff death jump, pushed inexorably by the surging mass from behind.

The letter was forgotten now as the warrior received the Hawken ball in the chest. *Hurry! In another stick figure remove one of the two pistols from the sash and place it in his hand. No! Hold the horse reins closer yet to the bit, force the terrified animal to serve as barrier between Smith and his mounted, circling foes, now pointing their long lances downward.*

Hasten! Hasten with grieving reluctance to portray the warrior leveling his musket, hitting Smith. Now he lies on the earth, transfixed by many lances. The exultant warriors scalp him, clawing his possessions, throwing the Bible into the air, scattering for a last time the notebook pages until the wind catches them up like cottonwood leaves in s'tcé:ei, *the eleventh moon of Autumn.*

Little Coyote's dulled knife point stopped. He was sweating. There was something else, too, a certainty untinged by any doubt as he lifted the slate tablet and dashed it against the cliff. The shards tinkled dissonantly as they bounced downward. Anger momentarily displaced awe as he kicked the restraining rock from atop the blank paper and Smith's and John Colter's letters. The breeze, striking the face of the cliff, wafted them upward; then, abating, it let them drift, rising but ever falling, toward the tree tops far below.

The raven-quill pen, caught up in a stronger gust of the same seemingly capricious breeze, sailed high above the cliff into the familiar medium of its now-dead owner. In falling, it scribbled its own indecipherable words into the empty sky, the only message this day the grieving Flathead could not comprehend.

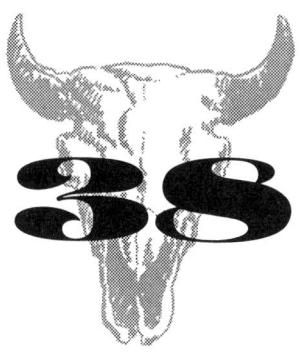

More lodges began rising like circles of mushrooms near a lake shore after the camas, bitterroot and onion harvest in the valley and elsewhere. Black Eagle, a Nez Percé war chief, arrived to lend his support for the trip to St. Louis for the Black Robes. Shoshonis drove in some of their best horses to trade, reporting that beaver were almost gone near the Snake now. They gladly accepted the older muskets, understanding the reluctance of the Flatheads to part with their rifles in the face of the growing ferocity and depredations of the Blackfeet, increasingly armed by the American Fur Company. Then Pend d'Oreilles, Kalispels, Kutenais, even a few Coeur d'Alenes, Okanogans and Spokans, arrived with their lodges—and a common concern. Hunger was beginning to stalk them as relentlessly as the Blackfeet. The ever increasing numbers of fur-takers, often accompanied by their families, were reducing the game—even the fish in some waters—to dangerous lows.

"A warrior should not eat snakes, poor fish, insects and roots. He should not eat his horses and most of his dogs in winter. His family should not starve!" Women—even children—crowding around the two great council fires echoed these words of Knife, respected sub-chief of the Kutenais. Spears Her Enemy, warrior woman of the Kalispels, said there must be longer hunts for the buffalo by greater numbers of well-armed people. So the talks went, all agreeing, finally, there would be more hunts by way of Hell Gate to the region of the great falls, with the Shoshonis, Nez Percé and Flatheads increasingly moving north to join their allies rather than taking the southern route. With more tribes involved, fewer hunters from each would have to go, thereby leaving protectors in their home areas. Other warriors could seek furs and follow the trappers for trade.

All, except the Nez Percé, left after agreements were reached for a great cow hunt that winter. It also was agreed that those departing would insist the Hudson's Bay people at much-visited Flathead Post trade them more and better guns, along with powder and lead.

"Exchange the tanned cow robes for lack of other furs," Tjolzhitsay reminded them, "even if the traders say they are hard to transport."

The chief's work did not end with his allies' departure north. Now, with the Nez Percé, they would prepare for the trip to seek the Black Robes, whose words about the Good Spirit and powers seemed needed more than ever.

"Smith is dead." No one challenged Little Coyote's flat statement. Rather, Tjolzhitsay, after expressing regret, explained, "When Smith talked to me about trade, he said the Good Spirit would be pleased if we would seek the Black Robes." So the only questions were: "Who will go, when, and who will they see?" Remembering Smith's information about Clark, the seer suggested the emissaries see the red-head first. He could speak with signs, perhaps with words. Big Ignace, who traveled much, explained that there were chiefs and sub-chiefs among the Black Robes. They should see Rosati, called a "bishop." The Iroquois said that while Smith and his men had treated them well, had urged they seek the Black Robes, and helped them get the rifles, they should accept the offer of Fontenelle and travel with the American Fur Company for protection. Big Ignace had heard that the fur companies might not bring trading goods to an 1831 summer rendezvous, so there could be difficulty finding another trustworthy party returning to St. Louis.

"In the meantime," Big Ignace said, "trap in higher mountains where some white men are more reluctant to go, where the beaver remain prime longer. Use this winter of 1830 to get as many furs as possible. Trade them for the Hawken guns, for you surely will need them."

When others urged trappers to go in force to regions such as Three Forks to get many beaver, Big Ignace, who also had lived among the Blackfeet, shook his head. "The great beaver catches from Three Forks have been taken."

Tjolzhitsay brought the talk back to the Black Robes. At length it was agreed. The Nez Percé would send Black Eagle, the war chief, along with Rabbit's Skin Leggins, No Horns on His Head and Smoke. Yes, Man of the Morning, the Flathead sub-chief, again would set out, as would Old Blanket and Thunder on the Mountain. Gun rode with the three Flatheads until they met with Fontenelle's party and the Nez Percé. Alone, he returned. Then, instead of voicing his sorrow in an ill-bred way that his infirmities had kept him home, he worked harder with the Iroquois to teach the people about the bad and good sides of life and what lay beyond when each would make the lonely journey to the sand hills. Many listened.

When early frost began whitening the grass until it crunched under the moccasins of the early-risers, the Flatheads joined their allies—including Shoshonis—for the great march that Little Bear Claw, chief of the hunt, led through Hell Gate to the buffalo lands beyond. Numerous scouts and flankers routed the few Blackfeet who lay in wait along the defile, perhaps expressing wonder at the hundreds of people and several thousand horses. Strict rules were in force. In the early stages of the hunt, at least, there would be no individual pursuit of the buffalo. Rather, the tribal leaders agreed the Flathead rules would apply; a band of warriors from all tribes would enforce them.

Though many hunters knew the locations of cliffs over which, in the past, they had driven great numbers of buffalo, Little Bear Claw said the Blackfeet, alerted by scouts, would defend them more stoutly.

"We can see the enemy and fight them more successfully on open ground," he said. "Nor, as we would butcher the kill below the cliffs, would we wish to become surrounded like the buffalo themselves."

The chief of the hunt led forth a superb buffalo pony. An ancient brave, seated firmly in the Spanish-type saddle, proudly raised his head, chin up, ancient eyes looking almost unblinkingly at the hunters—and far beyond. The Flatheads recognized him as Otter Tail, once a powerful member of the medicine band. Now, for the most part, he sat outside his son's lodge in the summer warmth and told the stories of the people to the younger children.

"There is a place," Otter Tail said. "It is near the great falls. There our people would go when we and our friends were many. Then we could resist the Blackfeet who swept down from the north. Now we are many again and well-armed. Little Bear Claw has listened. We can go there again. There we will find the land the Good Spirit shaped to help us feed our many people." Tired, the old man slumped forward, but found the strength to remain in the saddle as the great hunting party swung sharply northeast to face snow driven by cold winds.

When Little Bear Claw signaled they would stop, the lodges went up. At a good distance away, all began constructing a strong, circular pen where two long hillsides, generally running north and south, almost converged into a great V. More than one-hundred hunters would have had to hold hands to encircle the pen. They left the north side of the pen open as they wedged stout poles between large boulders that had been put in place in the long ago. Between the boulders and posts they piled smaller rocks, logs and brush. At each end of the open pen the people began constructing a palisade running north to south just below the two hillsides. They ended where the hillsides, tapering upward, joined the level plain. Now the hunters had a great funnel down which to run the buffalo to the pen.

The people agreed that aged Otter Tail should be leader of the pen ceremonies. Only he could signal the start of this hunt. The ancient man seemed to draw on deep wells of new strength as with much ceremony he erected a medicine pole in the middle of the pen and hung from it three of his most powerful charms. The suspenseful camp waited and watched for three mornings while the old man beat his shield-shaped drum, chanted prayers and called strongly on his buffalo medicine to determine the proper time for the chase. Each of those mornings he handed a ball of buffalo hair covered with hide to a noted hunter from the Flatheads, the Shoshonis, Nez Percé and Pend d'Oreilles. Riding one fleet horse, trailing another for a fast get-away from lurking enemies, they rode great distances in the four directions to locate the buffalo and estimate their numbers. Each day the four wearily returned; the encampment watched to see if one of their number would go to Otter Tail with the good news that the buffalo were out there. Meanwhile, Otter Tail could eat only the food killed within the bounds of the great funnel-shaped park and the pen. On the fourth day, gingerly, triumphantly, his bony hands grasping a fat porcupine's foot, the old man held up the plump animal's body. The Good Spirit had sent it ambling within reach of the ancient's club. Seated next to a small fire, he ate well.

"See, I have put the porcupine's head on the charm pole; soon the buffalo will come—I think this fourth day," Otter Tail confidently told Little Bear Claw as he proffered a well-cooked and oily leg and shoulder.

Little Bear Claw shared the old man's optimism with Little Coyote as the two warriors' families visited and waited.

Later that day, Antelope excitedly seized her mate's sleeve.

"See! The Pend d'Oreille buffalo-seeker approaches Otter Tail!"

Lance carried the news to Running Buffalo Bull and his grandmother. Soon, the family, shivering both in anticipation and in the freshening and cool breeze, walked to the park.

Otter Tail beat on his drum until the hundreds of onlookers were silent. Four criers, knowledgeable in tongues and with strong lungs, repeated the old man's announcement and admonitions:

"There are many buffalo, but less than a quarter Sun's ride to the north many fat cows and young bulls! See, the wind comes from the north! Even so, there must be no fires in the lodges to carry smoke to their keen noses! The warriors will mount their horses! The other warriors will seize their weapons and take their positions!"

Otter Tail continued to sit on his buffalo hide in the center of the pen, praying that the Good Spirit would strengthen the hunters and help direct the buffalo. He had set aside his drum now and cautioned that all should remain quiet until the buffalo were moving toward the pen. He called for Little Coyote to come forth.

"Little Coyote." The old man's eyes peered brightly at the younger Flathead. "The Good Spirit wisely has strengthened the *sumesh* in your younger body even as this one has grown old." He paused for breath and tapped his bony chest with one gnarled finger. "Your strengths branch out in many directions. As do our problems. The Good Spirit truly loves our people. Soon I will go to the sand hills. There I will hunt again with Three Eagles and see Shining Shirt. I had hoped to see the Black Robes. This I know will not be. I—, but you must go. Quickly, will you place the robe of the sacred white buffalo at the highest, strongest peak in the pen? There it will be safe from the hooves of the buffalo. Soon they will come. This I know." Tottering, he raised himself and touched the seer, who gently helped him sit again on the robe.

Little Coyote asked the four buffalo-seekers to help him securely tie the white buffalo hide to the post. Then the five of them galloped their horses to join the other mounted warriors moving far beyond the end of the northwest palisade. Running Buffalo Bull and Lance had joined those who had moved beyond the northeast palisade. Soon, both groups were strung out in two converging lines, single file, perhaps two miles from the outermost ends of the palisades. Now, armed hunters afoot closed the space between the palisades and the two lines of mounted warriors. Those afoot crouched down or actually lay on the cold ground.

Otter Tail continued to sit on his buffalo hide.

Broken Tooth, his horse and stout body covered by a large buffalo robe, slowly rode outward from the pen, past the slanting lines of hunters on foot, past the slanting lines of mounted hunters.

As he approached Little Coyote near the most northern end of the line from which he could view a large herd of buffalo, the sub-chief paused once again and wrenched some hair from the hide to test the breeze. The hair rapidly drifted southward. The wind was holding true.

Carefully maneuvering his horse to imitate a grazing, moving buffalo, Broken Tooth drew ever closer to the herd. Most were cows, calves, young bulls, but small bands of older bulls grazed nearby. Now the silent northerly horsemen closest to the herd could hear Broken Tooth's repeated, urgent cry imitating a buffalo calf. All the grazing heads jerked upward to peer toward Broken Tooth. Slowly, he began retreating, again voicing the plaintive cry. The portion of the herd nearest him began moving south toward him. He carefully maintained his slow retreat, keeping the same distance from the herd. Now some of the animals began running toward him, those nearest bellowing, agitating those behind to greater speed amid the louder drumming of heavy hooves on the yet-soft earth.

With great precision, the outermost lines of mounted hunters and, finally, those on foot folded in on the rear of the now wildly running herd of approximately six-hundred animals. The buffalo reached the palisades funneling into the pen. Some, hearing the long-pent-up shouts, screams and whistles of all the people in the lines, tried to turn. They no more could resist the pushing, crowding, surging mass behind than could a canoe force its way up the great falls less than a day's ride away.

Gun reports began rising above the melee; animals began going down from lead and the more silent, but equally lethal, hunting arrows and lances. The three-hundred or so yet-living buffalo neared the pen, more and more of their numbers dropping, the living mindlessly running against the stout sides of the palisade.

Otter Tail rose from his prayerful position on his robe and began to run as best he could toward the safety aperture between two boulders and a post. Those excited persons nearest him later related that he had paused, turned and hurried on old legs to retrieve his forgotten drum. Then, again, he sought safety. Too late! Too late! The frenzied animals were on, over and past him again and again, crashing against the rocks and logs. Some, especially the larger bulls, blood streaming from nostrils and wounds, tried lunging over the barrier, then fell, too, under the hooves of those yet living. Roars, bellows, shouting, the noise of the guns filled the air, diminishing gradually as more of the trapped beasts fell to the plowed-up soil. Then, at last, the noise died, immediately followed by shouts of exultant hunters giving expert lance thrusts into yet-moving bodies.

There was utter stillness until the four buffalo-seekers Otter Tail had directed so well returned to the pen and expertly turned up a plump cow for butchering. One, holding a large slice of dripping liver, ran about looking, shouting for Otter Tail. They found only gory remnants of the old man. With blood dripping down his arm, the buffalo-seeker, heeding the shouts of the hungry onlookers, carried it to Fishing Bird of the Kutenais, oldest of the four buffalo-seekers. He sat on his lathered buffalo pony near the pen entrance. Fishing Bird looked toward Little Bear Claw, who nodded. Then the warrior raised the bloody blob, lowered it for a huge bite, and handed the meat to Little Bear Claw. He, too, raised it aloft. The first hunt was over. The work and feasting would begin.

In less than two Suns, the carefully removed skins and meat had been divided according to tribe and number in families. There was much singing, dancing, story-telling until, once more, and then yet again, Fishing Bird sat in the middle of the repaired pen and erected his medicine post. The Kutenai medicine band selected another to join the three buffalo-seekers. They, Broken Tooth and all the others performed well, and there was meat and hides enough for all the pack horses. All the people agreed they should come back in strength to this "place of Otter Tail." The lodges came down. The encampment set out together for respective homes with much of the precision of the buffalo chases. The grizzly bears, wolves, foxes and coyotes scarcely sniffed at the great bone piles of the cows, calves and younger bulls. Even the birds found little to peck at there. Instead, all fought over and eventually consumed the largely untouched great buffalo bulls, which had been caught up in the races for, and the killings at, the pen but, almost completely, had been left behind.

Enemies tried to oppose the returning hunters then and during the next winter hunt. None succeeded.

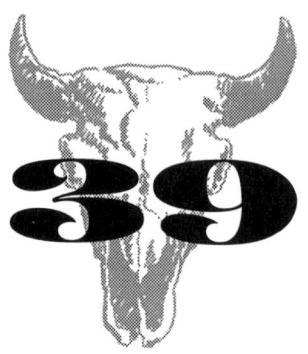

"Puls! *Puls! Puls!"* The first war cries pierced the tranquility of the Flathead and Nez Percé encampments more startlingly than an unexpected shower of silent arrows. As the second shrill "Kill! Kill! Kill!" tumbled over the echoes returning from the nearest mountains arcing Pierre's Hole, warriors began scrambling from sides or backs of their lodges. They were well aware a tomahawk might await their skulls if they chose the usual exit. Before the echoes died, each of the lodges at this western edge of the Three Tetons had produced at least one armed man or woman. Despite the surprise and resulting commotion, the stream's murmur remained audible while the warriors followed another long-rehearsed tactic. They fell prone, then scrambled on all fours to a protective cottonwood trunk or some screening willows. Quietly, they sought the source of the war cries, straining in the light of the near full moon to see any movement in this part of the great valley.

Little Coyote, Lance and Antelope, grasping her rifle/ shotgun, lay behind the base of a cottonwood near their lodge. From far off, they heard a screech owl, then even farther another— and a third. Lance brushed an ant from his neck; his movement sounded almost deafening, but was quickly forgotten as the tense listeners heard loud splashing in the nearby headwaters of the Snake.

Dog That Sits' feet sank into the muddy indentation near shore. Torn Ear, as erratically, splashed across to help him stand up. Dog That Sits slipped, then fell again, into the cloying mud, dragging Torn Ear with him. There they kicked, squirmed and wriggled, their mouths sucking and blowing like two beached sucker fish. With drunken grunts, disjointed words and considerable luck, they rose to their knees, and finally legs, to stumble up the grassy bank. When the men fell a third time, most people in the alerted encampments returned to their lodges, showering the inert bodies with ridicule.

Tjolzhitsay called to Pipe and Broken Hoof, two stalwart warriors who, like the drunks, usually lived in the north end of the Bitter Root Valley. They pulled the stupefied pair to knee-depth in the stream and roughly rinsed them up and down. When the cold bite of the mountain water partially revived the drunken men, Pipe and Broken Hoof dragged them to dry land. Voicing disapproval and concern, Antelope stepped near the men. When she detected blood seeping from wounds she and Little Coyote knew were in Dog That Sits' upper thigh and Torn Ear's side, she hastened for dry cattail fluff and wide strips of buckskin. Little Coyote struck a small fire to which Lance added dead willow twigs.

When the drunks could talk coherently, they disclosed they had obtained "whiskee" from two trappers who had arrived here early. The trappers had not joined the search for Bill Sublette. Sublette had agreed to haul trading goods here for the Rocky Mountain Fur Company's 1832 rendezvous and had not arrived. Later, when real whiskey loosened the two trappers' tongues, they would brag how they had shown great ingenuity and discipline by hoarding their precious supply of sugar to ferment a wine when the berries began to ripen in this more than thirty-mile-long valley named after dead Pierre Tevanitagon. While many men had searched for Sublette, the two had tapped the wine and taken a full canteen of it on a tour of the Indian camps to find a means of assuaging other long-pent-up thirsts. Dog That Sits and Torn Ear got the wine; their wives got the trappers.

"The whiskee. It stops the hurts." Dog That Sits raised his mud-plastered head and blurted the explanation with sour breath.

"It stops the hurts," Torn Ear agreed. Then, blearily focusing on this great truth, he began endlessly repeating it as though the minds of his listeners were muddled, too. He ceased when the vehemence of a foul belch, followed by a fit of vomiting, strained the wounded side.

Both warriors had taken musket balls several days earlier in yet another skirmish with the Blackfeet. The Blackfeet likely had been trying to avenge, among others, a recent major defeat in the Beaverhead Mountains that had cost them sixteen scalps. Nonetheless, the Blackfeet would keep trying. That promise had come from an alarmed Hudson's Bay agent. The Blackfeet had told him and some accompanying Pend d'Oreilles that the American Fur Company now had its fort on the Marias River.

"The Blackfeet are trading for many muskets, powder and balls," the agent had said, adding that they had boasted to him they soon "would wipe out the Flatheads and their allies so they never again can come in force to the buffalo grounds. We will make all the white men leave the land."

Little Coyote raised his hand and pointed. He and his family guided the drunken men out of the firelight. Little Coyote, Lance and Antelope could hear prolonged splashing sounds in the stream. Lance scrambled behind a bush and began crawling toward the water. He soon walked back and said to the men, "Your women are bathing." He returned to the lodge. Two women entered the firelight; they were pulling gowns over their bodies, which had borne several children to Dog That Sits and Torn Ear. The warriors stood up, gingerly tested the fit of the buckskin bandages, then started limping toward their lodges. The women docilely followed. Before disappearing into the darkness, they stopped to pick up some sticks for their cooking fires. Soon their children would want food.

"There will be more troubles! Perhaps so many of us should not have come here. Perhaps the Black Robes will not arrive after all." Little Bear Claw's comment ended for now his and

406

Little Coyote's families' talk about information they had received concerning another battle with the Blackfeet on the Salmon River. It had lasted two days and the Flatheads and Nez Percé had lost half their horses.

While the elk haunch and ribs roasted, the two families began watching some of the nearer white men who, seemingly from all directions, had begun sauntering between the lodges. As their numbers increased into the hundreds, so did their boldness. Four walked past the chief's family and friends as they prepared to eat. The whites stopped and openly gawked, the hunger in their eyes centering on Antelope, Young Willow and her son Fast Runner's mate, Warm Breeze, rather than on the food. The trappers were cordial enough, bowing profusely to the women, grasping Running Buffalo Bull's hand first, then pumping those of the other four warriors. They accepted the first large cuts from the haunch, then enthusiastically sliced off more with their own knives. Belly hunger sated, they again shook hands all around, promising "terbackee when Sublette jines us." They would keep their promise.

Lance and Fast Runner remained near their lodges while the other three warriors decided they also would walk. Two left with bows and arrows slung over their shoulders; Little Coyote carried the ancient lance. They listened and watched attentively at the outer circles of several small groups of men who had come from their respective company camps. Little Coyote soon could inform his father and friend that these were free trappers, Rocky Mountain Fur Company men and employees of the American Fur Company. Even some smaller firms were represented. One group was arguing, stopping occasionally to examine a wooden shingle. A mountain man had been perforating the shingle closer to the center of the charcoal-scrawled X each time he tapped his Hawken sights a bit more and fired at the target.

"Wisht we cud have a few more shootin' matches to wile away some of the time whilst we wait for Bill, 'n enough powder to burn thataway." The speaker pointed accusingly at three of the onlookers. "Yore sons a' bitchin' American Compny trades guns 'n powder 'n ball to the Blackfeet to kill us with, then has the sons a' bitchin' guts to folly us 'round the mountings to whar we finds the beaver, then come hyar to steal the trade from the free trappers 'n the Injuns!"

The irate trapper, knees and elbows protruding from holes in his worn and heavy woolen shirt and pants, paused for breath. Then he pulled off his floppy, woolen hat and threw it to the ground in disgust.

"You Rocky Mountain Company fellows ain't got all the answers!" an American Company trapper replied. "We got as much right to be here as you. Got licenses from St. Louis to prove it, our company has. Besides, Vanderburgh and Drips brought us here to wait for Fontenelle to bring in American Company goods, too—from Fort Union." The trapper reached into a droopy pocket of his less-worn, badly soiled woolen jacket and brought out a large twist of tobacco. "What the hell, there's gonna' be enough goods for all, and more furs than we ever can trap. Here, have a chaw. Where's Sublette or Fontenelle? Don't give much of a diddley damn which, so long's they bring the whiskey and terbackee. Here, Injuns. More where this come from. You can share some things with us, right soon enough!" He nudged one of the Rocky Mountain men in the ribs, popped the remaining bit of tobacco into his mouth, spat, tongued the chew into his cheek and laughed. "Look at Genous, here." He pointed to a shorter, stout man whose woolen shirt flared open to expose a heavy, vertical line of black hair above and below the navel.

"Where's your buttons, Genous? Lose 'em or trade 'em one at a time or all 'twunce? Lessee. One, two, three, four, five. And where's your knife, belt and hat? Why, you're gonna' slim that carcass down to nothin' afore this roundervoo ends. Well, almost nothin'. Better save your best parts. There'll be other roundervoos you can fatten up for like a bull elk at rut."

Genous grinned. He looked around to see who was listening. "Lissen, hoss. I see you got all yore buttons 'n other plunder. You waitin' to do a few little waltzes in the bushes with one 'a them Flathead *berdaches*, all garbed up like a woman? Maybe even that ain't possible for you neither. Hoss, you might as well let the Blackfeet shoot you next time around."

The men laughed loudly, including the trapper who now seemed content with the accuracy of his rifle.

The three Flatheads meandered among numerous other groups that were wrestling, story-telling, mending woolens or buckskins or snoring in the sun. All were awaiting the arrival of the trading goods for next season. Some had Indian women and children from near and far tribes joining in the work and play. A number of men were pressing company-owned beaver pelts into better packs of approximately eighty skins each. Elsewhere, loosely tied pelts, owned by the non-company men, lay scattered with other possessions under tents, trees or on the open prairie. There was no reason to guard them—until the whiskey kegs were tapped.

The only posted guards, Indian and white, were around the many herds of horses, from which some of the men extracted a few of the best to tether among their tents.

By now their slow walk had taken the three warriors up a gradual slope above the encampment. They drank from a tumbling creek that would end its merry song as its waters merged with the river. The trio clambered atop a large table rock warming in the sun, yet shaded on one side by a tall cottonwood. They counted eighty Flathead and one-hundred-twenty Nez Percé lodges below, agreeing there were approximately a thousand people at this site. Running Buffalo Bull and Little Coyote watched some distant horse races, the yells of the riders and onlookers reaching up to them. Little Bear Claw slid down the rock. He captured a grasshopper, baited a hook on a short length of line and, after repeating the process twice, soon had three plump trout impaled on green willow sticks and broiling over a small fire. He carried them to his companions; they ate while discussing Dog That Sits' and Torn Ear's misadventures with the "whiskee."

Running Buffalo Bull expertly began separating the skeleton from the remaining half of his trout. While doing so, he shook his graying head sadly: "We cannot tell everyone how to behave. We cannot have one warrior stand guard over another warrior— or his women. Our people have gone their own ways too long, except for matters of war and the buffalo hunt. Must we now include the rendezvous? Such freedoms and such fewer restrictions have been our strengths. Yet, most of the people frown on such silliness with whiskey, which, indeed, is *tciaimúl*, the clever seducer. Whiskey, for which a warrior will turn his mate into *nlkalkalcúl*, the prostitute."

They finished their meal in silence. Little Coyote stood to cut a small, leafy branch from the cottonwood tree. They drew the bough through their hands to remove the fish oil. "They make such trades for other articles, too," Little Coyote said. "Even buttons!" The seer raised the bough to whisk away several flies attracted by the fish odor. "As Tjolzhitsay suggests, we will listen to the messages on these matters from the Black Robes. Yet, do the white men listen?"

He tossed the soiled bough next to the fish skeletons, which had been thrown near the base of the tree. Flies began buzzing over the spot, then alighting until they covered the bones. While they fed, others tried to displace them, then hungrily settled on the bough. Numerous others buzzed around to await their turn at the bough; finally, the bones were bare, except for newly deposited hordes of maggots.

The sharp crack of a rifle came from a trapper galloping his horse across the meadow. His racing companion fired another shot.

"Ol' Bill's comin'! Ol' Bill's comin'!" Their exultant shouts were repeated by the nearest group of trappers, the men echoing the cry until the entire rendezvous was alerted. From farther down the valley came a ragged volley of shots. The eager trappers fired more shots as they began running toward a small stand of trees. There, some men had tied long poles to tree trunks to form a rough circle. This would be the trading post.

"Good ol' Bill! He's hyar!"

"Bill, whar's the whiskey?"

"Whadju do, crawl most o' the way?"

"How's the fur market holdin' out? Any truth to that 'air story that they's makin' hats from silk worms?"

"Bringed lotsa' goods, 'pears like. We's moughty thirsty...

410

an' hungry for lots o' things. Haw, haw, haw!"

The men crowding in around the circle picked up the laugh and pounded each other on the back, company rivalries momentarily forgotten.

The leader of the sixty men and their long pack train signaled a halt. He stepped off his horse onto one of the poles next to a tree, testing it to see if it would support his more than six-foot frame. Gripping a large protrusion of rough cottonwood bark, he removed his wide-brimmed hat and waved it above his sandy hair in a friendly greeting.

"Boys!" The strong voice reached out to the crowd, including the Indians at the outer edge. "Boys, Fitzpatrick came on ahead to tell you we were on our way! Isn't he here?"

At the loudly chorused "No!" Sublette quickly added, "We got held up along the Green by a brush with the Gros Ventre. They got a few of our horses, none of the goods. I can tell you the market's good. We have lots of goods—including damn good whiskey. Soon's I outfit the Rocky Mountain boys for the next season, we'll be glad to trade you goods for furs, whiskey for furs. And while you're having the first good snort on Bill Sublette right now, I've got to look into this Fitzpatrick business."

Loud yells drowned out Sublette's rapid instructions that four precious tin kegs be set up behind the poles. Sublette departed as men formed four boisterous lines, then began handing over a cup or a small cooking pot to the men tapping the kegs. As each free trapper received a generous swig, he stepped out of line for the next man and headed back to his camp to fetch some of his furs. These he would exchange for supplies, more whiskey and fooforaw to do a bit of trading, himself.

Amid this hurrying, jostling and shouting, Little Coyote felt a strong hand grip his shoulder from behind. Tull, probably smiling beneath the hair, burbled, "Howdy, Coyote!" The trapper stepped back for a moment, then, feeling that free round of whiskey, hugged his friend and bowed deeply to Antelope. They withdrew a short distance from the center of the pandemonium. Tull looked for an open space to spit, found none at all, so fired blindly between the legs of a trapper. The man stepped at exactly the wrong moment, but did not feel the misdirected shot.

"Varlet! Shoulda' stooded still." Tull wiped off the space between nostrils and chin with his sleeve. "Took'd off for St. Looey, I did, ta see th' goin' ons thar. Too many people, so I com'd back with Sublette." His voice softened. "Smith. He's gone under. Comanches killed him, they did. Got off one shot with his Hawken, 'n sent th' chief under, but th' rest a' th' sarpants got him with a fuzee ball 'n lances. His pistols 'n Hawken an' th' story a' th' fracas showed 'mong some Injuns in Santy Fee. Wull, already got ma gear fer next yar. Met Bridger yet? He 'n t'other booshways ownin' th' Rocky Mounting Compny 'er purty fear'd th' Blackfeet got Fitzpatrick. Hol' on."

Tull slipped under the pole circle and spoke briefly to one of the busy men minding the kegs. The man quickly marked something in a notebook atop a fast-growing pile of furs, then filled Tull's cup. The trapper offered it to Little Coyote and Antelope, who declined. Muttering, "Jes' as well," Tull gulped down a shudder-producing swig and directed them from the growing rabble toward two men talking under a nearby tree. They were Bill Sublette and his brother, Milton, who still was hurting from an Indian-inflicted wound. The two were cordial enough, but quickly excused themselves. Tull emptied and pocketed his cup. He next directed his friends toward a man who apparently was preparing for a long horseback ride.

"This hyar's Bridger. He's ben in Flathead camps afore."

The broad-shouldered, dark-haired man looked up from tying a small pack behind his saddle. Fixing steely gray eyes on the Flatheads, he gravely shook their hands. The tiniest hint of annoyance flickered across Bridger's face as Tull prepared to leave, but the man promptly grinned his appreciation at hearing, "Hol' on, Ol' Gabe, 'n I'll fetch somthin' ta wet yore gullet afore startin' out."

Tull hurried on creaky legs toward the trading area, his side-to-side roll surely reaching the limits of equilibrium. Bridger briefly conveyed in signs to the two Flatheads his concern about Fitzpatrick and the need to start a search.

"We understand. Our friend Jedediah Smith told us about

Fitzpatrick."

Little Coyote's reply, voiced loudly above the nearby cacophony of sounds and followed by Antelope's affirming nod and "Yes," surprised Bridger. His eyes centered more carefully on their faces. He would remember these Flatheads. Before he could reply, Tull returned with the half-empty tin cup. Judging from his loud song, incomprehensible to the straining ears of the Flatheads, Tull had wet his gullet with the other half. Bridger drank and handed the remainder back to a grateful Tull, who showed no such restraint. As the younger man signed *farewell*, mounted and hurried away, Tull spat, filled his mouth with tobacco and sat down. His friends left him then, his loud, even more incomprehensible song melding with the noise from the near chaos outside the trading corral.

A few of the hundred or so American Fur Company trappers held onto their furs through the first day or two of the revelry. Then they, too, capitulated after viewing the growing pile of beaver packs and diminishing stacks of goods inside the corral. They agreed they had no choice. With Fontenelle not showing, maybe gone under, they had to get supplies and whiskey somewhere—fast. Already, some of the Rocky Mountain Company men were "going on the books" against next year's catch. Soon there would be nothing left.

When Little Coyote and Antelope saw Bridger in a few days, he was somber. He remained that way even after Fitzpatrick arrived in the company of two Iroquois who had been sent to look for him. The Iroquois had found Fitzpatick sitting at the base of a large boulder, starving, almost naked, weaponless and beginning to babble like the crazy ones.

"He's Fitzpatrick, though with his hair turned white I scarce knew him when we found him," Antoine Godin explained. Bridger gently lifted his friend from the horse and easily carried him to a pile of furs inside the corral.

"He's not talking much," Godin continued. "Said the Gros Ventre took after him near South Pass. He had to leave his horses and hide out. Lost everything crossing a stream. Don't know how he lived."

Bridger brought the two Iroquois a cup of whiskey and clapped them on the back. "I'm eternally grateful."

Each day and night the craziness in the white men's camps boiled over into those of the Flatheads and Nez Percé. Dog That Sits and Torn Ear quickly became adept at trading their tired wives for watered whiskey. A growing number of younger women began stealing away from the drudgery of the encampments, usually in the darkness. Their punishment did not deter others. Some formed liaisons that would last beyond the rendezvous. The two warriors met this competition by centering on the most besotted trappers; their wives learned that the more quickly they could beguile their mates into becoming drunk, the sooner they could return to their lodges and children.

More warriors tried the whiskey and soon fights began breaking out. When one drunken warrior stabbed another, Tjolzhitsay and Tuekakas called a council. Some of their sub-chiefs were absent or incapable of lending wise counsel. Tjolzhitsay, at council urging, began to use the whip. It usually was ineffective and he put it away when drunken War Club tore it from his grasp. Fumblingly, War Club tried to lash the head chief, then held onto the whip despite terrible punishment at the hands of the frustrated leaders. Their thudding blows jarred pain-filled whimpers through his clenched teeth.

"Do this no more!" his woman shouted. His kin, friends and others also raised their voices in loud protest.

His punishers spent, War Club lay on his back, knees doubled up in pain. He grasped the whip handle as tightly as the squatting woman clutches the birthing pole as her child begins to arrive.

Some, following the lead of War Club's determined wife, moved their lodges away from the central encampment and closer to that of the Rocky Mountain Fur Company. Tuekakas, drawing on melancholy experience gained from his people's access to Fort Nez Percés, asked old Bad Leg to re-establish the patrol among the elderly warriors to discourage that segment from seeking the whiskey. Red Paint had a similar task with the younger warriors. More than enough of the latter were eager to serve, particularly

414

those who had found their women wearing a bit of ribbon or a string of beads that had not come from their mates.

Now an anger against some whites who supplied the whiskey began to take seed in the breasts of the warriors who would not drink; also in the breasts of the drinkers against the traders, who no longer would supply the liquor because the Indians had nothing left to exchange. The Flatheads adopted the tactics of their Nez Percé brethren with somewhat less success until a weary Tjolzhitsay acknowledged that "some fish always elude the nets." When furs and whiskey were gone in seven Suns, most of the Indians were eager to return home. They collectively voiced their disappointment that the Black Robes had not arrived.

Even before that, Bill Sublette began lining up the approximately six tons of furs for transport on seventy horses. Battered War Club's family and other kin remained outraged that the warrior had become the focus of the Flatheads' punishment. They struck their small camp and prepared to leave with Milton Sublette.

"This is not good; our people should not go different ways," Little Bear Claw tried to argue when he and several other equally agitated sub-chiefs went to the defectors' camp. "When our people have trekked as far as Fort Vancouver to trade, we have been weakened until they returned. When some of our people and our brothers, the Nez Percé, followed the fur-takers to St. Louis seven summers ago, they never returned. Nor have the Flatheads, Kutenais and Iroquois who did the same only a summer ago to also settle where the Kaw meets the Missouri River. Tjolzhitsay and others begin to think now we should have been saddened when the white chiefs Clark and Lewis made their appearance among us."

The defectors listened politely, but there would be no turning back. No matter that Milton Sublette would be trekking south then southwest, away from the Flatheads' beloved Bitter Root Valley. War Club's wife was correct. The people should "do this no more" to a respected warrior who had become crazy because of the whiskey. Fiery Howling Wolf seated his battered *i-sts-sókoi* on his pony and led the procession trailing after Sublette's small band. If they were lucky, they all would be out of this hole by night's camp.

They weren't lucky.

Learning to articulate into a formation that offered some protection against possible enemies took time. The Milton Sublette party camped after covering seven miles or so. This was lucky in a perverse way because their larger luck ran out when Sublette fixed his spyglass on two lines of horsemen next morning. More and more people began appearing on foot. They were a detachment of approximately one-hundred-sixty Gros Ventre, allies of the Blackfeet, ranging far ahead of a much larger, more heavily laden village. The Gros Ventre proved their unfriendliness by attacking Bill Sublette and trying to take Fitzpatrick's scalp. Also, they carried a British flag that John Work's Hudson's Bay outfit had not given up willingly.

Surprised, both groups halted. They needed time to contemplate their next moves. The Gros Ventre war chief took the initiative. Wearing a scarlet blanket and cradling a medicine pipe in his left arm, he rode boldly toward the smaller Sublette group.

Antoine Godin spat contemptuously. Seventy or so miles from here the Blackfeet had killed his Iroquois father two years earlier.

"They want to parley," Godin said. He looked at a doubtful Sublette. No one spoke for several moments until Godin murmured, "I will talk."

Godin looked at Howling Wolf. "Bring along your Hawken." Those nearby heard the ominous cocking sounds as the two men rode toward the Gros Ventre chief. The chief gazed at Howling Wolf and the gun. With a scarcely perceptible, contemptuous, downward movement of his lips, the chief raised the medicine pipe and held out his right hand to meet that proffered by Godin. Godin grasped his saddle pommel with his left hand as he reached forward to seize the chief's hand. Then he jerked the chief forward.

"Kill him," Godin said. Howling Wolf tipped the rifle upward on his own saddle and fired. The Gros Ventre's eyes widened as his chest took the bullet; before the gunsmoke dissipated, his killers had scalped him, remounted and were galloping back to safety. Godin waved the dead chief's red blanket in defiance of the shrill cries of rage and faster-moving musket balls.

With this treacherous grasping of hands, the battle of Pierre's Hole was joined. It was a battle that would be argued in the stories of the people long after the bones of the participants became dust with those of Pierre Tevanitagon, long after the battle site, itself, received white man's name of Teton Basin.

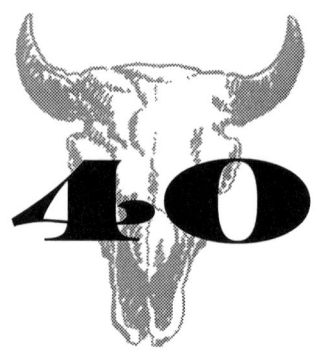

40

"Gun is dying. He calls to you from near his lodge. Marianne and Shield Maker remain with him."

Ignace Hatchiorauquasha signed an appreciative refusal to Antelope's instant offer of food even as the part-Iroquois spoke to Little Coyote this second morning after the departure of the Milton Sublette party. Hatchiorauquasha shook his head so vigorously his grizzly-claw necklace rattled when Little Coyote reached for the medicine box.

"He cannot get well. We only can help his spirit prepare for its journey—if we hurry!"

The medicine man shrugged. This John Gray, expert hunter-trapper, possessed what the often-exasperated fur company leaders called "too much white man's education." He did know many things. As for Shield Maker being with Gun, again the seer shrugged. Perhaps the wise old man had listened to Gun and other Flatheads who wished to learn more about the Black Robes. Perhaps Shield Maker merely wished to help Gun on his journey to the sand hills, too. These thoughts gave way to an important decision before the trio had walked five paces from the lodge.

Lance galloped his Appaloosa between the shelters to reach his own. Holding the Hawken gun, he nimbly leaped from the

418

animal before it stopped.

"Godin, Howling Wolf and two Sublette men rode down the valley past our horse guards!" Lance shouted. "They are fighting many Gros Ventres up the valley. Our enemies have sent out most of their families and now fight in a beaver swamp." Lance held his thin-scraped, translucent powder horn toward Sun. There was an ample supply. "Howling Wolf and others ask our help. We will go?"

Little Coyote glanced at Hatchiorauquasha. Only four months earlier Hatchiorauquasha almost had lost his life in a fight with enemy Indians. His partner, David Montgomery, had died, after which Hatchiorauquasha had escaped downriver in a boat he had constructed with his only remaining weapon—a pen knife. Even now his body continued to suffer from the ordeal.

"You will go," Little Coyote told Lance. "Antelope and I . . ." Again he looked at the part-Iroquois, who nodded affirmatively. ". . . All of us will attend Gun. He dies." Little Coyote and Antelope entered the lodge and picked up their weapons as Lance grasped his bow and arrows.

At Antelope's sharp, "A warrior must eat!" her son picked up a food bag. They watched him gallop past, brandishing his rifle, shrilling a war cry as he joined the ragged stream of noisy horsemen hurrying up the valley. Antelope spoke briefly to Running Buffalo Bull and Little Yellow Bird. They, too, trudged up the slight knoll toward Gun's lodge. From a distance they could see Gun reclining against a cottonwood root—seemingly a motionless infant in the giant lap of Mother Earth, her great breasts, the towering Tetons, beckoning them all in an eternally mysterious way. Nearer, the five looked down at the long, badly scarred face. It was slack and gray, only the single eye moving.

"He but hears and sees now." Marianne, Hatchiorauquasha's Mohawk-French wife, rose from her seat on a nearby rock she had been sharing with Shield Maker. "Before he quit talking, he clutched his chest and said his arms were dying. Now he can move no more. He voiced his regrets that the Black Robes did not arrive to help with the sorrow the rendezvous has brought us all. He wished to have the baptism, so I baptized him." She pointed to a canteen. "His eye tells me he seeks more. What it is, Shield Maker and I cannot discover."

She returned to her rock seat and continued her prayers.

Hatchiorauquasha and the two younger people knelt before the battered warrior. His eye moved to encompass them all. His lips, seemingly frozen into a crooked grimace, tried to move. Hatchiorauquasha peered closely into the eye, then leaned back.

"Marianne!" he said harshly. "The eyeball moves up, down, left then right in the form of a cross. Give me your crucifix!" Shield Maker stood now from his seat on the rock and approached the woman as she pulled a leather thong over her head and dangled a small crucifix before Gun's good eye. The eye moved downward to watch the woman place the crucifix in his paralyzed right hand. Once more the eye centered in the socket. The lips quivered slightly, but the grimace remained. Little Coyote placed his hand on his old friend's left shoulder while he, too, watched the eye. There were only a few slow blinks. The breathing was hard, more labored, and, yet, that eye, trying to communicate in a mortal way even as the immortal sought release. The plea: How it sought release ahead of the spirit!

Hatchiorauquasha spoke quietly into Gun's right ear: "Oh my God, I am heartily sorry for having offended Thee, and I detest all my sins because I dread the loss of heaven and the pains of hell. But most of all because they offend Thee, my God, Who art all good and deserving of all my love . . ." When the Iroquois concluded the prayer, he and Marianne made the sign of the cross.

Shield Maker pointed to Little Coyote's bow and arrows as the old man chanted a prayer that the Good Spirit soon would pull his friend into His presence and the joys of the sand hills.

Gun's eye slowly moved from Shield Maker and fixed downward on the bow and arrows. Now Little Coyote understood the plea, too. He moved the quiver to Gun's feet and closed the fingers of the warrior's near-lifeless left hand over the bow. The right half of Gun's upper and lower lips formed a slight smile as the eye dulled; the mouth opened in a final, drawn-out exhalation and the spirit of this Christian Flathead was free.

420

The seven people buried Gun in a tree above the small knoll, the crucifix and the bow still frozen in his hands. Her lips moving in prayer, Marianne fashioned a small cross from pliant willow and set it on the tree base. Little Coyote, his father and Shield Maker pushed in two of the best hunting arrows beside the cross. Leaving the two older warriors, Little Yellow Bird and Antelope returned sorrowing to the excited encampment. Shield Maker talked quietly to Little Coyote, his old face crinkling in deep thought as he told of Gun's struggle to convey his last thoughts: "Gun thanked the Good Spirit for letting him learn about these matters that most concern Him. 'I wish,' he told me, then repeated, 'I wish there had been more time to learn in my youth about the straightest way, yet harder, to do the wishes of the Good Spirit. As I die, I see more clearly and understand better the little I have learned: The Good Spirit loves all. We must love all. First the Good Spirit, then even our enemies. We must forgive our enemies, love them all. That is what the Black Robes say.'" Shield Maker walked away, shaking his head.

There was a brief flurry of conversation between Hatchiorau-quasha and his wife after the remaining three had sat there on the knoll for a time and watched Sun arc westward. Marianne stood, placed her hands on her slim hips and continued to talk. Little Coyote did not understand Mohawk, but there was no mistaking the woman's feelings. She concluded by vehemently wagging her finger at her silent spouse. As she flounced down the hill, Hatchiorauquasha's lean face bore an amused, slightly rueful grin: "If the priests do not come soon to the Nez Percé and the Flatheads, she tells me we no longer will live among them and others, but must take our family near St. Louis if we want to save our souls." The Iroquois nodded more to himself than to Little Coyote as he continued: "She feels very deeply the loss of Gun, with whom she worked hard so the people could learn more about the Good Spirit."

Tjolzhitsay and Tuekakas had prepared well should the Gros Ventre move down the valley. On one side beyond the encampment, many Nez Percé stood, sat or lay near their horses.

The Flatheads formed a similar flank on the other. In front of the encampment, men and women warriors moved behind hastily constructed log and brush piles. The packers Bill Sublette had left behind scarcely moved at all; they seemed content to let the Indians prepare for a possible fight, even when all others sprang into wakefulness as the eyes of the most watchful saw a series of mirror flashes come from far up the valley.

Tjolzhitsay and Red Paint, their sweating bodies streaked with powder residue and dust, galloped their horses down the valley to report to their respective people. Their short battle summaries were delivered hastily and accurately because soon the mountain men would be hurrying back to help protect their encampment. Tjolzhitsay first told how Godin and Howling Wolf had killed the war chief, after which the Gros Ventre had entered the swamp. Amid the noise of the battle the Gros Ventre had taunted that soon they would be joined by four-hundred lodges of warriors from their main body of people.

"Some of our white friends misinterpreted the enemies' taunts and war cries," Tjolzhitsay said. "Soon many whites and Indians were shouting that the great body of Gros Ventre was attacking their rendezvous encampments." Tjolzhitsay commanded silence so he could continue.

"The Gros Ventre hung blankets, lodges and robes, and piled dirt and mud in front of their fort. Most of us were not foolish enough to charge through the brush. Our movement would have given us away." A note of pride entered Tjolzhitsay's voice. "Instead, our warriors with rifles fired slowly and carefully from behind trees and logs. We shot many horses so the enemy could not get away fast. The Gros Ventre have good muskets." Now a note of sorrow entered his voice. "Seven of the Flathead and Nez Percé warriors are dead, as are five of the whites and a half-Indian. As many at least are wounded. Bill Sublette was shot in the shoulder. The same ball wounded a man who was kneeling behind him."

A great cry went up. Tjolzhitsay again commanded silence, signing hurriedly to Little Coyote, *Your son fights bravely.*

"We have killed many enemy," the head chief shouted above

the gradually diminishing hub-bub. "The whites wished to burn them out, but we would have lost the blankets, lodges, furs, muskets, powder and other possessions. Most of our warriors and the Nez Percé have not joined in the great ride back here. They continue to defeat the enemy."

The anxious assemblage gave way for a Nez Percé, who quickly rode up to Tjolzhitsay. The chief raised his hands: "The whites approach. Running Buffalo Bull will take ten warriors to the Nez Percé. They will send an equal number to the Gros Ventre fort. We must keep them there. If what the Gros Ventre shouted about the four-hundred lodges is true, our warriors and the Nez Percé will return here. Tuekakas agrees. We will fight any big battle at this place."

Little Coyote found Tull in front of his small wickiup. He was refilling his powder horn from a small keg.

"Them varlets fit us good," Tull said. "Bill tol' Ol' Gabe ta wait'll there's a leetle light come mornin' afore he heads us back. Suits me." He began cleaning his Hawken. "Jine us ifn ye wants." The seer left when Tull prepared to cast some bullets.

Small wisps of fog were moving ghost-like in the beaver swamp when Bridger led the men to the battle site at dawn. Water dropped from the cottonwoods and the stale odor of sulphur hung in the moisture-laden air. A wounded horse shrieked its agony behind the crude fort and, as the pain-laden echoes returned, the men could hear the animal thrashing about in the muddy water. There was much death here.

Running Buffalo Bull met the arrivals where the many trails leading to and from the swamp merged into one.

"There has been no firing since dark," he said. "We have warriors at the front and at both sides. The Gros Ventre wait for us to rush, or they are gone."

Bridger spread out the men in an uneven line before the fort: "Aim your guns low and directly in front of you so our bullets will 'specially cover the whole front of the fort."

Some Flatheads and Nez Percé joined in the ragged volley. Only the horse's weaker scream returned with the echoes.

"I reckon they're gone, but I'll take a look-see." Bridger crouched low and made a zig-zag dash forward from tree to tree until he was in the swamp. He returned soon, water dripping from his buckskins. "They're gone—the live ones, that is."

The Flatheads and Nez Percé rushed in as the whites began digging graves in the heavily churned-up area near the fort. While some of the Indians deliberated over claims to four of the scalps of the nine dead Gros Ventre behind the fort, others—mostly late-comers, including a few trappers—sought different battle spoils. At first there were few. Then the warriors began finding their own dead. Shrilling vengeance, they followed the Gros Ventres' trail along the creek and into the forest of another valley. The valley soon began echoing to increasing triumphant cries over the discovery of horses and other booty, as well as badly wounded enemy and abandoned corpses, including those of a few children.

The pursuers gathered together when one mountain man shouted, "Hyar's a squaw!"

Her leg was badly broken, the shin bone protruding like a splintered, white, lance point from the back of her bloody calf. Though sick with pain, weak from blood loss, worn out from trying to keep up with the fleeing Gros Ventre, the woman raised her head, lowered it, then raised it again and motioned for the trappers to kill her. She found sufficient strength to snarl her defiance as the Nez Percé and Flatheads approached. Dog That Sits reached her first. He climbed down from his horse. The woman tried to rise on her mangled leg, so he kicked her there. As she sank down in greater agony, he seized her by the hair and carefully sank his hatchet through her forehead and into her brain. He wiped the weapon on her gown and reached for his rusty knife. As he raggedly sawed the blade back and forth to remove her scalp, he looked up to voice his sorrow that Torn Ear was among the dead. His own *sumesh*, he claimed, came from the dog tail suspended on a thong around his neck.

Lance's familiar whistle brought his grandfather and father to the mid-point of a small, sloping hillside well away from the general direction of the flight. Many horses had converged here. Clearly, the animals had been widely dispersed before being herded up here for a faster retreat.

"Do they carry riders?" Lance unabashedly asked. Other riders gathered about Running Buffalo Bull, who told them not to destroy the story hidden in the tracks. Running Buffalo Bull dismounted and walked a brief arc at the nearer edge of the hoofprints. He entered the churned-up grass and leaves, then knelt with difficulty several times to examine the story more clearly. He mounted his horse: "They were brought this way by women before the fight at the fort. We will move carefully, for perhaps the fleeing Gros Ventre have circled this way and gotten them."

Others of these warriors found forty-two horses, including the two Fitzpatrick had lost, hidden in a small *cul de sac* with a brush barricade. Encouraged by his earlier discovery of the horses' trail, Lance sought and found one of the women who had left her track, too. She had hidden in a small, triangular cleft in the base of a rocky cliff. She emerged with a short spear. As she tried to run one direction along the cliff base, the warrior urged his horse ahead so he was waiting for her there. When she ran back in the other direction, again he was waiting. Back and forth, back and forth until she leaned, exhausted, near the cleft from which he had flushed her. He dismounted and warily approached, easily dodging the spear hurled by a tired arm. She was reaching for her knife when Lance jumped her. Not caring to risk a blade in the gut, he knocked her unconscious with a flat-handed punch alongside her head. The woman was tall and of perhaps eighteen summers; she was as well-proportioned as Fast Runner's Warm Breeze and, despite the grime of battle and her flight, was fully as desirable.

Lance bound her hands with a ragged strip of buckskin cut from her gown, boosted her onto his Appaloosa, tied her legs around the barrel and began leading the horse toward the noisy, growing assemblage near the swamp.

Each arguing or exulting small group stared as captor and prisoner passed by. Total quiet reigned as Lance stopped his horse near his grandfather and father.

Dog That Sits mounted his horse, grasped his hatchet and

shouted for Bird Wing and Thunder Cloud to come from the burying party: "Here is another Gros Ventre to kill and help avenge the deaths of these warriors we mourn!"

Running Buffalo Bull mounted his horse. His surprised demeanor at the arrival of his grandson and the captive changed to a darkness that even Little Coyote never before had seen.

"Take the woman to Tuekakas," Running Buffalo Bull said. "She is a gift!"

He bumped his horse into that of Dog That Sits. "Complete the burial of Torn Ear, your *i-sts-sokoi*, and the others. Bird Wing. You have performed bravely. We ask you to accept the honor to drive the horse herd Lance helped discover to Tjolzhitsay and Tuekakas for fair distribution. Yours will be the first choice of five horses after the man Fitzpatrick receives back his two. Thunder Cloud—" Running Buffalo Bull turned an even darker countenance on Lance. "Go!" he hissed. Little Coyote prodded his son in the side with his rifle. "Thunder Cloud," Running Buffalo Bull repeated. "You carry two fresh scalps of two Gros Ventre warriors. I step back for you to lead the procession to the encampment."

The return was both triumphant and sorrowful. Three Flatheads remained behind at possible great peril should the Gros Ventre return. Dog That Sits convinced two young, untested braves that his *sumesh* was strong and that the dog tail hanging from his neck gave both him and those nearby special protection. He pointed to the woman's scalp and to his almost healed wound as proof.

By now, all were anxious to leave Pierre's Hole. Bill Sublette waited for his wound to heal and to learn if the Gros Ventre would contest his return of the two years' fur take to St. Louis. The Flatheads and Nez Percé mourned their dead and talked much about Howling Wolf's and Godin's killing of the Gros Ventre chief. They seemed equally divided concerning treachery and boldness. One good emerged from all the discussion: The people who angrily had set out with Milton Sublette succumbed to pleas they not go again; there was no mention of the possibly lurking

Gros Ventre.

Two days before the Flatheads and Nez Percé left for home, Dog That Sits led a triumphant procession into the encampment. The warrior held a tether leading to the neck of an emaciated, stumbling and badly beaten white man. Two younger braves rode slightly behind and on either side of the tottery figure. One had tied a small, ham-shaped case behind his saddle.

"Be seated! Be seated!" Dog That Sits urged. "Be quiet. A great marvel will occur."

The younger braves carried a large chest to the center of the circle. Little Coyote, Antelope and Lance, his comments about the Gros Ventre maiden momentarily diverted, whispered among themselves. Surely they knew this prisoner. With a strong kick to the ribs, Dog That Sits encouraged the human wreck to climb atop the box. One of his captors opened the ham-shaped case. From it he withdrew a shiny, wooden instrument and a small, bow-shaped device. The white man's cadaverous head and face turned almost absently here and there on his dejected shoulders as though hoping to see a friend among these hundreds of curiosity-filled faces. Dog That Sits rapped him sharply on his legs with a lance, whereupon the creature began flexing fingers that evidently had been spared the beatings. The brave handed him the violin; in a few moments the music began to move out from the man on the box and over the audience—slowly, sadly, rising and falling in various voices like the muted and mournful keening of the women in the camps these past few days. Dog That Sits angrily poked the player in the belly. Now the sounds possessed a faster tempo, an entrancing beauty that rose to the sky and surrounded all. None had heard such beauty before, except Little Coyote's family at Lisa's fort, a few of the Nez Percé at Fort Nez Percés, and, before that, from the fiddle of Cruzat, one of the Clark and Lewis men so long ago.

The player, too, seemed overcome. Tears coursed down his hollow cheeks until he was forced to stop and free one hand to blow his soggy nose. That impertinence brought him a stout, upward jab in the crotch from the butt end of his master's lance. Curiously, instead of doubling up in agony, the creature energetically began playing a livelier tune, faster and faster, louder and louder, to the delight of all—except the three astounded Flatheads and Red Paint, who had walked over to join them.

"Yes," Red Paint murmured, "he fled with a small band of Arapahos when you threatened to kill him at Fort Nez Percés. He is Brandt."

Dog That Sits broadened his following among some of the people as he forced Brandt to play music at the end of each day's trek back toward the Bitter Root Valley. Except for an occasional thundershower, the weather remained warm with few winds. This spared the women from erecting the lodges. Water and wood always were near at hand. Thus, all who wished could sit on the ground and listen to almost-rapturous sounds so unlike their own music. Brandt learned quickly enough he could escape the club by limping amid the delighted audience, ankles rubbed raw by the imprisoning sinew hobbles.

One evening Dog That Sits again had savagely beaten the hapless Brandt for playing music appropriately fitting his woebegone appearance and dejected spirit. His owner's two assistants had held Brandt's hands so the club would not injure the fingers. When the master's arm had tired and the slave could howl no more, he played the liveliest music the encampment had heard. The people tried to hum the sounds and improvise words instead of voicing *i, a, e* in chromes.

"Now Dog That Sits trades more charms than anyone else to bring better luck among the people, from one end of the valley to the other," Lance said. "Like some of the others, he claims great cures for the sick and openly tells all that his *sumesh* is better than that of Little Coyote. He amasses many things he will trade for whiskey the traders bring, and he has taken to wife Torn Ear's woman for that purpose, too."

Little Coyote's son disgustedly spat a small bone into the cooking fire and reached for another part of a grouse. He no longer spoke openly of the Gros Ventre maiden, Swan, but his father and mother particularly noted his restlessness when Brandt's violin seemed to speak of joyous walks in the scented mountains, singing birds and waters and standing close in a blanket under the stars.

"I could not let the woman cause fighting among the angry and mourning people as we buried our dead," Running Buffalo Bull had told Lance after the Pierre's Hole battle. "I know our people would not fight Tuekakas, nor would he allow torture or killing of a gift." The grandfather's face had softened. "I told him that perhaps my grandson would bring good friendship gifts and, perhaps, in return, Tuekakas would throw away the woman. He smiled, but did not reply. He will not need horses."

Shortening days and early frosts turned the Bitter Root Valley red, yellow and gold. Tjolzhitsay began sending out calls for a great buffalo hunt. Those in the main encampment were briefly diverted when Fitzpatrick and Bridger brought a trapping party into one end of the valley. They would risk the Blackfeet and go to the headwaters of the Missouri. For this they wanted more good horses. Bridger had sought out Tjolzhitsay, Little Coyote, Little Bear Claw and Has Many Horses to learn, by using English and signs, how the Flatheads and Nez Percé had worked to obtain guns and build stronger alliances with other peoples to resist their enemies. When he learned that the Shoshonis had participated with the Flatheads and others, he nodded his head approvingly.

Those Snakes are good people, too, Bridger signed. He held out his right fist, with index finger extended, and moved it forward, indicating "Snake," the term most white men used for the Shoshonis.

"Honest, word's good," Bridger said. "They've still got some beaver over thataway, but their enemies, especially the Sioux, are trying to wipe them out. I'm planning to work more in that country. Maybe I'd better help them get guns—good guns."

Bridger and Fitzpatrick put a small, somewhat stooped, young redhead they called "Kit" to testing the likeliest animals.

"I wisely did not bring in my best three horses," Lance explained to his parents, proudly showing a good supply of powder and lead he had received for one animal. "The man Carson tested them well. He is a great horseman. He took the best of those I offered." The pride in the young warrior's voice changed to a pensiveness. "When I returned the other two horses to the herd, I encountered the sub-chief Insula's oldest daughter and Bridger sitting by the river." He fell silent then and carried his ammunition to his nearby small lodge, which he earlier and often had told his parents seemed too large for one man.

Soon thereafter Stone Pipe and Ram Horn Bow brought both a reason and a means for Lance to become one of the messengers to tell the Nez Percé about the plans for the hunt and, eventually, to return home with Swan.

The two warriors had joined in the previous great buffalo hunt, but did not attend the rendezvous. Instead, armed with Hawken guns and much courage, they had driven eleven swift Appaloosas to trade with the Crows on Tongue River.

"The Crows are most friendly," Stone Pipe told the council. "They had just danced with many scalps, guns and other equipment taken in a great victory over the Gros Ventre, who already had lost many warriors in the battle of Pierre's Hole and had little powder left for their guns. Very few escaped. Drum remains alive, though his hand is shaky. He pledges his friendship with our people. His son, Man Who Fights, now gratefully uses the long rifle gift of our chief. Drum remembers with gratitude Little Coyote and Antelope, who slew his brother's killers. There is much to tell about the great fire boat, which brought Rabbit's Skin Leggins and No Horns on His Head from St. Louis."

Thunder on the Mountain joyfully called out, "They live!" He quieted as others smiled and scowled at him. Some smiled because they knew he and Old Blanket from their people, and

Smoke from the Nez Percé, had returned home with much fever when they had left the mountains on their way to St. Louis. Some scowled because Stone Pipe, a good story-teller not given to exaggeration or excitement, would tell of a great fire boat.

This would be a telling of much importance. Tjolzhitsay summoned his wife and oldest daughter. The maiden moved amid the admiring glances of the council and listeners. She poured many of the precious coffee beans into a buckskin pouch, closed it and pounded it with a stone. Her mother carried in a great pot of boiling water. Soon the savory odor of coffee filled the lodge, calling back those who had gone outside to relieve themselves or talk. The head chief's wife poured in even more of the sugar. When all were drinking from her tin cups, Tjolzhitsay signed for Stone Pipe to continue. He looked at Ram Horn Bow, who nodded agreeably.

"Man of the Morning became sick and died in St. Louis, but not before receiving the pouring-on of water by the Black Robes," the warrior related sadly. "The war chief Black Eagle of the Nez Percé did the same."

During the silence, Tjolzhitsay once more gravely passed the pipe. When he put it down, Stone Pipe began relating their great adventure.

"The Crows told us that the American Fur Company also has placed a Fort Cass on the Yellowstone near the mouth of the Big Horn. Even so, with Drum and many warriors driving the Gros Ventre horses, we began a journey of trade to the Mandans." Stone Pipe began drawing a map in the air and facing the directions as he talked. "We trekked down the Yellowstone. As we neared where its waters join with the Missouri, we left gifts and smoked with some Cheyennes. They told us the white chief at Fort Union has declared the place a peace grounds, so some Crows, Crees and Blackfeet risked going there to trade, even though the American Fur Company also has put a Fort McKenzie among the Blackfeet.

"Drum led us east through great herds of buffalo until we struck and followed the Little Missouri. Soon its waters joined the Missouri. We trekked down that toward the Mandans. There was much good hunting and eating. One sundown we camped between two sloping hills where good water entered a bend of the Missouri. Many cottonwood trees and willows were growing in a small meadow in this bowl. While Crow scouts watched from the rimrocks, a great noise filled our ears and terrified the horses." Stone Pipe put down his coffee and cupped his hands together. When he blew between the thumbs, a sound like that of the last drawn-out wolf howl filled the lodge.

"We looked to the sky. Could it be thunder in a clear sky? Then Sky Fire, one of the scouts, fired his gun and raced his horse downhill to our camp. We sprang to our horses. 'A great fire boat comes up the river!' the scout told Drum. Now we looked to our weapons and hid among the trees as Sky Fire pointed to a plume of smoke rising above the rim of the hill and curve of the river and coming closer like a swirling pillar of black dust. Again came the great noise, sounding this time like the one great roaring of a herd of buffalo bulls. The front end of a great boat that could hold the people in this encampment came around the curve and approached us. We saw a pillar of white smoke and almost immediately again heard the roar, a long one, then two short ones. A small cannon, about the size of the one the Flatheads possess in a hidden place, fired over the water. When we shrank back in fear and had difficulty holding our horses, we could see that men aboard were amused. Two men then stood atop the boat and signed they were friends. White men and two black men tied the boat to a tree. More men came out of the boat's guts to chop dead trees and haul them for the fire.

"Then we saw Rabbit's Skin Leggins and No Horns on His Head. The Sioux had paid them great honor by dressing them in their finery at Fort Pierre below. We scarcely knew them. We embraced these two brothers and while the other men gathered wood they told us of the marvels at St. Louis, and the sadness there about the deaths of Black Eagle and Man of the Morning. St. Louis has many people and needs to get more Black Robes. Then they will send some. Many people call for them. We must keep calling, too. There was so much to hear that Rabbit's Skin Leggins and No Horns on His Head told us to bring onto the fire boat our four horses and the trade goods we had obtained for the Appaloosas. The chief of the fire boat agreed and told Drum they would protect us, too. From Fort Union we and the two Nez Percé could accompany one of their brigades out of the land of the Assiniboins. The ride on the fire boat was of much importance. The white men feel this is so. They gave the boat a name— *Yellow Stone*. I found it as long as forty of my great steps. The Assiniboins at Fort Union eyed us with much hatred, as did the Blackfeet. We watched our horses with care. We kept near the fire boat and while we slept, one of us remained awake with the guns close. We were pleased when we left.

"The brigade went up the Yellowstone River. On the way the lingering sickness in the guts of No Horns on His Head killed him. Some Nez Percé, who also were driving horses to the Crows, met us. They would hunt after their trades. This was on the lodge grass prairie near the Little Big Horn. There was much joy. Soon thereafter, the Blackfeet struck. Rabbit's Skin Leggins received a fuzee ball in his chest. He called to me and with much difficulty pointed to these two saddlebags." Stone Pipe reached down and held aloft the buckskin bags. "They hold seeds Rabbit's Skin Leggins received from the Black Robes in St. Louis. They are called 'oats' and 'alfalfa.' They are for the Nez Percé to grow with the good bunchgrass on which their fine horses prosper in winter. 'Have Gun or the medicine man, Little Coyote, take these to Tuekakas,' Rabbit's Skin Leggins said. Then he died while talking to the Good Spirit. Other Nez Percé and Blackfeet died before the enemy were driven away. We told the Nez Percé we would tell their people about these matters and carry the seeds to Gun or Little Coyote. Since perhaps two moons yet must pass before the Nez Perce come to join us for the buffalo hunt, we must take this story to the Nez Percé."

"Is Stone Pipe through talking?" Tjolzhitsay asked.

"There is more to tell, but some of the stories have mysteries I cannot fully explain." Stone Pipe seemed tired. Perplexity wrinkled his face. He rubbed it and then dropped his hands. "As No Horns on His Head lay dying, he wondered if the white man, Catlin, wounded his spirit by painting his image while on the fire boat. Rabbit's Skin Leggins had that thought after he got the fuzee ball in his chest. Shield Maker scoffs at this." Again Stone Pipe rubbed his face. "Dog That Sits says the man Catlin stole part of their spirits. There is another matter I do not understand at all. Perhaps Little Coyote will help us to understand. One day on the fire boat a black man who hauls the wood and feeds the fire talked to our Nez Percé brothers." Stone Pipe paused, then spoke ever so slowly so he would be correct. There was only Ram Horn Bow to help correct what he might say.

"The black man said one of the sub-chiefs on the fire boat secretly began drinking whiskey from the great supply brought for trade. His tongue loosened." Stone Pipe looked at Ram Horn Bow, who nodded encouragingly. "The black man said the fire boat sub-chief had been told that the councils of the Great White Father had agreed white medicine men should go with this fire boat. They were to take magic that would keep away the smallpox evil from all the Indians who would receive the magic." Again Stone Pipe looked at Ram Horn Bow. "The sub-chief of the fire boat said the Great White Father's powerful sub-chiefs, unknown to him, refused to do this." Stone Pipe's face brightened. "Perhaps they knew that the smallpox is worn out and, like the toothless wolf, can bite no more."

Ram Horn Bow nodded approvingly, then reminded his friend, "There remains the important matter of the buffalo robes."

"Yes," Stone Pipe agreed. "As we trekked up the Yellowstone, the white fur brigade sub-chief told us the fire boat can carry great loads of furs and buffalo robes down the Missouri. He said that if the Flatheads, Nez Percé and their allies would kill many buffalo near the Missouri, but away from the buffalo grounds of the Assiniboins, they could stack them up and wait for the fire boat to come along and trade for them before going on to Fort Union. They do not like for enemies to be brought together near the forts, and fear quarrels will break out over hunting the buffalo near the forts."

Now Ram Horn Bow spoke: "The fur brigade sub-chief said a good place would be where they had stopped for the wood and had let us go on the fire boat." The warrior lowered his head in deep thought. Slowly, the words came out. "The fur-takers said they do not want the unworked hides of bulls. Like the Indians, they find them much tougher to work. They want only the worked robes of cows and young bulls. They must have their heavy winter hair." The words came faster now. "They should be taken about the eleventh moon, as we know, and through perhaps three more moons. The boat can carry all we can kill and turn to robes. Yes, white man likes the robes. He also likes the tongues. One day when most of the trading with all the tribes was over and the robes had been taken onto the fire boat, a powerful band of five-hundred Blackfeet came to the fort. They demanded whiskey, but the fur-takers already had traded them for their furs and robes. With great splashing, the Blackfeet crossed the river. Before Sun had gone to rest, they recrossed the river with great bags of buffalo tongues. The black man told us the man Catlin counted the tongues as the wood-haulers put them in great, round, wooden boxes with much salt like we get in our treks to the great salt lake in the land of the Utes, or to the much closer Girdle Mountains. There were almost three tongues for each Blackfeet. The fur-takers gave them perhaps ten pots of whiskey. Much wildness followed, and the Assiniboins, Crows and Crees looked to their weapons. The black man told us to take our horses to the fire boat and stay there. He also told us Catlin said there now were on the fire boat five tons of tongues from Fort Pierre below and Fort Union, but the black man could not help me comprehend what a ton is."

Ram Horn Bow looked at Stone Pipe: "We are through talking." Ram Horn Bow drank his cold coffee.

With Gun dead, Little Coyote had no difficulty persuading the head chief to let Lance carry the alfalfa and oat seeds to the Nez Percé. He also was to ask them to join in the coming winter hunt, both for meat and good robes. They also could discuss with the Flatheads the plan for the great hunt for robes to trade to the people on the *Yellow Stone*. And, yes, Lance could carry the same message to the Shoshonis. Tjolzhitsay smiled and added to Little Coyote's suggestion, ". . . unless the Gros Ventre maiden,

Swan, demands his full attention."

Tuekakas had not mistreated the Gros Ventre maiden. Indeed, when Lance arrived, he learned the wise chief had counseled her to learn the language of signs; surely, Tuekakas reasoned, she would need to talk to the Flatheads in the future. And when Lance explained the story of the seeds, Tuekakas told him he would accept no gift in return for the woman.

"Our women were told to work her very hard, but not harm her, so she would be more willing to return to the Flatheads at the proper time," Tuekakas said. "Our only problem was convincing our own young braves that they were not to stand in the blanket with her. Tell Tjolzhitsay we will join in the coming meat and robe hunt, and will listen about the plan to take robes for the people on the *Yellow Stone*."

With much ceremony at a council meeting, Tuekakas had Lance tell the story about the adventures and deaths of No Horns on His Head and Rabbit's Skin Leggins. Then, amid the sorrowing, he presented the seeds. The chief then called the principal medicine man and asked him to work out a plan to grow, harvest, then plant again and again until all could share this goodwill gift of the Black Robes.

Tuekakas, himself, performed the ceremony for the mating of Lance and Swan. Swan accompanied Lance to the Shoshonis, who greeted the young couple with much joy and hospitality despite the poor condition of the tribe. The Shoshonis' situation stemmed from hardships in the hunts and constant depredations of Blackfeet and other enemies. Yes, they gladly would participate in the meat and robe hunts.

Lance and Swan returned to the Bitter Root Valley mounted on two of Broken Pipe's best Appaloosas. These drew the eyes of the Flathead people, but the eyes also lingered long on this comely woman whom Lance, son of Little Coyote and Antelope, had taken to wife. Lance smiled and no longer talked about his lodge seeming too large.

The winter hunt brought all who participated as much meat

and good cow and young bull hides as their many pack horses could carry. The people had hoped to save many arrows and much ammunition by using the ancient buffalo jump on the Madison River west of Three Forks. Despite Dog That Sits' boastful assurances his medicine had told him the animals were there, the scouts had found them many miles away between the Musselshell River and Sweetgrass Creek, where there was no jump. With much effort they constructed a pen; after many drives the people ate well and worked to preserve the meat, even some of the hides, while they were there.

As winter began dying in their beloved valley, the head chief summoned a council of all sub-chiefs. He had prepared well. Stretched on a pole frame was a large, blackened portion of an old lodge. Ram Horn Bow and Stone Pipe sat near it, the latter busily stirring a mixture of powdered white clay and water. Ram Horn Bow was pounding the end of a greening willow twig between two stones to make a brush.

Tjolzhitsay briefly told of the two warriors' experience on the *Yellow Stone* and the traders' plan for them to be ready with many buffalo robes when the fire boat came up the Missouri.

"I ask you to think about our not going on the big meat hunt during the warm season," Tjolzhitsay said. He held up his arms to silence the low murmurs that rose from the assemblage. "Hear me. I ask you to think about Little Bear Claw's suggestion we go near the Missouri with most of our equipage. This would be in the tenth moon. We would set up a great encampment with our allies and spend the cool and the cold months there, as well as the following spring—killing the cows and young bulls and preparing the robes. We must go where the buffalo are, or our spirits will die. We must think better than our enemies, with whom we have tried to make peace, or die."

Tjolzhitsay signed for Little Bear Claw to speak. Little Bear Claw looked at the silent, older sub-chiefs, the great hunters. Later he would tell Little Coyote that only the seer's slight smile gave him courage.

"We must kill the buffalo near the Missouri so we will not wear out our horses carrying the robes many miles," Little Bear

Claw told the council. "We also must avoid as many Assiniboins and Blackfeet as possible. We have little choice. Increasingly, the Blackfeet and their allies get the guns and powder and lead since they have allowed the Fort McKenzie to be erected in their midst. They also can go to Fort Union. I agree with Tjolzhitsay. We, too, must have the guns and ammunition and other of white man's marvels. We have few beaver and other furs.

"We would leave from the south end of the Bitter Root Valley." Ram Horn Bow dipped his brush into the clay paint and dabbed a large, white spot on the hide. As the sub-chief continued to talk, the warrior began drawing a few streams and a long, unbroken travel line generally moving east from the valley. "This will be one of the longest treks our people ever have undertaken. Learn where we must go, what we must do. We would go to the three forks, through the land of the Crows, ever toward rising Sun to the land of the Northern Cheyenne. We would acquaint them with our purpose and invite them to join us. The beaver are fast disappearing from their region, too. We would go in great strength to the sacred Medicine Rocks at the beginnings of Little Beaver Creek, which joins the Little Missouri. We would prepare buffalo jumps from the rimrocks. There we would remove the hides and have our women make them into robes until the river will permit the fire boat to come up it. We would take the robes down the Little Missouri till its waters enter the Missouri—where the fire boat found Drum and his Crows and Stone Pipe and Ram Horn Bow." The latter drew a white line through the unmarked space between the smaller and larger stream.

"Many Assiniboins, perhaps numerous Blackfeet and their allies, will be converging on Fort Union," Little Bear Claw continued. "We will be well away from there, and will get the trade goods first. We will be strong enough to fight any we might encounter. Our horses and people would face a long trip back. We must not wear them down. And we could hunt for meat when closer to our valley."

Tjolzhitsay nodded to Shield Maker, who carried forward a small, model bull boat he had made from Little Coyote's and Antelope's description of those they had seen during their visit to the Mandan villages.

"We would transport the dried hides in bull boats to the waiting place for the fire boat," Little Bear Claw said. "The people and horses would follow. When the trading would end, we would transport the trade goods back on the strong horses, as well as our equipage. We would divide the goods according to the numbers in the tribes that help this hunt."

Sounds of approval filled the lodge. Tjolzhitsay held up his arms: "If we do not do this, we must separate and work hard at perilous distances to get beaver and other furs while our enemies get the buffalo. We must have the trade goods. I would ask the people to honor Stone Pipe and Ram Horn Bow by having them be chiefs of the hunt."

There were no objections. Little Bear Claw agreed to send messengers for Tjolzhitsay to tell their many allies about the plan. Others, the head chief would travel to see in person. There was much risk here, also much opportunity.

In the seventh moon of Serviceberries the white men Robert Newell and Warren Ferris, who had done much trading with the Flatheads and Nez Percé for smaller furs, including deerskins, learned from the people about their plans for the robe hunt. In a moment of great truth over the pipes one evening, Newell revealed, with Ferris nodding his agreement, that, "White men all over aren't wearing beaver hats much anymore. 'Sides, the critters are fast disappearing all over, too. Buffalo, that's what shines. People want buffalo robes. Yep, take 'em to the Missoury for the *Yellow Stone* to pick up. But don't let the Blackfeet know what y'er doing."

Much encouraged, Tjolzhitsay, Broken Tooth and old Shield Maker set out on their finest horses in the earliest days of the ninth moon of the Harvest of Ripe Things to talk to the Crows through Drum and, in turn, have counsel with the nearest and friendliest of the Northern Cheyennes about the great hunt for robes. The warrior, Fast Runner, and three younger braves accompanied them. Theirs would be a leisurely journey, largely out of deference to Shield Maker. He, more than the rest, had good relations with many of the Cheyenne. Arrives With Spring, his long-dead wife, had come from the yet-powerful family of now dead war chief Kills With Club. The travelers carried on one of their fleet-footed pack horses three rifles of the five that Stone Pipe and Ram Horn Bow had received from the chief of the *Yellow Stone* for one of their finest Appaloosas. The boat's chief would take the animal to St. Louis. The weapons were much like the Hawken rifles, flintlocks with the name J.J. Henry stamped on them.

Yes, many Crows would join the hunt. Fort Union was getting better and more trade goods than was Fort Cass on the Yellowstone; the fur company would trade for more buffalo robes where the fire boat could go.

Shield Maker, using his short spear for support, entered the Cheyenne council lodge carrying a gift Henry rifle. He emerged much later, a rare smile dominating the wrinkles on his face. "Like the Crows," he said, "the Cheyenne wish to trade robes before the fire boat reaches Fort Union. And . . ." The old man paused, then wearily continued. ". . . the Cheyenne think perhaps they can join with the Crows to keep the Red River hunters out of their region. I will tell more about this. Now I will rest. The Cheyenne prepare us a feast. I must be there. Strong voices among these Cheyenne would rather raise the hatchet with the Crows than bury it."

Their alliances and plans completed for the robe hunt, Tjolzhitsay's group hastened back to the Bitter Root Valley. The warriors and sub-chiefs told of their many adventures and the extraordinarily long and arduous trek that lay ahead.

The great gathering began with the arrival in the valley of kin and others from the north and the west. The leaders explained that some of their people had gone to hunt buffalo with Francis Ermatinger, the trader at Flathead Post. Ermatinger had told them the Hudson's Bay Company increasingly was looking on buffalo robes with a pleasing eye and was working on better ways to transport them. He would try to get the rifled guns many preferred.

These arrivals moved southward up the valley, their long

lines filling the better trails until they encountered the Flatheads, Nez Percé and Shoshonis in the bowl where Shining Shirt slept. The cavalcade toiled generally eastward through passes and across valleys wide and narrow until it left the higher mountains behind. Now people began bunching up—large masses of seemingly disorganized, noisy women and children, horses, dogs and equipment in the center—yet maintaining tribal groups.

The various leaders had met to form a battle plan, which began with the placement of scouts who rode ahead, left and right and, always, behind.

The Crows met them near Pompey's Pillar on the south side of the Yellowstone River. Despite the lateness of the summer, great clouds of dust began marking the hunters' eastward movement across the now-more-open country. Soon after fording Rosebud Creek, the forward scouts of this mass of people and animals encountered the Northern Cheyennes. To help cement this somewhat uneasy alliance, the others showed the Cheyennes honor by asking them to take the lead. They crossed the Tongue River and unerringly pointed eastward until, by the latter part of the tenth moon of Half Autumn, three great circles of lodges stood in a somewhat round, shallow valley north of the Chalk Buttes and the Medicine Rocks. Wind and time had carved these structures into numerous grotesque shapes. The lodge circle of the Crows, near the beginning of Little Beaver Creek, was the largest. The circle of the Flatheads, their kin and friends, and of the Nez Percé and some Shoshonis almost rivaled in size that of the Northern Cheyennes. They would use perhaps three jumps, but not widely separated; all knew that the Blackfeet, who might be trekking to Fort Union, were so numerous they could outnumber them all.

Stone Pipe and Ram Horn Bow conferred with the chiefs of the other tribes, whereupon the people conducted separate meat hunts. They killed great numbers of buffalo with arrows and lances, but not for hides. These would be prime a bit later. The leaders came together again to agree on three possible jump sites. Yes, those chosen would do. The people would begin their preparation after they had dried their fresh meat. The buffalo would fall only the height of five or six tall warriors; much more of a fall would damage the hides and make for poor robes.

"How fortunate we are to live among the trees, the singing water and the mountains." Little Bear Claw's quiet voice seemed oddly lost in this vastness of open space. He and Little Coyote watched Sky Fire of the Crow people nudge his horse up the slope, dismount, then, after tethering the animal to a rock, run in a half-crouch to just below the rock-ribbed skyline above the Missouri River. Sky Fire squirmed forward on his belly until he could look below. At length, he signaled for his fellow scouts to join him.

"We were camping there when the fire boat arrived." Sky Fire pointed downward and toward the deep and narrow curve of the river. "Here the fire boat will stop to trade for our robes."

The trio watched the multitude of buffalo feeding into the slight breeze across the river, disjointing as they encountered the low, crumbling remnants of ancient rocky hills, coalescing once again after feeding around them. Already the cows and bulls were beginning to separate as they fed in numbers so great the warriors could smell them and hear their low grunting; the sounds of the great beasts could be heard above the chatter of cowbirds and other winged creatures perching atop or near them to feed on the insects they attracted.

The men hid their horses and camped that night amid the cottonwood trees where the small stream entered the river. At daylight Little Coyote would hasten back to the people to report that the scouts had found no enemy encampments between Medicine Rocks and here. Happily, the people could come here to hunt for the robes because there were more buffalo near the river than the Medicine Rocks.

There was much contentment as a very tired Little Coyote drew his robe about him and, certain he and his companions could find other jump sites, fell asleep.

Muted at first, the distant sound shrilled unrhythmically with increasing intensity into Little Coyote's ears until dreams segmented and blinked out in quick succession: Exciting buffalo hunts, Lance and Antelope in the tranquility of moon-flooded Bitter Root Valley. In their stead, as both the seer and Little Bear Claw threw off their blankets and seized their weapons, was one dominating memory—that of the braying mule that the Clark and Lewis people had demonstrated so long ago on their arrival in the valley where Shining Shirt slept. Were mules as numerous as the buffalo across the river collectively announcing their arrival by braying—loudly, piercingly, hideously?

Crouching, the two Flatheads examined the tethers on the three nervous horses. Then they looked about the cottonwoods for their Crow companion. Sky Fire signaled from behind a boulder on the hillside above the height of the trees. Perspiring from their climb despite the pre-dawn coolness, the two warriors soon were peering across the river at the source of the sound.

A few small bands of agitated buffalo were fleeing toward the river, then splitting east and west to join the distant, almost-solid, masses of the creatures. Preceded by a dust cloud and also coming from the north toward the river to fill the considerable space vacated by the buffalo were many long, widely separated lines of what Sky Fire said were "carts." All lines were staggered to avoid as much of the dust as possible. Hundreds of human figures, horses and strange animals Sky Fire called "oxen" meandered in front, alongside and behind the carts, each apparently seeking tiny, dust-free pockets of the prairie air.

"Ten lines," Little Coyote said as he gazed through his spyglass. "Surely forty carts in a line, and they weave to avoid the small, rocky hillocks." He lowered the spyglass. "The foremost cart carries a banner atop a long pole." He looked to Sky Fire.

As best he could, the Crow warrior explained this almost indescribable sight both with signs and a mixture of the Flathead tongue and his own. Always there were the intensifying shrieks of large, wooden axles rubbing against ungreased wheel hubs— shrieks that reached like invisible, jarring hammer blows across the water to set the trio's teeth to grinding. "They cannot put the fat of animals on the axles because the dust would turn it to rock and stop the carts," Sky Fire explained as Little Bear Claw jumped, then started sliding down the hillside to reassure the horses.

"They will stop by the river, and will go no farther," the Crow assured Little Coyote, "because here are the buffalo they wish to kill and carry back to their far-away home along Red River in Canada. This season, as in times past, the buffalo surely did not arrive near their homes. Our people have observed, even visited with them, when they have floated their carts across the Missouri River and gone up the Yellowstone to seek the buffalo in the land of the Cheyenne and Crows." He picked up the spyglass.

The cart with the banner stopped at the edge of the high river bank near a series of well-worn buffalo trails leading to the water. The other thirty-nine carts in that line formed a small arc on one side, leaving a space of perhaps three horse lengths between each vehicle. One by one the remaining nine lines expertly formed an additional arc until, at last, a gigantic circle encompassed the prairie in front of the three warriors watching from across the river. Mercifully, as each line of carts stopped, the unearthly screeching diminished until at last the three onlookers began hearing men, women and children shouting unnecessarily loud as though the carts still were moving. Interspersed were the sounds of horses and the strange oxen inside the circle. The dust cloud rapidly settled and tents began springing up between the carts.

"My father told me they are part-Indian; they call themselves 'Métis,'" the Crow explained as the spyglass revealed the men's elaborately beaded buckskin shirts and leggings, black pants and colorful sashes, and strange hats perched atop shaggy heads. Soon, some of the women, wearing dark dresses and highly beaded boots, were filing down the trails to the river and filling pails of water. Their noisy chatter sounded almost pleasant to the watchers' tortured ears. Other women gathered apronsful of older, dried buffalo manure, which dotted the prairie like huge, brownish-grey, stemless mushrooms. Soon, scores of small fires were roasting fresh buffalo meat. Like the dust cloud, the odor reached across the river to remind the trio they had meat of their own to cook.

The meal ended, the two Flatheads watched Sky Fire scramble atop the highest boulder at river's edge. He shouted twice toward the encampment. Almost instantly the Métis men seized muskets and assembled in ten lines in the center of the circle of carts. Ten men stepped out and faced the lines. An eleventh man, older and stouter, stepped ahead of them. The spyglass revealed he, too, was using a spyglass. Decisively, the man pushed it together and pointed his arm at the circle. Each of the ten men standing near him led one of the lines toward a one-tenth segment of the circle. They knelt behind the heavy wheels. Five men from each of the lines remained standing in the center of the circle before the man with the spyglass.

"There is much to learn here," Little Bear Claw said as he reached for the spyglass. "The warriors who yet stand would rush to the part of the circle most in need."

Sky Fire shouted once more and began signing that he was Crow—a friend. The leader with the spyglass waved back and the camp resumed its busy movements.

Yet another Métis carrying a spyglass sat next to a rock to watch the river until yet another warrior replaced him.

Just before Sun set, a Black Robe held a ceremony in the center of the circle while all present alternately stood, knelt or sat. Little Coyote watched the entire encampment walk forward and, except for the babes in arms, receive something from the Black Robe that they put in their mouths. Then people returned to their places to kneel again amid total silence while Sun sank into the prairie far to the west.

Before Sun reappeared Little Coyote watched several horsemen set out east and west. Dimly, through the spyglass, he could see many buffalo approximately two miles away. They were far more numerous than the smaller bands on his own side of the river. The scouts from the west returned on galloping horses before the night's heavy frost had melted in the growing sunlight. Before Little Bear Claw and Sky Fire had responded to the seer's signal and climbed the hillside, the Métis women had emptied their carts and were helping the men harness a horse to each one. The three warriors watched approximately four-hundred men, each holding a musket, mount their horses. The Black Robe slowly made the sign of the cross over the hunters.

"They seemingly listen to the Black Robes," Little Coyote said. He pondered dying Gun's last thoughts conveyed to Shield Maker, then to him: "I have had thoughts that this listening might turn them into children. I think I am wrong. I would not like to meet them in battle."

The Métis faced their mounts west and urged them outside the circle of carts.

"They are good horses," Little Bear Claw said quietly. "They seem eager for a hunt. Perhaps the—" His words were lost as the carts wheeled and began screeching their way behind the now slowly trotting horses. A single horseman moved perhaps forty paces ahead of the rest.

For a time, the night's damp helped hold down the dust. In the growing light the watching trio could see the black mass of buffalo. Most were continuing to feed, though the nearest turned to face the approaching throng. Now a few of the beasts began to run. The hunters raced past the lead horseman, closing the distance to the buffalo amid a few musket reports. The carts bumped ever faster over the uneven prairie, their individual screeches blending, finally, into one great, unremitting shriek. Again a dust cloud encompassed almost all movement; increasing distance mercifully muted the noise.

Sky Fire pointed west, down their own side of the river where the buffalo were beginning to respond to the agitation opposite them. Soon they had run from sight on the undulating prairie.

"The Métis will haul their fresh hides and meat back to their tents for drying if Sun is kind, and make much pemmican, too," Sky Fire explained. "They trade some of this pemmican to Hudson's Bay Company for further sale or trade."

The three ate cold meat and searched the remainder of the day among the cliffs near the river for three buffalo jumps. Next day before Sun arrived, Little Coyote hastened toward the Medicine Rocks. His two companions, ever on the lookout for enemies, began pushing small, sharpened, willow and cottonwood wands into the prairie. By the time Little Coyote would return with the many robe-takers, there would be a great V of wands extending for perhaps one white man's mile in front of each jump site. Each V would be perhaps eighty long strides wide near the cliff, and hundreds of strides wide at the mouth.

The robe-takers arrived in eight days and began erecting the circles of lodges above the river near where the fire boat would stop.

"We were watching the dust cloud of the departing Métis when we saw that which our people raised," Little Bear Claw said as he smiled at reunited Little Coyote and Antelope. "We have seen no enemies. As you can see, buffalo abound everywhere."

Little Coyote nodded. "All the way back to the Medicine Rocks. The tribes agreed that Fishing Bird of the Kutenais will conduct the ceremonies for the jump sites. A Cheyenne and a Crow will be callers at the other two sites. They will select their own buffalo scouts. Our caller will be Broken Tooth. He has selected a Nez Percé, Shoshone, a Pend d'Oreille and a Spokan to be buffalo scouts for our site. He emphasized there will be much responsibility to select the bands with the most cows and young bulls, for many of the older bulls, as you can see, still remain among them." Little Bear Claw again smiled, wider this time, at the approach of Willow Woman.

"I lack your powers, Little Coyote," he said, "but with confidence I can predict that if these buffalo remain near us, before Sun next appears we all will meet to erect the 'dead men.' Stay strong!"

Except for the vigilant scouts for all tribes, the encampment divided to erect piles of head-sized and larger rocks. These "dead men" were placed at each wooden wand that Sky Fire and Little Bear Claw had pushed into the prairie. Fishing Bird asked the various sub-chiefs to arrange for and instruct the people to crouch beside the rock piles and under robes. When the callers at the three sites, mounted on their fastest and wisest horses, would entice the buffalo into the wide mouths of the V's, the scouts would appear and begin driving the animals down the narrowing lines that ended at the cliffs. As the agitated herds would thunder next to each rock pile, those hiding would stand up, shout and wave their robes, driving the animals past more of the piles. When the caller would reach the cliffs, he hastily would hand his horse to a waiting friend and scramble into a protective rocky crevice at cliff's edge. The beasts would tumble past him to be killed or crippled on the rocks below.

Broken Tooth approached Little Coyote the day before Fishing Bird was to start his sacred ceremonies for all. Greeting the medicine man, he said, "I would be honored if you, Little Coyote, would say many prayers to the Good Spirit that I successfully will select and call many cows and young bulls to the cliffs."

"You have such prayers already," Little Coyote assured his older friend, whose smile widened to expose many teeth beyond the broken one.

They both looked up at the approach of Tjolzhitsay, Little

Bear Claw and Bad Leg and Red Paint of the Nez Percé.

"Our head chief greatly misses Three Eagles," Broken Tooth said. "Though Little Bear Claw is not his *i-sts-sókoi*, Tjolzhitsay proves his wisdom by leaning ever more heavily on this sub-chief."

Broken Tooth made one other request of Little Coyote: "Will you station yourself near one of the dead men closest to the jump so I can hand you the reins of my good buffalo horse? You can take it to safety while I seek my protective hole at cliff's edge to complete my work."

"That, too, will be my honor," Little Coyote replied.

Broken Tooth mounted his horse and prepared to leave.

"Stay, Broken Tooth!" Tjolzhitsay called. "We would use your wisdom here."

Soon the six warriors were seated in the lee of an almost-square boulder at cliff's edge.

Tjolzhitsay did not bring out a pipe. Instead, he looked toward Sun, which was still blessing them with warmth that late autumn afternoon.

"There is much for us all to do," the head chief said. "The council had no time to discuss the Métis. Tuekakas of the Nez Percé asked me to relate to you and others the lessons gained from observing the Métis lest they be lost, should I go to the Sand Hills."

As Little Bear Claw talked, he used a sharp rock to scratch the outline of the Métis' defensive system on the face of the boulder. Most questions centered around the discipline within each group of men under a sub-chief and the retention of a reserve force to rush to any weak point.

"I think we would like these Métis braves from Canada," Bad Leg said as he stood. He looked at Red Paint. "And our Nee Mee Poo will be interested that the Black Robes work among them, too."

Little Coyote complied with Fishing Bird's request that he erect the sacred white buffalo robe atop the highest crag at cliffside. Then he and Antelope stationed themselves between the last two dead men before the cliffs on the east line leading to the jump. Directly across from them in corresponding positions were Red Paint and his mate. They had brought two of their grandchildren—young boys armed with tiny bows and arrows. The boys flexed and unflexed their bows from atop the dead men, where they had climbed to peer excitedly southward for the buffalo.

Broken Tooth performed well as caller, just as he had done for the drive to the corral at the Place of Otter Tail.

"They come! They come!" The two boys' voices reached across to the Flatheads. Southward, a cloud of dust began rising above the two rows of dead men, which appeared and disappeared in the undulations of the prairie. Some of the people huddling beneath their robes began to stand and flap the garments to urge the terrified beasts to even greater movement and mindlessness. Loud shouts reached above the intensifying thunder of the buffalo hooves until the animals were almost upon them, leaving behind numerous pulped blobs of young calves on this narrow trail of death. Little Coyote stepped forward, seized the reins of Broken Tooth's lathered horse and led it outside the path of certain destruction as its owner scrambled inside a wedge-shaped fracture in a large boulder at cliff's edge.

The cracking sounds of horn against horn and grunts forced from colliding bodies intensified as the medicine man led the shaking horse to a tethering rock. The dust now had caught up with the doomed herd, which was pushed onward then downward by the frantic, irresistible mass behind. As he resumed his place beside Antelope, Little Coyote glimpsed a small arrow protruding from the black muzzle of a huge bull; another protruded from the animal's eye as he ran and was pushed from behind. The medicine man's attention focused on the whirring succession of eyes, the whites showing against the dark background of the animals, themselves, until all had passed. Amid the settling dust rose new sounds: Thuds, grunts, agonized bellows and the triumphant shouts of people who had rushed from safe places to work on the herd now on the rocks below.

Little Coyote and Antelope carefully picked their way down

the cliff. They stopped three times to lance a badly crippled cow, a calf and, finally, an old bull. The animals' bodies had wedged in the rocks instead of tumbling the entire distance. The bull evidently had landed on its neck and head, the impact popping out one eye and smearing hair, hide and flesh on the fractured rocks until little of his features remained—except for the one eye. Rolling in shock, the eye appeared to fix accusingly on Little Coyote. Pausing with uplifted lance, the seer seemed to see a composite of the accusing eyes of the thawing beavers in his small lodge at the hot springs so long ago, of the tortured Blackfeet, of the white buffalo bull and of Gun at their dying.

"Why do you hesitate?" Antelope's voice rose sharply above the agonized grunts and bloody snuffling of the suffering beasts and the excited voices of the people below. Again she called.

This time Little Coyote looked up. "The beaver are almost gone. Are the buffalo next, and then the people?" he asked. Antelope, only partially hearing, shook her head uncomprehendingly as the seer forced the lance between the ribs and probed downward to find the life. Soon afterward, Little Coyote began wandering among the hundreds of chattering, industriously working men, women and children. Some were using horses to drag carcasses from the piles; others already were removing hides from cows and young bulls, ignoring the dead, dying and other badly crippled older bulls. Gone was much of the usual arguing and tussling about who should do or get what, which so reminded Little Coyote of a handful of magpies disputing an oversized bite of meat. There were a few wondering looks and comments as he lanced the suffering animals, but mostly he heard the feeble voice of long-dead White Buffalo Calf during the peace-making days with the Blackfeet: "Our world changes. Perhaps I am too old, too tired, to provide wise counsel, but the buffalo is sacred to us. It has a life. We should not take that life unless we use all of the buffalo . . . What do we tell our sons? What pattern will they follow? These thoughts must be a part of our thinking now and in the future . . . ."

Again the seer's mind fixed on his earlier questions. Aloud, he said to himself, "The beaver are almost gone. Are the buffalo

452

next, and then the people?" But now he was approaching an old, smashed, yet moving, bull near the work site of Dog That Sits, his two wives and Brandt. Dog That Sits had brought in several horses; contrary to tribal customs and the agreed-on rules of division among the tribes, he was prodding a blood-smeared Brandt into throwing two hides onto a reluctant horse preparatory to leading it to some hidden place.

Little Coyote lanced the old bull. The crushed legs kicked a few times, projecting more splinters of bone onto the rocks. The frothy bubbles ceased issuing from the nose and mouth. Antelope caught up with her mate.

"Ho, Little Coyote! Has your woman no work to do? Can you not help?" Dog That Sits' taunting voice rose above the work of the knives and grunts of the women as they pulled on the hide.

Receiving no answer, Dog That Sits stared back, rapped Brandt with his lance haft and pointed to the two women. Brandt moved as quickly as the rawhide hobbles would allow and began helping dead Torn Ear's woman lift and pull while the other woman made deft, curving swipes with the knife blade between meat and hide.

That hide loaded onto yet another horse, Dog That Sits motioned toward a two-year-old bull that had landed on a rocky shelf just above the two skinned carcasses. Brandt, his jaw hanging slackly, raised his dull eyes upward; then, he wearily climbed to the animal and began tugging until more of its weight hung over the edge. The slave sat down and pushed both feet against the carcass. The jarring fall renewed the residual life in the bull's body; the beast ineffectually began raising and lowering its head. As Brandt painfully worked his way downward, Dog That Sits expertly slashed the testicles from the bull. Cackling, he held them to Brandt's crotch.

Little Coyote lanced the animal. As the head dropped from a seemingly frozen raised position, Brandt began screaming again and yet again on an ever-higher pitch. The sound rose above the others as though Brandt were spokesman for all these dead and dying beasts. Dog That Sits threw his handful into the slave's face and yet he screamed, the bloody hands reaching skyward in his despair. Then, Brandt's eyes focused on Little Coyote. They moved only as his head moved in response to Dog That Sits' jarring, brutal blows with his own lance haft. Dog That Sits raised the weapon as though to drive it through Brandt's bloody, bruised body. Brandt straightened then, seemingly welcoming the thrust. Instead, Dog That Sits kicked him sprawling toward the women, who had continued working with scarcely a glance upward since the screaming had stopped. Brandt lay there, his head rising and falling each time Dog That Sits pricked him in the buttocks with the lance point. Then, groaning, the slave heeded the women's insistent motions that he pull on the hide.

Little Coyote and Antelope silently searched for Running Buffalo Bull and Little Yellow Bird. Assisting them in the skinning were Lance and Swan. In their lodge, after the first day's hard work, Little Coyote and Antelope discussed how they had watched Swan offer tidbits of fresh buffalo to her mate. The gesture brought memories to the older couple of similar activities on their first hunt so long ago. Within the family, the warriors skinned while the three women fleshed and scraped, then smeared the hides with brains and liver mixed with certain parts of bushes and trees Little Yellow Bird and Antelope had packed along. Later, when the killing would stop, the lengthier robe-tanning process would begin.

Broken Tooth successfully called other herds over the cliff as the days shortened and became colder. Fewer bulls died because now they were more widely separated from the cows. Soon, scouts reported finding protected spots along the river that would afford cottonwood, beached driftwood and other fuel for winter fires and corrals for the horses. Even in colder weather they would have to be driven to the grasslands above for feeding.

The moons that followed were cold, long and hard, which helped reduce the possibility of discovery by the Blackfeet. Little Coyote, remembering his winter of aloneness with the beaver, called this "the winter of *spúmtse*, the buffalo hide." Warriors among the tribes willingly and unwillingly brought in wood; the women prepared the hides by stretching, washing, further scraping, heating and softening. They spent perhaps three days on each one. Before the buffalo moved to more protected areas, too, many more fell both for robes and meat, which the cold now would preserve. Younger braves brought in numerous wolf pelts and those from many smaller creatures that worked the great piles of meat and offal at the jump sites.

Dog That Sits, wandering from lodge to lodge, scornfully boasted of his two women and his slave. He made the obvious point that he and the few other warriors who had multiple wives need not do women's work. Ram Horn Bow, Broken Pipe and others in council agreed, but again stressed that this was a collective effort. There were loud sounds of agreement when Ram Horn Bow forcefully stated that, "Each gun obtained would be one less the Blackfeet would receive when the *Yellow Stone* would reach Fort Union." To this end, Dog That Sits' boasts turned to anguished howls when the council forced him to add his hidden robes to those stored in ancient lodges carefully erected above flood mark when ever beneficent Sun helped the Missouri conquer the icy grip of this "winter of *spúmtse*."

Part 3

The
Land-Grabbers

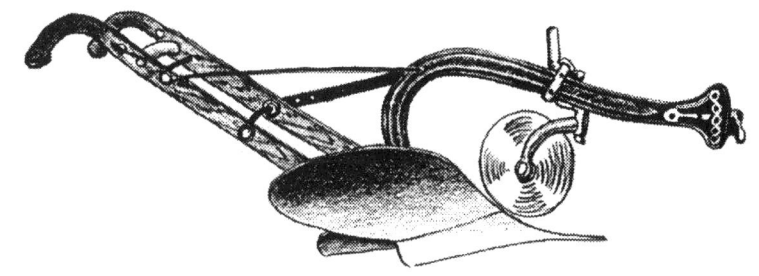

S un and warm spring breezes worked on the thick river ice, blending its seminal smell with the powerful death stench at the bases of the three jump sites. Wafting upward to the prairie, the odor-filled breeze danced through and over the pasqueflowers; other small flora competed in sight and smell with the wild rose, juneberry and dogwood bushes leafing out along the swollen small streams adding their snowmelt to the river. Cracks began appearing in the ice, heightening both restlessness and expectancy among the people awaiting the side-wheeler *Yellow Stone*. Over and over all the tribes had repeated the descriptions of the vessel provided by the three warriors; many people were certain her arrival would be the greatest event in their lives. The buffalo robes were ready near the jump sites, great piles of them, fairly divided between the tribes, and so marked. As the people viewed their accomplishments, there was great rejoicing that most of them had not heeded the plea from Ermatinger of the Hudson's Bay Company that they go with him for robe hunts the past two winters.

There was much rejoicing, too, on the day of breakup and during the seemingly interminable waiting while logs, trees, brush, dead buffalo, silt and other scourings from almost countless upriver streams swept by. Dog That Sits led his dejected slave from camp to camp; Brandt's merry violin spoke different musical messages to people ranging from sedate old to yearning young. The performance threatened to fail but once—on the brightest spring day when Brandt's instrument began lamenting its doleful owner's inner feelings, too. Dog That Sits almost reverently set the instrument aside and slashed off his slave's imprisoning hobbles. Now the haggard creature began a new form of entertainment by capering unrhythmically in a lively jig. He was encouraged by punishing pokes of his owner's sharpened stick. The jig was livelier yet when one of Dog That Sits' women viciously brought her longer stick into play; it was lively to the point of exhaustion when the second woman began belaboring Brandt's gaunt, bruised and scarred legs with an even weightier and longer rod as though Brandt, rather than Dog That Sits, was responsible for her and the first woman's dreary existence. The slave hopped, circled, jumped, even rolled, to the dissonance of his own loud howling. At length Dog That Sits shouted, "Enough!" and the three torturers gently guided the crawling, blubbering man toward the violin. The two women solicitously wiped off his arms and hands with a rabbit skin, knotted on new hobbles and helped him to a seat on a nearby rock. Once again the instrument spoke transcendentally of forests, flowers, dancing, yearning and love from distant, unknown regions to here along the serenely flowing Missouri River. Dog That Sits energetically hawked charms, cures and great promises in exchange for a growing store of pelts from smaller furbearers.

That night, secure in their own lodge, Little Coyote and Antelope talked much about Brandt's torture as the camp sounds dwindled to the occasional restless movement of horses and the fat dogs snarling over the yet-plenteous buffalo meat. Gun's dying face and the earnest words of old Shield Maker seemed to fill the lodge: "We must forgive our enemies . . . ."

"The ideal perhaps, but the doing!" a small voice seemed to whisper to the seer as sleep stole away all but dream thoughts.

Scouts pursued by a series of strange, loud noises raced to

inform the huge encampment of the fire boat's coming. Great cries went up, almost muting the noises from the side-wheeler. Some people leaped on their horses and fled along the river bank. Others fell down, afraid to look at this river monster seemingly ready to leave the water and pursue them on land. Yet others valiantly stood their ground as this smoking, steaming thing approached; still, they nervously looked left, right and behind as though seeking assurance there was space to flee should they need to do so. A few people cautiously moved forward as though to count coup on this threat.

"Not the *Yellow Stone*, this," Little Coyote told those around him. Painstakingly the seer and Antelope, aided by the spyglass, spelled out and pronounced the name painted on the vessel. *Assiniboin*! As this name began speeding through the awe-filled crowd, a cannon boomed from the bow of the vessel. Amid the sound and smoke, the chief of the fire boat stepped into view. He was clad in a black garment with two rows of shiny buttons and a hat with much shiny thread.

"Yes, the name of the boat honors the Assiniboins," the fire boat chief later explained. He used his hands and voice to quiet the deep, resentful rumbling among some of the people. "There will be other such fire boats plying the many waters. They will carry the names of other people like yourselves. Such boats will supply other forts we will build and fill with trading goods to exchange for robes and furs. Already we have stopped at forts down the river. The *Yellow Stone* fire boat became filled with such robes and furs traded from the Sioux and others. We have sent her back to St. Louis."

There were smiles now among the people standing on the long, sloping river bank and near the vessel, herself. Those on board the *Assiniboin* reflected this good will and expectation, except for two watching Blackfeet warriors who had come aboard downriver. Their visages were dark as the smoke belching from two great stacks towering above the vessel. The smile of the fire boat chief broadened as sub-chiefs moved among the throng urging the chosen ones to carry the robes from the old lodges. The fire boat chief signaled for several black men to begin offering firewater as a prelude to trading on the lower portion of the boat, which was covered with a huge array of goods. The sub-chiefs representing their particular tribes valiantly withstood the tempting drinks during the haggling with the traders assigned to them. There were flintlock trade muskets in plenteous supply, but there was a delay when the Crows and Cheyennes demanded some rifled guns. The Flatheads demanded caplocks. There were not enough rifled guns to meet the demand. At length, each of the three tribes received seventeen rifles, mostly Hawkens, a few quite similar with the markings of LeBeau, Gumpf, Gill and others. Twelve of the Flatheads' weapons were caplock.

Little Coyote and Antelope helped with trading matters. They noted the deference extended to a great white chief called Maximilian, who had come from a region far beyond the great salt water. Thin as a winter-gaunted buffalo bull and almost running, he excitedly moved among the interested throngs. He talked through a person skilled in the signs. Maximilian's deep voice sounded as though he were forming his words through a mouthful of tough buffalo bull meat. Accompanying him on his energetic forays was another white man called Bodmer. Bodmer freely drew many pictures until Dog That Sits began warning this was bad medicine; Bodmer, he contended, was stealing part of their spirit.

The firearms and ammunition trading completed, the chiefs received presents of awls, files, tobacco, beads and paint; the rest of the people lined up to trade their smaller furs for articles of their choice. The fire boat chief lessened their disappointment over the lack of many rifles when he informed the chiefs he had two gunsmiths who would repair all firearms brought to them while the *Assiniboin* was there. He would do this as a present because he was pleased with the people and their robes. "The *Assiniboin* will leave after the sun arrives next day," he cautioned.

The sub-chiefs' efforts to protect their own people were aided, as they had hoped, when those who drank the whiskey began vomiting, staggering and performing other stupid, unwarriorlike actions. One of the Flatheads' own who served as a warning example was Dog That Sits.

462

He elbowed his way to the front of a line. On either side, his women were dragging two bales of small furs. The warrior partook first of the free drink of whiskey, then began trading for a tiny keg and other articles. He soon was shunted aside when his inflamed brain comprehended that he lacked sufficient furs for another keg. In the growing darkness he immediately set his women to work in his lodge, specifying that they demand a good trade item from each member of the *Assiniboin* crew who chose to enter. He was tipsily shaking the final drops of whiskey into a tin cup some distance from these activities when Little Coyote and Little Bear Claw approached. They were lugging a larger keg between them. Securely tied to a cottonwood, Brandt looked up and stiffened when he recognized the medicine man. Expecting an outburst, Little Coyote heard only the growing clamor in the distance as the whiskey began its work on more of the people.

With exaggerated care, Dog That Sits placed his keg upright and eyed the two warriors. Little Coyote spoke: "Your slave looks tired. We would share our whiskey."

"Share it with me. Do not pour whiskey into a buffalo turd."

"We would trade this larger keg for your smaller keg, and for the buffalo turd."

Dog That Sits put his cup atop the keg, then unsteadily faced his tribesmen. His slack jaw tightened and his eyes squinted craftily as he stood there weaving.

"I have whiskey."

The two warriors stooped to lift their keg and walk away.

"I would have more whiskey. The buffalo turd for the whiskey." He hiccupped and drained his cup.

The two men began walking away.

"The buffalo turd for your whiskey. Because we are brothers, his music-maker will be in the trade. He is worthless without the music-maker, as a keg is worthless without the whiskey." Dog That Sits pounded the stopper more securely into his keg; he teetered, yet maintained a commanding tone in his voice as he repeated his offer.

Reluctantly, the two warriors rolled the keg back to the feet of Dog That Sits.

"We own the buffalo turd," Little Coyote said.

Brandt stood erect, eying Little Coyote's knife. He fell to the ground when the blade freed him from the rope and the hobbles.

"Do not talk." Little Coyote threw his blanket over the thin, stooped shoulders. "Hide the violin under your arm. Throw your hair before your face."

Brandt complied. He, Little Coyote and Little Bear Claw moved past several *Assiniboin* crew members noisily sitting in a ragged line next to Dog That Sits' lodge. Soon, the three men neared the boisterous crowd, at the fringe of which Antelope handed Little Coyote two small bundles. The three men walked up the *Assiniboin*'s wide gangplank onto the open foredeck, which extended almost a third the length of the vessel. A black man approached. He was carrying a candle in a fire-safe lantern. He steered them among the robes piled inside the covered portion of the lower deck. He explained the fire-blackened walls and, finally, pointed to a small hiding space among the bales.

Little Coyote's voice sounded muffled in the closeness of the space. "You will remain here," he told Brandt, "in the darkness, where few are allowed to come. The black man said that fire almost reached the gunpowder as they came upriver. The fire boat chief will take you to St. Louis. Even so, if you betray your presence before the boat leaves this place, you likely will die. We do this because we do not like slavery and we have been told that the Black Robes say, 'Forgive your enemies.' Perhaps they will help you. This black brave will feed you." The seer handed the black man a small bundle of furs and gave the other to Brandt.

The two Flatheads returned to the trading area on the open deck. Many of the *Assiniboin*'s crew members, carrying strings of beads, colored feathers and other presents, were leaving the vessel and heading toward the noisy people. Occasional reports and flashes of light from discharged weapons filled the night air up and down the river bank and from the prairie above. Only the two gunsmiths worked on in the light of three large lanterns and under the interested stares of the weapon owners, including Little

464

Coyote and Little Bear Claw.

Little Coyote sat before his lodge carefully examining, setting, springing and filing on his family's traps. In various areas around this place where Shining Shirt slept, many of the people were digging the important bitterroots. From distant places came the reports of rifles that, along with arrows, were taking many deer. He would be hunting, too, but for the need to ponder recent events and, like the traveler establishing landmarks to guide him, determine where he should go now and in the future. So! His mind would work as his hands tended the traps—but carefully, lest a hand get caught in these almost five-pound devices.

He snapped the first one and, satisfied, reached for another.

"Ross' Hole!" white man called this place now. It was named after the Hudson's Bay trader, Alexander Ross, whose appearance among the sand dunes near the Centennial Mountains probably had saved Little Coyote's and Lance's lives when they were forted up behind Not Afraid of Guns and Lance's Appaloosa and awaiting the next Blackfeet charge.

Snap! The file rasped on the metal of the next trap as deep thoughts began working in Little Coyote's mind. How long would his own people continue to call this "the place where Shining Shirt sleeps" while the white men used the name of a trader whose party foolishly had become snowed in here for almost one moon long ago?

Snap! At the sound of the trap the seer looked up, sensing, then affirming, that Antelope was peering at him from her fleshing position near the deer hide pegged to the earth. She smiled, her white teeth and dark hair catching Sun and radiating a loving warmth that closed the few paces between them. She rolled together the strands of flesh and fiber she had scraped from yet another part of the hide and tossed them toward the waiting dog. The animal knew by the changing sounds of the woman's motions that another bite was forthcoming. The jaws snapped closed and once again the usually watchful dog lowered his head between his forepaws to doze—and wait for the next tidbit.

Little Coyote filed away on the rustiest trap. Ross' Hole.

Here at the headwaters of the Ootlashoots—Red Willow River. Ross had called the stream "Courtine's Fork." Drouillard had told Little Coyote that a Patrick Gass among the Clark and Lewis people had called it "Clark's River." The seer had heard the trapper William Ferris call it the "Bitter Root." How imperceptibly these name changes occurred, perhaps because they seemed to merit little notice in the lives of the people as the people faced greater changes. He would have to contemplate this more deeply. Again he reached up under one jaw of the trap with the short, steel ramrod from his pistol. This pan required the most pressure yet before the jaws snapped. Again he filed. How many changes had to occur before people noticed, talked and then, perhaps, acted?

Tools, not names, marvels like these traps, the file, the pistol and its ramrod. All white man's articles. Perhaps even after much examination the change of names would be of little moment, but that persistent thought from years ago had grown to certainty: Acceptance of and dependence on things was noteworthy because such marvels were immediately discernible, highly useful—and there had become a discontent if the people could not get more of them. Further, there was a sweetness and a bitterness to this.

A sweetness because life became easier with such acceptance. Certainly his people, perhaps more than most, had learned long ago that adapting, shaping with conditions, helped keep their small tribe alive. Again, he pressed the ramrod on the pan. Snap!

A bitterness lay in the fact that a trap seldom lets go. Hidden in the acceptance of the sweetness of things was the fact that there was little deep thought about change, itself, until a comparison of the old *then* and the new *now* left the *now* wanting. He, Lance and Running Buffalo Bull only a short time ago had agreed yet again, while discussing the tactics of the Métis, that there was a far more discernible diminishment in the individual warrior's display of initiative, bravery, accomplishment than even among the Flathead people. Instead, the conditions of life now increasingly demanded group battle, firepower, greater loss of life.

The medicine man stopped his filing. The round pan of the trap pushed his straying mind toward different thoughts—thoughts as closely related to the others as were the chain, spring and jaws of the traps. He closed his eyes and no longer could see the pan of the trap. His mind began to see the eyes of the beaver, the tortured Blackfeet, the ancient and sacred white buffalo bull and, perhaps most accusatory, the single eye of the wasted bull at the jump site above the Missouri River. Would he soon add to this recurring procession the gentle eye of the deer that now were dying in great numbers, even this day, so the people could carry their hides to trade at the 1836 rendezvous at Horse Creek on the Siskadee? The word spreading among the people was that this would be one of the greatest rendezvous ever. Even so, if it were not for the hope the Black Robes would arrive there, Tjolzhitsay and sub-chiefs from both ends of the valley would avoid the rendezvous and go with Ermatinger for robes and other trade. There was much agreement the trading with him did not bring out so much of the dark side of the people. Well, perhaps they would go with him in 1837. Yes, there would be much talking about this.

Little Coyote opened his eyes. The accusatory eyes faded, disappeared, but his deep thoughts did not change course. Surely other tribes, or at least members within the tribes, were thinking as was he. Yes, white man's marvels exacted a price. Did white man, himself, often think about this? Yes, the marvels exacted a price, but, in honesty, the stories of the *Flathead* people emphasized that all of life before the coming of white man had demanded a price, too. Perhaps the process of change merely was accelerating as had the heavy boulder Red Paint had pried out to roll down the mountainside on the trek to the Nez Percé people so long ago. Would the stories growing out of today and told in the future be that much different? Yes, there had been traps in life before the Clark and Lewis people arrived.

He put down the file and moved the pan up and down. The rust was gone. The pan functioned freely now, Sun reflecting on the newly filed metal disk. Centered in each pan was a +, stamped out in the manufacturing process. It was one of the symbols white man put on his marvels as surely as individual warriors marked their arrows or other articles of the hunt, peace or war.

That +: Much like the metal cross Shining Shirt had worn. It was the shape of those the Black Robes wore, as described by those who had met them, and akin to Marianne Hatchiorau-quasha's crucifix buried with Gun. That cross had brought comfort to Gun, to others less close.

Again the sweetness and the bitterness, because only two summers ago the Flathead sub-chief Insula had led a large delegation of the people and the Nez Percé to the rendezvous at Ham's Fork on the Siskadee. All had hoped to meet the Black Robes. Yes, a white man of the Good Spirit was there, with four helpers!

"This Jason Lee was not a Black Robe," Insula disappointedly had reported to the council. "Jason Lee had told the white men he was sent to help the Flatheads. Many of the trappers told us this even before they began drinking, seeking the women and inducing some of the Flatheads and Nez Percé to drink, too, in exchange for the furs and women. We sought Jason Lee and found him amid much noise and confusion attending the trading, drinking and whoring. We shook his hand and told him we had waited many years for the Black Robes to help us in many ways through their closeness to the Good Spirit. We told him many of us were using Black Robe prayers. Jason Lee had been scowling at the drinking and whoring and a scalp dance. Now he smiled. He said words, approving words, but they were only words. We could tell. He was like the weak brave who does not forthrightly speak out as he seeks a good animal. He mouths polite words when he sees the animal. It is there; it is a horse; it has four legs, a head and a tail on its sleek body, but it is not the horse he has dreamed of. The refusal to trade already is in his eyes, though he still talks of trade. He never looks in the animal's mouth. He already has formed a judgment from the little he has seen. He rides away, promising perhaps he will trade. But the horse owner knows he will not be back. Jason Lee would not come to our camp. He rode away—to the Columbia River."

Little Coyote stood and stretched his back, as had the council after listening to Insula. There had been little discussion because many of those in the lodge also had attended the 1834 rendezvous and long since had expressed their disappointment. Still, the story had to be told because there had to be decisions about the rendezvous of 1835 near Fort Bonneville on the Siskadee. Despite the great drinking and whoring there, Little Coyote had no regrets he had joined the trek. There, Bridger had invited him to stand closest in a circle of many observers to watch a white medicine man, Marcus Whitman, skillfully remove a large, iron arrowhead a Blackfeet bow had loosed three summers earlier into the mountain man's back. Rid of the arrowhead, Bridger had married the oldest daughter of the sub-chief Insula before the people returned to the valley. They carried with them many kindly thoughts about the man Whitman, who, while not a Black Robe, was a man of the Good Spirit who had frowned deeply when told about Jason Lee. Whitman also did much to tell them about the Good Spirit and encouraged them to follow His ways. Another man of the Good Spirit, Samuel Parker, had furthered Whitman's teaching when some Flatheads accompanied him and some Nez Percé from the rendezvous toward the Walla Walla country. When the Flatheads left for a buffalo hunt, Parker sent his good words with them and promised to see them again, which he did when some of them later held a Good Spirit meeting in a camp with some Nez Percé.

Little Coyote stretched again before gathering up the traps. Antelope also stood, then bent over to remove the pegs from the deer hide. She shook the hide free of twigs, grass and dust on the hair side, tiny remnants of flesh and fiber from the skin side. The dog, too, rose and humped its back in a vigorous stretch. It yawned widely and began nosing about, smelling but scarcely seeing what a few ants already were tugging away.

Antelope hung the hide on the rack with four others that Sun and wind already had dried. The traders would take these untanned. As her mate returned the traps to the three lodges, Antelope stirred up the fire and put fresh venison and water into the large brass pot. There would be food when Little Yellow Bird and Swan finished digging the roots and when Running

Buffalo Bull and Lance returned from the deer hunt.

As Antelope stirred in dried roots and other herbs from the harvest of last year, Little Coyote pulled a stiff hide from the rack and sat on it. When he filled his pipe, Antelope handed him a burning twig.

"You prepare to contemplate even deeper thoughts than those that covered you while working on the traps," she said, laughing. Taking the twig from him, she threw it in the fire. She sat beside him. "Share these thoughts, and perhaps I will share the food with you."

The seer pulled deeply on the pipe and slowly blew out the smoke.

"I have thought of our disappointment that the Black Robes did not arrive two summers ago," he said. "I was preparing to think again about the promise the Bishop Rosati made to Big Ignace La Mousse last summer in St. Louis that the Black Robes will be sent. And I wonder if they will be at Horse Creek on the Siskadee when we take these hides there. Throughout my thoughts I pondered the worth of the marvels we seek."

He sucked hard on the pipe until the smoke again came freely. After a few moments he returned it to its tiny stand and picked up the metal cross he had recovered near Shining Shirt's destroyed burial platform.

"Let us eat. I must move from such thoughts to some doing. Little Bear Claw has asked me to bury the bones of Shining Shirt here."

"Quiver Hill." This was the name Little Coyote had given the somewhat rounded mountain behind Shining Shirt's burial site. The warrior would look toward this landmark each time he entered the great bowl. The stand of lodgepole pines had begun at its base and spread up the slope until the trees at the top resembled the upper shafts and feathers of giant arrows protruding from a quiver. He need not look now. With eyes open or closed he could see the place—a few black, skeletal fingers pointing despairingly to the sky, a large jumble of fallen, partially consumed trunks resting in the ashes of the others. Now those seeking lodgepoles to re-erect their shelters in this place would have to travel much farther to obtain them. The source of the fire was easy to detect: A badly scorched, crude, log cabin that someone had built near the protective cliff at the south edge of the burn. The prevailing southerly wind had wafted sparks from the even cruder stone-and-mud fireplace into grass, brush and trees to the north.

Two rough bunks indicated that perhaps a pair of hunters or trappers had built the structure. In their idle moments they had examined the platform grave of Shining Shirt and had chopped and shaken it down, as well as those of Three Eagles and others. Rodents had gnawed the scattered bones. Shining Shirt's skull, lower jaw detached, had been swaying to and fro on one of the yet-green willow stalks whose blunted tip had been shoved through the hole at the skull base.

The Flathead searchers had placed among the pile of bones the few trade beads they had found, but the dead seer's stone lance head was gone, as were the points of his decaying arrows. A few rusty iron weapons remained.

When the others had left, Little Coyote and Little Bear Claw had reassured themselves that the gold nuggets had escaped detection at the base of the now-burned trunk of the tree. And the cross? As the platform had plunged earthward, it had projected the now-rusty symbol far southward. Little Coyote had found it where it had struck and fallen at the base of an unscarred ponderosa pine. The two warriors had buried the gold there and had scooped out a small hollow to contain the bones.

This day while the people sought the roots and the deer, Little Coyote sent a long prayer to the Good Spirit, reverently placed the bones and the cross in the hollow and covered them with earth, including a few handsful of sacred soil taken from atop the graves of the chiefs. That done, he removed from his horse the stout, cedar chest containing the great flint axe, knife and spear point shown at the treaty with the Blackfeet. He buried the chest near, and more deeply, than the bones. During his slow return to the encampment, he listened to the people talk about the imminent departure of most of them for the 1836 rendezvous at Horse Creek on the Siskadee.

The seer almost walked his horse past his own lodge as he found himself pondering even more deeply the thoughts generated as he had worked over white man's traps.

44

Ignace Hatchiorauquasha removed his wide-brimmed, felt hat,
which had compressed his dark, silver-streaked hair, and
shadowed his bright eyes, thin nose and lips. Expressive hands
protruding from the sleeves of his slightly shrunken buckskin
jacket seemingly helped form his words, which stopped
momentarily as he took his turn at Little Coyote's pipe. The
lodge interior was beginning to darken as Sun slipped behind the
mountains on the west side of the Bitter Root Valley. From outside
came the prayerful voices of the eleven other mixed-blood families
that were preparing to leave the Rocky Mountains. They would
join those who earlier had settled in Missouri. There, for certain,
they would be among the Black Robes.

Hatchiorauquasha passed the pipe to Running Buffalo Bull
and slowly blew out the smoke as he began to speak: "Little
Bear Claw said he and your kin and allies will welcome our party
on the trek to the rendezvous, even to live among you again. I
am ready to do other things. The white chiefs now know about
these western lands where the Indians live. As you already have
seen, the white men have marvels that travel up and down the
water, and the land, too. The furs are going. White man will
now seek his money from the land. The chiefs and the sub-chiefs

already have become rich from the lands to the east. They and those who have watched them become rich are coming here— mostly to work the land. We had talked of going to that part of the Oregon country near what white man calls the Pacific Ocean. There is much fertile soil and the weather is easier on older bones. But the Black Robes are not there, either, and the Hudson's Bay people tell us that in the twenty years I have been trapping, white man's sicknesses have killed three out of every four Indians west of the Blue Mountains.

"We wish to escape that. Also, many whites already are moving to join the Bostons there, most lately the Jason Lee you told us about. The medicine man and chief, McLoughlin, of the Hudson's Bay Company at Fort Vancouver, helped him to settle in the Willamette Valley there. This is as hard to understand as would be a Blackfeet invitation for the Flatheads to move into the region near the great falls. Jason Lee is American. He is certain to bring many others. Already the British complain about the numbers of Americans moving into that area despite a long-standing agreement between the Americans and the British that both can go there."

Hatchiorauquasha looked questioningly at Little Coyote. Was he talking too long? Little Coyote motioned for him to go on.

"The strong displace the weak," Hatchiorauquasha continued. "Perhaps soon the Americans will force out the British, much as your people and others were driven out as the Blackfeet swept in from the north."

In exaggerated despair this John Gray, as many whites irritably called him, again raised his expressive hands: "Marianne and the others say, quite rightly, 'There is no escaping white man. We must move to the Black Robes if we wish to save our souls.'"

Both Little Coyote and Little Bear Claw, even Tjolzhitsay, acknowledged they could learn much from this part-Iroquois warrior if they remained near him during the trek to Horse Creek. He had been educated among white men and had lived among British and Americans many of his years. He very quickly could point out the lessons to be learned from the past and the now. He could speak and write white man's tongue and also stand up to white man with the same fearlessness with which he had killed many grizzly bears. Only four years ago Milton Sublette had learned that lesson when he insulted Hatchiorauquasha's daughter. The father's knife almost put Sublette under.

The Flatheads' trek to the rendezvous was leisurely, given to many ceremonies, feasts and much visiting as Shoshonis, Nez Percé and Bannacks joined the travelers. Some saved their victorious scalp dances until the greatest number could see them. Small parties of whites, some mixed with Delawares, Shawnees and Pottawatomies, put up their shelters, too. Finally, almost one-thousand-five-hundred Indians had erected their lodges near Horse Creek up the Siskadee to await the arrival of trade goods.

Perhaps because he found his Flathead friends genuinely interested and he sought conversations not given solely to trapping, hunting and immediate survival, Hatchiorauquasha— often assisted by forthright Marianne and greatly encouraged by much-loved Tjolzhitsay—often spoke in the early evenings. He spoke of religions, as all the peoples he knew of practiced them; of geography, as he had learned it; of politics, which existed in various forms everywhere; of great wars and of people who now lived—as well as of those who once were. He gave names to each of these broad areas of instruction and often used a sharpened stick to mark his lessons on the earth. The listeners were attentive, as they most often were with their own story-tellers. One mark Tjolzhitsay, Little Coyote and Little Bear Claw always would remember as they discussed these lessons was a long line Hatchiorauquasha said represented the Mississippi River. They also would remember even more vividly what their part-Iroquois friend said:

"The Great White Father Jefferson, who sent Lewis and Clark here and elsewhere, once suggested that all Indian tribes be removed across this Mississippi River to make room for the many white men. The Hudson's Bay people have told me that. Andrew Jackson now is the Great White Father and he began doing this. In the past seven years, through almost one-hundred of what the white men call 'treaty talks,' many, many Indians have been forced to move across that river."

Little Bear Claw and others attended these discussions as demands elsewhere allowed. Old Shield Maker and their head chief attended them all, listening quietly, shifting uncomfortably from time to time on their blankets. At their conclusion the head chief's sole remark, stated loudly enough for all to hear, remained with Little Coyote forever: "Though we often express our sorrow that we no longer are a tribe of many people, there is a value here in our small numbers, for the wisdom we must seek to live with white man can reach us all."

Little Coyote, considering this trek especially momentous, marked on his story skin a larger figure, one side of his face red, the other white. The figure was speaking to many smaller beings seated on the ground. As the seer painted, there arose the eternal question: Had the Good Spirit given Shining Shirt a far-seeing look ahead as through a great spyglass, of sorts, so he could both discern and comprehend this irresistible movement of white man from east to west—and caution not to fight them? Many late nights the warrior pondered his own same message received during his vision quest. Was he receiving the reasons for the message now, through Hatchiorauquasha in part? Who would follow him to remind the people of this same message as the westward movement of white man occurred at an ever quickening pace? Pondering these matters more deeply than ever, he linked together the earlier thoughts he had had while working on the traps—and the conclusion: The Flatheads and others lost much independence as they traded for white man's marvels, which made life easier, true. But as Hatchiorauquasha explained had happened elsewhere, could it be *possible* in these vast spaces to lose the freedom of movement over Mother Earth herself?

Abruptly, on the night of that lingering thought, Little Coyote sat upright on the furs, startling Antelope from deep sleep. He had seen the loop of a great lariat moving through the air to settle around the neck of long-dead Not Afraid of Guns. The horse had raced and bucked and pulled, ever tightening the noose until she toppled over, submissive, but the strong fires yet burning in the subdued body.

The seer reassured Antelope and, once more, she slept as, much later, did he. He awakened very tired with Sun, but somewhere from deep within a voice, a question, sought release: *Will I be the last seer needed to warn the people, "Do not fight white man?"* Would the noose tighten forever during his own lifetime?

Little Coyote concluded—and Tjolzhitsay later agreed with great solemnity and conviction—that, indeed, the Good Spirit had arranged for Hatchiorauquasha to help provide the lessons of conduct when white man would be everywhere. Determinedly, systematically, Little Coyote and Antelope spoke often in English. They retained the old tongue, true, but agreed that they must learn how white man thought. Little Coyote knew one thing: White man believed that Indians thought not at all beyond fulfilling the basic needs of each new day.

The best bowmen among the Shoshonis, Nez Percé, Bannacks, Flatheads and others were preparing to ride back to their lodges, rejoicing or sorrowing with their fellow tribesmen over the winning or losing of bets. Once again the powerful double-curved bow of sinew-backed horn had won over the others—in the hands of a Shoshone. What these less-rich warriors lacked in guns they made up with other weapons; this much-sought Nez Percé trade item was the "Hawken" among bows. Sun was westering now, making as its target the notch between two distant, snow-capped peaks. A cool, southwest wind had begun dispersing the heat waves that had shimmered over the shooting field almost from the start of the contests.

Now a new wave reached both contestants and onlookers, growing in excitement, intensity and mixture of voices as it moved from the most distant to the closest circle of lodges and tents: "The pack train is coming!"

Bringer of this news was Tull. He, his strong-limbed mount and a trailing pack horse had grown in size from mere specks in the vastness of this place to the full focus of attention as he steadily moved closer. Reaching the first small collection of shelters,

Tull stopped his horse, held up his left hand to suppress the excited voices and batted brown alkali dust from his hat. He placed it back on his head, then dusted off his long beard and clothing. He reached into a sagging pocket and withdrew a twist of tobacco.

"Sumna bitch, cain't ye talk, hoss?" Joe Meek, the nearest trapper, tall, talkative and clean-shaven, sounded the plaint of them all.

Tull aimed the tobacco twist at a spot about two-thirds the way down from the top of his head. The hair parted and strong teeth worried off a chaw. The hairy face moved up and down for a few more almost unbearable moments, then the loosed saliva splashed downward on a stone target.

"Howdy, Meek! Tom Fitzpatrick tol' me ta tell ya' all th' pack train crossed th' deevide on Indeependence Day. It'll be hyar in coupla' days." Tull waited patiently for the elated shout to echo back, then spat again. "Said ta tell ya' mebbeso ya'll be eager ta celbrate yore own kinda' late Indeependence Day—f'm weak tea 'n cawfee, even water." Again he held up the cautionary hand. "Ya' varlets better lissen. He's abringin' a coupla' what ya' ain't seed fur a long spell, nuther, a coupla'—"

He wanted to say more, but laughter, shouting, whooping and yells from the dancing, elated trappers continued until he lowered his hand. He shrugged, finished painting the stone brown with another spurt, then began looking for a shady place to picket his horses and lay out his gear. He looked up once and shook his head wonderingly when Meek, a few other trappers and some Nez Percé, perhaps a dozen in all, set out across the sage-filled Siskadee River Plains. They followed the tracks Tull and his horses had just laid down—tracks that the timeless breeze already had begun to obliterate.

The wait had become unbearable. Sun crawled toward the apex, reached it and seemed to hang there unmoving, high above the shimmering heat waves. Insects, birds, animals and man quieted, even among the trees. There the most impatient— thirstiest, perhaps, for whiskey and new activities—quietly cursed Fitzpatrick and praised him in almost the same breath.

"Fitz'll bring plenty tuh celbrate with. Why'nt he ashowin'?" They looked at Sun. "Past midway 'tween noon 'n dark, damn well is. Hell, let's go arter 'em!"

So they went, at least twice the number of the earlier Meek party, whooping, as had their predecessors, racing through the sagebrush, their horses kicking up tiny dust clouds that hung in the air for a time to mark their passage down a long-dry ravine and out of sight. Like the heat, their voices continued to fill this expectant tiny world of Indians and whites after the dust had dissipated.

A ragged volley of distant gun shots and a more prolonged reply indicated connection between friends and friends or foes and foes. Then, as though each human throat and gun muzzle had been stoppered simultaneously—silence. Total silence.

An almost-balanced number of the most wary and timorous in the encampment sought out Tull. He was snoozing under a small canvas stretched between two trees.

"Didja' cross hostile sign comin' hyar? What in hell is happening?"

Indignant, Tull sat upright. He refused to answer the jumble of questions until he had quenched his thirst from a canteen, stuffed some tobacco into his mouth, chewed meditatively, then spat far to leeward. He wiped off his whiskers with a half-closed hand and chuckled.

"I tried to tell thet first passel o' sarpants settin' out with Meek they was a coupla' ladies with Fitzpatrick. Yas, ladies. Wooden lissen. When they seen th' ladies, betcha th' tongues o' Meek 'n th' boys, like this latest passel o' varlets, was turned ta stone. Stone like Black Harris is allus claimin' he seed in a putrified forest he com'd ta onct. Yas, they's ladies comin' hyar, right quick now." Tull chuckled again, fingered out his chaw and put it in the sun to dry. Once again he stretched out under his canvas.

No petrified trappers here until well into the morning of the next day after liquor and exhaustion had done their work. While quiet reigned in the growing heat at the tent camps, there were no stone tongues in the more sober lodges of the Indians. There they wagged freely, loudly, even among the warriors, the most skeptical who had attended many a rendezvous now acknowledging there *really* were white women!

Whites and Indians had marveled as Fitzpatrick led the almost mile-long train into the encampment: Perhaps four-hundred mules and horses, eighty men, then, well back from these to escape the worst dust, a springless, two-mule cart transporting a wan Milton Sublette. Even Hatchiorauquasha had clucked sympathetically at the sight of his old adversary forlornly holding the sideboards to help take up the shock of each bump that transferred to his amputated leg. The sight of Sublette confirmed Marianne's sympathetic, "He carries the mark of death."

After a gap, an even-more-wondrous file: A well-loaded, small, springless, four-wheeled wagon, more horses and mules, beef cattle and, plodding most slowly of all, milk cows. Their bags endlessly swinging from side to side, the strange creatures would stop, bellow for the thousandth time the uselessness of this long trek, then, poked in the behind by two weary Nez Percé lads wielding sharpened willow sticks, resume their weary march, oblivious that they were the second most interesting sight to most of the watching Indians.

First attraction? The two white women—for Indians and whites alike.

The pair industriously had beaten the alkali dust from voluminous cloth skirts gathered at tiny waists before riding between two irregularly formed lines of hoorahing onlookers stretching across a meadow almost to the dilapidated log storeroom. The storeroom was a remnant of a trading post Captain Benjamin Bonneville had built four years earlier while on leave from the United States Army. The women's bearing was akin to that of very important visiting chiefs. They had sat sideways in curious saddles, exposing worn and scuffed boots. They had removed their hats and struck them smartly against the shoulders of their moving mounts in an apparent afterthought to remove that dust, too. But they did not replace them. Almost as a signal, this motion had quieted most of the onlookers and formed them up.

Both women were tanned, the taller of the two evidently worn from the travel. The smaller woman had finely formed features. Her bright eyes and ready smile demonstrated that she was enjoying the welcome; even the older male Indians grunted their delight as Sun caught and glistened in her reddish-golden curls.

Tull seemed to represent the attitude of most of the mountain men. Though he had seen the women before, had traveled a great distance with them, he, too, stood there gawking, holding his old hat almost worshipfully to his chest, his mouth so agape at times that Little Coyote could see the trapper's tobacco-stained teeth. Other whites who only a short time earlier had been cavorting with Indian women now pushed them behind and were staring upward. Even the most rowdy was silenced by the appearance of these two white women, the first many had seen for years.

Marcus Whitman, his broad, muscular body contrasting sharply with the lithe, golden-haired woman's, had helped his new bride from her saddle, their ready smiles attesting to mutual devotion during that brief interval between saddle and earth. Another angular man, clad in worn, baggy, dark clothing, tenderly had assisted the other woman, but there had been no such public display of closeness between them. Many of the onlookers almost had fought to help erect tents for the women, then had stood by silently as the pair had entered them even though Fitzpatrick's clerks as quickly had set out their trading goods fronted by four barrels of whiskey and a mighty collection of tin cups.

The silence that had engulfed most of the rendezvous gradually began breaking until, at last, whiskey and the appearance of almost-forgotten coffee, sugar, hardtack, bacon and other foods loosened most tongues and inhibitions. Now this gathering resembled most of the others—with one exception: Almost always, some mountain men, young and old, stood around the tents of the women or followed them like faithful dogs wherever they went. Sometimes the men silently formed a diversionary phalanx to shunt the woman away from some of the activities which, like whiskey and some white man foods, too long had been denied.

"She is Narcissa Whitman, she with the golden hair. The other, Eliza Spalding, also the mate of a man of the Good Spirit, though not a Black Robe."

Marianne Gray had pushed her way through the Indian women who increasingly were thronging around, touching, even kissing white-man-style the two white women. What she could not learn immediately from the mountain men she had learned by asking questions. Her questions were addressed to the women, themselves, then Marianne eagerly had returned to her lodge set up among her Flathead friends.

"She is beautiful, the golden hair," Antelope acknowledged as she straightened up from leaning over a large, brass kettle erected between her lodge and that of Little Yellow Bird. Antelope raised her large stirring stick and pointed it at her friends as she tried to focus her thoughts into one succinct sentence that would summarize her thinking since she had seen the two white women: "When white men bring white women to these places, they are here to stay." She paused as stew ran down the stick and onto her wrist and hand. All the men and women present looked up and would remember her words above all that would follow that day.

Willow Woman joined in the friendly laughter over Antelope's mishap before again thrusting her needle into the front of the buckskin jacket she was ornamenting with trade beads for Little Bear Claw. She clucked sympathetically: "The Spalding woman, she remains unwell from the journey and the bearing of a stillborn child. We have tried to make her comfortable here. She smiled for the first time when Antelope gave her assurances that more babies will come."

Willow Woman patted her own flat belly and laughed. "We did not tell her it might take much work. Little Bear Claw labored steadily, more satisfactorily than Eagle Claw, before that one came six summers ago." She pointed to Little Grizzly Bear Claw. Tired from long playing in the water, the boy was curled up on a deerskin. Willow Woman resumed her bead work. "Yes, but he was planted well, that one. He scarcely wanted to enter this world."

So they chattered until the food was ready. Before the women and children ate, Antelope carried stew to Little Coyote, Little Bear Claw, Running Buffalo Bull and Hatchiorauquasha.

They, too, had discussed each white member of the Whitman party, briefly, less animatedly, agreeing these were white men they liked. "Except one," Hatchiorauquasha had commented, a look of distaste on his thin face. "The man called, like myself, Gray. *William*, not John." They had laughed at this, agreeing that, in their brief observations, William Gray had stood aloof, disdainful of even those celebrating without the whiskey. He appeared to be ignoring the dancing, music, shooting with guns and arrows, racing afoot and on horses. Seemingly, he even disapproved of the friendliness of the Whitmans and the Spaldings toward everyone. All in all, he appeared a person who was neither, by calling nor by temperament, a man of the Good Spirit.

Then, quickly, the subject shifted as the four men began showing and discussing their trade goods from Fitzpatrick. They were of good quality; perhaps they would match those Lance and Swan, Fast Runner and Warm Breeze would bring back to the Bitter Root after deciding they would hunt with Ermatinger, who had brought Hudson's Bay trade goods eastward from the west coast.

That hunt had gone well. So said Tom McKay and John McLeod when, as the first excitement of the rendezvous began to wane, they belatedly brought their British trade goods and a letter for Whitman to this rendezvous of the Americans. The Flatheads and Nez Percé, once more disappointed that the Black Robes were not here, rode and walked to the Hudson's Bay trading center and listened with great interest to what McKay, McLeod and their people said. Whitman was disappointed, too. He had been waiting for the sender of the letter—a man of the Good Spirit who had spent much time with the Hudson's Bay people as well as with the Spokans, Walla Wallas, Pend d'Oreilles, Cayuses and others. Most of them had liked this Samuel Parker and what he said because he obviously liked them. He had wanted to take the long journey over the mountains to join the Whitman party at the rendezvous, but his bones were older than most and he was woefully tired. So, his letter revealed, he had taken the easier trip down the Columbia River to Fort Vancouver.

Words telling of the disappointment of the Flatheads and Nez Percé and of Whitman began going around the two quieting camps for chewing and re-chewing until they became as flavorless as one of Tull's discarded quids. Then the Whitman party and numerous Nez Percé moved to the Hudson's Bay camp. Now there was something fresh to chew on! The McKay and McLeod people soon would leave for Fort Vancouver; the Whitman party would accompany them to serve as people of the Good Spirit among the Nez Percé.

Little Coyote marked this notable event on his story skin by showing a man with a cross accompanied by a golden-haired woman, both with smiling faces, moving west from Horse Creek on the Siskadee, or Green River, as white man now was calling it. And Horse Creek? Some trappers claimed someone there stole a horse from Tom Fitzpatrick, seemingly a minor affair in the vastness of the land, but mighty important to a mountain man, where a horse, a gun and a dependable partner could mean life, itself.

The Flatheads rejoiced with the Nez Percé as the Whitmans departed. But at the close of the next year's buffalo hunt, the Flatheads learned of and shared the sorrow of the Nez Percé: Whitman had chosen to found a mission at Waiilatpu, closer to the Cayuses than the Nez Percé. The latter warned the men of the Good Spirit that the Cayuses had troubles with white man. The Nez Percé got the Spaldings, who settled in the Lapwai Valley ten miles up from the Clearwater's confluence with the Snake.

In the sixth moon of *Itxwe*, Camas, in white man's 1837, death
began moving north and west to the upper Missouri River
country while most of the Flatheads and many kin and allies
were trekking south, southeast and southwest after trading at
Flathead House. Some people later said, most fervently, "The
Good Spirit was our guide."

Some also credited their lives to the determination of
Hudson's Bay's much-traveled Francis Ermatinger to heed
McLoughlin's order that he strive even harder to keep the trade
of the Flatheads and their allies. Ermatinger's first argument
was powerful: "The Blackfeet are aware and angry that you and
your friends formed the great alliance to trek to the upper Missouri
River and become the first to obtain trade goods from the
Assiniboin. Your enemies have allied to prevent this from
occurring again. You have no second alliance. You would be
wiped out if you were to go in smaller numbers. Accompany us
to the rendezvous on the Siskadee."

The Flatheads and others had done so.

"This William Gray. Ermatinger told me he is not a man of
the Good Spirit like much-loved Whitman or the Black Robes,
but has a strong wish to be. He runs about like a bull elk trying to

keep his many cows away from other bulls." Little Bear Claw erratically moved his hand through the air. "Thus he alienates the other bulls—and disappoints the expectant cows."

The large circle of warriors laughed heartily. They watched as Gray once more harangued a patient Ermatinger to hurry, hurry. "I must get back to the States so I can prepare to establish a mission among the Spokanes." Little Coyote translated the message to their head chief and the warriors. Again they laughed. This time Gray looked toward and down at the Flatheads. He flushed and angrily strode away from the circle. Ermatinger shook his head wonderingly and moved his hand back and forth toward the Indians in a "What can I do?" gesture. Then he set about once more preparing his men to trek with most of the Flatheads. They should, on this last day of the fifth moon of the Bitter Root, enter the Big Hole Basin.

Except for Gray, there had been little reason to hurry. While traveling with Ermatinger's party this spring, Gray had encountered Henry Spalding, who had come from the Lapwai Valley among the Nez Percé. Quickly, the two had decided there must be a mission among the Spokanes. So, Gray had chafed for many days as Ermatinger and his trappers accompanied the Flatheads. They hunted buffalo well away from the Blackfeet, prepared bitterroot, and carefully trapped their way toward the 1837 rendezvous. They were careful because the Blackfeet were following parties converging on the site between Horse Creek and Big Fork on the Siskadee. Men again began dying.

Members of the Flathead-Ermatinger cavalcade spread out as they moved through the vast Big Hole Basin, setting a general direction for Deer Lodge Prairie. With cool weather, there still was some fur to be caught, a need for fresh meat, deer hides, elk.

The lay missionary, William Gray, determined to establish a mission among the Spokans, tagged along with the Ermatinger party. After the rendezvous, he would accompany the fur-trader to the States to get church permission for his undertaking. Gray held prayer meetings with many of the Flatheads and helped others with injuries, often aided in his talking by Little Coyote and Antelope. Gray's listeners liked his flute-playing and his voice, but.... Tjolzhitsay summarized the people's growing impression of this would-be man of the Good Spirit as they ate an evening meal after a prayer meeting on the first night of the sixth moon: "He wishes for us to change to his ways at once, yet fails to see we do not like all his ways—one of which is that his manner shows he does not really like us. If I had Little Coyote's powers, perhaps I could know what he marks in his book at the end of each day." The irregular circle of eaters laughed when the head chief stopped talking, chewed thoughtfully for a few moments, then, with a wide grin, added questioningly, "Does he truly believe we should change at once and not like *ourselves*?"

Their attention shifted to the excited movement and talk at Ermatinger's nearby camp. Silhouetted against the largest fire were two horses, one carrying a man leaning forward in his saddle, another being lifted from his. The eaters hurried toward them.

"Blackfeet hit our huntin' party, Frank," an uninjured man said to Ermatinger. "We lit out soon's we cud. Lots of 'em about. Tucker, here, got a ball off th' side his haid. Lucky, he is. Claudet, wull, as ya' c'n see, they's an arrer in his chest twixt th' shoulder 'n left tit. Moughty hurtin', he is."

"Here, help me lift him off." Gray had taken over. Claudet, a part-Iroquois, leaned far enough over his horse for three men to catch and place him face up on the ground near the fire. Gray tentatively moved the arrow shaft, then hurried to his tent. He returned with a bag somewhat smaller than that used by Whitman when the surgeon had removed the arrowhead from Bridger's back.

Once again Gray experimentally moved the shaft back and forth. He removed a small knife from the kit.

"What will you do?" Ermatinger's blunt question was what Little Coyote was prepared to ask.

"Widen the cut to pull out the arrow." Gray's voice was cold, determined.

"But—" Perhaps Ermatinger would have said it more diplomatically, but a trapper voiced the issue in very plain language: "Hell, maybe the arrer needs pushin' out, not pullin'. We knows *that*! These war arrers' er most often made so the sinew they's tied with will pull away from the haid an' it'll stay in."

"I'll do the doctoring," Gray, removing a cloth from the bag, said to Ermatinger and the others—except Little Coyote.

Little Coyote leaned over the Iroquois and spoke in Flathead. The man feebly nodded his head. Little Coyote and Antelope quickly split the man's jacket sufficiently for them to remove it despite the shaft. They rolled up the garment and placed it under the man's head and shoulders, then gently tested the arrow shaft.

Gray had recovered from his astonishment.

"Here, what are you doing?" He pushed away the Flathead medicine man's hands.

"What will you do?"

"Remove the arrow."

"Will you truly pull it?"

"After I widen the cut. Listen. No ignorant Indian is—" Gray looked up at the many heads peering down, the campfire flames shining on their faces, glittering in their eyes.

"Claudet has asked the medicine man to remove the arrow." The flames shone on Ermatinger's teeth.

"But—"

"Mr. Gray," Ermatinger said, "you had better watch."

"But—"

"Now! Stand back!" Ermatinger's voice was steady. He had handled many men, sometimes with much diplomacy and kindness, at other times with little of either and, if necessary, with his strong body. Hudson's Bay Company had trained him well. His grasp on Gray's arm appeared to help him to stand, but Little Coyote saw the fingers grip very hard, indeed.

Antelope had cut, then snapped off, most of the shaft. Little Coyote helped the man to sit, back to the fire. A hum carrying many interpretations spread among the onlookers when Antelope produced a small bottle of whiskey and gave Claudet a deep swig. She stoppered the bottle and replaced it in her bag. She would guard this well until Fitzpatrick and his whiskey arrived on the Siskadee.

Little Coyote calculated the location of blood vessels and arteries with his fingers. He began telling Antelope how to work, guide and push the shaft stub and arrow head. Claudet silently winced; he managed a wan smile backed by a surprisingly loud voice: "The arrow would move easier if I had another pull at that bottle."

Antelope gave the stub a final push; Little Coyote seized the tip of the head and pulled the missile clear as all but Gray laughed. Claudet got his second swig for his belly while the shoulder was bandaged.

Little Coyote drew on none of his powers as seer that night as he watched and knew what the would-be missionary/surgeon was writing in his journal by his own lonely campfire. The medicine man wanted to walk over and explain why he and Antelope had removed the arrow, but he knew there would be no understanding in this proud man. Gray walked to the edge of light from his dying campfire. He looked at *spqeni*, Moon, and appeared to be praying to the Good Spirit. Almost at once a heavy cloud blotted out Moon. Little Coyote pondered all this before falling into troubled sleep.

One morning when many of Ermatinger's men formed a large group to hunt deer and elk, the Flathead council met to discuss the appearance of yet another small group of Blackfeet who had begged for a truce.

"There is something they do not tell us. Why are they in little bands now?" Tjolzhitsay waited for an answer. He got none.

Earlier he had displayed wisdom by suggesting there be a great scalp dance to impress other Blackfeet continuing to lurk about. The people had danced for several days while William Gray fretted about hurrying to the rendezvous site so he could continue on his way to the East.

Ermatinger had other, more important, problems. He did not wish for his men, his trade goods and furs to be endangered by a great battle between the Flatheads and Blackfeet. He patiently had explained this to Gray while the exhausted celebrants had rested between dances.

When scouts reported a much larger group of Blackfeet

approaching, the hardy trader, armed with gifts and a persuasive tongue, set out to parley with them. Perhaps both cavalcades could pass each other without fighting as each went its own way. The Blackfeet, beginning to hear rumors of a great unknown calamity befalling their peoples near the upper Missouri, agreed to Ermatinger's suggestion.

"The Blackfeet are aware the many groups of whites and other tribes are converging on the rendezvous site," a concerned Tjolzhitsay told the council. "Their defeat in the Battle of Pierre's Hole still is a strong memory. They do not wish all these arriving people to join together and fight them while they await the arrival of the trade goods."

Then Little Bear Claw, at Tjolzhitsay's nod, told how thirty-two years ago the Blackfeet had honored such a truce following the release of the Blood chief, Owl. Even so, the traditional enemies watched each other as warily as two boar grizzlies following the scent of a sow in heat. Savage battles still lay ahead.

Other tribes had encounters with the swarming Blackfeet bands, too. They held their own scalp dances as they joined those nearing the rendezvous and, finally, at the site, itself.

Fitzpatrick would not arrive with the trade goods until July 18, so, in addition to these celebrations, there was much of the usual rendezvous betting, competitions and talk. The general conversation focused on the declining take of furs, the specifics on Gray's tiresome running from camp to camp to try to get up a party to join him on his trip "to civilization." There were no takers—yet. The fun really had not started, but it picked up with the arrival of McLeod's party and became downright lively when Andrew Drips came with his group—plus liquor. Tjolzhitsay called on the sub-chiefs to exert their influence to keep the Flatheads away from liquor and their wives and young women away from the trappers. Their efforts were moderately successful, helped by Dog That Sits' busy lodges; he had two now, with two more women to help him in this highly remunerative "work."

There was no sign of the Black Robes.

This fact helped Gray to put together a small party to leave well before Fitzpatrick would depart with his furs.

Would the troubled, greatly disappointed, head chief wish to send more messengers pleading for the Black Robes?

Yes, Big Ignace LaMousse would go again—and would guide. Grand Visage, the war chief, would send his two sons so they could learn more about white man and his religion. One more Flathead agreed to go, as did one Nez Percé. Few of his people had come to the rendezvous. They were staying with Spalding.

Little Coyote and Antelope rejoiced at the arrival of a large village of Shoshonis, preceded by more than two-hundred well-mounted men who put on a parade judged best of the entire rendezvous.

"Yes, the horse-trading remains profitable," aging Broken Pipe conceded. "The many white men want more of our horses. I work closely with the Nez Percé. Bridger is doing much to help us become better armed." Broken Pipe had brought five horses to Little Coyote and his family; it was during this presentation that Chalax, an older warrior/seer from the north end of the Bitter Root Valley, came to Little Coyote. Chalax stood beside his own magnificent horse while the two talked.

"The man, Gray, leaves for St. Louis," Chalax said. "Big Ignace asked me if I could foresee any attacks on them by Blackfeet. I could not do so. I urged Big Ignace to try to have Gray wait until Fitzpatrick leaves. Gray will not wait, despite warnings from Little Bear Claw, Drips, McLeod, Ermatinger and Fitzpatrick, himself." Chalax tapped his fingers worriedly on the seat of his saddle. "As I said, I could not foresee any attacks by the Blackfeet. But the Shoshonis say the Sioux get bolder, and many live where the Gray party must go."

"Gray would set his heart more firmly to leave would I approach him," Little Coyote said. "I, too, will talk to Big Ignace."

Chalax rode away still shaking his head despite Little Coyote's promise.

"Gray will leave," Big Ignace told Little Coyote. "Three whites—Barrows, Grimm and Callaghan—will go with us."

So they left, the forebodings Little Coyote shared with Chalax and the others lightened for now by Antelope's continuing joy over the presence of her family.

46

Before Broken Pipe's return to the country of the Shoshonis, his son, Pony Whip, and grandson, Lance, drew on the aged horse-trader's knowledge and support to form their own venture: They would drive excellent riding horses to the 1838 rendezvous set for Horse Creek and, because of dwindling furs, obtain trade goods to supply their own families. There would be risks, from the Blackfeet especially, but by now vague rumors that something was terribly amiss on the upper Missouri were beginning to take on more substance. This fact, coupled with the noticeably cowed manner of the wandering Blackfeet bands hanging about the 1837 rendezvous like wolves, convinced the two warriors they could depend on the speed of the horses and good scouting to reach the next rendezvous with their animals— and their scalps.

Broken Pipe looked at these two eager would-be traders and smiled. "If you had not considered the Blackfeet, I would not have considered the advance of some of my horses. Sons and grandsons are of value, but my *horses!* They are dearer than my life." Now he embraced them, adding, "Tell your people and others that a part-Iroquois who came down from the Canada country to obtain some of my best stallions for breeding told me the Métis, though greatly in need of meat, are staying away from the upper Missouri buffalo grounds because the smallpox is there. More, I could not learn. Do not go there!"

Broken Pipe nodded approvingly once again when Lance explained further that he and Pony Whip also would exchange some of the trade goods for even more horses from the Flatheads, Shoshonis and Nez Percé.

Their first venture was successful—barely, because mountain man Joe Walker had driven riding and pack horses from Mexico's land of California for the same purpose. But not to the Siskadee. Andrew Drips, leading the American Fur Company trek from Westport Landing near Independence, Missouri, decided to change the rendezvous to the 1830 site on the Popo Agie River, nearer to their Fort Laramie and not in the Oregon country shared with the British. Perhaps he thought this change would discourage the Hudson's Bay Company. It did not. Ermatinger reached the Popo Agie from the west on July 8, barely a week after Lance and Pony Whip had arrived with their horses, surprised they had met no Blackfeet at all. Other Flatheads who had taken only furs to the rendezvous told the same story.

The return of the two young traders to the Bitter Root Valley before the others provided answers to questions about the smallpox reports. Lance and Pony Whip also brought the tragic answer to the question of what had become of Big Ignace and the others who, once again, had sought the Black Robes. Which story would they tell the council first? They would tell of the loss of their own people, this time to the Sioux. Then what Ermatinger had told them, and others, about the smallpox.

Lance and Pony Whip had begun to tell their stories to the people even before Tjolzhitsay quieted the noise in the council lodge. Lance could speak English, so he had learned the most from the white trappers. He would speak to the council first.

"Four men of the Good Spirit had brought their mates to the 1838 rendezvous," Lance said. "One was newly married William Gray. We could not talk with him until we had traded our horses. This we had to do quickly because the trade goods were in much demand and there were more horses than we had anticipated. Also, the fur company was using more wagons and carts to bring their goods and carry away the furs. After the exchange, we could roam about. One of Bridger's drunken trappers saw we were Flathead and Shoshone." Lance screwed up his usually cheerful face and tried to communicate the trapper's language with his own. He failed miserably, although those in the council who understood some English roared at his efforts.

"He said to us, 'They's ta be mebbe a guttin' or a scalpin' o' Gray fer lettin' the Sioux kill the Flathead people who're frens o' our'n, too, ta save his own scalp.'"

Anger surged when Lance repeated this information and the rest of his story in Flathead.

"Other Flatheads joined us as we followed this man and three other drunken trappers toward Gray's and the others' lodges. As we walked, we learned many of the trappers were angry because Gray had not fought enough to save Big Ignace and the others when many Sioux surrounded them in the Nebraska country. There was a fight. Three Sioux were killed." Lance stopped and looked at his father, who, in turn, looked about for the war chief, Grand Visage. A long groan filled the silent lodge as Grand Visage leaned forward in sorrow. The head chief motioned for Lance to continue. "A white trader was with the Sioux. He talked to Gray. He said the Sioux would kill our people, but spare the whites. Barrows was not there. He had stayed at Fort Laramie. Big Ignace was dressed as a white and would have been spared, but he chose to die with his brothers. While Gray talked, they died.

"The drunken trappers could not find Gray. He was hiding in one of the lodges. The white women were much afraid until the trappers began to sing. Soon after we left these white people, Bridger arrived with his trappers. After they had drunk whiskey, they rushed to see the white women. There was much dancing around a Blackfeet scalp and rejoicing that smallpox had struck the Blackfeet. We talked about this with trappers who were not yet drunk. They said Bridger led them from winter camp on the Powder River to the Tongue, Little Big Horn, Big Horn, Three

Forks. They had one great fight with the Blackfeet up the Madison, then continued through Henry's Fork, Pierre's Hole and Jackson Hole. Almost all over the Blackfeet numbers were few because smallpox had struck them.

"Four days after these events, Ermatinger's party arrived with his British trade goods and more missionaries, but no Black Robes, either. While his clerks conducted the trade, he talked to many trappers to learn as much as possible about the smallpox so he could carry this information to McLoughlin. After but four days, he started back, accompanied by Gray and the others who had arrived with Andrew Drips. Harried now for time, but kindly as always, Ermatinger sought out all the Flatheads and their kin who were present.

"Ermatinger said to the Flatheads, 'The smallpox stories among your people still are strong as a leather thong. I wish to make them strong as the woven lariat which will hold the most untamed stallion.' We watched him shake his head almost unbelievingly at what he had learned."

Lance shook his own head in wonderment as he continued to relate what Ermatinger had learned: "Ermatinger said the American Fur Company's fire boat *Assiniboin*, carrying eleven-thousand buffalo robes and other furs, three summers ago wrecked and burned where the Heart River flows into the Missouri below Fort Clark in the Dakota country. There were noises of recognition among our brothers as Ermatinger spoke of this place. Ermatinger said that last summer, as the Flatheads traded and traveled with him, the *St. Peter's*, replacing the *Assiniboin*, came up the Missouri and stopped at Fort Clark, carrying many trade goods which the Mandans could see—and the smallpox which they could not see. The Mandans went aboard the fire boat despite the whites' warnings to keep away.

"Ermatinger said that soon the Mandans began to die in their villages. Even the mightiest warrior, Mah-to-toh-pah, Four Bears. He said that most of the Indians who caught the smallpox blamed white man, but that white man tried to keep the Indians away from the smallpox. He said that Four Bears, like the others, swelled up like a carp pulled from the river and left in Sun's light. Next came the pox, the hurt all over, the vomiting when there was nothing to bring up. Then strange visions changed the minds till the people babbled as with the voices of many evil spirits. Then the sick began dying—ten, twenty, more each day. The smell of their corruption was as great as that near a buffalo jump during the hottest days of the seventh moon. The winds carried this stench to the fort, itself. Everywhere there was dying—and always the stench. The people jumped from cliffs like crazed, pushed buffaloes. They cut their throats, shot others and themselves. Mates, children, friends. Others jumped into the river and drowned. Soon there was no one to carry out the ceremonies for the dead. Dogs, then foxes, coyotes and wolves, emboldened by the growing silence, fed on the almost uncountable corpses, as did the birds, great and small. There are perhaps but one-hundred Mandans living. This death by rotting visited the Hidatsa, the Arikaras."

As Lance recounted what Ermatinger had learned and revealed, Little Coyote thought briefly of his and Antelope's days among the Mandans early after the pair had mated—of the kindnesses of the people, some of their fears. Now, inwardly, he wept.

"Ermatinger said that those who fled the villages with few possessions carried death with them," Lance continued. "Now Sioux, emboldened like the animals, came to the villages, taking what the animals did not—the many scalps, possessions and the remaining corn. They, too, began to die there, as did many while trading at Fort Pierre far downriver, though not in as great numbers, for they lived in many places far apart from one another."

Here Lance emphasized to the silent council what Ermatinger had said at the Popo Agie: "The death seems to lie in the people who catch the smallpox, then in their possessions, whatever they touch—as flame consumes all but a few remnant ends of sticks at the fire's edge. Then, with time, this death threat is reduced to ashes. But where will the next lightning fire strike? Ermatinger said that life teaches us many hard lessons. He urged his friends to remain away from the Blackfeet, their villages, their possessions until the fire burns out."

There was much talk in the council lodge; the talk reached those seated around the lodge outside, for the circular base had been rolled high and tied against the summer heat. Now these many voices hummed, too, until Lance signed to Tjolzhitsay there was more to tell.

Before the chief could tell Lance to continue, Grand Visage stood and demanded in a strong voice that the council now consider taking up the hatchet against William Gray.

"This we will talk about after we hear more from Little Coyote's son," the head chief replied. Lance, to give the grieving Grand Visage some additional thoughts to ponder, quickly said, "The Flatheads and our kin at the Popo Agie prepared to seek out Gray after the drunken trappers reduced their threats to songs. Bridger, Drips, Ermatinger worked hard to dissuade us, and because many of us had refused the whiskey, our minds were clear. We reluctantly agreed."

Lance continued to tell what Ermatinger had learned: "The smallpox did not stop with the Mandans. The *St. Peter's* continued upriver to Fort Union. The white chiefs there kept the Assiniboins away. A few warriors stole two horses; some of the Fort Union people pursued them. They got back the horses and unwittingly left the smallpox in their places, because of the sudden sickness of one of the pursuers.

"Now, Ermatinger said, Fort Union became like stricken Fort Clark. Like the deer running with the strong-jawed wolverine clamped to its neck, the Assiniboins tried to outrun the death they carried with them. They brought this death to the Crees, who died like the fish in a pond cut off from the river and warmed by Sun.

"Few Crows died, though smallpox came up the Yellowstone to Fort Cass. The Crows were hunting in the Absarokas. When they heard of the smallpox, their story-tellers quickly reminded them of the great death that came to the Mandans before the Clark and Lewis people. So they stayed away from the fort."

Old Shield Maker suddenly interrupted Lance: "The trading forts surround us like the stones around our lodges, and the death enters in from all directions." He raised his gaunt features and spoke out as loudly as possible, then lapsed into his usual hunched-up posture, muttering, ". . . *kowacksqwéeltem klotaye. Komieetzegail*—but deliver us from evil. Amen!"

Lance waited once more for the undercurrents both within and without the lodge to die down. Tjolzhitsay again signed for him to talk.

"Drips tried to dissuade many of the Bostons from trading with Ermatinger, reminding them this Britisher was in American land," Lance said. "The late-comers, especially, traded with him because much of the best of the American goods was gone. Ermatinger approached Bridger, whose long-standing reluctance to talk in a friendly way with any Britisher faded with each gulp from Ermatinger's bottle of brandy. Liquor now was a rarity at the rendezvous. Ermatinger reminded Bridger that since he was known as a fair man so far as the friendly Indians were concerned, and he *had* married the daughter of a Flathead chief, perhaps if he would tell what he knew about the smallpox, this knowledge would help all their friends.

"Bridger told Ermatinger he had learned the most about the smallpox when his party found a small village of Blackfeet at Henry's Lake. The trappers prepared to kill them all, until a few warriors approached, begging peace. During the parley, Bridger learned they had outrun the disease as they fled from dying village to dying village to this great distance, but it already had caught them, too. With much satisfaction Bridger told Ermatinger that smallpox had reduced the Blackfeet to numbers 'most any party could now handle. They're fewer than the beaver now, and there's not much seed left!'"

Lance was tiring now from the strain of remembering such an important story and from the newness of speaking to so many silent people. He asked Pony Whip to approach from the outer part of the lodge. They conversed briefly above the excited murmurs inside and outside. Lance signed to Tjolzhitsay he again would talk.

"Bridger told Ermatinger how the dying had come about," Lance said. "Alexander Harvey brought the keelboat downriver from Fort McKenzie near the great falls to Fort Union. He filled it with trade goods for the Blackfeet. As they hurried back upriver, the smallpox caught up with an Indian woman and one of Harvey's men. Harvey stopped the keelboat at the Judith River and sent a man to tell Fort McKenzie there was smallpox in the keelboat. The fort people should tell the five-hundred lodges there. The Blackfeet were powerful. None could stand against them. Seemingly, they could not remember their stories of the smallpox.

"'Bring the trade goods,' they demanded. 'You told us to prepare buffalo robes for trade. We have prepared almost enough to fill any fire boat. Now you do not keep your word. Will you not bring us the guns and powder and lead we demanded to use against the Flatheads, our other—'" A loud murmur of satisfaction filled the lodge and drowned out Lance's words. A brief, grim smile touched Tjolzhitsay's stern face, then disappeared as he demanded silence. "'. . . our other enemies? If Harvey does not bring us the goods, we will send our warriors to take them!'

"Bridger said Harvey brought the goods. Two of his men died when the keelboat reached Fort McKenzie. The Blackfeet traded quickly and left, but the smallpox flew on fast wings with them.

"Bridger said a Blackfeet sub-chief who his trappers had met at Henry's Lake also revealed that whenever his people approached another Blackfeet village, the odor of death warned them away. As they continued to flee ever more distant from Fort McKenzie, they encountered the corpses of others who had fled—and left near them even more of their own."

Between Lance's re-telling of Ermatinger's story and preparations for a great autumn meat hunt, this time with fewer allies than usual, Little Coyote had time to contemplate the smallpox scourge and its implications. One certainty was that the disease had done what other forces could not do—break the power of the Blackfeet. There was much rejoicing about that, but Tjolzhitsay warned the council to remember a lesson from a grizzly-bear hunter: "When he thinks the bear is dead, the mighty creature sometimes comes alive again to kill the hunter. Is its equally dangerous mate still lurking nearby in breeding season?

Does it have an inexperienced, but lethal, two-year-old cub that could charge from any direction? Two such cubs? Three? Four? There must be much thinking and counsel about what yet is not readily seen—now we must continue to hold to past practices. A large group of the remaining Blackfeet and their allies still could strike us."

As could a dying rattlesnake, Little Coyote thought.

Later that day, the seer remembered how he so willingly had agreed to Little Bear Claw's request that he help the sub-chief's now eight-year-old son, Little Grizzly Bear Claw, prepare to deal with life. He sought out the sub-chief and asked him for guidance as to what was needed.

"I will teach my son to ride and shoot, as I did your own son, Lance," Little Bear Claw said. "I would wish that you teach my son to deal with varying people. By considering past events, those now, and those that lie ahead, Little Grizzly Bear Claw can make wise decisions to cope with the future—which could, with all the rapid changes, become more troubling, indeed. When most of us see a single raven circling in the big sky, we watch to see if other ravens will join it. If so, there emerges an almost certainty: There is a kill below, or something—man or beast—about to make a kill. We then must be more careful. Yes, a small event can lead to a great one. We understand, too, what the people of the various tribes do. There are some differences, and we learn those. But white man? We know so little. So much to learn."

Little Coyote nodded his head understandingly, aware that he had two reasons for doing so. The most obvious—he comprehended what Little Bear Claw was saying. Less obvious, unvoiced by both, there seemed a mutual need to talk, to allay, if even for the moment, the nagging worry: Where could the smallpox strike next? Back to the first reason: It truly would require much wisdom for their sons to deal with what rapidly was becoming white man's world.

"Yes, Little Bear Claw," the seer said, "in a somewhat like way in the affairs of people, I have been thinking about the extra wheel Marcus Whitman carried in his wagon to the 1836 rendezvous. I have been thinking that Whitman's wheel was strongly made. It can represent the unity of a single people, like ourselves, or of many tribes. Several strong spokes attached the outer wheel to the hub. And there was an iron band encircling, strengthening, all the parts. The four wheels on Whitman's wagon were well-used, greatly worn, but unbroken. One afternoon I watched two drunken trappers take this extra wheel, as yet unused, up the high, treeless hill near the encampment. They painted it red to be more easily seen. Then they fired their rifles so all could see them set the wheel to rolling faster and faster down the hill. How it rolled—effortlessly—graceful as a running elk, sometimes leaping into the air, but never losing its position, almost straight as an arrow down the hill. Even Whitman watched with much interest. Then the wheel struck a large boulder embedded in the base of the hill.

"Wooden parts of the outer wheel flew in many directions like a band of grouse, as did the spokes, some badly splintered. The strong hub rolled but a little ways more, then stopped. And the iron rim, badly bent, crookedly rolled partly uphill, then downhill. It stopped, then fell over, much like the elk whose heart has been pierced by a rifle ball.

"Whitman lost his smile while other trappers collected armloads of parts and returned them to the owner. Fitzpatrick showed the greatest anger and almost cast out the two drunken trappers. But Whitman searched about, with Fitzpatrick's help, and soon found two men to help the mechanic. They used some mountain wood, strong knives, hatchets and an iron hammer, fire and river water to put the parts back together. And they again had a strong wheel, though made of some different, not so strong, wood."

As Little Coyote ceased drawing shapes in the soil, Little Bear Claw nodded: "As one wraps the broken parts of a rifle stock with wet rawhide to be tightened by Sun."

"I think . . ." Little Coyote caught himself trying to grasp the end of thoughts he had not spoken before. ". . . perhaps the Flatheads, our children especially, could be the iron rim which holds the strong parts together. We must talk about this more, but now let us talk about the buffalo hunt!"

Some blamed the tragedy on bad spirits. Others laid it at the feet of Dog That Sits, who had not gone on the 1838 buffalo hunt. After hawking charms and cures for all ailments in the southern end of the Bitter Root Valley before the people departed, he returned to the northern end, where he usually chose to live. By now there should be many goods for him there, earned by his two women the scornful people openly called *nlkalkscúl*— prostitutes. Their sorry lodge was a stopping point for amorous wanderers from here and there; also, worn-down, white trappers inhabiting miserable hovels and eking fish from the river and few small furs from the land.

Dog That Sits planned to bring his women's earnings to trade for buffalo meat at the south encampment, where the hunters soon would return. Having come back to the valley's north end to gather trade items for another trip south, Dog That Sits discovered that smallpox had struck. Scattered remnants of his women and two younger braves he had left with them lay decaying in Sun's light. No one remained alive. Their goods were untouched. Stunned at what he had found, Dog That Sits nevertheless collected usable goods from the dwellings of the dead; they had no one on the hunt who might protest. Goods in hand, he had gone again to the south camp.

All this information came first to Pipe and Broken Hoof, the far-forward scouts for the returning hunters. Informants were the oldest survivors among fifteen children who came running from a hastily constructed, poorly supplied camp in a willow grove on the outskirts of the south encampment. "All are dead!" they shouted to an almost-unbelieving Pipe and Broken Hoof. Stiffly moving Little Yellow Bird and Running Buffalo Bull had forced Dog That Sits from this south encampment at rifle point when they heard him telling the people what had occurred at the north encampment.

Too late! Too late! Even as Little Coyote's parents had set up the willow camp and had started taking children there, the disease had struck with an awfulness the children scarcely could describe. They insisted that, "No one lives here or at the north camp. Dog That Sits lies among his goods by the river. The dogs feed on him and others."

Pipe and Broken Hoof scarcely could restrain themselves from hurrying north. They cautioned the children to remain where they were, then hurried to intercept Tjolzhitsay and the returning cavalcade. The head chief rode toward them after reading their signs they would talk with him alone.

"All are dead at the north camp," they reported. "We did not . . . take . . . our pregnant wives . . . and our children on this hunt. They remained at our north camp." Already the two mourning warriors had put on their black paint. "If we two could but die," Broken Hoof said. Pipe sat silently, motionless on his horse.

"Broken Tooth! The hunt is over! You have led it well!" Tjolzhitsay shouted above the growing tumult of the approaching cavalcade. "Stop the people! The guards are to let no one leave! I summon the sub-chiefs to help me!"

Though summarily divested of his authority, Broken Tooth immediately rode toward Tjolzhitsay, who had begun quirting his stallion to move back and forth across the broken front of the leading warriors and their families. Just as savagely, Broken Tooth and others soon were racing their horses dangerously close to the crowding near-rabble of people who could see no enemies. Now the people remained there, mounted and unmounted, eying this head chief who had fired his rifle into the air and demanded their attention.

The chief reloaded his rifle, then stood upright in the stirrups of his Spanish saddle. The northerly breeze brought the unmistakable, sickly-sweet odor of decaying human flesh. Tjolzhitsay asked Broken Tooth to shoot a cringing, fat dog emerging from the encampment to greet the throng.

"Shoot all dogs that approach! Hold onto your own!" the chief shouted. Then he said, "One warrior will enter the encampment. What he learns, he will shout to you from the small hillock back from the river. Perhaps there are yet some who can be helped. Let no one follow me!" Tjolzhitsay looked fondly at

504

his people; then, while the chief was handing his rifle to Little Bear Claw, Little Coyote saw Pipe and Broken Hoof suddenly divest their horses of all gear, save for a pistol and small leather bag. The two raced into the death camp. Flocks of large birds rose to mark their movements there.

Sun scarcely seemed to move at all toward the peaks as this part of the Flathead people and some of their allies from the more northerly regions, even beyond the Lake of the Flatheads, waited. Then a pistol shot, and two more. A wounded, emaciated Appaloosa began running crazily from the camp, trailing a tethering rope. Broken Tooth raced toward it. Another shot.

A great cry went up as Sun painted the eastern peaks blood-red, thinning out to pale pink as Pipe and Broken Hoof rode their horses to the hillock. The warriors tried once, twice, thrice to call out. At last they put their black faces in their hands and kept them there for a few moments. Then Broken Hoof, with the louder voice, called out. Distance necessitated short messages. Grief shortened them further.

"All are dead! From smallpox! Do not enter! Move away! We have dragged them into the lodges!"

Now a heavy smoke began rising behind the two warriors. They had fired the encampment.

"When Little Yellow Bird helped us carry food to the lodges, she said no one else was to come here," one of the dirt-streaked children said. "She returned to help Running Buffalo Bull and others who yet were not sick." As the people listened, Little Bear Claw and Little Coyote rode a bit closer to Broken Hoof and Pipe, minding that the wind was blowing away from the burning camp. The four shouted back and forth until the outpouring of grief from the stunned Flatheads and their remaining allies from north beyond the valley drowned out individual voices.

Two watchers remained near the hillock above the death encampment. They would report to the large, temporary camp established southward at the Lake of the White Moose. The leading sub-chief from the north end of the valley told the council he had sent two warriors to approach, but not enter, that death camp. They, too, would report to the council, now including sub-chiefs from far north.

"The people are restive," they reported. "They want to return somewhat closer to their homes."

There was much to do. All in council agreed there was good fortune that their problems did not include lack of buffalo meat. The Shoshonis and Nez Percé were well-laden when they had broken off from the hunting party near where Shining Shirt sleeps.

"The dead will not eat," a grim Tjolzhitsay responded when the watchers reported that Pipe and Broken Hoof no longer climbed the hillock. The two warriors sent to the north camp agreed that Dog That Sits had reported correctly; they had found no one alive, even at the widely separated trappers' hovels.

Chalax, elderly seer from the north camp, sat on the council, too. He spoke: "Less than two days west from where the Ootlashoots blends its waters with the Inmissouletka, two creeks also meet. As you know, nearby there is a great grass valley and grove of trees for horses. We have used it for encampments at times because it is not too far from the rest of our people. There are many deer, and there is much wood for the fires. And fish. The older among us remember the stone forts built against our enemies. Perhaps some of us should go there until the Good Spirit, with Mother Earth and Sun, once more drives away the smallpox, as in the past."

Changing weather hastened discussion of Chalax's plan. There were fewer women now, so some would accompany the people to help set up a winter encampment near the two creeks and big grassy prairie. Then they would return to the Lake of the White Moose. The children who had survived the smallpox would go to the new camp.

Cold northerly winds began disrobing the trees, which seemingly raised despairing limbs against ever-darkening skies. The skies began weeping, too—throughout the Bitter Root Valley and beyond.

506

L ittle Coyote lowered his arms as Sun began clearing the rim of the eastern mountain. A doe and twin fawns raised their heads to the light, as though continuing the prayers he had begun while stars in the graying sky were winking out like sparks in the scattered ashes of a dying fire. The smallest of breezes gently pushed ghostly steam figures from the hot springs toward the nearby trees.

Little had changed at the springs since that 1805 winter of *sqléw*, the beaver—or, for that matter, in the almost five years since he had retreated here after the 1838 devastating losses of his family to smallpox and the cruel battle near the two creeks.

Travelers to the hot springs had worn the main trail more deeply and scooped out larger pools in the warm water. Fire had burned over the cliff-walled meadow where he had corralled his horses. Many small dams were in various stages of disrepair or gone completely, like the beaver, though there were fish aplenty. Deer abounded at the lower elevations, mountain sheep and goats at the higher.

The seer stood there, facing yet another long day, sorrow scarcely diminished for Running Buffalo Bull, Little Yellow Bird, Lance and his Gros Ventre wife, Swan, and what would have been his grandson—carefully, proudly nurtured in Swan's body until torn out by the cruel knives of the Blackfeet. And the even more frightful mutilation of Antelope! Even now his mind dwelt so fully on this loss that his senses responded slowly to the awakening world about him, including the two horsemen cautiously emerging from the trees as though steam wraiths had taken on flesh. He had watched other people do much the same over the five years; mostly, he had ignored them, content that his lodge was well-hidden and he left few signs to follow. But the appearance of these two began evoking old memories that intruded on grief, then were sharpened into a growing certainty through the intuitive powers only the Good Spirit who had endowed them could fully comprehend. So the grieving mind focused on the horses as the pair ventured farther into the clearing, as distant as possible from any cover that could conceal an enemy. No other horses followed. Yes! The larger man, as in the distant spring of 1806, was Little Bear Claw! This time, too, his friend looked quickly upward toward the source of the sharp, closely spaced coyote yelps.

Soon bright-eyed, twelve-year-old Little Grizzly Bear Claw was grinning delightedly while his father and Little Coyote silently embraced as though each was afraid a single word would release an emotional torrent not even the stoutest warrior could control.

"My father is head chief!" The youth broke the silence with this fact uppermost in his mind as he quickly stripped off his buckskins and jumped into the largest warm pool to wash away the grime of hard, fast traveling. The two warriors stepped back to escape the splashing water. Even had they wished, they could not avoid talking of the past any more than they could have stopped the disturbed waters from surging over the pool's rim and hurrying downward in the small channel to the great river.

"Yes," Little Bear Claw began modestly, "so I must help shape the many changes that beset our people. I have missed you for so many reasons. I must leave here in two days. Most of our people have gone on the summer hunt near Three Forks. The Black Robe, Father Gregory Mengarini, remains there with the older people and children." The chief smiled. "While he is a very wise man in matters other than about the Good Spirit, he is not a warrior."

The first hurried communications over, the seer looked at the youth, lying now on the warm earth, naked, dozing, seemingly burdened with no cares, except to fill his belly when he would awaken. Possibly one day he would be bearing burdens that would outweigh all both warriors till now and in the future would carry. Drawing on his own experiences and much contemplation about what lay ahead, Little Coyote could have told this to the youth even before Little Bear Claw said, "Enough about my chieftainship. My son, Little Grizzly Bear Claw, sought and found his vision quest atop the great peak where you found your own, and which the great Shining Shirt interpreted. We ask you to interpret that of my son."

Little Coyote nodded agreeably. First, though, he wished to unfold the story leading to his isolation, for thus, with Little Bear Claw's young son listening, it would be in the stories of the people. The seer would get it out of the way and avoid much questioning so he could devote full attention to his friends during the short time they would be here.

Already there was a feeling of foreboding in his spirit, a sense he would like to avoid interpreting the vision, but he must do so. At that quiet acquiescence, his spirit for the moment, above all else, seemed once again to be with that of old Shield Maker, who had died in the battle near the grass valley and the two creeks. Standing near the grass valley and the two creeks in a heavy rain with the dead all about him, an anguished and stunned Little Coyote had heard Shield Maker repeat, word for word, what Lance long ago had told his father and the old man after his return from his vision quest. While Little Coyote was hearing Shield Maker's voice, the old man's body lay scalped and sprawled among others, a deep lance wound in the chest.

Little Coyote signed he would talk. Little Bear Claw tossed a pebble on his son's back to get his attention. Little Grizzly Bear Claw sat up as the two warriors sat down.

"I will tell here what occurred after our sorrowing people set out from the Lake of the White Moose," Little Coyote said.

"I will tell all this, then we will move up this mountain and leave these old events here. I will interpret your vision quest so we can move into the future as brave and warriors, not old men dreaming of the past, which provides us lessons for the future."

"My beloved Antelope, her face yet carrying the grief of loss of family and friends, came to me during the eating stop near where the noisy waters of the Ootlashoots heavied up before entering the Inmissouletka.

"With the help of a few kin, Swan and Lance, the fifteen yet-apprehensive children had been walking near the end of the pack train.

"Antelope told me she had the children clean their bodies with sand and water. She discovered that four were heavily covered with marks that might be the beginnings of the smallpox.

"Chalax and I dismounted to examine these children. We quickly agreed that they had slept too long among some of the dogs Little Yellow Bird had tied near the lodges to keep them away from the dead. The children's marks were but the bites of fleas.

"Yet, we could take no chances. Another warrior, his mate and I would remain here for a short time among the children. All other people would accompany the pack train that already was beginning to string out westerly in two watchful columns.

"I tightly held Antelope and told her I wanted us to be in our own lodge. Soon. Alone. Away from all cares for a time.

"'Soon. It will be soon,' she responded, embracing me so tightly I knew I would remember this forever. I told her that we two should go to the place of the hot springs, and reminded her that the old lodge was there. We could travel fast after we had helped the rest of our people settle.

"As Lance prepared to hoist plump Swan onto her horse, my mood lightened. I told Swan I would have to embrace a part of her at a time. I tapped her belly and told her she should bear a son. Yet, perhaps there were two girl swans there, which would double our joy. She turned away to hide her tears.

"Lance said he would see us at the place of the grass valley, then raced away to take his place as left-front scout, where he would be the first to die. But I am racing ahead of my story."

Little Coyote paused and looked at the changing patterns of the hot steam.

"Chalax told me that Lance's killer loosed a silent arrow into him as he approached belly-high grass near the new encampment site.

"Chalax had been the last to leave the rest stop at the confluence of the Ootlashoots and Inmissouletka. He would be rear scout. He dismounted from his horse as I watched my son disappear after circling a small grove of trees from a safe distance.

"'I do not like this,' Chalax said. 'The spirit within me says, *Blackfeet, watch for Blackfeet. Perhaps a large number of them have come this way to escape the smallpox, also knowing there is food and forage near the two creeks. Yet, there are our forts. We cannot be careful enough.*' A tight smile flitted across his strong features. 'Enemies everywhere,' he said. 'I choose Blackfeet rather than the smallpox.' He signed *farewell* and almost jumped atop his horse. As he left he said, 'Guard the flea-bitten children well!'

"He would return in three days, worn, hurt and bloody, with a pitifully small group, most hurting like himself, a few being pulled on travois, perhaps strong enough to make it back to the Lake of the White Moose.

"He said to me, 'We would not be here had the Blackfeet not become content with the others' scalps, horses and weapons— and meat. The Flatheads and their allies fought from the forts. The Blackfeet also appeared as though they wanted to avoid losing more of their own warriors. We placed many loaded rifles on two of the travois.'

"Chalax pointed briefly, whereupon they all agreed that the mate of the warrior who had remained with me should hasten to the Lake of the White Moose for help. There was some gladness that the children who had remained behind because of what truly were flea bites had escaped the Blackfeet.

"I remained with the survivors until help arrived. Declining the offer by Chalax to accompany me to the battle site, I tied his horses, save one, near those who were to be the new owners and that night quietly left the small encampment to find my loved ones. The grass valley and the two creeks, where Antelope and Lance now rest, is sacred ground to me forever."

Seer, chief and son silently watched the steam wraiths forming, changing form, disappearing.

"Now, Little Grizzly Bear Claw," the seer said, "while you are here I will tell you my son Lance's vision of long ago. Remember it well, because yours, I know already, becomes a part of his.

"My son, Lance, spoke thus: 'In my vision I saw many warriors fighting, and sometimes I fought too—and well. I remember well the final battle. I was helped with food and water and weapons by a woman I dimly perceived as Antelope, my mother. Hand in hand we left that battle in peace, followed at a great distance by an old man who leaned over so far from his heavy load on his back that I could not see his face. Then a lightning bolt struck the ground between us and the old man. When I again could see, he was gone. My mother and I saw down to eat with our people amid much rejoicing that we had returned.'"

Little Coyote paused, his son's words rekindling deep grief. Then he tapped himself on his chest. "This I know. My family is reunited with our people who have gone to the sand hills before us. Throughout my long stay here I have wondered how long I must bear these burdens before I join them there."

Little Bear Claw's face saddened. He nodded understandingly. "I know your grief. Willow Woman is dead, too. From a fast-growing sickness. I have a new wife, Agnes. You do not know her." The chief signed he would not talk about this now.

With much difficulty as he took this new arrow of grief, the seer shook his head as though to clear it of the past and come more fully to the present, to adhere to his determination to listen to his friends. He pointed up the mountainside. "Come. There is food in my lodge."

As Little Bear Claw took a quick bath in a pool, his son leaped on his horse and disappeared into the trees. He soon appeared again leading two other horses. Little Coyote accepted one and led the group almost directly upward until they reached the higher, tree-encircled clearing where, as a youth, Little Coyote had erected his lodge. They continued upward until they encountered a somewhat level game trail. They followed that for a time, then again moved upward through the trees, repeating this process until Little Coyote pointed to his mother's old lodge he carefully had cached after the Clark and Lewis party had left the hot springs.

"No guns, no horses?" Little Grizzly Bear Claw looked about wonderingly as he accepted the food. Inside the sparsely furnished shelter were two bows, arrows, an ancient lance and a shield, and another shield, somewhat oval-shaped, with a lightning bolt painted on one side.

"No horses; too easy to track," Little Coyote replied. "I gave my remaining one to a blind, old warrior and his woman who came to the springs one day after I returned from the Shoshonis, where I told Broken Pipe of our losses."

Little Bear Claw eyed Lance's shield, which Little Coyote had found amid the carnage near the two creeks. As the chief leaned forward to lift another piece of smoked trout from the bark platter, a crucifix that was hanging from his neck at the pool fell outside his shirt and swung back and forth. As he straightened to eat, he dropped the symbol inside his shirt. "Broken Pipe and his mate are dead. The warrior Pony Whip brought this word to my stepson Fast Runner and Antelope's sister, Warm Breeze, while on a horse-trading trip to the Shoshonis two summers ago. Those two are well. They have a son and a daughter." When Little Coyote made no comment, the trio ate silently, the seer noting with pleasure the discipline of Little Grizzly Bear Claw. He sat somewhat apart, only his eyes and jaws moving as he watched these two old friends.

Twice, Little Grizzly Bear Claw's eyes centered on Lance's shield.

"It is yours. Take it," Little Coyote said. He rejoiced as the youth gravely walked over to the shield, lifted it and, his eyes sparkling with delight now, promised, "I will bear it with much honor." Instead of rushing outside the lodge to examine the gift more closely, he carried it to where he had been sitting and listening.

At length the youth stirred. Clearly, he wished that he, instead of his father, could answer Little Coyote's question: "How could you know you would find me here?"

"My son has revealed to me only the last part of his vision," Little Bear Claw said. "An old man told him, 'Now seek Little Yellow Bird's lodge. The voice of Shining Shirt will speak further through Little Coyote.' Remember, I, too, knew of this old lodge." He reached backward and struck the smoke-blackened hide, then held up his hand. "But I ask that we not yet deal with my son's vision. Important events have occurred in the lives of all our people during your absence. Perhaps you should learn of them first because they might have much bearing on your inter-pretations.

"The Black Robes," Little Bear Claw continued, "now live among us and tell us the way to the Good Spirit. Most families were touched by the smallpox and the defeat near the two creeks. We had lost much meat and we had to risk our smaller numbers by sending a hunting party back to the buffalo grounds. Two of our adopted Iroquois brothers, Left Hand Peter and Little Ignace, led us in much prayer that these endeavors would be successful. Our hunters returned quickly, laden with much meat. They had kept close watch, but the Blackfeet were gone. They saw not one enemy, whereupon Left Hand Peter and Little Ignace, praising the Good Spirit, set out at once for St. Louis to again seek the Black Robes."

Little Bear Claw's face widened into the familiar grin. "Repeatedly, the Good Spirit helped us thereafter. Our two adopted brothers were able to travel in safety with fur-traders going down the river to St. Louis. They saw more great stores of buffalo robes coming down the river." He frowned. "Some of our warriors take more wives, like Dog That Sits, to prepare the robes. The Black Robes do not like this. But enough! While our brothers passed through the Iowa country, they heard a Black Robe named DeSmet was there. They sought him out. He was tending an abandoned, dying warrior. He gave them a written message to give to the Bishop Rosati at St. Louis. This Rosati promised he would send a Black Robe in the spring. Rosati spoke truth. Almost one-thousand-six-hundred of our people and Pend d'Oreilles went to Pierre's Hole to await the arrival of the Black Robe—DeSmet!

"DeSmet climbed mountains like the sheep and goats, kept walking when we were tired, cared for the sick and taught us prayers. He traveled with us to Three Forks, performed the ceremony of the mass as we had watched the priest do for the Métis, and baptized three-hundred-fifty of us. Among them was the head chief of the Pend d'Oreilles. My Christian name now is Victor, my son's Charlo, though white man puts a 't' at the end of his name, which, as you know, we pronounce as 'Mitto' in our tongue. Father DeSmet returned, then, to St. Louis and brought back eleven other people, including two Canadians who drove the three carts and the wagon that carried their possessions. That DeSmet, he is a man, as you shall see when we return to our valley."

Little Coyote's first impulse was to respond that they, not he, would be returning. Instead, changing thought to action, he stood as though to stretch his legs and body. The other two stood, then the three moved outside. From atop a crumbling outcropping they silently watched for a while the white steam emerging from the hot pools far below: Narrowing, widening, slowing, hurrying in ever-changing patterns, sometimes almost disappearing in a momentary quick breeze—but always returning.

Little Bear Claw's ". . . as you shall see when we return to our valley" lingered in the medicine man's mind as he again sat. He motioned for Little Grizzly Bear Claw to do the same.

"Tell me of your vision."

As Sun moved past its apex and tree shadows began lengthening eastward across the meadows, the youth and the seer talked. The chief of the Flatheads quietly listened as his son spoke: "As you know, Little Coyote, it is in the stories of our people that the great peak to which Shining Shirt and you went is a sacred place. I sought, and found, my vision there even as our people helped Father DeSmet and the others build a mission almost in its shadow. For three days I remained atop the peak. The few white clouds did not cover the face of Sun that first day, and I could see afar in all directions."

The youth paused, thoughtfully wrinkled his face, then sniffed. He stood and moved to where the sunlight was warmest. "I became hungry. I saw only a crow circling above some of the lesser peaks about me. Hungrier yet on the second day after a cold night, I saw that other crows had joined the first. Many white clouds began filling the sky, their shadows darkening our valley as they crossed Sun's face. Growing lonely, I leaned against a great rock and out of the wind. Again the night was cold. I awoke to find the clouds were covering the peak so heavily I scarcely could see. Cold and hungry I stood, walked about, then sat. I could see nothing. I heard only my horse nicker where I had tethered him, whereupon the gray world brightened somewhat. Soon I could see small patches of sunlight on the valley far below. They appeared at the south end first. Then, almost as if stepping, these patches began opening in an ever-northward movement, one patch closing up in the fog as the next opened. Finally, far in the distance to the north, the largest bright patch appeared and I could see the great white peaks beyond the Lake of the Flatheads. Then cold rains commenced and I could see only the great patch of sunlight to the north. Darkness fell and yet I sat, cold, hungry, miserable, feeling totally alone. In fitful sleep I saw small groups of our people gathering and facing northward. My father stood before them, striving to hold them back. They began moving toward the patch of sunlight. The crows were accompanying them. I could not see my father. Now I strove to halt the people, but I could not. 'Stay!' I shouted. 'Stay! Sun will return!' Only a few listened as the others trekked northward, though the light had lessened there, too. 'Stay!' I again shouted, but no one heard.

"I awoke from my poor sleep. The crows were gone. I thought of my father's lodge—warm with love and furs and food.

I wanted to come down the mountain then, but I knew I must stay. When I again half-slept, I dreamed I now was returning to my father's lodge. I could see it during times of light and dark. I tried to reach it, but always I lost it in the darkness. At length I saw a bright light approaching me. An ancient man carrying a medicine staff and accompanied by a coyote pup looked at me, his eyes reflecting in the light from his shirt, which seemed afire. He reached outward with his staff, as though to give it to me. I held out my hand. Now he removed from around his neck a metal cross and handed it to me. Such a heavy cross. I scarce could lift it. Alas, it fell from my hand and buried itself in the earth. Some Black Robes appeared, each with a smaller cross hanging from his neck. They helped me dig up the cross and lift it, for it had grown to great size. Many of our people now came and helped me carry it, though some tired quickly and left others to bear the burden. I know we groped our way northward through the clouds to a new patch of light. At times people of many tribes showed in the lightning bolts which set the sky afire. As we moved away from the old man with the shining shirt and the coyote pup, he shouted a last message: 'Now seek Little Yellow Bird's lodge. The voice of Shining Shirt will speak further through Little Coyote.' They disappeared then, the old man and the coyote, and my vision ended as we continued to move north."

Little Grizzly Bear Claw looked expectantly at Little Coyote. Little Coyote again stood, then looked at the youth's father.

"This Father DeSmet. The other Black Robes. Did they say why they came?"

"Father DeSmet told my father they wished only to help us save our souls."

The chief stood: "When I ponder his words and those our Iroquois, Nez Percé and other brothers have told us for many years, I, as do they, believe."

As he had begun the day with long prayer, Little Coyote ended it—long after Little Bear Claw and his son gratefully had stretched out on the lodge furs to scarcely move as they slept away their tiredness. The seer's prayers began only after he had sat on the outcropping and, under the light of the waning moon, battled himself. One voice, strengthened by an almost-five-year-old resolution, demanded: *"Stay here!"* The other voice, conceived during his own vision quest so long ago and strengthened by Shining Shirt's words, said: *"Return to your people. Remember the great resolve you formed during that long winter of the sqléw. You told Little Bear Claw before the two of you left this place of the hot springs that perhaps you were destined to tell the people how to use the marvels of the white man wisely to shape the change you foresaw as more white men arrived."*

The first voice countered: *"You have done your share. Let the Black Robes take over."*

"But they are white men, too," the second voice persisted. *"Do you truly believe that the Good Spirit created only white men to show the red men His ways and only after the white men found the red men? Before the scourge of the smallpox, you promised Little Bear Claw you would help his son prepare to deal with life. Did not Little Bear Claw keep his word to do this for Lance? You have not used your voice for the people for almost five years. Is the value of Little Coyote's word becoming nothing?*

"You loved only your own family among the people? Shining Shirt lost his beloved wife, but returned to help his people. You, Little Coyote, must do the same, as you might know when you have interpreted the vision of Little Grizzly Bear Claw. Father and son need the help of the Good Spirit and of you, Little Coyote."

The seer prayed in the moonlight until his groan of submission brought both father and son from the lodge, their weapons ready to deal with wild animal or foe. They saw only the seer, seated on the outcropping above the moonlit world below. His arms clasped his knees, on which he had leaned his head as though in great pain. He began speaking—slowly, with long pauses between his mournful utterances, as though he was repeating only what someone else was telling him.

"You, Little Bear Claw, now known among the growing number of white men as Victor. You, Little Grizzly Bear Claw, known as Charlot, have, with the support of the Good Spirit, accepted white man's religion. I tell you now the wisdom of Shining Shirt and what I believe the Good Spirit directs my tongue to say: Never fight white man. Like the white clouds that surrounded the great peak and filled the valley, the white man will be everywhere. He will abuse you; he will, in Little Bear Claw's lifetime, try to drive you from the valley. In Little Grizzly Bear Claw's lifetime all will be forced northward from the valley. As the sky fills with lightning bolts and thunder during the great storms of summer, there will be greater battles than ever before among Indians and Indians and Indians and the whites.

"But the Flatheads will survive. The Black Robes, like the crows, which in your vision flew above the people, will help you with things of this world and the next. They have no great magic, as many of our people had hoped, to instantly change all bad things to good. Even so, most of our people will heed them; others, disappointed, will not. Yes, Little Grizzly Bear Claw, like the Christ the Black Robes tell about, you will carry a great cross—whether or not you continue to listen to the Black Robes. Stay on the side of the Good Spirit. I can tell you that within somewhat more than the years between our people meeting Clark and Lewis and being forced to leave our valley, your fortunes will equal, perhaps surpass, those of white man who forced you out. But hold to the Good Spirit."

Now the seer raised his head from his knees; Little Grizzly Bear Claw stepped back, recoiling from an unexpected mask of grief on Little Coyote's face.

"I can say now that if you reject the Black Robes, your lives will be harder," the seer said. "Do not use weapons against the white men. Use your mind, yes! I will help." He straightened as though a great weight had been lifted from his back.

"Now I, too, will sleep."

The warmth in the lodge awakened Little Coyote; he had slept late into the morning. For the first time since he had arrived here he felt greatly refreshed, as though much of his mind's burden of personal grief had burned away like pervasive morning mist. The odor of broiling meat filtered into the lodge with the quiet voices of father and son. Little Coyote stepped outside. Atop a large rock was the head of a year-old mountain sheep lamb. Leaning against the rock was Lance's shield. Painted in fresh lamb's blood on the blank half opposite the lightning flash was a large cross, slowly turning black in the warm sun.

Little Bear Claw halted his horse atop a high hill west of the Ootlashoots River. He dismounted and waited while Little Coyote and Little Grizzly Bear Claw worked their horses upward through the heavy tangle of willow. They, too, were glad to rest the horses and themselves. Their return from the hot springs had been rapid, shortened even more by the youth's enthusiastic descriptions of the Mission and activities there. The seer had begun wondering if the Mission surpassed in magnificence the white settlements he had seen or heard described: Fort Union, Fort Nez Percés, McLoughlin's great Fort Vancouver. Perhaps even St. Louis, itself, though the medicine man doubted that.

The chief pointed across the river. "That is St. Mary's Mission. The Jesuit fathers also have given this name to the valley, the great peak and the river, partly because of visions our people and others have had about Mary, the mother of Jesus."

Little Coyote would ponder that second sentence later, as well as the reverence with which this strong warrior uttered it. For now, the most compelling fact was that he was home.

On a flat part of the valley floor almost centered among a few lodges were some small log huts and one larger structure, the latter surmounted by a cross. Little Coyote exulted at the sight of a few figures busily moving about, some evidently working on the soil and others carrying poles toward a low palisade surrounding the buildings. Sounds of pounding and children's cries rose faintly above the quiet murmur of the river below the trio. They forded the now-shallow stream near a slight bend and approached the west end of a large area surrounded by a wooden fence.

"Like the Mandans, we grow food here," Little Bear Claw explained. "Already, we have eaten much of it. The Black Robes say there will come a day, soon they think, when the buffalo will be gone." He rose in his stirrups. "Brother Claessens!" he shouted. He waved to a slightly built, white man clad in tattered, black clothing, shiny as old buckskins. Seemingly with some difficulty walking, the man was leading a horse pulling a travois toward other workers in the garden. A large box was secured across the two poles.

"Victor! Charlot!" The man stopped the horse and carefully stepped across the intervening rows, a broad smile lighting his face. The trio vaulted the fence rails, whereupon the man hugged father and son. Then, bright eyes sparkling, he turned toward Little Coyote.

"Brother Claessens is one of those who accompanied Father DeSmet here," Little Bear Claw said.

Little Coyote gravely shook the work-worn hand and wanted to communicate with the man, but a small crowd of older men and women, some weeding, others harvesting the vegetables, had recognized Victor's Appaloosa.

"*Slem-cry-cre*! Little Bear Claw! Victor!" The chief hastened to an untilled portion of the field lest they trample the crop.

Little Coyote shared in the embraces of old friends there and elsewhere as all joined a constantly growing procession while leading the trio toward the church.

Brother Claessens, after vigorously blowing his nose, began loading part of the harvest from among the carrots, beans, corn, peas, turnips, potatoes and other domesticated varieties of vegetables.

Though very tired, Little Coyote looked about the lodge some older women at St. Mary's had erected for him well away from the others, as he had asked. Their welcoming greetings had been as warm as the lodge fire's bright flames. The flames revealed his story skin, Shining Shirt's medicine staff and pipe, and his own medicine box, which he had left with now-dead Willow Woman before hurrying to the grass valley. With these articles and the other simple equipment he had brought from the hot springs, he was content. Certainly he was comfortable as the Black Robes in their mean structures and would be more so in the cold of *siistc*, though winter was yet far off, this being . . . yes, only the middle part of *slá'ko*, the seventh moon of Serviceberries. Now he felt, most of all, a need to join the buffalo hunt, to help procure food, true, but in the chase solidly integrating himself once more in so many ways among his people. He was glad he had returned.

Brief introductions to the other white men had been interspersed this long day amid the hurried look at the Mission, the joyous welcome, the many questions asked and answered, the expressions of joy—and sorrow. Two other Jesuit brothers, like Claessens, had waved and called down a friendly "*a*," from a ridge pole they had just put in place on yet another hut. One was Charles Huet, a few years older than Claessens and called a "blacksmith," Little Bear Claw explained. The chief said the other was Joseph Specht, "as clever with tools as was Shield Maker. Brothers are holy men, too," Little Bear Claw continued as they walked on, "but they do not hold the mass, as do the priests." The seer had seen white laborers. They were cutting down and limbing trees, then dragging them with horses to the building site.

While his fire in the newly erected lodge waned, the seer focused his thoughts on the Black Robe Mengarini, whom they had found on the sunny side of one of the huts. He, too, was clad in the worn, shiny clothing and was busily drying many vegetable seeds.

The priest had straightened from his task and approached the two Flatheads. The seer's first impression was that, had this man been of darker skin, surely he would have resembled the sub-chief, Big Eagle, when he was perhaps thirty years old. There was an instant outward impression of leadership here—in bearing, piercing eyes, generous nose and mouth. Yet, there was a . . . an inner spirit, the seer sensed, masterfully curbed so that outward strength and inward genuine love shone forth, much as the warrior had detected early and found re-enforced later in Marcus Whitman. There was one instant and obvious difference: This Black Robe had both greeted and haltingly, but correctly, begun speaking in their own language. When Little Coyote had replied in correct English, the priest had raised his face skyward and voiced a very audible "*Laus Deo!*"

"I praise God because I wish to learn and write down the stories of your people, how you have lived and now live," the priest had explained. "This I have found hard to do, because few seem to care about this, and, of course, I have not been diligent enough to learn to speak your language better and more quickly."

Before the medicine man returned to his lodge, he promised the priest he would help him prepare "a Salish dictionary."

"If you will wait." Father Mengarini had disappeared into the hut and quickly returned. He held a small, flat, buckskin bag. "I understand you are keeping a story skin and hope one day to have a white man's book about your people. I believe that you will want this; open it when you have rested in your lodge after greeting all your friends."

Little Coyote stirred the embers of his lodge fire. The pieces of charcoal glowed separately now, some brightly, some scarcely at all, with no merging of their light. His familiar action, performed alone for so long at the hot springs, helped to uncover the thoughts that had lain almost dormant since Little Bear Claw and his son had found him. At the retreat there had been few intrusions on his thoughts, which became strongest when the body he had tired sought rest. Thoughts about Antelope, Lance, his father and mother, his people, but always circling back to Antelope. Here in the valley there were many thoughts, all seemingly emerging at once, like the sparks when much wood remains on the fire. How should he assess the changes already wrought and yet to come at the Mission? He had little doubt they would soon be of the magnitude Little Grizzly Bear Claw, with his as-yet-limited experience, already felt them to be. How interesting that the younger people, with little experience, could more readily accept rapid change. How dangerous if they were unwilling to draw on the wisdom gained from the past and be guided by it. He must think more on this! Should I join the buffalo hunters at the killing grounds? When? When I meet the priests DeSmet and Point, will I care as much for them as I like Father Mengarini?

Remembering the buckskin packet the priest had handed him, the seer placed a few small sticks on the fire. The packet held a three-page letter, very carefully printed. The seer looked at the bottom of the last page. Father Mengarini had written it:

Little Coyote, I hope one day to know as friend:

Chief Victor, his son Charlot, so many others have told me so much about you in the short time I have been here. I have learned you are a keeper of the history of your people. I do not know when you will return to the Bitter Root Valley. Victor told me he thinks he knows where you have been for well past three years now. I do not know when I might be sent elsewhere. For this reason I wish to tell you about the death of a good woman, Charlot's mother, your dear friend Victor's first wife—Willow Woman. Perhaps I am writing this in too fancy words. The hour is late. The stubby candle is flickering.

Willow Woman, baptized Helena, after St. Helena, who found the true cross, came to our cabin this evening, again bearing warm food. Surprisingly thinner, seemingly almost breathless from her walk, she no longer radiated her old wit and bantering manner I am certain you know so well. Heavily, she sat down and soon was breathing more easily. During my years as a priest I have seen and heard ill people shortly before their death speak with great eloquence and strength. So it was with Helena. She smiled once and began talking as I started to eat.

"Perhaps Father Ravalli has told you I have what he calls a fast-growing cancer. He says I will get weaker, get thinner and die, very likely not without pain, although Father said he can help that."

The candlelight intermittently cast and removed shadows on her kindly, sagging face.

"Like most of us, I do not fear death. I am grateful for many things—my new faith and my family, especially."

She looked at me as I silently continued to eat.

"And friends. I would speak to you about my family. I have few worries about my son, Fast Runner, and my daughter by Eagle Claw. My thoughts are of Victor and Charlot. I thank God they have such a good friend in Little Coyote. I know that as strong a bond as i-sts-sókoi *has existed between Victor and Little Coyote since their youth. Some of us, such as I, are but small shadows that appear with morning Sun, grow, diminish, then fade, forgotten, into the blackness of night. You have told me, Father Mengarini, others are gifted by God to take more solid form and influence the destiny of others. Yet, all of us are loved equally by God. There is much I do not know, but of this I am certain: Such persons of destiny must be strong, and they need the strength of others. My husband and our son face far greater problems than any chief farther back than even Tjolzhitsay."*

She paused, breathed deeply, winced and placed a hand upon her chest.

526

"I am caught up too much in my own talking, but I wish to continue because I have given these matters much thought. Perhaps Victor and Charlot face problems even greater than did the chiefs, their names forgotten, in our stories, who brought our diminished people here when driven from the buffalo grounds. Many of Father DeSmet's reasons for seeking peace with the Blackfeet are the same for which we fashioned our short-lived truce before the Black Robes appeared here. But Father DeSmet gives another great reason: 'You must prepare yourselves for the disappearance of the almost uncountable buffalo, and the appearance of almost uncountable white men!'"

Helena sadly shook her head.

"This seems unbelievable. Totally unbelievable, but I accept its truth with faith, as I have the teachings of the Black Robes we sought for so long."

Again the warrior woman paused, looking long into my eyes. I can assure you, long before this I had ceased eating to better concentrate on this dear woman's words.

"I think that as God has created men of destiny, he has given to a few the power to see far ahead. I believe that Little Coyote, more than Father DeSmet and in a different way, is such a one. Father Ravalli has said that perhaps I am right. I can see but a short distance with the same certainty, and in matters that concern only myself. My body feels and my spirit knows I will be dead before Little Coyote returns. I have prayed that he would return before my death. Tell me, Father Mengarini, that you will tell Little Coyote I hope he will help guide them, and I will sing a happy song as I die."

Her eyes spoke the question:

"Will you tell Little Coyote, Father? And, will you encourage Victor to find a good woman soon for his wife?"

I nodded, wanting to say more, wanting to deny the look of death I saw there. She arose heavily, placing her hand on my shoulder for momentary balance. Erect, she strongly gripped my shoulder and, gathering up two of the empty brass pots, stepped outside. The quiet song, like her happy laughter in the past, began almost instantly. It ended when the bell-like calls of the dropped pots summoned me and others to where she had fallen beside a stout willow prayerfully lifting its bare branches to the cold, sparkling sky.

All persons at the Mission, including a few visiting Kutenais, Kalispels and Pend d'Oreilles, attended the funeral mass, and she was buried at the newly cleared far edge of the cemetery. Afterward, Father Ravalli cut down the willow where she had died. Next morning those who went to pray at the grave site walked away exclaiming over the exquisitely carved willow cross, so placed that all could see the figures excised in the smooth bark. One represented St. Helena. She was touching one of the cross arms to the shoulder of a Flathead woman. Later, these excisions should slowly fill in as the willow takes root to flourish even to the day you receive this letter.

I hope you will count me a friend.

Fr. Gregory Mengarini

Society of Jesus

The brightest embers faded. Little Coyote sought his bed, saddened by the contents of the letter, the loss of this good friend.

At length his thoughts once again centered on Antelope until, long after the ashes had turned cold, he finally fell into dream-tossed sleep.

The woman scratched the lodge flap with her knees, shunted it aside with her hips and stepped into the shelter. She set down a pot of food and some new buckskins, then again stepped outside. Little Coyote threw off the light furs and sleepily donned the long leggings and shirt. When she re-entered, she spoke before the seer could do so.

"I am called Agnes now, since my baptism." Her voice was low and there was much dignity there. "Victor asked me to get you the new clothing. I am glad it fits. I did not see you come to the Mission yesterday because I was catching fish from the pools below. Victor only told me: 'If Little Coyote were an equally skinny horse, I would either fatten him up or chop him up for dog food. He looks as though he has not eaten for more than four years.'" Her laugh also was low, but merry. "Yes, the buckskins fit. We are pleased you have returned." She looked directly into the seer's eyes, her kindly face reflecting the sincerity of her words. "Charlot said you have no guns, use no white man's marvels, save the spyglass and medicines. We are grateful you interpreted his vision, but we are fearful of its contents." She crossed herself.

Little Coyote stepped outside, his eyes sweeping the sky, valley and mountains. As he briefly prayed, a few cloud wisps scurried up and behind the great peak. Magpies settled into a nearby cottonwood to gossip, their movements sending more of the heavily dew-drenched leaves fluttering downward like broken-winged butterflies onto the golden-carpeted earth. He breathed deeply of the cool air, then stooped to wash in the nearby seep basin, which had settled during the night. He straightened at the brushing sound of the lodge flap. *This persistent woman*, he thought, then softened. *Of course she fears for her husband, her stepson, our people, as I do.* He washed while she stood there, then she followed him back into the lodge.

"Victor said you foresee much sorrow for him and for

Charlot. We expect that, too, for a chief and his son. But you see more." She would watch him eat.

He chewed for a while, then answered her earlier questions about living the old way: "I have resolved to remain Indian as much as I can for as long as I can. Perhaps I should serve as a reminder of our old ways to help our people carefully choose each new step they take into white man's world, help them hold to the most important old ways, because once they step fully across that line . . ." He stooped and drew a line in the as-yet unpacked soil of the lodge floor. ". . . there will be no turning back. Little Bear Claw and Little Grizzly Bear Claw must make the choices the growing presence of white man demands. I will help them as I can, as I am asked."

The woman's jaw tightened, the friendly smile fading. "Yes, even if we chose to take no steps into white man's world, he would continue to take longer strides into ours, the land, at least. We welcome the Black Robes, many, many of us hoping their closeness to God—and ours—will protect us. I was among the more than two-hundred older people, including Willow Woman, Father DeSmet baptized on St. Francis Xavier's Day during the last twelfth month of Continuous Snow. Our Nez Percé friends came to see this, and at the Christmas time thirty of them received the baptism with one-hundred-thirty more of our people. We had learned our prayers well. My prayers now are that the Black Robes, who seem to have the respect of most white men, even the more dissolute womanizers and drunkards, will sway white man's mind to treat us well. Part of my spirit within me says we should fight all who would harm us, fight them as we do the Blackfeet. But we must survive—and pray!"

She remained silent while he completed his meal, then she picked up the old pot and clothing. "Soon Victor and Charlot will be going to the buffalo grounds. Victor asks if you will go."

"I am grateful for your help. Tell *Little Bear Claw* and *Little Grizzly Bear Claw* I will go." Now her face softened into a smile and her voice was bantering, almost as had been Willow Woman's. "I will tell *Victor* you need much fresh, buffalo cow meat to help you hide your bones. Perhaps you, too, need a mate. There surely is the right one among the many women who have lost their men to the Blackfeet. Perhaps you would thank me for helping in that hunt." Her laughter continued until it merged with the other sounds of life at St. Mary's Mission.

"You missed Father DeSmet by one day," Little Bear Claw told his son and the medicine man as their horses stopped near the chief's lodge. "Upon his return here, he remained but two days, then left with the hunters Brown Bottle and Bead. We will find them near Three Forks."

True to his long-ago promise, Little Coyote immediately had begun helping direct the growth of Little Grizzly Bear Claw. As a preliminary to the buffalo hunt, the two had ridden to the lakes south of the great peak. There, the youth killed a deer with his bow and arrow. Only then did the warrior let him shoot his rifle at an elk. He hit it with his first shot, but because he had sighted too quickly with the unfamiliar and heavy weapon, he had to track down and kill the bull with an arrow.

Little Bear Claw had shown the rifle to Little Coyote before the seer and youth left for the hunt. "It is a vision quest gift," the chief had explained. Tull, more hairy and talkative than ever, had brought three pack horses loaded with rifles to the valley the spring following the defeat near the two creeks.

"Figgered ye'd need weepons arter what th' sarpants did ta ye at th' last big fracas, so I com'd hyar," he had explained to Little Bear Claw. "F'm th' way this hoss's laigs is hurtin', gotta stay 'way f'm th' cold criks, not thet they's many plews thar anyway. Tradin' I'll do with frens, I says to me, so hyar I be. I c'n trade 'em ta ye fur few pelts each cuz Hellinhouse is jest astartin' out, 'n his weapons be gud as Hawkens makes."

Before leaving the lakes, Little Coyote, spirit joyous over his efforts with Little Grizzly Bear Claw, aching over thoughts of Lance, also began instructing Little Grizzly Bear Claw in the mysteries concerning white man's writing. He started with the markings on the rifle: "F. Hellinghaus, St. Louis" on the lock; "St. Louis" again on the top barrel flat, and "Remington Cast Steel" underneath the barrel near the breech. When the pair returned home, the youth also had learned the other eleven letters of the alphabet, plus numbers up to ten. His greatest problem was remembering that his language lacked B, D, F, R and V, so he had to substitute P, T, L and M for these.

"You will learn to use these symbols on paper just as you bind together, with strong but fine sinew, the wooden shaft, the feathers and point to make an arrow that flies true," the seer assured his somewhat mystified, but willing, charge. "And you will learn to speak both the white man's language and that of our people. There also will be instruction in the wisdom of *when* to write or speak. Often," now he grinned, "a chief can learn much more if he feigns a certain ignorance and listens to those who talk much. Then the listener's few words can, like that well-made arrow, fly true and hit the mark."

Little Bear Claw's eyes flicked ever so briefly over Little Coyote's ancient lance, bow and arrows while he handed his friend the reins of an Appaloosa mare and the lead rope of a strong pack horse.

"They are yours," he said as his son joined them. The trio began moving up the deeply worn trail leading south well before the Mission's Angelus bell awakened the people to prayers and mass.

Little Coyote chose to ride in the rear. His spirits rose with each movement of his horse carrying him to higher elevations toward the pass—and more of his people. There, southwest breezes began sighing warnings of colder days ahead and showering horses and men with golden larch needles. The hunters halted by a spring where white-bark pine towered above low bushes hanging with delicious berries. While they roasted some of Little Grizzly Bear Claw's venison and elk meat, the seer savored sight and haunting sound of geese flying south in irregular wedges as this year's hatch learned the mysteries of earth and sky from their elders, too.

"The priests, do they hunt well?" Little Coyote asked.

Before answering, Little Bear Claw took the final bite of hot meat from his roasting stick and impaled another raw slab on it. "Father Point is a willing, but poor hunter. He can draw pictures as well as you and his prayers are strong. Father DeSmet? I do not know. On last winter's hunt by two-hundred lodges of our people and the Pend d'Oreilles, Father Point almost died during a long snowstorm in which all suffered. Their luck was better against the Blackfeet, who also were forced to hunt in the deep cold. One day sixty of our people surrounded seventeen of them and were prepared to kill them all. Father Point placed himself in greater peril than from the storm as he argued against their death. This was after they had cried out, 'Black Robe, do not let us die!' There was much anger, especially from people who had lost so much near the two creeks. Even those who had most wanted the Black Robes to come raised their voices against him, but, amid muttering and threats, he prevailed and our hunters had to watch the hated Blackfeet ride off.

"The mutterings increased as the buffalo remained hidden amid the snow and cold. 'At least, we should have taken the Blackfeet horses to use and eat,' some of the angry warriors said.

"'Clear your minds of enmity so we properly can ask God to show us the buffalo,' Father Point said. Desperate, even the most angry did so. After fervent prayers, Sun appeared. Our hunters saw many buffalo and killed one-hundred-fifty-three."

Little Bear Claw tossed his roasting stick into the dying fire and walked toward the horses. "Father DeSmet told me he favors the priests accompanying the hunters so they can learn more about the ways of God while the priests learn about our people. I think the hunts are poor times to do this, unless organized like the Métis. Perhaps some day we all can hunt in peace. A few of the Piegan we have found to be friendly have accepted baptism. Perhaps in time there will be peace among us as we have tried even before the Black Robes came."

Little Coyote, remembering much, too, shook his head negatively at first as he recalled the wooden cannon Brother Claessens had erected in the fort, of sorts, around the Mission. The seer resolved to replace it with the brass cannon the Flatheads had buried so long ago. And he gained a further insight into this much-talked-about Father DeSmet when Little Bear Claw, riding beside the seer as the trail permitted, related how the cold and skulking Blackfeet had made life hard on all who stayed at the incomplete Mission.

"That DeSmet. As I told you at the hot springs, he is a man. He even put rifles into the hands of kindly Brothers Claessens and Specht and told them to shoot if the Blackfeet came too near, either to harm the Mission or drive off the horses in the corral where our people also were on constant watch."

The trail narrowed now and the chief moved ahead. Little Coyote's Appaloosa swiveled her ears toward the ponderosa pines, which were becoming more numerous as the hunters began descending the pass. A squirrel scampered up a moss-grown boulder, dropped a cone from its mouth and scolded these intruders; a fat woodchuck continued to lie in the wide band of sunlight striking the rotten log from which the creature tracked with bright eyes the passage of lead to rear horses. Growing flocks of alpine birds chattered between flights from spot to spot, balancing primordial urges to stay and enjoy the bountiful now against future deep snow and death.

Perhaps the hunters already will have enough meat to last the people until the winter hunt. This thought lent a certain urgency as Little Coyote nudged his horse to quicken her pace. Little Bear Claw had trained her well. She would be a good hunter, too, else he would not have received the gift.

Amid these sights and sounds, Little Coyote's mind flitted like the birds from thought to thought, balancing first that of his people stooping over the vegetables at the Mission with memories of buffalo chases in which the endeavor, itself, transcended the importance of the meat. Even those white and other trappers he respected had acknowledged that more than the lure of beaver had brought them here. Their coming had created change, but the more thoughtful often regretted it; in their regret, perhaps they exhibited a certain kinship with the red man. And what impulses drove the Whitmans, the Black Robes, others? Certainly there were easier tasks for them elsewhere. And those promises to the Good Spirit! Poverty he could understand, even practice. Chastity. This thought began nibbling at a portion of the old

534

wounds over the loss of beloved Antelope. Obedience. To a certain point. No more! What changes would these Black Robes make?

Yes, wiser people than himself, knowing they could not stop change, could, as he had agreed long ago, strive to shape it for the good, yet, strangely, all the while being a part of that change, too. Would this continue among all mankind everywhere, forever? How often his mind had centered on this strangeness, especially during his long, self-imposed exile at the hot springs when he had contrasted his present views with the youthful self-discoveries during the long-ago winter of the beaver.

So long ago! He sighed. Regretfully, the people could not, like those alpine birds, fly to new lands of perpetual summer, escaping the effects of change, the ever encompassing white man . . . "till we go to the sand hills," he said aloud.

Little Bear Claw stopped his horse.

"You called?"

"No, no. Like old Big Mouse, in my loneliness at the hot springs I began to speak my thoughts aloud."

Little Bear Claw motioned for his son to scout ahead. The chief smiled as the youth slung Lance's shield on his shoulder to better grasp his rifle in instant readiness. Little Coyote brought his horses abreast of his friend's in the widening trail.

"Did the seeds for the food come with the Black Robes?"

"With ten of our warriors Father DeSmet journeyed to the Hudson's Bay post at Fort Colville on the Columbia River. With money he begged at St. Louis he bought the seed, and tools and beeves and cows. He travels much. On his most recent trip he went as far as Fort Vancouver and the Willamette Valley to see how he could help people there. The Indian people are eager to see him and told him they want to become Christians—the Kalispels, Kutenais, Coeur d'Alenes, Spokans—" Little Bear Claw's Appaloosa shied as a chipmunk darted from a rock pile and ran across the trail. Yes, the chief had given his friend the better-trained horse.

"Have you thought much about the growing chain of forts?" The question appeared as unexpectedly as had the chipmunk.

His horse under control, the chief looked briefly at his friend. "I have."

"Will there be a circle of missions within the forts?"

"I have thought much about this." The chief once more smiled as he waved to his son, who was waiting near a bend in the trail.

Now Little Bear Claw's face lengthened as he moved his horse ahead of the seer's.

"Yes, I have thought about all this, but have not yet spoken much about it. Perhaps such heavy thoughts will move past my lips, too, like old Big Mouse and my much younger friend, Little Coyote." He pulled back on his reins, looked obliquely at his friend and managed another smile.

Little Bear Claw spoke more loudly now above the clatter of hooves against many rocks littering the trail.

"I begin to think, not say yet, that perhaps the missions will become forts of one kind against the forts of another. Soon we will see Father DeSmet. Without his speaking so, his spirit around him has told me that those are his thoughts, too."

Memories of Marcus Whitman's splintered wagon wheel crept into the medicine man's mind as he waited for the chief's horses to pick their way through a jumble of small rocks. Again, the seer sighed and once more voiced his thoughts aloud as he set his horses into motion. "It was put back together again, but with different, softer woods in its many parts." This time the Appaloosa twitched her ears ever so briefly. Only she had heard.

Far below, Little Grizzly Bear Claw had dismounted and was carefully helping his horses find their way downward through a heavy rockfall. Once again the youth hitched the shield with the lamb's blood cross more securely on his shoulder, then disappeared from view.

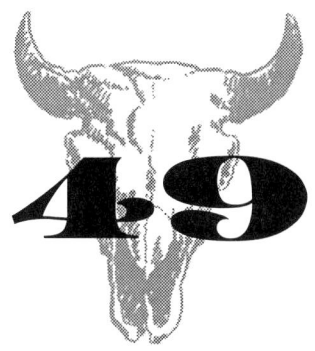

49

Little Coyote limited his story skin representation of Father Pierre Jean DeSmet to that of a stocky, black-clad figure with a large crucifix stuck in a band encircling his ample waist. Not shown on the rough hide were the priest's powerful shoulders, strong hands and long, grayish hair, cut almost straight across his broad forehead. And how to portray the Black Robe's piercing eyes? After much thought, Little Coyote finally painted a tiny arrow projecting from each eye, as though from a bow. Those eyes! They set the beholder to wondering whether the Black Robe looked into the future, the now and the past. As though to keep others comfortable, the Black Robe's wide mouth seemed poised always to break into a ready, warm and reassuring smile, despite whatever unpleasantness remained a certainty ahead, existed now, or had just been undergone.

"If Dog That Sits, even wise Broken Pipe, were alive and prepared to trade a good horse for all this Black Robe owned, they would walk away empty-handed, yet content, had the man but pierced their souls with his eyes, then smiled." So said Little Bear Claw to his son and Little Coyote as they arrived early in the morning at their people's encampment near the Madison River fork, where Chalax had said they would find the buffalo. The hunters were busily preparing to chase three widely separated bands of the animals. Even so, there was much rejoicing over the trio's arrival. Old Cougar was war chief for the hunt. He quickly allotted the chief and his son positions in the group that would hunt closest to the encampment.

With regret, Little Coyote decided not to hunt when he learned that Father DeSmet would remain behind this time. Father DeSmet had asked Little Coyote if he would come talk, but first the priest had to remove whiskers, buffalo blood, dirt and grime accumulated during active participation in an earlier successful chase.

He was twisting water from his other black robe when the seer arrived at his camp, which was between great boulders. The priest hung the clothing on a tree branch, then shook out his buffalo robe before asking his guest to sit.

"Bless us, Lord, and these, Thy gifts, which we are about to receive from Thy bounty, through Christ our Lord, Amen."

Father DeSmet ended his brief prayer and placed broiled buffalo meat before his guest. As they ate they could hear, but not see, the busy people who had remained behind to care for the meat acquired the day before. Twice the eaters could hear distant gun reports, indicating there soon would be more meat to prepare.

"I join the others in rejoicing you are here," the priest said. "I also rejoice that you speak English." The smile became almost boyishly rueful. "I have not yet learned your language. Victor and others have told me how you aided the efforts of our Iroquois brothers, Gun, Shield Maker, all the others, to invite us here. I soon must travel once again to distant lands. That is why I asked you if we could talk this day when I know you, like my interpreters, would rather be hunting. I would ask you to help in our endeavors. There is so much to do."

The seer listened quietly while the priest spoke in detail of many matters Little Bear Claw briefly had disclosed.

Already Little Coyote felt he could, without offense, carry out his resolve formed while traveling from the hot springs. He would test this man who agreeably had accepted his place in the hunt without questioning Chalax's vision of where the buffalo would be. Would the Black Robe, like many white men the seer had met, scoff at and reject the red man's revelations from the spirit world—revelations that helped him to order his life? Little Coyote began by recounting his interpretation of Little Grizzly Bear Claw's vision. The only indication of its effect on the Black Robe was a slight waning of his ever-ready smile and an almost-cadenced, barely perceptible, affirmative nodding of his head.

The priest sighed. "Our arrival, among the many white men and sought for too long by your people, is good and it will be helpful. God has told all of us that. Three times last year at the Mission there were visions over which we all rejoiced." Now Little Coyote nodded, remembering that Little Bear Claw had mentioned them only briefly.

"At the request of a dying Flathead girl, our Iroquois brother, Pierre, baptized her because I was gone. She received the name of Mary, the mother of Jesus, whom she saw in her vision. She told your people we are the true Black Robes and pointed to a place, saying, 'A house of prayer will be built there.'

"On Christmas Eve, Holy Mary appeared before the orphan boy, Little Paul, and almost instantly he knew his prayers so he could be baptized with others. I looked as carefully into this matter as do the buffalo scouts before reporting to the war chief of the hunt. The vision is true, as true as that of our Cree brother, Michael, who, earlier on the feast day of St. Francis Xavier, saw an apparition of this saint. All three of those who had these visions could truly describe varying clothing and other matters they had never seen nor heard about."

Father DeSmet leaned over and gripped Little Coyote's shoulder in his strong hand. "The God of us all rarely opens the lodge flap to permit us to look into His world beyond, or for the good souls with Him to return to our world with messages. Yet, when He does, He is equally generous to all of our brothers and sisters of all colors. I do not question, Little Coyote, that in this way He has favored you more than me."

They drank sweetened coffee, which the priest called "recent gifts from Dr. McLoughlin at Fort Vancouver." Any imaginary barriers between the two men dissolved as readily as the sugar.

"You say there is so much to do, yet you again will leave soon?"

An almost undetectable look of sorrow flitted across the priest's face. As he responded, Little Coyote remembered his talks so long ago with Drouillard, Colter, Jedediah Smith, even Tull.

"Dr. McLoughlin told me, and I could see, that ever increasing numbers of white men are coming to, and remaining, in his part of the Oregon country. Most are Americans now, who perhaps soon will drive out the British. This is no vision. I have seen this done elsewhere. Your people have seen Americans moving into the Rocky Mountains, and a few remaining even as the beaver are disappearing. There are few in your valley now, but we can learn from what has gone before. Here the weather is mostly good. There is much water, and grasses for animals. As you can see, your people can grow food. And the Flatheads do not fight white man, as do many tribes elsewhere—to their sorrow." The Black Robe paused, then added, "To their *unimaginable* sorrow. For these many reasons, there will be more white men coming here before they move into the flatter buffalo country now roamed by the Arikara, Blackfeet, Crows, Cheyenne, the Sioux and others. White men will graze great herds of cattle and horses and other animals. They will break the soil to plant crops that will stretch farther than the eye can see. Again this is no vision. All this has been done elsewhere, to the eternal sorrow of God's red men. So, I fear for you—much like Dr. McLoughlin fears at his Fort Vancouver, from where most Indians now are gone. There are few Black Robes, yet I feel I must try to build up missions throughout the Oregon country. Yes, I must leave again to seek men and money and supplies. I have promised the God of us all that I will bring faith and justice to his red children. There is so little time, so much to do."

Too soon, Sun began to set. Calls of night birds began replacing those of magpies and crows, which had quarreled incessantly while the encampment had worked at the meat. Numerous fires sprang up and the tired people gathered around

540

them to roast meat and talk. A few sought their lodge furs when messengers from two of the hunting parties rode into the encampment almost simultaneously to report good kills. "We have opened up the carcasses, but must have help when Sun returns." They eagerly accepted freshly broiled meat and began telling about the hunts.

A young brave raced toward the fires from his guard position atop a small hillside darkly silhouetted against the dying pink of the western sky: "Seven of our warriors return quickly with Old Cougar. The other five he led afar to hunt come more slowly with Father Point. They bring extra horses."

Even as the messenger spoke, the seven warriors, shrilling cries of victory, raced into the encampment and began circling the fires. Old Cougar brandished his quirt and a knife from which hung a bloody scalp. Three held aloft their guns, one a lance, two their bows. All weapons had scalps affixed to them by their long hair. The exultant warriors pulled up their horses as the excited people, tiredness gone, piled more wood onto the fires. Sparks rose high above them and began drifting north.

"The power of the Black Robes is strong!" Old Cougar roared. "We sought buffalo and found Blackfeet."

Now the sleepers in the lodges ran outside to hear each of the seven tell his story amid exultant cries of his listeners, which died only so they could hear another. Old Cougar had made the first kill with his knife after jumping from his horse and quirting his enemy, who had fired his musket and missed. Those with scalps affixed to their guns had killed their enemies who, after firing their muskets, began racing toward two lodges hidden in a willow thicket. The other Flatheads boasted how they had killed three prisoners taken at the lodges—two women and a small boy—with arrows and the lance. "There was no torture," each boasted. By now all the scalp-takers were moving in an impromptu dance. Soon they circled the largest fire and were dancing more energetically when Father Point and the five remaining hunters entered the camp. The captured horses carried Blackfeet booty, which the latecomers piled near the fire before joining the circle around it. Now the watchers began swaying to the chants of those around the fire and crooning jubilant words. Father Point rode unsteadily toward Father DeSmet, who was approaching with his Cree interpreter, Gabriel Prudhomme. Father Point dismounted and, holding onto the saddle, leaned over and tried to vomit. The coughs wracked the priest's thin body again and again, but nothing more would come. He raised his long, gaunt face and cried out both in French and English as though pleading with all present.

"The two women and the boy! Killed even as I pleaded for their lives! Butchery! Butchery! They didn't listen at all! At the death of each they became more drunk with passion! I tried to stay the arm of the warrior with the lance! He struck me aside and skewered the terrified boy as he bent over his dead mother!"

Father DeSmet looked toward the fire. Now the people were jumping up and down, some firing shots into the air, the muzzle flashes lighting for an instant the savagely working faces covered with hastily smeared paint. Light from the fire flickered over Father DeSmet's inexpressibly sad face. He placed his arm on the other priest's frail, sob-wracked body and almost shouted above the wild chanting.

"Come, Father. Seek some rest. We must begin the new day by setting the only example they will understand. We will bury and pray over the dead."

"Father DeSmet pointed this way and said to me: 'Just follow your noses and you will find the stone houses where the furs are bought and stored.'"

Little Coyote set down his heavy bundle of furs and leaned his lance against the small structure in which he and Little Grizzly Bear Claw had spent their first night in St. Louis. The seer placed his hand reassuringly on the youth's shoulders before helping him adjust a somewhat smaller pack of furs and sling his bow and arrows. The late October air blowing in from the fog-shrouded river carried a mixture of odors as confusing as the place, itself. The seer and his charge had gazed in wonder as they had stepped off the fur-laden steamboat the previous early afternoon and ridden in a wagon with Father DeSmet and his small group to the rectory buildings near the cathedral. Little Coyote had watched them all offer thanks at the altar to St. Mary before receiving instructions about housing and meals.

When the Black Robe had prepared to leave the buffalo hunts to visit the Crows, he had sought out Little Coyote, Little Bear Claw and his son among the disappointed Flatheads.

"As I have said, I must seek more money and people for the missions. You might learn much about the white man and his ways if you would go to St. Louis. We will help as we can."

The chief had suggested to several warriors they accompany Father DeSmet, Ignace and Prudhomme to the country of the Crows. All agreed before their departure that Little Coyote and Little Grizzly Bear Claw would journey to the Missouri River after the hunts and trade furs for a steamboat ride downriver. They were overjoyed when Father DeSmet also had signaled for a ride only a few days after they had come aboard. Truly, they beheld great wonders and many Indians trying to cope in various ways with white man, as Father DeSmet had described, during the forty-six days they spent with this black-robed fellow traveler aboard the steamboat.

The priest immediately was caught up in a myriad of activities in St. Louis. These included begging men, supplies and funds for the already-established missions. Later he would do the same in many great American cities before leaving for Europe to obtain more money, men and women for Oregon missions.

So as the two Flatheads resolutely set out to follow their noses, they almost immediately began encountering a bewildering variety of sights. They paused often to gawk at wagon yards, piles of lumber, homes, horse and mule barns, and into windows of many small shops displaying goods in far greater numbers than the wonder-struck pair ever had seen at trading posts in their land.

Twice, Little Grizzly Bear Claw pointed delightedly at two signs he could read almost immediately as the Flatheads moved from structure to structure and street to street: "J. and S. Hawken, Gunsmith." "Frederick Hellinghaus, Gunsmith." Understanding these signs seemed to make comprehensible to the young brave many more new sights which, as the morning wore on, included a growing, jostling crowd of trappers, boat hands, blanket-clad Indians, workers in a variety of clothes. Occasional steamboat whistles echoed above all the noises. From open spaces between buildings the Flatheads could see the vessels splashing into town both from up and down the Mississippi River. They were racing against time and possible freezeup, which could bring traffic to a halt.

Heavy wagons rumbled by in the streets, deferring, seemingly, to the passage of much lighter wheeled vehicles carrying cleanly dressed men and women. These people looked straight ahead as if through their long exposure they had become oblivious to the turmoil surrounding—and supporting—them.

"We will come back here," Little Grizzly Bear Claw said, pointing to the Hellinghaus sign, and to the horses. He wrinkled his nose like an eating rabbit and, for the first time since stepping off the steamboat, his deeply buried humor emerged through a wide grin: "First, though, we must follow our noses."

When some of the women in the carriages began holding tiny, white cloths to their noses, the two Flatheads stopped and breathed deeply. Then, catching an unmistakable scent, they headed down the nearest street leading toward the river. Soon they could see numerous structures sprawled across a flattened hill. Wagons were transporting to long, wooden buildings the goods taken from three steamboats that had come upriver. Other wagons were hauling to the nearby yellow and gray stone buildings loosely tied bales of furs and buffalo robes disgorged from two boats that had come downriver. As quickly as the wagons were empty, teamsters would load and haul carefully separated and securely tied large and small bales of robes and furs from the stone warehouses to the steamboats from which other wagons were continuing to take the newly arrived and as-yet ungraded and unsorted furs.

Now the breeze shifted, picking up in its passage directly over and around the stone warehouse area a magnified odor akin to that from a sun-drenched buffalo jump and butchering site three days after a successful drive. "The smell of a large, winter encampment in the first warm days of spring," the medicine man said aloud. Little Grizzly Bear Claw turned to look at him briefly, then began watching trappers entering a wide, glass-paned door.

The pair followed the men into the structure and stood in the shortest of the three lines. Like the other men, the Flatheads began loosening the rawhide thongs binding their furs. The Indian standing directly in front of them held a string of carefully prepared muskrat furs. He reeked of the vomit and excrement that stained his old, woolen pants and shirt. Outside, a sad-faced Indian woman with three rag-clad children peered anxiously through the nearest window. Ahead of the reeking brave, a heavily bearded mountain man sat on one large bale. He was puffing contentedly on his pipe, which he held by its short stem to his lips. His other hand, resting on a second bale, was holding a large, unsheathed Green River knife. His bright eyes centered on a younger mountain man dealing with the clerk.

"Yu ain't payin' whut thet-air sign says! Ah ain't no Injun yu can cheat this-a-way!"

"Can you read?" The clerk's voice expressed both disdain and challenge.

"No, but by thunder ah kin lissen whut t'others bin gettin'!" He pointed to the other busy lines. "Ah jest know muh furs air wuth more'n thet."

"Well, if you want to argue, step out of line and we'll discuss the matter after we've helped these other, um . . ." The clerk's eyes flickered over the rest of the line. ". . . people." His arm began sweeping all the furs toward a large bin; it stopped abruptly when the older trapper's knife sank into the counter just behind the clerk's hand.

The trapper lowered his pipe. His voice was soft: "Settle fairly with the gentleman—now, or do I settle with you? I figure you owe him four-hundred-seventy-eight dollars and twenty-seven cents, exactly one-hundred-seventy-eight dollars and twenty-seven cents more than you paid him."

The clerk paled. He looked about as though seeking help; finding none, he re-focused on the bearded trapper and began counting out the money. The trapper stood there slowly puffing his pipe after the younger man had voiced his thanks and departed and the Indian with the muskrat pelts had received his money and staggered out to his waiting family. The clerk hastily counted and graded the mountain man's furs, marked the information on a paper, then handed him the money. People, meanwhile, had joined all the waiting lines.

The mountain man knocked the ashes from his pipe onto the sawdust-covered floor, leaned against the counter and slowly refilled the pipe while the two Flatheads as quietly lifted up their furs. They were good ones. After grading them, the clerk began counting and marking on the paper. He paid the yet-silent Indians and said, "Next!"

The mountain man removed his pipe. As he prepared to speak again, Little Coyote handed the money to Little Grizzly Bear Claw, then extended his hand toward the clerk.

"You counted seven beaver pelts, marked down five. You counted twenty-three weasel skins and marked down nineteen. You counted three wolf pelts and marked down two. The other counts and payment are correct. You now will pay me for two beaver pelts, four weasel skins and one wolf pelt—all prime." He pointed to the sign and carelessly tilted his lance point dangerously near the clerk's throat. The man gulped, leaned back and silently handed the money to Little Coyote.

"Now I will talk to the chief clerk." The lance point quivered. "We will fetch him."

The mountain man touched Little Coyote on the shoulder. "Name's Owen, Frank Owen, from up in the Shoshone country. Been meaning to get up the Bitter Root way ever since I left Pennsylvania. Let me fetch the chief clerk. You just stand by with your warrior here. Keep the two piles of money separate. Do you understand? Yes, I'll hold onto the tally sheet here and fetch the chief clerk." He pulled the knife from the counter top, opened the gate and disappeared through a door leading to the building's depths, from which issued the greatest stink yet. The clerk, sallow face sweating, took his eyes off the lance point, swallowed nervously and looked at his fellow clerks. All ignored him.

"What have we here?" The large, well-dressed man who returned with Owen looked briefly at the tally sheet, as quickly at the clerk and the lance head. Then Étienne Brandt's eyes widened as he looked directly into the unmoving eyes of Little Coyote.

50

The startled seer's wonderment at Brandt's transformation from tortured human wreck to well-dressed and well-fed trader began fading as the man's eyes politely moved briefly to Owen. The eyes spoke of the dishonest clerk, then went back to prolonged, almost unblinking, stares at Little Coyote. What lay behind those glittering eyes? Hatred? No. Nor was there the seeming all-knowing and indescribable sadness that had appeared so long ago in the remaining eye of the tortured Blackfeet warrior near Saleesh House, and those of the white buffalo bull the medicine man had killed during peace talks with the Blackfeet. Brandt's most prolonged stare yet, as though the trader had lost interest, caused Owen to falter in his explanation. Now Little Coyote realized he was seeing in Brandt's eyes a reflection of the window through which the Indian woman and her children earlier had peered as her near-stuporous mate had sold the muskrat skins. Centered in the reflection were the two cross-shaped pieces of wood that held the four panes of glass.

Yes! Those eyes looked out on the world much as did those of the dying, crucified Christ in the large painting Father Point had hung near the altar in the crude chapel at St. Mary's. They were eyes that, having seen the world, pitied it for the cruelty, the pain, the hardship amid His own suffering, yet continued to hold a vision of something transcending all this as the spirit prepared itself to flee toward that promise. A part of Brandt had died; a greater part of him lived in the expectation of something better ahead. Now the trader spoke; his words partially confirmed the medicine man's conclusions.

"Marner, last year you pleaded for a job so you could help your wife and child. You worked hard in the warehouse, moving upward quickly from the dumping bins to the sorting and then the classifying tables, and now here. I can only assume you sought to cheat for yourself and family." The clerk nodded dumbly, awaiting his dismissal.

"Those skills remain. Once again, you will start at the dumping bins. One can think many thoughts while surrounded by stinking hides. What lies ahead, I cannot tell. This is an honest company. Be gone!"

The clerk seized his coat and fled, almost stumbling in his eagerness to return to the noisome depths of the warehouse. Brandt motioned for those waiting in Marner's line to divide and join the others where the clerks busily continued to trade or pay for their furs.

"Thank you, Mr. Owen. I hope we can do business again." Brandt held out his hand, which the trapper briefly shook. "And you." Brandt shook the hand of a somewhat surprised Little Grizzly Bear Claw, then stepped from behind the counter to do the same with Little Coyote. The hand was soft but the grip surprisingly strong; the eyes were kindly now, the words memorable: "Yes, one can think many thoughts while surrounded by stinking hides. To you, Little Coyote, I am forever in debt."

The trio stood outside a moment while Owen lighted his pipe. "Good man, that." He nodded toward the trading room, obviously wishing to say more, but trying to cover his curiosity with long pulls at his pipe. "Well, maybe I'll see you in the Bitter Root. Have to talk to my brother, John, about it." He shook hands with the two Flatheads and began striding purposefully toward the busier, shop-lined streets.

The Flatheads walked more slowly in the same direction,

both expressing their satisfaction when they moved through the invisible line separating stench and invigorating cold air. The youth exclaimed over each new sight, scarcely noticing that, except for an occasional affirmative or negative grunt, his companion's mind was elsewhere. The seer was pondering a medley of thoughts that moved beyond Brandt's physical transformation. He was trying to grasp how Brandt now possessed some inner power the medicine man had discerned in dying Gun, old Shield Maker, Tjolzhitsay, who was ninety summers at death, others of his people, some of the Iroquois, Whitman, DeSmet, the other Jesuits. Whatever the power was, it moved beyond the quality of their being likable persons, yet it was different from the things he loved about now long-dead Antelope and Lance. Yes, there was something in the spirit that could grow, even radiate, beyond the bonds of the physical body.

Could this something within the spirit also diminish? Evidently so, else how could a once-noble warrior like Dog That Sits become what he had? What was there in man to choose the path? Indeed, why had the seer resisted his first impulse to kill Brandt after the man had tried to rape Antelope? Why had he castrated him, instead, then later saved his mind and life?

Now, when Little Coyote, as before, seemed almost ready to grasp the answers to the questions he was asking, he must wait. Little Grizzly Bear Claw's instincts had brought them to Morgan Street between Fourth and Fifth, and the shop of Frederick Hellinghaus, Gunsmith. Here, too, was Frank Owen. Soon, he and the younger Flathead each owned one of the strong, plainly made, percussion rifles and an extra complete lock at Owen's strong suggestion. Once again they were saying good-bye.

The bespectacled gunsmith had shown as much interest in the youth's fine Nez Percé bow and the seer's ancient lance as they had in his rifles.

"I haven't been in St. Louis long enough to obtain a good collection of Indian weapons," Hellinghaus said. He vigorously wiped his oily hands across his apron when Little Coyote explained to Little Grizzly Bear Claw that the gunsmith wished to examine the bow. Hellinghaus strung it, pulled back on the string, relaxed it, examined the laminations of sheep horn, nocked an arrow and again pulled back. He unstrung the weapon and handed it back.

"I'll give him three dollars trade-in toward the rifle. I plan to move to California soon to cater to the trade that's growing there, as well as in Mexico." He pointed to the array of Indian weapons hanging on the wall. "I'd like to get more such weapons while it's still possible, while the Indians still are making them." Little Grizzly Bear Claw made the trade.

The two Flatheads saw little of Father DeSmet as he traveled that winter of 1842 to other great cities to beg funds for St. Mary's Mission. As the priest had predicted, the pair learned much about white man and his ways. Though grateful for the shelter and food, they soon tired of vegetables and craved wild meat over beef and pork. Purchasing two fair-grade horses, Little Coyote and Little Grizzly Bear Claw set out to find the alcoholic Osage Indian, Old Fire, who still was trapping a few muskrats and pulling on the bottles of cheap whiskey their pelts bought.

Greeted profusely, the Flatheads seated themselves about the small fire in Old Fire's wretched lodge of grass, reeds, saplings and ancient hides. While his dispirited family scavenged for more fuel and ate the food the visitors had brought, he readily agreed in broken English to show his new acquaintances where the muskrats lived "in numbers as great as the buffalo my father once had pursued as a youth and warrior."

On the first and succeeding trips to the marshes, Old Fire carefully took the horsemen around a then frost-rimmed, later snow-covered, stubble field. Politely, his guests did not point out that the most direct route was through the field. On every trip they caught muskrats. Other small game stepped into the traps and snares or fell to rifle, an ancient sawed-off musket and arrows. The pot in Old Fire's lodge began steaming day and night, even on Sundays, because Little Grizzly Bear Claw could attend one of the earliest masses in the church before riding afield. Soon the children became playful and Old Fire's dolorous wife even smiled.

Then, early one morning, mind slightly befuddled, Old Fire led the trappers through the stubble field and into one of the greatest lessons they would derive from their trip to St. Louis.

Birdshot whacked into the frozen ground in front of the lead horse before the trappers heard the shotgun boom.

"Damn Indian! I told you to stay off my land. Instead, you bring two more!" The voice came from behind a small straw stack. Soon, a man clad in a decaying buffalo robe coat and floppy, felt hat stepped into view. He paused to replace the ramrod under the double barrels of his shotgun, then strode closer toward the watchful trio. His thin, whiskery face was working angrily. "I've half a mind to plug all three of you, and I will if'n I see you again. I'll let you off easy this time, but I'm gonna' burn that filthy place you live in, so you'll have to leave." He swung the menacing muzzle toward Little Coyote as the seer shifted his lance downward. "Don't you threaten me, damn Indian!" The man spat tobacco juice toward the horses.

Old Fire, his mind clearing, kicked his horse closer to the farmer.

"No more! We will come no more. We go that way." His arm swept around the field.

Little Grizzly Bear Claw pointed to the farmer's small house and outbuildings as he spoke to Little Coyote.

"None of that gibberish. What'd he say?" The white man turned his head toward Little Coyote as Little Grizzly Bear Claw nudged his horse away from the others.

"The great chief's son from the shining mountains asked if white man's lodges do not also burn. I agreed with him that they do, day or night."

A woman had emerged from the house, two small children clutching her skirts.

"Mr. Culpepper!" she shouted. "Now mind you, be careful! Think of the young uns!"

Little Coyote pointed his lance toward the trail in the snow.

"We will backtrack, then continue to the marsh. We will not return over your land. Now, do not point the shotgun at me and the chief's son will not point his gun at you."

552

The farmer's face sagged, tobacco juice dribbling from the corners of his mouth as fear took over. He lowered the shotgun and uncocked it. He again spat, this time at his feet. Then he nodded at Old Fire.

"If this one rides across here in winter, he'll do it when next year's crops are up. It's little enough land we have. I had to clear off the brush, and all of us, even the little ones, picked out the rocks. Too many people coming here. Thought there was lots of good land when we came down the Ohio River and up the Mississippi to here. I've told this Indian all this before. We got to have the grain and vegetables to live. It's a hard life!"

They left then for the marsh, Old Fire and Little Coyote riding close together, the younger Flathead apart, until they were well out of birdshot range.

Before entering the brush that fringed the marsh, Old Fire turned to look backward at the land. Now he straightened on his skinny horse and, cradling the old musket in his left arm and across his chest, swept his right arm from left to right. His voice strengthened as he proudly raised his head, his companions seemingly forgotten.

"Once Indians lived all over this land. We tended great fields, strong enough to go to the nearby buffalo grounds. I have a paper with the marks of William Clark on it. When he was what white men call governor of the Missouri Territory, he gave the paper to my father, Marks His Arrows Blue. My father served as peacemaker with many tribes, trying to keep them from fighting among themselves and with white man, who took over our fields. My father knew more Indians would die than white men, even when the soldiers moved most of the Indians to the Oklahoma country. The paper says Marks His Arrows Blue and his sons and their sons forever can live here. Then in white man's 1821, Clark no longer was governor, and Marks His Arrows Blue was dead. The paper remained good, but I had to move from place to place. My lodge was last where Culpepper put his house. There is no land, except where I have put my lodge. The farmers even ploughed up the bones of my ancestors: War Horse, my grandfather; Always Smiles, my grandmother; Marks His Arrows

Blue, my father; One Beaver, my mother. Others. So many others. Gone. All gone!"

Old Fire again slumped forward and kicked his horse into motion. "Clark died here four years ago. Is our paper still good? Where will we go?" He turned to face his silent Flathead friends. "Come. Let us see how many muskrats have stepped into *our* traps."

The Flatheads were looking northwest, toward the land of the shining mountains.

"Yes, we know Old Fire and we will ask our supporters to help him," Father DeSmet promised early in April when he visited the Flatheads in their small shelter near the church. He glanced at the drying muskrat skins. "Mr. Étienne Brandt has organized a group that does much to help such unfortunates, red, black or white. He plays his violin sometimes during high mass and has helped collect musical instruments for St. Mary's Mission. He says some Indian people and a black man once extended Christian charity to him.

"Well, now. How would you like to return to the Bitter Root Valley with Fathers Peter DeVos and Adrian Hoecken and Brother Peter MacGean?" He smiled, pleased as the Flatheads responded by standing up. "I must travel across the great ocean to Europe to get men, women and money for the Oregon missions. Father DeVos will be superior at St. Mary's Mission. I cannot delay." The smile disappeared as Father DeSmet went on.

"Thousands of white settlers are preparing to go to the Oregon country over what they call the Oregon Trail. You have seen the many white men living in St. Louis. More come every spring. You are learning what numbers mean. More than four-hundred-thousand white men live in Missouri now. Why, that could be half the number of Indians living in all of America!" The priest began holding up his fingers. "That's three times the number that were here only ten years ago.

"You are the son of a chief, Charlot. You likely will lead your people one day. You, Little Coyote, are a great leader, too. We have hoped your experiences here would lead you to help us to help your people.

"I have learned this since I came to America, and I will tell you now: It is the way of the white man to come where the Indians live. For a time they remain peaceable. Then they want more land. So they make treaties with the Indians. The Indians give way. The white men are content for a time, then, as more come to the Indian country, they, too, want land. They break the treaties as easily as they break a clay pot. The Indians fight. They lose, because there always are more and more white men.

"White men no longer will halt here in Missouri. They are ready to spread out like the buffalo following the point animals of a great herd, too many to count, too powerful to stop. Soon, too soon, the never-ending herd will split three ways to go to the Columbia River country, your valley and north and east, and to the California country."

As new greenery began displacing the dead grasses of winter, the two Flatheads grew as restless as the myriads of waterfowl in the marshes. In late April, before he left for Europe, Father DeSmet accompanied the three Jesuits, the Flatheads and a motley collection of other travelers westerly along the Missouri to Westport. On the banks of the Kansas River they joined a growing assemblage of land-seekers easily as eager as had been the fur-takers at the now-dead rendezvous. There were many greetings, including those of Marcus Whitman, too busy just then to more than warmly greet Little Coyote and his companion. The minister had agreed to help lead the almost one thousand people, their great herd of cattle and numerous wagons through South Pass, the Oregon Trail.

"Father Mengarini has instructions to meet you when the time comes to split off and travel to the Bitter Root." With this reassuring word, Father DeSmet embraced, then blessed, the Jesuits. The two Flatheads, astride better horses and each trailing one of their earlier mounts as a pack horse, accompanied Father DeSmet to a long, low hill from which they watched the widely dispersed people, wagons, cattle and horsemen begin to articulate. When all were in motion, the priest blessed the Flatheads and also bade them good-bye.

Little Coyote watched his companion push a large stick into the soft earth, then load and fire his new rifle several times. The seer reviewed the many events of this trip to St. Louis, which he might never see again. His mind, like a pack horse, was carrying to the Bitter Root many worries that had accumulated with each new experience. He had thought about seeking John Colter's wife and son, if they yet lived. But to what purpose? Discuss the silent grave he had searched out in the hilltop cemetery above Sullens Spring? Thirty years and the elements had worn almost indecipherable the markings on the headboard, which tilted in the soft ground like Little Grizzly Bear Claw's target.

The memories, even the face of John Colter, remained strong as those legs that had carried him as fast as the years that had sped by since his departure from Three Forks in 1810. *Colter, Drouillard, Lisa, Jedediah Smith, Little Yellow Bird, Running Buffalo Bull, Broken Pipe . . . .* Little Coyote shook his head. *Enough, lest the two dearest faces, the timeless sorrow, return yet again.*

"Enough! Let us go!" he shouted at Little Grizzly Bear Claw.

The youth placed a cap on the nipple of the reloaded rifle, mounted his horse and fired at the base of the stick, knocking it to the earth. He reloaded and inserted the weapon in the untanned elk-hide scabbard affixed left of his saddle, alongside Lance's white shield. The black cross glistened from the new coat of more permanent paint its owner had bought in St. Louis.

As the two began moving up the left side of the strung-out column, they were surprised to see Culpepper, his wife and children sitting proudly in the seats of a well-worn and filled sturdy wagon. Behind the wagon were a milk cow and several horses. The farmer reached down and lifted up his shotgun to wave it in a friendly fashion.

"Hi you! Hi you!" he shouted. The pair warily drew closer, well separated. "Brandt at the fur company bought us out for three-hundred-fifty dollars, he did! Threw in this wagon and the milk cow to boot. Damn fool *gave* our place to that Osage, he did." Culpepper loosed a stream of tobacco juice at the fly-encircled rear end of one of his draft horses and prepared to bite off another chew. "The Osage, well he's grading furs and hides in one of them stinking warehouses."

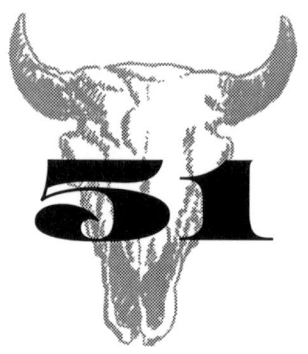

T ull's deep, rumbling snores continued unbroken as he thrashed about, then turned in his blanket, sounding as though he were wrestling a black bear. Little Grizzly Bear Claw stirred uneasily on his bed by the pile of equipment near the lodge entry. Though Little Coyote was tired from participating in a successful elk hunt, his mind moved back and forth over the events of the long trek from Westport and during their four-day stay among the Shoshonis.

Yes, the decision to leave the wagon train after its first crossing of the Snake River had been a good one. Had Young Ignace not accompanied Father Mengarini from the Bitter Root to guide the Jesuit newcomers there, the two Flatheads would have done so. Instead, the seer and his companion had sought out the Shoshonis, both to see kin and to put the chief's son in better touch with these friendly allies. The Flatheads had spent most of their visit with Antelope's brother, Pony Whip; though a sub-chief now, Pony Whip lacked much of Broken Pipe's solemnity, but none of his trading instincts. He was richer in number of horses than had been his father, though many were not of the same high breed.

"The white men coming over the trail now want strong horses

for their wagons," Pony Whip had said. "Many care little what they ride. The bones of their horses and oxen mark the trail as do those of the buffalo after a great chase."

Tull had arrived only this day.

"Howdy, Coyote!" The old trapper's greeting at the lodge the Flatheads were occupying had been brief, but hearty. "I'll look ye up soon."

Bridger had sent Tull out with a small pack train of "more rifles, powder 'n sech t' trade t' th' Snakes," who by now were becoming well-armed, indeed. Better led, the chiefs of the smaller groups were much heartened by the example of Chief Washakie of the large eastern band. No longer would they seek almost instant flight from the ever-more-numerous and wide-ranging Sioux.

Trading completed for the day, Tull had walked to the savory pot suspended over the outside cooking fire serving both lodges and filled his bowl. He politely had saved his talking until he and the two Flatheads had sought their beds.

"Bridger 'n me 'n some t'other boys was at Fort Laramie yarnin' 'bout slim fur pickins 'n figgerin' how ta get more buffler robes when we heerd th' biggest party o' pilgrims yet was comin' up th' Platte. If'n I'd knowed 'bout you bein' thet clost, woulda' look'd ye up, I would. Fort Laramie's moughty busy tradin' with Indians 'n sech. When Bridger seed all them pilgrims, 'n heerd how skeerd they was o' th' trail, trappers 'n Indians 'n sech, he got an idea. Tried it out on a young army feller there, name o' Fremont, who tol' him he was gonna' map thet trail clean t' th' Columbia River. Said they'd be bigger parties o' pilgrims in '44 'n '45 fer shore.

"Wull . . ." Tull looked around the lodge, creakily scrambled to the flap and spat outside. "Wull, Bridger made fast tracks ta Black's Fork on th' Green 'mong th' friendly Snakes, 'n whar most o' th' pilgrims will be pullin' through. Gonna' team up with ol' Looey Vaskiss 'n set up a fort 'n work his ol' trade o' blacksmithin', 'n tradin', maybe even guide fer th' pilgrims. They got cash money. Said he mought take me in ta help out, seein's these ol' knees er clost ta givin' out. That'd leave him 'n Looey some free, me bein' there 'n all."

Tull had fallen silent, snored tentatively, then had awakened with a choking snort. He spoke once more in the darkness.

"Say, Coyote. 'Member when we was in th' Three Forks kentry 'n Henry buried th' two brass swivel guns?"

"Yes, I took one to Henry on the north fork of the Snake and hauled out the other. I buried it among the rocks in the Bitter Root Valley."

"Not usin' it, eh?"

"No. The Black Robes have a big cannon in which they fire only powder at night to warn away the Blackfeet and a few Bannacks who lurk about to kill or steal. The Black Robes do not like to do that because they say it's a waste. They now furnish us, as well as the Indian people at the other missions, with some of our powder and lead so that we can hunt better. This is much help because with the beaver and many other furs hard to get, some of the people otherwise would go hungry."

"How 'bout me tradin' fer th' swivel? Maybe Bridger cud use it at thet fort o' his'n. Probably wud like me gettin' it fer 'im. Cannons 'r gettin' harder ta find, cus 'pears there mought be some fightin' with th' Mexicans 'n Britishers, too."

"It is a good thought. There are fewer furs to trade for guns, and even our women must carry them when they work with our warriors in the fields. I will talk to Little Grizzly Bear Claw here, and his father, Little Bear Claw."

For a moment Little Coyote thought Tull was asleep, then, "Wull, see you come mornin'." This time the snores did not stop.

The seer, sleepy now, focused on what Young Ignace hurriedly had told him about St. Mary's Mission as Father Mengarini was greeting the other Jesuits: "Some of the younger braves are challenging Chief Little Bear Claw. They say the Black Robes' magic is not working strong enough to keep the Blackfeet away. They have attacked us several times, and we had one good fight." Young Ignace's face had brightened momentarily. "The crops are doing well." His face had sobered. "The Black Robes talk of carrying the faith to more of our kin and friends to the north and northwest." Young Ignace gravely had shaken his head. "There were many angry words when Father Mengarini said the Black Robes wish to go to the Blackfeet, too."

Matters sorted out and partially weighed now, the seer concluded they must leave the Shoshonis soon. On that unsettling thought, he let sleep take over until he heard Pony Whip's wife breaking sticks for the morning fire.

Tull fingered the final bone from his bowl of meat; he eyed it for a moment before giving it a final suck and tossing it to one of the dogs expectantly standing outside the eating circle. He wiped his hand across his buckskin jacket just below his flowing beard. Little Coyote recognized the signal. Tull was going to "speechify," make up for his virtual silence during the meal the night before.

"Eny more idee 'bout tradin' fer th' swivel gun?"

"Little Grizzly Bear Claw and I agreed our people would wish to trade it for five good Hellinghaus rifles, or Hawkens, each with a mould, two pounds of powder, two-hundred caps and eight half-pound bars of lead."

"Fair." Tull nodded his bushy head. "I'll 'member. Whar 'n when do we meet? Cain't make it in '44 or '45. Th' boys at Fort Laramie and I figgered we'd head inta th' better buffler kentry 'n pile us up a heap o' high-quality robes ta have one o' them paddlewheelers float ta St. Looey. Try ta find us some Indian women who's makin' th' robes good 'n far f'm th' forts th' traders is settin' up 'long th' Mizzoury 'n Yallerstone. Must be clost ta a hunnert o' 'em thar now ta get th' robes. 'N tongues. Smoked buffler tongues. They's fetchin' a moughty high price in St. Looey now. Nope. We'd better not figger '44 er '45. Sides, Bridger's fixin' ta get young Choteau in St. Looey ta send tradin' goods up th' Mizzoury ta stock up th' fort, 'n 'pears, dependin' on how th' robes go, I'll be helpin' ta bring th' goods up th' trail f'm Westport, er hep mind th' fort while Bridger does it. Is th' late fall o' '46, 'fore snow, 'greeable? Mebbee in—le's see." Tull held out his bowl for another horn ladle of meat, rolled his eyes upward in appreciation, took a bite, chewed it twice and swallowed. "How 'bout September of '46 at . . . um, th' Sentinel Rock at Camas Meadows? 'Pears that's half-way. I'll make that a sort o' turn-'round spot f'm 'nother tradin' trip. Thet'd make it wuthwhile even if Bridger gets a swivel er so f'm Choteau. Wull, allus c'd use 'nother." Tull chortled. "Er mebbe he cud sell it at a 'tarnal high price ta one o' them scared immygrant trains."

When Little Coyote nodded agreeably, Tull bit off a great chew of tobacco. So it was settled; the Flatheads prepared to leave. As Tull shook their hands, Little Coyote told him to give greetings to Bridger and his wife, the daughter of Insula.

"She went under." Tull shook his head. "Good woman, that. Bridger up and married a Ute."

"Victor, perhaps we can wash off the blood before we cross St. Mary's River."

Father Anthony Ravalli agilely hoisted his two-hundred-pound body atop his sturdy horse which, with those of Little Bear Claw and Little Coyote, impatiently had whisked its tail at the flies buzzing on the shady side of the small log cabin while the priest and seer had saved Packrat's life. Much of it had drained out before he had staggered to the priest, assisted by the oldest of his three wives and trailed by their children.

"He drank whiskey at the big man's place there." The woman had pointed toward the slough and three cottonwoods—Skrellings' place, where he traded whiskey and a few trinkets for furs, women's favors and horses. Packrat's wife had clamped her now-bloody hand firmly over the spouting artery after the knife fight and held it there while seeking help. Little Coyote had minded the tourniquet while the priest, intently squinting those gentle eyes, had lanced, probed, seized, clamped and, finally, sewed.

"I thank God for the seeming contradiction that the very whiskey that caused the problem spared Packrat much of the pain I was inflicting to save him." The priest smiled, then left a streak of blood on his prominent nose as he brushed at one of the flies drawn to the feast. "But the problem of Skrellings and those others remains." With Flathead words and a few signs, he instructed the woman to have the pallid-faced warrior lie down in the building beside two other patients. Here he would be fed and cared for.

They scoured off the dried blood with sand and creek water. Little Coyote thought of the cleanliness he had seen and, with Antelope, had practiced as far back as his early experiences at Lisa's fort. He suppressed again that persistent deep pang of sorrow by vigorously shaking off the water and remembering Father Ravalli's delight when the seer had shown him his medicine box.

Medicinal herbs: Those, as well as the opportunity to learn even more about and from each other, had drawn together Father Ravalli, the tribal chief and the medicine man this early summer of 1846. Ever since this Black Robe's arrival at St. Mary's only a year ago, he had worked as busily and incessantly as does the beaver before freezeup. He had remained at St. Francis Xavier Mission on the Willamette River when his superior, Father DeSmet, had returned from his 1843 begging trip to Europe for helpers and money for the expanding Northwest missions. Next, Father DeSmet had assigned Father Ravalli to work among the Kalispels, where he quickly had learned their dialect, which closely resembled that of the Flatheads. Too, he had worked hard to help and come to know other tribes— Okanogans, Crees, Kutenais, Flatheads, even more. Soon after building a chapel among the Shuyelpi, or Colvilles, near Fort Colvile on the Columbia River, he had been sent to help Father Mengarini at St. Mary's Mission on the death of Father Zerbinatti there. Father Mengarini was the superior there now because Father DeVos had been sent to work among the Shuyelpi.

Long before this search for herbs, the chief and the seer had agreed to speak to the priest in English as much as possible. He would use their language, as would Father Mengarini, who, with Little Coyote's help, was compiling a dictionary. Thus, all would learn.

"We will follow this well-worn trail to the base of my medicine mountain—St. Mary's Peak," Little Coyote explained, "then up an old path to a small, steeply sloping meadow. There we will find the plants."

They staked out their horses at meadow's edge. Little Coyote patiently began describing the growing plants before picking a few of each, tying them together with a long grass stem, then putting the small bundles into a basket until it was full.

Father Ravalli removed the larger basket he had tied behind his saddle and withdrew thick sheets of crude paper, pen and ink. Little Coyote was surprised at how well the Black Robe had remembered what he had been told. The seer nodded affirmatively as the priest identified each bundle of plants, placed it between two sheets of paper and marked its name and use on the top sheet.

"*Hasx's*," the priest said, pointing to the roots. "*N'calé*. For bellyache. Boil or chew it." He stripped off some fir needles from an overhead branch. "*S'kélpu*. For coughs. *Mtce éus*. Use the leaf for boils or sores."

So it went. As Sun lowered, the seer's great respect for the kindly priest's wisdom increased. Father Ravalli had earned Little Coyote's respect when he had vaccinated the Flathead people against smallpox with vaccine he had brought from Italy and was keeping alive even now. The tribal skeptics who had agreed to receive this medicine had lived. Not so, many of their Nez Percé allies who had not been vaccinated when the scourge again made its deadly visit.

Yes, Father DeSmet, busily moving from mission to mission, had chosen well.

"Shall we eat here?" the Black Robe asked. The three halted on the last high knob overlooking the Mission below and across the river. The priest opened a woven willow basket and distributed cold pork, chicken and rough bread baked from flour ground at the water-powered mill he had designed and others had helped him construct. They ate while the mountain shadows slowly crept across the grain fields and gardens and reached the many lodges. Soon the shadows began encompassing the Mission, itself—the small church building and eleven houses, plus that of the Black Robes. Construction had been made easier by the output of a water-powered sawmill, the blade for which Father Ravalli laboriously and ingeniously had made with fire, water, hammer

564

and file from the iron tire of an old wagon wheel. There were other structures, including granaries, which had held thousands of bushels of vegetables, potatoes and wheat, and soon once again would be filled. The distant mooing among the forty head of cattle reached up to the eaters; as the cool, evening breeze arrived, they watched guards drive the cattle and numerous horses closer to the village—an unsettling reminder of the ever-present danger from roving enemies.

"So beautiful, and seemingly so peaceful. It almost could be a worldly paradise." Father Ravalli arose and dusted the bread crumbs and meat particles from his hands and lap onto a small anthill. The ants scurried about at this unexpected gift from above, some, in their excitement, pulling larger crumbs this way and that. Again the priest looked at the Mission. This time he sighed, the ready smile flickering on and off as though trying to choose between the joy of his good soul or apprehensions about the world surrounding them all.

He mounted his horse and again looked at his two companions.

"As I have told Victor, there is a far-off land called Paraguay. There the Jesuits have helped build what we call 'reductions' among those wandering people. We wish to help them acquire a strong faith, a respect for those in charge, and a strong liking, almost a love, for hard work." The impatient horse pranced about, anxious to depart. "And, Victor, how much you are helping to lead your good people to reach these three aims, too, despite opposition from jealous warriors, some of the younger men and those who do not wish for us to try to help the Blackfeet now and against the changes that surely lie ahead. Which leads to the fourth aim. And here I worry the most. We can more fully reach the three by staying away from the often-evil people and forces of the world."

The priest waited for Little Bear Claw's horse to take the lead before he loosened his reins. "I fear. Yes, fear Skrellings and others who are here or are sure to come." He turned to look at Little Coyote. "Our prayers together to our one God the Indians largely have believed in long before white man came must be constant and strong, stronger than any other force. Our prayers have helped us to accomplish much already. They will help us in the tasks ahead. We shall endure."

As the priest turned his horse toward the sloping trail, Little Coyote observed the right hind hoof of the animal drag briefly across and demolish the southern arc of the ant hill. He paused briefly to look down at the chaos resulting from this unintentional devastation. He tried to move his mind from a sense of foreboding to a happier plateau. Yes, with much work, surely prayers to the Good Spirit, the Flatheads had prospered in many ways. Then he, too, set his horse into motion, wondering momentarily about St. Louis and how his Osage friend, Old Fire, was faring.

Little Bear Claw and his son brought a small pot of food to Little Coyote's lodge, which was set almost equidistant between Skrellings' hovel and the last cluster of other lodges.

"Agnes," Little Bear Claw said with a grin, "continues to worry about your belly." The chief smiled. "I about your soul." He nodded for the young brave to set down the food and gripped his old friend strongly by the shoulder. "You know the prayers. You like the Black Robes. There will be three baptisms, two of Kalispels and a Nez Percé, after prayers tonight. You could prepare yourself for baptism in a few days."

"Not yet. There are many things I yet must ponder. However, on another matter . . ." This time Little Coyote grinned. ". . . I accept defeat. You are the victor." He frowned as though undergoing great pain, yet in all honesty regretting the thrust of his next few words: "From now on, because it is your preference, I will call you by your Christian name, unless circumstances require that I do not. Come, *Victor* and *Charlot*, let us step outside where I will eat."

As he ate the yet-warm food, Little Coyote heard bird calls blending with more distant coyote songs. Nearer, the voices of his people rose in joyful song to the accompaniment of musical instruments. Visualizing the shape of the wind instruments reminded the seer of the swivel gun. He was waiting when the people filed outside the chapel and, amid animated talking,

566

dispersed to their lodges.

"Will you help me bring the swivel gun to my lodge?" he greeted Victor and Agnes. He looked about for Charlot.

"He goes to guard the horses," Victor responded. "Come, I will help."

The two warriors lifted aside some of the flatter rocks from the pile laboriously hauled from the largest garden plot, then hauled out the badly tarnished swivel gun. The old piece of tough buffalo bull hide still was tightly bound around the touch hole and barrel. They poked around inside the barrel with a willow stick and dumped out the loosened dust and dirt before hoisting the weapon atop the pack horse.

There was much talk that night around the swivel and tiny fire in Little Coyote's lodge.

"I would like to go with you to meet Tull." Victor's downcast mouth emphasized his regrets. "There are many new tasks I am called on to do. I have thought much of that journey of Father DeSmet's to Canada, from which he returned only this spring. Though it was a failure, I understand why he tried to make peace with the Blackfeet, and to stop their attacks on St. Mary's. Perhaps it was good that he did not find them, for even the Hudson's Bay people had warned him the Blackfeet would kill him and his three Indian companions." The chief's lips drooped even more. "Now he will seek the Blackfeet again, even before you seek Tull. I find Father DeSmet's new plan even more difficult to explain to our people."

Little Coyote listened. He had swallowed his own wish to try to dissuade Father Mengarini from accompanying many of their people on this past spring's buffalo hunt. Four had died in a furious battle—as had twenty-four Blackfeet. Little Coyote had learned that the priest had persuaded Victor to call off the fight and even return some captives and booty. Oh, how the people had talked, their grumbling persisting to this very day.

Victor picked up a long, dry ponderosa pine twig and slowly began breaking it into tiny pieces.

"I continue to learn more about Christianity every time I am with the Black Robes," he said, "but others of our people do not mix so often with them. They believe, some of them such as Agnes, very deeply. But many yield to temptations too readily because their beliefs have not worn deeply yet.

"I have spoken to Father DeSmet about this. He said the Black Robes have hurried with the baptisms because what has happened to Indians elsewhere is beginning to happen to them up the Missouri and in the great buffalo lands. He said, 'We seek to avoid this as much as possible.'

"But Father," I said, "if the white man is Christian, why does he make the Indian suffer?

"'All people are born to suffer,' he replied sadly. 'Even Christ. So we try to help the whites, too. I agree, for now the Indians suffer more. We must work harder to stop this.'"

Victor tossed the bits of wood onto the lodge fire. "I must send warriors, including my step-son, Fast Runner, now John, with Father DeSmet, and keep others here. As you know, Broken Bow, called Francis, and Stone Rattle, now Robert, have had their vision quests. They would go with you to meet Tull. They will serve you well, for they are the sons of Kills With Lance and Wild Horse. Only two years ago when our people were returning heavily laden from the buffalo grounds, these two warriors set up the great ambush of the Blackfeet in the canyon above Big Prairie on the south fork of the River of the Flatheads. Charlot also would go. Yes, take my son, too." He worriedly pounded his hands together. "Our sick become well, more warriors are settling for one wife. More of our children survive birth. They receive better care from their mothers. Most of us do not drink the whiskey. The fields yield much good food. I use my whip less, though I do this because the Black Robes frown on such punishment. We eat much better than before when most of the buffalo meat is gone.

"We must make peace with the Blackfeet, though we often kill many—as in the ambush at Big Prairie. We agreed long ago that we can lose four warriors, they twenty-four, and yet their people will survive, for they and their allies are more numerous despite the smallpox. We could disappear. I understand this. We number between five-hundred and six-hundred souls. The

Black Robes are right. We must seek peace. I must work harder to convince our people of this. Yes, trade the swivel for good guns. The Black Robes still will not put shot into their cannon. Father DeSmet has told me he would move the Mission before he would kill great numbers of our enemies."

The downcast lips formed a half-smile. "Though we might all lose our lives, we will save our souls. This I firmly believe." The chief crossed himself. "My son must become more learned than I. He must spend much time with you and the Black Robes for what surely lies ahead."

He arose and, before departing, clapped his friend strongly on the shoulder. He was grinning now, the moodiness gone, the light from the tiny fire revealing his strong, white teeth.

"On my way back to my lodge I firmly desire to drive a war arrow into the buffalo turd, Skrellings. Here." He put his finger to his throat. "But, you, my friend, have told us from the days of Clark and Lewis: 'We must not fight the white man.'" He left the lodge shaking his head. "Interesting, not to kill such a one as Skrellings causes us to fight among ourselves."

52

Victor accompanied the cannon-traders a half-day's journey southward toward Ross' Hole, resting place of Shining Shirt and others. He and Little Coyote lagged behind while Charlot proudly preceded the pack train he had organized. Two sturdy horses alternately would carry the swivel. There was an extra horse for each of the four Flatheads, plus five more animals carrying buffalo robes for trading. Charlot would have to remember what Tull exchanged for the robes and horses because only the swivel-gun trade would be a community venture.

Little Coyote grinned as the procession wound past the old forts he and Willow Woman had defended against the Blackfeet. Then his thoughts centered on Agnes as he remembered her repeated insistence since he had returned to the Mission that he seek another mate. In the ancient ways of the people she had spared no graphic and alluring descriptions of the many gratifications that would result.

"Some matters flow easily from her imaginative mind." He spoke so Victor would hear.

"Are you comparing various women?" There was a hopeful note in his voice, too.

"No. Only of one I never would marry."

570

"Who? And why not? Agnes said she repeatedly has talked to you."

"The very woman I spoke about. She is the wife of a great chief."

"Sometimes she speaks like the chief, even to the Black Robes, most lately arguing with them that the council and I have done right to start using the whip again on the drunkards and most licentious. 'Confession,' she says, 'is not enough.'" Victor again looked behind, left and right, finally far ahead to assure himself that the three others were following instructions to maintain contact. "When I returned to my lodge last night, several young warriors—two older who should have known better—and some women had arrived to argue that Father DeSmet should not again seek the Blackfeet. I had no chance to speak out. Agnes, hard to believe, was just thrusting two fingers almost into the face of Flint Arrow—Joseph, who seemed to be leading the group. Others, attracted by the uproar, laughed when the complainers sneaked away just after this great insult. Yes, she takes care of me in many ways." They rode on silently. Charlot, always-smiling Francis and the more solemn Robert were waiting for the two warriors as they topped a sloping hill well above and back from the now-shallow river. Here, tall trees gave way to short brush. The sky was blue as a trade bead, except for a few high clouds serenely sailing east, enticing the watching group to follow.

The chief looked somberly at the party. He must hurry back to the Mission and its myriad problems. He nudged his horse alongside his son's.

"Pray for the souls of Shining Shirt and the others when you reach his resting place. Go with God." He clasped his son's arm, then pointed east, not north. "Remember Little Coyote's interpretation of your vision. If ever you have to leave this valley, try to go east, not north. To the east is the land of your people, too, as well as that of the Pend d'Oreilles, Kutenais and our friends the Shoshonis." He let go his son's arm as the others filed down the hill. They looked back before entering the trees. The chief waved once as they disappeared from view.

Charlot signaled *danger* when he began skirting the northwestern fringe of a large meadow barely a half-day's ride from Ross' Hole. Francis, long hair flying, waving his old cut-off Hudson's Bay flintlock musket, galloped his horse back to Robert. They waited until Little Coyote rode up.

"Charlot signaled *four white people*," Francis explained while Robert spilled a few grains of powder in his haste to reprime the musket his father had given him as a vision-quest gift.

"Francis," Little Coyote said. "Seek the edge of the trees, so the whites will not know how many we are. As I approach them, ride your horse into view. Robert, take the pack horse string into the trees. When Francis shows himself, do the same." Little Coyote loosened his bow in its case, raised the old lance higher and approached Charlot while the two youths hastened to comply.

"They have built a cabin much like that of Skrellings," the young brave explained. "I saw a man, two children and a woman. They watch us carefully."

Little Coyote used his spyglass before slowly approaching the white people. He rode around a garden patch scratched out near the small creek and enclosed with lodge poles. Willow had been woven between the posts to keep out deer. Closer to the cabin was a small pole corral into which a barefoot boy hurriedly was driving two cows and a young bull. Four scrawny horses were picketed in the meadow in front of the cabin. The medicine man raised his arm in greeting as the white man approached; the man was carrying a smooth-bore, caplock musket with a sling made from an old bridle rein.

"Howdy." He nervously glanced back at his family. "Are you Nez Percé?"

"Flathead."

The man's taut face loosened. He almost managed a smile as he hastily spilled out his story.

"We're the Enfingers. Some trappers at Fort Hall told us how to get here. They warned us about the Blackfeet. Said the Flatheads and the Nez Percé were most friendly. Perkins, he was my partner, he came part way with his family, then scared out.

Said he'd go on to Oregon. Do you understand?"

Little Coyote nodded. "My friends will approach. You need not be afraid."

While they broiled a gift of fresh elk meat, the seer watched the woman. Though pregnant, she was skinny as the horses, with great shadows under her eyes. She seemed unable to sit down to rest, all the while whispering to her twin boys, perhaps eight years old, to do this and that. Though Sun had warmed the land, she wore a red, knitted cape with three metal buttons over her thin shoulders.

"We came up the Mississipp from Tennessee," Enfinger said. "Wagon broke down before we reached Fort Hall. We didn't have the cash money to buy a good one. We figgered we could make it here. We've lived off the land afore. We can get a start by trading hides and furs. That's what my daddy did in Tennessee, but somebody else owned the land." His voice now held half pride, half challenge. "This is ourn!"

Little Coyote pondered telling Enfinger about the safer Bitter Root Valley. He thought of Skrellings, the others. No, more whites will find the valley soon enough.

"Many Blackfeet come this way."

"My boys and I can shoot; so can the woman."

Leaning against the cabin near the door were an old shotgun and two large-bore, flintlock muskets similar to those Little Coyote had helped trade for more than forty years earlier.

"You would do well to leave. You could get out before the heavy snows come. We go to meet a trader who will return to Fort Bridger. If you hurry, you could join forces."

"But we have the land, the garden."

"Mr. Enfinger." The woman clutched the cape more closely about her shoulders. "I think the Indian is right. We have to think of the young-uns. Us, too, fer that matter."

"No, woman. We've got no money. Here we have our land and the chance. Others will come, and with more we'll be safer. Think of that great valley we looked at first, the one the trappers marked as Ross' Hole." He shook his head. "No, we'll never leave."

Charlot put the cavalcade into motion before leaving to scout ahead. Once again Francis and Robert diligently began looking left and right, even upward as they rode. Little Coyote remained in the rear. He slowly rode past the spindly corral, the scrawny, picketed horses, then abruptly returned to the cabin. This time the family walked over to his horse. He looked from the nervous Enfinger to the silent twins and, finally, at the cavernous eyes of the woman.

"In maybe two or three days' journey for you and your animals northward on the trail and down the river," he said, pointing, "you could reach St. Mary's Mission. There are priests there, others. The Blackfeet come there, too, but you would be safer than here."

The woman bent forward to look at her man; she wanted to speak more.

Now Enfinger eyed her and their sons, then the land. His face stiffened as when Little Coyote first had seen him.

"We thank you kindly, Indian, we surely do." He shook his head. "No, like I said, we're staying here."

At Ross' Hole, the Flatheads prayed at the graves. The young braves listened intently as Little Coyote told them of this place, from his earliest memories till now. While Francis and Robert eagerly sought some fresh meat, Little Coyote took Charlot to the ponderosa pine where he and Victor had reburied the bones, the large ceremonial flint weapons, and gold nuggets.

"Your father and I grow older. We agreed we should tell you about what lies buried here. The gold should only be used at a time of greatest trouble." Little Coyote dug up the nuggets, let Charlot heft and rebury them, then spilled pine needles over the site. In the doing, the medicine man explained how gold turns the white man's head like whiskey.

"Even the priests fear its effects," he warned. "Victor told me to caution you that what I say now should only pass your lips to the person who would be next chief after you. While our people were bringing Father DeSmet into our valley five years ago, he told about wandering alone and prayerfully along a creek in the deer lodge valley, perhaps two or three days' trek from our valley.

There he found some nuggets like these. Even when he most greatly needed supplies and other help for the Mission, he did not offer the gold or tell about it and how some more likely could be found.

"Father DeSmet told your father: 'While we Jesuits recognize that bodily needs must be met, we labor for the spirit. Gold would draw white men to this place with the rapidity and destructiveness of a mindless buffalo herd.'"

The triumphant halloo from the two youths brought the seer and young brave back to their camp. The welcome deer meat, procured with an arrow, took them most of the way to Camas Meadow and Tull.

"We seed ye comin'. This be Kniffen." Tull pointed his walking stick at the tall, thin, salt-and-pepper-bewhiskered man hunkered over a fire and broiling a slab of elk meat. The man looked up, grimacing against the contrary smoke, but waved a friendly greeting. Tull eyed the heavily laden horses drinking from the small pond. "Pears ye brought th' swivel, shure 'nough, 'n robes." His bright eyes centered on the four Flatheads. "Hosses?" The hairy face parted in a grin wide enough to disclose some of his brown teeth when Little Coyote nodded. "I'm relieved. Them Shoshonis loaded up my critters with a fine harvest o' furs. Wull, sit 'n have some vittles." He added more water and tea leaves to the blackened pail.

The mountain man was expansive. Kniffen ambled over to the base of Sentinel Rock with his meat and seated himself on the next largest fragment of the low and heavily fractured granitic upthrust. When the trading ended, Charlot divided the goods into recognizable piles so each of the robe owners would get his due. Francis and Robert were examining the goods, then bundling them into tanned deer hides; they also were walking past and eying, whenever possible, the two Hawkens and three Hellinghaus caplock rifles and accouterment lying on a piece of canvas.

"Lucky ta git 'em, 'n had a helluva time holdin' onta 'em." Tull spat and extinguished a small tongue of flame threatening to creep into the dry grass surrounding the campfire. "Bridger shore wanted th' swivel. He's . . ." Tull paused. ". . . But ta get back ta th' rifle guns. "'Bout fifteen-hundred immygrants com'd up th' trail in '44, 'n Bridger calclated three-thousand er more in '45. Ever'body wants rifle guns, includin' th' red men.

"When th' beaver went, I figgered I'd had th' best o' it, 'n with these cussed knees I wuz gonna' get th' wust o' it." He spat again. "We gone ta war with Mexico. Thet's helpin' keep folks outta Californy. They's comin' hyar. Th' British 'n us settled the fracas 'bout th' Oregon kentry, with th' Britishers pullin' out mostly. Seems ever' pilgrim in creation wants ta travel up th' Oregon Trail. Bridger 'n Looey Vaskiss shore 'nuff wanted my he'p arter t'other fellars, includin' Kniffen thar." Tull swiveled on his butt to face and again point his walking stick. "Kniffen 'n me cleaned up on th' buffler robes 'n tongues shore 'nuff.

"Kniffen's squar, he is. We made a 'greement thet if him er me goes under, what we got goes ta th' Black Robes in St. Looey, who 'er heppin' take keer o' hosses like me whose laigs don't work much, 'n 'er findin' it hard ginerally. Bridger, he's holdin' onta our cash money 'n all.

"Why they's shure 'nough work ta keep me agoin'. I ain't had time ta spend much cash, 'cept fer— Whut in tarnation's pesterin' Kniffen?" Tull dug his walking stick into the earth, grunted and pulled himself erect.

Kniffen was holding the back of his fully open left hand toward the campers. He rubbed it from wrist to knuckles twice with his right hand, then repeated the gesture. *Indians!* Now he held his half-closed hands to the left and right of his body and moved them in vertical curves downward and upward. *Many!* He clambered behind the rock.

"Stay low among the rocks so they can't count us all." That said, Little Coyote seized his spyglass, bow and arrows. Kniffen didn't need to point. Perhaps seventeen, yes, seventeen horsemen. Little Coyote moved the spyglass from left to right across the irregular line, stopped before completing the swing, then moved back. That flash of red! He focused more carefully. The warrior was wearing the red cape that had covered the thin shoulders of the Enfinger woman near Ross' Hole!

Even before the seer signed for *moccasin, black* and *seventeen*, Tull and the three Flatheads were picketing their horses more securely and somewhat apart among the scattered rocks. Tull then began directing the three youths to place the bundles of trade goods in a number of widely separated piles a short distance from the rocks.

Little Coyote hurried back and repeated to Tull what he had just told Kniffen about the Enfingers: "Before the Blackfeet killed them, I am certain they learned we are four Flatheads, and how we are armed."

"Glad ye tol' us. I knows whut yore thinkin', Coyote," Tull said coolly, "but th' wind's comin' f'm th' south. Them varlets won't try ta burn us out, 'n lose th' robes 'n hosses, bundles, too, 'less there ain't no other way."

Little Coyote nodded, then directed the youths to help him carry some of the bales of robes near five of the largest rocks for greater protection. "Line up the rest near the rock where Kniffen is, so the Blackfeet will think that's where we'll be waiting."

"Gittin' closter!" Kniffen sang out.

Little Coyote's mind centered on the red cape as they worked. He linked those thoughts to Father DeSmet's disputed reasons for seeking the Blackfeet again. *If we kill Blackfeet here without being killed, ourselves,* the seer reasoned, *any survivors will tell about their losses and hamper the Black Robes' attempts; the rage here would spread widely, never mind their presumed killing of the Enfingers and the attempts to kill us.*

Yes, these Blackfeet, blood up from an easy victory over the Enfingers, scarcely would care to parley, considering their numbers, the prospective booty and scalps.

Little Coyote glanced at his bow and arrows, his lance, the untested youths, crippled Tull, seemingly capable Kniffen. For an instant he weighed Father DeSmet's journey to the Blackfeet against the Black Robe's decision, despite provocation, not to use the cannon for slaughter at St. Mary's. Once again the seer looked at his weapons, then at the swivel gun, finally at expectant Charlot, the chief's seed.

Win or die! Little Coyote threw his robe over the swivel

gun and directed the youths to carry it to Kniffen's rock. The warrior brought up flasks of powder and some of the soft bar lead. He set a determined Francis to chopping the lead up into bullet-size pieces. After loading the weapon, the seer again threw his robe over it and directed the youths: "Wedge the post of the swivel securely into a tight crack in this rock. Pound it with a smaller rock, if you must. Mind the robe. We want the Blackfeet to think we've only put one more bale atop the rock."

Little Coyote looked at Kniffen. "Have you fired a swivel?"

"I have, on keel boats from time to time comin' up the Missouri. Yep, I can handle that 'ere swivel . . . if you can use that bow and arrers."

Tull loaded the rifles he had traded and put one by each fortified rock. "Coyote, tell th' young fellers ta 'range four o' them bales so they c'n skeedaddle behint 'em ifn' th' sarpents come f'm whichever derection. 'N tell 'em ta keep their haids down, asses, too, behint th' rocks should we have ta turn th' swivel their way." He put two pistols in his sash, picked up his Hawken and limped toward the swivel. The Blackfeet had formed into three small and silent groups, well out of accurate rifle shot.

Tull gave Kniffen a drink from a small metal flask, took one himself and handed Little Coyote a small twist of tobacco. "Knows ye don't like speerits, Coyote, but fer these two ol' hosses, wull, there comes a time." He bit off a big chew of tobacco, rolled it around in his mouth, spat and moved it to his cheek. "Yep, there comes a time." He looked around. "Wull, we got water, ammynition . . ." He looked at the remainder of the elk and the horses. ". . . 'n meat." He glanced at slightly westering Sun. "Now we waits fer th' varlets.

"Say, Coyote," Tull said with a grin, "how 'bout you 'n t'others steppin' out in front o' th' swivel fer a looksee so th' sarpants'll know they's on'y four o' us?"

Charlot, Francis and Robert energetically belly-crawled to the bales near the swivel gun. Tull and Kniffen sat down. Then the four Flatheads sauntered singly, weapons in hand, in front of the bales as though for a closer look at their enemies. The three braves, armed with the new rifles, looked at each other for reassurance. Finding it, all grinned and experimentally sighted their guns toward the Blackfeet.

"Wull," Tull said, looking at Charlot, "Jed Smith tol' me onct in a fracas, 'Th' more ye kin git in light, th' fewer ta fight near night.' Clost ta thet anyways. Young feller, d'ye figger ye c'n cuss th' varlets 'nough ta bring 'em tord th' swivel, stid o' comin' in f'm all three sides?"

Charlot glanced inquiringly at Little Coyote. The seer's face was impassive as he translated Tull's own brand of English.

Charlot picked up Lance's shield, carefully leaned his rifle against a bale, then walked a short distance toward the Blackfeet while Kniffen struck a small fire and placed the ends of several long, dry sticks in it.

Charlot's first barrage of insults, almost matching those of his dead mother in descriptive powers, but slowly spoken and brief, reached outward—then mockingly echoed back. Inspired by this discovery, Charlot became even more creative and selective. He ended by asking the warrior in the red cape if he dressed like a woman because he could fight only women. This created noticeable movement among some of the horsemen. Charlot walked back to ask Little Coyote how to put the same meanings in Blackfeet. Before the insults in the Blackfeet tongue echoed back, a cacophony of shrill cries reached the six in the rock field. As their echoes arrived, the groups of wildly yelling horsemen coalesced and rushed toward Charlot. He scampered behind a bale.

"Use your rifles first, then smooth-bores for closer work," he told Francis and Robert. They nodded. Jaws set, the two tried not to wince as they saw and heard the destruction racing toward them.

"Well, here goes." Kniffen reached up under the robe to pour some powder over the swivel's touch hole. Then he handed his powder horn, wiping stick and bullet pouch to Tull. The warrior in the red cape was racing ahead of the others, striking his horse, then extending the quirt outward like a lance to count coup. He held his rifle in his other hand. Kniffen's bullet almost knocked him off the horse. He dropped the rifle but held the lead until he was close enough for Little Coyote's arrow to take him in the face between two parallel lines of red paint. Kniffen had handed his rifle to Tull for reloading and picked up one burning stick. The tightly compacted, frightfully yelling warriors were perhaps seventy feet away now, their horses colliding and grunting as they maintained footing and momentum amid the uproar. Kniffen coolly stood erect, whisked the robe off the swivel and seized the traversing and elevating bar extending from under the breach. Despite hastily fired shots at him, he lowered the muzzle, swiveled it toward the most densely packed mass of shrilling men and horses, then put the ember on the touch hole.

The effect was stupefying, fearsomely lethal.

Stupefying because the murderous, single-minded intentions of the horsemen seemed to melt in the fire and noise of the explosion. Fearsomely lethal because the downed horses and their riders caused others—dying, wounded or unscathed—to stumble or veer away from or continue to rush pell-mell among the rocks. There they fell, or crazily ran ahead amid grunting, screaming and the snapping of bones. Now the methodical pop-pop of rifles and two booms of muskets punctuated the chaos. Little Coyote, his arrows almost gone, stopped for an instant to look at the writhing, suffering, screaming mess. Appalled, he nevertheless seized his lance to assist in the closer work. Tull was hobbling forward with pistols and hatchet.

Kniffen had clambered atop the rock and found it in himself to urinate down the swivel barrel to extinguish any residual sparks. He dumped the now-black liquid and hastily reloaded. The horsemen who had survived the run through the camp and jumbled rocks had not regrouped. Kniffen methodically aimed the swivel at the nearest and largest mass of yet-struggling flesh and again let fly. The horrific roar outraced the sulphurous smoke and added its diminished echo to the equally lowering screaming, shrieks and groans. Finally, the defenders could hear each other speak.

The six would have been better served had Kniffen directed his second ministration of hell at the smaller huddle. Fate, in the thunderous charge, had nudged that group to the extreme left tip of the swivel's V-shaped swath of destruction. One horse there was dead; another dumbly stood with its hooves entangled in the ropy, roiling guts hanging from its belly—that drawer opened as by a sharp, giant knife. A third horse was gone, but the three silent riders were lying there.

The six defenders looked around. They had not made a count in the carnage, beyond these three. The remnant Blackfeet who looked toward the defenders from the south were far fewer—three, four, five. Silent, again beyond accurate rifle shot, they were examining horses and human bodies.

Tull had laid down his weapons and was fingering his hairy ears and shaking his head as though to hear better. He pulled another small flask from his baggage, took a deep swig and hobbled toward Kniffen. Spent, he was leaning against the rock as though he single-handedly had cut down the mass of flesh with many swipes and chops of a giant scythe. His pants remained unbuttoned and a black and wide ribbon of powder residue covered his left cheek and right hand as though he, too, had painted up for the battle.

Tull took one more nip, handed the flask to Kniffen, reloaded his pistols, then stuffed a small twist of tobacco into his left cheek.

"Wull . . . " His eyes centered on the gutted horse, tottering now, ready to fall. The old mountain man pulled one of the pistols from his sash and rocked toward the dying beast as Little Coyote also started with his lance.

Three more shots and a climactic flurry ended this battle of Camas Meadows. The horse, shot through the ear, dropped. Tull, shot in the belly by the Blackfeet warrior lying alongside the other dead horse, did not drop. Instead, he doubled up, swayed almost as had the gutted horse, steadied, then pulled his second pistol. The warrior, sitting now, threw his tomahawk. He took Tull's shot in his chest as the hatchet lodged between Tull's neck and upper chest. Tull crumpled quietly, raised his head once, then looked wonderingly around until the angling hatchet handle stopped all movement. The hairy head dropped; both crippled legs kicked as though aiding his spirit in its race to join Drouillard, Jedediah Smith, John Colter and others in the far-off sand hills.

Little Coyote, startled in the instant he saw his old friend double up, knew immediately that Tull, indeed, had had the best and the worst of it. There was also a flash of wonder if the same applied to himself as one of the other three Blackfeet sprang to his feet and shot the seer in his left arm. Failing to drop him, the Blackfeet slashed at Little Coyote's dodging head; he tomahawked the seer in his right shoulder and upper arm before Little Coyote could even try to ward off the blows with his lance. Dimly, the medicine man saw Charlot and his shield racing toward them, knife, not gun, in his free hand lest a hastily aimed shot kill the seer. The Blackfeet seemed to hesitate for the briefest instant at the sight of the black cross on the white shield; then he stepped back and made a sweeping swing at the young warrior. Too late. Charlot, agilely holding the shield above him, ducked under the tomahawk and, springing forward, plunged his knife into the man's upper belly. The tomahawk dropped. Once again the stabbing thrust, this time, more accurately, into the heart.

L ittle Coyote tried to move his head away from the force that was trying to open his eyes. Still, there was the thought that perhaps opening his eyes would dispel the visions of Indians of many tribes racing toward destructive swivel guns fired by giant white men. There was hurt, which, combined with each short flicker of light, did halt the visions and give some focus to his hearing, too. He also began to feel the sharper edges of the rock he was leaning against. He could hear Kniffen saying, "He's comin' 'round" and see the man's eyes peering into his own. Then Kniffen said, "Well, Tull wouldn't mind this." The medicine man could feel a finger forcing open his mouth, inserting something metallic between his teeth. The whiskey gagged him. He wanted to retch, but lacked the strength. The fiery cascade continued. Tears clouded, then cleared, his vision; he could see the anxious faces of Francis, Robert and Charlot, the latter holding one of the trade packs of needles and thread and a heavily blood-stained cape.

"Hold him like I said." Kniffen's voice was soft. The seer felt someone sit on both his legs and someone else grasp one arm. The right and most hurting one, he concluded as Kniffen poured whiskey over the shoulder and upper arm. At its bite, there again was the impulse to wrench away. Then he could take the pain. By slowly moving his head and swiveling his eyeballs until they hurt, too, he watched Kniffen wipe off blood with the cape. Kniffen sewed, wiped and sewed the badly chopped shoulder, much as a woman draws together irregular rents in an erect lodge covering.

With pain clearing his sight and hammering in his head, Little Coyote looked up, beyond the stitching. Segmented thoughts, beyond the painful, now grew more real. Or was the whiskey causing drunken visions? No. He was certain he could see the backs of three broad figures astride their horses—one near the front of the pack train ready to leave, the two others at the rear. The three faced south, almost unmoving as Sentinel Rock, itself, except when their impatient mounts twitched.

"Well, that's that!" The medicine man felt a final tug at his shoulder as Kniffen, showing the same detached efficiency with which he had wielded the swivel, knotted the thread, cut it, handed the needle to Charlot and stood up.

"Can you hear?" While he waited for the answer, Kniffen drank the remainder of the whiskey and flung away the flask. Little Coyote could hear a metallic sound as it struck a rock.

"I . . . can . . . hear." He tried to look up.

"There's five Blackfeet somewhere around, in mostly good condition. I want to light out for Fort Bridger, with swivel and all, before they gather up some friends. We've propped up old Tull with rope and some sticks, as we did with two of the Blackfeet, after cuttin' off much of their long hair and ornaments. I'll bury Tull where he'd like it. You got three live ones, damn good fighters, and fewer horses to manage. But I ain't lightin' out unless you say so. Can you make it back?"

Little Coyote could feel the whiskey at work. He wanted to wave his arms in dismissal. "We can. We are most grateful."

"Yeah. That's what Charlot here said. Well . . . " Kniffen knelt down, grasped, but did not lift, Little Coyote's right hand. "Well, take care." Kniffen picked up the lead rope, mounted his horse and began moving south, Tull and the others stiffly and unrhythmically moving from side to side, forward and back, as their mounts picked their way through the rocks and moved onto the uncluttered meadow toward the closest stand of trees.

Little Coyote awakened. For an instant he lay there, eyes closed, pondering the persistent memory; it was so strong he almost could see the assorted Indians' charges into the belching maw of the cannon. There was blood, so much blood it clouded the eyesight. He opened his eyes. He was lying on his back in a buffalo robe with low, westering Sun striking his eyes. He closed them and slept.

He next awoke in darkness, the blood gone, the vision of another charge at the cannon fading as someone lifted his head and repeatedly put broth-soaked camas bread into his mouth. At length he whispered, "Water." Receiving it, he gratefully drifted off again.

The blended stink of human and animal death surrounded the seer and set him struggling to sit up. Was he contributing to this great stink? Weakly, he sniffed his shoulder. No. He heard Francis shout, "He's awake!" Then he could feel the young warrior reach around his body and help him sit against the rock. Three smiling faces peered down at him. Each of his Flathead companions leaned on a good rifle and had knotted a Blackfeet eagle feather into long hair.

Charlot approached with a cup. Little Coyote tried to reach for it, but his right arm was bound to his body. He held out his left hand and Charlot helped guide warm soup to his lips. Between sips and while chewing tiny bits of meat, the seer looked beyond the yet-grinning warriors.

Assorted muskets, four rifles and a shotgun were piled on a blanket close by. One converted caplock musket had a bridle-rein sling. Enfinger's. Also the shotgun. On another blanket, laid out for packing, were quivers of mostly steel-tipped arrows, bows, two short lances, three pistols, powder horns and flasks, bullet pouches, bar lead and an old sword similar to that the drunken Mandan chief, Shahaka, had worn almost thirty-nine years earlier. Intricately beaded designs, some blood-scabbed, had been cut from garments and equipment for later reworking in Flathead patterns.

"I owe you my life." Little Coyote looked at Charlot, who squirmed uncomfortably. The seer put aside the empty cup and weakly beckoned for him to bend down. "How would I have explained to Victor had you died?"

"How would I have explained to my father had I not fought?"

"You are dearer than a brother, but Victor's son only." Little Coyote painfully grasped Charlot's right wrist. "You are young, but you are *i-sts-sókoi*, war friend dearer than a brother."

Charlot's eyes widened. "You must know—" He stopped so the seer could speak while strength remained.

"With your assent, I will proclaim this at the councils."

This most compelling matter attended to, Little Coyote wearily sorted out the order of things that must be done. He closed his eyes and reviewed the battle. The memory of Kniffen's deadly use of the swivel began to dominate. Yes, as the mountain man had led away his ghostly cavalcade, the swivel was roped to the horse directly behind his own mount. The white man's priority of values was evident in the way he had lined up the laden horses behind him: The swivel gun, dead Tull, packs of food, ammunition and camp gear, bundles of furs, the bales of robes and, finally, the dead Blackfeet.

Again the seer gathered his strength to speak to Charlot. "I will ride on a travois for two days until the flesh mends better. Select the two best horses and hasten to the Mission. Relate to Victor all that has occurred, even if you must go beyond the Mission to find him already accompanying Black Robe on his peace trip to the Blackfeet."

The young warrior's eyes widened in surprise. "I will do so, but you must know—" He stopped when Little Coyote impatiently moved his head. "But I must tell you that when you were bleeding so much I feared you dying or dead and, after I killed the Blackfeet warrior, I poured water over your head and—" Again, the seer impatiently interrupted.

"Later. There is much I must say. Give Victor this message: Little Coyote foresees . . ." He paused. "Yes, Little Coyote foresees many Indians of many tribes fighting the increasingly more numerous white men as we once did the Blackfeet, always armed with better weapons. We must strive to preserve all Indian lives, lest tribes die in great numbers as though struck by repeated attacks of smallpox. We have won a fight with the Blackfeet here, but we must look beyond our victory. We must seek ways to wage lasting peace, not war—if we also can preserve our lives and honor. If your father also should talk of peace with the Blackfeet, he would like to have my thoughts. Do you understand? I will move to our valley more slowly with two proven warriors to assist me."

"I understand." Charlot grimly smiled while his two companions drew themselves upright, awkwardly trying not to betray their prideful feelings.

Charlot and Francis angled their horses across the great meadow to strike the nearest trees. There, Francis felled three lodgepoles, which his horse quickly dragged to Sentinel Rock. While he and Robert began chopping one pole into equal lengths and fashioning the pieces into a small platform across the other two, the medicine man reviewed his words to Charlot: *"Little Coyote foresees . . ." Yes, surely the Good Spirit, during this present illness, is sending a strong message for me to reveal to the people. He has extended the message from my vision quest— "Do not fight white man"—to now say: "No Indians can wage a successful war against white man." It is interesting that the Good Spirit also sends messages to others, helps them, and those people accept these kindnesses without pondering or acknowledging the source.*

Even more content now, the seer let his two companions help him to the padded platform of the travois, the two small ends of which they had fastened to the sides of a sturdy horse. With trade goods and booty packed on the other animals, they all began picking their way through this stinking place, rousing the quarreling birds into short, scolding flights. Little Coyote noted that scalps remained on the intact heads he could see from his flexible conveyance.

That night he awakened several times, feeling better, less stiff and weak. From the direction of Sentinel Rock, the cold night breeze brought occasional sounds of coyotes, perhaps signaling their kind to hasten to the site of the fallen Blackfeet and their horses.

After another night's rest the warriors had moved beyond the charred, skeletal outline of the Enfingers' cabin and the scattered bone fragments of two adult humans. The younger warriors searched while Little Coyote walked a bit with the aid of his lance haft. They found no trace of the Enfinger twins.

Father Ravalli murmured sympathetically as he examined Little Coyote's wounds. He peered at Kniffen's handiwork and said, "I will leave the stitches in until you have moved about more. The musket ball wound is of little consequence, *Laus Deo*, because the bone and important veins and arteries were not struck."

Extremely worn from the day's journey, wanting only rest, Little Coyote had sought no answers to many questions in his mind after Francis and Robert brought Father Ravalli to his lodge. He was grateful the priest had not suggested he be brought to the infirmary, and for the care provided by many friends, including Agnes.

Little Coyote slowly regained fuller use of his right arm, aided in part by Father Ravalli's ministrations and a determination to use it in repeated and gradually more strenuous tasks. The priest nodded approvingly when he found the seer loosing arrows from a light bow toward a distant, grass-filled sack. Few had struck the target, but Little Coyote was cheerful as he relaxed and set down the weapon.

"Fast Runner and Warm Breeze . . . ," he began. He stopped, remembering Agnes' strong views, then continued. "Rather, John and Louise returned during last night's cold rain with a few others from the hunt on the Yellowstone River with the thirty lodges of Nez Percé. Has he talked to you?"

Father Ravalli shook his head.

"No." His face brightened. "Did they get much meat?"

"There was a good kill. He continues to mourn deeply the

death of his mother, so I encouraged him to come to my lodge and tell about the hunt. He told me much I have wanted to ask. To avoid telling you what you already know, what word did you receive from our people who returned after escorting Fathers DeSmet and Point to seek the Blackfeet?"

"After they trekked through Hell Gate and up the Deer Lodge River, they encountered Blackfeet sign." Father Ravalli picked up the heaviest bow and admiringly ran his long fingers over the ram's horn laminations. "At the insistence of the Fathers, most of them returned here, though a few warriors went even farther. They returned, except for Victor, himself. He told them he would join the Flathead hunters who, with the Nez Percé, had gone to the region where many Crows are friendly to us."

The priest's voice quickened, so much so that his next question was in garbled Flathead. He started over, more slowly.

"Did John bring word of Victor? What of Charlot?"

"They are well." Little Coyote signed *wait* and slowly walked to gather the arrows and target. Father Ravalli put each arrow into the quiver after the seer had examined it, then helped carry the weapons to the lodge.

"I have some of John's freshly roasted buffalo meat warming by my fire," the seer said.

"I can offer only a good appetite."

"And grace over the food."

Knowing the priest had many duties, Little Coyote cut the meat into thin slices against the grain so they more easily could eat and talk.

"John and Fathers DeSmet and Point, and Charles and Gabriel, their interpreters, found the Flathead and Nez Percé hunters in the Yellowstone Valley soon after the others had been sent back here." Little Coyote took another bite, chewed, swallowed, then added, "A few Blackfeet had set up their lodges near our hunters."

The priest's face brightened. He hurriedly swallowed to joyfully exclaim, "Our prayers are being answered already!"

"In part, perhaps. The Blackfeet, like us, seek to maintain old alliances and form new ones. Especially since they were so scourged by smallpox. The St. Louis fur-traders and others said the Blackfeet and the Assiniboins already are forming such bonds with the increasingly powerful Sioux. They are moving ever west from the upper Mississippi. They have fought through the Arikaras, the now-few Mandans of the Dakota country, our friends among the Crows of the Powder River country, others, and into the Big Horn Mountains. Even now the Sioux ally themselves with the Northern Arapahos and Cheyennes." The seer stretched his right arm as far out as he could, then shortened his reach to grasp another slice of meat. "Victor worries about the effect of these alliances on the enemies of the Sioux, such as the Pawnees, the Crows, and especially those Shoshonis who have strong bonds with us. But back to what John told us. Perhaps that will increase your joy.

"Father DeSmet had sent his interpreters ahead to the hunting encampment. Before they arrived, a great band of Crows who were unfriendly to the Nez Percé and hated the Blackfeet prepared to fight the smaller groups. The Flatheads kept them from attacking, partially because of their announcement that the Black Robes approached.

"Among the Crows were many young braves who sought battle honors. They attacked soon after watching the Nez Percé and Flatheads make great prayers. There was a good fight. The Crows lost heart after fourteen of their warriors died. Only one Nez Percé was killed."

Father Ravalli had stopped eating and was listening raptly.

"John told me all these Blackfeet came to Father DeSmet's lodge and pledged their friendship to the Flatheads and assumed that we had no friends among the Crows. Our people did not enlighten them on this matter. The Blackfeet asked Father DeSmet to put them under the protection of God, which would make them stronger in body and more brave in battle."

"*And* be good for their souls," Father Ravalli murmured.

"Yes, John said Father DeSmet greatly tired Gabriel and Charles by having them stress this over and over, but . . ." Little Coyote paused longer than he wished as he sought the words to enable him to add, as delicately as possible, "there seemingly was some uncertainty about what the Blackfeet deemed the most important reasons for seeking baptism."

This effort was not lost on Father Ravalli. His gentle smile seemed to light up the lodge. "Yes, well . . . hmm. We Jesuits often are accused of not insisting a people immediately cast aside all former beliefs—no matter how long held or, as often is the case, their genuine merit—before being baptized." He selected a substantial slice of the meat. He would interrupt no more.

"John returned here just before the Blackfeet prepared a great dance for the Black Robes. More, he does not know. I feel this bodes well for the priests' safety, and that of Victor and Charlot, as well."

Little Coyote again stretched his right arm as far as he could, then shortened his reach. He, too, grasped a thick slice of the meat. They ate in silence until the priest offered profound thanks after their meal. On his departure, Little Coyote hung the uncased light bow near the two stronger and cased weapons on the rack.

54

leased, Little Coyote relaxed his heaviest bow and hung it beside the cased light and medium weapons on the rack inside his lodge. Yet again, the shoulder, arm and hand had worked well with the eyes. Most of the arrows were hitting the mark. Now he must practice from his horse. Soon his body almost could forget the Camas Meadow Massacre. Father Mengarini had supplied that word "massacre." The seer had told the priest he needed a word to best describe what had occurred three years earlier. He hung up the quiver of arrows beside the bows and stepped outside to bathe in the seep pool he had dug nearby. His arms were tired, but this was because of advancing age rather than the after-effects of the musket and tomahawk wounds.

He was . . . yes, thirteen summers when Clark and Lewis had arrived in that ninth month of 1805. Now it was late spring of 1849; he was fifty-seven. He danced energetically for a moment to shake off the water drops. Then, as he stood quietly and waited for Sun to dry him, he raised his eyes and mind to the Good Spirit for making his body strong again.

He had felt a great restlessness during his prolonged recuperation, partly because he, like Chalax, had encouraged

592

ailing people to go to the Black Robes rather than having him treat them.

Both men had agreed that too many warriors, unwilling to hunt, trap or work in the garden, had begun fashioning strange regalia, rattles and charms and actively were seeking the ill to deprive them of their hard-won possessions in exchange for a dance or other worthless ministrations. As a consequence, Little Coyote had become poorer in worldly possessions. He was content with that, though, because he gave much to the needy, anyway. He had continued to interpret vision quests, sometimes even for youths sent by the Black Robes. Such cooperation led to new directions.

Father Mengarini, himself collecting legends and studying the ways of the Flatheads lest the lore be lost, had persuaded Little Coyote to begin writing about his life and that of his people. "Over the years you have come to speak better English than many whites," the priest said. "Thus, your convalescence can be most fruitful. The story skin will remain a very valuable summary."

The priest encouraged the occasional use of unfamiliar big words, for example stressing, "The chronological narrative is the easiest and, perhaps, most interesting way to tell the story." Then he explained what he meant: "The merit in what you write will provide an insight into your people's lives that we late-comers here never could properly capture, particularly prior to our arrival. It would be interesting, however . . ." The priest chuckled for a moment. "Lord, forgive me, yes, interesting to compare what you write about us as all of us send letters and reports to St. Louis and elsewhere about you and others. Be assured there will be much written from all this, for that is the white man's way. And much of that written could favor the white man. For that reason, perhaps, and that is for you to decide, you should concentrate more on what occurred before the Jesuits' arrival than after." Again he chuckled. "Be assured the white men, mostly, will write what favors them."

The priest's dictionary, which he had started in 1846, continued to progress. Little Coyote and others helped as they were able.

Body dry, the seer looked at Sun. Yes, high, warm, certainly right for him to bring his rack and the story skin outside. That done, he flexed his right fingers—needlessly, he remembered: If they could help him accurately aim the arrows and write the white man's language in the thick, gray, ledger book given him by Father Mengarini, certainly the fingers could paint with the tiny instruments. He sat outside on an untanned deer skin, raised his food to Sun and began eating. He contemplated which symbols would best portray the most notable events he had selected from the many that had occurred in the three years since the massacre.

While making the selection, he thanked the Good Spirit for one of Black Robe Mengarini's suggestions. The priest had said there was less need to dwell on the Black Robes' activities among the people because others were telling about those. After much thinking, however, Little Coyote had concluded he certainly would not ignore them. They merited better treatment. The seer also could not ignore some of the distant events because of the lessons provided by the long progression of friends from the time of Drouillard, John Colter and Jedediah Smith. The lessons led to the present, and were strongly re-enforced by his adventures on his trip to St. Louis.

He and many other people, including those outside his tribe, fortunately had learned that what occurred distantly might affect them sometimes as fast as human legs, horses, small boats, steamboats or wagons could travel. He also must be selective in the actual portrayal of the events, too, because, as Father Mengarini wisely had pointed out, "The symbols on your superb story skin can serve as reminders of chapters for the events you will write about in your autobiography. Fortunately, you have progressed more in your story-skin telling than the writing of your chronology. Merely elaborate on the symbols. Tell the stories on paper as your elders have spoken them almost from their beginnings."

Little Coyote quickly completed his meal. After all this contemplation, he was anxious to paint. He would start with the events after leaving St. Louis with Charlot. For those, he had prepared a larger supply of dark paints than at any other time.

One of his most dominant symbols for 1846 was of a swivel gun belching forth death to charging Blackfeet. Some of the missiles were going through bodies and reaching a great distance to strike indistinct, almost ghostlike, Indians of other tribes. He depicted himself lying on the ground bleeding, seemingly viewing the carnage. Next most dominant was the figure of the Black Robe, DeSmet. He held aloft his crucifix, from which radiated beams of seeming light. A Blackfeet was facing the light directly, a Flathead obliquely, and a Nez Percé hardly at all.

Victor's face had been more haggard than ever before when he and Charlot had come to Little Coyote's lodge during a heavy December snowfall. This was because of a great unpleasantness that had occurred at the Mission on the return of the buffalo hunters—usually a very festive occasion. Adding to Victor's woebegone appearance had been his worn and torn, but clean, buckskins; he would wear them for a year to mark his mourning for Helena. Rather than talk of most recent events, the chief had begun recounting his and Charlot's experiences with the Black Robe after the chief's stepson, Fast Runner, had returned to the Mission. Anxious though he was for an explanation of the unpleasantness, Little Coyote had asked no questions.

"Hate flowed among us like a great river when Black Robe drew some of the Blackfeet, Flatheads and Nez Percé together for the peace agreement in the buffalo country," Victor had said. "He had stayed many days with the Blackfeet. So eager were they for Black Robe's great medicine, they readily agreed to peace. Reluctantly, we did so."

"And the Nez Percé?" Little Coyote had asked. He had shifted his gaze to Victor from a very quiet Charlot, noting the marks representing two Blackfeet warriors to the left of the cross on the warrior's white shield. The Blackfeet eagle feather, or another like it, still hung from Charlot's hair.

"The Nez Percé were more reluctant than we." The chief's face had brightened for a moment. "Some were of the band of Tuekakas, who said he has a son of two years in their Wallowa Valley. He is Hinmatooyahlatkekht, Thunder Rolling in the Mountains—Joseph. Tuekakas sent you greetings. He and sub-chiefs say the peace will not last at all, but they did not want to offend Black Robe before his departure in the ninth month toward St. Louis."

"And Father Point?"

Victor's mouth had tightened: "Father Point will spend the winter with the Blackfeet and Gros Ventres at Fort Lewis, which the American Fur Company chief, Alexander Culbertson, built among them on the Missouri. It is far to the west of Fort Union and honors the Lewis who, with Clark, came among us in 1805. Father Point might go to Canada thereafter."

Victor, looking worried, had shook his head: "We did not bring back as much buffalo meat as we will need." Again he had compressed his lips. "After the peace, the Blackfeet stole more than one-hundred of our horses. We would have pursued them with great vengeance, helped by our Nez Percé allies, perhaps even that band of Crows we had helped the Blackfeet to fight, so much do they hate the Blackfeet, had we not wished to avoid distressing Father Point. This was very hard for me to do. Some of our younger hunters said loudly to others, so I could hear, that perhaps I was afraid." He had raised his head. "They are young, hard to control like ungelded stallions, so I remained silent, because, also, Father DeSmet already had given to these Blackfeet the tobacco he had promised to us."

Now Victor had come to the unpleasantness of the night before: "For all these reasons the returning hunters gave no meat to the Black Robes and others at the Mission when we returned. That is why most of the returning hunters were able to persuade those who had remained at the Mission during our absence to join with them in setting up their lodges away from the Mission."

A faint breeze had begun ruffling the lodge. The occupants had heard distant shrieks and yells of long-unheard war dances. They knew that Skrellings, quick to profit from these lapses, had traded whiskey for the few good robes brought to the valley. The whiskey also had brought the companionship of drunken warriors' wives for himself and five other dissolute whites.

Later, a brisk wind had begun pummeling the lodge, strengthening more until its howl drowned out the more distant human ones. Snow had continued to fall, the wind sweeping it into great drifts throughout this central part of the valley.

Yes, Victor and Charlot had said they would stay the night. Lying in his furs, Little Coyote had exerted no visionary powers at all when he concluded, long after his guests were asleep, that the Flatheads were in for a bad winter.

Little Coyote stepped back from painting the symbols for 1846. He noted the appropriateness of Black Robe DeSmet's tiny, distant figure. It symbolized the priest's departure for the east after the already-fraying peace attempts and Father Ravalli's gentle disclosure to the greatly diminished number of Flatheads attending a mass early in 1847 that, "Father DeSmet will not return to serve at St. Mary's Mission." The worshipers had greeted this disclosure silently, but as they had filed from the chapel their expressions ranged from grief to wonderment. Why had he seemingly deserted them? Word had soon reached the larger number of lodges still set away from the Mission. Fathers Ravalli and Mengarini had spoken on the matter during visits to the lodges of the faithful that long winter of 1846-47. They also had spoken to those who seemingly, by their conduct, were indicating they remained displeased with the many things the Black Robes had done or left undone. Some, rallied by Victor, Charlot and others, had given the Black Robes dried buffalo meat when the heavy drifts cut off resupply pack trains to the Mission. A few Flatheads had sold or traded meat if they could obtain more from the priests than from the dissolute whites.

"How Skrellings and the others are jeering and spreading more discontent because the priests are trying to provide a feast for the band of peaceable Blackfeet who came here last night." Charlot had put down his almost-empty pack and removed his mittens and outer robe. He had stepped closer to Little Coyote's lodge fire. "None of our people will give food."

With some difficulty, Little Coyote had removed a frozen hind quarter from the high meat rack outside. Charlot had looked up questioningly as the seer bent over to put it into the pack.

"My arms works better," Little Coyote had said. "I

snowshoed a day's journey east and killed the deer in a heavy willow thicket. This is a gift to the Black Robes. They will mix it with their vegetables. I do not like the thought of Blackfeet bellies carrying away what I spent three days relaying here."

He had poked a roasting stick through two slices of thawed venison and handed it to the young warrior. Drops of juice had begun sizzling on the coals as Charlot spoke.

"There will be a great buffalo hunt and raid for horses as soon as the snow will allow it. We will bring back from the less-peaceful Blackfeet more horses than they ever have taken from us. Many people are willing to go, including some Pend d'Oreilles, Kutenais and Kalispels. The plan is first to get the buffalo. Chalax says they will be between the Teton and Marias rivers. The horse-takers will be sent to the Blackfeet north of the Marias River. When they get the horses, they will drive them to where others of us wait with the buffalo meat. We will then load up our pack horses and set out with the Blackfeet horses, too, leaving them with few to pursue us. Our allies will drop out with their shares as we return here."

Charlot had bundled up, lifted the pack and signed thanks as he prepared to step toward the flap.

"Will they avoid Fort Lewis?"

Charlot had shrugged the robe off his head, then nodded, a confident smile replacing his excited look as he had told of the plan.

"My father said to tell you that you could help him if you once again would attend the council meetings. He argued against going that far northeast. He does not wish to imperil Father Point. Of course, if we get many horses, the displeasure of the Blackfeet owners will spread to others who will agree that the Black Robe magic is not working very well. We can do nothing about that." He had set down the pack. "My father wished to go, but he fears the Blackfeet coming here, so will remain with some good warriors. Chief for the hunt will be Little Chief, uh, Michael, who, my father says, is a far better Christian than himself. My father seldom is incorrect, but he is a little incorrect here. He is being very careful not to have the Blackfeet, who will eat your venison, move around the Mission or talk to those of our people who drink the whiskey for fear our plans will depart with the Blackfeet. My father already has set up warriors to prevent this." Again Charlot had prepared to leave. Throwing his robe about him, Little Coyote had accompanied him outside where the air was so cold there was a gap of almost a bow's length before the smoke became visible to rise feather-like and straight above the lodges.

"Tell Victor I believe him very wise to urge the people to select Michael," Little Coyote said. "There could have been no better choice, for Michael truly was a great hunter and warrior, who did not boast of his prowess. He was so renowned that the Nez Percé had asked him to become their chief." Charlot nodded agreement. As he had walked away, the seer, disappointed his body could not support his strong wish to participate in the hunt, again had looked at the lodges dotting the quiet world close to, around and far from the Mission. The varying distances represented the degree of the inhabitants' disaffection with the Black Robes. The one solace was that none were so distant that the inhabitants could not quickly band together as the fighting Flathead people. Yes, Victor had been very wise to set them all to thinking about that hunt for the horses and buffalo in the spring of 1847!

Pleased with the portrayal of the 1846 events on his story skin, Little Coyote waited only two days for the paint to dry before he set about portraying the events of 1847.

He began by painting many horses surrounding a long pack train bearing meat and buffalo robes arriving at St. Mary's Mission. The well-planned horse raid and buffalo hunt had been highly successful. On the hunters' return, the Black Robes understood better why some of the most devout and supportive Flatheads had responded coldly to the feast provided the visiting Blackfeet and why, at a later date, they had remained even more aloof to another visiting group—even firing their guns at the sky as the Blackfeet departed. Despite the religious devotion of the Blackfeet, who could blame their former enemies if they had learned about and relayed to their wise and fierce brethren even one word about the pending horse raid? Then, too, long-time enmities and regrets at sharing the long-sought Black Robes died hard, too, among the Flatheads.

Little Coyote put his finger on the newly added 1846 symbols and traced it backward ten years to 1836. Here! Yes, here were his symbols showing a man with a cross and accompanied by a golden-haired woman moving west from Horse Creek on the Siskadee—Marcus and Narcissa Whitman, who had founded their mission at Waiilatpu, close to the Cayuses. Both these figures had smiling faces.

Little Coyote looked at the figures closely, sorrow again welling in him. Carefully, he duplicated these figures next to the 1846 symbols. But no smiling faces, no cross carried high. He dipped a tiny, chewed, willow brush into the black paint and blacked out both faces. The Whitmans were dead, murdered, the cross broken and on the ground. There were other sorrows to portray for 1847 and 1848.

A grim-faced Tuekakas had brought the first of this information to the valley with his wife and their now-more-than-two-year-old son, Joseph. Tuekakas' band had added much strength to preparations for the 1847 winter buffalo hunt, again near the Teton and Marias rivers; the Blackfeet no longer could resist such numbers.

Tuekakas had said little about the Whitman murders in the council, which Little Coyote once more had begun attending. What he had said had been grim: "When yet another party of the immigrants passed by the Mission, they left the measles behind. The disease killed almost half the Cayuses, greatly enraging the remainder who, for too long now, had watched the Bostons move into the country and not move out. The Cayuses, as do most of us, know about the Bostons taking Indian land far to the east. Thus enraged, worrying about their land, too, they blamed the deaths on sorcery by the whites.

"Some of the Cayuses killed Whitman with three blows of a tomahawk, the golden-haired one with three gun shots." Tuekakas had patiently waited for the expressions of sorrow to die down.

"Before they were through, the Cayuses had killed thirteen people and taken many captives. We fear white man will quickly take revenge. We hope they will remember, and we have told them, not all the Cayuses did this. Some opposed the killing. It is, perhaps, best we are going after the buffalo."

When the council had ended, Little Coyote had sought out his Nez Percé friend, Red Paint, heavier now, a chief, hair almost silver, but the smile yet ready to furrow his cheeks.

Remembering the wagon train he and Charlot had seen setting out from Westport, the seer had asked, "Do many immigrants still seek the Oregon country?"

Red Paint's smile had vanished. "In ever increasing numbers, by white man's thousands, like the migrations of a growing herd of buffalo. They bring their cows and horses and families and put up homes where our horses graze, where there is much good land to raise food. Some even place their homes along the rivers where we get our fish." He had shaken his head. "The younger braves in many bands are hard to control. Perhaps the trouble among the Cayuses will come among us."

Fathers Ravalli and Mengarini had voiced deep sorrow when told about the killings at Waiilatpu, but had said nothing when they learned, after the buffalo hunters' departure, where they would hunt. Before their return in February with a great quantity of meat, Father Ravalli had, somewhat obliquely, remarked to Little Coyote that Father Point had been sent to Canada and perhaps much time would pass before there again would be Black Robes among the Blackfeet.

In late March of 1848, Victor and Little Coyote had waited quietly for the priests to pour some tea. They had been invited to Father Mengarini's quarters two days after delivering more dried and frozen meat to the missionaries. There had been some delay while the firewood crackled and the cabin logs popped in the cold of a savage storm that had rushed in from the southeast. Soon, someone had stomped on the roughly sawn boards outside the cabin to rid himself of snow. Before entering, the visitor had shaken off his robe. He was Has Sharp Eyes—Damian—son of Broken Tooth, the latter now very old, infirm, but yet wise.

The greeting had been cordial, with a hint of some surprise, for Damian had absented himself many months living and hunting among the Nez Percé to acquire a few of their best horses to build up his own large herd.

Damian had grinned, looking much like a younger version of his once-powerfully-built father, save for strong, intact teeth. He had wearily held his hands to the fire before Father Ravalli had given him a cup of tea.

"Damian has come on snowshoes from among the Nez Percé of Tuekakas' band," Father Mengarini had explained. "He carries word from Father Brouillet at his recently established St. Ann's Mission on the Umatilla River near Waiilatpu. Two days after the killings there, Father Brouillet came to the Mission." Father Mengarini had put down his tea, his expressive hands helping to accept the horror of what Damian evidently already had told him. "Father Brouillet, though sickened at the sight and moved to tears by the entreaties of the many captives, knew that if he upbraided the Cayuses, he, too, would die, with his death, perhaps, inciting them to fall upon the captives. He was able to get away and warn Reverend Spalding and his wife at their Lapwai Mission that they also were to be killed. They fled." Father Ravalli had picked up his tea cup, but did not drink until Father Mengarini served a second cup to the others.

"The Hudson's Bay Company sent the man Ogden to seek freedom for the captives," Damian had begun. "They were traded for ammunition, guns, clothing, blankets and tobacco."

"Tuekakas said he feared white man would take vengeance." Victor had leaned forward, his tea forgotten.

"Yes. It began soon after he brought his people here before the hunt. The whites in Oregon demanded vengeance, and more than a half-thousand formed what they call a 'militia' to fight the Cayuses. The chief was Gilliam. The Bostons also formed a three-man council to try to keep the other tribes peaceful. Gilliam would not listen to this council. Tuekakas had told me that Gilliam was a preacher who had fought the red men to the east and who did not like them.

"Only a short time ago, before I set out on snowshoes,

Gilliam attacked the camp of the Cayuses who had no part in the killings at Waiilatpu. His soldiers killed maybe twenty-five. Those remaining then attacked Gilliam and killed three. The peace council sought to restrain Gilliam. He would not listen. When the peacemakers asked for a few soldiers to accompany them on their mission, Gilliam took all the soldiers with them. They and the peacemakers tried to talk to the Nez Percé, who mistrusted their intentions, holding as they did the pipe in front and the gun behind, with Gilliam saying he had come to fight the hostiles and he would."

"So the invaded are the hostiles!" Father Mengarini had shaken his head wonderingly. His "Tch, tch" had filled the tiny room.

"Soon some of Gilliam's soldiers took Palouse cattle, thinking the owners were the Cayuses, whereupon two-hundred-fifty Palouse attacked the soldiers, who fled to Waiilatpu. Ten were wounded. Most of the Cayuses now hide among the many Nez Percé bands, who are showing anger along with the Palouse, as do the Umatillas and the Walla Wallas." Damian had looked at his tea cup, but had asked for no more because the kettle was empty. "Father Brouillet says he worries about all this, and to be sure to say that this Cayuse war is prompting the Great Father to erect more forts for his soldiers in the Oregon country."

All had sought their beds. While they slept, the storm had shifted direction. Coming from almost directly west, it had swirled with unabating fury throughout St. Mary's Mission and soon the entire Bitter Root Valley.

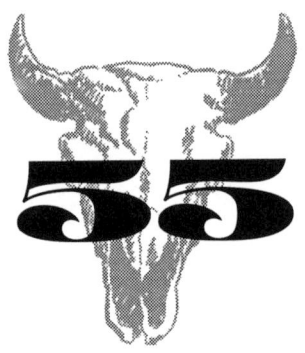

55

Sun remained friendly, bright and warm during the next several days of that 1849 early summer as Little Coyote prepared to add to his story skin his representations of the events of both 1848 and 1849. Many thoughts about those for 1848 had taken root in his mind and grown until, again, he was certain he was ready to paint. He was eager to see what the creative process would add, too. All of his ideas disappeared when the Good Spirit, to make him think more deeply about this record he would leave for his people, sent ants, one of the least of the Good Spirit's creatures. They came to the bark dish of crumbled camas bread the seer had left almost untouched near the deerskin as he mixed his fresh paints.

When Little Coyote sought to eat, he discovered many dead, dying, partially dismembered red ants scattered about or in the food dish. A few were scurrying away, pursued by larger ants. When he knelt to peer more closely, he could see that a narrow procession of the larger ants was carrying away bits of this rich, seemingly inexhaustible, find.

He traced the line of ants over the dry, almost bare, ground toward an old tree. The ponderosa pine was leaning northeast from the prevailing southwest winds that had buffeted it ever since it had taken root, perhaps about the time the people had sought refuge in the valley. Near the tree base, and somewhat protected by its branches, was a huge, cone-shaped ant hill surrounded by tall grasses. The hill was many times larger than the one west of the river over which Father Ravalli had dusted his luncheon crumbs while on the search for medicinal herbs. The very size of this second ant hill seemingly demanded that its almost-countless inhabitants, always abuilding, forage ever more distantly for sustenance.

Little Coyote watched the food column triumphantly begin struggling up the hill and past the roving soldiers. Others, greeting the bearers, were dropping short lengths of grass and other less important burdens and helping them. The seer watched the food disappear underground via many routes. He observed that a communication process had commenced among the food carriers that reappeared and the growing numbers excitedly scurrying atop the heap. Soon a line of foragers, including those that already had brought in their burdens, began resolutely moving down the hill and paralleling those struggling upward with their booty.

Now there were two ribbons of ants, one moving somewhat irregularly around various obstacles from food to hill, the other from hill to food. Several times the warrior, ever more absorbed with this phenomenon, painting forgotten, stepped carefully to avoid crushing the industrious, single-minded army. In doing so, he entered a scattered series of much smaller cone-shaped ant hills composed of sand excavated a grain at a time by these industrious and smaller red ants. These ants also were agitated; indeed, in small and larger groups, they were scurrying toward the food-carrying column of ants moving around a large, lichen-covered stone embedded in the bank near the seep that fed the warrior's bathing pool. Excitedly, the small groups of red ants attacked immediately; they were trying to seize the food their kind had discovered, but were failing because of the size and number of their opponents.

Soldier ants accompanying the food chain seized legs, antennae, any available part of the red attackers. They pulled off their appendages, systematically crippling or dismembering them like the ants near or in the dish. Soon this first wave of red attackers was almost annihilated, but more rushed in. Their numbers and fierce attacks disrupted the food column and enabled them to seize some of the food; then the soldier ants from the great heap arrived in sufficient numbers to form an erratic line between the column and the attackers. This permitted the food carriers to work almost uninterrupted as the battles, large and small, continued with growing ferocity, the jaws of the soldier ants steadily winning over the smaller opponents. Gradually, they fell back, the intact and some of the crippled valiantly trying to carry off the bodies of their fallen.

Now the larger ants carried the war to the smaller hills as though they had done this before. They annihilated all red ants that rushed to the fray. A few scattered, tried to return, fought, lost and died. Strangely, in the final frenzy, the red ants even attacked, crippled and killed some of their own.

As a small boy on hands and knees, Little Coyote had seen such battles before, but never of such magnitude and ferocity. He waited at the scene of carnage, expecting a line of workers to begin carrying off the bodies of the fallen. When he returned to his food, he found it visibly diminished from the efforts of the now-greatly-widened ribbons of workers. Interspersed among them were the soldiers, some missing a leg, two, a portion of an antenna, but continuing to function with those who had not joined the fray.

For a moment he felt an urge to move the food away from the army and throw it into the pool, then, like a towering giant, grind the ribbons into the soil and fire the great ant hill. Instead, while his mind began moving backward and forward over the more memorable events of his adult life, he dragged his deerskin aside, sat on it and mused long in the light of now-westering Sun while the forgotten paints began drying in their small birchbark containers.

Sun neared the peaks to the west. Little Coyote arose from the deerskin when the shadow of the ponderosa pine next to the ant hill reached out and touched him. Other long shadows encompassed the Mission buildings and scattered lodges. Some wild cries from the direction of the Skrellings place reached his ears; they dominated other human voices from the lodges. His eyes saw the mean hovel; his mind reached out as quickly to visualize the house and corrals near Ross' Hole for which at least the adult Enfingers had died, and the Culpeppers' structure near St. Louis, wrested from and defended against the seer's Osage friend, Old Fire.

Little Coyote held onto the thought of the Culpeppers while he looked at his food dish. It was empty. The ant hill was a seething mass as the last of the food carriers hoarded away their booty. The remnants of the red ants, assisted by some of the cripples, were struggling to carry their dead away from all their hills.

Yes! The Culpeppers! They were among the myriad of whites who had gone into the Oregon country, enraging the Cayuses and others, causing much of the apprehension voiced by Tuekakas and Red Paint. Perhaps . . . no, *surely*, they had helped to cause Little Faro and other Flatheads to speak out against the Black Robes.

In the early twilight, Little Coyote examined the container of black paint. Scraping away the dried surface he found enough remaining liquid to draw what he knew must solely symbolize the events of 1848: A large heap of white man's gunpowder kegs, lead bars and many guns. He painted a cage around these, with a white soldier standing guard at the gate.

The cage represented that the Cayuse War, seemingly so far away, had reached the Bitter Root Valley, with an agitated Father Ravalli explaining to the more upset Flatheads there would be no powder or lead to distribute here or at the other missions.

"The new Oregon Territorial Legislature, an important council of many white chiefs, has forbidden the distribution of guns and ammunition to all Indians," the priest had said. "Our thirty-six guns, three-hundred pounds of birdshot and buckshot, fifteen-hundred pounds of lead balls, and more than one-thousand pounds of powder have been seized by the soldiers at The Dalles. None of our missions will receive these supplies."

The seizure had its bad and good effects. The bad effect, as Victor and Little Coyote viewed it, was that it set some of the already-disaffected Flatheads even more against the blameless Black Robes. The good effect was that the tribal council ruled guns and ammunition would be used for defense only. This required many of the people to make new arrows and bows and practice old hunting skills with and without their horses. The 1848 winter buffalo hunt had produced more animals than had the hunts of the previous two years; the hunt was aided by continued good alliances and successful use of old jumps. And this time the people had arrived home safely, most of them giving thanks at the chapel that illness and death had not struck them as they had the previous year—perhaps from bad drinking water. There had been more work involved than ever before, however, in finding the animals; all people conceded, "The buffalo are not always coming back in such great numbers to the old places."

During the council meeting following the hunt, some of the younger warriors had said the reason the buffalo were so hard to find was that the Good Spirit had begun turning against the Flatheads since the arrival of the Black Robes. Little Faro, a brave warrior who sought to become at least a sub-chief, had said more: "The Good Spirit's face seems to shine only for the white men."

Victor had defended the Black Robes well. He had pointed out that Father DeSmet had asked that he not be made an important bishop, choosing, instead, to live and work among the Indians he loved. And gentle Father Ravalli, worriedly awaiting the outcome of this council, had come from a rich family, indeed. With his many abilities, he could have prospered anywhere. "And where did he choose to come? Whom did he choose to serve?" The chief had become weary as the night lengthened, until, finally, Little Coyote had stood. Silently, the seer had walked to the white buffalo robe, which was rolled up and suspended on the large wall of the lodge. He had untied the rawhide strings, causing the white robe to hang there like a great white blanket. His first words had been scornful, indeed, spoken while his unwavering gaze focused on Little Faro.

"There are those who would become chiefs through strong words, not brave deeds. Does Little Faro choose now to become a chief by fighting the Black Robes, who are not warriors? Why does he look about, always trying to find some fault to charge against the Black Robes?

"Why does Little Faro speak only about the buffalo being hard to find? Why does he not say that after they were found, the people brought back as much meat as they could use? Why does Little Faro not speak of the many good things the Black Robes have done? They are men of the Good Spirit. They are not the Good Spirit. They make mistakes. I, who have not joined with the Black Robes as have you, see the good they do. Perhaps they have made a great mistake in speaking out against the chief's ancient use of the whip, for stealing, adultery, drunkenness and other such actions. Perhaps this confessing becomes easier in the Flatheads' minds than enduring the whipping, so they do these evil actions more often. But I will not make the mistake of saying that the Good Spirit has turned away from the Flathead people because of the presence of the Black Robes among us. Who dares say that our Iroquois brothers, who helped lead the Flatheads to the Black Robes, had no troubles equally as great as ours?"

Little Coyote had told the council the story of Brandt and how the Good Spirit, through the teachings the Iroquois had received from the Black Robes, had turned the heart of Little Coyote and Victor. Also how thereafter, Little Coyote had turned the heart of Brandt, who now helped the Indians.

"Tell me," the seer had challenged, "why did the Cayuse War end so suddenly?"

None knew, though Little Faro, his blood still up from his earlier words against the Black Robes, and Little Coyote's words against him, had tried to explain. He had become so absurd the listeners had laughed. Humiliated, he had fallen silent.

"No," Little Coyote had said, though he didn't need to. "The Black Robes and many of the Indians they had helped prayed for the war to end. The Good Spirit listened and cut down Gilliam, who was leading the war. After the Palouse warriors chased the soldiers to Waiilatpu, Gilliam prepared a rope to stake out his horse. The Good Spirit set the rope to the trigger of Gilliam's gun. Carelessly, he pulled the rope once more. His own gun killed him. Soon thereafter, his soldiers lost heart and went to their homes. That is what we should do now."

Victor and Little Coyote, with Charlot intently listening, had talked over their pipes after the lodge cleared. They quickly agreed that the Good Spirit had shown the Flatheads should not become so dependent on trade goods that whites could control even their destiny by merely caging all supplies.

"We always must keep a goodly store of ammunition and the best guns, even if we have to forego other marvels," Victor had emphasized. He had looked hard at his son who, ready smile gone, solemnly nodded in agreement.

Little Coyote sought out Victor next day after painting the caged guns and ammunition.

"I have asked the story-tellers to keep the denial of the guns and ammunition strong in their memories and tell it often," Victor said approvingly. He waited for his friend to speak more urgent thoughts.

"Only yesterday," Little Coyote began, "I had a vision in front of my lodge and near the great tree. The Good Spirit told me in His own way that the troubles that beset our red brethren to the east, south and west move toward all of us who use the buffalo country. The troubles approach as rapidly as the lead buffalo that irresistibly draws the herd to its death at the jump. My thoughts are that we must talk about this. Our people must avoid joining those who leap to their destruction. I sent Charlot to find you after I participated in the Camas Meadow massacre with the swivel gun, urging you to try to make peace with the Blackfeet. Indians must not seek the destruction of Indians. White man, I fear, will do that easily enough. There are many Gilliams about."

Victor sought out Charlot. Both warriors silently listened as a much-troubled Little Coyote, substituting Indians for ants, explained the vision the Good Spirit had sent through some of His least creatures.

"We will see Father Mengarini," the chief decided, "after

prayers tonight in the chapel."

Father Ravalli greeted the trio that night. He lighted a candle and ushered them into the tiny study and asked them to be seated on the sturdy chairs he had made.

"Father Mengarini will join you very soon," the priest said. "We are discussing with others the plans we soon will suggest to you for the harvest of the pumpkins, squashes and potatoes, which will begin soon. May I, too, return and listen?"

"We would be most grateful." Victor walked over to the tiny window. Charlot joined Little Coyote in looking at a simple, but complete, map generally outlining the whites' political borders and the regions inhabited by the various Indian tribes. In the right corner were the initials "P.J.DeS." In greater detail, which Little Coyote explained to Charlot, were sketched the various missions, as well as stations established for instruction. The Flatheads had heard all their names before, had visited most, but seeing representations of them all at one time sufficiently impressed Charlot that he called Victor to "Come see, and hear."

The seer traced his finger from the west first: "St. Paul's near Fort Vancouver; St. Peter, near Fort Colvile; St. Mary's, Bitter Root Valley."

"And what is this?" Charlot pointed to a smaller map to the right of the large one, then answered his own question: "St. Mary's, with all the buildings, corrals, fields and such."

The seer delightedly clapped Charlot on the back, then resumed the listing: "St. Ignatius, west of the Lake of the Pend d'Oreilles, and St. Regis Station nearby; St. Joseph's; St. Paul, again, near Fort Colvile; Sacred Heart, and St. Ann's."

The three were examining the more detailed sketch of St. Mary's Mission when Father Ravalli returned, followed by Father Mengarini, receding hair turning gray, cheeks gaunt, the eyes shining brightly above his strong nose. He warmly greeted them before sitting down and folding those excitable hands in his lap as though he was prepared to remain in that position all night. This latter action told Little Coyote the priest perhaps had something momentous to say, but first he would hear his Indian friends.

Victor opened the talk. He quickly pointed out that Little Coyote wished to tell of his recent vision, which re-enforced in an ominous way that which the Good Spirit had given him far back into the time of Clark's and Lewis' coming to the valley. "But Little Coyote will tell you about this," Victor said simply, his face troubled, his hands in his lap, too, almost as though glad others could speak for him.

"I have told the Black Robes of my vision quest and the message we should not fight white man," Little Coyote began. "My white and part-white friends have warned us against this, too. I thought . . ." The seer paused. ". . . that not fighting the whites would be easier to do than it is because I did not know, could not know, that we must remain peaceful toward them while they do not remain peaceful with the Indians. We fear for what lies ahead. While the Black Robes and others seek to bring us closer to the Good Spirit, and we try, we often question if there perhaps is some way we also could try to bring white man closer to the Good Spirit. Clark and Lewis told us the Great Father in Washington would treat us well. He has not. And he has not made his trappers, traders, soldiers and others treat us well, though some do, and they have been like our brothers. I ask why this is so."

There was silence before Father Mengarini began speaking slowly, wanting to say much with few words. Both Father Ravalli and Little Coyote helped to make the messages understandable to all.

"Yes, white men need to listen to the word of God as much as the Indians. Like the Indians, they sometimes do not. And they sometimes do not obey when they listen.

"Victor's and the council's power sometimes weakens the farther away they are from the people in the valley. The Great Father's power weakens the farther away his people are from Washington. He has many matters that demand his attention. The American people do not like reins on their actions. They have not fully caught the idea they are one united great tribe. They move far away to avoid such control. So, we find it hard to accept that while the whites wish to be free from controls, they wish to control the Indians even when they come into the Indians' lands." The priest looked at the Flatheads. They understood.

"You have been told by your white friends and others, you have seen and heard for yourselves, that white man seeks land and the riches the land can provide. Unfortunately, he will fight, kill, to obtain land, to hold onto it. You ask if, perhaps, there is some way the Indians could seek to bring white man closer to the Good Spirit."

Father Mengarini stood, walked over to Victor and gripped his shoulder. "There is no gentle way to say this, my friends, but as more white men pour into the Indian lands, they justify their actions toward the Indians by calling them heathens. Heathens, they say, who would prevent them from occupying what the whites often call 'our promised land,' because they view themselves as God's chosen people above all others. Nonsense! Absolute nonsense, but we have found no way to change all their minds."

The priest released his grip on the chief's shoulder, walked over to the window, looked up at the darkened peak, then down to the part of the Mission visible from the window. Centered in his view was the chapel.

"You have seen what has happened between 1804 and 1849. In those forty-five years the fur-takers discovered the furs and trapped them. Now, few furs remain." He touched the lighted candle to another, as though having thus summarized the era of the fur-takers, he would now, as succinctly, summarize with his next words what the Flatheads had been undergoing and what yet lay ahead.

"Believe me, God loves all people alike, else He would not have created them. We Jesuits, as well as other good ministers, firmly believe this. Thus, we work among you as well as others in many parts of the world. But we do so in a protective sense, too." He spoke quietly, forcefully, then, turning away from the window, pounded his clenched right fist three times into his left palm. "The whites learn about the land, they settle on the land, they will do so until it is all taken, and they will fight to do so. Yes. We sought to form our missions protectively around you because the time rapidly approaches when the whites will ask that the Great Father, as he has elsewhere, send his soldiers to the northern plains, the buffalo country, to form forts protectively—for the whites. The Jesuits at St. Louis and Father DeSmet remain interested in the Rocky Mountain missions; I am certain Father DeSmet especially is interested in St. Mary's, though he now is treasurer for the Missouri Province."

Father Ravalli quietly left the room and soon returned with tea and sugar. They all drank reflectively, then Father Mengarini put down his cup.

"We fear greater changes," he continued. "Last year gold was discovered in California. Great amounts of gold, and fairly easy to obtain. White men are going there in as great numbers as the buffalo, from many places, by many routes. The fathers in St. Louis have sent us word that perhaps forty-thousand in this 1849 will go to California just by the River Platte Trail alone. Gold sets man's mind aflame more than does the land. He will stop at nothing to obtain it."

Little Coyote looked at Victor. The chief had straightened up in his chair, his cup part way to his mouth. Yes, he, too, was remembering how the gun-seekers had exchanged gold so long ago, the whites gladly trading the best guns.

"Already," Father Mengarini continued, his face even more grave, "this rush to the gold fields causes the Jesuits to shift much of their efforts from here to the Indian people and others caught up in the problems brought by the gold-seekers.

"We will talk more. Will tomorrow at sunset be satis-factory?" When they nodded, Father Mengarini drank the rest of his tea, walked to the largest table and pulled the homemade chest from under it.

"Father DeSmet thinks of his Flathead friends." He lifted two small, wooden boxes from the chest and placed them on the table. Around each was a piece of string to which was attached two small keys and a piece of cardboard. Written on one was "Victor," on the other "Little Coyote." Father Mengarini set both candles on the far end of the table, well away from the two warriors as they inserted keys in the locks and lifted the lids. Inside each velvet-lined case was a six-shot, fourteen-inch-long, Dragoon Colt, Model of 1848 Holster Pistol, percussion caps, a double mould for casting both a conical and ball .44-caliber bullet, a copper powder flask and a combination screwdriver and nipple wrench.

Father Mengarini smiled broadly for the first time that evening. "I am told people would exchange much gold for such a weapon. Yes, Father DeSmet has many contacts, including a man named Brandt. Father does think of his Flathead friends. He is certain you will easily learn to use such a weapon."

Victor delightedly raised the heavy weapon, sighted it through the window, then almost lovingly rubbed it across his buckskin coat before handing it to eager Charlot.

Little Coyote, too, displayed great interest in the gift: "I will be gratified if you will thank Father DeSmet for this great gift when next you send messages to St. Louis. He always will be strong in my memories." To the astonishment of all, the seer handed his gift to a stunned Charlot: "This now becomes a gift to my *i-sts-sókoi*."

Before he slept, Little Coyote stirred up his lodge fire and prepared two paints—black and yellow. In the flickering light he painted two small symbols for 1849 on his story skin. One was the chapel at St. Mary's, topped by a cross larger than the structure, itself. To the southwest he drew a simple line representing the California coast. Slightly inland he painted a yellow nugget larger than the chapel and cross, then added yellow rays of light emanating in every direction from the nugget. Stepping back, the seer looked at his handiwork. As an afterthought, he painted a few rays emanating from the cross.

B rother Claessens pulled his old, black coat more tightly about his thin body as though he suddenly was cold on this warm, early-summer morning in 1849. He began pointing his work-roughened hands in all directions as tears formed in his large eyes and slowly ran down his gaunt face.

"Destroyed, all our work destroyed." Beseechingly he looked skyward. "All our work, the seeds, the young plants. Our hopes for a good harvest. All gone. To what purpose?"

Chief Victor, Charlot and a few well-armed Flatheads accompanied by Father Mengarini briefly turned from looking at the destroyed gardens and fields. Streaming from the Mission area were Father Ravalli, Brothers Bellomo and Savio and most other people who had not gone on the buffalo hunt. Crippled old Broken Tooth carried his rifle as he joined others who were carefully moving between the garden rows and along the margins of the fields.

Blackfeet raiders, throughout most of the night, had raced their own horses and a stolen band again and again over the young crops. They were aided by light from two burning haystacks remaining after the long winter. There had been plenty of ineffective firepower in the first volley from the Mission and palisade to re-enforce what the scouts evidently had told the Blackfeet before the raid: "The bands of best horses are here, here and here. Avoid an assault on the Mission."

Father Mengarini patted Brother Claessens' shoulder. "We have lost much," he agreed, "but we have not lost everything." For a moment a look of deep sorrow flitted across his face, too, its startling intensity exceeding by far that of the Jesuit brother. Even the most disaffected Flatheads, who had refused to work in the fields, murmured sympathetically as they viewed the destruction. There would be little to harvest from this rocky land this year. There was reassurance, however, in a recently arrived messenger's announcement that the hunters were returning with enough meat to last until the fall hunt.

"Trouble rides double," Father Mengarini commented as all, except Brother Claessens, began leaving the gardens and fields. Those accompanying the priest between two destroyed rows nodded in agreement. Yes, Father Mengarini's three words did aptly link with the other message greatly distraught Stephen had included as he had told about the hunt.

He had killed two good buffalo, but had secreted his wife, their child and his share of the meat in a well-hidden ravine and hurried to the Mission to seek out Father Mengarini.

"I am Stephen," he had told the priest on his arrival. "You do not know me, Father. Father DeSmet baptized me and my family before your arrival, and I have been living among our Pend d'Oreille brothers. God directed our large party of hunters to many buffalo, but during most nights after each day's trek homeward there was much debauchery, dancing and coupling, exchanging of partners, even more lewd acts by those the guards forced to forego whiskey until after the hunt. I tell you this so you will be prepared. I will return for my family and the meat." Thanked by the distraught Black Robe and Chief Victor, the young warrior had hurried away after a brief rest.

"*Yes-tcilptsáscin em!*"

Victor spat out the threat as the young warrior's horse galloped into the trees.

Father Ravalli looked questioningly at the chief. Father

Mengarini coughed delicately as he caught the meaning—"I threaten to urinate on his forehead."

"Victor, Victor," he said gently, "there is trouble enough already. Do promise me you will limit your reproach of Little Faro to words only. I will talk to him again, for he continues to be a great disappointment in so many ways, especially that he . . . that he scoffs even in the chapel, itself, at what we try to teach. He could help so much because he had enough support to be chosen chief for the hunt."

Victor, his anger subsiding, shook his head agreeably, though reluctantly, and muttered loudly enough for all to hear that Little Faro would be "*tckcn'm epilei.*"

Little Coyote translated for the priests: "A person under trial by a chief."

And that's where, as Father Mengarini later would put it, "Trouble tried to ride treble, with almost-disastrous results for all."

"Habit dies slowly. Witness how carefully the people stepped through the destroyed fields." Such was Little Coyote's response to distraught Charlot's report that some of the returning hunters were trying to insist that Little Faro not relinquish leadership after returning to the valley. "Most of the people will support Victor, and he will devise a stratagem to bring them to the council he has called." Thus, the seer spoke indirectly to Victor through Victor's son, both to further the education of the young warrior and preserve the chief's authority and diminishing self-esteem. Chief and son then employed habit and curiosity to bring the sub-chiefs and leading warriors to the council in such numbers that Little Faro scarcely could remain away.

While the hunters were gone, Victor and Charlot had practiced sufficiently with their Colt six-shooters that they now could hit targets at a good distance. While disaffection within the tribe probably would not lead to such past agreements that all provide furs and robes to collectively obtain weapons for the most capable few, Victor had no doubts warriors would want to obtain some.

"Though we disagree strongly among ourselves, we yet fight the common enemy," the chief grimly told Little Coyote while the criers announced the mid-afternoon shooting exhibition that would precede the council meeting. He also had set the target posts so they scarcely stood upright; thus, he would achieve greater effect when the impact of the bullets knocked them down.

Victor allowed himself a rare smile: "I remember well how Clark and Lewis set Drouillard to breaking the mirror with the air gun, and how he used his rifle to knock down the poorly set post on which the ram's skull was perched."

In front of the assemblage outside the council lodge, the chief employed one further stratagem—this one to lessen some of the animosity toward the Black Robes. Victor spoke solemnly, with much authority, holding up both weapons as he did so: "Last winter the Black Robes presented these wondrous guns to this chief, Little Bear Claw, and to Little Coyote. They were the gift of the Indians' friend, Brandt, in St. Louis to Father DeSmet, and carried here by Frank Owen, another friend Little Coyote and my son, Little Grizzly Bear Claw, met in St. Louis. Owen, too, was here briefly before the winter snows fell. Little Coyote gave his Colt to Little Grizzly Bear Claw."

The murmurs of appreciation following that final statement multiplied with each shot the chief fired. While he reloaded the six-shooter, Charlot's shots proved effective, too. Any wavering council members succumbed completely when Victor, after the two had fired twenty-four shots, announced the council would discuss ways to get more such guns.

A measure of harmony reigned through the early part of the meeting as Victor slowly demonstrated loading the six-shooter, then firing through the open smoke vent. The dominant questions were, "How soon can we get more? What must we trade?" Victor explained that Frank Owen had told him there were few such guns, and many demands for them. "Frank Owen spoke thus to me after he had met with the Black Robes: 'I have a brother, John. He sells provisions to the soldiers near Fort Hall, thus knows the ways to obtain guns and other marvels. We look about for a place to build a trading fort.' Little Grizzly Bear Claw said

Frank Owen treated him and other Indians fairly at St. Louis. I only tell you what Frank Owen said about John Owen."

"This John Owen is known to me." Fast Runner spoke boldly from the outer circle in the lodge. Baptized as Ambrose, he successfully insisted that all but the Black Robes call him by his tribal name. He had gained such stature, not as stepson to the chief, but from the golden beads he continued to add to one of the strings about his neck. The beads denoted his fast-growing and usually safely hidden herd of fine horses. His battle exploits with Blackfeet thieves had cost them five warriors.

"John Owen's woman is the Shoshone, Nancy. She told my wife, Warm Breeze, while we were among the Shoshonis, that he seeks to set up his fort among more peaceful people—perhaps the Flatheads."

There were murmurs of approval. A fort and trading post nearby! More such murmurs when Victor said: "Frank Owen told me that he fears it will be impossible to get such six-shooters soon because most are going to soldiers. But there are other earlier-made Colt guns of many shots, called Patersons, he might be able to obtain."

The amity in the meeting began breaking down when Victor strongly declined to pass the Colts around for closer inspection, yet he and two older sub-chiefs argued for setting aside some robes and furs to effect a trade for the Colt guns. The trio also argued that, as in the past, most guns should go to the best shooters and more proven warriors. The majority opposed this plan, each wanting one for himself. Little Faro quickly sided with the majority. He began to rise as though to seize and inspect one of the Colts. Victor stopped him with his eyes.

"We will talk about this later when we know more about how we can get the Colt guns." The council deferred to Victor's statement on this matter. But the younger majority, its ranks not yet decimated by smallpox, other diseases and war as had been the older, began exploding almost like both six-guns firing at once when Victor, finally, sought to employ other old customs and upbraid Little Faro for dissolute actions after the hunt.

Little Faro stood. He was a medium-size man much younger

than Victor. As yet keen-eyed, he was a proud, brave warrior. He also was ambitious. Many of the people were ignorant, as yet, that he had become eager lately for the whiskey Skrellings always could find when he, too, wanted something badly. Secure in the backing of so many, and reckless from a visit to Skrellings' before the shooting exhibition, Little Faro raised his hands for silence rather than deferentially allowing the chief to do so. Nor did he sign now that he wished to speak.

"We brought back much meat from the buffalo grounds," he began arrogantly. "Where was our chief? The chief remained in the valley with the older people, the Black Robes and the women. Has Victor become a woman because he no longer has as mate a warrior woman?"

Almost all in the lodge gasped because this insult partially was directed against a highly respected and brave dead woman who often had sat in the council lodge, as well as against Agnes, held in high regard by all who knew her.

"*Etss 'tciltsuút?* What kind of manners has he?" many could hear Kills With Lance and Wild Horse ask aloud. These two warriors, who had set up the great ambush of the Blackfeet along the south fork of the River of the Flatheads, signed that they would speak now.

No gasps from Fast Runner. At this insult to his dead mother and to his step-father and step-mother, Agnes, he scrambled upright and would have reached Little Faro had he not stumbled on his robe. The moment provided time for others to grasp and hold him, but his first hot words reached out like an arrow.

"*Empíle, you!*" he shouted contemptuously. Then he launched the war arrow, insulting this insulter through his own woman: "*An-ulu elts enmisten your* whore!"

Those in the circle nearest Victor, seeing Little Faro's eyes center instantly on the reloaded Colts, desperately restrained the warrior until he quieted. When they released him, he slapped the chief.

The earlier near pandemonium became total silence. All present froze, as though early spring, instantly giving way to deepest cold, had turned them all to ice.

Little Coyote later concluded that most warriors present would have supported Victor had he shot Little Faro then and there, or, more appropriately, stabbed him with the ancient tribal stone knife. Perhaps he would have done so—certainly there was a momentary look of intent there—had not one person stood and waved his shield from the very outer circle of the council. This was Charlot, present because of his position as *eltilimigum*, or heir-apparent, and unquestioned because of his performance during the Camas Meadow massacre.

Silently, Charlot waved the shield above his head, holding it to cover the symbols depicting two fallen Blackfeet warriors. Only the much larger cross showed. Twice in the continuing silence Victor's gaze moved from the shield to Little Faro, the guns and knife. At length, the chief's clenched fists opened; he reached down, silently grasped the whip and pipe and strode from the lodge.

Charlot called from the darkness before he entered Little Coyote's lodge. Both six-shooters were in his sash. Over the years, the seer approvingly had noted, indeed had encouraged, Charlot's considered diminishment and final parting of the lines between irresolute youth, eager brave and proven warrior. More difficult had been encouraging the retention and use of the wisdom acquired in each stage. Manifestly, the lines between warrior and growing leader had strengthened during the altercation in the council lodge that day. The flickering light of the feeble lodge fire revealed in this now twenty-one-year-old warrior a stronger, unwavering resoluteness of countenance, a more commanding presence, suggesting strength to defer as appropriate to the deserving—all requisites of a chief.

Quite expectedly, then, Charlot's first question was: "When events were going so well in the council, why did my father not let them all inspect the Colts?"

The seer's response was to ask for one of the six-shooters, whereupon he stirred up the fire, leaned near it and motioned for Charlot to see.

"I suggested to your father that if we were to remain peaceful toward the whites, and wanted to encourage good whites such as Owen to build a fort here, we should not show the pictures you possibly did not examine that are drawn into the steel on the outside of the cylinder. Do you not remember?"

Slowly, the seer revolved the cylinder to disclose the soldiers armed with Colts and fighting Indians.

"I don't think the Black Robes examined these gifts closely," he said.

Charlot returned the Colt to his sash, slowly shaking his head in comprehension.

"I set the horse guards in place long ago, and with Francis and Robert have been seeking my father at the Mission and various lodges. I will go to Skrellings' place to deal with that *sgo élenem* Satan."

"To what purpose?" Little Coyote uncased his medium bow.

"When I leave there he will be *estcoaúkan*, a gambler down to his last robe."

Charlot would not kill, so they set out. Their quiet talk became whispers. Soon they neared the large, crudely erected, pole fence surrounding hovel, corral and outhouse. The two men could see the remnants of the bonfire that had drawn the revelers through much of the evening and early night. Now only a few coals were glowing, then hiding in the gray ashes, as the fitful night breeze lamented through the willows and smaller trees. A feeble candle light shone dully through the hovel's single, translucent, scraped-hide window. Through the widest cracks in the dilapidated door the warriors watched Skrellings remove his shirt and bare a chest as hairy as his face. He was unbuckling the belt of his unbuttoned trousers when Charlot kicked open the door. Startled, the man whirled, the action bringing the trousers down over his ample, sweating belly and about his hairy legs.

"Whatcha' want, Indians?" The voice was half snarl, half contempt and challenge. But he closed his mouth, sat and obediently kicked off his trousers when Charlot aimed one Colt at his head and pointed to the bench with his club.

Little Coyote threw a stinking blanket over the naked, drunken woman sprawled on the pole bunk. He helped her stumble outside the hovel, her thick voice incoherently rising above those of the nervously moving horses inside the corral. She sank to the ground near a stuporous brave leaning against a large tree and snoring.

The two warriors tied Skrellings to a sitting position on the bench. His fearful whines became shouts bordering on screams when they quietly touched the candle to the bunk. Then they ignited the haystack outside, pushed over the outhouse, opened the corral gate, led and tethered one horse to a tree near the two drunken Flatheads. They closed the gate on the other horses; the animals' terrified screams began blending with those of Skrellings as Charlot threw a handful of burning hay into their midst. The horses destroyed the flimsy fence as they scattered into the night. Skrellings had scrabbled to the door of his burning shelter, but the wide bench held him inside. White froth clung to his beard; his noises continued while Little Coyote and Charlot solicitously turned his bench and body and guided him through the doorway. Roughly, they hustled him toward the privy, where they suspended him above the reeking pit.

The fearful bellowing started again as Charlot brought a torch of twisted hay. By its light they cut the restraining rope and stepped back. The screams ended with a slurpy, muffled thud as Skrellings fell butt first into the mess. He was sitting there, almost paralyzed, as Charlot, holding the torch high, handed one Colt to Little Coyote. Skrellings raised his dripping countenance upward, his eyes rolling fearfully in the light.

Charlot's voice was cold: "Will you leave this place, or . . .?" He had to repeat the question before the man quieted and dumbly nodded yes. They waited beyond the reach of the firelight until a strange creature hoisted itself from the pit, argued savagely with the protesting horse, then raced eastward toward the nearest similar encampment, perhaps two miles away.

Three days later, Charlot and Little Coyote, still seeking Victor, passed several hovels such as Skrellings'. All were vacant, all showing signs of hurried, unplanned departure. Not so the disaffected buffalo hunters. In the early light of the day after the confrontation between Little Faro and Victor, they had lowered their lodges and set up another encampment perhaps eight miles away.

When Father Mengarini attempted to arrange a meeting with them, one warrior appeared: Little Faro. Once again he was drunk.

57

L ittle Coyote focused his spyglass at the top of the small cliff above Lake of the White Moose, then silently handed the instrument to Charlot.

"My father." Puzzlement and relief colored the young warrior's voice—puzzlement that Victor evidently had come to this distant food-gathering site to pray, relief that their search of many days had ended. The pair had ridden to the places where, in the past, the medicine man had accompanied the chief when he had sought a vision. On those occasions, in the ancient ways of the people, the seer would go first to the exact location. There he would pray for good medicine and a vision for the pair, then bring the chief there. Thus, Little Coyote and Charlot had ridden first to *Cqe*, the place with the horn in a tree. Here they had found three other Flatheads camping, fishing, hunting and praying at intervals near the good medicine pine tree in which was embedded the horn of a great Rocky Mountain sheep. The searchers found many offerings of tobacco in tiny buckskin bags, rifle balls, beads and other ornaments hanging there, but no Victor. Searches of other locations had been equally fruitless, including *Ckwelkwelqéy*, red mountain top; *Epltemtemné*, place has graves, and *Nlpapá*, place with cliffs.

At this latter place in the southern end of the valley, Little Coyote had thought of the Lake of the White Moose. There, long ago, he had gone to write his letter to Jedediah Smith; the Good Spirit had told him his friend was dead.

Fish were dimpling the northeast and closest end of this lake. An eagle drifted above the water on motionless wings, perhaps eying the ducks which, honking their protests at the approaching horsemen, had paddled into the protective reeds at the lake's end. Trailing the ducks were energetic flotillas of ducklings. The two men heard a large body slowly moving northward through the trees and undergrowth and toward the two beaver dams. The nervous horses' swiveling ears and snorts told the warriors a bear had been searching the lake shore, too.

Little Coyote nodded in answer to Charlot's inquiring look. Yes, they should go a bit farther before tethering their horses among the trees, then head for the cliff on foot. Charlot dismounted, pushed a fresh percussion cap onto the nipple of his rifle lock and shouldered a small buckskin pack. The seer would carry only his bow and quiver of arrows. As they began clambering upward in the brush-covered scree, several grouse flushed, their wings beating against the smaller branches as they arced northward. Soon a new sound began rising above all others, faintly at first, growing louder as the warriors continued their ascent—somber, widely spaced beats from Victor's personal religious drum. As had the grouse, the men moved slightly northward toward an arrow-shaped part of the slope swept free of brush by a recent slide. Victor should have seen son and friend now, but the throbbing drumbeats continued. Charlot, waiting for Little Coyote to catch up, pointed. The chief was holding his white drum out from his chest, the white-tanned buckskin streamers around its rim jerking to each beat. He wore his headdress, white-tanned buckskin clothing, and ornately beaded, high moccasins. The prayer song in Flathead was ending; it was an ancient one, calling for the Good Spirit to point the singer to new ways that would enable him to forget old sorrows and face up to and surmount present tribulations.

Rested, Little Coyote signed he was ready. They climbed

around the base of the largest crag, momentarily out of sight of the chief, and re-emerged slightly above and behind him. Little Coyote, again breathing heavily, sat down, resolving to exercise more.

"Perhaps I should not listen to his prayers?" Charlot whispered.

"By hearing him, we can help," the seer responded. "I have heard this prayer. It is ending." Surprisingly, then, the chief's new song reached upward.

"It is from the Bible," Charlot whispered. Soon the short prayer ended with:

> *Like a flower of the field, he blooms*
> *The wind sweeps over him and he is gone*
> *And his place knows him no more.*

Victor, too, remained sitting in utter silence, head bent abjectly forward as though awaiting the blow of a war club. Bees busily worked the yellow, white and blue flowers; a mouse rustled in the matted, dry grass below the sparse new growth. A bluejay called down from atop the nearest tamarack, towering perhaps two-hundred feet.

The two men ate, each saving a portion for Victor, then continued to observe, pray and think while Sun neared the tamarack, hid behind its high branches, then re-emerged lower. Victor's hand moved then, but only to place his large, wooden-beaded rosary atop his drum.

"May we approach?"

At Little Coyote's query, the hand again moved, listlessly motioning them downward. The chief raised his head when they sat to his left, away from the drum. His face was haggard, shaped by fasting and sorrow, his eyes dulled as he had, in this solitude, communicated with his inner self and sought to do so with the Good Spirit. Clearly, there had been no answer.

"How can I lead our people as they are blown in all directions?" Victor asked. "Who can divine all the contrary winds of change? Even faithful and brave sub-chief Moise, after I was slapped, said, 'I don't listen to Victor anymore.'" Again, he lowered his head.

Little Coyote called on wisdom gained from the years that had passed between his youthful winter of the *sqléw* at the hot springs and his retreat there after the loss of Antelope and Lance. He set the drum and rosary atop his friend's crossed legs.

"You prayed for an answer," the seer said. "We appeared. I point to your answer."

Father and son followed the sweep of his arm toward the tamarack. As he did so, the bluejay, as though waiting only for this moment, screeched, then silently glided downward and out of sight.

"Perhaps by joining our arms and hands together we could reach around the tree," Little Coyote continued. "See how the other trees surrounding it seem to seek its protection—the smaller white pine, the firs, the spruce. Observe closely the thick, reddish-brown bark near the base, bark the Good Spirit colored like our skin. Note how the bark becomes more thin and brown as the tree grows ever higher to the sky from which comes the storms it must face through life.

"Father Ravalli once showed me how to tell such a creation's age when he explained his sawmill. A tamarack log I quite easily could reach around was more than two-hundred years old. The one we view now is perhaps seven-hundred years old. Yet, like a brave chieftain, it surely began growing from a special seed, a single winged seed that, before snows came, had dropped from another stalwart tamarack now long turned to dust.

"The Good Spirit spoke to me as you sat here praying. The tree began growing when enemies in greater numbers than our people forced us into this valley. The tamarack prospered while our chiefs helped our people seek and find food and safer living here. While they began to deplete the game, the tree continued to grow. And it became ever stronger as our people held council with our chiefs on how they could go back to the buffalo grounds. Braver and wiser chiefs grew up in their midst and formed alliances that successfully fought their way to and back from the buffalo grounds against ever growing enemy forces. The tamarack prospered, too, despite hardship, which the Good Spirit provides every living thing to make it strong. See the great streaks of black bark high up, the stubs of the great branches? There lightning struck and the tree survived. Great storms tore off stalwart branches. See the fire-blackened bark extending from the great base to a height almost equal to that of the surrounding trees? Great fire swept up the mountainside, perhaps many times, destroying the lesser trees, which always grew back from the ashes. But the tamarack continued to stand. In size, in strength, it is chief among all the trees on the mountain. No one can deny this. Yes, it looks bare, almost dead, after all the needles fall in the cold winds of winter. Yet, new life comes with each warm wind of spring. New needles form and help it to grow stronger. The chiefs of our people have, like the tamarack, survived the lightning, repeated storms and fires of hundreds of years.

"The Black Robes claim that the Good Spirit, who promised, 'I will not send more than you can bear,' molded and helped most chiefs to grow, to perform best during their times at their places to help most of the people to do the same. Can you say differently? Is this not a proper message for all our people for all time?"

Little Coyote motioned to Charlot, who grasped one of his father's hands. Together they pulled him upright, whereupon Little Coyote placed his hands on the chief's shoulders.

"Remember, you told me at the hot springs, 'The people need you.' I say, perhaps through the Good Spirit you called upon in your loneliness, that if you view your problems as greater than those faced by any other chief, that you are the chief ordained to deal with them. Can you, as chief, say the Good Spirit has not given you many friends who can help you to lead us through our problems?"

Almost as an "amen," Charlot added, "And Father, you have the even greater faith in God explained by the Black Robes. You are rich, indeed."

Little Coyote handed the food to Victor. While the chief ate, the seer told him that the aged Blackfeet sub-chief, Two Horns, waited at St. Mary's to talk.

"He is oldest brother of Tree, who parleyed with Three Eagles and our council many years ago at the buffalo grounds to free Owl, the Blood chief." Little Coyote paused sufficiently long for father and son to look inquiringly at him. Very slowly then, the seer spoke: "You surely remember the bravery of Tree, who walked alone into our midst seeking the release of his friend. He never changed his name."

"The Blackfeet again come to the Flatheads." For the first time, Victor smiled, briefly as a small cloud scudding past Sun, but the smile was there.

"Two Horns says he wishes to talk about the growing strength of the Sioux," Charlot said. "More and more people crowd to the buffalo grounds from the growing pressure of the whites moving in. Father Ravalli said Two Horns is powerful among the Blackfeet and their allies."

This set the trio to talking about the buffalo now. Who would lead the fall hunt?

"It is not unknown for the chief of the people to lead the hunt," Little Coyote said quietly. "Tjolzhitsay and others have done this in our time. There would be much to be gained in the doing."

Again Victor smiled, more grimly, then looked at Sun, which, threatening to hide behind the mountain, had cast the shadow of the great tamarack over them. As the warriors descended toward the lake, Little Coyote suggested, and Charlot immediately agreed, they could catch their next meal at the beaver ponds. Victor nudged his horse slightly north, then followed the stream bank from which spring floods over the years had cleared most of the brush. Before they crossed the creek, Little Coyote looked backward once; he noted that setting Sun's rays were climbing higher in the ancient tamarack's pale green, shining branches. Soon they would be gone.

Victor signed grizzly bear and pointed to the more-than-man-size tracks in the wet sand. The horses sniffed the evening breeze flowing down the stream channel. Goaded by repeated heel kicks, they reluctantly plodded ahead, ears twitching, nervously fighting the tight reins. When they would move no more, Victor leaped off, placed a fresh cap on the nipple of his Hellinghaus and motioned for Charlot to move abreast with him.

Little Coyote tethered the horses and followed behind.

The bear was huge—and very old. He stood in the lush vegetation near the foot of the lower beaver dam, weaving, sensing more than seeing, that danger was approaching. He dropped, then again stood, facing the hunters. Bare patches of skin extended far up the gaunt hind flanks; others were near the front shoulders. His great maw partially open as though he were laughing, he exposed broken teeth and gaps where others had been. Victor tossed a few blades of grass upward. They drifted south. The contrary breeze favored them—for the moment.

The chief raised his rifle as though aiming it. He touched Charlot's right shoulder. Again he aimed his rifle, lowered it and touched his left shoulder. Charlot nodded understandingly and moved away so Victor would have a better shot at the right shoulder. Again the bear dropped to all fours, looked about uncertainly, then stood. Victor raised his rifle, looked to assure himself that Charlot had done the same, then carefully sighted. The two weapons went off almost simultaneously; the bear roared fearfully and, squealing like a great boar hog at the Mission, began to bite at both broken shoulders. As the hunters reloaded, the bear quieted, listened, then tried to charge at the sounds. Roaring, grunting in pain, he flexed his strong muscles and began humping, sometimes belly-crawling; pushed by those powerful hind legs, he tried to reach his killers. One of the next two shots plowed through his slavering mouth and toward the brain; the other entered below the jaws and went into the neck where the head joined the spine. The grizzly slumped, his hind legs kicking and finally quieting as had old Tull's at Camas Meadows. Even after reloading, the two men sat watching while Little Coyote built a fire. Father and son sat there in the dusk while the medicine man, holding bow and arrows in one hand, crept behind the bear and pelted him with stones. Finally, Little Coyote reached out and touched him. Four times the medicine man pulled out a pinch of the sparse hair, cast it in the four directions, then silently thanked the Good Spirit that He had used the old bear to strengthen the heart of a chief the people needed perhaps more than ever before.

632

They cut out the two long slabs of tenderloin along the spine of the old boar and broiled parts of it, examining each piece in the brightest light to assure it was thoroughly done. While eating, the men relived the hunt, the placing of the shots; then, sated, the two hunters removed and kept the claws from all paws. They took no other parts of the thin, old body. Piling large logs on the fire, they picketed the horses upwind from the carcass in good grass, then sought sleep.

Little Coyote called a last message from his robe: "While you've been gone, Little Bear Claw, Agnes daily has prepared food for you. You ate part of it near the great tamarack."

Victor's muffled grunt conveyed he, too, was awake, eager to return home. As Little Coyote found sleep, he imagined he could hear Antelope's joyous laugh rising above the lulling sounds of the water spilling over the brimming beaver dams.

Vigilant horse guards fired a rifle shot to alert St. Mary's Mission that warriors approached. Soon Fast Runner galloped his horse toward Victor and the others. He stopped a short distance away and waited until all three had reached him. The welcoming sign was sincere, his voice troubled: "Only Father Ravalli and Brother Claessens remain at the Mission. Father Mengarini traveled to see the Jesuit chief after sending Brothers Savio and Bellomo to perform tasks elsewhere. Because the Blackfeet continue to steal our horses, I have controlled the guards. Two nights ago they ran a Blackfeet thief into the field like a scared rabbit and shot him."

Fast Runner, knowing his listeners would respond, chopped his hand up and down, signing for them to wait. "The Blackfeet visitor, old Two Horns, who came in peace, fearing for his life tried to hurry to his horse. Big Cap shot him. He lies dying under Father Ravalli's care."

Six watchful eyes focused on Victor. Resolutely, he strode to his lodge, seized his whip and, routing Big Cap from the shade of his own lodge, whipped him toward the dispensary until the man lay gasping at its door. Father Ravalli, alerted by Big Cap's gasps, ran out as though to stay the chief's hand. Wisely, he walked between Victor and Big Cap and motioned for Little Coyote and Charlot.

They carried out dead Two Horns, his head yet wet from the baptism Father Ravalli explained the old warrior had requested. With the curt acquiescence of the chief, the pair helped Big Cap to the dead man's cot. Victor departed. While the distraught Black Robe applied medicated bear grease to Big Cap's lacerated shoulders and back, he spoke hurriedly, briefly, as though to himself, except the message was in Flathead.

"I greatly fear that when the Blackfeet learn of Two Horns' death, the troubles with them here will intensify. When our superiors learn of that and of the increasing dissension here, they will order Father Mengarini to close the Mission."

A resolute Victor had planned well for the 1849 buffalo hunt. If the people would get much buffalo meat and preserve it while Sun remained warm, there would need be only a short winter hunt with lesser numbers for fresh meat, which winter cold would preserve. Accordingly, the chief had sent Fast Runner and Charlot to persuade Shoshonis and Nez Percé to hunt with them before the deep snows. On the appearance of those people, many in Little Faro's camp had insisted they join with the others. As the great procession of warriors, women and children moved northward, other kin and allies had added their strength. Not even the Sioux could have stopped them had they tried. Nor had the Little Faro faction protested when Victor was named chief of the hunt. The hunters had obtained all the meat they could carry.

Trouble had started after the return southward, after kin and allies had detached themselves to return to their regions and, finally, when the Shoshonis and Nez Percé had headed for Lolo Pass, wishing to camp near the hot springs for a well-earned rest before continuing homeward. Lolo Pass was a more arduous route, but, perhaps, free of possible enemies.

Some Flathead hunters challenged Victor when he firmly said, "We must rest our heavily loaded pack horses. They are worn. True, we have less than a full day's trek before we reach the Mission. If we ruin these horses, are you sure the Blackfeet, who dared not attack our hunting party, will have left us good ones at the Mission? I continue to fear too few of our warriors remained to guard the Mission, the old people and children, our horses and lodges when the remainder of Little Faro's camp, after saying they did not wish to join the hunt, later caught up with us."

When the dissidents continued to mutter among themselves, Victor appointed strong warriors to enforce his decision. The muttering died as all sought sleep, except the guards—and Little Coyote. After picketing his black horse in a grassy area between two trees, the seer had wrapped his robe about him and sat against the base of a tree. The uncountable bright stars scarcely lifted his spirits. His dream of the night before continued to disturb and puzzle him. He could understand the first part: All the rejoicing people traditionally welcoming the hunters home. But in the puzzling second part, many of the people almost immediately were grieving as another heavily laden pack train moved outward. Well . . . He pulled his robe more closely about him and laid down. The problems appear so often now the people must choose which to deal with—like trying to lasso one mustang in a stampeding herd.

The tiredness that began to claim his body vanished momentarily as he countered the worry about the dream with the more-pleasing reality of only two days earlier. That is when Victor triumphantly had reasserted his leadership. While the Shoshonis and Nez Percé still had been trekking with the Flatheads, the guards had sighted almost sixty Blackfeet driving a large herd of horses northward. Some of the Blackfeet had remained behind on a hillock, watching the meat-hunters, arguing, Little Coyote could tell through his spyglass, whether they should attack.

Some of the more impetuous buffalo-hunters immediately had begun clamoring to pursue the Blackfeet, for they undoubtedly were driving Flathead horses.

"My own son, Charlot, is at the Mission!" Victor had thundered, "as well as the sons of Kills With Lance and Wild Horse. Do you think we are not fearful for their safety as well as for the others, our women and children? We will not risk the women and children here, our meat, our horses, our lives. The Blackfeet are crafty, wise to the ways of war. Perhaps they have attacked the Mission. Can we help them now if they are wiped out? Who among you knows they did not wait to drive the horses in the view of our scouts, and now hide with a stronger force to attack us here or those who would set out in pursuit?"

Thus, Victor had maintained control of the hunting party. When some of the dissidents had continued their clamor, hinting that perhaps their chief was afraid, Victor had looked contemptuously at them, then galloped his horse toward the Blackfeet.

Immediately, a warrior astride a magnificent Appaloosa had thundered downward from the knoll, his war cry reaching the watching warriors.

Victor had leaped off his mount and run toward the Blackfeet. The warrior, waving shield and rifle, had done the same, whereupon Victor, raising the Hellinghaus rifle that had performed so well on the hunt, had shot the Appaloosa. The Blackfeet's shrill cry, rising above the scream of his struggling, dying horse, was a mixture of rage and triumph. He had lengthened his stride almost to a run, eager to close on and shoot this foolish Flathead before he could reload. Again Victor had done the unexpected. He had raised the Dragoon Colt, executed a quarter turn away from the charging warrior and fired two quick, ineffective shots toward the watching Blackfeet horsemen. Ineffective because he had hit neither horses nor warriors, but quite effective in halting the warrior's charge. He had stopped, started to raise his own gun, then lowered it as two bullets plowed the earth on either side, followed by the sounds of the two explosions that had sent them there. Again Victor had fired, this time the bullet striking a few feet in front of the Blackfeet. The warrior had turned and scampered back to the protection of his now-dead horse. Victor had watched while calmly reloading his Hellinghaus and the five empty chambers in the six-shooter's cylinder. Again he had begun walking toward the Blackfeet, who had scuttled up the hillock to rejoin his wavering companions. Victor had hacked off the Appaloosa's magnificent tail and remounted his own horse. Then, holding the flowing trophy above his head, he challengingly had ridden back and forth a short distance from the base of the hillock. One by one the Blackfeet had hurried away. Last to depart were the dead Appaloosa's owner and another warrior with whom he was riding double. Their loudly shouted imprecations ever more faintly reached the gaping hunters. As the hunters resumed their homeward trek, perhaps only a third of Little Faro's faction had accompanied him to the encampment north of St. Mary's Mission.

Despite this triumph, Victor later had confided to Little Coyote, "I acted like a stupid grouse by not sending more warriors back to the Mission when the remainder of Little Faro's faction joined us for the hunt. I have a feeling something is greatly wrong at St. Mary's Mission, something far exceeding what occurred there when I sought the help of the Good Spirit at the Lake of the White Moose."

Eager to reach the familiar meadow near the Mission, Little Coyote's black horse tried to move out ahead of the plodding pack horses loaded with dried buffalo meat. When the bullet struck with a sharp "thwak," the horse stumbled and fell; the sound of the shot arrived just before the seer grunted on impact with the earth. Struggling to his feet, the horse screamed in pain, agitating other horses in the train. He erratically began galloping toward the Mission buildings, crashed into the palisade and fell again. There was one more shot; Little Coyote blearily saw the animal's canted neck and head instantly drop and two armed figures racing toward the pack train.

They were Francis and Robert. Even before they reached the leading horsemen, shouted exclamations began filling the cool, afternoon air. "Our lodges! Many are pulled down!" "Where are our old people, our children?" "The haystacks are burned!" "The fences are pulled down!"

Victor's pistol shot and "Hold!" rose above the clamor; the milling horsemen stared down at the two young warriors.

"Old Broken Tooth shot the horse!" Francis looked solicitously at shaken Little Coyote while the last of the pack animals caught up and stopped. "His weakened ears and eyes

638

told him you were the Blackfeet returning. It was they who raided the lodges and threatened all who were fervently praying within the stockade. Uncertain of our numbers there, they departed with many horses after shooting one youth. Even now, Father Ravalli says the funeral mass. Father Mengarini, worn out like an old moccasin, remains at the Coeur d'Alene mission."

Evidently Father Ravalli had abbreviated the funeral mass, for by now the pent-up people were streaming toward the pack train, their distant, accusatory voices growing louder and, finally, drowning out Francis' attempts to explain. Throwing up his hands, Francis greeted his father and they began leading three pack animals toward the Mission.

Little Coyote's lodge had escaped the depredations, perhaps because of the symbols painted on it or its distance from the Mission. Charlot hastened to the seer soon after the boy's burial. The warrior, his stern face a younger version of his father's, was leading a fine Appaloosa behind his own.

"Fast Runner sends this gift, though some of his best were among the band the Blackfeet stole. I put the bullet into the ear of your horse after he struck the palisade. Broken Tooth is much shaken that his bullet was intended for you. He says he now will use only his old lance to help him hobble and to kill any enemy close by. Had the hunters not returned with the meat, we gladly would have eaten your horse because our food within the stockade was almost gone. We had eaten many dogs and my older mare."

With meat aplenty, the Flatheads resolutely set about sharing their lodges and helping to repair or replace the damaged ones. Other people began fashioning replacements for stolen or destroyed essential equipment. After a time Victor summoned the council. He opened it with the traditional pipe ceremony. Then, for the first time, he crossed himself, bowed low from his seated position and said The Lord's Prayer amid such muttering as, "The Black Robes' medicine is no better than Little Coyote's, Chalax's, others'." "We do not need this." "Get on with the meeting, if it is important!"

Charlot began explaining how Father Ravalli and Brother

Claessens had helped him, Francis and Robert, even old Broken Tooth, protect and feed the women and children. Those who had been clamoring quieted when Charlot had answered many questions about the raid. The people who had been quiet before began demanding they assemble their many allies and wipe out the Blackfeet.

Again, Victor broke with tradition. Rising, he strode into the very center of the assemblage. His gaze, angry at first, softened to sadness as he viewed the council. Some were clad only in buckskins, others in some buckskins and old white man's clothes, a few completely in ill-fitting and old woolen pants and shirts sent up the Missouri to the Black Robes. All continued to wear moccasins.

Now the sadness in his voice matched his expression and filled the lodge. Never before had he spoken so forcefully, so well.

"'Wipe out the Blackfeet,' some of you say. Yes, our people are brave. This we all know from our stories and the exploits of our warriors even now. They are good hunters. They breed good horses and can match the Blackfeet in acquiring them in other ways. But look about you. Where are many of our great warriors? Dead, gone to the sand hills too soon from incessant war, white man's diseases and whiskey. Many of you are young, as my son is young, brave, as my son is brave. Yes, we could fight the Blackfeet yet again. But to what end? Even they, their numbers dying, too, skulk about us like abandoned dogs. Our allies have suffered as we have suffered. Their numbers are much smaller, too. Our people never have gone to war with white man. Some white men have helped us; some have not. We have learned much from them."

Victor paused, thoughtfully rubbing his thumb and index finger downward from the ends of his lips as though this motion had molded them into the dominant feature in his now perpetually sad face. Again he stared downward at the oddly garbed listeners.

"Perhaps the most important lesson is that those Indians who fight white man are almost wiped out, the remainder herded like jaded horses to what they call 'reservations,' till today they scarcely survive as tribes. We are few now, perhaps always will be few. But we will survive. Hear me well. To do so, for now and forever, we must work together as in the past, keep together, change more of our ways to new ways, as does the coyote in its particular family—cunning, wise, ever watchful, always finding enough to eat and raise its young. As the seasons come and go, the coyote, too, changes its coat, but it has remained the wise coyote since the days of creation.

Victor's voice softened. "Some of you speak against the Black Robes, even say they want to take over our land. We gained much from seeking them out. I always will thank them for their help amid success and failure, which would have arrived even if the Black Robes had not. They are our friends who have brought us a richness I always will be able to carry because it is in my soul. A deeper faith in the Good Spirit—God. A certainty that one day we all will be under His full protection amid the company of our chiefs, our warriors, our braves, our wives, our children, our friends.

"Yes, and our past ways, bound and glued together like the arrowhead and sinew to the shaft, with the Black Robes' teachings, will help hold us together now, even though the Black Robes say they are almost certain they will close the Mission and leave."

The chief held up his hand to still the loud murmurs that filled the lodge. "While we hunted, the Black Robe, Michael Accolti, arrived to tell Father Ravalli to pack up and leave." Now, amid loud exclamations ranging from deep sorrow to satisfaction, Victor strode back to his usual position in the council and picked up the pipe and whip. All gave way as he departed.

More lodges went up around the Mission as winter progressed. Some were newly made, others skillfully patched. The Little Faro faction moved closer, too. For fresh meat that spring of 1850 the people seemed content to depend on elk and deer that moved into the valley to escape deep snow in the mountains.

As snow runoff in the side streams diminished and the river returned to its main banks, various white men began drifting into the valley. Their arrival continued throughout the summer. Plans for another great buffalo hunt scattered like a flock of grouse when Frank Owen again returned to the valley, this time in company with his brother, John, and John's Shoshone woman, Nancy. She was erecting two large canvas tents, hurried in her efforts by the snowfall moving down St. Mary's Peak and toward the Mission, when Warm Breeze eagerly sought her out. Yes! Nancy was from the same band as was dead Broken Pipe's family and could tell Warm Breeze about kinfolk she had not seen since the last trip with Fast Runner to obtain more Appaloosas.

About the same age and size as had been Willow Woman at her death, ever smiling Nancy also was equally as talkative, except when men were around. As Warm Breeze helped Nancy with the tents, Nancy chattered about how her band had prospered since joining with the large one of Chief Washakie. She also began telling why her recently acquired mate had come to the Bitter Root Valley.

That same day the Owen brothers were introducing themselves to Father Ravalli and recently arrived Father Joseph Joset. A few days later the Owens were meeting with the Black Robes about a far more serious matter.

"As I told you earlier, we are planning to abandon the Mission, at least for now," Father Joset began. "I was ordered here to carry out the task. Perhaps we *could* sell our holdings to you for a trading fort, and leave soon thereafter, because most of our belongings already are packed."

At Father Ravalli's suggestion, Father Joset had invited Victor and Charlot to be present. Two others were there: Little Coyote, as Charlot's *i-sts-sókoi*, and Agnes, who served the tea and sugar provided by the Black Robes, and the many hard ginger cookies the Owens had brought in their pack train. During the small talk over refreshments, the three Flathead men often spoke with their eyes as Father Ravalli carefully provided any needed interpretations to all, including balding, heavy-set Father Joset, whose shrewd eyes seemed at odds with his ready, friendly smile.

Yes, like Father Mengarini, Father Ravalli should have been resting, perhaps among the Coeur d'Alenes, too. His shiny and patched robe hung on his emaciated frame like the worn-out clothes over the crossed sticks of the scarecrows in the destroyed gardens. Agnes astutely only half-filled the cup he held in his shaking hand.

Little Coyote liked what he saw in John Owen, a man perhaps in his early thirties. Owen explained that he, like his brother, had come from Pennsylvania and most recently had served as sutler, or provisioner, to a rifle regiment.

"While we were spending last winter near Fort Hall, Frank, here, convinced me the Bitter Root would be a good place to end my hankering for my own fort." Owen centered his bright eyes on Victor's. "I'd treat you fairly; I can say that, and I've saved my money to buy such a place as you have here. This is a good location, well away from most other such forts, good weather, generally, with lots of people passing through . . . and maybe staying."

Father Ravalli placed his cup and three cookies atop a small table. "May I, Father?" He looked at Father Joset. "I want our Flathead friends to most clearly understand." He touched the cookies. "These are the other buildings." He moved his hand back and forth across the table top, then spoke in English, then Flathead. "This table top is Flathead land. We do not, cannot, sell it, nor would we if we could. The law of the United States protects the Flatheads' rights to the land through what is called 'immemorial occupancy.' Do all understand?" Victor gravely nodded his head.

Father Ravalli rocked forward twice in his chair to gain his feet. He grasped the back for a moment before walking to Victor. He looked down at the chief, then placed one of his hands on the chief's shoulder.

"Before the United States was, before anyone thought what it could be, wise men, or philosophers, and priests, yes . . . medicine men, in Europe understood to even greater depths the meaning of 'immemorial occupancy,' how no one justly can take away the land from those who earliest held it. They used these Latin words to express these rights and many other thoughts, even to the miraculous act of God's creation of the land and all its inhabitants, something only He can do: *'Nemo dat quod non habet,'* meaning 'No one can give what he doesn't have.' Are you sure you all understand?"

Victor, Charlot and Little Coyote talked for a moment, as did the Owens, before the chief gravely nodded his head yet again: "This land rightly remains ours till the world is no more."

Father Ravalli's face broke into the familiar, all-embracing, loving smile. He sank into his chair with a grateful sigh: "God love you always, friend. No one can put it better."

"We are striving for precision here, Mr. Owen, and I think we can sell our holdings to you," Father Joset said with a smile. "Please realize that Jesuits are humans, too. Their leaders change. Events which one leader hears about at one time which lead to his decision might have changed somewhat when a new leader takes over and wishes something else. Would it be satisfactory to you if we put into our contract a period of, say, two years in which the church could get back its improvements here should it wish to establish another mission?"

John Owen stroked his long, gray-flecked beard. "We could agree to that, Father. By that time the chief here and I could know how the fort would work out for them, for others and for me."

"We can complete our packing and depart by November 5, if the weather permits, Mr. Owen. Shall we put that date on the bill of sale?"

"Agreed again, Father."

Thus the sale came to be. Little Coyote inserted a copy of the sale document in his ledger book.

While John Owen was counting out the two-hundred-fifty dollars, Frank examined the map Father DeSmet had drawn and hung on the wall—the one showing the rough outline of boundaries of the various Indian nations and the locations of the Jesuit missions.

"John, look at this." Frank pointed to the map. He put his finger on the St. Mary's Mission site. "Here's Fort Owen, Major!" Exultantly, he pounded his brother on the back.

John's beard parted in a wide smile. He looked at Father

Joset. "Could this go into our bargain, Father? It would remind me of my limited domain, but also help me to understand the wider ones of so many people."

"A persuasive argument for me to say, 'yes.'"

"Reminds me of something else Jim Bridger told me about Broken Hand . . . uh, Tom Fitzpatrick, now Indian agent for the Upper Platte and Arkansas, when I went to get Nancy at Chief Washakie's encampment. Jim said, 'There's word getting around these parts Broken Hand is arguing that a great rendezvous be held, maybe at Fort Laramie, to lay out a great treaty respecting the boundaries of the different Indian nations, keep them from fighting and so forth. Seems a mighty important thing to do, so long as it is intended to keep the Indians from fighting among themselves, or the white men who just haven't a good record of respecting the Indians' boundaries.' Jim also said eight nations most likely will be there: Gros Ventres, Sioux, Arapahos, Cheyennes, Assiniboins, Crows, Mandans and Hidatsa. He also said . . . uh, excuse me, Fathers, 'They haven't mentioned the Shoshonis yet, but by damn they're sure as hell going to be there!'"

Frank Owen turned from looking out the window at the large, wet snowflakes silently falling over the Mission. He re-lighted his pipe and, between the first deep puffs, looked at the three Flatheads.

"Maybe the Flatheads ought to be there, too. Anyone with half an eye can see there's going to be trouble. All those immigrants and California gold-seekers coming up the Oregon Trail along the Platte are dividing the buffalo into two great herds—north and south. And the south part, others, as anyone can see, is filling up with whites faster than the buffalo are disappearing. The Indians know who is responsible." Owen shifted his gaze to Charlot and Little Coyote, then back to his brother. "Be to the advantage of the Flatheads and their friends to know what's going on, yours, too, John, as much as anyone's. Maybe I can arrange to go with some of them, invited or not, and work out things to bring back a pack train of supplies with us."

Again John Owen pulled at his beard. "Sounds reasonable." He looked at Victor. The chief's countenance was grim for the first time that afternoon. It remained that way until Agnes came in to serve a final cup of tea.

Brother Claessens trudged through his beloved garden plots, seemingly oblivious to shouted farewells, bawling cattle and church music raggedly issuing from a tiny knot of undirected horn-blowers. He moved around the laboriously gathered piles of stones, stopped to examine some fence rails and berry trellises that had escaped Blackfeet depredations, then peered closely at a few unharvested potato vines, cabbages and turnips enmired in the wet snow and deep mud splashing onto his old, black robe.

He would be carrying away more than mud this day from the Bitter Root Valley. He skirted the edge of a large crowd assembled near the chapel and began waving good-bye with his handkerchief each time he blew his nose or dabbed at tears running down his thin face into his sparse, gray beard.

Most of the Flatheads and other Indian visitors were watching the three heavily loaded carts and four wagons stringing out before moving north from Fort Owen. Trailing them would be numerous work cattle, some cows and a few good horses. Fathers Ravalli and Joset already were in the wagons; the latter called down a final, "Remember, Major, your promise to burn the chapel to avoid desecration if we don't return by January 1,

1852!" Owen, who had taken on the title of "Major" with the purchase of the Mission, nodded agreeably. He moved so two Flatheads could help Brother Claessens step up to a wheel hub. Brother Claessens kicked some of the mud off his shoes, slowly clambered into the wagon box and settled onto the seat. As the procession started, only he did not look back.

Father Ravalli had asked Victor, Charlot and Little Coyote to meet with him the day before the Black Robes' departure.

"The two Coeur d'Alenes who came here with Father Joset will escort me to the Sacred Heart Mission at the Coeur d'Alene River," the weary priest explained. "Brothers Bellomo and Savio will go to the Willamette. Because of the animals and baggage, Father Joset and Brother Claessens will have to set up winter camp somewhere near the fork of the Jocko River and the south fork of the Flathead River. We understand that other later-arriving Hudson's Bay Company free trappers have kept up a cabin Jocko Finlay built there in 1808. Father and Brother will try to stay there. We will worry about their safety, but God will answer our prayers."

"They will be safe! Many of us will see to that," Victor assured the delighted priest. "If we could accompany the Black Robes here for our good, we can help them depart in safety. You leave us much enriched and greatly saddened."

Before their tea cups were empty, Victor had agreed he would lead as many lodges of people as possible to spend the winter with Father Joset and Brother Claessens. Charlot, Little Coyote and a few others would remain at Fort Owen, both to assist and help protect the new owners. Then a small party would attend the great smoke at Fort Laramie, if it were held.

"If Bridger plans to take the uninvited eastern Shoshonis there, perhaps we could borrow some of their clothing for a time," Charlot suggested, grinning widely. "Or, Owen's woman, Nancy, and Warm Breeze could fashion us some here during the winter."

Now Victor laughed. "However you wish to plan, do so. If you magically could go as an eagle, that would be better." He sobered at once and added, "Be watchful, and mindful of our efforts to smoke the pipe with the Blackfeet. The whites will work magic, indeed, if they can succeed in getting such enemies as Crows and Sioux and others to smoke. We will strike our lodges once the Black Robes depart. I am mindful of your Osage friend at St. Louis. Truly, why does white man want the big smoke? But enough. Perhaps John Owen would allow those who remain here to use some of the cabins not yet needed for trade goods and the men he brought with him."

Father Ravalli could only nod in agreement. Finally he managed to say that in the most desperate times he and Father Mengarini had wondered if the Flatheads worth saving and serving had died since the Black Robes' arrival. "How quick we are to judge," he said, then corrected himself: "Misjudge." Tears streaming from his gentle eyes, he blessed the three as they departed.

Warm Breeze would not be assisting Nancy in making Shoshone clothing for Charlot and Little Coyote, perhaps others.

When Victor headed north and northwest for the Jocko with thirty lodges of people, Warm Breeze accompanied Fast Runner in the opposite direction. Fast Runner had left his best horses to the care of the Owen brothers in exchange for three mounts; he received some trade articles for others so he might get better animals from the Nez Percé. The warrior would try to confer with Chief Washakie and other Shoshonis, perhaps Bridger, too, and remain among them for possible later arrival of Charlot and Little Coyote.

Any needed proof that Father DeSmet remained interested in the Flathead people reached Fort Owen in the late spring of 1851.

"Some trappers brought up this message from St. Louis along with a larger and better saw blade and other supplies I ordered." Major Owen scarcely looked up from the crude table piled with papers, supplies, rough construction plans and a large ledger book in which he was entering some sales for the day. He handed a strong parchment envelope to Charlot. "It's for Victor, but since he'll be on the Jocko for a while yet, I figured you ought to get it. Coyote, here, can help you figure it out. If not, Frank and I could help." He motioned for the two warriors to sit on a bench and began examining and testing the strength of some adobe bricks Frank had lugged in and piled up next to some robes.

Charlot handed the envelope to Little Coyote as though it were a hot camas cake.

Greetings, Victor:

Herewith is a copy of a letter Thomas Fitzpatrick, Indian Agent for the Upper Platte and Arkansas, sent last September 24 to Mr. D.D. Mitchell. He is Superintendent of Indian Affairs at St. Louis.

Little Coyote looked up. Yes, Charlot was comprehending. Major Owen was listening intently, his long eyebrows, like wings of a bedraggled bird, arched as though poised for flight. Frank leaned against a wall and silently was refilling his pipe.

The letter asks that a great smoke be held. This should interest you and your people, and your kin and allies to the north and west of the Bitter Root Valley. You might wish to share the information with John and Frank Owen, too.

Here, also, is a copy of Mr. Mitchell's April 4, 1851, Circular to Indian Agents, Traders &c. It says, yes, there will be a great smoke. It will be held between Indians and whites at Fort Laramie in the Wyoming country on September 1, 1851. Mr. Mitchell has asked me to carry his letter throughout the great region south and west of the Missouri River and north of the Platte River. If it is God's will, I will see you and your people while I am thus employed. I have been told the following nations will be at the great smoke: Sioux, Cheyennes, Arapahos, Crows, Assiniboins, Mandans, Gros Ventres, and Arikaras.

I regret this letter is so brief. Perhaps you also should discuss this Circular with one or both of the Owens. I have sent John Owen one by the same messengers who brought yours. As you read all this, you might do well to recall what we have talked about in the past.

God Love You All,

P. J. DeSmet

Little Coyote looked up at Major Owen. Owen was stroking the long, drooping ends of his mustache until they formed part of the outer edges of his long beard. The seer handed him Fitzpatrick's letter.

"Yes, I received the copy of the Mitchell circular," Owen explained, "and I'd have talked to you about it before taking my pack train to The Dalles for goods." He quickly read the Fitzpatrick letter and handed it to Frank. "They're pretty much the same. Fitz asks for the smoke; Mitchell calls for it."

"There are many words," Charlot began somewhat hesitantly.

"The white man's way," John Owen said bluntly, "but look for the few real meanings in long letters, just as you Indians do in your eternally long speeches." His wide smile separated his mustache ends from his beard. "Writing words does not always make them any more true than saying them, though Indians have believed otherwise, usually to their sorrow, maybe because not many Indians speak with forked tongues."

"You distrust such letters?" Charlot asked.

"Sometimes yes, sometimes no," Owen replied. "Depends on who's writing. But since you've asked me, and Black Robe requested me to help explain, here's what I think. Both these letters say in many words they are mainly interested in holding the smoke because the Great Father wants to reward the Indians for the white destruction of game, timber and such, and give gifts because of the Indians' kindnesses shown to the many whites passing through their regions. Briefly put, I think the whites are trying to get the Indians to sign a treaty to quit fighting among themselves, which imperils the whites, and to protect the Oregon Trail and maybe the Santa Fe Trail to the south from raids. It's going to cost the Indians some, and . . ." He looked directly into

Little Coyote's eyes. ". . . I reckon that's what Black Robe means in that letter to Victor when he says, 'you might do well to recall what we have talked about in the past.'"

Seer and trader maintained unblinking eye contact until Frank Owen quietly spoke: "Fort Laramie is a long ways away, but what is done there will affect you some, too." He began picking up the bricks. "I'd bet my horse that one of these years you'll be called for treaty talks here, too. What the Indians have to remember is that the talks are supposed to be a give-and-take proposition. Seems to me it's been mostly 'Indians give and whites take' in the past."

Frank paused, then put down the bricks: "John, let me read that last part of Mitchell's circular again. Knowing how those fellows think, just because it's last doesn't mean it's not the most important." He began reading aloud, his voice strengthening with each added word: "'It is hoped, among other beneficial arrangements (intended for the permanent good of the Indians) that we will be enabled to divide and subdivide the country into various geographical districts, in a manner entirely satisfactory to the parties concerned. This, if accomplished, will go far toward extinguishing the bloody wars which have raged from time immemorable—producing such a horrible waste of human life and innocent blood . . .'"

Again Frank Owen began picking up the bricks. "Me, I'd watch that part about . . ." He bent over to read it from the circular, which he had placed atop the crowded table. ". . . 'The many objects so fondly hoped to be accomplished are, however, too numerous to be stated or commented upon in this brief Circular; they will *all* be fully explained around "our council fires."'"

Now Frank's eyes locked on Charlot's, then Little Coyote's. "You are wise, indeed, to plan to attend the big smoke."

The two Flatheads signed their thanks and prepared to leave. They could discuss later with Frank if he wanted to accompany them.

Owen's Delaware hunters, Jim and Ben Simonds, strode into the room, both towering above a short, thin and wiry man between them.

"Major, this fellow says he is a good blacksmith," Delaware Jim announced. "Want us to try him out?"

Soon the clanging of hammer and anvil began resounding throughout the busy fort site as had the ringing of a bell for so long such a short time ago. Little Coyote thought briefly about how, in the early days of the Mission, he had watched Brother Huet cleverly shape the different pieces of red-hot iron into the many-shaped objects useful to everyone. That night several scattered shots and some wild yells and rapid hoofbeats startled newcomers to the community. At dawn they determined their losses were fourteen horses to the Blackfeet raid. John Owen concluded that Frank ought to stay at the fort when he set out for The Dalles.

Chief Washakie leaped from his war horse and agilely clambered atop a box-shaped boulder embedded in the almost-grassless slope of the high hill. Sun dully highlighted his impassive, bronze face as he patiently waited for the fan-shaped procession of women, children, travois, pack horses, dogs and mounted rear guard to draw closer. Several hundred more Shoshone warriors dismounted and held their horses between the chief and the near spine of the hill. As most movement ceased, the panting dogs sought the shadows of the patient work horses. When the dust cloud of their ascent had swept over the hilltop, Washakie raised his rifle for silence.

"Scouts tell us our brother, Bridger, approaches," the chief said. "He will help interpret at the great smoke. The lodges of ten-thousand friends and enemies, including the Sioux, are on the prairie below us." When his vastly outnumbered people remained silent despite this dread news, Washakie's face broke into the usual friendly smile hundreds of immigrants passing through the Shoshone region had come to know.

Though the chief and his people had helped the immigrants, the Shoshonis were arriving at the great smoke uninvited by the Great Father. Invited by Bridger, they seemingly were receiving no protests from their accompanying white agents, Mr. Rose and Major Holman. Somewhere along the way, these uninvited/

invited Shoshonis had decided they should make sure the Great Father's chiefs did not get too liberal with their territory. Bridger wouldn't own up to *that* thought, though his words packed the power of a horse's hind legs with the Shoshonis; he recently had married a Shoshone after the death of his Ute wife and was chiefly responsible for arming them with good guns. At the end of the big smoke the Shoshonis would lose out, too, though it did not seem so at the time when there was only a paper to show it.

A scout atop the hill signaled. Bridger would reach them when Sun was directly overhead. The people fell to resting, talking and eating while the warriors changed their travel-worn garb for their best. A great cry went up as Bridger's silhouette joined that of the scout on the ridge. The warriors unsheathed their guns and all the Shoshonis followed Washakie upward.

Fast Runner was riding with Charlot and Little Coyote on the left flank of the well-ordered procession. He gasped: Widely separated circle after circle of lodges came into view as the trio neared the hilltop and veered away from the warriors surrounding Bridger. Even Charlot and Little Coyote, who had seen St. Louis, wonderingly shook their heads at the number of lodges.

The color and discipline of the Shoshonis had become widely known at the rendezvous; they would show it all now as they began descending the hill. A few of the American dragoons, their total less than just the Shoshone warriors, responded to the bugled "Boots and Saddles" by detaching themselves from the main body and cantering their horses out to meet these impressive late arrivals.

A Sioux warrior's shrill cries of old enmities and vengeance picked up the dying bugle notes. Waving bow and arrows, he raced his pony toward the Shoshone chief and other leaders now well out on the prairie. Little Coyote, yet descending the hillside, instantly thought back nineteen years to Antoine Godin's shooting and scalping of the Gros Ventre war chief, precipitating the battle of Pierre's Hole. But there would be no killing here.

Washakie held his rifle aloft and signaled peace. The great mixture of thousands of warriors, enemies and allies, moved restlessly like the buffalo agitated by the first lightning strike.

An interpreter kicked his superb Nez Percé steed into motion; all eyes focused on the life-or-death race between pony and Appaloosa while Washakie continued to close the distance between both. The Sioux lost the race but kept his life. The interpreter pulled him to the ground, leaped off his Appaloosa and snatched away the bow and arrows. He aimed his gun at the fallen warrior. Though few Sioux owned a gun, the message was clear.

"Where do we camp?" Washakie asked Bridger. As the mountain man led the way, every Shoshone warrior was pointing his gun upward, the butt resting on his right hip. The precision brought murmurs of admiration from the disciplined lines of two-hundred-seventy dragoons—and a sharp snap of disapproval from the troopers' apprehensive commander, already sharing the other leaders' concern over lack of food, forage for the horses, and the delayed arrival of the wagon train of presents.

Most people at the great smoke agreed that the interpreter's quick response to the Sioux warrior's ride for revenge and glory probably saved the meeting. Complaints over the lack of presents diminished during the encampment's move more than thirty miles down the Platte to near the mouth of Horse Creek. All Indians fully understood this necessity to be close to game and grass. They also credited Fitzpatrick, Mitchell, the Black Robe and others with the great accomplishment of bringing so many nations together.

Little Coyote and Charlot communicated but once with Father DeSmet, one of the busiest men of all. *We will meet later*, the Black Robe had signed while helping to settle yet another dispute. All chiefs wished to sit closest to Mitchell and Fitzpatrick for prestige; no one wanted to be shoulder to shoulder with ancient enemies. After a prolonged smoke ceremony, Bridger and the other interpreters began patiently repeating what the super-intendent sought and what the chiefs were willing to concede.

The chance communication with Father DeSmet resulted from one of the sudden wind gusts that occasionally struck the great assemblage. This one suspended all talk and scattered papers from a small table. Many people scrambled to recover and hand them to the Black Robe, who carried them to a man who was doing much writing. The man carefully rearranged them, crumpling and tossing away two in the process. One remained inside the circle of talkers, the other, unheeded, blew away in the dying breeze like a dry thistle clump. Little Coyote scrambled after it and, after pressing out the wrinkles, was pleased to see that one side was blank. While all were stretching, talking about whether the Crows would arrive, or walking behind a long, canvas wall to relieve themselves, the seer asked a mystified Charlot for one of his conical-shaped rifle bullets. After a few expert poundings with a rock, Little Coyote had produced a pencil. With but one piece of paper, the seer would not write until the final agreements were reached.

The Crows arrived on October 10. The smoke and prolonged opening remarks were repeated.

One week later, when birds were beginning their awakening calls through the low fog covering the yet-dark treaty grounds, Little Coyote and Charlot began walking quietly through the Shoshone encampment. They regretted that these friends, unlike most others at the great smoke, had spared their barking, snarling dogs during the hungry period preceding the move to Horse Creek. Free of the noise at last, the two warriors washed in a tiny creek, filled a water bag, then trudged toward the sentries patrolling the treaty grounds. The Flatheads chose one of the sitting places closest to the table. They ate their meat and prayed, then, as the sky turned from light pink to red, began pointing out to one another the tribal affiliations of others who also had chosen to arrive early this momentous day to watch the chiefs sign the treaty. As with Charlot and Little Coyote, none arrived singly; all carried weapons. All were talking among themselves, the tongues varied, the subject the same: There was astonishment that, despite the long days of arguments, there could be agreements of sorts on the major points Mitchell had wanted, but had not mentioned in his circular. As the two Flatheads listened, Little Coyote found himself shaking his head in dismay over the degrees of understanding—misunderstanding, really—about what the agreements really meant.

Soon the people were arriving in great numbers. The chiefs made their appearances, too; the medicine man could understand some of their talk, most of it centering on a very practical question: How can such agreements be honored when they are so opposite to tribal history, customs, experience and present and future need? "These white man matters are not easy to understand. Does white man try as hard to understand us? Does Mitchell think these matters can be easily settled by his just saying, 'Your condition is now changed from what it formerly was?'"

The Arapaho chief, Nehunnutah, The Storm, carefully spoke these questions, too, in Flathead as he pulled his blanket about him: "I think not!" he grunted as he sat down and impassively began eying Charlot's and Little Coyote's faces and then the Shoshone clothing.

As Sun began warming the land, Little Coyote carefully withdrew the piece of paper from his quiver, smoothed it once again over a flat rock and again conferred with Charlot. What the medicine man had printed in English was the briefest summary of the major points of the proposed treaty. Would all sign?

1. *The Great Father can build forts and roads in the hunting grounds.*
2. *There will be peace among the tribes, and with the whites. The tribes will repay the whites for any damages they do to the white man.*
3. *There will be boundaries for all the tribes, and each will have one chief.*
4. *The tribes will receive annuities of various needed articles for 50 years.*
5. *The United States bind themselves to protect the Aforesaid Indian Nations against the depredations by the people of the said United States.*

Little Coyote waited until all were assembled and the treaty provisions once again read and interpreted before he was able to get the precise wording of the fifth point.

There was new excitement preceding the signing of the treaty. A white messenger brought word the wagon train of presents was very near. Indian scouts brought word many buffalo had appeared on the south fork of the Platte River—only three days away from the hungry encampment.

Mitchell and Fitzpatrick signed for the Great Father. Two chiefs each made their marks for the Arikaras, Gros Ventres, Assiniboins, Mandans and Crows; three for the Arapahos; four for the Cheyennes; six for the Sioux.

There. White man was pleased. Now would come the presents. Then the people could hurry after the buffalo, except those various warriors Mitchell had requested from each tribe. They would go to Washington to see the Great Father. On returning, they would, among other things, tell their fellow tribesmen " . . . what they had seen of the strength, power and number of the white men."

Charlot, Little Coyote and Fast Runner easily would be able to catch up with Warm Breeze and the Shoshonis at the buffalo grounds. Father DeSmet had brought a basket of food. As he sat by the new fire, he was tired. His walk had been slower; there were dark areas under his eyes, yet the ever-ready link between the warmth of the eyes and his smile remained. For a brief time, these Flathead friends would receive his total attention. Expressions of gratitude for presents and a discussion of the past, though unhurried, were brief so they could get to the important thing—the future. With the greatest solemnity, the Black Robe had promised, "When I cannot say, but I know we will return to St. Mary's Mission." The Flatheads believed him.

The treaty?

Father DeSmet looked carefully at Little Coyote's piece of paper and praised him for the accomplishment and the accuracy. The priest's smile vanished at the two questions the seer asked: "How can this treaty be fair to all? How can it last?"

"As I have said, Little Coyote, God has provided you with the power to look ahead at times without providing you with the reasons certain events will occur. Because of this, I believe you already have the answers to your questions. God has enabled me to say certain events will occur because I have, over time, gotten the information that helps me to make the prediction, somewhat like Fast Runner's Warm Breeze shapes from many collected beads a grand design on his ceremonial shirt—a design she already has formed one bead at a time in her mind."

Little Coyote nodded. "You heard Mitchell tell all at the great smoke: 'Your condition is changed—and the Great Father desires you prepare for the changes that await you.'"

Father DeSmet spoke slowly now into the dying fire. "The whites want a map showing the boundaries of the various tribes. Because of my travels, Mitchell and Fitzpatrick have asked me to prepare the map. If I do not do so, others with less knowledge will prepare the map. So I have agreed. I will try my best to show on the map the regions of the tribes that did not come to the great smoke, that did not sign the treaty. You, your kin and friends, and the Blackfeet, will be on that map.

"The Indians, by agreement or force, will be kept away from where the white man travels now. Remember that even if I most carefully and fairly show on the map the regions of the various tribes, white man in the past has made much smaller boundaries and forced the Indians into them. He calls them 'reservations.' Certain chiefs signed the treaty for tribes made up of many bands. This is not the Indian way. They will not all agree to this new way, nor can the chiefs force them to do so—even if they would wish to do so."

Gloomily, the priest asked a question of the fire, its vanishing smoke, the great sky: "And how will the white men under the one Great Father force all white men to agree to the treaty and follow it? I must go."

Father DeSmet gave them a final embrace, blessed them and picked up the empty basket. "I can promise you we will return to St. Mary's Mission."

He kicked apart the dying ashes lest the forming late-afternoon breeze blow sparks into the dry grass of the treaty grounds and start a great conflagration. The breeze carried the fine, gray ashes a short distance until, widely separated, they no longer were visible or presented a threat.

So they parted as two soldiers came to disassemble and carry away the treaty table. With Charlot and Fast Runner animatedly talking abut the forthcoming buffalo hunt and all the good meat, Little Coyote's mind focused on what he had overheard one sentry say to another when he and Charlot were earliest arrivals at the treaty grounds: *"Hell, Billy, why there's such a fuss 'about the Oregon Trail, I can't figure. I heard Colonel Cooper tell Major Chilton that seventeen people have already died for every mile of the trail—from disease and hunger and one thing and another, even losing their way. I can't see the worth of the trail and all this talk."*

Finding he had lagged behind his companions, Little Coyote nudged his horse into an easy lope.

Who, he wondered, *would measure the cost to the Indian?*

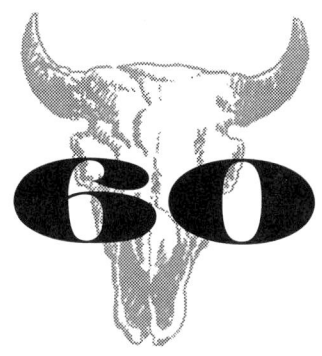

60

"The Skrellings crowd couldn't help us. They're dead. All dead. Killed near one wickiup where they were playing cards." Frank Owen reached under the counter for the whiskey bottle, poured a drink and sat down. He eyed Victor and Charlot, who had been talking to John, then tossed down the whiskey, got up and joined Little Coyote in peering out the window of the newly constructed section of adobe building inside the compound. In the growing darkness of this September 15, 1852, evening, the two men could see the other Flatheads who had ridden in with them walking toward the whites and Indians clustered around Pierre Baptiste, one of the horse guards. Frank turned around.

"Damn Blackfeet didn't just kill and scalp all seven of them," he said. "After other work with their knives they cut off their privates and stuffed them into their mouths." He grimaced and shook his head as though to clear it of the memory. "One poor bastard had the worst of it and for the longest time. He . . . ah hell! They're buried. Tracks told us there were too many Blackfeet for us to tangle with. They'd joined up with those who took our five horses yesterday. Why all the ruckus outside?"

"Dodson's dead, Frank. Wish I'd never brought him from

Fort Hall." Now John reached for the bottle. "He and Pierre were hauling in a load of hay today when about fifteen Blackfeet jumped them. Pierre managed to cut loose one of the horses and hightail it back here, but they scalped young Johnny. We saw it all happen before we could do anything about it. Fired a new haystack, too. Dammit! With the other big forts or trading posts so far away, we could make a good living here, especially since the Jesuits haven't come back and the place is mine."

Major Owen held out the bottle, then poured himself another drink when Frank declined.

"Victor and I've been trying to figure out what more we can do until the fort is built. If we can't handle them when they come here, we can't stay. Simple as that. My money's mostly gone."

Winter cold of 1852-53 did what the Owens, their workers, the Flatheads and the few remaining whites could not do. Few Blackfeet showed, but they returned in greater numbers with increased fury in the spring and summer. The Flatheads cooperated with the Owens as best they could by leaving some warriors behind with old people and children when the rest went after buffalo with their allies. Even so, when the hunters returned from the spring hunt, the Blackfeet had struck again, killing cattle, running off horses and burning two buildings. The Owens were preparing to leave.

"Well, Victor, I kept my bargain and you kept yours by helping us. And I've got to say that Sam Caldwell's been a decent sort, too. Sorry we can't trade for your robes. Maybe the Hudson's Bay people will take them. They've moved from Thompson's Falls to Fort Connah, north of here at Post Creek."

John Owen had asked Victor if he could come to the trading rooms for a smoke. He handed his visitors some tea.

"We're going to be hard put to take all our stock with us to the coast, part of the goods, too, but some of your warriors are welcome to the rest if they'll go with us, say, as far as the Spokane country. That'd pretty well be out of Blackfeet range. I just can't afford to lose my stock."

662

Yes, Owen had kept his bargain. Early in 1852 he had found some gold, and soon thereafter Caldwell had panned some out of Mill Creek, across the river from the fort. Both men had discussed their find and, after considering gains and losses, had agreed to share the information only with the Flathead chief, his son and their principal medicine man.

"There's probably not enough to make mining worthwhile," the trader had explained. "That's looking at it from all sides. We've seen what a stampede to even a poor strike in California could do to the Indians, game, fur and countryside. I've concluded, and Caldwell has gone along, we'd all stand to lose more than we could gain, especially if we'd have to mine out where we'd be more open to Blackfeet attacks than in the fields close to the fort. Really no choice at all there."

Told of the Owens' pending departure, the few whites who had not arrived with them would go their separate ways—south to safer country, north to as far as the Pend d'Oreilles and Kutenais. The Flatheads would allow three to live with them.

Eleven warriors under sub-chief Adolph would go with the Owens to the region of the Spokanes. Victor asked Little Coyote if he would go, accompanying Charlot, who needed to know that region and the people. The chief's countenance was brighter these days despite the Blackfeet problems and the Owens' pending departure. The last hunt had been good; there was ample food and another group of hunters in the Musselshell country most likely would have equal success. Also, many of the people were living as the Black Robes had taught them. While Major Owens liked a drink of whiskey, he forbade its sale or trade around the fort.

Delaware Jim Simonds and Little Coyote were scouting the south side of the extensive, almost square, lava table that rose above the undulating expanses of the Spokane country. John Owen and Adolph had agreed that Ben Simonds and Charlot should scout around the table's north side. The Flatheads had come to like these two powerfully built Delaware Indians. They could speak several tongues, including Flathead, almost as easily as they could find something to talk about or that was humorous under almost any circumstance—like now.

"When I attended mission school, there was a teacher who always found time to play games with us," Jim told Little Coyote, "if we had worked hard at our lessons. This nun would put six stools under the table and have seven of us walk around and around it, clapping our hands and singing." The huge man began singing in a deep, bass voice and nudging his powerful horse into a canter. He circled around Little Coyote, who stopped his mount.

> *Around the table we go—and*
> *around, around.*
> *Around the table we go—and*
> *around, around.*
> *Around the table we go—and*
> *then: Sit down!*

Laughing heartily at Little Coyote's amused reaction, Jim again pointed his horse west.

"In this game one of us always would wind up without a stool, and she'd pull away one more after each song. Soon there'd be two players for one stool. The winner who got that last stool could name the next game. When we get to the west end of this table rock, I'm going to name the next leg of the route we take. We'll get into real desert country soon enough after you Flatheads drop out. It's going to be back to the trees. Getting monotonous and hot here in the open already. I agree it's harder to drive stock and pull wagons through scattered tree country, but it's closer to water and cooler going, even though slower. Right now I'd settle for just another palaver with some more Coeur d'Alenes, or maybe Spokanes."

Unless there were some compelling reason, the Flatheads would be returning east next day. They would miss their friends, most of whom were camped a dozen or so miles behind them awaiting the Simonds' recommendation for the next leg of the trek.

Jim tilted his head back to take a swallow from his water bottle. He lowered it and jammed the stopper back in with a smart tap before pointing ahead and slightly upward with the same hand.

"It's Ben and Charlot. Signaling . . . *People coming*. Let's see. *Fifty or so*." Simultaneously the Delaware and Flathead guided their horses behind a badly weathered lava slab. They watched Ben and Charlot head for a long, east-west depression, then race toward them like large bugs while Little Coyote adjusted his spyglass. The heat waves rising from the hot rocks and earth distorted the view, but the seer could make out what appeared to be an almost-equal number of mounted soldiers and non-soldiers moving toward them with a large pack train.

"I'm Lieutenant Rufus Saxton." The deeply tanned young officer beat the dust from his sweaty shirt and pants with his hat. Others in his party inquired about water, game and forage, as though they could get more satisfactory information from the Flatheads and Delawares than from their guide, Antoine Plante. This wide-ranging, part Gros Ventre and French trapper knew the country well enough. He and his Flathead wife, Mary, now lived on their cattle and garden farm in the Spokane Valley.

"Well, sir, I'm bringing these supplies from Oregon," Saxton said. His voice was polite and decisive, yet a bit puzzled. "My orders are to proceed to Fort Owen and set up a depot for a railroad survey party."

The Delawares and Flatheads guided the Saxton party of fifty-two to the Owen encampment near some trees and a small, shallow lake. Before Sun set, the officer explained his particular assignment and the broader plan. Like the early-spring prairie flower that opens to Sun one petal at a time, Little Coyote discerned another long-hidden meaning in the enduring, ever unfolding, vision-quest revelations that had begun on the arrival of the Clark and Lewis expedition forty-nine years earlier.

The United States government wanted a transcontinental railroad. While the lieutenant continued his explanation, Frank Owen quickly and quietly explained to his Indian companions what that was. To do so, he used a few marks in the earth, laying parallel on them two long sticks used for oxen goads; he pointed to the wagons and called to his listeners' minds the guts that moved the stern-wheelers. All had seen these vessels puffing up the Missouri, most lately almost to Fort Benton, which Alexander Culbertson of The Pierre Choteau Jr. & Company had established at the head of navigation below the great falls. All the Flatheads did not fully understand nor seem to care much, really, what Lt. Saxton said next, but the Owens listened attentively.

Plans called for four surveys to determine which would be the best all-around rail route from the middle west to the Pacific coast, "because great changes are under way." With some pride, Lt. Saxton explained that his chief was Isaac I. Stevens. "He was made governor of the new Washington Territory, including from the coast to where we're standing right now, the Bitter Root Valley and more. We understand that next year the eastern part of this huge region of mountains and plains will be included in a Nebraska territory. Governor Stevens is leading the northern route survey. Near the end of September, Major Stevens should be reaching Fort Owen after working west from St. Paul to Forts Union and Benton."

Having firmly established the rank of his leader, Lt. Saxton, as had Frank Owen, used the earth and one of the gods to scratch out the directions various sections of the Stevens survey party were taking. Long before the lieutenant had completed his talk, John Owen had concluded his prospects were far better back in the Bitter Root than in Oregon.

"We're returning home with these folks come morning," he announced, jovially thumping Charlot and Little Coyote on their backs. "I'll make it right with all of you for your help. I think I see some answers to those plague-taked Blackfeet."

The warm night breeze laden with the perfume of trees and sagebrush whispered over Little Coyote as he lay on his robe apart from the busy camp of the Owen and Saxton forces. Tired from the day's scout, he slept briefly, then awakened to heavy thoughts that kept him alert through two changes of the guard. John Owen was seeing answers to his problems in the arrival of the United States Army. What should the Flathead people see? Centering at length on the notes he had taken at the Laramie great smoke, his mind linked with then and now; he remained awake until a soldier's horn aroused the entire camp.

Fort Owen became busier than ever as teams of the survey party began arriving: The Major Stevens group on September 28; Lt. A.J. Donelson's, September 29, and Lt. John Mullan's, September 30. The latter was accompanied by the successful hunters he had encountered in the Musselshell country. The Indians watched these soldiers and civilians with much interest, often expressing astonishment at their rapid coming and going, with little discussion, when Saxton, Donelson or Mullan spoke. These three men, in turn, moved faster yet when directed by Major Stevens, who clearly was an impatient man. He sent Lt. Mullan, perhaps twenty-two years old, to Victor with the request he bring the sub-chiefs to a meeting inside the fort. Victor and Charlot notified the others and arrived almost immediately clad in highly beaded new buckskins. Moses, Ambrose and Adolph arrived soon thereafter, and Michael and Henry, or Arlee, a bit later, the latter two groups graciously asked by friendly Lt. Mullan to hurry. There was a small table in the room, and four crude chairs, little else because John Owen evidently had not had time to return the fort's furnishings to their former places.

Lt. Mullan ushered the chief, sub-chiefs, Charlot and Little Coyote into the room. They leaned their rifles against the wall for easy access should the Blackfeet attack again. They stood until Mullan ceremoniously escorted and seated Lts. Donelson and Saxton. Mullan then sat. After a brief wait, one of the officers snapped "Ten-shun!" All stood as Major Stevens strode into the room, resplendent in his blue uniform with two vertical rows of bright metal buttons running almost to the high collar. Above it was the face of a man in his mid-thirties; he had a neatly trimmed beard and mustache, a modest nose and piercing eyes akin to those of Victor. His long hair was neatly trimmed and parted into a slant across the left side of his high forehead. The major prepared to seat himself, aided by Lt. Mullan. Seated, the major raised his hand and signed for the Flatheads to take their seats—evidently on the floor. Victor spoke quickly in Flathead.

They remained standing as Charlot departed and soon returned with a crude, Mission school bench. Charlot placed it against the wall, withdrew and returned with a slightly smaller one. Victor ceremoniously sat, as did the others. Little Coyote, waiting till last, seated himself on the floor and leaned against the wall. Throughout this activity, the major drummed his right fingers on the table top.

Now Gabriel Prudhomme walked in and introduced the officers, in order of rank, to Victor. Victor gravely stepped forward to shake their hands. Prudhomme evidently had been instructed to introduce each of the sub-chiefs and Charlot hastily and without the hand-shaking. He began with Arlee, recently designated second chief, who would have been content to remain stiffly seated. Again Victor spoke. Arlee arose, walked to the table and waited until the officers again stood; then he gravely gave each a single vigorous handshake and returned. Prudhomme then introduced Adolph as third chief, then the others in turn, ending with Charlot and Little Coyote.

The major stood once again, ready to speak for Prudhomme to interpret. He paused, a hint of annoyance flitting across his face as Victor stood, walked past his sub-chiefs and handed his pipe and tobacco pouch to Little Coyote. Gravely, the chief returned to his seat, then said to Prudhomme in English, "Now."

The officer's voice was quick, decisive, his eyes moving with each major thought to a different listener. The Great Father and the Congress wanted a railroad to be built across the nation to bind all the different people and lands together with a belt of iron and steel. He described a railroad and Prudhomme passed around a print of one so all would understand. Jefferson Davis, Secretary of War—the major had Prudhomme repeat the name and title—would see that the railroad would be built. As the major had moved west from St. Paul with his scientists, engineers and soldiers, they had looked for the best places to build the railroad, as had these other officers and their men. The major had spoken to various Indians who often had fought with one

668

another. They had said they were willing to sign treaties not to make war, and to agree to the railroad coming across the land. At Fort Benton near Great Falls, the major had spoken to Alexander Culbertson and some of the Blackfeet chiefs. The chiefs were willing not to make war with the Flatheads if the Flatheads also wanted peace. "The Blackfeet will stay out of the Bitter Root Valley," Stevens said.

The major paused, evidently expecting some response to this revelation. When there was none, he forgot for several seconds to employ the individual eye contact. "Are they stones?" he asked Prudhomme, but told him not to interpret that. He paused again when, for the first time, he noticed the high quality of the Flatheads' rifles. This time he whispered something to Mullan, who made some marks on the paper at the table.

Culbertson had agreed to go to Washington to ask the Great Father to allow the major to return to make the treaties. He thought the Great Father would agree to this. Meanwhile, the major's people would do more work elsewhere, and all must leave October 7 to begin. He would talk to other Indians. Would the Flathead people, as had others, say they were willing to sign a treaty with the Great Father? The major looked steadily at Victor, Arlee, Adolph and the others.

"Why does the Great Father build the railroad?" Victor asked Stevens through Prudhomme.

"To bind together all the people, as I have said."

"Who will use this railroad?"

"All the people." Again that hint of annoyance.

"The Indian people?"

"Of course!"

"They do not often use the fireboats."

The major stood. He walked with a slight limp to the rifles. "But the boats bring you good rifles. Other marvels." Smiling, he again sat down.

"The white men carry out many furs, robes, buffalo tongues, good horses. Will the railroad do this?"

"Yes."

"Will it bring many white people?"

"Yes."

"And the Blackfeet greeted this information by agreeing not to fight more white men, nor the Flatheads and their allies?"

Major Stevens slowly walked to the small window. He stood in the bright sunlight, then turned to face this persistent interrogator. The light slanting across half his body reflected off one row of buttons and highlighted the tiredness on his face. Little Coyote closed his eyes momentarily to adjust them to the grayness of the rest of the room. He heard the major resume his seat.

Victor turned away from the table and looked down at the seer, the chief's eyes asking the question: The Fort Laramie Treaty?

The seer signed affirmatively.

"Tell Stevens this," Victor told Prudhomme. "I, too, will speak slowly so Stevens will understand. Yes, once again the Flathead people would like to have a lasting treaty with the Blackfeet."

Stevens smiled.

"At the Fort Laramie great smoke, the Great Father's chiefs asked the chiefs of many tribes to agree that white man would be able to do what he already had been doing where the Indians live."

Stevens frowned.

"If the Flatheads and their kin and allies, or the Blackfeet and others did not want the railroad, would Stevens take all his men to Washington and not have the railroad built?"

Stevens' face reddened as though the high collar suddenly had become tight. He frowned, then quickly smiled.

"I am not the chief who can make that decision. If the Great Father asks for treaty talks, we can answer such questions. Would you attend a treaty talk?"

"To be held soon before the railroad comes? There was no treaty before the fireboats came."

"Yes."

"We would attend a treaty talk."

Major Stevens left Lt. Mullan and a few others behind. The

lieutenant named their camp near Fort Owen "Cantonment Stevens." He led his men on many exploratory trips through late fall till early spring. Between such trips he visited Fort Owen and the Flathead encampment. All soon grew to like this friendly, inquisitive, energetic, young officer.

He was ambitious, too. As the days lengthened and grew warm, an idea began to sprout and grow. There should be a wagon road from Fort Benton, at the head of navigation on the Missouri River, to Fort Walla Walla, head of navigation on the mighty Columbia!

61

L ittle Knife sifted his fingers through the patch of ashes he had stirred up with his long scratching stick. Almost at once he found another long, fire-discolored, squarish nail. Before burning the church and Mission building, one of Major Owen's workmen had removed all visible nails and spikes. Though few had been used in the construction, each one salvaged meant one less to be packed from afar or hammered out by the blacksmith.

Owen, preparing for a supply trip to The Dalles, had handed the young Flathead a piece of sugar crystal, then told him what he wanted: "Clement, I understand you're a hard worker and have good eyes. You fill this box with nails and I'll give you a whole string of sugar crystal."

So this bright day of March 1854, the youth was searching systematically, examining larger pieces of unburned wood before throwing them outside the fire area, which he roughly had divided into large squares. His eyesight had become the talk of the ever-vigilant encampment. He plopped a nail into the box and again picked up his stick.

Something was moving through a distant patch of snow. Clement watched the next closest patch. Yes, there was movement

672

across it. A wagon? Yes. And horsemen. Clement looked toward the trading post. Major Owen's wagon was there. Besides, this wagon was larger and coming toward the fort. Who had such a wagon in the valley? The youth stashed the nail box and stick between two blackened logs. Wiping his sooty hands across his thighs, he hurried toward the Flathead encampment.

"You are a good watcher, Clement," Victor said. "Tell Owen." The chief strode toward Little Coyote's lodge, wanting to grin about the five black "war streaks" across each of Clement's thighs, but sobered by what message the wagon and horsemen might bring.

"There are four of our people on horses. They lean far forward in their saddles. A soldier and Lt. Mullan ride the wagon. They all move slowly, too slowly. I do not like this." Little Coyote collapsed his spyglass and he and Victor began striding to the encampment edge. Too soon the curious group gathering there was plunged into deep sorrow, which spread like fire in dry buffalo grass. In the front end of the wagon were five neatly gutted deer carcasses. In the back end under a fly screen of tree boughs were the bodies of six savagely mutilated and scalped Flathead hunters.

"We hunted the brush patches on the hillsides east of Cantonment Stevens," Big Elk explained amid the loud keening of the women. "My brother and the others," the grieving warrior said as he nodded toward the wagon, "rode higher up to hunt and perhaps drive any deer toward us. There were a few shots, and we said, 'They have found deer,' then many shots, so we left our deer and hurried upward. Late. Too late. We found one dead horse with Blackfeet trappings, and these." He pointed toward the wagon and despairingly dropped his arm. "Lt. Mullan had just brought this wagon from Fort Benton. He offered to help us." Big Elk joined the loudly grieving throng. Victor sent for a canvas on which to reassemble the wagon's tragic cargo.

Grim-faced Victor waited patiently till the first loud outcries for vengeance died down in the council lodge. One by one all spoke, their demands ranging from mounting a great war party of Flatheads and allies against the Blackfeet to the employment of several well-planned and simultaneous raids.

Their initial grief and anger thus vented, Victor said there would be a meeting after the burials to select and plan which retaliatory measures to take. Had the powerful sub-chiefs Arlee and Adolph not accompanied the trading party Major Owen had sent to the Shoshonis, there very likely would have been a great battle. Victor was determined to carry the hatchet to the Blackfeet.

This time, however, outside the council, he found opposition from three sources: His son; the chief medicine man, who was his closest friend; and Thomas Adams, an assistant topographer who had served with Major Stevens and, after discharge, had remained in the valley. Little Coyote had come to know and like the map-maker while Adams had watched the seer sketch two more years' events on his story skin.

Lt. Mullan had pleaded earnestly with the angry chief not to seek out the Blackfeet. "Stevens could send his soldiers to punish your people if you should punish the Blackfeet," the officer said at last. Then he and Adams had sought out Charlot and Little Coyote.

"Stevens quit the Army last year to become a governor with much more power." Mullan showed the two Flatheads a paper signed: Isaac I. Stevens, Governor of the Territory of Washington. He had appointed Adams as special agent to the Flathead Indians.

"Adams speaks for Governor Stevens," Mullan explained. "These men do not want the Flatheads to fight the Blackfeet. The Governor prepares important meetings with the Flatheads, Blackfeet and many other tribes. In the councils the Governor will tell you again he does not want the Blackfeet to raid the Flatheads and others." The lieutenant paused momentarily, then carefully added, "I ask you not to think up a fort against what I now must say. The Governor can call many soldiers to enforce his wishes. As your friend who must leave in September, I hope that when I am gone you will listen to Thomas Adams."

Other forces also helped deter Victor. Word came from Tuekakas that, since the Fort Laramie Treaty, the Nez Percé were having even greater troubles trying to cope with continued incursions of whites to their regions. Washakie's Shoshonis had lost much of their range from Wind River to the Big Horn. The Crows were the winners there. Then, too, came word that Fathers Adrian Hoecken and Joseph Menetrey were moving their St. Ignatius Mission among the Kalispels or Upper Pend d'Oreilles to a better location that Chief Alexander had shown the Black Robes and said the people desired. This was the Jocko or Mission Valley, roughly sixty miles north and west of Fort Owen. Most Flatheads were reluctant to jeopardize their Pend d'Oreille kinfolk by stirring up the ever-simmering fury of the Blackfeet, who might center their attention on the newly forming Mission and make the builders wish they never had left the poor prairie land above the mouth of the Clark River. Five lightning-like Blackfeet raids on Flathead horses in widely separated parts of the Bitter Root Valley convinced any remaining Flathead proponents of war that they would wear themselves out just trying to find their enemies.

When the tracks of a sixth, then seventh, Blackfeet horse raid in September 1854 led toward Mission Valley, Victor, Charlot and a few other determined, frustrated pursuers visited St. Ignatius Mission. They found it as bustling as had been St. Mary's only a few years earlier. There was solace that the Kalispel kin were so near, and much delight that a visitor to St. Ignatius was Father Ravalli, newly named Superior at Mission of the Sacred Heart among the Coeur d'Alenes!

One pleasant evening just before the priest was to return to his Mission, the Flatheads invited him to a quiet feast on the fattest elk they had killed in a grassy meadow almost in the shadow of the mighty Mission Range of mountains. The priest's smile had returned; his body no longer appeared starved; his hands were steady, and even his tattered, old robe had been replaced by an almost-new one. He expressed relief he could converse in the Flatheads' tongue, because "I am more secure in this one than the others."

Thus, his grace over the food could range afar in but a few moments: He thanked the Good Spirit that the chief of the Flatheads and many others always had kept their faith. Some of the most dissolute had mended their ways. Most had freed their slaves. "Your faith, like my smallpox vaccine, stays with you."

The Black Robe expressed certainty the Good Spirit would heed the collective pleas of a delegation sent to Father Mengarini in California, and to Father DeSmet and others, to send the Black Robes back to the Bitter Root Valley.

After a period of silent eating, Father Ravalli lowered his broiled elk rib, chewed for a moment longer and swallowed. He looked up to the Mission Range, centering his gaze, finally, on a small waterfall that was white against the side of the darkening peak.

"This Mission Valley is beautiful, indeed, as is the country of the Coeur d'Alenes. I, too, pray that I will be among those who surely will return to our Bitter Root Valley. Two months ago, Major Owen visited here. He said, 'The only way we're going to survive in the Bitter Root Valley is to build my fort big and strong, which I'm doing, and have Stevens force the Blackfeet to stop their attacks.'

"Of course," Father Ravalli continued somewhat musingly, "if the people moving through the valley and making purchases at the fort find the place safer, they might be inclined to stay." He carefully placed the rib on a piece of wood near the fire, then looked at Victor. "I also am told how you spoke up to Major Stevens for your people. I am somewhat aware that Major Stevens soon might seek treaties with the various tribes. I remain mindful of Father Mengarini's statement: 'As white man moves in, the condition of the Flatheads *versus* the whites threatens to become the condition of Indians everywhere.' I fear that Major Stevens, much as did the Jesuits at first throughout the great Northwest, is trying to do too much too quickly—but particularly, in his case, to remain ahead of events even as he helps to precipitate them. And, of course, this forces the Indians to try to cope immediately with the results."

For a while the priest bit off and chewed the remaining meat. Finally he threw the bone into the fire while seemingly saying to himself, "I sometimes wonder if the so-called savages are thought to be unable to perceive what white man's aims are, to discuss them and form opinions, too."

The priest looked at Little Coyote. "And what of you? Are

the people well?"

Little Coyote chewed longer than necessary, too, as he pondered what his reply should be. Father Ravalli had ranged afar before approaching the subject of possible treaties. This discerning white medicine man could see for himself that, during his absence, Victor had regained much of his self-assurance and authority since his lonely flight to the cliff above the Lake of the White Moose. The priest could not know that the chief calmly had been accepting the many views, even those of his son and best friend, opposing his proposal to punish the Blackfeet.

"Mostly, our people are well," Little Coyote said. "Victor insists his people keep a clean encampment, and Major Owen does the same at his ever-growing fort. As yet, we eat well. There have been a few deaths from the smallpox among people who did not get your vaccine. Also, the pneumonia often keeps many of the people coughing as does a herd of elk during a hard run."

There. Now he, too, could speak to the possible treaties, for here the total well-being of the people was at risk. But his words must be to his own people who were listening, too.

"You mention treaties. We remember well the Fort Laramie Treaty! In the Oregon country are medicine men who, during and after the Cayuse War, urged their chiefs to return to the old ways, cast away all that is white. This cannot work. Frank Owen told me that largely because of that war the Great Father and the Congress gave Oregon a territorial government, and set up more Army posts. And the white men were told they could come and take the land."

Little Coyote picked up the battered, old, rectangular basket that had held the camas cakes served with the elk meat.

"When Victor suggested that Chief Tuekakas perhaps bring the Nez Percé to help fight the Blackfeet, he said the troubles with whites who sought their land were keeping him busy enough. Father Ravalli fears that Stevens, like the Black Robes, is trying to do too much too quickly. There is a great difference. Long ago we learned the Black Robes sought changes to help the Indians. Stevens seemingly seeks only to help the whites. Tuekakas says more. 'Chief Peo-peo-mox-mox of the Walla

Wallas says Stevens wishes to move all Indians to reservations like corralled, gelded horses, where they will be out of the way and not bother white man and his plans.'"

Little Coyote held the old basket aloft and turned it. The flickering firelight seemed to give movement to the horse design on one side, a large cross on the other. Now the seer turned the basket on its side so all could see the sturdy ribs inside and the base made from split willow.

"I know this basket," he said. "It was old when my mother, Little Yellow Bird, gave it to Willow Woman when she married Little Bear Claw—Victor. Then there was a yellow bird woven in the grasses on its side. As this wore away from use, Willow Woman wove a grizzly bear on one side, a willow tree on the other. In turn, Agnes replaced the old grass patterns with this horse and cross."

Little Coyote suddenly threw the basket to the ground. It bounced and rolled out of the firelight.

"You see, the basket, itself, remains strong. Only the weaker portions wear out. These can be replaced with new patterns. The whites increase. They encircle us. They come afoot, on horses, in great fireboats and wagons. Stevens wants the railroad. If immigrant trains have split the buffalo into two great herds, what will this railroad do? We carefully must ask such questions, seek answers and weave our lives among the whites, holding to important, old ways as new ways irresistibly help shape the now and the forever. Only thus can there be a forever for our people. These must be our thoughts if we ever talk about treaties."

The medicine man looked at the silent listeners. Father Ravalli's jaw had drooped; for a moment longer he continued to look at Little Coyote across the fire. Then the priest stood, dusted off his robe and stepped outside the firelight. He soon returned with a large coffee pot and a pail of water.

"Working out treaties can be like making coffee that pleases all." He poured some water into the pot. "The Indians supply the good water." He reached deep into a robe pocket for a bag, then dumped the contents into the pot. "White man provides the coffee." The priest withdrew a smaller bag from his other pocket.

678

He untied the drawstring and carefully began pouring some of its contents into the pot. "One must be vigilant not to destroy the coffee taste with an over-abundance of sugar—which I fear the Indians have come to like too much."

Amid continued silence, he stirred the mixture, then placed the pot on the fire, where soon it began boiling.

"Old Wife!" Major John Owen had shouted for Nancy. "Will you get Victor and Charlot, maybe Little Coyote, if you can find him? I've got to tell them a few things about handling themselves before the Flatheads leave here for the Hell Gate meeting with Governor Stevens." Owen was mildly drunk, peevish and hurting—drunk because of late he had sought to find temporary solace from his many anxieties in the bottle; peevish because the early July 1855 heat shimmering on the well-packed earth at Fort Owen was pouring through the open windows of his office, making him uncomfortable, indeed; hurting because his now-loosely-bandaged arm hampered him from performing some of the many jobs the abuilding fort demanded. Instead, he had to depend on others, Indians and whites alike, many of whom, though willing, lacked the experience the tasks demanded. He wanted to go to Hell Gate near the mouth of the Bitter Root River, too, but his brother, Frank, Flathead Charlie and his son were in the Nez Percé and Coeur d'Alene regions. The three men would complete the trading trip the major was engaged in when that damnable horse had kicked him. The animal's iron shoe had displaced a slab of his upper arm till a part of it moved like a roughly cut initial slice into a ham. The major had sent Charlie to the Coeur d'Alene Mission for help. Father Ravalli had responded quickly, accompanied by another priest.

"The bone is badly bruised, but not broken," the Black Robe reported after washing away the moist moss and tobacco leaves the trader had plastered over the wound. The priest had sniffed the flesh, given the major some laudanum, snipped away some questionable edges of flesh, then had bound and sewed the slab in place. He had stuck around the crude camp for two days, tending his patient, closely examining the injury by sight, touch and smell, then had said he must return to the Mission on the third day. During those days a very grateful Owen had learned much more than medicine from this gentle priest.

That spring the Black Robes serving in the great Rocky Mountain region had met at Colville. Then Father Ravalli had started for the city of Vancouver ". . . which like others—The Dalles, Portland, Walla Walla—had sprung up during the ten short years since I had left the Willamette. I heard the plans to construct a railroad between the large cities of San Francisco and St. Louis." Owen had shaken his head understandingly when the Black Robe had expressed concern about a possible railroad in the Rocky Mountain region.

Learning that Governor Stevens was holding a meeting at Walla Walla with chiefs and others from upper northwest tribes, the priest had gone there. The Governor was pleased at Father Ravalli's appearance, displeased with the information he brought. The Coeur d'Alenes and Spokans would not be attending; the Walla Wallas would deliberately arrive late, if at all.

As gently as he could, Father Ravalli had explained that the Indians were becoming increasingly hostile because of the ever-increasing incursions of whites and the Governor's insistence the Indians withdraw to reservations.

"The Governor will be holding a great council at Hell Gate next month," the Black Robe had said while shaking Owen's good hand and arm before they had gone their separate ways. "He has asked the various Jesuits to help as they can." He paused and looked meaningfully at Owen, gripping his hand more tightly. "I wish there were some way I could communicate to my beloved Flatheads, the Upper Pend d'Oreilles of the mountains, and the Kutenais the Governor's intent—namely to place all three tribes on the same reservation." He paused; his sad look deepened. "As well as the Coeur d'Alenes and the Kalispels, or Lower Pend d'Oreilles! What changes I foresee; what miseries, too." He had dropped Owen's hand then, and prepared to ride away.

"Yes, I know generally about the meeting, Father," Owen had replied. "Tom Adams is getting the tribes together for it. I'll talk to them before they set out. Damn well better. Uh, excuse me, Father, but right now most of them are thinking the main purpose of the meeting is to figure out a way to deal with the Blackfeet problems!"

"Victor, Charlot and Little Coyote will come," Nancy announced, then she hurried away to bake biscuits to serve with tea to their guests. Owen, remembering the apprehensive look on Father Ravalli's face at their good-bye, took one more swig from the bottle and placed it under the table. Then he picked up and re-read the message Frank had sent from the Nez Percé country with Charlie's son: "Agggh! What a son-of-a-bitchin' world this sometimes is!"

On the seventh day of the seventh month, Victor urged his superb Appaloosa into the space between the equally fine horses of Alexander of the Upper Pend d'Oreilles and Michael of the Kutenais. There had been jealous moments among the three chiefs until they finally had agreed at this council, just as on buffalo hunts, they must try to work together for the good of all. Then they had cooperated so that now, pridefully, the chiefs could watch several hundred of their warriors form a great circle on this flat area of Old Grass Valley near where Little Coyote had lost his family in the battle with the Blackfeet. Governor Stevens' party, its pack string and a few beeves entered through a small, open arc, which the horsemen immediately closed. The whites stopped in the center, whereupon the chiefs raised their arms then simultaneously lowered them. More than three-hundred rifles, muskets and pistols boomed at once, the powder smoke continuing to swirl above them all. Now the circle of horsemen segmented into three arcs that quickly became long, straight and motionless lines.

Again the chiefs dropped their arms. The Pend d'Oreilles, shrilling their war cries, raced abreast to the far end of the field, then stopped. Next were the Flatheads, then the Kutenais. With great precision the horsemen and women formed a tightly packed circle that began moving, ever widening, around, around, larger and larger till once again the white men were in the center, restraining their own mounts and other livestock.

At a third hand signal the circle melted away and the chiefs solemnly, pridefully rode forward to greet these twenty-two visitors to their land and escort them to the Indians' camp on the Hell Gate River.

The Stevens party would camp a short distance away. After the ceremonial pipe in Stevens' tent, the chiefs agreed that, since the next day was Sunday, all would rest. The talks would begin the next day. Stevens said he was grateful for the rest, explaining that the travelers had a bit of sorting out to do. The crossing of the flooding St. Regis River to the west had been perilous and could have ended in disaster had not their packmaster taken things in hand. Stevens pointed to Christopher Higgins, whom the Flatheads had come to know when he had been wagon master for Lt. Donelson two years earlier.

"I would like for you three chiefs to decide which one should do most of the speaking," Stevens said. "Yes, we will talk about the Blackfeet. And a treaty, as well. I have recently signed one with the Cayuses, Umatillas, Yakimas and Walla Wallas, and your friends, the Nez Percé."

Frank Owen's letter, which Major Owen had read to Victor, Charlot and Little Coyote, told about that treaty—and far more:

Isaac Stevens has been working out a treaty with the Indians in this neck of the woods—Cayuses, Umatillas, Walla Wallas, Yakimas and many bands of the Nez Percé. Surprisingly, out of the 5,000 warriors, who put on quite a show, 58 chiefs and sub-chiefs signed it, including Lawyer of the Nez Percé, Looking Glass and Joseph. These three were the first to sign. I will bring you a complete description of the reservation the treaty would set aside for them, so you can include it on that map you have of the various tribes—the one Father DeSmet left at St. Mary's Mission. Near as I can figure it, the area is about 150 miles long by maybe 115 or so wide.

They didn't want to sign, especially Looking Glass.

682

Most of them probably didn't fully understand what they were doing anyway. But there's a lot of anger over Stevens coming right out and telling the most reluctant ones they could accept the reservation idea peacefully, or refuse and he'd force them. Damn fool left no room for natural pride. Maybe he's got it all! And there's more anger over the number of whites pouring in and settling everywhere. Maybe some of the signers figure that at least the reservation will keep out the whites there. The treaty does say '. . . nor shall any white man, excepting those in the employment of the Indian Department, be permitted to reside upon said reservation without permission of the tribe and the superintendent and agent . . .'

John, there's trouble already here. You know as well as I do that among the Nez Percé the 'tribe' is made up of so many bands roaming so many valleys and elsewhere they don't recognize any one head chief as do, say, the Flatheads in their one valley. Dr. White, the missionary who became sub-agent for Oregon Territory in 1842, created the position of head chief and had most to do with getting Ellis to fill the job. He never was really recognized as the top chief.

There's a fuze leading toward one powder keg here: Whites are moving into the reservation area before the ink on the treaty is dry. And Congress has to approve it, in maybe two years at the most, taken up as they are about slave and non-slave states.

My trip here among the Nez Percé is a bust already. Why? Too many traders moving in, setting up little cabins for posts.

And here's the match to light that fuze: Stevens told the Indians they could stay where they are until Congress ratifies the treaty. One trader here showed me a newspaper with an article signed by Stevens that the lands are open for settlement. The paper was dated 12 days after the Indians signed the treaty!

Well, maybe with this information you can give some

good advice to Victor. Stevens is heading for a meeting at Hell Gate.

I've done better in the Coeur d'Alene country, but not enough to keep Charlie's son busy. That's why I could spare him to bring this letter.

I understand that Stevens will be going to the Blackfeet for a treaty after the Hell Gate meeting. I don't put much hope in his prospects.

Take your pipe out of your mouth, so you don't bite it in two, and consider this: One of Stevens' men told me that the Governor came to the Walla Walla meeting with the treaties already worked out, pretty well settled in his mind, and Stevens already has a rough draft of a treaty he'll work out at Hell Gate, and one for the Blackfeet after that. This latter rough draft supposedly reads that the Nez Percé and other tribes 'residing west of the main range of the Rocky Mountains' won't go after the buffalo in what will be the Blackfeet hunting grounds.

Never have seen yet a treaty that would work for fairness to all—except the whites. Only the Lord Almighty could say on paper, and enforce, that the bear, catamounts and wolverines shouldn't fight. And when it comes to saying who can and can't hunt buffalo where, well only the Lord is all-powerful there. But don't try to tell Stevens that.

Yr. bro.

Frank

As he had put down the letter, Major Owen had looked intently at Victor and spoken as though he were a ghost from the distant past: "Chief, as you ponder all this information before going to the council, remember that white man is more numerous than . . . well, all the service and other berries coming on now in this and Old Grass Valley."

Then he had, as he later would put it, "fired the second barrel of my verbal shotgun at Coyote, and it scattered to hit Charlot, too:

684

"Coyote, Agent Adams says the Hell Gate meeting will be in a stand of lodgepole pines he's calling 'Council Grove.' You and I've talked about the Osages and your friend Old Fire. So has Frank. Do you know the name of the place where the Osage treaty was signed? Well, I reckon not. It was called 'Council Grove.'"

L ittle Coyote would mark the Hell Gate Treaty on his story
skin with a large figure of a white man in a high-collared
shirt pulling with his right hand a lasso encircling the necks
of three small figures with Flathead, Pend d'Oreille and Kutenai
identification—all struggling to move in different directions. The
white man held a small cannon, rifle and revolver in his left hand.
Behind him was a small serviceberry bush with nine branches,
representing the ninth day of the seventh month.

On that day Governor Stevens impatiently looked at three
empty chairs.

"Mr. Adams!"

The Indian agent's chair squeaked.

"Did you tell Alexander and Michael I wanted them here
when the sun reached the height of that tree?" He pointed to a
tall lodgepole pine growing from a sloping hillock and somewhat
isolated from the grove selected for the council.

"Yes, sir. Victor is here. I don't know why the others aren't,
though I suspect each wishes to show his independence." Adams
pointed to Victor and several sub-chiefs seated on the ground in
front of the table and chairs. Many Flatheads quickly stood or
sat directly behind their chiefs. There was space on either side to

allow the same arrangement for the Pend d'Oreilles and Kutenais. As at Laramie, Little Coyote and Charlot had arrived early. The pair sat near the front two of four poles supporting a sunshade of interwoven tree boughs over the table and chairs.

"Send one of the criers after the others. They've got much less to do than we!" The Governor ran a finger around the inside of his high collar. Then he said something to his thirteen-year-old son, who was seated behind him next to Father Hoecken. The youth was flexing and unflexing a small bow he had been given as a present.

Adams stood and spoke to one of the three criers who would shout the interpreter's words during the meeting. The man set his horse galloping toward the encampment.

Stevens drummed his fingers on the table top, then looked at Victor.

"Who will speak for all the people?"

Victor continued to sit somewhat impassively next to sub-chiefs Moses and Arlee. Stevens pointed his finger at Ben Kiser, the white interpreter, then to the chief.

"Chief Victor. Who would speak for—"

Victor held his flat right-hand palm outward above his shoulders. He moved it sharply to his front and downward, stopping it with a suddenness that jarred the blanket from his shoulders. As bidden, Kiser halted and looked questioningly toward governor, then chief. A warming ray of sunlight, which much earlier had chased away some early-morning fog, pierced the grove and broadened to encompass Victor and Adolph.

"I understand Stevens. Tell Stevens he must understand that I cannot speak for the Kutenais and the Upper Pend d'Oreilles without their assent any more than Stevens can speak for the Canadians." Father Hoecken was shaking his head in dismay at the ineptness of Kiser's interpretations. The priest had told the chiefs that a white man, James Doty, would mark down what was said. They must think about speaking carefully.

"Where are the chiefs of the Coeur d'Alenes, the Lower Pend d'Oreilles?" Victor continued. "Will Stevens speak of matters concerning them? They are not here. Why are they not here when the Kutenais are here? The Kutenais are our friends now. They have added their strength to some of our buffalo hunts. Only one band lives near the Lake of the Flatheads. They are not Salish. Their other bands, their kin, live far away. Even in Canada."

Stevens looked at Agent Adams as though to inquire about who had talked of his plans to include the Coeur d'Alenes and Lower Pend d'Oreilles within the contemplated reservation. Too much was coming out too fast here, and the council had not yet started. To hear better, many Flatheads seated far back had begun moving closer into the space reserved for the non-arrivals.

"I ask Kiser to speak carefully what I say now, so Doty can write it down," Victor said. "Of course, the Kutenais, too, understand the most important reason we are here. Stevens is here to talk of a treaty to restrain the Blackfeet, and perhaps get us to agree that a railroad can come across our homelands. He will tell how the Blackfeet can be stopped. While you were gone, Stevens, the Blackfeet killed twelve of our people. They steal our horses, destroy our gardens. We even call this important entryway to the buffalo grounds 'Hell Gate' because the Blackfeet always try to kill us when we come from our valley to kill buffalo. This must stop. Or others will stop the Blackfeet despite fear of what your soldiers might do to us. The Flatheads will stop them. The Pend d'Oreilles. The Kutenais. The Coeur d'Alenes and many others. Of that, all can be certain." Victor held his fists in front of his body and a few inches apart. He repeatedly pumped one, then the other, forward and backward. *War!*

Songs of the birds high in the trees, and the buzzing of a few widely ranging bees, filled the almost-total silence. Finally, people turned toward the sound of hoofbeats drumming softly on the valley floor.

Stevens appeared more relieved than impatient when Chiefs Alexander and Michael rode up with their sub-chiefs. The Governor invited the three chiefs to sit at the table. Soon the Flatheads began moving back behind their sub-chiefs to make room for the slowly moving files of the other arrivals. This could be a long and hot day.

Amid the hub-bub Stevens stood, stretched and indicated by a head nod he would speak to Adams. They sauntered to the opposite side of the pole where Charlot sat.

"Adams, you told me Victor probably would be the easiest to handle of the three, even though I doubted it, given my experience at Fort Owen."

"No, Governor." Stevens' warm face flushed even more at the contradiction, but Adams spoke on. "I said he would be the best to work with, given your aims for the treaty. If you appoint one of the others as spokesman, you'll find that Victor still will insist his people's views be heard. He seems quieter than the others, only appears less energetic. You can bet it was Victor, much as any, who ran all those Indians through their maneuvers before they greeted us. He's a superb horseman. Generally, he commands high respect. He's a listener. I discern these tribes already feel threatened. This will draw all of them together, even the sub-chiefs with whom he has had some disagreements. If you can persuade him, he will have much influence on the others."

Stevens shook his head impatiently. "He seems to know more about my plans than I thought."

"Governor, I've even heard them talking about the treaty you proposed last February at Gray's Harbor for the coastal Indians. Remember, you brought the two Nez Percé observers with you here. Many are close allies of the Flatheads. When the warriors here greeted your party, I am certain they were copying what they had heard even earlier about the one-thousand who charged around you in a more aggressive fashion at Walla Walla. I'm certain they know you proposed several different tribes be put on the same reservation during the Gray's Harbor talks."

"Well, I'll . . ." Stevens looked at the latest arrivals. Only a few remained to settle down. Now perhaps fourteen-hundred sets of eyes were focusing on him. "I'll wait a while to name him spokesman, but he's going to accept both the position—and the treaty terms. And I'm taking off my gloves. No coddling."

"Governor, as I said, people who are made to feel helpless draw closer together. Perhaps you'd better consider—" Stevens was returning to his chair. No more advice.

Charlot had crowded next to Little Coyote before the Governor and Adams had reached their chairs. The medicine man's hands worked quickly for Victor before Stevens again spoke.

"I have talked with Great Father Franklin Pierce since last I was here. He holds you close in his thoughts and wants to help you. He said he is glad I am Governor and, so, the Superintendent of Indian Affairs. Thus, I have much power to help you, too. Many things are happening. Old ways change."

The Governor waited for the interpreter and the criers to work out and speak their messages. "I have brought presents with me, and Agent Adams has brought more from Fort Owen. We have brought beeves and much coffee and sugar and flour, so you will have a great feast of friendship during this treaty council that will concern the Blackfeet and the lands where you live."

There! The certainty of reservations was out. Stevens again waited for the criers, then eyed the imperturbable chiefs seated near him. He seemed to expect them to react as to a bee sting. Not so. He plunged on.

"The Great Father has told me to have a treaty with the Blackfeet, too. Thus I will keep my promise to you. This treaty will keep the Blackfeet out of the Jocko and Bitter Root valleys. The Blackfeet will be told that if they do not keep the treaty, I can send many soldiers. Soldiers could force them to keep the treaty. They, of course, will ask if there is a treaty saying where all of you will remain. I must be able to tell them this is so."

There was much talk then, the Governor with his people, the chiefs and sub-chiefs among themselves. Sun heated Old Grass Valley; soon all blankets were either under the people or hanging from their waists. Most of the whites seated under the sunshade shifted uncomfortably. Stevens ran a handkerchief inside his collar, wiped his face, then stood. He placed the tips of his right-hand fingers over his lips and moved his head forward. Again there was silence.

"The Great Father can help you best by our agreeing here that the Flatheads, Upper Pend d'Oreilles and Kutenais, at least, will live on one tract of land where life will be much easier for you than it is now. The Great Father will provide you with many of the marvels you have come to know and need. He has at his command more soldiers than all the people here if he ever should need to protect you because your numbers are small."

Sun reached its zenith and began driving its rays among the trees from the west while all three chiefs reacted with anger that the council would deal with a reservation. All voiced their opposition to it. Victor spoke last, trying to avoid repeating what Alexander and Michael had said, but often expressing their thoughts in his own way.

"The stories of our people tell how we once roamed freely, how we lived and hunted where we wished. Now we live in the Bitter Root Valley, where the bones of our chiefs and people lie. Nakarty, the Chinook chief, told you at Gray's Harbor that Indians do not wish to go away from their own homes. Like white man, they wish to bury their dead where their ancestors are buried. You heard much the same at Walla Walla." Stevens looked quickly at Adams, who returned stare for stare. "My people often travel to a second valley to the north—the Jocko, where our kin now live. When we have wished, most of our people, strengthened by the presence of others, have moved freely to chase the buffalo and other animals, often setting up our encampments to live near them. To cage the buffalo is unthinkable. To cage us away from our ancestors' graves is equally unthinkable. Even white man knows that our souls grow in the wildness of the land. Our souls would diminish if denied this. We also have learned this by watching and talking to the white men as they move ever westward to escape the sameness where their souls were dying. You have had wars afar with other tribes, nations, because the white man moves to live. Closer, you have had the Cayuse War because the Indians oppose this movement while they are caged. Will you put reservation fences around all Indians while white man puts fences around the land? Perhaps the Indians can share some of their lands, but will whites occupy all the Indians' lands? Where, then, will go the wildness that feeds us all, that feeds all our souls? For now, I can only agree with Alexander and Michael that we cannot share one reservation, but I must think even more about this."

Victor shook his head, his voice lowered and he seemed to be far away: "I think back to many years before Governor Stevens was born. Then I saw the first few white men. One, a chief called Lewis, spoke thus:

"'You have a great father called Jefferson. He is the chief of all the chiefs and of the people. He has made a great trade with a very distant people called French. Now this land where you and all the other people live is the Great Chief's land. He cares for his children, all the people here and there. He has sent us to know you, to find ways to help you, even if he must use the thunder sticks called "guns" for your protection. Traders will follow us to bring goods to exchange for your furs. We wish for all to dwell in peace. And now we depart in peace.'"

Victor held up a large medal. "Lewis gave this great medal to Chief Tjolzhitsay. On one side are these words: 'Peace and Friendship.' Should the chief of the Flatheads keep the medal? Can there only be peace and friendship if we let white men take our lands? Should I now, as chief, throw away the medal? Should it be fashioned into a lance point?"

Victor stood. He strode from under the roof of branches and pointed to sun. His voice strengthened to reach everyone. He paused so Kiser could tell the white men what he said.

"I have watched Sun for sixty-five years. Now Sun seeks the western hills. There will be night. Then Sun will rise above the eastern hills. I know what Sun will do. Sun's journey is fixed by the Good Spirit, who does not place one color of man above or below the other, because He created them all. The Great Father is not the Good Spirit. The Great Father is man. He has given some power to Governor Stevens. I have learned he recently made the Black Robes American citizens. But the Great Father and Governor Stevens do not have the power of the Good Spirit. The Black Robes have told me there have been eleven Great Fathers since Jefferson. Because they have been men, they have not always agreed. On one thing they have agreed: The Indian must give way. All have broken the pledge brought us from the Great Father Jefferson, and we mostly have remained silent, have greeted most white men as brothers. No one till now has tried so greatly to break the pledge Lewis brought us from Jefferson."

Stevens had stood. He waited till the hum of approval over Victor's words had died.

"Tell him, Kiser, that I have said many things are happening. Old ways change. This council will deal with the lands where the Indians will live. Victor may speak, but I expect him to speak like a chief, not an old woman who endlessly repeats the same words over and over!"

Again there was a hum, a louder one from all the people. Victor responded by standing. "I repeat," he said again looking at Stevens, "there have been eleven Great Fathers since Jefferson. There have been other chiefs since Tjolzhitsay spoke to Clark and Lewis. They, too, have been men. But they also have all agreed on one thing—the Flatheads must remain in their Bitter Root Valley. Yes, I repeat what I say. I must think deeply about this reservation idea. If we lose the freedom to roam freely, we will lose the wildness that feeds our souls. We must not lose our souls. No, I cannot say in one day—in my lifetime—I agree to leave our Bitter Root Valley."

Victor turned to look at Stevens, who again had stood. Adams and Father Hoecken were shaking their heads.

Stevens pointed to the lone pine. "Kiser, tell the criers to announce that because the sun gets lower, we will meet tomorrow when the sun reaches the top of the time tree! The chiefs can talk to their sub-chiefs about the reservation, then we will talk about this matter tomorrow. Tell them to choose one spokesman." He strode away, accompanied by his son.

The other whites mixed with the Indians for a while, then left when Adams, his lean jaw set grimly, suggested that perhaps the chiefs might wish to talk before Sun set. He walked away from all the people, stood alone for a short time, then returned to the encampment.

Long after Sun had set, the chiefs and sub-chiefs continued to talk. A large fire soon brightened the darkness, but not their spirits, because all agreed that Stevens was as fixed on the idea of a reservation as were the roots of the trees towering above the council area. His repeated mention of soldiers also had not gone unnoticed. Weary in body, sad in mind, they returned to their lodges. Stevens would have his reservation. They were as certain of that as they were that Sun would be in the sky when they awakened. Well . . . yes, Victor should be spokesman.

Charlot would accompany Victor to the council grove. Little Coyote would go there early, then share his vantage point with Charlot. Ominous dreams, only segments of which the seer could remember, had awakened him from a short sleep so close to the two creeks where the Blackfeet . . . . Finally, ancient lance in hand, he walked to the grove, almost hidden in dark shadows as the partial moon competed with high, ragged clouds stringing northward. Fog again had crept from the Hell Gate River to invade some of the valley's depressions, a quivering, gray blob seemingly trying to absorb all life in them before returning to its source.

With part of his mind yet trying to recall/reject the dark dreams, the seer walked to "the time tree." He stood on the sloping hummock at its base and lifted his arms toward the dark, eastern sky. His prayers were fervent, his central plea arising from Victor's mention the day before of chiefs who had preceded him.

"Good Spirit," the sixty-three-year-old medicine man concluded, "let the years that lie ahead be good for my people. Lighten the burdens of Little Bear Claw. Help him as you have helped our other chiefs, for he must lead our people on the paths the powerful white men already have decreed he must follow."

Still tired, Little Coyote wrapped himself in his blanket, stretched out on the sloping hummock and again sought sleep. It came. With it returned the segmented earlier dream. Hatchet in hand, he was creeping up on Governor Stevens, who held lifetimes of heavy misery in the thin sheaf of papers he repeatedly and impatiently had glanced at during his first confrontation with the chiefs. Now Little Coyote was raising the hatchet, then struggling with the bony hand and arm of Shining Shirt reaching from the fog, his ancient voice crackling, "*Ta! Ta! Ta!*"

The final "No!" trailed away as the seer again fought his blanket. He awakened, finally, gazed wonderingly about, then centered his eyes directly above him where, on a whitened, dead

694

limb, *mla*, the raven, was voicing its challenge at this moving, grunting, human lump below his tree. Perspiring heavily, the seer sat upright; the sudden movement sent the raven into silent flight toward the graying, eastern sky. The seer watched thin, pink streaks darken to blood red. He pondered how sleep had exposed his mind's cruel desire to kill because of pending cruelty; awakened, his mind could provide a lifetime of reasons why he could not.

Distant barks of the ever-vigilant dogs told him the encampments were awakening; horse guards were changing. He ate the food Agnes had provided the night before, then sought the creek to drink and wash. As he straightened to shake off the water, he saw Governor Stevens, evidently in deep thought, sitting on one of the chairs he had carried from under the canopy of boughs.

Little Coyote returned to the time tree. The Governor placed a board on his knees and studiously marked some papers. He moved once for better light from the brightening sky, then again bent forward, equally oblivious to two Flathead eyes and gray fog. Pushed by the gentlest of breezes, the fog had begun to encircle the grove as quietly as a Blackfeet raiding party.

The seer pulled his blanket more closely around him, his gloomy thoughts focusing, finally, on this man as a first tendril of fog detached from the rising main bank and crept between the time tree and the chair. Here was no blustering militia officer—and preacher—Colonel Gilliam, who had brought from the East to the Oregon country his notion that killing Indians, warring or peaceful, was the way to settle problems. Among surviving Indians, many of whom had adopted white man's religious beliefs, came another notion that had extended from Cayuse country to the Bitter Root Valley and beyond: The Good Spirit had arranged the gun trigger and circumstances so the Colonel would die.

Just before the closure of St. Mary's Mission, Little Coyote had watched Father Ravalli apply his many skills to keep life in a whiskey-sodden warrior who had fallen from his wildly running horse into a patch of fractured sharp rocks. The priest had completed his bloody task, then washed his hands and arms. Now he would wait ". . . for God's will to work." Priest and seer had talked then on the worth of a life, the latter agreeing, finally, that the most dissolute man could change. He had cited the story of Brandt. Seated now, next to the restless fog in Old Grass Valley, Little Coyote again pondered the depth of the priest's reply. "Often the least of God's creatures, His human creations, can help shape the will of man to work for the good of all, and we do not always see, as in the case of Brandt, the results in our own lifetimes. So, one must have much love and patience that extends toward eternity."

The priest had concluded their discussion next to the battered warrior by agreeing that "patience can be coupled with just anger." He cited the story of Christ angrily driving the money-changers from the temple with a knotted rope. The priest had smiled and renewed their discussion when the seer had countered: "But cannot just anger bring a bloody response? How would the money-changers have reacted had they possessed Colt revolvers?"

"Little Coyote, you are warrior, medicine man and seer. I firmly believe God, with affirmation from Shining Shirt, warned you never to fight white man for two principal reasons. The first is that killing is as useless as it is wrong. White man, while often professing the first reason, conveniently forgets it, as many are doing now, as they move ever westward to claim the lands where the Indians live, and killing them if they resist.

"I believe the second principal reason God warned you is that the Indians could never survive if the United States, itself, took up arms against them."

Little Coyote acknowledged that in the swift passage of years, often marked by much sorrow, he had learned patience. A consequence of that was better understanding, but he could feel the same deep anger he knew Victor, Alexander and Michael shared. In their frustrations the night before, they had turned on one another—minor, long-standing differences growing into great ones. The seer had stressed calmness, mindful of the nagging admonition of John Owen: ". . . remember that white man is more numerous than . . . well, all the serviceberries in this and in Old Grass Valley."

696

Undoubtedly, the Good Spirit also had put these words into Owen's mouth to remind the seer, especially, of the almost identical message received in his vision quest so long ago. Then he had been but an ignorant . . what was the word Father Mengarini used? Stripling. In the intervening years the Good Spirit had directed his moccasins to places, people and events that had helped him form certainties he sometimes reluctantly had to express as seer when his warrior nature said, "Fight!" No, the people must never fight white man with such weapons as lance, bow or gun. With words. Yes. Now. He had decided on that before John Owen, his sore arm and testiness much improved, had sought out the seer and Victor on the day of the Flatheads' departure for Hell Gate.

"Frank and I know something about the Army, though neither of us is connected with it any more," Major Owen had said. "And we know a bit about politics. Done a lot of talking about both. Generally, the Army doesn't get into politics. Governor Stevens still thinks Army. He's in politics, and he's ambitious and smart. Just remember that the United States have added on most a million square miles in the last few years, and there must be near a quarter-million more Indians in those miles, with the Army remaining about the same size—maybe about ten-thousand or so, and the lower ranks aren't much to brag about. But they've got good weapons, generally, and something the Indians don't have and likely never will. They can stick together, when the Indians won't. Too, these people moving west, most with bibles in their trunks and guns in their hands, as some have said, want land. Don't forget that they want land so badly they'll fight to get it, kill to keep it. I'm not saying you should unite to fight. You need to think on all these things. Speak up, but if you want to live, don't draw a fighting line in the sand. You'd lose. There'd be bloody hell, but you'd still lose."

For the sixth time now, fog had moved in and obscured Governor Stevens sitting there, surely shaping *his* words to deal with the Indians' resistance to the idea of reservations.

Little Coyote stood, mindful yet again that the years had exacted more of a toll on body than mind. He flexed the arm carrying the old scars, then the other limbs, leaned backward and forward a few times, then again sat down.

Yes, the reservations. By now, Stevens had gained much experience with shaping reservations for Indians, strengthened by the reassurance soldiers or militia, perhaps other Colonel Gilliams, were available elsewhere to enforce what he demanded here from all these warriors. The dominant demand among some of the sub-chiefs and noted warriors after the Stevens party left the council grounds the day before had been resistance. Fight. War.

Victor asked Little Coyote to explain to the chiefs and sub-chiefs the warning from his vision quest, which had paralleled that of the great Shining Shirt and those of John Owen. But Victor's most persuasive argument had been the graphic detailing of the effects of the Cayuse War. These effects surely had been in the minds of the brave Nez Percé and others when they reluctantly had signed the Walla Walla treaty.

And for those who yet wavered, who would raise the hatchet? Charlot had related in detail the lessons he and Little Coyote had learned from their Osage friend, Old Fire, near St. Louis, and how, despite the efforts of his peacemaker father, Marks His Arrows Blue, his people and others had been forced from their homeland.

"I tell you," Victor had said at last to these chiefs, "we must accept the reservations as a newly broken stallion finally accepts the bit. We must hold to one hope. Stevens has not demanded we be moved from our homelands. While we disagree among ourselves which valley it will be, we must not disagree too much in front of Stevens. Rather, we must argue, forcefully, on another matter. Remember, Stevens next will talk treaty to the Blackfeet. We must continue to fight, perhaps even threaten white man this time, to have access to the buffalo grounds."

A single gunshot sounded its message that all awaken in the whites' encampment. Little Coyote dropped his blanket to his waist as warm Sun, higher in the blue sky, drove all fog from the field, including the seventh and wispiest tendril that had separated the seer and Stevens. But this time the Governor was gone, silently

698

as the fog itself, his chair carefully replaced for this new day's meeting.

Little Coyote's mind moved to new levels as he slowly walked toward the place where he would sit for the meeting. What as yet inexplicable forces had brought him here so early to the time tree, the raven, the fog—and Stevens?

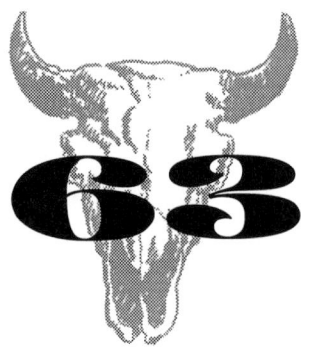

63

"Yes, I will be a voice for the people here. Alexander and Michael say this should be so." Victor turned his head from the resolute countenance of Governor Stevens and toward the two chiefs. They solemnly eyed each other, then voiced their agreement of the night before—an unenthusiastic "*Uné.*"

At this "Yes," Victor struck the table with his fist, then stood. "So be it, then." Again he eyed Stevens. "I will not readily agree to anything that was decided for us before you came to Hell Gate." He pointed to the Pend d'Oreille warrior, Big Canoe, noted for his skills on the waters of the lakes and rivers. "Governor Stevens. You have asked us all to speak what is in our hearts. Many have spoken. You have heard them. You have not said much about what they have said. I regret that you did not reply to Big Canoe's suggestion that we need no treaty. The people here have lived well with the white men who have come to our homelands in peace. That is our way. As I talk here I cannot feel as secure as does Big Canoe when he moves through the most turbulent waters.

"Instead, I am made to feel that I am standing on an Indian rock and a white man rock in the very deep and swift Missouri

700

River above the great falls. I cannot step backward to the safe shore. It is spring, the time of much change. The creek and rivers flood. There are many things in the water. I cannot see the depths because there is much mud in the water. Nor are there other rocks to stand upon. I can feel the small stones and clay, which have held the Indian rock securely for so long, washing away. It trembles. Perhaps I could hazard trying to quickly bring my leg and foot to the white man rock without tumbling into the water. But the white man rock is slippery. I reach above for the cross-shaped branch hanging out to me from the solidly rooted great tree. I will hold onto it forever, if need be, until my spirit flies above the water and the tree, itself. So, as I hold to the tree, I speak for the people. As in time past, I want them all to eat, and to save their souls."

Victor looked downward at Stevens. The Governor had placed his left elbow on the table, hand cupped loosely on his cheek bone. Like most of the whites, he appeared sleepy or tired. Sensing the scrutiny, the Governor asked: "Have you agreed to live on one reservation?"

"My people do not wish to live in the homeland of the Pend d'Oreille. The Pend d'Oreille and Kutenais wish to live near St. Ignatius Mission, not in the Bitter Root Valley. We—"

Stevens stood. He picked up his papers and motioned to his son.

"We will meet tomorrow when the sun reaches the top of the time tree. You chiefs need to reach further agreement." He strode away, trailed by most of the white men.

When Victor revealed next day that the Flatheads would not move from the Bitter Root, Governor Stevens abruptly stood and started to point his finger accusingly at Father Hoecken. He lowered his finger, but not his voice: "I have asked you priests to assist us in helping the Indians to adjust to the demands of the times. Do you think by secretly urging the Indians to resist reservations you can better guarantee success of your missions? You were here for the first meeting. Did you think by absenting yourself from the others, the Indians would appear to be voicing only their own views? You have had your try at missions. We will have our try at reservations. They will succeed."

Father Hoecken stood, tall, ascetical, his usually half-smiling face stern, those penetrating eyes fixed unwaveringly on his accuser.

"Governor," he said, "we have cooperated with Mr. Adams and others in trying to assemble the Indian people for this meeting. Because they are people trying to understand white man's world, we have answered their questions objectively, just as they have tried to answer the questions of white men trying to find their way about this land. Yes, at your invitation I attended the first meeting to assist you all. Since then, I have spent much time attending cholera victims at St. Ignatius Mission, hardly as pleasant a task as sitting under a sunshade in a grove of trees. But now I become angry. I—" He threw his hands into the air and sat down. There was a hum of approval from those who had been able to follow his rapidly spoken rejoinder. Stevens remained standing.

"These hot days are trying for us all." The Governor smiled broadly and told Kiser to tell the criers to walk among the people, inviting them to a great feast on the morrow.

High clouds and a gentle breeze helped make the feast a great success. During the festivities Alexander expansively told Victor he would come with his Upper Pend d'Oreille people to the Bitter Root Valley. Victor continued to chew his beef, raising his eyebrows in an expression of seeming surprise. Then he shifted his eyes to Red Wolf, one of Alexander's sub-chiefs, who spat out his half-chewed beef, then his words.

"You say you will go to the Bitter Root, Alexander. I will not go. Our people will not go. Do not let this beef, which cannot rival buffalo, cloud your mind."

Instead of replying, Alexander pretended to be chewing a tough bite. He had lost face the previous day when Stevens had told him, "I reject your claim that you represent the Lower Pend d'Oreilles as well as the Upper. Saying does not make this so."

Little Coyote closely watched Victor swallow, then worry off the last bite clinging to the portion of rib. Chewing that, Victor reached for a portion of roast elk from one of the animals the Indian hunters had brought to the feast. He would not humiliate Alexander further.

Stevens and his men appeared everywhere during the feast. As the people began to become full of the good food, Kiser helped Stevens spread the word that the whites were willing to place a hospital and a doctor for a score of years on the reservation, whether in the Mission Valley or the Bitter Root. During that time they also would have a trained farmer, a wheelwright, a blacksmith, a gristmill and sawmill. Best of all, there would be a school. Each person would receive farm equipment. And, they no longer would have to fight the Blackfeet!

Contemplation of this latter promise, capping all the others, brought many people to talk to Victor. He asked the Pend d'Oreille and the Kutenais: "Would you move to the Bitter Root Valley?"

"No," most said. "We must think more about this."

Next day Stevens and his people spoke of the friendship feast; there was much good feeling until the Governor looked at Victor, smiled and asked if the chief and his people now were ready to move to the Mission Valley. Interpreter Kiser was improving his translations somewhat.

With Stevens still smiling, Victor stood and thanked the Governor for the great feast and for the many fine promises if the people would agree to live on a reservation. "There would have been food aplenty if none of the hunters had gone out for the deer and the elk, but no, I cannot agree to move to the Mission Valley."

Stevens stood, throwing down his papers as he did so.

"You bitch dog!" he shouted. "What do you think you stand to gain by talking but not agreeing?"

Victor remained standing, scarcely moving, while Kiser looked questioningly at Stevens as though to ask if he should request the criers to announce these words.

"You are the interpreter; speak what Stevens has said," Victor demanded, eying his son, who had leaped to his feet and was looking alternately at Stevens and Little Coyote's ancient lance.

Kiser and the criers did their duty, whereupon with great dignity Victor stalked from under the sunshade while Chief Alexander's words to the Governor reached all ears: "You are a man with a double mouth!" Victor mounted his horse and, accompanied by many of his people, returned to his lodge.

Saturday, a grim-faced Charlot stiffly delivered word to Stevens that Chief Victor had not changed his decision. Sunday passed. Stevens had said Monday would be the end of the Hell Gate meeting.

When all were gathered, Stevens looked at Victor. The chief looked at the Governor. At length Victor stood and spoke: "Stevens has called me an old woman. Stevens has called me a bitch dog. Without our women, our people would not continue to exist or, existing, live as comfortably as our conditions allow. Without our dogs, we would not be forewarned of many dangers. I think Stevens does not like me because I speak from my heart as Stevens has asked me to do. Perhaps he is unhappy because we, who are fewer, have not as readily agreed to his demands as have Indian people in far greater numbers elsewhere with whom he has signed treaties. Or, has he simply threatened them more?

"I now speak only for my Flathead people. Alexander and Michael do not agree with what I will say now. We often have been told, again even here, that the Great Fathers, Jefferson in the time of Tjolzhitsay to Pierce in my time, care for their children. I ask that the Great Father Pierce come see the Mission Valley and the Bitter Root Valley. I then will agree to live where the Great Father decides is the better place."

As had Father Hoecken in response to the Governor's accusations earlier, Stevens threw his hands into the air. His momentary silence quieted all present.

"Very well," he responded. "For now the Kutenais and Pend d'Oreille will live near St. Ignatius Mission. The Flatheads can remain where they are until the two proposed reservations are carefully studied and the decision made."

Stevens proposed that the chiefs and sub-chiefs now sign the treaty he had brought with him. Victor glanced at Charlot and Little Coyote, who repeatedly and gently moved their right hands, palms outward, up and down.

"I ask that we wait for a while so we can see the treaty beyond what Stevens and Kiser have told us," Victor requested.

704

In the short time grudgingly allowed, the chief and others could see that the treaty was the draft the Governor had brought with him, with a few changes penned between lines or in the margins. He also had written in a description of what the reservation boundaries would be. The Indians were to cede all their lands and the tribes were to agree that Victor would be chief of a "nation" of Kutenais, Pend d'Oreilles and Flatheads. With their approval, other tribes could be placed on the reservation. White people could move onto lands the Indians were not living on. The Great Fathers would pay the nation $120,000 during twenty years.

When Stevens told Kiser to announce the time had come for signing, Second Chief Moses asked Little Coyote and Charlot to read the conditions once more. While the whites waited impatiently, the pair complied. Moses silently returned to his seat close to the table and chairs. One by one, then, Kiser repeated Governor Stevens' call for the chiefs to come forward and make their marks where the secretary had written their names. All complied, except Moses.

Instead, he continued to sit, closely watching the signers, scarcely moving at all, even when a bee fled the commotion near the table and settled on the warrior's knee. Secretary Doty handed the document to Stevens, who glanced approvingly at it, then, scowling, looked down at the second chief.

"Moses," he asked chidingly, "does your mark as second chief mean nothing to you, along with the names of all the others?" Moses placed his curled index finger next the bee, quietly watched the insect crawl upon it, then raised his arm high above his head. He snapped the finger open, catapulting the bee into flight above the assembly.

"Moses, will you sign!" Stevens gestured for Kiser to walk directly in front of the warrior to ask. The interpreter respectfully stepped to his side, sat down beside him and asked the question. "Moses, the Governor asks, 'Will you sign?'"

Moses grasped the haft of his lance and used it to help push himself up. "Governor Stevens." The warrior held both arms upward and outward, his richly colored blanket spreading fan-like on both sides like the wings of a giant butterfly.

"My brother lies buried on land you take," he continued. "I did not think white man would want to take that land, too. No, I will not sign. Before I received the baptism from the Black Robes, I learned much about the man they named me for. He led his people from slavery. How can I agree to your taking our land and leading my people to slavery? The Black Robes have taught us to free our slaves even when we knew other white men had slaves. I have thought long on this, ever since I, Victor, Little Coyote, ancient Broken Tooth, others saw York, the black man, the slave, come into our beloved land with Clark and Lewis. No, I cannot sign. White man wants the land, even where our people lie buried. And white man will enslave those who live."

Moses turned his back on the treaty table and with great dignity strode away, leaning at times on the ancient lance. Stevens left the table and walked behind the canvas that screened the privy pit from the assemblage. He returned soon and with unaccustomed joviality began giving presents to the chiefs. When he handed a colorful military coat and sash to Victor, he called him "head chief of the Flathead nation."

"I will go with Moise," many said, scrambling to their feet. As he followed his father, only Little Knife, or Clement, he of the sharp eyes, looked back. He and his father soon were talking to Moses.

Victor looked at the seventeen other chiefs and sub-chiefs who earlier that day had signed the treaty, and at Moses who had not. Because the night was warm, all sat well away from the large council fire. Occasional moths and other large flying insects attracted by the light swept in from all sides and plummeted into the flames. Victor had removed the military coat and sash and wore much-used buckskins. A single eagle feather hung midway from one of his two braids of graying hair. His Colt revolver was near the ceremonial pipe. Just outside the circle, Clement sat between Charlot and Little Coyote.

"We will hear from Clement," Victor said, "then he will return to his family lodge."

"My father and I followed Moise from the treaty council." The youth looked downward at the many staring faces, then toward Little Coyote, who nodded encouragingly. "I looked back to see if others of my friends were following. We soon would replace the horse guards. I saw two of our people returning from the privy pit. When there was no one there, Stevens hastened behind the canvas as though he would not reach the pit in time. In seeming great anger, he kicked one of the poles holding up the canvas. He kicked it again and again as though it was an enemy. Then he strode back to the table and chairs. My father and I concluded Stevens was very angry because Moise had talked about slaves." The youth looked about, seemingly relieved that there were no questions, then returned to the encampment.

"When Sun again reaches the top of the time tree, Stevens will call us together to learn if we will accompany him to the treaty talks with the Blackfeet," Victor told the council. "Let us talk about this now." While they did so, Charlot and Little Coyote returned to Victor's lodge to talk with Father Hoecken. He again had left his cholera patients, this time to study the signed treaty. He sat quietly drinking the tea Agnes had provided, the copy of the treaty spread out on the elk hide nearby. He stood as the two warriors entered, his eyes dark-circled above the tense, unusually gaunt face, the smile almost gone. He listened quietly as Charlot recounted what was occurring at the council fire. The priest appeared especially interested in Clement's description of Stevens at the privy pit. At length, Father Hoecken placed his index finger on his lower lip, then thoughtfully began pinching his chin. He spoke musingly, as though to himself.

"Let me see. Stevens was born in Massachusetts. He is known to be violently anti-slavery." The priest looked up. "Let me see, how shall I put this? Some of the United States have slaves. Others do not. Washington Territory, which includes this region west of the mountains, is against slaves. Last year the Congress included the region east of the mountains in Nebraska Territory. Kansas also became a Territory. Some day these great territories will become two or even more states. The Congress said that the people of the two new territories would be able to decide for themselves whether they should come into the union slave or free. Already whites are fighting whites in Kansas over this matter. I fear that the dispute that will attach to the lands becoming public with each new treaty of cession, such as was signed near here today, threatens the very peace of the United States far more than do the dispossessed Indians."

"And the Indian inhabitants of these lands are given little thought, are of little value?" Charlot asked bitterly.

Father Hoecken put down his cup. "Among some whites they receive much thought, are of as great value as any of God's creatures," he said soothingly. "And also among some politicians, though I admit they seem few. Sam Houston of Texas is a powerful man. While the Congress talked about the Kansas-Nebraska Bill last year, he reminded the Senate they had approved treaties saying that almost all of Kansas and Nebraska were to be the Indians' for 'as long as grass shall grow and water run.'

"We priests are not the only ones who disapprove of the way treaties are being forced upon the Indians, largely through intimidation." A troubled look crossed the priest's face. "As God is my witness, I wish to stir up no trouble, but I, too, have a duty.

"General John Wool is the chief of the Army's Pacific Department. He openly opposes the way Governor Stevens, and Governor George Curry of Oregon, treat the Indians. When the Cherokees were forced to sign a treaty and relocate to the west, General Wool had to enforce the treaty. He openly opposed it, saying he would like to move every Indian beyond the reach of white men 'who, like vultures, are watching, ready to pounce upon their prey and strip them of everything they have or expect to receive from the government of the United States.'

"I strongly suspect that Moses knows nothing about all this, but by some means he evidently managed to make Governor Stevens at least begin to look upon his treaty-making process, and effects, in another way."

The three men talked then about the various treaty provisions, centering, finally, on the promise of a school.

"I believe the Governor incorrectly accused me of trying to

influence the three chiefs against the treaty," the priest explained. "I also believe it would be useless, tragic, to oppose the treaties, even the reservations—for they will be. Our task now is to help you make the best of it. Yes, while the schools must teach white man's ways, so the Indians can learn better to cope with white man, I believe it is so important that . . ." He looked steadily at Little Coyote for a moment across the fire. ". . . the Indians hold on to the good that is in their culture, too. Someday all Americans will appreciate how much you have lost, how hard you have striven to hold on to your good ways, and what you have contributed to us all."

Father Hoecken handed the cup to Agnes and thanked her. "Wash it well in boiling water," he cautioned. "I would grieve if I brought cholera to your lodge." He blessed them and departed. Soon they heard his horse galloping off into the night.

Little Coyote resolved to remember this night for all the lessons in it. Remember it he would, especially five years later when John Owen obtained and let him examine one of the ten-thousand extra copies of the book Congress published embodying Governor Stevens' reports of his explorations, surveys and other activities from 1853-55.

> . . . we will now part with our Flathead friends, with whom we made a treaty of peace and cession—every man pleased and every man satisfied; and this satisfaction has continued to this present hour. We left them on Wednesday, July 18, to move forward to Fort Benton.

64

A scarcely audible rustling in the dry grass intruded on Little Coyote's reverie as the seer sat beside dying Broken Tooth. The old warrior was facing Sun and lying on his blanket above a small cottonwood grove fringing the creek. The stream's muted song seemed to be pleading for freshening autumnal rains. When a few tall grass stalks began dipping their seed-laden tassels, the seer's mind moved away from thinking about the long cavalcade of loved ones and friends who had taken their lonely journey to the sand hills. The spirit of this fearless warrior soon would hasten there.

A mouse peered from the edge of the grass forest and fixed his trade-bead eyes on Broken Tooth's wrinkled hand, firmly closed around his lance. Wrinkling his nose, twitching his whiskers, the creature leaped onto and began running along the stout lance haft, its end badly worn and splintered from long use as a walking stick. The mouse reached the hand, then scampered up the unmoving arm, to sit, finally, on the heavily beaded shirt front. When something had happened inside Broken Tooth's body and he had fallen from his horse, he had insisted his kin clothe him in his finery and leave him behind with Little Coyote despite his son Damian's strong protests. The others should continue trekking toward Fort Benton, where Stevens would sign a treaty with the Blackfeet. A few Nez Percé, Walla Wallas and Coeur d'Alenes were scattered among the Flatheads' seventy or so lodges on the move, as were Pend d'Oreilles under Alexander. Word had gone out for more to come.

"It will be a big smoke," both Kiser and Adams had assured the Indians before accompanying them under Stevens' orders to keep them peaceful. They would hunt buffalo away from Fort Benton until the treaty council began. "If you locate the Crows, bring them, too," Stevens had ordered, then more quietly had sent Dr. R.H. Lansdale in another direction. The outraged Flatheads would learn about his assignment on their return to the Bitter Root Valley.

Before the arrival of the mouse, and while the people were moving from sight down an undulating series of low hills, Little Coyote had brought water from the creek. He had tried to make Broken Tooth comfortable and had listened to the warrior's death songs. Broken Tooth had loudly voiced The Lord's Prayer and a petition to the Blessed Virgin. Then, as so often occurs among the lucid dying, he seemingly had revived, as does a drooping prairie flower after the Good Spirit sends rain.

At first Broken Tooth had spoken of many things—happy adventures, mostly, his early manhood, marriage, exciting hunts, his grandsons. From his blanket bed he had gazed wonderingly up the trunks of the tall cottonwoods; in the long silence that had followed, he had rolled his head as though trying to decipher the creek's voice. His mouth had closed over the yet-strong teeth and the gap of the missing incisor. The lips had moved, then they quieted and became almost lost among the folds of his ever-sagging face. When the warrior's breath became raspy, the medicine man adjusted the saddle-bag pillow to ease his breathing.

"I do not die yet, Little Coyote," the old man had said. "I think now of the Blackfeet treaty, and what Stevens forced us to sign. My silent prayers have brought some answers already. Not all the answers. Some of the answers. As I began thinking of what lies ahead for our people, I spied the cottonwoods, and the Good Spirit reminded me of my long-ago visit to a distant but friendly band of the Hidatsas in the Dakotah country."

Broken Tooth had signed for more water.

"We agreed we would talk trade for my horses in a cottonwood grove near the Missouri River. Before we passed the pipe, Old Bull Boat, the chief, prayed beside the greatest cottonwood. 'Help us, shade of the cottonwood,' he implored. 'Help our people to grow in numbers—stronger as we gain many good horses from these, our Flathead friends. Help us to resist our enemies. We, who only too well can feel your predicament, will pray that the Good Spirit Above All will divert the river away from you and the others, who surely silently weep as they reluctantly are torn, one by one, from the land and swept away in each new spring's torrents.'"

Broken Tooth had cocked his head sideways to look at Little Coyote more directly. "Strange. The river channel had changed next time we came to trade. Many more small cottonwoods were springing up in the silt of the old channel. But Old Bull Boat's Hidatsas were gone. The smallpox had swept them away."

The warrior's voice had quieted as he began murmuring, seemingly to himself. "I think now how our people have survived the many dangers, often with prayer. Is there the hidden certainty we have done so, only to be forced into a small corral of land where our bodies might live, but our spirits die? How I wanted to see and hear, learn and think more about these things while among the Blackfeet. But if our people are to be corralled, it is well I depart now. I also would like to have a Black Robe with me as I do so. But I had them to help guide all of me as I became old and crippled, so I can die in the good company of Little Coyote. Others will guide my soul, for I have tried hard to merit this. Perhaps had I not been so old, it would have been harder for me to be a Christian, for the Black Robes told us that to be a Christian is to love all people. Being old, I could overlook that many white men who say they are Christian do not love all people."

Broken Tooth became so silent that Little Coyote would have thought him dead, but there was no last breath. After a time Broken Tooth again spoke, strongly, with wonderment in his voice: "The light begins to enfold me. Yes, yes." He murmured and remained motionless, even when the mouse appeared and finally stood on his hind legs to peer inquiringly toward the sound of the breathing.

The terrified creature bounded off Broken Tooth's chest and scurried into the protective grass as the old man unexpectedly kicked his legs and held out his arms. With surprising strength, he used the lance to raise himself to his knees. Little Coyote helped him to stand, tottering. His voice was strong. "I enter a bright cave. Many hands of my long-gone chiefs, fellow warriors, my wife, beckon me. I leave you with a vision, Little Coyote, in exchange for your horse I shot when my eyes were dim as you returned to the Mission: The light that envelops me will carry away Stevens in as many years as there are days in white man's week. He, like Old Bull Boat and his Hidatsas, will be gone, but our people, like the seedling cottonwoods, will survive great adversity and will grow as did the stalwart cottonwoods from which came the seed. I can say this with as great certainty as Little Paul had when the Blessed Virgin appeared to him that first Christmas at the Mission."

Wonderingly, the seer watched. He accepted that the Good Spirit sent visions to link with the old and extend to the future. Then, Broken Tooth began hobbling downward into the creek shallows.

"The old Blackfeet chief, Nicholas, and his family were baptized that Christmas. The Blackfeet will accept Stevens' treaty." Broken Tooth halted, standing like a newly born buffalo calf. "There will be less fighting as they share our common adversary—white man." Broken Tooth turned and shook his lance admonishingly. "Our people must learn, and use, the power of the white man's paper. Do not fight!" He stumbled, fell and died, the old lance head striking a large stone and breaking in two.

Little Coyote put Broken Tooth's blanket on a small, concave shelf of rocks well above the creek. After placing the body on the blanket, he closed the dead man's fingers around the lance and pressed the broken half of the blade in the other hand. He tied the blanket securely and covered it with rocks. Mounting his horse, he easily found and began following the trail of his people. Less easily, he pondered the old warrior's last words.

"He is Fast Runner—John." Little Coyote corrected himself aloud and, admittedly, with some relief, when his spyglass disclosed the familiar Appaloosa of Victor's stepson. The other three? Broken Bow and Stone Rattle. Again the voiced corrections—"Francis and Robert"—as the seer laughed aloud. His horse turned her head sideways and peered inquiringly at her rider. And the fourth horseman? The spyglass was no help there, except the rider was close to Fast Runner's years, had a poorer horse, and carried an old Pennsylvania long rifle. "I soon will know," the seer said. "Yes! Increasingly I talk to myself, like old Broken Tooth." The momentary sadness was replaced by elation as the trio of younger warriors signaled recognition and began galloping their horses toward him.

There was much to tell, but first Fast Runner pointed to the stranger.

"Low Thunder, sub-chief of the Little Robes, sends his son, Circling Hawk, to also escort you to the council at Fort Benton."

The warrior nodded in a friendly way. Aware Little Coyote's eyes were on the rifle, he placed it across his thighs. His hands worked eloquently in the sign language: *Yes, I am Circling Hawk, son of Low Thunder, who is the son of long-dead Wise Owl, who spoke well for many years of New Blade of Grass, Little Coyote, Little Bear Claw, other Flatheads and Nez Percé. They had directed the Little Robes to the lake of the Pend d'Oreille almost half a hundred years ago when they, too, sought good guns from the white traders so our small tribe also could continue to exist. Our people even procured three of these guns.*

Circling Hawk pointed to the long rifle and continued to sign: *Our people honor Little Coyote. Perhaps after the big smoke at Fort Benton all people can speak openly of their friends.*

The seer bowed his head and body in agreement and signed his thanks by extending both flat hands, backs up, in an arc toward Circling Hawk, then downward.

"Adams says there are maybe more people coming to Fort

Benton than the ten-thousand we saw at Fort Laramie. All have pledged to refrain from war." A grin flitted across Fast Runner's face. "The provisions and presents were delayed reaching Superintendent Mitchell at Fort Laramie. They have not yet reached Fort Benton, though Stevens does not take the delay of the steamboat as did Mitchell the wagon train."

"The tribes grow impatient, too," Francis added. "So many people: Little Robes, Blackfeet, Bloods, Gros Ventres, Piegans, even Chief Broken Arm of the Crees. And horses, so many horses, as numerous as a great buffalo herd. I have never seen so many horses!" Francis paused, apparently certain Fast Runner had even more important information. With a wide smile, Fast Runner delivered it. "More than one-hundred lodges of Nez Percé are there, and perhaps forty lodges of the Shoshonis, all camped near our people and the Pend d'Oreille. Among the Shoshonis are the kin of Antelope and my wife, Warm Breeze! They scarcely wanted me to leave, but relented when I told them who we would seek."

Little Coyote nudged his horse forward as he spoke. "I rejoice." And he did, despite the resurgence of old sorrows.

There was much visiting, much talk about Stevens and his treaties. Also the shortage of food, made worse yet as the buffalo moved toward the Yellowstone, then Judith rivers. Soon the people, like the buffalo, began to move out.

Determined to hold a council despite the problems, Stevens sent word to the scattering tribes that the council would be downriver where the Judith flows into the Missouri, east of the White Cliffs. There he hoped to intercept the much-delayed supply boat.

With peace possible, the Flatheads and their traditional allies felt safe to hunt in smaller, sometimes mixed groups—wherever the buffalo led them. One small herd led a party of twelve Flatheads, eight Nez Percé and six Shoshonis up the Yellowstone to old friend Jim Bridger and a bounteous gift of meat, which they accepted with well-concealed anger.

Red Paint of the Nez Percé had suggested the makeup of the party. Gray-haired, yet lean in body and with almost unlined face and neck, he had grinned delightedly as he greeted Little Coyote's arrival at Fort Benton. "We can hunt the buffalo and talk about our great trek for the guns so long ago," he had exclaimed, eager to show the seer his newest Hawken caplock. He had nodded understandingly when the seer had replied he would use the bow and arrows.

"Tuekakas honors me by having his son Hinmahtoo-yahlatkekht, Thunder Rolling in the Mountains, learn the ways of people and the hunt." Red Paint pointed to a stripling, perhaps eleven, a close pattern of the Nez Percé chief, trying to restrain his eagerness and excitement as had Little Coyote when called to the Flathead council after his vision quest. All agreed that Pony Whip, the Shoshone brother of dead Antelope, would be chief of the hunt. Charlot would lead the three scouts from the three tribes. It was they who found Bridger.

"We saw many dead buffalo scattered closely together on a slight rise above the river," Charlot told the hunting party. "They were bloated, not yet stinking, and the wolves had eaten upon but two.

"*Esuwéci*, lightning, I told the others, remembering the band of dead elk my father had pointed out to me when I was perhaps the age of Joseph there." Charlot pointed to Thunder Rolling in the Mountains, who had accompanied the scouts. "But lightning did not kill these buffalo. Soon we found others, two shot through the eye, as well as behind the front quarter, as had been some of those earlier. A great bull, a cow and a calf had been skinned. We found many horses' hoofprints. Joseph found two sets that were well-shod. Both were near those of buffalo that had run hard but had died. 'Could that be the Crows that Adams and Kiser could not find for the council?' we asked ourselves. But no. They would not cut out tongues, a little of the hump meat, then abandon the remainder."

The hunters pondered this strangeness while eating a fine elk dropped with an arrow in a wide, timbered ravine.

Early next morning they set out, more cautiously now, with a broad line of six widely spaced scouts. Soon two came pounding back on lathered horses. White men mounted on fine horses were shooting many buffalo near the Yellowstone River.

From behind a small spine of yellow rocks the party watched these men join the leader in another chase. He was mounted on a superb white horse and seemingly carried a double-barreled rifle that sounded like thunder. When fourteen buffalo lay on the ground, a heavy cart drawn by four oxen emerged from a grove of trees near the river bend. These were not Métis. They did not kill animals in this fashion. The cart wheels were small and did not shriek.

While four men began skinning the two largest dead bulls, the man riding the white horse waved his large hat high above his head. A horse-drawn wagon carrying six more men emerged from the trees. The wagon halted under a tree closest to the skinners. The occupants set up a large table and spread a white cloth across it. Next they placed some seats similar to those Stevens had used at Council Grove. Soon a fire was burning and the four shooters sat down. Another rider emerged from the trees. As he dismounted and sat down near the table, Little Coyote closed his spyglass with an unusually loud snap.

"It is Bridger."

"I will have the Shoshonis take the lead as we ride there," Pony Whip decided.

Still thin, steely eyed, Bridger arose and put down his brandy glass. His rapid stride showed he was genuinely glad to see the visitors. When he grinned, the skin tightened around a pouch-like lump on his throat—a lump Father Ravalli once had called "a goiter" when he saw it on a John Owen worker. No need for this mountain man's hands to talk to these twenty-six Indians. Pony Whip, Red Paint, Charlot and Little Coyote could translate for their respective tribesmen.

"Seen ya up in the rocks. Figgered you'd come down soons ya had us figgered out. Sit. Ya fellows there . . ." He motioned to the gaping cooks and stewards. ". . . dig out some more cups an' give these friends some coffee an' lots of sugar. An' fetch some roastin' sticks." Before the Indians dismounted, Bridger pointed to a stout man seated at the end of the table. The man was watching this encounter with a friendly smile on his face.

"This is Sir George Gore. He's a chief in a place called Ireland. He'd been huntin' in the Black Hills and mountains when I met him at Fort Laramie last year. I stayed there last winter, too, seein' Brigham Young and his Danites stole all my goods an' my fort and was lookin' to peg out my hide. I'm takin' George here on a great hunt."

Still smiling, Gore rose from his chair, wiped his face on a napkin, strode to Pony Whip's horse, reached upward and shook the warrior's hand.

"Yes, sit," he said jovially. Then he told one of the men hovering around the table, "Open up some tinned hams for them to eat while they are roasting some buffalo meat."

Along with meat and coffee, the visitors swallowed some of their anger about the wasted animals. Pony Whip, Red Paint, Charlot and the medicine man politely, perhaps wisely, did not convey to their somewhat mystified brethren some of the composite knowledge gained from the fragments of conversation that moved back and forth like the wine bottles between the men at the table. The talk began when Gore opened a small book and made some marks in it.

"My count shows almost eighteen-hundred buffalo so far, including those today." Gore closed the book and poured another drink.

"Mine's still the largest of the twenty-eight grizzlies so far. I've been keeping count, too."

"I still claim my elk's the largest of the hundreds we've bagged."

"What about my buck deer?"

"Yes, but my antelope has the longest prongs!"

Only Bridger restrained himself with the bottle and enthusiastic bragging. Later, after Pony Whip's party had set all the available meat to drying, they counted for themselves the size of the expedition in the cottonwood grove: Forty men, more than one-hundred horses, twenty-four oxen, perhaps a dozen strange dogs called "hounds," six wagons, twenty more carts— and remarkable weapons.

The weapons drew the visitors more than any of the other marvels. Soon, all were crowding and jostling around the three men cleaning and oiling the heavy weapons used earlier in the day. Obligingly, the workmen spread apart so the Indians could move from one operation to another.

Bridger ambled over from Gore's tent, his springy walk that of a man far younger than his . . . yes, fifty-one years. Little Coyote remembered that the trapper had told him he would have gone with Lewis and Clark, "except I was just born the year they set out."

"Made in England, across the great salt water," Bridger explained. "Each one is worth a helluva lot of horses, if ya could get them. Made by Manton, Richards, Purdy, a few others." He pointed to a single-barrel gun one of the men was cleaning. "Few of these here. British like the double-barl. Straight shootin', close in an' far out, big bore, good killers, but they use up powder an' lead somethin' fierce, so you almost need a wagon to supply them. Had me a double Shuler onct, .49 caliber, same as pore Tull got onct, too, but traded her off." He hefted his own rifle. "I stick to the old Hawken, here, for the two-legged an' four-legged huntin' I have to do.

"I ain't much for shootin' the animals an' lettin' them rot," Bridger explained lamely as he handed his Hawken to pride-struck Joseph to carry. He picked up two cloth sacks and accompanied the Indians to their camp at the edge of the grove. Bridger's face brightened when he added that many hides were being dried or wrapped with salt so later they could be mounted for people in distant lands to see.

Cooperating to make the best of an embarrassing situation, Pony Whip nodded understandingly. "Yes, my father Broken Pipe . . ." Bridger nodded in recognition. ". . . was in the band of Shoshonis who attended the rendezvous at Bonneville's Fort on Salmon River."

"In '33."

"Yes. Broken Pipe talked much about the chief, who also had many fine horses, wagons of much strange food, good guns, a generous heart, and did much shooting."

"From Scotland," Bridger replied promptly. "Sir William Drummond Stuart. Jined right in with us on that almost ten-day soiree, he did. Coyote, you saw him at the '35 rendezvous on the Green when Dr. Whitman carved out that cussed Blackfeet arrerhead I'd been packin' for three years. Married the Flathead sub-chief Insula's oldest daughter, I did."

Little Coyote nodded as Bridger handed the sacks to Pony Whip.

"There's a flask of powder an' a box of caps for every one of you. From Gore. For the animals." He shook the hands of each warrior, slipped a wondrous pocket knife to astonished Joseph, then ambled toward the brush near the base of the cottonwoods. He turned near the edge.

"I heard Stevens was over at Hell Gate an' you had to sign some papers. Well, for your sakes I hope they don't stick. Ever'body wants the Indians to give ground." He spat. "Remember who the winners an' the losers was at Fort Laramie. Some whites are going to be permanent losers, I can tell you. Last I heerd comin' from Fort Laramie was that the Yakimas and others east of the Cascades, an' some of the chiefs in the Oregon Rogue River country, are poundin' war drums. But don't fight. You'd only lose. I still don't cotton to that cussed Blackfeet song: 'It's no good to live to be old; it's better to fall young, a warrior fightin' his enemies.' Well, maybe they'll have to change their tune when they sign papers, too." Bridger signed *farewell friends*, then disappeared into the brush and deepening gloom.

Pony Whip's party reached the confluence of the Judith and Missouri rivers with well-loaded pack horses and many adventures to relate.

"The council will begin October 16," the translators and criers notified the slowly gathering assemblage, which had shrunk from approximately twelve-thousand to four-thousand.

During the wait, Little Coyote unrolled the sacred white buffalo robe, which had figured so heavily in the truce with the Blackfeet so long ago. He carried it to a table-like white cliff slightly south of the confluence. There he prayed fervently that the Good Spirit would help all the people in the treaty that was certain to follow. That done, he sat next to the robe and peered north toward the Bear Paw Mountains, east toward Dog Creek, far south toward the gap between the Big Snowy and Little Belt Mountains, then, in his mind, southwesterly to the Bitter Root Valley. His mind was on Broken Tooth's dying visions when Victor and Charlot, after waiting a respectful time, signaled up to him with a sharp whistle. Carefully re-rolling the sacred robe, he descended. As Sun flooded the land, they ate buffalo meat and some of Agnes' camas cakes.

Serious talk gave way to light. Charlot, his face sobering, told how Joseph, in his narrations of his adventures with the Nez Percé, had come at last to Bridger's explanation that Gore would mount some of his trophies out of the thousands shot so people in distant lands could see them.

"'Huh!' Yellow Bull of the Nez Percé had snorted. 'Such killing and waste! Must we stuff prairie grass into a few old hides so our children will see buffalo, too?'"

Charlot did *not* laugh when he said that many *had* laughed at Yellow Bull's question.

65

"*Slaxt!*" The single word intruded on Little Coyote's pre-dawn prayers near the tiny waterfall merrily emptying into the Judith River. The word *friend* in his own language was reassuring, though he did not recognize the voice. Nor did he know the speaker, Piegan, surely, his powerful, almost-naked body covered with the holy red paint. His teeth and eyes showed white as he spoke and glanced at the sacred white buffalo robe draped over a willow tripod. His voice was deep and respectful as he uttered a prayer, then emptied a small, reddened buckskin bag on the low fire burning well away from the seer's willow-and-hide shelter.

"I am Stamyekhsascicay, of the Piegan. Little Coyote is known to this chief, Lame Bull, and others of us since the times of Tree and Owl. I come here because I wish it, as do others: Hacatusheyehu, Star Robe, chief of the Gros Ventres, and their great war chief, Thketepers, The Rider; Sakuistan, Heavy Shield, great warrior of the Bloods and kin of Owl."

Little Coyote signed: *Pipe?* Lame Bull signed this would come later.

"Culbertson of the American Fur Company's Fort Benton, other whites, but mostly their smallpox, have prepared the

722

Blackfeet well for the treaty council," Lame Bull said. "Culbertson talks to us of tending cattle and sheep, besides our many horses. And growing food in the ground as did the Mandans who once were." Bitterness and scorn edged the chief's voice. "Much like you were prepared for *your* people's treaty. Now, more than long ago when your warrior, Gun, sought peace, we share a strong reason to have it. We will open a sacred Medicine Pipe Bundle to pray for all the Indian people, even the Teton Sioux, who have moved into our buffalo country west of the Missouri. We ask you to add your prayers to ours that all will fare well." Lame Bull's eyes again moved from Little Coyote to the white buffalo robe.

So it was that Little Coyote would paint a Red Medicine Pipe Bundle on his story skin to note that memorable October 14, 1855, ceremony two days preceding the Blackfeet treaty council. The council he would mark with a small, black, death mask most tribes would know. The huge quadrupled lodge was jammed with great chiefs and warriors, including women. There were Keepers of the Pipe, drummers, others. All wore the paint, redder than soon-to-rise Sun, toward which the lodge opened. Heavy Shield had smeared but one side of Little Coyote's body with the red paint, the Blood's eyes glittering as he covered the seer's large body wounds with an even deeper red. There was utter silence as the Flathead had erected his tripod among the crowded bodies and, in turn, said his fervent prayers while Sun broke over the eastern hills. In the sacred lodge he thought of the people's silence during the most solemn part of the Black Robes' masses at St. Mary's Mission.

From deep, deep within him arose the ancient mix of hatred/sorrow that were a part of him as surely as had been Antelope, Lance and Lance's wife, Swan. They were among the many these people had killed. As others took up the prayers, the seer thought of long-dead Gun and how the old warrior had urged forgiveness and peace long before he departed for the sand hills. Next, the seer thought of the living—of Victor, Charlot and others who had tried to explain to him how, at the mass, came the post-communion deep peace; also, the certainty that eventually, in eternity, all matters would be right.

Then Heavy Shield solemnly conducted the seer through the crowded bodies and outside while the Keepers of the Pipe waited for the Blood chief to return before they removed the last wrapping from the Medicine Pipe Bundle.

As Little Coyote slowly washed off the red paint, he pondered the significance of the extra layer Heavy Shield had applied to the Blackfeet-inflicted wounds. The seer knew that but one thin layer of his own strong will separated his Flathead identity from oneness with red people everywhere—yes, in these times, even the formerly hated Blackfeet.

Not so Antoine Plante, though Gros Ventre blood coursed in his veins with the predominant French. "They tried to kill me long ago, though I told them we were blood brothers," he had informed the Flatheads often enough, most recently when he had guided Lt. Saxton to Fort Owen. His arrival at Little Coyote's camp above the Judith River with Victor, Charlot and Thomas Adams the evening preceding the Blackfeet treaty council surprised the seer almost as greatly as had the visit of Lame Bull.

Plante's shrewd bright eyes lit up with pleasure and he shook Little Coyote's hand before the seer prepared the pipe. "Through you," Plante said, "the Blackfeet have paid the Flatheads much honor." While Plante's wife, Mary, and Agnes placed fresh grasses in Little Coyote's shelter and lit a separate cooking fire, the men, except for Adams, talked of people dead, adventures and hunts long over. Charlot, perhaps impatient or more greatly worried about the possible consequences of the treaty that would open on the morrow, respectfully asked Plante if he would repeat the reason he belatedly had come to the treaty site. Plante sucked deeply on his own short-stemmed pipe, blew the smoke upward and watched the breeze whisk it away.

"Troubles are coming on the coast and eastward," he said. "There will be killing. I warned Stevens, but I don't know how much he listened. He was feistier than a wounded catamount. His son told me that Stevens' leg that picked up the ball in the

Mexican War is sore as a boil again." Plante sucked again on the pipe, tamped the tobacco downward with his brown, sinewy index finger, and puffed again. "Trouble is, I don't think Stevens is listening here, either. I agree with what Father DeSmet said last year at St. Louis about the president running out of remote lands to force the Indians onto. Considering that fact, Stevens had better let the Blackfeet have some mighty good conditions—a mighty big reservation. They aren't going to take lightly to the suggestion they use all those horses of theirs, and their young people's wild spirits, to chase around on a small reservation. Eventually, though, I reckon it'll come to that." Plante looked at Adams, for whom he had been translating the essentials of the talks. "Looks like you'll be a mighty busy Indian agent for a long time."

Adams threw a small stick into the fire. "Not me! I want a farm and to raise cattle while I do a bit of what I'm trained to do best." Worry lines on his forehead and face seemed to disappear as though, at this moment, he had made a decision and, with great relief, was spilling it out.

"Major Stevens plans to name Dr. Lansdale agent to the 'Flathead Nation' he cobbled together, and I don't like what he's been doing, though it soon won't be any of my business." Perhaps it was the puff of ashes the stick had stirred up that caused him to wink one eye as he looked across the tiny circle at Chief Victor. "Talk to John Owen about that. The Blackfeet Treaty papers already are made out, the same, mostly, as they were for the Flatheads and others."

Adams grasped a handful of dead ashes from the edge of the fire, looked toward Mary and Agnes, talking animatedly while their pot boiled, then stood away slightly from the other men.

"We know the breeze is coming down the Missouri River from the west. We know when I throw these ashes into the air the breeze will carry them east. Agreed?" He waited until all had solemnly nodded their heads or signed yes. "If I say the ashes will move west into the breeze, you will think me *qwew*— crazy. The treaty will say the tribes will remain separate, and free to parley as such with the Great Father. Yet, the treaty also will say the tribes must . . . depend—hang onto—the Great Father. *Qwew!* The Blackfeet will be told the treaty says no one can come into this land for ninety-nine years. But the treaty will read that white man can go through their lands, live in them, make roads, put up the telegraph, the singing wire, which gets closer and closer—and forts. *Qwew!*"

Adams raised the handful of ashes, opened his fingers and shook them vigorously. The five men silently watched the ashes float away, separating in the process until they no longer were visible. The men knew the ashes continued their journey east and, in the vagaries of the current, even a little north and south.

"It's a damnable business and I've learned enough at this agenting work to know there's trouble ahead, maybe for the whole area," Adams said. He pointed in all directions. "I don't know what will bring it to a head, or when, but it's coming."

All ate, silently, agreeing they would see one another at the council next day. As the two women and four men began scrambling down the slope, Plante paused, then returned to Little Coyote.

"That Adams, he spilled his guts like a butchered buffalo. Probably feels better for having done so, but me, considering what I came from to tell Stevens, and from the stink that's coming, I don't feel comfortable at all." He signed farewell, friend, and hurried to join the others.

Despite the certainty of gifts, perhaps only a quarter of the twelve-thousand Indians who first had assembled near Fort Benton remained for the treaty. That set Little Coyote to thinking about his trip with Jim Simonds and Simonds' story of the game of stools the nuns had taught him. "In this game one of us always would wind up without a stool." Would those who signed the last treaty get none of their land at all?

There were no Crows here, no far-northern Blackfeet. Stevens, noticeably limping, told the assemblage that the Great Father wanted the people to live on farms, raise animals. "Like Mr. Antoine Plante here, as some of the Flatheads near Fort Owen. We want you to be peaceful, and remain at your homes, except when you want to trade or hunt."

Chief Alexander of the Pend d'Oreilles spoke up sharply when Stevens proposed the tribes share common hunting grounds in the Blackfeet country, as had been stated at the Fort Laramie Treaty Council.

"All Indians must have the buffalo," Alexander said, waiting until the Flathead interpreter, Ben Kiser, and Gustavus Sohon had translated his words. "Without them, we would die. You would close the Marias and Cut Bank passes, as you call them. Our people have used them for as long as we can remember." The chief remained standing, defiantly facing Stevens until Little Dog, a powerful Piegan warrior, also stood—erect, silent, proud. Little Coyote, closely observing the three men, at length saw an almost-imperceptible slump in Little Dog's shoulders as he carefully chose his words: "We will let him come to the buffalo grounds from the two passes."

That point settled, Alexander tried once more.

"Stevens," he said, "we have been told that after the Cayuses killed Whitman and others, the white chiefs in Oregon said the Cayuses had lost their lands as punishment. We try to understand that. But other Indians in the Oregon country told us that five summers ago the Great Congress said that all land there can be taken by the whites, no matter what the Indians claim. When you have all your treaties will white men have all the lands?"

Stevens quickly stood up, the smile brought by Little Dog's offer wiped away.

"You are talking about the Oregon Donation Land Law. Yes, it calls for all land there to be open for settlement. But that should not concern you here." He pointed to some of the Nez Percé. "See. They do not ask such questions. Why should you?" Stevens sat down. Alexander looked about. When no one raised his voice, he, too, sat. He remained silent throughout the next two days, during which peace was agreed to, the treaty signed and gifts distributed. Harmony, and disquietude, prevailed.

After two more days, Stevens told the chiefs he must return to Olympia in two more. Hunters from several tribes had found a small band of buffalo cows and calves between the Judith River and Dog Creek. That night Stevens and his staff wound their way around the cooking fires dotting the treaty sites, all feasters insisting the whites try this delicacy and that. Sated, their meat gone, the encampments slept till Sun rose. For a time the people were not hungry. Soon, however, many began picking around the remnants of the great feast, only to find that the numerous dogs had done this most efficiently while their masters slept. A few people shared what dried meat they owned; some caught fish. By next day, all were ready to move out for buffalo.

While the Stevens pack train prepared for departure to the west, a horse guard reported a great Blackfeet column was approaching from the south. Soon the onlookers could see perhaps two-hundred-fifty horses silhouetted on an east-west ridge; slowly, like a huge snake, they descended into a great depression, the head re-emerging close to the onlookers. Here was meat! In the ways of the people they would share, so the greetings were especially joyous. The column stopped near the river.

Immediately, the women wearily began unloading the animals—hide after hide until the onlookers openly were asking one another: "But the meat?" There was little of that, scarcely enough to feed the hunters for a few days. No matter, they would camp here while the women began taking the first steps to turn the hides into robes. With luck, the hunters would catch more buffalo, so they would share the meat now. Yes, there would be many robes to trade.

Adams bade the Flatheads good-bye as together they watched the Stevens party pull out. The Flatheads had named the sub-chief Bear Track to conduct the hunt south up the Judith to the Musselshell, and in the prevailing peace spend the winter there.

"Get some robes and save some meat," Adams said earnestly. He shook his head. "More than two-hundred of those Blackfeet pack horses brought in nearly six-hundred hides. I counted them. Figuring seven-hundred, eight-hundred, say, seven-hundred-fifty pounds of meat each, the varmints and scavengers got fat on two-hundred-twenty-five tons of meat." He reached out to shake hands. "Chief, as I said, the Indians have a problem with white man pushing them from all directions. So've the buffalo, with Indians and whites pushing them. I'm glad I'm out of it. If they're going to kill off the buffalo, I *know* I'm going to raise cattle."

Even some of the plodding pack horses moved with less urging as the Flatheads entered their Bitter Root Valley. There had been buffalo aplenty along the Musselshell throughout the winter of 1855, but now horses and people were glad to be home. An April shower pelted the long cavalcade as it began stringing across the first wide meadow. A small band of elk began running toward the weary travelers, then abruptly swung west toward the nearer mountains where black clouds obscuring the peaks hinted of snow.

Two scouts ranging ahead reported a lone rider observing the tribe from a small knoll.

"The Delaware, Jim Simonds. He, too, looks through his spyglass."

Little Coyote returned his instrument to the saddle bag. The scouts again set their horses galloping, this time past Simonds, who waited until Victor, Charlot, Little Coyote and others drew abreast of him. He waved before joining them. The big man would accompany them to their encampment area near Fort Owen.

"My brother Ben's at the other end of the valley," he explained above the chatter incited by his appearance. "With all that's happening around us, Major Owen's taking no chances." He motioned they could talk better away from the pack horses and people.

"Heard the Blackfeet signed their treaty. Governor Stevens isn't pushing for any more, I can tell you, at least for a while. He's got himself some wars going from the ones he already forced—in southern Oregon's Rogue River country, and the Columbia Basin. The Walla Wallas, Yakimas and others want to keep the whites west of the Cascade Mountains." The man stopped and silently watched the procession move past. "Stevens also has a war of words going with General John Wool. He's the chief of the Army's Department of the Pacific. He calls Stevens and Oregon's territorial governor Curry 'war governors,' saying they started the war to plunder the Indians and spend the Great Father's and the whites' money.

"The regular army has tried in some instances to protect the Indians from the volunteer soldiers," Simonds explained patiently. "There's going to be more hell to pay for sure. Some of the Oregon militia set up a peace talk with Peo-peo-mox-mox of the Walla Wallas. They shot him dead and sent his scalp and his ears to their homes to show to other white people."

Now Victor shook his head. "And what are Owen's fears for our valley?"

Simonds drew his pipe from a pocket. There was much more to tell. Victor would hear it now. They sat under three ponderosa pines dominating the meadow.

"Owens doesn't know what to expect. More whites and Indians are coming in here. Whites are sticking. You'll see them soon. The Crows are fixing to attack whites and Indians coming into their neck of the woods. Even though they weren't bound at the Blackfeet Treaty Council near the Judith, they ought to be smart enough to learn from the Sioux."

Victor signed he understood about the Sioux. He told Simonds how some trappers near the Musselshell had pieced together that story for them. One of Chief Brave Bear's warriors, High Forehead, had put an arrow into an ox as some immigrants passed by their encampment near Fort Laramie. Lieutenant John Grattan came to the Sioux camp with thirty soldiers and two cannon. When High Forehead had refused to give up, Grattan had fired on the Sioux encampment, killing Brave Bear. His warriors and other Sioux wiped out all but one of Grattan's party. He died of his wounds at Fort Laramie.

"Well, you got the first part right, and it's bad enough, but I reckon you didn't hear the second part," Simonds said. "General Harney and six-hundred soldiers attacked Brave Bear's people. Little Thunder was new chief when Harney marched up the Oregon Trail to their village along Blue Water Creek. Eighty-five of the band died and seventy children and women were taken captive. After shows of strength in Sioux country, Harney forced them to sign a peace treaty."

Simonds drew in a deep breath until his barrel chest threatened to pop the wooden peg fasteners on his elk-skin jacket. He tapped the ashes from his pipe, exhaled, then added grimly, "We'll all be hearing more of these messes."

Victor got up and slowly walked to his horse. "You say more whites are moving into our valley. Yes, I am certain we will be hearing more of these messes."

Victor and Little Coyote watched Charlot hang his bow, arrows and Lance's shield on his Appaloosa's Spanish saddle, then re-enter his small lodge to return with his rifle, bullet/cap pouch and powder horn. Sensing the scrutiny, he waved, grinned and set off toward the south end of the encampment. Margarite, daughter of Pilchimo, raced a powerful sorrel to meet him, her hair and the animal's red tail streaming behind like the flag atop the Fort Owen pole on a windy day. As the pair began moving up the hill where Willow Woman and Victor had intruded on Little Coyote and Antelope so long ago, seer and chief sighed. Then they watched the 26-year-olds disappear from sight.

"They would produce good sons," Victor grunted. Just before the Black Robes had come to the Bitter Root, Pilchimo had saved many of his fellow warriors from a great war party of Blackfeet. "But let us go. John Owen waits."

Soon they neared the fort, astir with outdoor activities that largely would stop with the first heavy snow. Emanuel Martin, "Old Manwell," grinned at them as he loaded his wagon with adobe bricks. He had helped make them during summer's heat for Owen, who was determined "This place damn well is going to have adobe walls, barracks and bastions, seeing there could be troubles all around." The west barracks wall was partially completed already. While the Flatheads had been attending the Council Grove and Blackfeet Treaty meetings, Martin had proved he could bring his wagon into the valley over the well-worn Indian trail at Ross' Hole, then over the hills south of Rye Creek. Van Etten, the Mormon trader from near Salt Lake City who twice had brought wagons of trade goods to Fort Owen, only recently, with great difficulty, had come over Martin's Trail with two huge wagons, each pulled by four yoke of oxen.

Frank Owen sauntered over from an adobe wall Al Tallman was constructing as Victor and Little Coyote dropped their horses' reins next to the office building. Owen's greeting was cheerful, the smile masked now by a bushy, black beard and mustache. His facial hair contrasted sharply with his brother John's, which, as it grew more white, long and pointed like the Flatheads' horn cups, increasingly merited him the name *I-mool-tzen*.

"If Tallman proves he can lay bricks, John will hire him come spring to build two of the fort's flank buildings and work on the new sawmill," Frank said. "Some of your people might like to learn how to make adobes come spring. John pays one cent each—if they're good ones, and he'll need a passel of them.

"John can see you soon. He's working on a deal with Neil McArthur to haul some more lodgepole pine for the rig that makes jack-leg fences. Louis Rabboin and Henri Chase are working on it now."

Theirs was a difficult task, and they seemed glad to rest a moment to greet the trio. Chase and Rabboin, with Tallman, recently had fled to the Bitter Root with their families. The Nez Percé, furious about the increasing numbers of white settlers and broken treaties, were beginning to threaten, in some instances raid, property. They wanted the whites to get out.

Rabboin and Chase had peeled the bark from a great quantity of long, small-diameter, lodgepole pines. The men were sawing them into four more piles—the greatest diameter into fence-post lengths; posts of the same length, but smaller diameter; pegs approximately sixteen inches long, and, finally, rails approximately twenty-two feet long. The workers had rigged a large-diameter, iron auger so a horse, walking in a circle, could power it to bore three equidistant holes at the same upward angle through the fence posts when they were held firmly in place by large plank clamps.

Nearby was a model of the fence for the men to imitate. It consisted of two fence posts leaning back at an angle supported by a leg and the weight of three rails hung across three projections. The lesser-diameter posts, or "legs," of the same length, had been driven to project approximately a foot through the top hole in the post. Two pegs had been driven through the lower two holes to project upward and outward the same distance.

"John plans to put up a second grist mill next year," his brother explained, "and he hopes to use one of the axles of the water wheel to power the jack-leg drill." He looked up at the sound of a moving wagon. "Well, McArthur's leaving." They started walking back to the fort. "Several settlers just east of here are willing to rent one of John's wagons to haul their own logs here for drilling. The way others are starting to settle well away from your encampment here, I'd wager a pound of tobacco they would hire some of your people to saw and drill the logs when the other mill goes up."

As he spoke, Frank looked closely at his two Flathead friends. There was no noticeable reaction on their faces until he added, "John has told the settlers to stay out of that big stand of lodgepole you people use." Now both the chief and the seer appreciatively nodded their heads as Frank strolled over to watch four Flatheads working at a wood pile to feed the fireplaces and stoves when the snow moved down from the white-tipped peaks.

Nancy was clearing away coffee cups when the two Flatheads entered John Owen's office. She smiled in welcome; clearly, she was more cheerful since Owen had made a marriage contract between them a short time ago. Almost immediately she served well-sweetened, steaming coffee to the visitors, then handed a third cup that was not steaming to her husband.

Before drinking, he removed a weapon encased in an elk-skin scabbard from the elk antlers fastened above a large map behind his desk. He pulled off the scabbard to reveal an English double rifle. "I got it for Frank," he explained as he handed it to Victor. Little Coyote had seen its counterpart in Gore's and Bridger's camp along the Yellowstone. "He's sticking around here more than he really intended, and if I read the wind right, I'm going to need him more than ever." Owen drank, put down the cup and stroked his pointed beard. Little Coyote could smell the whiskey. "Doc Lansdale took off from those Indian Agency cabins he built near the junction of the Jocko and Flathead Rivers. He's on the Pacific coast." Owen pointed to the map. "And he has been told the Indian troubles make it unsafe for him to return here." The trader arose this time and handed a paper to Little Coyote.

"As you can see, I've been asked to become special agent to the Flatheads. Now hold on!" He held up both hands as if to ward off his two friends. "I've hardly got a strong enough stomach to accept. Indian Bureau seems to be filling up with maggots. Their greed, fraud, deceit and lack of know-how is one of the main reasons many Indians are on the warpath. You know that. Besides, I've got more than I can do here, especially with so many whites coming into the Bitter Root on account of the fracases elsewhere—some of them figuring the best way to get a new start is to become wagon-box traders, despite Stevens forbidding them to come in."

Owen took another drink from his cup. "And I won't say I'll not encourage whites, good ones, from settling here, despite the agreement you have with Stevens so far. I figure, given your size, you need friendly ones. So do I. I sure as hell won't take the job if you have any objections at all. If I've got Doc figured right, he doesn't like his work, and sooner or later will leave for good, though the job won't go with him. Just as well say, too, you might get someone you'd like less than me." Owen slowly stroked his beard, chuckled, then added, "Or Doc!"

Owen and the Indians could laugh now, but their anger on learning of Dr. Lansdale's activities since Stevens had appointed him greatly diminished their elation over the Blackfeet Treaty. Owen had shaken hands with the Flathead leaders as they had entered the outer trading room soon after their return from the Musselshell. Except for coffee, there had been little ceremony. True, they would see the display of recently stocked trade goods, but there was a deeper reason for his invitation.

"While you were on the way to the Blackfeet Treaty, Stevens sent Doc Lansdale to inspect the Bitter Root and Jocko valleys to report which would make the best reservation. I went with him to St. Ignatius Mission." Owen spoke slowly so the chiefs could communicate his words fully among themselves. "Doc really only looked at what would make the best farm land, since Stevens plans for you, the Blackfeet and others to turn into farmers, quick as a whipstitch. By others, I mean the Lower Pend d'Oreilles and Coeur d'Alenes. Yes, Stevens still plans to put them in with you, the Upper Pend d'Oreilles and Kutenais. And continue to call you the Flathead Nation.

"Forty or so of the Lower Pend d'Oreille families already are farming in the Jocko, but the Black Robes are furnishing everything from seeds to tools because the Senate hasn't agreed to last year's treaty."

Owen had motioned for Nancy to refill the coffee cups. She did so, then brought in a great, black pan of molasses cake. The Flatheads quietly watched her begin to slice it into generous chunks.

"There's been no government survey, but Stevens evidently plans to call Doc's quick look-see the survey the treaty calls for. Doc told me he recommended to Stevens the reservation be in the Jocko. Doc also told me that Stevens informed Father Ravalli that St. Ignatius Mission is where the reservation will be." Owen shook his head. "Damn fools. When it comes to understanding Indians, Stevens and Doc don't know 'Come here' from 'Sic 'em!'"

Because they were guests, the chiefs quietly put down their cups almost as quickly as had Victor, then stalked from the building. For a time Owen silently watched them sit on the unfinished adobe wall near the south entrance and, one at a time, speak their thoughts. He returned to his desk and began attacking the pile of papers. As he neared the completion of a message to Fort Benton that he would be there soon for two more wagons of trade goods that had come up the Missouri, he sensed the presence of three people who quietly had entered the office. Without looking up, he completed the message by assuring Andrew Dawson, resident trader, that "if you fear I might bring the smallpox that most lately has been striking down many Flatheads here, I am most willing to have you deliver the goods to a safe pick-up point, where we can load it ourselves."

Owen looked up at Victor, Little Coyote and Nancy as he sealed the envelope.

"There are voices among us who urge following the example of the Yakimas, Walla Wallas and others," Victor explained. "We have quieted them. We will not fight white man, but these voices ask: 'Who can we trust?' We agreed we trust John Owen and the Black Robes. We will go now to talk more, but we wish to talk more with you, too."

Owen nodded understandingly, whereupon they left, declining the molasses cake Nancy carried out to the Flatheads who still lingered near the adobe wall. These, too, shook their heads, so she carried it to the white workers. They eagerly and quickly consumed it all.

Part 4

The
Dispossessed

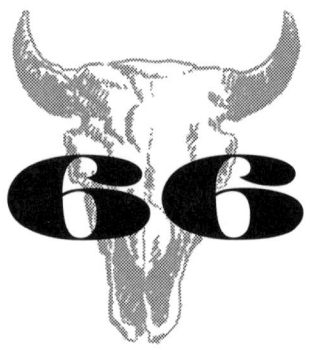

66

"Hell, John, trade 'em the ammunition. Like they said, they're not going after white man. They want to trap!"

Frank Owen stood up from the bench in the trade room, put his pipe on the small window sill and walked to the counter. Charlot's voice had remained polite, quiet, until John had replied, "Governor Stevens' orders" to the warrior's, "Why not?" Then Charlot's voice had become a forceful, mixed torrent in his own tongue and English until the trader held up both hands as though to ward off the vehemence.

"Dammit, Frank, stay out of this! I've already told Victor I can't do it for any Indians for any purpose—even buffalo hunts. If I trade guns or munitions to Charlot here, and the others, word'll get around; in fairness to all I'll have to do the same for everybody. Stevens says none to Indians while the wars are on, even if they say it's for hunting and protection. I don't doubt Charlot's word at all when he says it is. I reckon he knows that."

"They could get the goods at Fort Connah near St. Ignatius, Hudson's Bay would like to get the business. And some of the wagon-box traders who keep drifting in here will sell, too, if they figure they can get away with it—with treble prices, like they

738

have with illegal rotgut."

"And as I've caught them, I've given them hell!" John pounded the counter top. "I've explained to Charlot that, as Indian agent, I have to follow orders. I don't want the damn job, but if I don't keep it, these people could be in for far worse than now. Hold on." He walked into the tiny adjoining room and returned almost instantly. When he resumed talking, Little Coyote could smell liquor. "I'm doing what I can. I want the Flatheads to get furs. I don't have to tell any of you that! Even Doc Lansdale, give him his due, hasn't been able to get treaty goods into here, though the Blackfeet have gotten them, and there's likely to be a tough winter ahead."

"Tough winter ahead." Little Coyote appreciated the trader's honesty. Owen's last three words triggered the seer's musings of late about how the trader likened natural seasonal changes to the condition of the Flatheads. *In the spring of their lives—youth, joy, regeneration, unlimited promise provided by the Good Spirit in the usually bounteous land; summer—the actuality of the promise; autumn—growth, joy yet, but with darkening skies, hints of hard times ahead—winter! In the eternal cycle, should not spring continue to lie ahead, beckoning after cold, hardship, danger always, and suffering often?*

One answer to this question emerged from his memory and those of others; the answer was confirmed on his story skin and in the ever lengthening manuscript: Yes, since the arrival of Clark and Lewis the seasons had begun racing even faster toward that seemingly eternal winter.

Victor had not known about the restrictions on munitions when he had called a council meeting to discuss the next spring's buffalo hunt, as well as events occurring in the Bitter Root. Always, the council seemed to ponder these subjects and, as Father Ravalli would say, "with added dimensions." The sub-chiefs were there, but few other warriors. Some were hunting hard for the ever-decreasing game in the valley or in more distant places; others worked the gardens. A small number had traded off all worthwhile they possessed to passers-through for rotgut, or had stayed near their tattered lodges and gambled, seemingly resigned to seek only the here and now as best they could with little effort.

Quite the opposite were most whites, save for the dissolute. The whites increasingly were arriving, some to buy or trade, even proselytize, and move on; others were settling, erecting cabins—and fences to surround the earth and claim what was on or under it.

The council meeting was long, with the story of Victor's stepson, Fast Runner, or John, summarizing the many told by others:

"The man, Lenter," John began. "Oh, how he wanted our help cutting the lodgepoles, using hand augers to bore the holes, then erecting his jackleg fence around the great deer and elk meadow above Scattered Creek." Anger had mounted in John's voice. "When the fence was up, Lenter walked with us outside it to our horses. Owen had said, 'Ask for one dollar each a day.' Joseph would have returned for his axe near Lenter's cabin. Lenter said, 'No, I will get it. Now, I must keep people outside the fence.' Joseph, ever the impetuous one, would have replied, but, given the axe, we hastened away.

"We met Lenter's neighbor, Scotten. This good man was leading Damian's Appaloosa that had gone missing. Scotten said, 'That strangely spotted rump told me the horse was Damian's, and he led me a great chase before I caught him. I heard you boys were working for Lenter, so I brought him up here. Guess I'll go see the fence. Don't know that I could afford to hire you to help build mine.' We told him we were grateful, and watched him ride through the gate. Lenter brought a jug from his cabin and both men raised it after Lenter proudly had pointed out all the far ends of the fence.

"On the trail we saw the man, McNeale, and his woman, who came over Martin's Trail with a small wagon to 'Settle down hereabouts,' White Pony Tail heard them tell Owen. We made room for them on the trail and all greeted them. They drove on past, ignoring us as though we were old horse turds."

Others wanted to say more about these matters; Victor allowed it for a time until he said they should talk about the buffalo.

"We must not be like the confused buffalo herd, running this way and that until a new danger sends them in another direction, then another. Yes, many white men seem to lurk behind the rock piles to spring out and steer us over the destructive jump. I, who detest Stevens, swallowed my pride and sent him a message through Owen that we never would fight them, hoping, thereby, he would know we would keep our word, but would expect him to do the same. We live in confusing times. White men treat us in confusing ways. Old enemies sign treaties, and old friends war with our other friends. Stevens says bear oil *will* mix with water, so forced us into the 'Flathead Nation.' And, yes, we see ragged white men, like starving wolves, come to our valley. Suddenly some, not all, treat *us* as the skulking wolves. Even John Owen, who likes the Black Robes, sometimes speaks out against them, but I have noticed he most often does this because the whiskey is talking. We can remain strong if we always work together to get the buffalo, our striplings emerging as braves, even warriors, if the need arises."

Finally, all agreed there would be the spring buffalo hunt. Perhaps the Nez Percé, a few Spokanes and others who had come to the valley would accompany them, also many from St. Ignatius.

Four warriors had remained to eat at Victor's lodge when the council ended. They were Charlot, wise Kills With Lance, Wild Horse and Little Coyote. Agnes served a stew of mountain goat and potatoes brought over by kindly Sits Outside The Lodge, Louise.

Victor passed around his tobacco pouch, tamped some tobacco into his pipe, lighted it and blew the smoke upward.

"I will tell Kills With Lance and Wild Horse, who also have warrior sons, what Charlot, Little Coyote and I talked to Antoine Plante about near Judith River. As in the council, we exchanged views about wars and white men, the diminishing game. 'I have seen all this elsewhere,' Antoine said. Then he smiled, wearily, true, as he began telling of a hidden place of much beaver and other animals, including the great bear. 'I tell you this because I have lived among you as my brothers. If I were younger, I would go back there always, trap many animals and always leave seed.'

"Antoine jabbed a stick into the river sand. 'Go to St. Ignatius,' he said. 'Follow Clark Fork west to Thompson River. Follow that north till you see the great peak west of Thompson River. There are many peaks, but seek the greatest peak. There are many creeks. Follow the greatest one. You will find many lakes and beaver ponds. There are valleys where a few can be hidden for years if they do not make a great horse trail. Someday, surely, the lakes will be known as well as now Lo Lo Hot Springs.'

"My son, Charlot, prayed hard for answers there at the Judith. Thus, the Good Spirit sent them."

The faces of Kills With Lance and Wild Horse brightened as they absorbed Victor's words.

"Tired, distressed like most of our people over the turmoil in our rapidly changing valley, our medicine man talked to Charlot, his *i-sts-sókoi*, about going immediately to this region. But Little Coyote remembered the loneliness of his exiles at the hot springs, and he mentioned his wish to help his people as best he could at sixty-four summers.

"I must say this, too. Little Coyote lives simply, holding to what he considers the best of the old ways. He has not sold charms to bring good luck, which he has sought through prayers, too. Nor does he accept others' pathetic magical claims that the total rejection of white man's marvels will assure continuation of the old ways. He has received scorn at times by warning we never must battle white man. He accepts that our people will change. But there must be time, with appreciation for our tribal and individual dignity. Here his thinking is no different from that of the Black Robes, the great Whitman, the Owen brothers, even our new neighbor, Scotten. The young colt does not become the great stallion overnight. Like the great stallion, our Indian brothers everywhere, even the Blackfeet, must not be subdued through castration.

"So, Charlot and Little Coyote mixed their thoughts like two small creeks to make a greater stream. They agreed that when the people would return from the Judith, and the hunt along the Musselshell, Charlot would propose he and Little Coyote take their many traps to where Antoine had suggested. A few younger members of the tribe could accompany them and return to trade the furs at Fort Owen. Then a new group of younger people would return to the trapping grounds. Charlot and Little Coyote would teach them the ways of the forest and plain—and of our people. They could pass this on to their children and others, even while they tried to farm and, perhaps more successfully, raise more horses to trade to the settlers and others. White men like to use horses, many horses."

Now Victor had looked at Kills With Lance and Wild Horse. "Charlot and Little Coyote know and respect the prowess of your sons, Francis and Robert. We ask you to counsel them about these matters. If they wish to become the first to go to Antoine's hidden valleys, with their mates, the party of trappers will meet at John Owen's trading room when Sun rises tomorrow."

After that first disagreement with his brother over the munitions, Frank Owen returned to the window sill for his pipe. After lighting it, he signed *trust me* to Little Coyote and sauntered back to the trade room counter.

"Charlot, what would you trade John here for the supplies?"

"Good, well-worked robes. Your brother sells them for four dollars. Good horses. He sells not as good ones for thirty-six dollars."

"Will you give them to me?"

Charlot, puzzled, looked at Frank, then glanced at Little Coyote ever so briefly.

"They are yours, Frank Owen."

Frank nodded agreeably and reached for the supplies list.

1,000 caps @ 1 cent	*$10.00*
40 # powder @ $2	*80.00*
50 # lead @ 25 cents	*12.50*
50 # salt @ 25 cents	*12.50*
25 # tobacco @ $1	*25.00*
50 # coffee @ $1	*50.00*
10 # tea @ $3	*30.00*
100 # flour @ 15 cents	*15.00*

50 # sugar @ $1   *50.00*
10 bx. matches @ 50 cents   *5.00*

"Dammit, Frank, this won't work!"

"Now, John, don't ask for trouble here. How in hell can you run a trading post if you don't trade with white men, even your brother?"

The trader grumbled, but later, quite willingly, let Little Coyote place his story skin and manuscript packet atop his well-stocked bookshelves for safe-keeping.

That afternoon, eight mounted Flatheads headed north with their pack string. They hoped to camp by nightfall at Travelers Rest. There, they decided that Charlot and White Pony Tail would ask Father Hoecken at St. Ignatius Mission to say mass for them at a camp hidden in willows before they headed west. The eight were Little Coyote; Charlot and his wife, energetic Margarite; always-smiling Francis, son of Kills With Lance; his wife, sober-faced and pregnant Little Owl; solemn Robert, son of Wild Horse, with his wife, tiny and bashful Rainbow. White Pony Tail was the son of Second War Horse and Tall Woman, a beautiful Nez Percé who so long ago had many Flathead warriors complaining their sons had pursued her to her own country after a hunt and seemed never to return. One at a time they had, but there had been but one victor. Only White Pony Tail had survived the smallpox of last spring.

"Moon Face," many whites called this sixteen-year-old as he worked about the fort. The handsome survivor's face was pitted as one sees the rising moon, full and silver-red, poised atop the Sapphire Mountains. Shy and industrious, with Charlot's help he had asked Owen to credit him with his dead father's many horses—save three, a remarkable Appaloosa and two roan pack animals. White Pony Tail carried his father's Hawken and newly purchased Nez Percé hunting bow and quiver of arrows. All family property, save the horses and gun, had been burned in the death lodge.

North winds began raggedly tearing at the Flatheads as they

moved from the Clark Fork to a ridge along the Thompson River. Grateful there was no snow to leave tracks, they remained hidden to watch a group of Pend d'Oreilles toiling east on the Clark Fork. A scout galloped his wretched pony back to the bedraggled band when he spotted sign of the Flatheads' passage. His people stopped to talk and look about indecisively until a second scout galloped in and pointed up the Thompson. A warrior cut the throat of an emaciated horse; the people roasted and ate part of the meat, packed up the remainder, then resumed moving eastward. They were more orderly now, with watchful warriors on the flanks; the children traded turns on the horses' backs.

Perplexed but pleased, Father Hoecken, who kept many secrets, had told the trappers in his brief homily during the willow camp mass that more than a thousand persons were at the Mission now "drawn by common faith and adversity, including even a few Creeks, Iroquois, Spokanes, Flatheads and Blackfeet." He had spoken approvingly of the Flatheads' earlier request that Lt. Mullan try to get them a Black Robe again. He also had approved of the trappers' idea of rotation with Flatheads who remained in the Bitter Root, so as to cling as long as possible, in a practical way, to the better parts of the old life. "Alas," he had added, "I tried to impress upon Governor Stevens that the mixing of these increasingly harried tribes also kills their distinctness, their own cultural values." Fixing those deep-set eyes on Little Coyote, the priest had repeated essentially what the earliest missionaries had said, and the Flatheads certainly understood better now: "If we could have securely established the missions long before white man arrived, perhaps we better could have prepared each of the tribes to cope with the . . . well, what most white men like to call 'the inevitabilities of history.'"

There was considerable discussion about Father Hoecken's meanings long after he had blessed the trappers and all had departed. The group felt gratitude toward the priest: As White Pony Tail had helped tie the Black Robe's tiny mass kit to his saddle, he had been directed to empty the bulging saddlebags of sixteen pounds of tea and some precious sugar.

Late that night Charlot shared only with Little Coyote what

the Black Robe had revealed while the chief's son and White Pony Tail were accompanying him back to St. Ignatius: The same day Governor Stevens had signed the Council Grove Treaty with the "Flathead Nation," he had sent a letter to Washington, D.C., saying that if the Jocko were chosen for the reservation, he felt there would be no further problems with Victor and the others.

Stormy weather began plaguing the trappers as they moved west up the largest creek flowing into the Thompson, drawn always by the white-capped peak dominating the land. Abundant game fell to the arrows. One evening the travelers considered setting up permanent camp in a grove of trees back from a fish-filled lake where myriads of ducks and geese noisily flapped in to feed and rest before continuing south.

"Yes, there is food, beaver and some small meadows, other furs, and we've found no sign of other people," Charlot agreed. He shifted his gaze from wet, tired companions to the great peak where snow had descended ever lower earlier that day. "We need more meadows for our horses. Antoine warned of deep snows, a burden as well as a protection." Charlot divided the group into three, asking that next day they seek a smaller lake, if necessary, but larger pastures and stands of trees.

"Look well. We will return here in three days. Little Coyote has agreed to remain with our supplies and extra horses."

"White Pony Tail found perhaps the best place of all. Thus, we were the last to return." Robert's face broke into a rare grin as he reported on the fourth day. Warm again, all sat on logs before a great fire; they roasted fresh venison, screened by a canvas tarp erected against a cold, northerly wind.

"Rainbow and I rested in a valley not so good as this one," Robert explained. "White Pony Tail, trailing his horse, climbed the next high ridge to the north and descended into the valley. It is wide, with a lake, beaver, game, and many trees and meadows. We could travel there in two days. Others have searched well, too, and found the valley. No," Robert hastily added, noting his listeners' consternation, "I believe they are dead. But White Pony

Tail should talk."

The youth gravely walked to his blanket roll and returned with a small, birchbark box crudely sewn with cedar-root strands. Placing the box on his lap, he looked self-consciously at his companions, the firelight alternately darkening and lightening the deeper pits in his face.

"I rode up the valley, then circled around the lake, near its northern end. The valley is as Robert said. In the forest behind the lake I found the stump of a tree chopped down, then some distance away another and another. The chopper did not want anyone to see from a distance man had been at work. Soon I found the old and scattered bones of two horses, then, before a small, well-made cabin, a rock-covered grave with a tilting cross." He swallowed nervously. "A grizzly bear had torn the rawhide hinges off the door, which then had fallen. There were great scratch marks, but they and other sign were old. Cautiously, I opened the two small shutters. Varmints had eaten most of the scraped skins through which some light could pass. Holding my Hawken gun before me, I entered the gloom." Again, he hesitated, then laughed. "When a great owl flew past me screeching its anger, I almost freshened the bear droppings before the cabin. There on one of the two bunks such as John Owen has for visitors, I found the skeleton of a . . . a man perhaps the size of myself, for I ventured to throw aside the stiff, moldy furs and measure it with my Hawken wiping stick. One upper leg bone was splintered, the smaller pieces on the fur. White hair clung to the skull. I found a poorly made and a fine Blackfeet bow, arrows, a good, but rusty, knife, and an axe. Little more, except the box." White Pony Tail handed it to Charlot.

Four messages painstakingly had been scratched into the underside of small birchbark squares. Charlot and Little Coyote tilted them to better catch the firelight:

I
we be Peter Paul Enfinger
blackfuts killd paw maw
tukd us

II

we stold horse gun an such
comd hyr

III

grizel killd Peter
an horss in II yer

IIII

grizel has killd me
shur in III yer

The Flatheads found a loaded, much-shortened Hudson's Bay flintlock musket and an almost-empty powder horn under the furs next to the skeleton. They buried the bones near the other grave, placing the cross between the two before cleaning the cabin and restoring the hinges. The structure would serve for storage. They erected their four small lodges nearby. White Pony Tail would share the seer's.

During the first snowfalls, they secured the horses nearby, scouted and began trapping the dams. As the freeze set in, much deer, elk, mountain sheep and beaver meat began bending the high poles well away from the camp. Marveling at the many animal tracks, each person made a set of snowshoes, remaining watchful always for fresh bear sign before the hibernation time. As the winter progressed and more snow lessened the likelihood other humans would enter the valley, the trappers pursued larger animals by trap and, occasionally, rifles. Soon there were many furs on the cabin bunks.

Especially heavy snowfalls sometimes transformed smaller conifers into multi-shaped snowmen; the branches of the larger trees drooped in seeming despair that they ever would spring upward again in this increasingly white world. These were joyful times for the Flathead trappers, who limited their actions to caring for the horses, working the furs, feeding the fires and talking.

Little Coyote encouraged the younger people to tell of their exploits, or the stories of the people. Often he found himself explaining the wisdom he had learned thus far in life, and interpreting as best he could the puzzlement resulting from the mixing of the old ways with the new. Such a burden forced him to present his thoughts in a more organized way; he was careful to allow his listeners to question, in the light of their experiences, their looks into the future. The major benefit, of course, was that the present instruction far exceeded that introspective period he underwent during his own lonely, memorable, long-ago winter of the *sqléw*.

Often, lying in his blankets after such talks, Little Coyote asked the Good Spirit to put this question into the minds of Stevens, the Great Father, even the Lenters and others in the Bitter Root: Were white men asking for too much in demanding that a single generation of red men, such as these young companions, understand white man's mystifying ways—if they fully understood them, themselves?

Spring of 1857 came early. Chinook winds began melting the snow and ice in the creeks and dams. Also triggered by some primordial force far south of this mountainous region, ducks and geese began halting their unerring northward flights to seek open parts of the lake where fish competed to seize baited hooks.

While all the men were looking to the traps far away one night, Little Coyote sat alone in his lodge awaiting word from Margarite. She had remained in camp to attend Little Owl, who was eager to deliver her baby prior to the Flatheads' return to the Bitter Root.

The seer leaned forward to brighten his fire, then sat back on his willow rest. He was holding the birchbark box of pitiful messages left by dying Paul Enfinger. The warrior had thought about the box as he began summarizing the highlights of this winter, preparatory to marking them on paper. Later he would transfer his recollections to his story skin and, ultimately, to his manuscript. Should the youth's four messages have been buried with his bones? Brief and tragic as they were, they did encompass the last portion of the twins' short lives. Certainly, the more detailed information Little Coyote had written in his manuscript about the encounters with the Enfinger family prior to the murders and kidnapping might be of some solace to the Enfinger clan in distant Tennessee. *But where in Tennessee?* The senior Enfinger had said his partner, Perkins, had gone to Oregon. Perhaps Perkins' bones also lay along the Oregon Trail with the many who had died of cholera, accidents and other causes. If not, perhaps Perkins could get a message to Tennessee. Should the medicine man send word to John Owen to copy the Enfinger information from his manuscript, put it in the tiny box and send it to some caring white leader in Oregon to seek out Perkins? The whites did seem to place as much importance on the dead as did the Indians.

But why the effort? Well, to concede there was little reason, little value in the doing, would be to question if there also was little purpose in the seer summarizing the events of his life and many others', encompassing the entire tribe and beyond, on his story skin and expanding these symbols into the vastly enlarged manuscript. The Black Robes had explained the meaning and importance of "history." Thus, the Flathead people's lives might become better known and understood by themselves and others. So, why not the whites' lives and those of the Enfingers? Yes, he would send the request, along with the birchbark box and its contents, to Owen.

Again, he brightened the fire. Margarite had told him she, in all likelihood, would need no help in delivering Little Owl— but he had agreed to be nearby, if needed. Now his mind moved beyond the symbols that would go on the story skin to their greater explanation in the manuscript. It was time to begin thinking more fully about what broader views, conclusions, he had reached— perhaps his people would reach—from someday reading his efforts at story-telling white man's way. Yet, perhaps he should acknowledge that the Good Spirit might grant him more years of life yet; conclusions reached now would be modified by the ever-accelerating pace of change that till now had overtaken the land and the people.

He heard a moan rising above the calls of night birds, the muted music of the gentle wind. He listened. Again the moan, ending as the cry of a newborn Flathead arose from the nearby lodge. Welcome! Persistent! To the seer, Margarite, and certainly the mother, the cry carried a sure message: Our people will endure!

Margarite met Little Coyote mid-way between the lodges.

"Francis and Little Owl have a son." She smiled and raised her arms in thanksgiving. Returning to his lodge, Little Coyote continued his musings: If he could, what would he tell this totally inexperienced new-born baby were the certainties he would face in the years ahead? In the way that dying Paul Enfinger had done on the bark, the seer, with little effort, carefully summarized that answer on white man's paper:

I

Yes, our people will endure. Largely, they have
survived as a small tribe by working together.
Even with the whites who, like Lenter, now seize
the earth.

II

Reviewing the certainties formed by my lifetime,
immeasurably strengthened this winter by close
experience with some of the next generation of
Flatheads, they, too, must freely share in
the land.

III

As long as possible the people must avoid the
reservations, which would spring closed like
the death grip of a great spiked bear trap on
mind, body and spirit.

Little Coyote stepped outside into the darkness. Like Margarite, he raised his arms skyward. "Great Spirit," he prayed, "guide us well so this son of Robert and Little Owl always will have the important parts of what You have given us in the past and even now."

He returned inside, knowing, but not fully liking, that this tranquil place soon would become lonesome for him, indeed. Thinking thus about Charlot and the others, there came the thought his war friend confidently had mentioned after they had helped to uplift gloomy Victor's spirit at the Lake of the White Moose: "The Black Robes tell us Our Lord promised He never will send more burdens than we can bear."

The seer slept until returning Charlot and White Pony Tail yipped their approach to camp.

L ittle Coyote had built his small fire between two rocks, mostly because there was a third and larger one nearby on which he could sit. He had walked much this day, trailing his horse over the ridges, riding in the small valleys as the creeks, willow and other growth permitted. He was weary! He spitted the grouse and placed the green stick across the rocks. Soon he was leaning forward to turn the stick and smell the delicious aroma.

The years scarcely had lessened his appetite. Nor memories. So easy to carry, undiminished by the years but increasingly invoked to vividness by familiar smell, sound, touch or sight. How often he had thanked the Good Spirit for the bitter/sweet of these. How often Antelope had prepared such birds during carefree days riding in the Bitter Root and elsewhere. And, later, both increasingly had shared their bird with Lance until, all too soon, he had wanted his own. Yes, and quickly learned to supply them. Perhaps memories of the good times strengthened the nearer one approached the sand hills and the sharing of new ones with all who had gone before. *How wonderful that time near the Lake of the White Moose, when the grouse had flushed toward the trees to the west and—*

The mare stomped nervously, snorted and tautened her picket line. The warrior carefully leaned the stick and grouse against one rock, then seized his bow and arrows. Now the horse was facing north, unchewed grass ends dropping from her lips as she lifted her head and tried to see and hear what she smelled to arouse such fears. Little Coyote rubbed his thumb and index finger in dead ashes before selecting a broad-head arrow from the quiver. Now the horse was pulling at her line, tiny squeals of fright rising above her snorts. The rope held. Tensely, she watched a grizzly bear emerge across the brush-filled gulch, then continue moving up the slope, ignoring some gopher hills in its path. When an errant breeze struck, Little Coyote could see the brownish-black hair on the bear's left side rippling like the grass through which it was sauntering. The creature stopped on a small rise, where it was silhouetted. The warrior could see that almost all the short, left ear was missing, evidently bitten off in a fight. Boar, old one, and with a full belly, the hunter judged. He returned to his own meal.

He had seen three other bears, working berry patches on the higher hillsides, during his many days' absence from the trapping camp at Enfinger cabin. As he had sought more beaver and other animal sign, numerous mountain sheep had curiously peered downward from their craggy heights. Coyotes sang at night, often quieting when deeper wolf howls took over. Lynx and rabbits abounded, evidently near the peak of a cycle. Small elk herds had fled from the lower meadows; deer fed without concern until horse and rider directly approached. Then, white flags up, they bounced out of sight. Yes, there was much fur and food—as there once had been in the Bitter Root Valley. The warrior sighed deeply and continued eating.

Soon he kicked dirt back into the shallow fire pit and placed the grouse bones on a rock where earlier the jays had fought for the guts. They were quarreling loudly as he began leading the horse downward toward a meadow where more elk were feeding near the base of a dirt, leaf and needle-covered snowbank receding ever more rapidly in the late August warmth of 1858. The elk fled upward, caught the grizzly scent and veered east, the bulls gracefully threading their heads and antlers between the trees. They, like the grizzlies, wolves and other plains animals—even some buffalo—increasingly were seeking safety in the mountains as more people entered this vast region. Seemingly, all were trying, as Frank Owen, long-dead Jed Smith, Tull and others had observed, "to get the most the fastest." And what of the people who lived here before Clark and Lewis had appeared?

More grimly now, as the elk disappeared, the medicine man caught the . . . what had Father Mengarini called the word? Yes. "Irony." The irony was that the seer, only too well, knew some Flatheads and others who were being forced to do the same: Flee like the very creatures they were pursuing. Where were other hidden valleys like these? When this way of life was gone, the whites could control the red man as surely as the hidden bit on the bridle of a horse controls the animal. Some bits were cruel, indeed.

But now he was lagging! Before the next group of Flatheads arrived, he wanted to be at Enfinger camp—almost as much to learn of events that affected his beloved valley as to see his people. At least here we are observing some vestiges of ancient ways and restraints, he acknowledged as he began thinking how Charlot had remained in the Bitter Root last fall.

Surprisingly, sub-chief Ambrose, with his wife, had led the party of three younger couples. All were highly compatible, eager and industrious, and their fur catch had equaled that of the first expedition of '56.

With the hurt yet glistening from his heavy-lidded eyes, Ambrose had confided to Little Coyote he "wanted to be with young hunters like my son, killed by the Gros Ventres despite treaties soon after you came to this place." Other information, discussed at great length among all nine Flatheads during heaviest snowfalls, had been the meanings and implications of what John Owen had said about Governor Stevens being elected Washington Territorial Delegate and going to Washington, D.C., and Dr. Lansdale briefly returning to the Flatheads, then again going to the Pacific coast.

"So now Owen is agent, and might be for the Bannacks and

some of the Shoshonis, too," Ambrose had revealed. A smile finally elevating all the careworn lines in his face, he had added, "We rejoice at this," though Owen had said, 'Stevens will work harder in Washington, D.C., to have Lt. Mullan build his road from Fort Walla Walla to Fort Benton.'"

One stormy night when all but the seer and Ambrose and his wife were in their sleeping furs, the sub-chief grimly had summarized many reports that travelers had carried from the Kansas country into the Bitter Root about a General Sumner. He punished the Cheyennes who had turned on the many white settlers in Nebraska. Looking directly across the lodge fire at Little Coyote, Ambrose had said, "The Cheyennes' medicine man said if the warriors would wash in a certain lake, bullets would not strike them. Sumner's three-hundred horse soldiers used sabres to attack as many mounted Cheyenne warriors, most of whom fell. Now those who fought in the Yakima War, as well as the Sioux and Cheyenne, know soldiers are to be feared, as well as the settlers they seek to protect."

Yes, there had been many furs to work and much to discuss around the lodge fires that winter of 1857—and think about till now.

As he neared Enfinger camp, Little Coyote vainly listened for the tinkling of the small, brass bell he had hung round the neck of his pack horse as he had begun his trip to find more beavers and other furs.

At length the mare stopped and, goaded by the warrior's heels, reluctantly moved a short distance along the ridge above the lake and camp. Then she stopped again and stood there until the warrior heard jays and ravens arguing in the meadow below. He, too, smelled old death, as briefly as an arrow's passage up the slope. He dismounted to focus the spyglass on the birds. There were two mixed flocks, the smaller near what seemingly was a torn-up hide, the larger at a pile of brush, grass and earth near the meadow's edge.

Closer inspection disclosed that the grizzly evidently had rushed and knocked down the pack horse while she had fed. The grizzly had feasted, then slept and gorged until it could drag the carcass toward some brush. It had covered the kill, unearthing and eating portions until the remnants would interest only smaller rodents and these birds. The bear had dragged the hide a short distance from the stinking jumble, then abandoned it. Little Coyote recovered the bell from a pile of almost-dry gut contents, cleaned it, then hung it from his saddle. It tolled each full step of his horse till they were home.

Second Chief Moses headed the trapping party to Enfinger camp in 1858, but warned, "I will leave for St. Ignatius after first snow to lead people from the Bitter Root and Jocko on a great buffalo hunt." Before his departure, accompanied by eager White Pony Tail, Moses told of stories brought to the Bitter Root by assorted tribesmen after the Yakima War.

"Wars seem to come ever closer to us," he said. "Now there are two forts in the Palouse and Walla Walla country—Simcoe and Walla Walla. Chief Kamiakin remained angry over the killing of Peo-peo-mox-mox of the Walla Wallas during that war. The general, Wool, who also could see Indians when he considered justice, was removed. A General Clarke became white man's war chief. When Kamiakin again protested the coming of more settlers, and gold-seekers going to Colville, he began telling the tribes east of the Columbia they must resist white man. Another war chief, Steptoe, set out from Fort Walla Walla with one-hundred-sixty-four soldiers, with cannon, to intimidate the Palouses and Spokanes, even our friends the Coeur d'Alenes. They put on paint and defeated Steptoe. He fled back to Fort Walla Walla. Then, just before we came here, we learned that the general Clarke sent out Wright. At the Great Spokane plain, the whites' rifles and cannons that could shoot very far defeated more than six-hundred Indians.

"After that fight, Wright killed fifteen more Indians." Moses shook his head sadly, his gnarled fingers grasping and loosening on his pipe stem. "Wright's soldiers put ropes around their necks and pulled them into the air, where they kicked like lassoed stallions until they were dead. Kamiakin, who once hid amongst us for a time, was injured. He escaped to Canada. Owhi, his brother-in-law, came to Wright to ask for peace. He was told he would be killed if he did not call his son, Qualchin, to the camp. When Qualchin came, he, too, did the rope dance in sight of Owhi. With his heart broken, Owhi tried to escape; a fast bullet killed him. I do not foresee more wars there. The people will accept the reservations, which will kill their spirits."

Shaky from the telling, Moses lighted his pipe, puffed reflectively, then put it down as though the tobacco had lost its taste.

"I would not sign Stevens' treaty. I told him that. I could foresee trouble, not like you foresee trouble, Little Coyote." Moses looked at the young people quietly sitting in the lodge. "We see where beaver cut the trees and make their dams. We know if we put our traps a certain way we will catch and skin them. So, we now must judge actions of white man. He sees the land. We now know he will grab the land. When the Indians protest, white man will build forts, then fight the Indians. I hope I do not live to see army forts go up in our land."

Again the old chief looked at his silent listeners before lighting his pipe. He puffed a few moments, then smiled briefly. "We must look for blue patches in the ever-darkening sky. John Owen said the wars stopped Mullan's plan for his road. In the seventh month, and again in the eighth month, Father Menetrey came to the Bitter Root. He said he will ask Father DeSmet to help him build another mission in our valley."

The industrious trappers and hunters were bringing in good furs before Moses and White Pony Tail set out for St. Ignatius. There was much rejoicing the day Hawk Flying By and Stephen brought the hide of a perhaps three-year-old grizzly to camp. It had been shot with Hawkens, true, but two arrows first had found its neck. The women prepared a feast.

"This is good." Moses set down a piece of cooked beaver tail. The others politely stopped feasting. His message was short, again telling where his mind was: "Life is harder for our people in the valley. They do not often eat like this. How strange. Many of the whites coming there tell John Owen they seek to escape the crowdedness found elsewhere. Many are good people. Yet some now grow angry that we resist going to the Jocko. The trapping, the hunting, the preparation of the furs. Yes, it is good. John Owen provided our people with many needs in exchange for the furs. He did not ask where we found them." The old chief laughed. "And we gave furs to Frank Owen. Yet again, he bought powder, lead and caps. He then gave them to us to bring here. We must hold to such tasks as you perform at Enfinger camp. Little Coyote and I know that we must have important things to do to remain strong. Important tasks for the day." He looked at the grizzly claw necklaces of Hawk Flying By and Stephen. "And important tasks for us all to work on together in the times ahead. And so, we leave for the buffalo hunt!"

Having left seed among the beaver and other fur-bearers nearest Enfinger camp, the trappers of 1859 once again were able to work near their shelters. It was well they could do so, for cold came down from the north after great snows, forcing everyone to work much harder with the traps and at keeping the horses alive. These creatures often huddled together in a great shelter constructed of tree boughs and trunks after pawing for grasses in the meadows with the least snow. Thus the bunks in the cabin would hold fewer furs than before—until earliest spring. Day and night trees popped in the intense cold like near and distant gunfire. Numerous small rodents crept into the lodges, supplying their bodies as bait in the traps for the larger creatures. Constant fires kept the lodges warm. The meat poles, which were hanging heavy after earliest freeze, plus an occasional deer or elk, supplied much good food. Flatheads and melt waters departed the valley together, all singing their varying songs in the grand release of spring. The somewhat smaller 1860 trapping party, though forced to roam afar, could do so in a surprisingly open winter and carry out an even greater number of skins, among them many of deer, wolves and two more grizzlies.

Charlot put his own saddle on Little Coyote's mare and helped his *i-sts-sókoi* painfully clamber into it. Shaken, he grasped the pommel as Charlot unsuccessfully tried to adjust the stirrup so there would be some degree of comfort for the medicine man's left leg as they left Enfinger camp this late spring of 1862. Finally, the warrior cut a lengthwise band from an almost-board-stiff elk hide, very wide in the center and tapering at both ends. He slit one end and pushed it over the pommel. Another Flathead trapper began raising the medicine man's splinted leg until he indicated the pain mostly had stopped. Charlot bent the leather band under the leg, slit a hole in the other end and pushed it over the pommel, too. With this stiff sling supporting the leg at the proper height somewhat parallel with the ground, Charlot set the pack train into motion. Little Coyote, chewing a mouthful of willow bark, signed he easily could catch up. He turned his horse and, for a final time, looked beyond the graves of Peter and Paul Enfinger to a third one. That grave had an old Hudson's Bay musket pounded barrel-end into the soil. Tied to the musket was a fleshed and very large grizzly skull.

The warrior nudged his horse to the edge of the meadow where lay the scattered bones of his horse and the bear. Reaching up, he broke three small pine boughs from a great tree and returned to drop one atop each grave.

So sudden had been the grizzly's attack, so great Little Coyote's pain following his brief, ineffectual attempt to fight, so sorrowful the outcome that even now the warrior vividly and almost instantaneously re-lived the entire sequence.

The fur take of twelve Flatheads that winter of 1861 had been substantial. Weather and snow depth had permitted wide-ranging travel, often on horses. By that early spring the Flatheads could supplant hard work with easier living, some riding afar to hunt, fish, explore. So it was that only Little Coyote, White Pony Tail, Charlot and Margarite were in camp, the latter two deciding that morning to try for large trout in a beaver pond a short distance away. Smoked, they would be good food for the return to the Bitter Root. White Pony Tail, carrying the old Hudson's Bay musket loaded with birdshot, would compete with Little Coyote and blunted arrows for a meal of grouse. Loser would cook and serve their prizes.

The hunters had slowly begun working their way across the

meadow toward the thicket of budding willow. Before entering the brush, White Pony Tail enthusiastically waved both arms as though a grouse, then motioned he would move slightly to the right so each would know where to direct birdshot and arrows.

The old grizzly had raised his one-eared, massive head above the bushes, his growly snort jarring into a cough as he fell to all fours directly facing the seer and charged. The blunted arrow stung him to greater fury and hung from his neck as Little Coyote reached for a stone-tipped missile. The collision with this savage monster, which outweighed the Flathead more than three times, knocked the air from Little Coyote's lungs and set him rolling. Belly down, he ineffectually reached for his knife; then, as he felt the huge bear atop him, he feigned death though his tortured lungs forced him to draw in air. Now, events had tumbled one over the other in an instant. The bear slapped the warrior's body face-up and closed his jaws on the upper left leg. Little Coyote felt the pain, tried to rise, blearily saw White Pony Tail place the musket on the bear's neck and heard the muffled explosion. The bear had squealed like a Mission pig, tried to stand, then had crushed the young brave's head with a dying blow of his heavily clawed forepaw. Jarringly, the beast fell partially atop the medicine man, raking the injured left leg with his claws before rolling off in his dying struggles. Gasping with pain, the warrior began crawling past the valiant, young brave's body and toward the trail, where perhaps Charlot and Margarite would find him. His mind was a maelstrom of thoughts as he tried to override pain; finally he settled on the question: *Why White Pony Tail and not me?*

Between his finding the trail and his *i-sts-sókoi* finding him, that question's answer had begun to form in a shapeless, yet somehow distinguishable, composite of Shining Shirt, Lance, Antelope and Gun. Between the knowing and not knowing of his mind, an answer began to come from that composite of his greatly loved ones: "Our people will need the wisdom from your vision quest till they leave the Bitter Root. Then others with as strong a spirit as White Pony Tail will arise to help guide them through a new way of life."

Abruptly, the seer set off his mare to catch up with the pack train.

That evening Little Coyote chewed more willow before Margarite tended his leg. Charlot helped him to his sleeping robes under a large tree. They talked for a time about who should lead the trappers back for next year's season; then the younger warrior opened his bullet pouch, poured a handful of balls onto the edge of the robe, extracted one and held it out.

"When we cut away the hide and flesh from the grizzly's head and bared his worn, broken and rotted teeth, we found this musket ball," Charlot said. "The lower inside jaw had partially grown around it." Little Coyote examined the ball. It would fit the bore of the old Hudson's Bay musket. "How strange the events that ball, perhaps cast by a Blackfeet and fired by the Enfinger youth, represents," Little Coyote said. "Some would say 'good medicine' or 'very bad, indeed.' Give the ball to Adolph's son. He now possesses his father's old musket."

"But the answer to all the events?" Charlot insisted.

"The Good Spirit knows."

"Yes. . ." Charlot's face softened much like Victor's, which so often had betrayed his deep love for the medicine man. "Yes. Sleep well." He strongly gripped Little Coyote's shoulder, then returned to the growing light of the campfire.

Weather remained good throughout much of the trek back to the Bitter Root. The group made frequent stops to accommodate Little Coyote. Twice Charlot cut off new strips of elk hide to provide stiffer supports for the seer's injured leg. Where the big creek raced into the Thompson River, a very puzzled young scout hastened to report he had watched three white men scooping gravel from the creek and twirling it about in large pans.

"They peer into the pans, their frowns growing longer and longer as they let the gravel wash over the edge and back into the water. When the rocks are almost gone, these white men put their faces into the pans. They cock their heads this way and that, like a robin seeking a worm, then, shouting obscenities, they scoop up more gravel. Perhaps they are crazy?" The scout shook his head in bewilderment. In the silence, he defiantly said, "I *did* see this strangeness!"

Charlot's look at Little Coyote went beyond questioning again if he was ready to travel. Were the gold-seekers coming to the Jocko and Bitter Root, too?

On his return to Enfinger camp, White Pony Tail had told of the frustration and anger some of his Nez Percé kin had vented during their most recent visit to the Bitter Root. An Indian trader had sneaked into their reservation and found gold near the western end of the Lo Lo trail. In December 1860 the trader then had brought more than thirty miners from Walla Walla.

"Their camp is very near our camas-digging ground at Wieppe Prairie," White Pony Tail's kin had explained.

Any apprehension Little Coyote had about gold-seekers diminished for a time as the pack train followed the Clark Fork and the Jocko. They bypassed St. Ignatius Mission, then, as they moved southward, they avoided the Indian agency that Charlot said John Owen had moved some distance up the Jocko River in 1860. Henceforth, Little Coyote began confronting solid realities that had occurred during his absence.

One such was a two-story cabin on a small hill overlooking a large meadow. Two men briefly gazed at the pack train, then continued shaping logs for the next course of a smaller structure. Near an unnamed creek meandering through yet another meadow, a pole corral forced the Flatheads off the old trail and made them walk around a larger cabin. Closer yet to Hell Gate were cabin, corral and jackleg fence, inside of which were seven horses, two cows, a bull and a large wagon. Smoke rose serenely from the cabin chimney to drift northeast. A man, woman, two boys and a girl stepped from the cabin to wave a friendly greeting before re-entering the structure. They patted the large, black dog for his vigilance and warning.

"They call themselves the McDannels," Charlot said. "They walked out and gave us some tobacco and bread when we came by here on our way to Enfinger camp." He had waited for Little Coyote to catch up. "McDannel helps the men Worden and

Higgins. They have a trading post and store at Hell Gate now. We will not go by there. I wish to keep their friendship, thus would not want them to inquire about our furs, which must go to John Owen. We must help him. He says he no longer will be the Indian agent if the Great Father does not keep his promises to send the treaty goods. He also frets that if the Mullan Road does come, it will bypass Fort Owen."

They camped late that evening at the Place With Bull. Again there was a cabin. With extra effort, the pack train would reach the encampment near Fort Owen by sunset next day. There were two cabins at Place of No Salmon, three near Place of Dirty Apron.

Worn, the injured leg throbbing, Little Coyote asked Margarite to fetch him the small bottle of laudanum from his medicine kit. It had been untouched throughout his years at Enfinger camp. Sleepily, he commented about the cabins to Margarite as she propped the leg upward before he slept.

"Yes," she agreed, "and when our people move past Fort Owen and ever south, we encounter cabins at the places of: Red Mountain Top, With Big Cottonwoods, To Gamble, With Willows, Yellow Pants, To Put a Baby to Sleep, Where a Rock is Lifted, With Cliffs, Has Valerian Root, With Horn in Tree, With Little Trees." Little Coyote remembered her saying "Main Gambling Grounds" just before the opium put him to sleep.

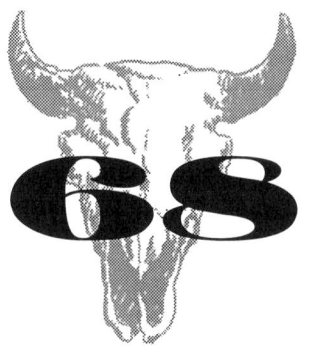

"**S**ons of bitches! If those damned, crooked bureaucrats in Washington, D.C., can't get a load of treaty goods right for this almost-forgotten neck of the woods, how in hell can they expect to win the war between the states?"

His cheeks flushing above his beard, John Owen glanced at the growing number of curious Flatheads assembling around their chief. Again, he looked at the bill of lading the lead teamster had handed down to him. Jamming the paper into his pocket, he clambered into one of the wagons and began sawing his Green River knife across the knot of the cord binding one of the large bales. He pulled out a shawl that fluttered momentarily in the cooling breeze. He threw down the garment; muttering "one-hundred-twenty dozen of them!" he climbed into another wagon. He pulled a flimsy, blue blanket from a bale and held it toward partially obscured Sun, which streamed thin shafts of light through the loose weave. "And they sent six-hundred-thirty of these!" Another wagon was loaded with more than eleven-hundred yards of thin flannel, some of the bolts mildewed from poor handling. In other wagons were rice, coffee and hardbread. "Tons, all sent at forty cents per pound freight rates," Owen fumed. "Another pay-off among crooks!"

Seemingly overwhelmed, he sat atop a barrel of hardbread in the last wagon while Emanuel Martin stood by, patiently listening and awaiting further instructions.

"I didn't order this shit," Owen said. "If I had been allowed to put in an order, I'd have requisitioned what the Indians have told me they could use, plus American brood mares to breed with their horses, and a helluva lot of heifers and a few good bulls. Instead, I'm supposed to take anything those crooks can get a rake-off from, including the freighters!" He stood and peered down at Victor. "I just can't keep on giving my own supplies to you folks. I haven't been paid for more than a year. Well, this is it! I'm not going to take any more."

As he came down from the wagon box, thunderheads from the southwest hid Sun as they moved into the valley and piled ever higher. Resignedly, Owen pointed to the two-story bastions at the south entrance to his completed fort. "Better get all this shit under cover, Old Manwell. Keep track of the work the Flatheads do, and I'll make it right. Victor, we'll give your people their share of this in two days, after we get it sorted out for here and elsewhere."

The word got around and people began leaving. Owen headed for his office. He was wiping his right hand across his bewhiskered lips when Charlot and Little Coyote slowly entered, the latter carrying two crutches Owen had insisted he borrow.

A smile lit up Charlot's somber face. "I thank you for telling my father you will have a cabin built for him near the fort. He and Agnes are clearing rocks from the ground."

Owen waved his hand. "He deserves it. Won't be able to get started till about snow time. Short-handed. So many of the workers have taken off for that gold strike Johnny White made at Bannack."

That word "gold." Now it caused a hasty exchange of looks between the two Flatheads. Till now the seer had hidden in his mind the implications of the scout's report of the gold-panners along the Thompson. There had been the problem with getting well, and his growing wonderment at the changes in the valley. He looked at Owen. "Thank you for the crutches. This gold-seeking. Is it important?"

"Sure is. Some of my best workers, even some of the earliest settlers here, have gone to the Deer Lodge Valley. There's going to be more activity there, too. Those teamsters outside say three steamboats loaded with mining gear and people have arrived at Fort Benton. This gold business has just gotten started. Sit down." Owen pointed to a bench.

"But you are busy." Charlot looked at the many papers on the desk.

"Day's shot. Damn politicians. Do sit down. Wonder if it was worthwhile for Caldwell and me to keep our mouths shut in '52 when we found that gold just west of the fort. Troubles are just starting for your people. Maybe we can keep the school going we started last year. I'll help as I can, but I truly feel I can do more for you, and myself, in the long run if I don't have to fight the government crooks. Guess I could give you and Victor some lessons there. While you were trapping the past several years, I've been stepping into snares, traps, pitfalls and deadfalls the bureaucrats have erected from Bannack and mountain Shoshone country to here and St. Ignatius and beyond. I can't begin to tell you the problems. Well, I'm quitting as Indian agent soon as I can."

"What can we do to help you remain as agent?" Charlot asked. "We trust you, John Owen. Can we—"

A flash of lightning lit up the office; thunder drowned out Charlot's voice. The three men looked out the small windows. The wagons were rolling toward a cottonwood grove. Old Manwell was urging his workers to greater efforts. Again the lightning, brighter yet, closer, and a sharp "craaack." The bolt had struck the top of the ancient tree towering far beyond the adobe walls where Little Coyote had watched the warring ants so long ago. The teamsters stopped their wagons in the open, set the brakes, hurriedly put rocks in front of and behind each wheel and crawled underneath. Owen strode to the door, waited for the thunder to echo away, then, as a few large rain drops began pelting down, shouted to Old Manwell to pull some tarps over the goods and get under cover, too.

Nancy Owen quietly had appeared with tea, sugar and molasses bread. Owen smiled for the first time. He picked up the crutches and held them out to Little Coyote.

"Why don't you run out there and get us some of that hardbread? I'm sure you'd rather have that than Old Wife's molasses bread." His smile faded. "I don't know what to do with those weevil-ridden rocks. Too large for musket balls. Too small for my howitzer. Throw them out on the other rock piles, maybe." He caught Little Coyote's glance at Nancy as she departed; now there was concern in his voice. "Old Wife is feeling poorly. Wish we had Father Ravalli here." He nodded toward the warrior's badly scarred leg. "Glad to see the meat has mended, and you can walk some."

"Yes. Now I will work on my story skin and manuscript."

The rain drummed loudly on the long, sloping roof of the east barracks and ran in sheets onto the wooden walkway below.

The trader started to reach for the top of the bookshelves and the medicine man's property. Instead, he withdrew a book with a grass stalk marking a page. "I remembered where I'd read what I wanted to tell you the other day when I was explaining this damn Civil War to you and Victor and Charlot." He opened the book. "Back in '32 when Rabbit's Skin Leggins and No Horns On His Head were returning out here from St. Louis, a Frenchman named De Tocqueville, a . . . well, I guess in a way he was sort of a seer like you, Little Coyote, anyway, he was visiting America, including the North and the South. Here's what he prophesied: The 'inevitable separation,' he called it, of the two sides." Owen held up his molasses bread and slowly broke it into two pieces, some of the ragged ends threatening to separate one way, then remaining hanging on the other piece. "Now it has come, and a lot more De Tocqueville couldn't see. And it's going to hit us here for sure, one way or the other.

"The whole situation reminds me of what makes gunpowder. Saltpeter, sulphur and charcoal: Saltpeter is the war that will make it harder to send soldiers out here. Sulphur's the gold rush bringing a lot of frenzied people to seek it. As in the California rush of '49 and in Oregon and Idaho, these'll include a wide range of people—from absolute scum to farmer types looking for land. A little too dark, maybe, but the charcoal's the Indians, already on edge enough, with some of them fighting just the people who've been killing off the game, putting them on reservations and grabbing the land. Who's going to light the match?"

Owen put the book rack on the shelf. "I'm no prophet at all. But I sure can smell trouble. All this might be good for my business. Is already. But it sure won't be good for you." The drumming rain increased its tempo and force for a moment. Owen sat down. He looked at the ceiling for leaks, then, as the noise subsided a bit, sighed. "Before that grizzly killed White Pony Tail, you know I had him working around here. I asked him to trap the mice that had invaded the bastion I was using for a granary. He live-trapped some of them and started putting them in a box, feeding them so the little tad would watch them. Old Wife and I would watch the tads. I got to noticing that the more tads crowded around the box, the more they got to wrangling who could stand to get the best looks. Also, the more mice that went into the box, the less food there was. Less space, too. The mice started fighting. One morning lots of them were dead. They'd killed each other. From then on White Pony Tail just trapped them and fed them to my dog."

Owen grimly shook his head as he put the story skin on the counter and handed the manuscript to Charlot. "With your permission, I've read through this, and mostly it's good, Little Coyote. It's a lot more important than this Cheyenne brag book I picked up during a trip to Fort Laramie." He handed an old ledger book to Little Coyote. Some warrior, perhaps named Spotted Shirt, had drawn a series of pictures of his exploits. The warrior always was clad in a spotted shirt. The trader waved at his books. "These all tell us that no nation, large or small, overseas or here, even Stevens' so-called 'Flathead Nation,' can continue to hold together unless it's got some kind of written account of what it has done, and has kept believing in, despite the sometimes hell of change.

"With the Indians' old ways going, the story-tellers dying off, you'd better keep working on your story, and the next generation better keep track, too. More of the whites coming in to settle are keeping records of one kind or another of what they're doing, just as I am." He pointed to the ledger book on the counter and to another on the lowest shelf. "I figure, Little Coyote, it's important for you to tell what the Indians have done and are doing, and how what the whites have done and are doing affects your people. Yours will be the most honest account. But don't be scornful if we try to help you by doing and telling what is in our hearts. And, increasingly, it's important to remember there are whites with Indian blood and Indians with white blood. We've all got to be careful when we cross that raging stream on a mighty small log." Owen shrugged. "You're the story-teller. Well, the rain has stopped. I guess we all have work to do now. I'm going to be busy as hell the next few days getting rid of all this stuff the teamsters brought. But bring Victor and some of the sub-chiefs over, say, in four days. Might as well use these books to tell you a few more things about the whites, since I'm not going to be agent much longer." He stuck his head out the door.

"Manwell!"

The now-always-present edges of worry began filling Little Coyote's mind as he carried his manuscript and story skin into his lodge. The people had erected the lodge apart from the others, a few of which were poor cabins. He kept his mare nearby. The extra horse Victor had given him was in the main herd, well guarded against Blackfeet raiders, other Indians who, destitute, had fled wars elsewhere, and the whites who increasingly were moving into and through the valley.

How much had happened since he had gone to Enfinger camp! Before he sharpened a pencil, made tiny brushes or mixed paint, he conceded he must devote more of his mind to focusing on the future than winnowing through past events that had shaped the now.

Had he accomplished much? How often he had asked himself this question as conditions changed! Yes, he did so because he needed reassurance, as do all persons. Despite many provocations, the Flatheads had not fought white men who increasingly were threatening to outnumber the berries in the valley with so many hungry people picking them. Yes, the people could be worse off than the starving Bannacks and Shoshonis who earlier had come to the valley, driven from their own lands by miners and others. Owen had helped them from his personal stores because, as he had explained to those Flatheads who complained about their presence, "They've passed the point where they can help themselves. They seem to have no future."

Yes, the now and the future would affect the Flatheads' very lives more than ever before. Had the Good Spirit protected him from enemies, disease and the grizzly more for others than himself? How should he devote his remaining time, aging body, mind and strength to help his people both to cope and achieve?

The future: Something is struggling to emerge here, but I cannot grasp its many threads. Good Spirit, help me to see! For what purpose have you spared my life? As he prayed, Little Coyote now could see the seldom-smiling faces of Victor and Charlot. Charlot, his *i-sts-sókoi*. With certainty above the hot springs so long ago, the seer had interpreted young Charlot's vision: ". . .In Little Grizzly Bear Claw's lifetime all will be forced northward from the valley . . . There will be greater battles than ever before among Indian and Indian and Indian and whites . . . But the Flatheads will survive."

Yes, to survive, the Flatheads must hold together despite all sadnesses because their future lay ahead in the Jocko. Little Coyote had not seen himself in Charlot's vision. So the seer must learn more to help the people toward their future with white man.

Now more overwhelmed than had been Owen on the arrival of the wagonloads of unrequisitioned treaty goods, the seer sat on the floor of his lodge. He faced the story skin framed on the willow tripod and held the manuscript in his lap.

Soon after returning from Enfinger camp, Charlot had helped the seer to sit on the bench in Owen's west barracks trade room waiting for the busy trader to lend him the crutches. The two Flatheads had watched this wise man, who knew what was in books, use his scales to carefully measure goods against weights to achieve fair balance. Yes, this wise man used the best instruments to gain answers and, yes, the Flatheads could rely on this proven friend to help them. If so, soon, for, as he had said, his involvements possibly could, of necessity, change his perspective on the Indians he had worked so long to serve. Then, too, he was beginning to like the whiskey too much.

Little Coyote galloped his mare to the fort and unobtrusively sat on a stool outside Owen's office while the trader was talking to two men. Soon they picked up their gear and lugged it toward the dormitory room as Owen lighted a candle and his pipe, then picked up a small, black book. At Little Coyote's firm knock, Owen said "Enter" and motioned for his friend to take the chair next to his yet-piled-up desk.

"Two days remain, John Owen, before you will talk to Victor and the sub-chiefs."

Owen nodded.

"You have the school for children. Can you make the council like the school, tell us more of what lies ahead? What will we face? Light many candles to dispel our great darkness. Those of us who know white man's language well could interpret to those who scarcely know it, or have learned some, but pretend to comprehend little so while among white men they will hear more."

Owen smiled. He filled a small clay pipe and held it and a candle out to his friend. They thoughtfully smoked for a time while sounds of clumping boots in the dormitory, and a few halloos from men moving about the fort's grounds, broke the silence. The trader looked long and hard into Little Coyote's eyes.

"I will do this. I have learned from your people, too, strangely, perhaps, more about the Black Robes' religion through your chiefs and their example. The Black Robes and I often disagree about . . . well, seemingly more practical matters, but I am inclining toward their religion. They have put out some good books, too. More importantly, I'm learning they mostly live as they write. They help others. Yes, I will do my best at the council. I will tell you this. As I said before, the main reason I have held onto this agent's job so long is I figured I could help you more. It has been a losing battle for me, too. With Victor's cabin nearby I'll be able to help with advice as I can. Trouble is, some of your people again aren't listening to him."

"Thank you, John Owen. You make a good teacher. We will profit much from *this* council with white man."

Again their eyes met. Both smiled. "Ummm. We'll see." Owen moved the candle closer to his chair and once more picked up the black book.

Fourteen sub-chiefs and leading warriors were seated in the dormitory room when John Owen arrived for the council. There were more cordial greetings for his brother, Frank, who again had returned briefly from one of his trading trips through the mountains.

Flatheads who did or did not understand English savvied maps. They drew them often in earth with stick, knife or finger and from memories that stored a particular stream, stone, cliff or hill, valley or mountain. John had tacked up three maps to catch the light coming through the windows from westering Sun. He had left sufficient space between them so people could gather about them if they wished. Little Coyote, Victor and Charlot would assist the trader's explanations.

The major pointed to and explained the first and most easily understood map—that drawn by Father DeSmet and which Father Joset had tossed in "to boot" during the Mission sale to the trader. The map showed the rough outline of the boundaries of the various Indian nations and the locations of the Jesuit missions.

Sun scarcely had moved when Owen pointed to the next map outline, boldly drawn as the Northwest, on a large piece of packing paper. Onto this he drew and described "the probable outline of a future territory and state people were talking about naming 'Montana.'" Sun descended from the top row of window panes to the second while Owen spoke of politicians and of gold rushes and land rushes, territories and states within the nation of the United States. He remained on these matters until the room darkened a bit and until all minds were at least somewhat enlightened. Though tired from the day's hard work, the trader answered many questions.

The third heavily outlined map also was in the shape of the possible Territory of Montana. But it was blank. John Owen handed his brother the stick of charcoal, then re-tacked the map in better light. "Frank, here, is going to talk now. He knows much of your language. Lately, he has been traveling much more than I have—the Northwest, even back East." John raised an admonitory finger. "Listen well." He disappeared into his office, but quickly returned, seemingly refreshed, as Frank slowly started his talk.

First, he drew in the general outlines of the various reservations they had learned about during the treaty talks: 1851—Assiniboin, Sioux, Gros Ventre and Piegan; 1851—Mandan, Arikara and, again, Gros Ventre; 1851—Crow; 1855—Blackfeet; 1855—the hated Flathead reserve, and south of that, including their beloved Bitter Root Valley, public domain and the Flatheads, Pend d'Oreilles and Kutenais. Frank's charcoal stick had divided off all the map now, except a large area south and east of the last named division. He resharpened the charcoal and, amid growing rumbles of discontent, marked in and explained: 1855—Blackfeet, and hunting ground for all. The map was full.

"*Hoy!*" There was silence then at Victor's command to quit, and, after a time, some laughter that they all were inclined to be unhappy at this white friend of theirs who was only outlining, trying mightily to explain, what others had done.

"I am happy that you left your arrows and lances outside, because here I go again." Frank laughed now as he again sharpened his charcoal.

He told about the familiar Mullan Wagon Road route from Walla Walla to Fort Benton, then represented it by a tiny line of arrows entering the outline of Montana at Mullan Pass to the west, eastward to the Missoula country and continuing to another Mullan Pass, arcing north and northeastward to Great Falls then Fort Benton. Now Frank moved to the eastern border edge of the map and said, "Fort Union," which all present fully understood. "Major Alexander Culbertson's old road," he said, and began sketching in a tiny line of lances pointing ever west, up the Milk River until it curved south to Fort Benton, too.

The Flatheads' interest grew, and Frank heightened it by asking them to name their old familiar trails that white man now was following, ending, finally, with Old Manwell's through Ross' Hole into the Bitter Root.

Silently, the Flatheads looked at this stark, visual representation of this place that likely would be called "Montana."

"Might as well tell them about Captain Raynolds' and Lieutenant Maynadier's expedition in '59, Frank." John had returned from another trip to his office.

"Raynolds and Maynadier were sent to locate the best trails into the Montana and Idaho country from these central plains here." Frank made a large charcoal X on the wall below the map. Again the charcoal lines on the map. "Captain Raynolds said wagons can go from the Platte River along the Bighorn Mountains, down the Bighorn River to the Yellowstone and over to the Judith River, then also to Fort Benton." Several of the Flatheads nodded. They had encountered some of these military explorers. "Raynolds said the best way is from the Platte, through the Bighorn Mountains to Three Forks, to Hell Gate Pass, here, to join with the Mullan Road."

Sun sank. The maps began to blur. From outside came the voices of three newly arriving whites inquiring where the dormitory was. The Flatheads stood, ready to depart.

"Hold on!" John Owen stood, steadying himself against a bunk. He reached for the charcoal. "Frank, tell those pilgrims to hold on for a while." The trader motioned for the Flatheads to step closer to the third map. "Don't forget Stevens. Remember, he came here first to see where a railroad could run." The trader drew a final, heavy line across the map. "Yes, there is much to think about. Don't know if this has helped much, but we had to try. A man has to live with himself."

The fourteen Flatheads silently walked outside and past the three white men waiting for Frank to admit them to the dormitory. The Indians stood together for a time, then silently broke into smaller groups and disappeared into the gloom.

After a restless night, Little Coyote trudged from his lodge to John Owen's office. The healing leg needed the exercise. He wanted to borrow the maps and study them before working further on his manuscript and the story skin. Perhaps he could dispel many questions clouding his mind like that bank of fog rolling in from the south.

Old Manwell greeted him as he opened the fort's south gate and drove a wagon toward the river. The office door was closed. All else was quiet. Little Coyote sensed the pair of eyes watching him from the top floor of a bastion. Tired, the seer propped his old lance against the building and sat down on the wooden walkway, leaned against the structure, drew his blanket more snugly about him and dozed, vaguely aware of the sounds of the awakening courtyard.

"Damned, lazy, no-good Indian!" The words struck Little Coyote's ears as the speaker stumbled against his outstretched legs. At another time, before the grizzly attack, the warrior would have been on his feet and confronting this white man. Instead, he threw back his blanket and looked upward at the long, unkempt hair, bewhiskered face and badly sunburned, peeling nose and ears. The sour whiskey smell on breath and filthy-clothing odor reached downward.

"Well, move! Get off this walkway!" The man prepared to kick.

"Lay off, Cal. Don't blame this Indian, here, because you got drunk last night on that damned rotgut you picked up south of here." The man's two companions seized the drunk's elbows. He struggled, boots pounding a tattoo on the walkway.

"Yes, get that scum out of here!" Owen had opened his door. He extended his hand to Little Coyote and helped pull him up. They walked inside. Soon, they walked out of the office, the maps under Little Coyote's arm. The three whites were riding out of the fort and toward the trail along the river.

"Sorry, Little Coyote."

"Yes, John Owen. I understand. There is much sorrow in the world." He shook the agent's hand. "For all of us."

"Yes, well . . . *adios*."

Little Coyote's plan this day to ponder the marks on the maps, what they meant now and could mean in the future, was not to be. He could walk slowly, unerringly, through this silent fog to his lodge, but his mind strayed onto this trail, then that, as increasingly it was wont to do.

"How do you think, my friend; rather, what *do* you think?" John Owen had asked him soon after his return from Enfinger camp. The trader proudly had waved his arm to encompass all his fort. With a grin, Little Coyote quickly had replied, "Like all others, John Owen, Indian and white, to answer your first question. To answer your second, events are occurring too fast for me or my people to understand all the white man knows, and expects without, mostly, trying to understand us."

With effort, the warrior could have scrambled upright at Fort Owen and put the ancient lance head against the insulting drunk's throat. At the instant of that impulse, another part of his mind had told him the penalty for that silliness to assuage deeply injured pride would have been an even greater limp in the mending leg. The drunk was not worth that.

As Little Coyote neared his lodge, he acknowledged he had failed to fully awaken at the drunk's approach. True, he was tired from little sleep after thinking about the Owen brothers' words, but the greater truth was the fact that his body was seventy years old! Not like that of Lance at Fort Nez Percés so long ago when Brandt had attempted to crash the heavy gate against him. The young brave had protected himself by hearing Brandt's approach, quickly scrambling out of the way and . . . But enough!

The medicine man heard his mare nicker. Soon he could see her, facing him and pulling at the rope as though anxious to greet him, to urge the two forget rope and bitter/sweet memories this day. He gave her a reassuring pat on the neck as she sniffed the maps. Soon she was bearing Little Coyote and a saddlebag of food and the carefully rolled maps toward St. Mary's Peak, yet well hidden this . . . yes, first day in the ninth Moon of the Harvest of Ripe Things. "White man's 1862," he said aloud, and the mare momentarily slowed as though trying to respond to a puzzling command. He spoke reassuringly in their tongue and, while giving her free rein, part of his mind seemed to be trying to tell the rest that some great truth, some revelation beyond those told on the maps, was trying to emerge as surely as was Sun rising now, though obscured by the valley fog. He had had such feelings before, but not so persistent, strong as this horse under him that was slowing and beginning to veer off the road. He gave the left rein a gentle pull to guide her back to the road—and himself to a trail of what white man might call "coincidence." He would follow it throughout a long day indeed.

"*E*, it is you, Little Coyote. You, too, are restless and tired, or are we both groping in this fog as though searching for the unknown trail to the sand hills?"

Chief Moses' voice was strong though a bit slurred because of the missing teeth. He stood there, holding his blanket around his old shoulders and leaning heavily on his lance.

"Not the sand hills yet, Moses, for either of us. I ponder the words the Owen brothers spoke at our meeting."

"I, too, think mostly of the second map showing the reservations from the Stevens treaty I would not sign. As I walk this road, I pray to God, to His Son, Jesus Christ, that I never will walk from our valley forever. And you go to the mountain to do the same?"

"Yes, I will pray there, too. But not all the way up the mountain. You, though older, walk better than I."

"This going to the mountain is proper. Before Clark and Lewis came, the Mandans, now mostly gone, told us mostly the same story the Black Robes tell about the great flood and how the great boat landed on a mountain with Noah, his family and all the live animals. Too, the Black Robes told me that the first Moses went to the mountain for God to give him the command-ments all should follow. I tell the people this, but many say, 'If white man would follow them, our lives would be easier.' Yes, Jesus prayed on the mountain, and died on a small one. Yes, the mountains are closer to God. And He has spoken to me there, too, in His mysterious way."

"Yes, Victor and Charlot have told me. I have food in the

bag."

"No. I will return to my lodge before others come to seek me. I do not think I have settled my anxieties on this walk, though I have prayed hard for many things I have received and have not received. Yes, even for Stevens!" The old chief spat, then signed deep thanks and farewell. He walked into the brightening fog that flowed thinly, then heavily, about him until all but the face was a shadow that turned a final time and, in the blink of an eye, disappeared.

Little Coyote and his horse drank at the river, crossed it and began climbing almost immediately. The animal stopped above fog level to blow. The seer dismounted and led her up the trail until he could go no more. Wearily, he carried the saddlebag to a large, sloping boulder from which he could look down on the grayish-white sea. He pushed the bag under his head. Yes, he would drowse. Fast-warming Sun would clear the valley and awaken him.

Fog. Out of the medley of old and new thoughts—growing, disjointing, merging, changing during the seer's state of half-awake/half-asleep, the fog predominated. His mind told him: *Sit! Awaken!* Contrarily, another part of the mind joined forces with his tired body and kept him there to fix, at last and inexplicably, on Stevens. Stevens, about whom Owen, shaking his head, had said, "created your reservations and now is fighting to free the slaves during this damned war." Stevens, who had limped to his chair to sit alone in the pre-dawn at the Council Grove treaty site a long seven years ago. Council Grove: So close to where Antelope and Lance rested in Mother Earth. How grateful Little Coyote was to the Good Spirit that, frequently, He had let their spirits join, though briefly, with his own. Six times fog had enveloped and moved past Stevens there at the grove. Then his seat was empty when the fog had swept away for the seventh time.

The seer struggled to awaken. He must get up. But he could not, as had dying Broken Tooth seven years earlier in prophesying the death of Stevens. Was Little Coyote's mare nervously nickering, whinnying, joining with a band of screaming horses now, the sound intensifying unbearably while distant lightning and thunder seemed to flash and roll ever closer, terrifyingly crashing until it was all about him, threatening to strike this very boulder and trees as earth exploded upward?

He sat up, hearing himself shouting "*Stem*? *Suwe*?" There was no answer to his "What?" But as he sat there bewildered, in the last large cloud of fog wafting upward and past him, he would be able to tell only himself with certainty the remainder of his life that the astonishing response to his shouted "Who?" was the figure of a soldier holding aloft a shiny sabre the instant before his face turned toward the seer, then bloodily erupted as Stevens fell from his horse.

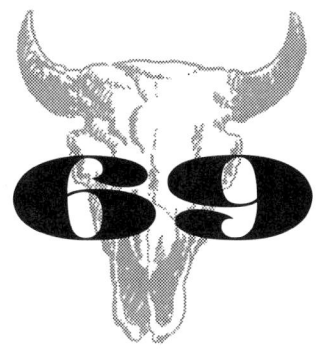

T he Indians peered beyond their fire into the growing dusk as the slamming, kicking sounds reached them from the wretched two-room cabin serving as the Jocko Indian Agency headquarters. John Owen's cuss words reached them, too, as he emerged from the structure. He gripped the door pull with both hands. Lifting the door as he kicked its base, he forced it back into the crude frame amid muffled protests from two of the other six whites who would participate in the pow-wow. The remaining four sleeping in the Indian lodge remained silent, but some crows, disturbed by the racket, settled on the walls of three decaying, roofless structures and cawed reproachfully as Owen neared the fire. He stopped in an abandoned, weed-strewn garden plot.

"Victor, Ambrose, Little Coyote."

Chief, third chief and seer approached him, closely watched by Isaac, Adolph, Arlee, Alexander and Stanislaus. Owen wore clean clothing, his beard was neatly trimmed and he had walked with a sprightly gait despite the heavy bag slung over his shoulder. He lowered the bag next to the agency's plow. With broken beam and missing share, the implement was rusting in a weed-grown furrow. Owen swept his arm to encompass the agency. "Dear

God, is this all that Stevens' 'Flathead Nation' has to show in the twelve years since his treaty?" Had the major looked at two bright stars glittering in the darkening southeast sky, the words would have seemed a prayer.

Owen reached inside the bag and handed a smaller one to Victor, its contents clinking during the transfer. "I'd be grateful if you'd stash this with your plunder until after the pow-wow. I'm going to have a hard enough time declining Wells'." Victor gravely accepted the bag. As he turned to carry it toward a tree, Owen said, "If you'll wait a moment." He looked toward the fire. "I reckon you're pow-wowing with Chief Alexander and the others about what you'll say tomorrow?"

"Yes, Ambrose will talk most for us. The whites know I refuse to leave the Bitter Root. They will listen better to others in the hope they will persuade me. We have little hope John Wells will be any better agent than Hutchins and Chapman, who lived in this . . . this place." Victor nodded toward the ruined buildings. "Alexander says the Pend d'Oreilles and Kutenais on the reservation continue to depend on St. Ignatius Mission for help, as we do the Black Robes at St. Mary's—and with the good help of our friend, John Owen. Alexander tells us the people here stopped listening to Wells almost as soon as he arrived three months ago." Victor shook his head. "He is to be pitied, for he appears *qweu*." The chief shifted the whiskey bottles to his left hand, made a fist with his right, raised it to his forehead and moved it in a small circle to the left. "Yes, crazy. But come, smoke with our brothers."

Major Owen smoked the pipe before passing around three loaves of bread, a crock of huckleberry jam and thick slices of roasted elk meat. Those from the Bitter Root ate almost ravenously while Owen talked.

"I've learned Wells has been a clerk in the Indian Office in Washington, D.C. He doesn't know the situation here, except there's nothing to work with despite all the supplies sent and money spent. He might have some power in Washington."

"He fears animals seek to eat him," Alexander grunted between bites.

"He told me the man without legs, Shaaft, is his son, who came here, but quickly departed." Ambrose, who could lead with easy humor and strong will, shook his head pityingly. "Isaac saw him talking to the flag when he carried it from the cabin."

Isaac swallowed. "Yes, I helped him hang it atop the lodge, and he again was talking inside the empty lodge, as I departed."

The men resumed eating while Owen lighted his pipe. "Wells is a friend of the Great Father, Johnson, but I suggest we consider talking more to the other whites than Wells. Fitz Stubbs is one of his workmen. You all know Angus McDonald from the Hudson's Bay post. He's some of the competition that's ruining me, but he's married to a fine Indian woman and is honest. Thomas Pomeroy and Jasper Rand—well, they're judges and I don't know much about them. Supposed to represent the whites in Montana Territory, to listen for them. Whatever we say might go to the Territorial Legislature, but I don't think they've got much power yet, or understanding for the Indians. Politics in the Territory are more mixed up than a bull elk with twenty cows during the rut. Another reason I didn't go to Virginia City when I was elected to the Legislature last year."

Owen started another loaf of bread around the circle, looked at Ambrose, then grinned.

"Are you 'Canterbury Pilgrims' still planning to talk on the things we discussed with Father Giorda while we were traveling here?"

Ambrose's ready laugh further broke the solemnity of the circle.

"Yes, Alexander and the others agree this is a good plan. I, the Knight, will talk of the Stevens treaty and the growing disaffection even among our own people, and the changing face of our Bitter Root Valley. Father Giorda, the Nun's Priest, will tell about the missions, beset by a growing lack of funds at a time of our people's greatest needs. And you, John Owen, will be the Pardoner, to talk of the effects of the increasing lack of buffalo and the difficulty getting to them, as well as emphasize the quality and commitment of government agents. And the wars. The council will, indeed, be glad to hear us!"

Owen tapped ashes from his pipe and, in this rare instance, laughed aloud.

"I will." He pulled a small, narrow ledger book from inside his coat. Holding it between thumb and index finger, he flipped it up and down. "My sermon is in this. I thought about it while we rode here and wrote it down during rest stops. There are no women among us, so there will be no Wife of Bath." He pushed the bag of food nearer the dying fire. "Here's some grub for morning, and I've got more for tomorrow. See you at the lodge. I'll try to have Wells do mostly listening soon as he opens the pow-wow. All he's got are words. There's nothing else here." Owen signed *farewell*.

More promises. There was silence around the glowing coals—then some laughter when pounding and rasping noises came from the direction of the dilapidated cabin. Sudden silence, then Owen's cuss words rose above all, followed by a mighty wrenching sound and the crash of the falling door. Candlelight and argumentative words still were issuing from the cabin as the eight Indians sought their blankets. One by one they fell asleep as Little Coyote answered questions about Father Giorda's references to the Canterbury Tales after they had set out from St. Mary's Mission. Soon the seer was talking only to Ambrose about even more serious matters.

A smile had flitted across the care-worn face of Father Joseph Giorda before he mounted his horse to set out northward with the delegation to the pow-wow. Such satisfaction that he again had brought here beloved Father Ravalli and Brother Claessens! They and recently arrived Father Jerome D'Aste had joined with the many Flatheads to wish them a safe journey filled with many accomplishments. Then the well-wishers had trailed behind ailing Second Chief Moses to attend mass in the new chapel they had constructed with the assistance of Brother Claessens while the whites were building a town nearby. The orators had proclaimed the town's name would be Stevensville, to honor General Isaac Stevens who, near the moment of victory, had been shot in the head on September 1, 1862, while bravely leading a charge amid a great thunderstorm at Chantilly, Virginia.

Victor had halted the delegation near Travelers Rest. While the people were feasting on trout thrown from an almost isolated pool of the river, Father Giorda had likened their party to the pilgrims on their way to the Shrine of St. Thomas à Becket. "All life is a pilgrimage," he had recounted often enough during strenuous travels in Washington, Idaho and Montana country. His toil had taken such a toll on his health that for a time he had been relieved as Superior of the Rocky Mountain Missions, overwhelmed by the problems occasioned by the mighty influx of people moving ever-west to where Sun set in the western sea. As the hungry Black Robe had put down the skeleton of one small trout and begun roasting another, he had nodded agreeably to Victor's statement, "We must plan for this pow-wow Wells has called."

They had begun doing so soon after continuing northward from the tiny settlement of Missoula. There, Father Giorda had entered the store of Frank Worden and Christopher Higgins, who had served as packmaster for Stevens. The priest carried out a bag of food, then greeted each Flathead and handed him three twists of tobacco. The Flatheads silently accepted this offering as one of peace—or shame, perhaps. They well remembered that only a short time earlier Higgins allegedly had persuaded some of the Bitter Root settlers to ask Governor Green Clay Smith to give them guns so they could resist the Flatheads, who were said to be setting fire to their fields and hay throughout the valley and beyond. Smith, recognizing the allegation was based on a lie, had refused, as much to the satisfaction of many of the white settlers as to the Indians, themselves.

On the opening day of the pow-wow, Agent Wells hastily emerged from the cabin with suspenders over his underwear. After a prolonged stay in the outhouse, which slowly was sinking toward the west, he re-entered the cabin, pausing to look briefly at the fallen door.

A wisp of smoke rose from the chimney and soon Wells carried a basin of water outside, where he washed and shaved.

He was dressed in a crumpled, black suit, apparently a new shirt and cravat, and was perspiring mightily as he hurried to greet profusely each small group beginning to assemble near the lodge on loan from a Pend d'Oreille family. The old American flag, blue almost faded to white, hung dispiritedly from the lodge.

Wells brought the meeting to order by banging a pan with a rock, and equally as unceremoniously opened it by stating he "thought the people should come together to talk and see what was needed for the good of all."

The white delegation appeared friendly; those in it were good listeners during the early part of this first day. As Father Giorda started speaking, Sun began to warm the lodge, so the Indians rolled up the walls a bit to disclose listeners from St. Ignatius and elsewhere seated outside the shelter. Father Giorda stressed the work of St. Ignatius Mission, the many activities of which now included a boarding school taught by nuns and the newly re-established St. Mary's, "where we serve the Flatheads and the increasing number of white settlers. Unfortunately," he said, "treaty goods seldom reached the Indians because those who purchase, ship and distribute them have forgotten the seventh commandment. Those the Indians do receive are ill-suited to their needs. Consequently, the missions are performing what this . . . this Indian Agency should be doing.

"Last year," the priest went on, "we had to close our St. Peter's Mission among the Blackfeet because more Sioux began moving into their hunting grounds." The Black Robe shook his head wonderingly. "These new breech-loading rifles the whites trade to the Indians cause fearful destruction, and many tribes now have them. The Blackfeet have killed perhaps fifty men from the confederated tribes in the past two years. Because our poorly armed people here now must face renewed savagery when they seek the buffalo, we are aware that more than a dozen of our people have starved to death this year alone! As they labor in the Mission gardens and fields for their daily bread, they are not impressed by the agrarian example this place has received both funds and equipment to set." The Black Robe looked at his clenched hands and, almost abruptly, sat down.

Wells then languidly pointed at Ambrose, who at first spoke carefully, quietly, then increasingly heatedly, about the oft-broken treaty.

"Soon the whites will outnumber us in the Bitter Root Valley," Ambrose said, "and while many are friendly and often helpful, we must carefully pick our way around fences and seek permission from some to cross the valley bottom land—even the settlements along the creeks and hillsides, too. Father Giorda spoke about repeating guns. There is the whiskey, too. Four years ago, I had to lead our warriors against some wagoneers carrying whiskey. We killed no whites, but we had to restrain our younger braves from doing so. There are many who are angry. Blackfeet, others, including whites, coming and going, have stolen hundreds of our horses. At another time we would have ridden out well-armed and brought them back, their manes decorated with the hair of the thieves."

Ambrose clapped his hands together in anger, startling Wells, who had been slowly and unevenly swiveling his head as though tracing and retracing the contour of the rolled wall of the lodge. "Yes, Father Giorda has told you in truth about our needs. The agent, Charles Hutchins, who followed John Owen, got us very little, though he talked much. He asked Sidney Edgerton, who you called Governor of the Territory of Montana, for money for goods. How did Edgerton respond? Hutchins told us Edgerton said he hoped the government would kill all Indian titles to land so it can be sold!"

Seemingly encouraged that his first loud clap had stimulated the listeners, Ambrose again clapped, this time more loudly. "Yes," he said, "and how much help did we receive from . . ." Ambrose paused, then carefully pronounced "Augustus H. Chapman?" The chief began strutting about the center of the lodge until all the Indians and some of the whites put their hands over their mouths. "Augustus H. Chapman. He talked big and promised much, but did little because Hutchins sold the agency animals and other property to white men. Chapman told us he had asked for more money for the agency. Then the marshal named John X. Beidler, who carries revolvers in his pants, came this spring to arrest Chapman for doing what Hutchins had done!"

Judges Pomeroy and Rand sat erect in their decrepit chairs and whispered momentarily when Ambrose walked first in front of Wells, then approached them.

"Why did the man who acted as governor, Thomas Meagher, come to our Bitter Root Valley while Edgerton was seeing the Great Father in Washington, D.C.?" Ambrose was strutting again. "Why did Meagher boast that he had one-thousand militiamen to fight the Sioux, if they went to war? We are not the Sioux here. We are not the Sioux in our Bitter Root Valley! Our Indian brothers told us this Meagher hurried all over Montana to show he is a great warrior. We are told he was—in the Civil War. So were many others. Now more of them come here. Do they seek to battle the red men now that they have set the black men free? Do they seek to battle the whites who steal our land and start to kill off the buffalo? After seeing us, if Meagher really saw us at all—sick, poor, hungry—he told our friend John Owen that almost all the land the Stevens treaty set aside for the Indians should be taken by the whites. We remain friendly to the whites, though many abuse us. We learn from the past. Cannot white man do so? The Cayuses, Yakimas, Palouses, Spokanes, Coeur d'Alenes and others could not bear to be caged on reservations, then watch the white men come into the cages and demand the gold there, and the animals, now even the cages.

"My heart saddens for our friends, the Nez Percé, with whom we long have hunted. Recently the great chief Tuekakas, Joseph the Older, of the Wallowa Nez Percé, sent some of his band to again strengthen our hunt for the buffalo. This band have signed no treaty with white man. Tuekakas did not come, because he is sick in body and in spirit. His son, Hinmahtooyahlatkekht, also Joseph, of twenty-three summers, did join us. And we also came to know better his brother, young Ollokot."

Angus McDonald stirred and quietly signed to Ambrose the whites were becoming tired.

"Tuekakas told us many bands of Nez Percé are angry. More than fifteen-thousand white men, most of them seeking gold, have moved onto the Nez Percé reservation. They even build towns in that reservation, too."

Wells sat upright. "Better get on with it, man," he said, and again sat back.

"Now the miners are here—in the Deer Lodge Valley, Bannack, Virginia City, Butte, Helena, Diamond City, the upper Yellowstone, the Musselshell forks, elsewhere."

Again Wells sat erect.

"I *will* say this!" Ambrose again spoke more quietly, carefully. "Now I speak for our chief, Little Bear Claw, who said Chief Tuekakas recently told these words to his son, Hinmahtoo-yahlatkekht: 'Always remember that your father never sold his country . . . A few years more, and white men will be all around you. They have their eye on this land. My son, never forget my dying words. This land holds your father's body. Never sell the bones of your father and mother.'"

Ambrose prepared to sit down. "Little Bear Claw has repeated these words to *his* son, Little Grizzly Bear Claw."

Victor was looking straight ahead, stiff, unmoving, his head high, jaw set, lips curved downward as though frozen—never to smile again.

Suddenly, Little Coyote felt cold, despite the heat inside this lodge.

Wells did not awaken the camp the second day. John Owen did—an Indian at a time, then the whites simultaneously. Victor started the process by touching Little Coyote's lips, to signal to awaken silently in the pre-dawn. Both men leaned on their elbows to watch the trader walk toward the Indians' equipage piled near the tree. He lifted a bottle, began walking rapidly in the direction of the privy, then, silently observed by eight pairs of eyes, resolutely strode back to the tree and replaced the bottle. Moments later he was flailing away at some of the boards that had fallen off the ruined barn. Rusty nails began shrieking their resistance to the hammer claws, then bang, bang, bang, he straightened them on a flat rock. Picking up the fallen door, Owen eyed it and then began hacking off long shavings with his knife. He held the door to the frame, evaluating both before leaning the door on the cabin and hammering nails into various parts of the frame. Satisfied the door would fit, he put it on the ground, drove more nails into the three leather hinge straps, replaced the door, then nailed the other ends of the straps to the frame and cabin wall. The door swung easily. He fitted it with an inside wire hook; he added a nail, bent into a circle on the inside frame, to hold it. Satisfied, he tossed the hammer into an old pan and strode to the creek.

He broke open a small bale of dried beef. While he and his Indian friends waited for it to cook, he sought out Father Giorda, who was reading his breviary nearby. Red and white, they ate meat and raisins and drank strong coffee, for Owen many cups of coffee—black!

Soon he was carrying a kettle of water and his small kit of eating utensils toward the lodge. Quietly, he built a fire and chopped up considerable dried beef. When it was cooking he made a large pot of fresh coffee and sliced several loaves of bread. He mixed a batter of water, flour and salt and stirred it into the kettle.

"Breakfast!" he shouted as Sun broke through pink and golden clouds hiding the highest peaks of the Mission Range. As he began serving coffee and the beef and gravy on bread to the sleepy delegation, Victor grunted, "You watch John Owen. When he does woman-work, he has a plan."

The trader carried the chairs outside the lodge and arranged them in an arc near the fire. He evidently made the same remark to each guest as he sat down, because they talked as they ate instead of pondering individual sleepy thoughts. Owen dropped the empty tin plates into the kettle and again served coffee, beckoning for the Indians to come for more, too. They sat somewhat apart, quietly listening to talk of Crazy Horse's victory at Lodge Trail Ridge, the Indians' defeats in the Hayfield and Wagon Box fights, and, finally, this year's disastrous campaign by General Hancock against the Sioux and Cheyenne across Kansas. There, a lieutenant colonel named Custer had worn out his 7th Cavalry trying to corral and whip them.

"Let's wait and see what comes of the peace commission Congress appointed in July." Judge Pomeroy waved his hand, declining more coffee. He lit a cigar. "The three generals will hold treaties at Medicine Lodge Creek in Kansas and at Fort Laramie. If they can't get those Indians to accept reservations, there's a real possibility the problems will spill over into our Territory."

Owen remained silent, except to urge the delegation to finish the coffee, "before Mr. Wells starts the pow-wow."

The men carried this distant treaty talk into the lodge along with their chairs. Wells, cravat askew, sat impassively, a hand atop each knee. When the discussion ended and all looked expectantly at him, he pointed to Owen: "Major Owen will talk to us."

The trader moved his chair to face the whites on theirs and the Indians on their buffalo robes. He stroked his beard before he began speaking, easily, confidently, gently, as though he were in his Fort Owen office.

"Talk around coffee this morning seemed to center on reservations, and I reckon that's proper, but apparently Mr. Wells wants us to set our sights on the Flathead Nation the late Major General Stevens established with his treaty. I know you gentlemen"—he looked at the whites—"have traveled rather widely. You understand most of the problems arising from the whites' interest in land, gold, commerce and peace, and wish to learn more about the problems arising from the notion most whites insist Indians be 'concentrated,' so the whites' plans can go ahead. I'd say I'm pretty well acquainted with this historical process elsewhere. I came from Pennsylvania, where it started soon after Penn landed. Matter of fact, I was sutler to the army there.

"You're probably tired of hearing the problems that arose from the Stevens treaties, because the Cayuse and Yakima and other wars came pretty close to home. Now we face similar problems all around us here in Montana Territory. Try crowding a grizzly that's been free to roam all his life and he either will kill you or you will kill him or, put too many mice into a box and they'll fight one another, and bite your fingers if you put them within reach."

Owen looked at Judge Pomeroy. "We hope the Medicine

Lodge Creek and Fort Laramie treaties General Sherman will conduct will solve many problems. But we need to keep our sights on, seems to me, why we're here. I take it we're to learn what can be done for the Flathead Nation, and show them we're grateful they've remained peaceful despite obvious neglect." Owen swept his arm to encompass the agency area. "And there's the fact that the wars elsewhere have funneled all kinds of people with all kinds of problems into this neck of the woods, intensifying the burdens of the people in the Jocko here and in the Bitter Root."

Owen began to reach inside his coat pocket, then evidently changed his mind. Now he looked briefly at Little Coyote, then at Wells. "I don't want you gentlemen to misunderstand me now. I have had the opportunity, while in the Bitter Root, to study the proud history of the Flathead people. I have no doubt that, despite the small numbers Father Giorda gave you, thousands upon thousands of other Indians from Idaho, Washington, Montana and elsewhere would follow that man seated right there, along with his chiefs here and in their valley." He pointed at Victor, seated on the buffalo robe, old army pants covering his lower body, an old, buckskin shirt the upper, head crowned by a floppy hat under which hung two braids of silver-streaked hair with a single eagle feather tied in. But the face! Unmoving as though carved from granite, the eyes staring straight at all the whites as though looking through them into a future that only he could see.

In the silence, Pomeroy threw away his cigar butt and ignited another. Owen quietly filled and fired his pipe. Ever so slowly, the smoke curled upward. Seemingly grateful for some movement to break the silence, the whites lifted their heads and watched the smoke whisk outside.

Owen reached into his coat and brought out his small ledger book. He slowly waved it up and down, much as had Father Mengarini his willow baton when directing the children's choir at St. Mary's so long ago.

"If I've learned anything about what needs to be done, it's that the settlers have to see things at least a little through the Indians' eyes; most *whites* demand the *Indians understand them*— or else! I keep journals of my experiences. Maybe someday someone will be interested in them. I'm going to read what a white pilgrim from Salt Lake City told me four years ago:

"'That Shoshone chief, Bear Hunter, ought to a knowed he couldn't keep the Mormons from moving north from Salt Lake City, and folks from coming to the gold strikes here in Montana. Damn good that Bear Hunter and more'n two-hundred of his Shoshonis got it good at Bear River. Can't keep white folks cooped up. Trails through Utah to the Boise River and Beaver Head are open, and they're acoming through!'"

Owen turned a page. "Here's how another pilgrim answered that first statement in my office: 'Yeh, and the Navahos and Apaches learned the same lessons. Gineral Carleton sent ol' Kit Carson after them Apaches, and he told him not to do any palavering with them. Kill the men and capture the women and children. Seems a good lesson to tell all the Injuns.'"

A couple of chairs creaked, and "*te, te*" came from the buffalo robes. Owen, understanding the "bad, bad," nodded and turned another page.

"I wrote this down after one of the many settlers in the Bitter Root, who likes the Flatheads and gets along with them, beat hell out of one of the newcomers who said this. He was standing in line behind some Flatheads to trade with me. The newcomer objected because, with me, it's first-come-first-served, Indian or white. Here's what he said while he still had most of his front teeth:

"'These damned Flatheads need a few Minnesotans or Coloradans to teach 'em their place. Put 'em on their reservations, and see that they stay there, or else. The Santee Sioux shoulda' stayed on their reservation along the upper Minnesota River. Cost more'n eight-hundred whites their lives when the Santees busted out in '62. Thirty-eight of 'em wuz hung, and there woulda' been more, three-hundred or so, if President Lincoln had kept his nose out of it.

'And they shoulda' caught and hung the Santees that took off for Dakota to infect the Teton Sioux, Cheyennes and Arapahos, and get 'em to fightin' cuz they didn't like the gold miners comin' up the Missouri to Montana. Injuns claimed they wuz afraid they'd have to trade *their* huntin' grounds for reservations. Hah! Their huntin' grounds. Them Coloradans didn't get fooled. We sure as hell didn't! There wuz old Chief Black Kettle at Sand Creek, claimin' he wuzn't fightin' whites. Runned up our American flag and a white one, too, when Colonel Chivington come up with seven-hundred or so of us in '64. Them howitzers sure showed 'em. Yes, sir! Minnesotans or Coloradans could sure teach these Flatheads what for. So could Owen. He could clean out this place mighty fast for white folks with that howitzer of his!'"

Owen clapped his book closed with both hands and returned it to his pocket. He nodded toward Angus McDonald who, though friendly enough, generally had remained silent the past two days. "Angus there most likely would agree that Indians are going to continue to object to construction of such trails as the Bozeman from the North Platte to the gold camps here, and to the erection of Army forts such as C.F. Smith on the Bighorn River, and Camp Cooke on the south shore of the Missouri just west of the Judith River. The whites are compressing the Indians more and more. There could be hell to pay if they keep this up." Owen again looked at McDonald as though for affirmation, the gaze lingering until all heads turned, whereupon that trader grimly nodded.

Owen turned his chair as though preparing to sit down. His right hand began shaking the chair. He suddenly looked completely spent.

"Gentlemen, all the plains tribes that the whites are trying to ring with forts, trying to force into signing treaties, and trying to put on reservations are going to look at the Indians who already have signed. They're going to see how they are treated—how the promises have been kept. Other Indians respect the Flatheads, and will see if the whites do. Look at them here and in the Bitter Root after following a trail of broken promises since '55. They're hungry, poor, diseased, increasingly discouraged and stolen from. Yet, they've never fought white man. If the Black Robes and some of the decent whites in the Bitter Root weren't helping them when others won't, they'd virtually disappear." Owen raised his shaking arm and pointed at the delegation. "If you right now

794

were, say, a Sioux, a Cheyenne or a Comanche, how would you judge the worth of treaties?"

Owen walked from the lodge and headed for the Indians' pile of gear.

Later, when Wells concluded the pow-wow with the astonishing comment he was pleased to see the Flathead Nation doing so well, Little Coyote and Victor sought out Owen. They found him sitting next to an old tree stump, facing the now pink-colored Mission Range. He was drunk.

"John Owen," Victor said quietly, "your voice and McDonald's nod helped our spirits, though we question if the other whites will remember any words when they leave the Jocko. We are grateful."

Owen lolled his head back until it touched the stump. He fumbled in his coat pocket. "Take thish ledger book, Coyote," he said, slurring. "Maybe you can use it. 'N Victor, I've owed your people shomething. I've encouraged shome whites to settle in the Bitter Root, ones I figured were good, because I know that eventually, if I were there or not, they'd come in anyway." He pulled at the half-empty bottle. "An', an', with the Mullan Road and othersh, the stores shpringing up at Stevenshville and Misshoula and elshwhere—all you Flatheads and me, we're being bypasshed by chivilizashun."

The chief and medicine man left him there. As darkness fell, they poured the whiskey from the bottles and covered his prostrate form with one of their blankets.

70

"**O**ld Manwell is in from his farm. I'll ask him if he'll haul your crate in his wagon. The 'sundries' in it are almighty heavy. Probably a good idea to open it inside your cabin. Even the teamsters who brought the crate here with my stuff from Fort Benton were curious."

John Owen led the Flatheads to the ground floor of one of the bastions he used for storage. He pointed to a coffin-shaped wooden crate set apart from the others. Painted on top center was:

TO
Chief Victor of the Flatheads
Care of Major Owen
Fort Owen, Montana Territory

In one corner was:

SENDER
Étienne Brandt
St. Louis, Mo.

Contents: Seeds, Blankets, Tools & Sundries

Emanuel Martin's face wrinkled from friendly grin to puzzlement as he helped Victor, Charlot and Little Coyote lift the crate into the wagon. He grinned again, bowed low, removed his old hat and swept his arm toward the wagon, inviting the Flatheads to get in, too, for the short ride. They set off at a brisk speed as Owen returned to his office. His gait had slowed, his drinking had increased and business had decreased since the death of Nancy the year before. Both she and Second Chief Moses now rested among the slowly growing number of plots in the small cemetery near St. Mary's chapel.

Agnes brought Victor the axe, cautioning him to pry off the crate's top boards with care.

"I will line and cover it with cloth for little Mary Running Horse," she said. "She died last night from the consumption."

Atop a blanket inside was a brown envelope containing a letter:

> *St. Louis, Mo.*
> *September, 1869*
>
> *Greetings, Chief Victor:*
> *Father DeSmet told me of your people's needs. I am pleased to send you these gifts. The fur trade brought me money. I share. You maintain friendship toward white men despite great injustice. Endure. During the tragic Civil War, these Triplett and Scott seven-shot carbines were made in Connecticut for Kentuckians to help General Sherman during the Atlanta campaign. Few were used. Sherman moves fast. I obtained many of them for trade after the war.*
> *Here are five with the 30-inch barrel and five with the 22-inch barrel. Here are 1,500 cartridges. You should be able to obtain more, because .50 caliber is common in single-shot and repeating guns.*

Good buffalo hunting with these guns! Greetings to Little Coyote, Charlot and the Owen brothers.

Two cartridge boxes are heavier than the others. Use their contents carefully for the good of all, too. Share one with the Black Robes.

Your Friend,

Étienne Brandt

"A fine weapon," John Owen remarked next morning. He handed the carbine to the farmer clad in faded, clean clothes, who had nodded a friendly greeting to Victor and Little Coyote. "I believe you have one, Lige."

"Had." The man's smile faded. "That ne'er-do-well Bykes took it when he lit out of here. We saw him on the Willow Creek trail while looking for three of our pigs we feared a bear had gotten. Gun was gone when we returned home. Good thing I was packing that .52 caliber Sharps carbine I bought from you, or it would have been gone, too." Lige Chaffin nodded toward the heavy scabbard hanging from his saddle. The Flatheads recognized the horse as one of the eleven the Chaffin clan had bought from young Robert Has Many Horses. "Going to use the gun on a buffalo hunt, Chief?"

"Next spring."

"Yes, a fine weapon. Not as handy, to my mind, as the lever action." Chaffin depressed a latch behind the hammer, then turned the barrel in a circular motion until it lined up with the magazine, which protruded from the buttstock. He turned the barrel to its original position, then tapped the buttstock with a work-hardened finger before handing the carbine to Victor. "The boring for the tube magazine weakened the buttstock a little here. Shrink some rawhide over this part, and the gun will last you like a crowbar. With practice you'll learn it's a straight shooter, powerful, too.

"Tell you what, Chief. If you have a good hunt, bring the Chaffins a bale of dried meat and I'll let you have the three-hundred-fifty rounds of ammunition Bykes missed in his hurry. I've got no use for them. John, give Victor that number now, and

I'll bring mine to you next time I come through. I reckon the chief and his son would like to fire the gun a bit."

Owen began putting the bullets on the counter. Victor gravely extended his hand to Chaffin.

"Like we said, Chief, that wooded area southeast of my place remains reserved for you folks only. You always seem to find a white-tail deer or so."

Victor almost smiled. "Yes, and we will only use arrows there, Elijah Chaffin."

"I know. You fellows are mighty quiet. Sometimes I find a hind quarter and the back straps hanging under my porch when I get up. Why doesn't my dog bark?"

"He's also a good friend, who likes deer meat." Now even Victor smiled.

Sunlight and songs of meadowlarks, robins and more-distant red-winged blackbirds were flooding the Bitter Root as Victor and Agnes left St. Mary's chapel this early June day of 1870. New snow had fallen on the highest peaks bordering the valley, bright reminders that winter had been long, cold and filled with hunger despite the gold Brandt had sent in the two cartridge boxes. The buffalo hunters' spirits seemed to elevate as each small group joined the others near the chief's cabin. Surely this hunt would be more successful than the terrible one only a few months past. Then, the people had encountered smallpox killing the Gros Ventre; Flatheads and their allies even had fought their former allies, the Crows, over horses and hunting, the conflict, like disease, taking many lives.

Many who would remain in the Bitter Root straggled over to converse quietly with the hunters. While Victor saddled his horse, Agnes re-examined each pack animal. She handed the lead rope up to Victor and tightly closed her hand over his.

"I should go."

"No, we all again will need our gardens if this hunt is no good. The sons of Fast Runner and Has Sharp Eyes say buffalo are near the Three Forks. There will be a good hunt. Pray hard!" Victor looked down at her a last time, then began counting the horsemen: forty-four Flatheads, seventeen Pend d'Oreilles from the Jocko, more than one-hundred pack horses, plus extra mounts. And now they would join the eleven Nez Percé camping near the river.

Little Coyote rode behind, his musing over Victor's reference to Fast Runner and Has Sharp Eyes linking with thoughts he'd had when Owen was pleading the Indians' interests before Wells and the others at the Jocko agency. Owen had referred to Sioux, Cheyennes, Shoshone warriors by their Indian names, not the baptismal, as Flatheads mostly were wont to do. Yet, when Victor had given the carbines to carefully selected Flathead warriors and to Lean Elk, the Nez Percé who lived among the Flatheads, he had used their native names, even for his son. Somewhat reluctantly, some of the warriors also agreed to take along their bows and arrows. Very pleasing was the presence among the hunters of some of the most dissident warriors and braves, who often had little good to say about their chief, the Black Robes and others. The certainty of a hunt truly had transformed them, for now.

The medicine man winced as a long, willow bough, bent by the preceding horse, snapped back against his shoulder, pulling his thoughts to the now. He smelled the Nez Percé campfire. Well, he concluded, many of these good friends, and others brought into closest contact with white men, also had baptismal names. But most remained strong warriors, too!

Young Joseph seemed older than his twenty-six years when he solemnly greeted his friends. His eyes seemed to brighten when Victor gave him a carbine and one-hundred rounds of ammunition for his father, Tuekakas. Joseph's younger brother, Ollokot, eagerly examined the empty weapon and almost instantly began working its unusual action and aiming at a rock in the river. Closely resembling his brother, Ollokot's eagerness and cautious assertiveness achingly stirred Little Coyote's memories of Lance.

"I will care for it," a grinning Ollokot said to Joseph, who smiled agreeably. While Charlot began explaining to Ollokot the merits of the carbine as he had learned them, Joseph quietly spoke to Victor and Little Coyote: "Tuekakas sends his greetings. He dies slowly, mostly from an illness our medicine men and the white doctor cannot fully name. It is his spirit, like that of an eagle we once saw caged in the whites' Lewiston on the Snake River. The 1855 treaty agreed the Wallowa Valley was ours. Our band refused to sign the 1863 treaty, but settlers move in to take it away, just as they do here." His arm swept to encompass the Bitter Root from north to south. Noting the look of sadness deepening on Victor's face, Joseph quickly gazed at Charlot and Ollokot. "Come, the gun talk must wait. We have prepared much good food to eat before we hunt the buffalo!"

They ate then, and for a time Little Coyote and Joseph talked about Tuekakas, while others listened to Arlee, chosen chief of the hunt.

"If he could come here," the seer ventured, "perhaps the Black Robe Ravalli could help him. He again is at St. Mary's, from the Mission at Hell Gate."

"Little Coyote. Good friend." Joseph carefully chose his words. "Your own chief, Victor, has the same caged-eagle sickness that afflicts my father in the Wallowa Valley, perhaps an illness even the good Ravalli could not cure." Joseph looked toward Victor, who was eating somewhat apart from the others. The inexpressibly sad mouth changed only as he bit into and chewed his food. "I fear both men only will find cause in the sand hills to laugh again."

Young Fishing Bird, grandson of long-dead Fishing Bird of the Kutenais, was a good buffalo-seeker. The sons of Fast Runner and Has Sharp Eyes led the hunters to where they long had found buffalo at the jump site near the Madison River. There was sign there: Tracks dried in early-spring mud; manure somewhat soft inside; closely cropped grass; bones recently cracked and scattered, but no animals. Young Fishing Bird looked about, then pointed to a pile of old skulls above a small, rock cliff near the head of a coulee.

"Blackfeet," all agreed. Arlee signaled the distant scouts to be more watchful for them and the widely ranging Sioux. Young

Fishing Bird examined the top skull, its empty eye sockets peering unseeingly eastward. He examined the base. The skull recently had been moved.

"Yes," he said, "there will be buffalo on the rolling hills and in the valley near the lower part of Gallatin River."

The buffalo were there, but not in numbers to meet the needs of so large a party. Arlee, son of a Nez Percé father and Flathead mother, had planned well. No one disagreed when he proposed, "We should stay together for protection as we move afar. We will proceed with our earlier plan, then return this way if we are not successful. Perhaps by then more buffalo will be here, and closer to our homes."

He sent out hunters who returned with elk and deer carcasses. They ate well, carefully packed the rest of the meat, and began heading north and east through the Judith Gap between the Little Belt and Snowy mountains. They would hunt in the great Judith Basin between Arrow and Wolf Creek west of the Judith River, striving to avoid other roving hunters, horse thieves or people with the smallpox.

"Especially take care," Arlee warned the scouts, "lest you lead us toward vengeful River Crows, still mourning Chief White Head, who we killed in the first hunt this year."

The scouts easily found buffalo, great numbers of them, perhaps twenty miles south of the Missouri. The warriors' ears did not hear them; their eyes did not find them; their noses detected them on the third day of their absence from the hunting party.

"North Wind brought the great stench. Soon it became almost unsupportable." Young Fishing Bird wrinkled his nose and face in distaste when he reported back. "We rode almost three miles southeast to escape it. Trying to remain upwind, we approached the source of the stench, pausing, finally, atop a small, rounded hill. In all directions, except behind us, were dead buffalo, dotting other nearby low hills and level places.

"Great clouds of flies rose from the carcasses as we approached. Some carcasses looked like someone had spilled white man's rice over them. Maggots pulsated through carcass parts till they seemed to move. Our horses struggled to get away.

Always we could see the carcasses, on and on toward the Missouri. Only scavenging birds, coyotes, a few wolves and two bears moved."

Again Young Fishing Bird paused, shaking his head wonderingly, though all listeners' eyes and stern mouths silently were demanding, "Why? What?"

Little Coyote watched Blue Bird Feather of the Pend d'Oreilles stir restlessly, his bright eyes flicking from Young Fishing Bird to Arlee and Victor. How the young brave wanted to blurt out the answer to this great discovery on his first big scouting mission.

"Every buffalo carcass was intact, except for meat reserved by the scavengers," Young Fishing Bird continued. "All had been skinned—calves, cows, even the most ancient bulls. Most had been shot through the lungs, so they would stand there and slowly die, rather than thundering across the prairie, setting others to flight."

Cautiously, the scouts had followed the great stink ever closer to where the steamboats sometimes stopped near the meeting of the Judith and Missouri. "You'll remember Camp Cooke was there until last year, when the soldiers went to Fort Benton. Blue Bird Feather carefully guarded our horses among some willows and cottonwoods." The young brave stood straighter now as all eyes briefly flicked toward him. "We would need them in an instant if danger lay below us. We worked our way to a cliff to peer down at the river. Many white men, assisted by Crows, hurriedly were collecting buffalo hides Sun had dried. They were in great bundles. Soon a steamboat coming downriver stopped to pick them up and add to the great stacks already being carried. When the boat again swung into the current, we returned."

The hunters ate the last of the elk and deer meat that evening amid much talk. "Why," they asked, "did white man and Crows kill so many buffalo, waste the meat and take even the hides of great bulls, which did not make good robes?" Well, that answer would come, perhaps, but now the hunters would have to return to the Three Forks area if they wished to eat meat instead of catching many meals from Arrow and Wolf creeks.

All scouts, except tardy Blue Bird Feather, brought good reports soon after the hunters crossed the Musselshell. They had seen no enemies, and there were buffalo on the prairie north of the Cayuse Hills. Many thousands!

Amid this rejoicing, Blue Bird Feather galloped in to announce, breathlessly, that he had followed strange wagon tracks coming from the northeast.

"They led me to Métis, perhaps two-thousand Métis!"

Victor and Charlot, Joseph and Ollokot, Young Fishing Bird and Little Coyote rode toward the great ring of Red River carts somewhat hidden in a deep depression. Blue Bird Feather would remain outside the encampment, should he need to seek out Arlee and the other hunters. They reluctantly had agreed to remain behind during the planned what-to-do talks. Lowering Sun was threatening to hide behind the clouds serenely moving between Conical and Crazy peaks as three outer Métis guards pulled off their round-crowned hats, scratched their heads and communicated in Cree, English and French. Then the oldest guard escorted the visitors toward the center of the circle, where children, women and men momentarily eyed them before again devoting their attention to the Black Robe and the mass. Victor, Charlot and Young Fishing Bird reverently received communion; as the mass ended, one of the men who had served at the crude altar signed the visitors should wait while he folded the white altar cloths and packed them and the holy vessels in a nearby chest.

As the Métis neared the delegation, Little Coyote thought of his long-dead friend, Drouillard. Same handsome, dark face, but more delicately formed nose, surely as compelling eyes. The man was clad in exquisitely beaded buckskin shirt and high moccasins. A colorful sash encircled his slim waist and the band of his black trousers. His smile was friendly as he greeted the visitors; his eyes seemed to peer into their souls. Dominic Bonneau's Salish proved surprisingly good. His words received the greatest deference in this busy camp, where the men had returned from mass to continue tightening up with buffalo rawhide and wood the many carts loosened by their long journey from the Red River country. There were many, many carts, seemingly far more than this number of people ordinarily would need for meat and pemmican.

Bonneau pulled a pouch from beneath his sash and tamped tobacco into a large-bowled pipe with a long, willow stem. He passed pipe and a burning stick to Victor. After the pipe had made the circle, widened by the arrival of an older and younger Métis who reported briefly on the movements of the buffalo, Bonneau asked Victor to speak. The chief did so, politely and in detail about his people's need for the meat. If they were to hunt now, Victor said, the Métis might lose out. Bonneau nodded his head almost rhythmically that he understood very well, indeed. At length, both a broad wave of his arm and his carefully chosen words encompassed the encampment, then ranged to parts of the Dakota country and Minnesota; then even more afar into the recently confederated Dominion of Canada—to the North and South Saskatchewan rivers, to Lakes Winnipegosic, Winnipeg and Manitoba. Finally, his words focused on the Red River.

"All people have wanted the buffalo where so many Métis live, too. Perhaps you know that Hudson's Bay defeated North West Company in a war over who would get the meat for pemmican. The buffalo mostly are gone now as white men increasingly move into our Red River country, as they do elsewhere into the lands of our Indian brothers."

Bonneau tamped tobacco into his own pipe after handing his pouch and short, white, clay pipes to his guests. They smoked while the pounding and tapping of the workers and the noises of hundreds of horses and people gradually began fading in the dusk. Bonneau pointed to the smoke rising above each smoker before it coalesced, then disappeared.

"We are Indian with you, partially in our blood, totally in our adversity," he said. "Will our way of life disappear like the smoke? We, like you, must have the buffalo, and our land in which to roam freely as God created us to do."

He pulled deeply on his pipe, raised his head and blew a stream of smoke into the air. All watched it widen then, caught by the quickening northeasterly breeze, disappear. "We must make pemmican at the Musselshell to eat and sell and trade it to Hudson's Bay. But we will not fight our brothers for it, as some of the beleaguered tribes south of the Missouri now are doing. Yes, perhaps you could hunt before we do, but should the buffalo stampede, they could go beyond where we could take our carts."

Silence and darkness descended on the group. Bonneau grunted as he leaned far forward to toss willow on the glowing coals. The wood hissed, steamed and smoked before bursting into bright flame; the flame heightened the darkness of Bonneau's face, and reflected in his eyes and from his teeth. Now he seemed brother, indeed.

"No. We would not fight our brothers. Our people have been crossing from the *Dominion*"—he emphasized the word—"of Canada into the United States long before they were known as such. We do not recognize a line drawn like this." His quickly drawn knife slashed an east-west furrow into the hard-packed earth. "We have watched the forts go up south of the Missouri, the soldiers come in with the settlers. We know about the wars. Discontent moves ever northward to this very country." He crossed himself and his words became a prayer. "God help us. The white Canadians press in from the east. What must we do? There is an almost priest who has returned to live with us. This Louis Riel, who has visions perplexing to us, talks of rebellion even now against these invading whites. The Métis, others, no more escaped *pekopuyewin*, the smallpox, than did you. All the others. What must we do?" Bonneau, seemingly forgetful now of the circle of men watching him, looked about the encampment, almost quiet in the sheltering blanket of darkness. "Why do most white men believe that part-Indians, all-Indians, do not think, do not talk, do not feel, do not suffer? What must we do?"

As most of the visitors silently continued to eye this Métis leader, Victor was leaning forward as though, for the first time, completely weighted down by his eighty years. Slowly he began sitting erect. He crossed himself, then stood. His hand reached downward across the low fire to grasp Bonneau's. "I will talk to our chief of the hunt. We will hunt the buffalo near Three Forks.

We will find them there." He looked at Joseph, who signed assent. "We will go."

As the visitors began moving toward the circle of carts, Little Coyote turned to wait for Victor. Bonneau was walking with him, talking animatedly. Bonneau stopped once to move both arms as though sighting a rifle again and again. He threw up his arms in a gesture of despair, signed farewell and returned to the fire. Once again, he seemed to be praying.

"I should have gone to the Métis! The buffalo are *here*!" Arlee angrily swept his arm west, north and east.

"Yes, I should have had you accompany us, not as chief of the hunt, but as second chief among us." Victor's voice was conciliatory, yet the firmness was there, too. He motioned they sit. "I think we must talk about sending back to the Bitter Root for more horses."

Arlee's voice was guardedly sarcastic. "You are so certain we will find more buffalo at Three Forks?"

"Hear me. Bonneau told me why his people brought so many carts, why our scouts found the great stink. Arlee, do not be angry. White men have found many new uses for all buffalo hides. They have found a way to quickly turn them into leather like that in some of our saddles and other articles. They no longer want just the soft robes our women work so hard to make. Bonneau said a great army of men, many loosed from the war between the south and the north, prepare to come to the buffalo country to kill for the hides. We will kill for the meat, but we will trade the hides to John Owen to haul over the Mullan Road to Fort Benton."

There was much talk then, with Arlee directing most of the speakers. Victor remained silent. Before all sought sleep, the chief stood, looked toward his blankets, then muttered absently to himself, "They sought the furs. They seek the gold. They take the land. Now the buffalo." As had Bonneau, Victor crossed himself, then said more loudly, "God help us. What are we to do?"

Scouts reported many buffalo along the Shields River in a valley west of the Crazy Mountains, so well known in the stories of the people. Arlee so carefully deployed the hunters that not an animal escaped the arrows, lances and efficient Triplett and Scott carbines. Soon the throats of those who had questioned Victor's decision among the Métis were filled with much fresh meat. Amid great rejoicing, and a sincere reconciliation between formerly much-worried Arlee and Victor, most hunters set out for their homes with fully laden pack horses. A few would remain behind with Victor. Arlee would send fifty pack horses to the chief's party near the Madison buffalo jump early in the seventh month of *Slá'ko*.

Charlot and Lean Elk led the hunters on a scout into the valley south of the jump site. Weary Victor and Little Coyote carried their buffalo ribs farther down the coulee and toward a large shale shelf slanting into singing Willow Creek.

"Aiii, my bones are tired." Victor gratefully sat on the rock shelf in the warm sunshine. He offered thanks while the medicine man held the ribs toward Sun, thanked the Good Spirit and threw a few bits of meat into the clear, deep and gently swirling pool on the riotous downstream side of the rock.

Numerous minnows swam from beneath the rock to nibble at the bits moving into the quickening current. Some minnows, hunger overcoming instinct, entered the heavy current and were swept downstream.

While Sun neared its apex, thoughts and talk traversed the span of almost seventy years of deep friendship. The worry lines of Victor's face stretched variously into smiles, frowns and laughter—registering spoken memories of happy, sad, joyous events. The chief rose and brushed the meat crumbs from his lap into the pool. A few high, wondrously white clouds momentarily cast shade, enabling the two warriors to better see the renewed competition between the minnows for the buffalo meat. Again, some were swept downstream. As Sun broke from the clouds, Little Coyote rubbed two of the rib bones over the water. Several fat rainbow trout darted upstream to gobble up the remaining minnows, then meat, while droplets cast into the air by the arcing trout sparkled ever so briefly like the best trade beads.

Bellies full, the two men tossed the rib bones below the pool where the trout yet lingered, cleaned their hands and again sat on the rock. Surely as the needle on John Owen's compass always centered on north, so did their talk of the Jocko, where all agents after Wells had insisted Victor take his people, and where the ramshackle agency, itself, despite continued flow of funds, had changed little since that memorable meeting.

Yes, the agents! Victor tugged at a loose lens of shale that time, water and weather were separating from the boulder. The Indians remembered most that the agents seemed mainly interested in what they could get from the impoverished tribes; Wells, recalled to Washington, D.C., where he had shot himself; Washington J. McCormick, an attorney, who, on temporary duty, had built himself a home in Missoula with Indian lumber; Michael M. McCauley. "Yes, McCauley." Victor gave a mighty wrench to the small, shale slab. "Never did he talk with me." The tenacious slab pulled free. Victor plunked it into the pool, scattering the trout downstream. Almost immediately, an even larger trout swam into the pool from upstream and began moving about in ever-widening circles. "William J. Cullen," Victor said grimly. "He who came as a special agent with many gifts to successfully lure tribes to give up their other lands and go to reservations—Gros Ventre, Blackfeet, Bloods, Piegans, Shoshonis, Bannacks, Crows. He, who before his departure, made us believe we would at least keep our valley south of Lolo Creek."

The two friends fell silent, perhaps both thinking about what Cullen had said. The new Indian superintendent in Montana, General Alfred M. Sully, had signed such an agreement with the Flatheads, so long as the whites already there could stay. Would the Great Father Grant allow this? Would the new Flathead agent, Major Galbreath, abide by it? This Grant, a great warrior, seemed to be putting more Army chiefs in positions to handle Indian matters. Well, they did seem to be more honest.

Little Coyote, watching the current catch the trout and begin to shunt it downstream, sensed he should look upward. He touched the chief's shoulder and pointed.

"*Stáma!*"

Yes, seven buffalo had browsed their way into the shallow coulee above.

"Do you want trout or more good meat?" Victor looked toward the horses, a grin widening that sorrowful mouth, the old body tense as a newly strung bow.

"Meat!"

"I will run them downward, lest they frighten others that might be out of sight above us. I will kill but one, lest Charlot and the others have found no buffalo this day. We must have meat until Arlee sends the pack horses."

Victor seized his bow and three arrows.

"Yes, I will kill but one fat animal." He began scrambling off the rock. "There will be a great feast tonight!"

Little Coyote walked to the top of the rock and sat. Immobile as the boulder, itself, he could view the entire coulee. Victor stripped tassels from grass and tossed them into the air. Hurriedly he led his horse upward through the screening willows. At their edge, the old man looked to the sky, made the sign of the cross, then set his horse pounding into the coulee well below the top, forcing the buffalo to flee downward, tails raised, into the least brushy area to the seer's left.

A cow took one arrow without pause; the second brought her to her knees, her momentum rolling her over and over. As she tried to stand, Victor leaped from his horse and hurried over to place the third arrow into her heart. The chief's triumphant yell reached above the noise of the animals splashing through the creek to labor upward on the other side.

Again, Victor yelled, exultantly pumping the bow above his head. Then he crumpled next to the cow.

The medicine man grasped his lance and carefully picked his way upward. Victor lay on his side, head uphill, his dying eyes centered on the cow. The animal's tongue protruded from her mouth; blood coursed down the black nose and into the grass.

Little Coyote gently turned his old friend onto his back and helped him retract his tongue. Victor swallowed again and again.

"It is a good kill," he gasped. "For us both. Have Charlot

say the prayers after yours."

Then, after a time, the old chief asked, "Why do not our people come with the pack horses? The buffalo are here. I come, Tjolzhitsay, Gun. Where are the pack horses? The day. What is the day?" The right hand rose, then dropped.

Little Coyote closed those eyes staring into eternity. He slowly began walking downward for his horse and his knife. He looked to the blue sky.

"It is the fourth day, your independence day, too, Little Bear Claw."

And so it was marked in the Book of the Dead at St. Mary's in his beloved Bitter Root Valley.

L ong before Sun rose, Little Coyote tethered Charlot's best buffalo horse outside the council lodge. Hanging from the saddle was the cross-adorned shield, its scalps long ago affixed to the lance and quiver. Most of the approximately five-hundred-fifty Flatheads remaining in the valley examined the horse and these trappings while waiting for the leading warriors and sub-chiefs to name a successor to beloved Victor. Charlot had entered the lodge last, carrying his father's pipe. He had re-emerged soon thereafter, grim-faced and more heavily burdened with his father's title.

A few days later Charlot and his war-friend dearer than a brother set out for the Place of the Sunflowers to pay the last of his father's debts. Later, he would aver that his father's spirit "surely accompanied us so two of his living white friends would add to those things I, as chief, must think about, but which could not be told to me from the other world."

As Charlot and Little Coyote approached the Place of the Sunflowers, they returned the friendly wave of B.F. See and his wife, "Aunt Mag," hard at work in their large garden. Now the men could guide their mares and pack horse with less care than they had used for the past several miles, during which they had

had to weave their way around the small, scattered farms. As in the past, the settlers' attitudes had ranged from friendly or tolerant to unfriendly or hostile. Meadowlarks and flocks of other birds, great and small, sang joyously of their freedom. They could rise above these fences and wing southward, well ahead of the snows that soon would whiten the land. The two warriors, amused, watched a little girl with carefully braided blonde hair jump from her swing dangling from a pine bough and scamper barefooted between two garden rows toward Elijah Chaffin and his wife, Elizabeth. The Chaffins were digging potatoes while two older children shook off the dirt and put them in tin pails. A yellow and white dog greeted the Flatheads with two sharp barks then, vigorously wagging its tail, ran toward them.

While the girl shyly peered from behind her mother's skirt, Lige Chaffin looked at Sun, then spoke to the others, who carried the pails toward a pole bin by a cottonwood next to the house. Elizabeth jabbed her potato fork upright into the soil, shook dust from her clothing, then shooed the girl and dog ahead of her.

"Chief and Little Coyote." Chaffin reached up to shake their hands. "Almost time to eat." They followed the rail fence to the house, where the farmer dusted off his clothing and ruefully examined his rump-sprung trousers. "Either I'm eating too much of our produce or these britches I wore from Kansas in '64 finally have given out."

Charlot grinned. "My father owed you a bale of meat for the cartridges, Elijah Chaffin. Perhaps you'd prefer I have Margarite make you some buckskins." The grin faded, the chief thinking, perhaps, of Margarite's sickness, which scarcely responded at all to Father Ravalli's and Little Coyote's gentle ministrations prior to and after the joyous arrival of her new son.

"I'll take the meat." Chaffin glanced briefly at Lance's shield hanging from Charlot's saddle, then helped him carry the bale to the porch.

"What's this?"

"Three apishamores to put under the saddles of the horses you bought from our people."

Charlot handed the buffalo calf skins to the farmer, whose

strong face brightened in appreciation. "We got them on a good hunt near Three Forks after my father died. I thank you for coming to the mass for the dead at the Mission."

"A great and good Christian leader, Charlot. History will treat him well, even if white men did not. How's the new agent working out?"

"They come and go like wandering horses. The Great Father does not select and train them as does the warrior who carefully picks his horse from a great herd before seeking the buffalo."

The friends took turns at the pump and wash basin, then sat on the rough-sawn steps and looked across the twenty acres of grain and vegetables. Soon they were discussing other changes in the valley—Chaffin from a perspective gained in Tennessee, Wyoming, Kansas and Oregon. In the distance the men heard someone, perhaps from another Chaffin family, beating a pan to announce dinner time.

"Yes, we've worked hard here," Chaffin said. "Made a lot of improvements after we bought out Jack Slack." Then, almost to himself: "Hmm. Mostly, we whites get the land for no money, but when a white gets it from another white, there's some money to seal a mutual agreement. Well . . . at any rate your father sure enough steered Jack to a good place. One of these days you'll be eating some apples and cherries from those trees. They've got to grow some to produce, but growth is a fact of life everywhere. There are single farms, ranches, small settlements, villages, towns, cities. There are the paths, trails and roads, wagons, steamboats, steam locomotives. They're coming, all coming, but this time I reckon too many are coming. That's what Nick Sondergast said when he sold me his small spread not long ago: 'When I can hear my neighbor's bacon frying, it's time to move out—if I still can find a place to go.'" Chaffin spat, raising a small puff of dust that brought a chicken running. It stopped, looking intently for a grasshopper or other large insect the other watchful barnyard fowl had missed. "Where's the possibility for you folks? Farms? You've got some good, small ones. Horses? You're ahead of all of us there, and we surely need them."

Chaffin shook his head while Charlot's mouth momentarily

tightened downward, then straightened, as Elizabeth appeared at the doorway.

"And there are carrots, potatoes, hot gravy, cold pork ribs and sauerkraut, hot coffee and sugar." She opened the screen door.

Elijah stood. "You might see Wilson Harlan next time you head up near Lake of the White Moose. He's looking for some good horses. He'll treat you square. You're welcome to stay to supper and the night, too, in the bunkhouse."

"We thank you. We will go to Stevensville tonight. Frank Owen is leaving the valley in two days."

"So I heard, Chief. A shame, particularly when John . . . well, needs him more than ever."

The farmer asked Little Coyote to thank the Good Spirit for their food. They ate silently while the many bright, little eyes around the table asked dozens of questions.

"So!" Frank Owen put down a box as the two Flatheads entered the small, rough building surmounted by a large sign:

GENERAL MERCHANDISE
F. Owen
Prop.

"Charlot and Little Coyote." Each gave his hand a quick shake up and down, then sat on the bench facing the open door and windows.

"John Owen said you are leaving. We came to tell you we will miss our friend since the long-ago in St. Louis."

Owen selected two clay pipes from one of the few small boxes of merchandise remaining on the shelves. They smoked silently for a time while wagons and horsemen moved down the dusty road and a few people passed the store.

"I'll be doing some meandering around St. Louis, but expect to be in Pennsylvania before heavy snow comes," Owen said at last. "As I told you before, I'd sort of planned to set up shop along the Missouri somewhere, and depend on the steamboats to bring supplies. But the buffalo plains are almighty hot, what with the Bloods, Blackfeet, Piegans, River Crows, Sioux and Northern Cheyennes raising hell from time to time among themselves, often with white man, like along the roads, Camp Reeve, Fort Buford, the last three years. Isaac Stevens, others before and after him!" Owen shook his head wonderingly. "Including the Indian Bureau and War Department. All trying to deal with the tribes as nations, then forcing them to live together on reservations, which any self-respecting Indian is going to hate worst of all. Hell, one white farmer often can't agree to live peaceably with another. Words fly. Shotguns sometimes come out. Fences go up. Just look around here."

He re-lit his pipe and puffed reflectively. "If ever the tribes get together, particularly the Sioux and Northern Cheyennes, who have crowded the others into what the whites are claiming, well! Better I'm out of it."

"Father Ravalli tells us these problems, too." Charlot's voice was tired, as though it came from a very tired body. He moved to another seat to escape the bright sunlight coming through the window. Increasingly, sunlight had been affecting his eyes, despite the wide-brimmed hat the priest, who had labeled it "iritis," had suggested he wear. "We would like for Father DeSmet to be here now as he was during the battles with the Yakimas and others."

"Yes, well . . ." Owen arose to greet a bonneted woman who hesitantly had entered the store. She looked about, then asked if the large bolt of blue twill cloth and buttons she spied would be cheaper, "seeing you seem to be closing out."

"I can let you have the cloth at thirty-seven cents a yard, ma'am, and two dozen buttons for another four bits."

The woman eyed Charlot, then Little Coyote, centering, finally, on the latter's feet. She reached inside her bag and withdrew two pieces of string.

"My Robert, he said, 'Try to get two pairs of Indian moccasins this long and wide.'" She held out the strings. Frank reached under the counter and easily lifted up a large box. He untied the cord and rummaged inside, producing, finally, three sets of Flathead moccasins. He returned one ornately beaded pair to the box.

"These'll fit. Really hadn't planned to sell these; I was going to take them back to Pennsylvania. I'll let you have these two pairs for six bits a set."

"Fifty cents."

"Seventy-five. Firm price."

"Well . . . seems mighty high." She sniffed, and began counting the coins onto the counter. Owen looked around for a wrapper, settling finally on a copy of *The Missoula and Cedar Creek Pioneer*. Little Coyote's eyes caught a headline Father Ravalli already had shown him: FLATHEADS MUST LEAVE THE BITTER ROOT. When the woman departed, Frank dropped the coins into a black cash box.

He wrote "Out of Business" on a piece of paper and tacked it on the outside door frame. "Shouldn't have sold those moccasins. Wanted them and other Indian gear I've collected to, well, remind me of the west and my friends."

Charlot abruptly walked from the store. Frank's puzzled look deepened when the chief returned with the shield old Shield Maker had made for Lance so long ago. The trader eyed the black cross on the repainted white background. He listened respectfully as the two Flatheads told its story; his pipe almost dropped from his mouth when Charlot concluded, "This is the gift of two war friends dearer than a brother to our friend, Frank Owen."

They ate then, cold pork ribs and buttered bread sent by Elizabeth Chaffin, and freshly fried eggs and hot coffee.

"About John," Frank began. He hesitated, eying the cross on the shield he had leaned against the packed boxes. "He wanted more than four-thousand dollars to hold onto the fort and all. For his own good I wouldn't help him out. So he mortgaged it to McCormick. John'll lose out. Sometimes he can't remember what happened the day before. It's as though the mile or so separating us is a hundred. He quit coming here a year ago. I've visited him often enough, but forgetfulness, worry and the rotgut have taken over. The other stores and trading posts, merchandise brought upriver and over the Mullan Road, have put him and the fort in the backwater." Again he eyed the shield. "When Nancy died he said that someday he wanted to join your church. Strange, when his head's right, he mostly praises and helps the Black Robes. When it isn't, he sometimes near damns them. I talked it over with Father Ravalli. He agrees that dreadful whanger John got on the side of his head from the windmill while you were trapping in the Thompson River country might have something to do with his problem. Over the years we've sent money to Pennsylvania in my name, and I did pretty well prospecting with Major Blake in '67. John won't leave with me, and I've talked with some of his friends. They'll get him to St. John's Hospital in Helena, and I've offered his return of passage back home, if need be. Won't leave the valley. He wants me to stay, help operate the fort. I've never backed losing propositions."

Little Coyote's almost 79-year-old body was tired; he wanted to return to his lodge along the river, only a short distance away. But Owen truly wanted them to stay, as though they represented his last hold on the life he loved. Charlot cared for the horses and the Flatheads slept on two buffalo robes in the store. After breakfast, Frank carried a number of books from his bedroom into the store.

"Mind taking these back to John? We've had our good-bye of sorts some time ago, and I've got a chance to drive a team to the Missouri. With the unrest there I'm glad there will be a number of us going together."

Little Coyote read the titles as Frank carefully wrapped and put them into a box: *Annual Report of the Commissioner of Indian Affairs for the Year 1868: Olmstead's School Philosophy*, inscribed: "Francis B. Owen from his uncle, B.T. Curtis, Phila, June 15/55."; several volumes of Richard Hildreth's *History of the United States, 1854*.

"Much wisdom here," the trader commented, clearly wishing to delay the final good-byes. "How is your manuscript coming along?" He nodded approvingly on hearing from Little Coyote, "It's up to date." When Charlot helped him re-roll the buffalo robes, Owen said, "I want to keep these." He began tying cords

818

around one. "Gold and land. Buffalo are caught between these forces, like the Indians, so the buff will go. Your people, perhaps sooner than you think, are going to rejoice you're in a somewhat sheltered valley, despite your problems and the attitudes and actions of some whites." Owen looked up before he tightened and knotted the second cord. "I'd stick together closer than ever before, even to the placing of your lodges, so you'll simply be together in what you do. Like I said, there's a storm coming in the buffalo country. Americans aren't as tolerant as Canadians. Last February, they let the rebelling Métis elect young Louis Riel, who set up a government, of sorts, in the Red River country. I doubt that it'll last as more whites come crowding in. You're all part of the same mix being compressed everywhere into an ever-decreasing space, their hatred for those damnable reservations and the dishonesty of so many of the agents. The Indians are going to get over-confident, like I've seen them do elsewhere. They'll figure President Grant is weak because he can't keep the agents honest. I can tell you he isn't. Neither are his generals. They're looking for jobs to do now that the War of the Rebellion is over.

"And now the immigrants are coming over the Mullan Road and settling in the great hunting valleys of the Dearborn River, the Sun, Teton, Marias, others. There's nobody trying to coop *them* up, except the Indians, and God help those who try to keep them out. It's almost a religion with them, believing God Himself wants them to settle and enlarge the republic. I should know. I've been one of them—up to now."

Owen put his weight on the second robe, drew up the cord and tied the knot. "The higher the whites develop, the lower, it seems, the Indians must sink. Someday . . ." The trader tossed the robes onto his pile of baggage, then loudly clapped his hands. "Boom!"

He removed a recent copy of *The Missoula and Cedar Creek Pioneer* from a carpet bag. "This says that the new 1870 census shows there are twenty-thousand-five-hundred-ninety-five citizens in the Territory, plus many soldiers, and eighteen-thousand Indians. All of the Indians are outnumbered now, Charlot, and white men still are coming. I've seen it all before. Some sort of spark is going to light a great prairie fire and, like I said, 'Someday boom!'"

Frank placed two empty boxes on the counter. "I hoped one or the other of you, or both, would show up." He removed the boxes of .50 caliber cartridges from the shelves; also the clay pipes, almost all of the tobacco, and the remainder of the bolt of blue cloth, "For Margarite."

They loaded the boxes onto the patient pack horse.

"Well," Frank Owen said. He shook their hands. "Well . . . hell!" He embraced them both. "I'll see you." He returned quickly to the store building.

The friends silently rode toward St. Mary's Mission and the cabin of Charlot's stepmother, Agnes. After unloading the pack horse, the 39-year-old chief moved as though his shoulders were weighted down by the bale of meat they had left only two days earlier with their friend, Chaffin.

"I will remain with John Owen. Yes, you should fetch Father Ravalli."

Charlot leaped on his horse and set her galloping toward the Mission while Little Coyote gently began leading the trader toward his bedroom in the fort's east barracks. Hesitantly following them were the two oldest workers who had not joined the hundreds of people stampeding to the recently discovered gold diggings at Cedar Creek in western Missoula County.

"We just came to ask the major what our work should be for the day. He started giving us hell because we weren't putting up the south entrance to the fort." The old man looked bewilderingly at Little Coyote. "Hell, I helped put that up in '60! It's more than the rotgut. When I got him to sit down, he looked at us and asked, 'Do I know you folks?'"

The oldsters followed the seer through the rubbish-strewn courtyard to his horse, then back into the office. They watched him put the box of books on the desk, then the oldest of the workers picked up the plaint.

"The major looked up onct an' said, 'You men go to the

bastion an' put the rest of the furs in one wagon, the remaining flour in 'nother, an' haul 'em over the Mullan to Fort Benton. Min' you, get the best price,' he said. There ain't no furs an' there ain't no flour. I dunno what we're agoin' to do!"

Father Ravalli drove his buggy to the shaded side of the well house, then began washing caked, purplish paint from his hands.

"He was mixing a paint of berries and white clay for the wooden statue of the Blessed Virgin he carved," Charlot explained. The priest entered the bedroom. He held the whiskey bottle toward the window. Hearing the swishing liquid, Owen got off his bed. When the priest put down the bottle, Owen walked into the office.

"Jenks," the trader said, "you and Matt better dig the rest of the potatoes and put them in the root cellar. We will be having a mighty hard winter. Well, Father, I appreciate your visit. It has been mighty quiet here. And Charlot and Little Coyote." Owen motioned for them to be seated, then lit his pipe.

"What's this, Charlot?"

"Frank Owen asked us to return these books."

The trader put down his pipe, opened the box and began removing the volumes. While quietly reading the titles aloud, his demeanor began to change. More rapidly now he began searching through one of the history books.

"Ah, there we are." He placed his pipe between the pages and hurried out the door.

"Jenks," he shouted, "Matt!" He beckoned vigorously, then directed the two panting men to sit on the bench.

"We forget these things," he began imperturbably. "Victor." He looked at Charlot. "Here's what I was looking for some time back, and Frank had the books. It's all right here." He held up the volume. His jaws and chin began trembling under his beard. He stroked the beard with his left hand, pulling slightly upward and outward. He leaned against the desk, at sixty-two looking at least fifteen years older than equally bald 58-year-old Father Ravalli. The trader possessed none of the priest's brightness of eye. Nor was there any hint of the Black Robe's ready, gentle smile. Owlishly, Owen looked at him.

"Mr. Speaker," he began solemnly, "I decline to take the oath of office as a legislator. I'm much too busy at Fort Owen. Now that's the business reason. And people aren't ready to follow what it says here!" His voice rose as he again held up the book. "That's the moral reason." He cleared his throat and turned to get more light on the page.

"'A declaration by the representatives of the United States of America, in Congress assembled.'" He muttered for a moment, running his index finger down the page. "Yes, yes. 'We hold these truths to be self-evident—that all men are created equal; that they are endowed by their Creator with certain unalienable rights; that among these are life, liberty and the pursuit of happiness. That, to secure these rights, governments are instituted among men, deriving their just powers from the consent of the governed.'"

Father Ravalli caught Charlot's sign for crazy to Little Coyote as Owen rambled on. "Not really," the priest said aloud. He arose and clapped. "Major, we applaud the reasons for your decision. Right now, however, there are things we need to discuss at the Mission. I brought my buggy, and I'll take you there. I'll help you get a few things in a bag. And you must bring your book. Perhaps Charlot and Little Coyote will accompany us, should you wish to instruct us more."

Before driving his buggy out the south entrance gates, Father Ravalli briefly reassured the two workmen: "Please remain here and take care of the place. I think the Major will be back, at least for a time. He will be in the Mission infirmary, if you need to see him. I don't know who will pay you. I understand that he has little left. He has given to friend and stranger alike for a long time. But we'll try to work out something—perhaps with Mr. W.J. McCormick. He is a kind man." The Black Robe raised the reins. "And it *might* be best if you dig those potatoes."

Charlot and Little Coyote rode on either side of the buggy, talking above the clatter of wheels over stones. Owen proudly sat upright, the history book in his lap, a finger marking the page with the Declaration of Independence. He spoke but once, happily assenting to Little Coyote's request he be able to copy the portion the trader had read. For the remainder of the ride he sat quietly, as though attentively listening to an orator.

Father Ravalli explained the great joy with which the people of Philadelphia, "Mr. Owen's home," greeted the news that the Congress had adopted the Declaration of Independence. "July Fourth," the priest added, slowing the buggy as Charlot changed places with Little Coyote so the chief would be on the driver's side. "You might wish to know we recently learned that Father Nicholas Point, who came to the Rocky Mountains with Father DeSmet so long ago, died on Independence Day two years ago in Quebec. Little Coyote and he exchanged ideas about sketching, painting—and mixing paints." Charlot crossed himself and rode silently until they neared the Mission, where people were certain to greet the four men.

"Father Ravalli."

At the tone of Charlot's voice, the missionary halted the buggy and looked up at the new chief. Charlot's face reflected a mixture of sadness and perplexity, yet strength.

"I have thought much of this independence the white men talk about, practice and put in their books. I have learned since my father's death that a leader should strive for independence for his people as Elijah Chaffin, Frank Owen, John Owen and others have told me since Victor died. This is my wish. But I think deeply and, most lately, wonder more if my people and others suffer, are punished, because there is so much to learn of white man's ways and we remain ignorant of them. We have tried hard, from the days we accepted the faith, renounced the torture and other evil ways. What more must we do?"

Tears formed almost instantly in the priest's eyes. He placed the reins in his lap as though wishing to reach upward to embrace his questioner.

"God love you all the more because you do so well with as-yet limited knowledge of white man's ways. If only others, including whites, would do so well. As Major Owen has so correctly reminded us, all people should have the same rights.

As we have striven to help you, we have reminded the whites how much you have done for them within your ability to do so."

The priest again picked up the reins, saying with great conviction, "We all must pray even harder—and have faith. God will answer our prayers. We must talk more about the lives of the saints. All had faults; all had problems. Yet their lives prove that God loves you and your people, and knows your problems. He will help, but perhaps not instantly. Perhaps in years to come. And then you'll look back and see that what you prayed for then was not what you really needed, that His denial of part of your petitions actually helped you at a later date to acquire a greater good."

The Black Robe again looked at Charlot. "Perplexing? Yes, to me, too, at times, but it works out that way."

He rippled the loose reins across the horse's rump.

L ittle Coyote again looked up from the story skin to watch the pair of ravens silently circling over the large trout erratically splashing through the broad riffle of the Bitter Root River. The river had been shallowed by lack of rain throughout most of the eleven months of 1871. Sometimes the rainbow's struggles put more water under its belly so, helped by the current, it soon would reach greater depths and freedom. The seer returned the tiny paint brush to the pot. By balancing his seventy-nine-year-old body with his lance, he could catch that fish. But no, he had eaten one for the morning meal; the four halves of two more hung from willow sticks over a slow, smoky fire. Perhaps this larger one in the water was meant for the ravens.

Again, he returned to his story skin, so covered now that the ever-spiraling and widening circle of symbols soon would reach the outer edges. Many of the important events detailed in his book manuscript were not on the hide. On the outer edge small cannons symbolized each new Army fort in Montana Territory; a tiny house with a line of smoke emanating from the chimney represented each new settlement in the valley. There were many of these.

The medicine man put down his brush. The woodpecker's

rat, tat-tat on the wind-sheared top of the dead aspen was muffled. The bird flew to a pine that had died for want of soil and moisture atop a small, rocky cliff. The trout had reached freedom in the water that heavied up below the cliff and sped around the bend out of sight of his lodge. This time the rat, tat-tat-tat was prolonged, sharp as the sound of a tightly stretched little dance drum. The bird cocked its head. A reply came from the direction of Fort Owen. The woodpecker repeated its query and listened; as soon as the answer began, the bird flew east.

How much easier to communicate among one's kind, but how important to try to understand others. He, Charlot and others were trying, greatly helped by the Black Robes and John Owen, who generously shared their books, tracts, magazines and the growing number of newspapers reaching this now-almost-settled valley in the territory. As the seer washed his brushes at river's edge, the lingering impact of the woodpecker's signals set him to thinking about the significance of a news story he had read four years earlier in an 1867 *Helena Daily Herald*. The story was about the telegraph reaching Virginia City from Salt Lake City, then reaching Helena. This singing wire also helped to bind the whites more closely; perversely, their growing strength weakened that of the Indians.

The seer put the brushes on a rock to dry and moved the skin and frame behind his lodge out of yet-warm Sun, but in a growing breeze. He brought into the lodge his manuscript from the tin box hidden among the rocks near the base of a large cottonwood. The Black Robes often tried to hide from him the growing number of thin novels with vivid illustrations that most virulently attacked Indians generally; also the Montana newspapers that more specifically railed against the Flatheads.

John Owen had hidden neither novels nor newspapers; he gathered many, sometimes deducting part of the lodging costs to travelers if they would leave their printed matter brought from many regions.

"It's best if you know what's going on," he had said time and time again to Victor, Charlot, Arlee, Adolph, others. "You'd better know what's in the minds of the bastards who'd take the last of the little you've got left! Many of them flat don't want you here," he had added one afternoon in 1869, only a few months after Nancy's death. That was amid the growing clamor echoing from settlement to settlement, newspaper to newspaper, that Indians had further to give way. They hold too much land!

The trader, chin whiskers working angrily, had hurried toward Victor, seated on a bench outside the west barracks. With him were Charlot, Abel Adams, Louis Vanderberg and Little Coyote. Some of them had helped Grizzly Bear Far Away bring more horses from his Nez Percé people.

Owen had thrust into Victor's hands a copy of *The New North-West* from Deer Lodge, referring to the Flatheads as "a band of mongrels, numbering bucks, squaws, papooses and dogs only three-hundred or four-hundred, not twenty of whom are Flatheads." The lie also had elicited outrage among numerous discerning non-Indian inhabitants of the valley and the Territory, itself. Many of these people soon would be sending deep condolences to the Flatheads over the loss of their illustrious chief, or attending his memorial services.

Yes, numbers seemed to be the special focus of white men. "All of the Indians are outnumbered now, Charlot," Frank Owen had said before his departure from the valley, and there was ever-growing understanding of his friendly suggestion the Flatheads stay together, work together more closely than ever before, both now and in the future.

Yes, white men's actions and words increasingly were focusing on the Flatheads' numbers, the highest ranks of territorial officials lying about them in their attempts to force Little Coyote's people from their homeland.

"You see, Charlot, and Little Coyote," gentle Father Ravalli had explained one day, "the settlers in your valley *know* that the Homestead Act of 1862 does not apply here. They cannot get a patent, for title, a paper showing they own the land. If you are not here, then they will be able to get the Congress to extend the Act to your valley."

Long ago the seer had recognized that bitterness and tendencies toward hatred were corrosive as water to the inner workings of a fine rifle. He often prayed to the Good Spirit to help him in these weaknesses. Yet, as he resumed writing in his ever-enlarging manuscript, he again found himself heartily wishing *he* could focus on trust and friendship, good hunting, the well-being of the people instead of their betrayal, their ever-deepening poverty when virtually all they had left was their homeland. And, as John Owen had said, white man would dispossess them of that.

"If they get the last of that, don't let them take your togetherness, your pride!"

The trader remained interested in his fort and his Flathead and other friends when he entered St. John's Hospital. In one short note he wrote his mind "at times seems to wink on and off, like the moon through low-lying clouds whisked through the Bitter Root Valley by our strong southwest wind."

While his mind was shining through the clouds, Owen had sent Little Coyote copies, or summaries of the contents, of some interesting letters "for your manuscript, and perhaps some peaceable communication, if need be. I regret I am not there to help you."

The letters had been written by a trio that earlier had come to the valley after their visit to the Jocko Agency. The Flatheads had not been impressed by the trio's importance at the time, largely because the people were hard put to find food, and so many agents and other officials had arrived in the sixteen years since the signing of the badly broken Stevens treaty. These three, however, were different in one major respect: "You must leave the Bitter Root Valley!" they had demanded after very short civilities, "and immediately."

The trio included Territorial Governor Benjamin F. Potts; Jasper A. Viall, Superintendent of Indian Affairs for Montana; and William H. Clagett, recently elected Territorial Delegate to Congress. Governor Potts' September 8, 1871, letter to the Commissioner of Indian Affairs in Washington, D.C., urged the immediate removal of "the remnant of the Flathead Tribe of Indians from the Bitter Root Valley to the Jocko Reservation." Despite the St. Mary's Mission's records showing five-hundred-forty-eight Flatheads in the valley, Potts claimed the tribe was almost extinct. The valley in a short time would be filled by settlers to its utmost capacity. Most of the tribe were absent on their hunts much of the year. The isolated Jocko "is covered with game and is the proper place to protect the Flatheads from the vices."

How Catholic Charlot's frown had deepened as he had read "The Agent of the Confederated Tribes, as well as the Catholic Flatheads, have expressed to me their strong desire that the Flathead Indians be removed to this Reservation." Potts further had declared that the Bitter Root Valley raised most of the grain and vegetables which feed and support nearly "one-half of our people."

Potts' letter admitted that the President had not carried out the provisions of the 1855 Stevens treaty, which had forbidden white settlement, and that the whites' presence was a trespass. Nevertheless, he urged that the President now make the necessary survey and, with the assurance of a predetermined outcome, authorize the Superintendent of Indian Affairs for Montana immediately to remove the Flatheads to the Jocko.

The letters of Superintendent Viall and the Delegate to the Congress also portrayed the Flatheads as "remnants," and demanded their removal. "There's more," John Owen had written. "Clagett took off for Washington, D.C., armed with a memorial from the Territorial Legislature in Virginia City demanding you Flatheads leave."

As Little Coyote found it necessary to explain some of the meanings to Charlot, the latter's sadly curved mouth had tightened into the same grim line and response that he adamantly had made to the three officials: "I will not go!"

Little Coyote re-wrapped the manuscript and pencils in the buckskin and returned them to the tin box in their hiding place. His fingers were cold. They warmed as he removed two halves of trout from above the smoky fire. Sun disappeared behind dark clouds sailing in from the northwest. Perhaps the long delayed snow would come soon. A large pile of broken branches and a stack of split wood between two sturdy cottonwoods were reassuring. Two of his three horses were in Charlot's band, well-guarded by his son. Two long ropes with heavy stones at their ends criss-crossed a stack of dry, meadow grass and assured food for the animal; he must go to Charlot's cabin for the dried buffalo meat and some of the vegetables Agnes and Margarite had set aside for him in their rock-lined root cellar.

The horse told Little Coyote that someone was near. Soon the warrior, too, smelled the mixture of sweat, dirt, tobacco smoke, urine and whiskey. A man, to the northwest, most likely white, screened by the wild currant bushes that months before had yielded their fruit to industrious Agnes.

"*A,*" the seer said, then more loudly, "Hello!"

The man carried a Triplett and Scott, 30-inch-barrel carbine. His ragged trousers were dust-covered, stained; the filthy shirt was torn at the shoulder, worn at the elbows; his Shoshone moccasins scarcely hung together at all. Close-set eyes above the hairy face darted about the small camp, lighting, finally, on the fish. Little Coyote shifted the lance to his left hand and gestured for Bykes to eat. Bykes put down his skin bag, then stood wolfing the fish, spitting or fingering out an occasional bone, always watching, carelessly holding the carbine on his host. He wiped his oily hand across his beard, the trousers, finally down the bark of a small poplar.

"What else yuh got, Indian?"

"No more food." Little Coyote leaned heavily on the lance, feigning deference, some fear—uncertainty.

"Had food. What else yuh got, old man?" He faced the lodge and, as a robin tweeted twice, pushed the lance aside with the carbine barrel, centering the weapon on Little Coyote.

The heavy bullet thwacked into and through the poplar inches above Bykes' head. The heavy lance haft knocked the carbine from Bykes' grasp in the downward stroke and caught him under the chin in the upward.

He awoke gagging blood, hands tied, a rope around his neck and Charlot nudging him with the carbine while the seer hoisted the partial bale of buffalo meat onto a tree platform.

"We will take you to Elijah Chaffin tomorrow," the chief

said. Most unwillingly, Bykes stumbled after the mounted pair until they reached Charlot's cabin. They fed him, tied both legs, too, and tossed him into the small hay mow with two sweaty apishamores for warmth.

"Cast your bread upon the water," was part of grateful Chaffin's remarks next day. Also, "But what will we do with a skunk?" The farmer's face twisted in distaste. "Well, the family'll talk it over."

Charlot's appearance at Little Coyote's lodge had had a purpose besides bringing the meat.

"Father Ravalli has received word from Helena, Virginia City and St. Louis that he wishes to share in two days with our people. I have called together Arlee, Adolph and others, numbering nine, from parts of the valley."

They met in the Fort Owen dormitory room, gratefully standing in front of the fireplace after removing their blankets and capotes, all commenting on the snow that had moved down from the mountains. Soon they could hear the crunch of Father Ravalli's buggy wheels. Charlot hastened outside to welcome him and to shelter his horse with the others in the northwest corral. Accompanying the priest was Sacalee, son of Peteter Clark, who recently had returned from St. Louis. Sacalee brought in a large box containing tobacco, tin cups, a bag of raisins, fresh bread, honey, sugar and a great coffee pot. The warrior immediately hung the pot over the fire. Soon, amid much happy talk after grace, all were sharing this welcome food and the tobacco. There was silence as Father Ravalli prepared to share his information.

His face had thinned over the years, the cheeks somewhat hollow now, the bright eyes peering from below the prominent eyebrows, the nose seemingly longer, thinner. But the ready smile was unchanged; it was there as he began to speak.

"The Black Robes have many friends who pray for them, provide them with food, other supplies and sometimes information, good and bad. I have been asked to share some now." He lifted a newspaper and slowly read in English, then put it into Salish:

President Grant signed an executive order on November 14 that the Flathead Indians in the Bitter Root Valley, Territory of Montana, be removed to the Jocko Reservation to the north. He has asked the Congress to appropriate more than $50,000 to recompense the Indians and pay for the removal.

The President's office explained that a survey has been made of the Bitter Root . . .

"Tamuné! Yóqwey! Te! Te!"

Father Ravalli leaned against the fireplace as "False!" "Not telling truth!" and "No good, no good!" rose from the listeners, several of the older standing in their agitation. Muttering, they sat down after Charlot signed, *Let the Black Robe speak.*

Shaking his head in dismay, Father Ravalli continued:

. . . a survey has been made of the Bitter Root Valley as required by a treaty of 1855, and, the valley not found the best for the Flatheads, they have been ordered to move at once.

The President said he will ask the Secretary of the Interior to appoint a special commissioner to negotiate a contract with the Flatheads for their removal.

There was much talk then, all the warriors saying essentially the same thing, while Father Ravalli sat on a bench and ate the remainder of his bread and raisins. At length his thin, expressive hands told Charlot there was more to say.

"We looked at the sky yesterday, then at the angry clouds covering St. Mary's Peak. We felt the cold breeze. These signs told us to put more firewood in the lodges and cabins. And the snows came. In the same way we feel the warm breezes, see snow melt, and look for the flowers and grasses of spring. I have looked into your eyes, your throats, listened to your heartbeats, and asked you questions. Thus, I have helped you, as has Little Coyote, with your sicknesses. We must look at white man's words on paper, listen to them from his mouth to understand his thoughts. I tell you these things to help you, not to make you angry or white man angry. I tell you because we care for you, because we love you, and perhaps we can help."

The Black Robe paused as a murmur of approval filled the dormitory, then he read from an older, much-worn eastern newspaper.

Before he became president in 1869, Grant had told the writer about a new policy he would establish to deal with Indians. It would be fair. All Indians who wished peace would find it. Those who were not peaceful would face a severe war policy. The Indians would be taught to farm, given food and clothing, and be Christianized. If they did not remain on their reservations, they would be treated as enemies.

Again murmurs, mixed, most disapproving.

"We believe he will make his plan a law before Christmas," Father Ravalli said as he managed a grin. "If those who have been most peaceful merit best treatment, surely the Flatheads, as well as your kin and friends at St. Ignatius, will be treated most fairly of all. The president will assign ministers of different churches to the reservations. Our church has had missions on forty of the seventy-two Indian agencies. Again, we should expect fairness there, which should enable us to help you all—and so many more. Yet, we must look ahead, look to the peaks, discern if storms are building. If so, we must prepare. I think we must try to learn who will be the special commissioner President Grant will send here. When General Sully was Superintendent of Indian Affairs in Montana two years ago, you agreed with him that if you could keep the valley south of Lo Lo Creek, the whites could have the rest—if you also would allow the whites already there to remain. Many settlers were very angry. The Congress did not allow this. Will the new commissioner also be inclined toward generosity when he learns the truth about the Stevens treaty?

"Zachariah, may I please read the letter you brought from St. Louis?" Sacalee, looking more like his explorer grandfather, Lt. William Clark, than his father, Peteter Clark, removed a thick, buckskin envelope from inside his shirt and gravely handed it to the priest. First, Father Ravalli extracted a very short letter.

"This tells us that the Jesuits in St. Louis have heard the commissioner might be General James A. Garfield, a congressman from Ohio, a great hero of the Civil War." He replaced the letter in the envelope, then held up another, which clearly was longer. "We ate before I read this one. I think it will take much time to explain." His face saddening, the physician/priest began:

Dear Father Ravalli:

Enclosed is part of a speech General Garfield made in the thirty-eighth Congress when he first became a congressman. A Mr. Alexander Long, of Ohio, had argued it was useless to try any more to coerce the South, defeated in the Civil War. One might gain useful insights into General Garfield's character by reading this portion of his reply to Mr. Long about this matter of forcing or compelling.

. . . I ask him, Mr. Long, for one moment to reflect that no statute ever was enforced without coercion. It is the basis of every law in the universe—God's law as well as man's. A law is no law without coercion behind it. When a man has murdered his brother, coercion takes the murderer, tries him and hangs him. When you levy your taxes, coercion secures their collection; it follows the shadow of the thief, and brings him to justice; it accompanies your diplomacy to foreign courts, and backs the declaration of the nation's rights by a pledge of the nation's power . . .

Discussions grew out of explanations. Arguments led to agreements, finally, as frost began forming on the dormitory's small windows. Warriors brought wood from the other two fireplaces in the east barracks. A tired Father Ravalli tapped the last coffee from the pot and sat sipping it as Sacalee strode to the wellhouse to refill it. Charlot asked for shortly stated views. The group provided them, the consensus being that all hoped the rumor about Garfield becoming commissioner was rumor only. Father Ravalli choked on his coffee, and hastily covered much of his face as he wiped it with his handkerchief, when astute Arlee loudly observed, "This President Grant. Owen told us he was the greatest chief when the north and south went on the warpath. Then, Grant had other good generals to win that war. I think Grant will choose this General Garfield to move us out. General Sully did not do so, and *he* was moved out." With great sarcasm, Arlee concluded, "And that was before Grant said what his peace policy will be."

Heavy, wet snowflakes tumbled down the chimney and hissed on the lowering fire. Some warriors would remain in the dormitory for the night. Others would leave for nearby homes after a final cup of coffee.

Father Ravalli, recovered from his choking spell, looked across the silence at Little Coyote. Help me help them, he was thinking. He stood.

"If Arlee is correct, I can say, 'Let Grant have his Garfield.' We have the power of prayer in at least equal measure. We have told you of the lives of the saints. All had faults. All had problems. I implore you always remember this. God loves you and knows your problems. Through prayer, He will help you, perhaps not instantly. Maybe in years to come. And you will look back and see that if you had gotten all you wanted then, you would not be as greatly helped in the future when your need, perhaps even different, was greater. All must understand this—and pray."

Little Coyote spoke with equal conviction: "The Good Spirit told me on my vision quest we must not fight white man. We have not done so. While we are poor, we have not been killed. I will tell you this, for some of you do not know. Thus I interpreted the vision of my war friend dearer than a brother. The white man will be everywhere. He will abuse you; he will, in Little Grizzly Bear Claw's lifetime, try to drive you from your valley." The seer paused and looked into Charlot's stricken face. "In Little Grizzly Bear Claw's lifetime, all will be forced northward from the valley. As the sky fills with lightning bolts and thunder during the great storms of summer, there will be greater battles than ever before among Indians and Indians and Indians and whites. But the Flatheads will survive!"

Some of the listeners started, as though to speak. Little Coyote quickly cleared his throat as he held up his hand. His old voice must not sound like the thin piping of a curlew. The increasing hissing in the fireplace filled the silence.

"Dying Broken Tooth, who is so strong in our people's stories as well as the spirits of his kin, told me in his death vision during the treaties with Stevens, 'I think now how our people have survived the many dangers, often with prayer.'" Little Coyote felt Father Ravalli's eyes on him. They were tear-filled. "'He, Stevens, like Old Bull Boat and his Hidatsas, will be gone, but our people, like the seedling cottonwoods, will survive great adversity and will grow as did the stalwart cottonwoods from which came the seed.'

"And I will say now. Resist what this Garfield calls 'coercion.' But do not fight as others will yet fight—and die."

Little Coyote sat down, closing his eyes, yet seeing Charlot's face.

"Charlot," Arlee said loudly, "as I believe Father Ravalli, I believe Little Coyote. The warrior within me, as I know is within you, says 'fight!' We are not known as cowards, but we must think of others. Now you must believe me, *all* of us. You must live for a long time."

73

"Aa—i—eee!" The thin cry expressed surprise, exultation and, perhaps, a tinge of fear. Or was it relief—vindication? Shining Shirt pointed his long medicine crook at the startled youth: "It is as my visions have told me. It is *Sin-sch-ch-leh*. Yes, it is Little Coyote."

Little Coyote wearily opened his eyes and, yet again, watched the dream figure dissolve into the mists creeping low across the slopes half-way up St. Mary's Peak. For a few moments longer he lay there, the repetitive dream fragments dissolving…dissolving….

The fear arrow struck: Its impact brought him to a seated position. "Umhhh!" He groaned as his ancient bones and joints complained about the effort required.

"Did I wait too long," he murmured, "to tell Little Grizzly Bear Claw that the spirit within me tells me, as does Shining Shirt, that my last trip to the peak must be a few days after this…tenth month of…*s'tcutes-tce:ei*, Half Autumn of white man's 1891? Oh, Good Spirit, how could I tell what I did not know until now?"

Fearfully, reluctantly, the seer opened his eyes. He turned toward Sun, pondering that, this day, ancient Shining Shirt had remained near him a bit longer than during the previous six nights of pained, fitful sleep. Yes, Shining Shirt again had scolded him: "You are like the frog, the snake, the lizard! Can you not move until Sun fully warms you? Hasten back to the valley!" This seventh time there was an insistent "Now!" since, once again, he had laid down.

The seer groped here and there. "Ahhh!" His fingers reassuringly closed on the haft of the ancient lance. He would arise…soon. Sun revealed the patient, old pack horse loaned to him by Little Grizzly Bear Claw, his tortured *i-sts-sókoi*. The animal was cropping grass next to the tiny spring beyond which Little Coyote simply had lacked the strength to climb.

Two more fear arrows! *The story skin? The manuscript?* Again, Little Coyote struggled to sit up—then slowly laid back. Yes, they were there; they had shared his rabbit-skin blanket that long night. *Story skin completed. The manuscript? Soon. Soon! And soon, life itself.* "Umhhh"! Any movement, though slight, caused pain.

On his arrival here to complete the story skin and manuscript, he had made a small rock firepit and gathered wood. From his blanket he could reach out to strike the fire and boil a pot of dried venison and a turnip, beet or potato. Eagle Whistle and One Horn Bull had been generous. The fire burning now, he again laid back to gather strength. The mists Shining Shirt's dream figure yet again had entered continued to fade. Soon, tiny heat waves would undulate up the mountainside while he, as he had done for at least ninety years, pondered this life, soon to end. With little space remaining on the story skin, and little life left for him, he had had to be selective about subjects—as selective as the hunter with one arrow closing in on one particular buffalo amid a great heaving mass of the animals racing at full speed over uneven prairie. "Umhhh!" Yes, pain had become almost as big a factor in the selective process as events, themselves.

While yet a stripling, No Name, later Little Coyote, had discerned the differences between pain of the body and pain to, and of, the very spirit within him. In his earlier years he had known more of the former.

There were extremes: Pain of the Blackfeet who Gun had helped to torture—something Gun had regretted the remainder of his life; and now, the pain of Chief Little Grizzly Bear Claw. His was the worst because the cause, his ever-growing burden, was the cumulative bodily and mental sufferings of his tribe. Charlot's pain also stemmed from what had to be an almost resigned, helpless acceptance of the fact that he could do nothing further to alleviate his people's agony.

Little Coyote had heard his *i-sts-sókoi* pray: "Oh Christ! I can withstand this near-crucifixion, but I suffer more because the whites will not change their ways. Yet, they demand we do so in but one lifetime. The white man carries his bible in his hands when he comes to our land, but seldom in his heart."

Even many of the chief's sincere, protective and generous white friends had urged him to depart to the Jocko, to alleviate the suffering of his hungry, dispirited and, therefore, increasingly contentious, people.

Though grieving inwardly over Little Grizzly Bear Claw's great anguish, the seer, somewhat banteringly, had suggested they pray together.

"When the Blackfeet killed our much-loved friend, Tull, and chopped me up, and we became *i-sts-sókoi*, you baptized me because you thought me going to the sand hills. Black Robe Ravalli told me I am Christian. Come let us go to the chapel."

Both silently had prayed while viewing the crucifix at the altar. At length, the weary chief had slept on the bench and Little Coyote had stepped outside to pray until Sun hid behind the great peaks.

But enough! "Umhhh!" Carefully, Little Coyote put down the pot and hoisted it to the spring with the haft end of the lance. Next, he placed the haft end on the ground next to him and grasped it a short distance upward. "Umhhh! Umhhh! Umhhh!" Hand over hand, he raised himself erect. Gasping, he hobbled to and leaned on the old horse.

"You will not carry me downward," he said as he patted the animal on the neck. "I cannot get on your back. But you will be my staff for four suns. Faster than that, I would be too worn to return soon to the peak high above us with my *i-sts-sókoi*. I must as carefully measure out my strength as does the salmon returning to its birthplace. I will spare you that trip, so your bones will not be with mine when Little Grizzly Bear Claw descends. Toward the end of each day downward, I again will look at the last symbols on the story skin to remind me what I must amplify in the manuscript."

The horse tried to nuzzle the old man as he continued to rub the animal's neck while softly speaking.

"John Owen said, 'Write your story over, over and over to improve it. I go over my ledgers each day, and often I find I charged too much, or too little. Thus, I remain correct—and honest. Yours is far more important than money, Little Coyote. It is the story of your people that *must* not be lost.' He retreated to the other room, refreshed his tongue from the bottle, then repeated, 'It must not be lost.'"

The seer slowly rolled his food sack and blanket. He tied them on the horse, with the pot, then tied the story skin and manuscript to the load.

"There is contentment, horse, that now white men are putting down words, too, more honest histories about themselves and the remnants of our people. There is much satisfaction in that. It also will make my final words much shorter, for I must hurry. I have little time now. Let us go."

Old man, old horse began their descent, both certain where they were going. During the trek the seer would write in his manuscript as he was able, and, thus, finish it....

I am grateful my story skin is full and I am now ending my manuscript.

I think, on this first late afternoon of my and old horse's descent toward our valley, that perhaps I was lazy between 1872 and 1891. I leave that for others to judge. I spent even more of my time during those years trying to use the strength of this torn and aging body to help our ever-more suffering people. Too, great troubles continued to occur when I sought peace for my spirit in the ancient lodge secreted high above the hot springs. I have forever grieved, as in the way of our people, that Antelope could not share this place with me because of her and Lance's deaths near what now mostly is called LaValle Creek.

During that long, solitary time, I had no heart to work on the skin and manuscript. Later, great events were occurring: The death of Little Bear Claw and the helpful works of the Black Robes—even my i-sts-sókoi *becoming head chief. Younger then, I did record these events, but only when I accompanied Little Bear Claw and Little Grizzly Bear Claw back to the much-changed Bitter Root.*

My symbols on the story skin were easiest to do, though I regretted always that I had put many large ones there before Antelope showed me how to make them smaller.

Explaining the symbols for white man in the manuscript always was harder—more so now on this first of four evenings old horse and I descend the mountain.

Yes, again I find myself thanking the Good Spirit that John Owen showed me that some white men are writing their histories, many as fair as were the judges who ruled on our horse races or the division of the buffalo meat and robes. These writers do not always look upon the truths as do I. Some have sincerely tried, though they cannot fully grasp the lives that were ours. And now, I lack the strength, as well as paper, to write at great length. Consider:

November 14, 1871. I was 79 summers old.

The Great Father, Grant, signed his order that my people be removed from our Bitter Root Valley. He did not know the truths. He knew we were Indians. I give him his due. Frank and John Owen said he was a great fighter to free the slaves like York, who came to our valley in 1805, and to keep all the states from being broken up, as were the Indian tribes.

August 22 to 26, 1872.

I was 80 summers old when Garfield came to our Bitter Root Valley and the Jocko Reservation to (here I use white man's names for our people) make our First Chief Charlot, Second Chief Arlee, and Third Chief Adolph sign the Agreement to leave our home.

With Garfield, who we learned was a brave fighter to free the slaves and preserve the Union, were more great white chiefs: W.G. Clagett, J. d'Aste (a Black Robe), G.A. Viall, Territorial Governor B.F. Potts, and Baptiste Robwanen, interpreter.

On August 26, Arlee, who earlier had told Charlot he wished for his chief to live a long time, and Adolph, after much persuasion and promises of gifts for the suffering people who would leave the valley with them, made their marks on the Agreement. Charlot refused to sign, not wishing for his people to be forced from their homes, and remembering that Stevens' coerced Hell Gate Treaty, and the great Fort Laramie treaty of 1851 which affected so many tribes, had been quickly broken. And all over, of course, treaties were being broken, tribes who always had roamed free were fighting white men because they did not wish to be corralled. But unlike these other tribes, the Flatheads always had helped white man, never had fought nor killed them, as the mountain men in my manuscript would agree.

Garfield knew all this, and that Charlot had refused to sign the Agreement. Our people were coerced to leave the valley.

Arlee was named the head chief of the Flatheads, and soon thereafter, as did Adolph, left for the Jocko with many of our dispirited, desperate people. To be thus cheated and humiliated hurt Charlot forever. He told me it would have been better for Grant to have killed him. He never spoke again to Arlee, who would die in 1889.

It was upon their departure that Charlot and I went to the chapel to sit before the crucifix. Before I left him on the bench, he whispered we also should pray for the largely Catholic Métis, with whom we had hunted the buffalo. They, too, were being hounded in Canada. Later, a leader, Louis Riel, would be hanged.

And in the beautiful spring of 1873, up and down our valley and far, far away, peoples of many colors and beliefs in the Good Spirit prayed to Him for much-loved Black Robe DeSmet, who most said, with truth, "He wore out his body for the souls of all!"

I was 85 summers in 1877 when great, much loved Chief Joseph of our Nez Percé friends, and the remnants

of his people, came through our Bitter Root Valley. It was not to join us in the buffalo hunt, as they had done for so long. They were trying to escape the soldiers who were chasing them. Some whites had been killed when Joseph's people could take no more from the whites who had begun filling up the Wallowa and Grande Ronde valleys, breaking all treaties. Old Joseph, a strong Christian, had told his sons never to leave their land. Our friend had to, or die. He sought to live among the Crows, or perhaps, in the desperation of his cold, hungry people, go to Canada. Our chief met him on behalf of fearful whites. He told Joseph he would have to fight him with a broken heart, if he hurt the whites. Meantime, my i-sts-sókoi consulted with me about the last of Shining Shirt's gold. Often, he had been tempted to trade it for food and other needs of our people. He gave it to Joseph to help his homeless people on their way.

"I cannot give you horses, Joseph. We keep them mostly for our own needs now, for white man taxes us for the few things we own, including horses and our own land to make us move. Even some white men shook my hand when they saw in the April 16, 1876, Weekly Missoulian what I said about taxation."

Joseph later surrendered, and like the Flatheads, was dishonorably mistreated. Joseph and many of his band were transported like cattle to hot Oklahoma where many died. There were many stories about this valiant, honorable man in the newspapers.

Yet again, I accompanied our chief to the chapel. He could thus pray to the Good Spirit, as he had for his betrayer, but not enemy Garfield when he was the Great Father and was shot in 1881 and, as our chief said, suffered for a long time, as greatly as Christ on the cross.

The years 1883 and 1884, when I was 91 and 92 summers old, three more important events occurred that brought some smiles, and more sorrows, on the face of my i-sts-sókoi—and my own.

The Senate in Washington in 1883 sent Senator George G. Vest of Missouri and Major Martin Maginnis, territorial representative from Montana, to study the dishonest events concerning the Agreement Garfield had forced on our people and Charlot said he did not sign.

After many meetings and looking at all the papers, these two honest men wrote: "We are compelled to admit there was much truth and justice in his (Charlot's) statement. That his name was falsely published as signed in the Garfield Agreement is unfortunately true as shown by the original."

Little Grizzly Bear Claw and Peter Ronan, our Indian agent we said was the straightest arrow among them all, went to Washington, D.C. in January of 1884 to see the Great Father, as many tribal leaders had done. They would talk about the rights of the Flatheads and others who were increasingly hungry, poor and desperate. Accompanying them were Michel Revais (interpreter), Antoine Moiese, Louis Vanderberg, Abel Adams, and our Nez Percé friend, John Hill.

"We held many talks," our chief told us upon their return. "Gentle Father Ravalli told me he lacked the medicines and instruments to operate upon my eye that disliked Sun's bright light, and often was weeping. He called it 'iritis.' The doctors of the Great Father fixed my eyes. I no longer wept. So I saw much on that trip— even some hope."

In October of 1884 both eyes of Little Grizzly Bear

Claw and many others, Indian and white, were weeping above the body of our beloved Black Robe Ravalli, whom my spirit tells me as I write this, again amid tears, I soon again will see. If we had not sent for the Black Robes, there would be few Indians alive. This I know.

Charlot looked up from his bench beside his cabin. Hurriedly, he tied a half-knot in the section of the old lariat he was re-braiding. Little Coyote, leaning on the white mare, had limped in so quietly that the tiny songbirds in the cottonwood tree continued twittering and the three scrawny chickens kept scratching in the nearby corral. The sorrel, pinto and two other horses remained in the tiny noon-time shadow of the old wagon stacked high with family possessions. The almost-full bag of dried venison and a small, woven string bag of wrinkled vegetables remained on the pack horse. Earlier, the seer had relieved her of the story skin, blanket, and manuscript back at his lodge near the curve of the ever-shallowing Ootlashoots. There, he would make the last entry before Sun would set.

Without a sound, the sixty- and ninty-nine-year-old *i-sts-sókoi* embraced.

"You planned well," Charlot said. "Isabel soon will come

from the Chapel. My small arrows dropped two squirrels and three meadowlarks to boil with the cracked wheat."

Children's eager chatter quieted the birds. For the first time Charlot smiled: "Isabel brings the five orphans two days sooner than she thought. They will eat."

All ate, fully, from the large pot of vegetables, venison, birds and squirrels. Reminding the children to return before Sun set, anxious Isabel turned them loose.

"They will ride with us to the Jocko," she reluctantly explained. She said no more, apparently wondering how long the two warriors had spoken before her arrival.

Again grim-faced, Charlot said, "You and I must leave for St. Mary's Peak tomorrow, Little Coyote. Our people all over the valley are prepared to leave for the Jocko in four days." He bent over his empty food bowl as though he was speaking to it. "What I most wish to take on this unfortunate journey to Jocko, next to Isabel, is you, *i-sts-sókoi*. Do we leave too early for the peak?"

"No, Little Grizzly Bear Claw. My spirit within this worn body says it must be there in two days. I…I cannot walk."

"We will ride as we agreed earlier, but now we will ride to your lodge." He looked toward his cabin. They could hear Isabel's quiet sobbing.

"You will return with three large trout I caught and put in the rock pen in the river," Little Coyote said. "They will be for Isabel and the children tonight. The venison will take you to the Jocko. Also, there are a few possessions I wish for you to have."

The two warriors set out. Tomorrow, Sun, as always, would not be late.

Epilogue

AUTHOR'S NOTE: *On the morning of October 16, 1891, a dejected Chief Charlot of the Flatheads led the last of his hungry, destitute followers out of their beloved Bitter Root Valley and northward toward the Jocko Valley reservation. On a Sunday afternoon in the following year, 1892, a Montana newspaper correspondent named Arthur L. Stone met and talked with Charlot on the reservation. Stone later became editor of the Missoula, Montana,* Missoulian *daily newspaper, which, on September 9, 1911, published a feature he had written. Titled "Charlot's Last March," the historical piece was one of several by Stone that in 1913 were compiled in a book,* Following Old Trails. *Stone founded the University of Montana School of Journalism in 1914 and served as its first dean. He died in 1945. A year after his death, in 1946, "Charlot's Last March" appeared in the anthology* Montana Margins, *edited by historian Joseph Kinsey Howard. In a note preceding "Charlot's Last March," Howard wrote this: "'Manifest destiny,' impelling the United States to the conquest of half a continent, had weapons other than guns to use in extermination of the aborigines. One was starvation—the deliberate elimination of the buffalo on which the Indian lived.*

849

Another was fraud; it may shock some readers to learn that a man who subsequently became the President of the United States resorted to it and thus helped rob an Indian tribe of its home and wrong a great chief. . . ." What follows is Arthur L. Stone's 1911 feature "Charlot's Last March." It is a fitting epilogue for this novel.

Perhaps there are more beautiful trails in this world than that which leads from old St. Mary's Mission at Stevensville, in the heart of the Bitter Root, to the valley in which the Jocko Agency nestles at the foot of the mountains that rise abruptly from its fertile slope. If there are any trails more beautiful than this, I have never seen any of them. Certainly there are few trails anywhere that possess the sad associations that cluster about this road.

It was along this trail that grim old Charlot made his last march. After years of determined and, at times, defiant, struggle against the inroads of white settlement, the stern and embittered chief yielded to the inevitable and with the little remnant of his people turned his back on the valley that had been his ancestral home and marched to the place allotted to him on the Jocko reservation. Charlot is dead. Next Monday (October 16, 1911) his people will travel back over the old trail to Stevensville to join with the people of that town in their observance of the twentieth anniversary of the departure of the Indians.

This week I spent a good deal of time along portions of this trail. The splendor of autumn was over the towering mountains, the glory of the harvest time was upon the valley. The breeze that wafted down from St. Mary's Peak was tingling with the crispness of late summer. The water in the river was clear as crystal as it murmured along beneath overhanging trees. The incomparably beautiful Bitter Root landscape was never more appealing—grand mountains, rolling valleys, broad meadows, dense groves, the bluest sky that spans the earth, the brightest sun that shines upon it and the intoxicating atmosphere of this western realm.

On just such a morning did Charlot, chieftain and the son of chieftains, bid good-bye to the valley that had always been his home as it had been the home of his fathers. Looking over the scene the other day as I walked from the mission over toward Fort Owen, I could easily understand the bitterness that filled the heart of the old man as he marched away from all that was dear to him, to make a new home for himself and his people in a place he did not like and under conditions that were humiliating to him and that broke his old heart.

His father had refused to leave the valley. Old Victor had fought with all his Indian wily diplomacy to retain the dwelling place that he and his people loved so dearly. And with the fight against the removal of his tribe there had been interwoven a struggle for his supremacy as the titular head of the people he ruled. To both of these struggles his son had fallen heir when he inherited the symbols of tribal authority; bravely had he maintained the contest.

Deceived by agents of the government, betrayed by special representatives of the president, conspired against by some of his own people, trusting only the few whites who were his close neighbors, the odds were heavy against the sturdy old fellow, but he resisted steadfastly. As Victor had sought to retain his home in argument with General Stevens in 1855, so did Charlot maintain the struggle in debate with General Garfield in 1872.

But, in the end he was beaten. It was not, however, the argument of the white man that convinced him against his will. It was not the threat of the emissary of the Great Father that daunted him into submission to the government's will. It was the suffering of his people, the wails of the starving children of his tribe, their destitution, their nakedness and hopelessness that touched his heart and led him into acquiescence with the will of the Great Father at Washington.

And, as he marched forth from St. Mary's with his people, with the benediction of his priest upon his head, with these memories in his mind and with the bitterness in his heart that came from a consciousness of the deceit that had been practiced against him, it is not to be wondered that he was sore and sullen.

It was the year after this exodus that I first saw and talked with Charlot. He would talk to me of everything except the Bitter Root; of his old home there was no word. I had gone to him with the approval of Mrs. Ronan, whom Charlot revered for her tenderness, and he knew that I was friendly. Whatever else I asked him on that Sunday afternoon in the Jocko Valley, he answered readily enough. But of the Bitter Root, no word. Nor would he, to the end, have aught to say of the beautiful place he had left. It was a painful subject to him and no one who knew him ever pressed it upon him. During his later days he softened somewhat. He came to regard Fred Morgan, superintendent of the reservation, as a trusted friend and his last days were the most peaceful he had known.

But there was none of that peace in his heart when he set forth that October morning, 20 years ago, to lead his people to their new home—a home prescribed by the government and made necessary by the impoverished condition of his tribe. His good-bye had been said to his old friends at Stevensville; he had severed the ties. He said he would never return. As nearly as I can learn, he never did return, except once when he was brought to the valley as a witness in a lawsuit over a water right in which his old friend, Abe Mittower, was involved. It is said that he did not go to Stevensville then; he went with his friend to look over the ground on the hills.

Down the river he marched his people. Through the fields where they had played as children and had hunted as men, fields that they had never stained with white man's blood, fields on whose bosom they had been nurtured and beneath whose breast their fathers slept, they marched in solemn train. Not in haste, not in disorder, not in an uproar, but slowly, with dignity and in silence they moved out from the mission. Out past Owen and across the river and then down the valley, ever amid scenes that had been their daily environment for a life-time, each step reluctant and each mile a pang. There was a night camp in the Missoula Valley and then the march to Jocko was resumed in the morning so deliberate was the retreat of the vanquished warrior. In the afternoon the Flatheads entered the Jocko Valley. Charlot's last march was ended.

The events that led to this departure are interesting. They reveal the utter lack of honor that characterized many of the government representatives in their dealings with the Indians; they make plain the duplicity that too often governed the negotiations with the reds; they awaken sympathy with the Indian and they furnish ample reason for the bitter hatred that Charlot bore to everything that bore a Washington postmark and to everybody who hailed from the capital. . . .

It was in 1855 that Stevens concluded his treaty with the Flatheads and their kindred tribes at Council Grove, below Missoula. Victor, the father of Charlot, had ceded, in this treaty, a large area in which is now western Montana; on yielding this region, Victor had insisted that his people retain that portion of the Bitter Root Valley above Lolo Creek. But there had been an alternative clause agreed to that empowered the President to make surveys and to determine from them whether it was better for the Flatheads to remain in the Bitter Root or to go to the Jocko Reservation. Until 1872 there had been no survey made nor had the government kept its promise to send carpenters, blacksmiths, artisans and school teachers to the tribe as had been promised in the treaty.

Consequently the Indians resisted a presidential order, made in 1871, that declared that the Indians should be transferred to the Jocko Valley. Congress appropriated $5,000 to defray the expenses of removal and in 1872 General Garfield was dispatched to the Bitter Root to arrange a treaty covering the removal. It was in August 1872 that Garfield came to the valley. He said in his official report that he found the Indians unwilling to move because for 17 years the government had taken no step to carry out the provisions of the Hell Gate Treaty. However, General Garfield prepared an agreement, which was published as having been signed by Charlot, first chief of the Flatheads; Arlee, second chief of the Flatheads; Adolf, third chief of the Flatheads—these as principals—and William H. Claggett, D.G. Swain, W.F. Sanders, J.A. Viall and B.F. Potts, then governor of Montana, as witnesses.

This treaty contained the provisions that the Flatheads should move to Jocko; that the government should build 60 houses for them; that 600 bushels of wheat should be delivered to the Indians the first year; that land be broken and fenced for the Indians and they be given agricultural implements; that the $5,000 appropriated for their removal be given to the Indians; that the sum of $50,000 be paid to them in ten annual installments and that the Indians should move as soon as the houses were built for them at Jocko, except such as chose to take up land in the Bitter Root Valley in the regular manner.

Charlot was outraged when he learned that it had been published that he signed the treaty. He declared he had never signed it and that he had told the commissioner that he would not sign it, and that he would never go, alive, to the Jocko. His sense of honor was wounded, his dignity was shocked, his last bit of trust in the whites was shattered.

Meanwhile, the houses were built near the agency at Jocko. Arlee, with his personal following, who had recognized the Garfield treaty, moved to the reservation. Arlee was designated by the government as chief of the Flatheads. This added to the resentment of Charlot. He persisted in his declaration that he had never signed the treaty and that he was not bound by its provisions. And he held the fort at Stevensville.

Major Ronan had become agent of the Flatheads. He sympathized with Charlot, but he recognized the futility of the continued resistance of the old chief and sought to dissuade him from his course. The Bitter Root was settling rapidly. The hunting grounds of the Flatheads were gone. They were starving. More than that, the crowding of the settlers called for their removal. The matter got to Congress.

Senator Vest of Missouri and Major Maginnis, Montana's delegate in Congress, were named as a special commission to investigate conditions. They visited the Jocko agency and then went to Stevensville. They investigated conditions. They listened to Charlot's story. They heard Father Ravalli's account of the case. They concluded that Charlot was absolutely correct and they forced from General Garfield, later, the admission that Charlot had not signed the treaty. The original document on file at Washington did not bear the old man's mark. Garfield's explanation of the publication of the treaty as having been signed by Charlot was that he deemed it best to proceed as if Charlot had signed, as he felt that Charlot, when he saw the work progressing, would conclude to join with the "other chiefs" and keep the tribe unbroken. It showed how little Garfield knew Charlot.

Vest and Maginnis were much impressed by the honesty and dignity of Charlot. Their report expresses regret that Garfield committed the act of misrepresentation, as it had wronged the chief and had doubly embittered him, especially as the act of the department had placed Arlee, whom Charlot characterized as a "Renegade Nez Percé," at the head of the tribe. The commission-ers talked earnestly with Charlot, urging him to accept the terms of the treaty and promised to do all they could to see that he was treated right. But the old man was too bitter and sore at heart.

In 1884, Major Ronan took Charlot and five of his sub-chiefs to Washington for a conference with the president and the secretary of the interior. There were further promises made to Charlot if he would consent to the removal, but he would not yield. He was told that he might remain in the Bitter Root as long as he was friendly with the whites—this he had always been; he had saved them from dire disaster on more than one occasion. The expedition returned with no better result than a clearer understanding on Charlot's part. He had learned that Major Ronan was his friend and when, a year later, there was a distribution of supplies to the Bitter Root band, he softened considerably. Wagons, horses and plows were also issued and an attempt was made, through Ronan's influence, to give the Indians a chance to make good on their located lands.

Time wore on. The Indians were not successful farmers and their condition became deplorable. General Carrington was sent in 1891 to try to induce Charlot to move. Arlee had died and conditions were such that it was felt that the old chief might at last consent. And this hope was, it proved, well-founded. Charlot talked with Major Ronan. He also called in some of his Bitter Root friends. He consulted with Amos Buck and with the father of Dave Whaley, who gave me this account of Charlot's speech after the old chief had reached his decision:

"I will go—I and my children. My young men are becoming bad; they have no place to hunt. My women are hungry. For their sake I will go. I do not want the land you promise. I do not believe your promises. All I want is enough ground for my grave. We will go over there."

Immediately the arrangements were made. Charlot's last march was begun. In the afternoon of the next day, October 17, 1891, he reached the new home of his people in the Jocko. Major Ronan had hastened ahead and was at the agency to greet the old chief, whose people also received him with proper demonstration. Mrs. Ronan, who witnessed the reception, gives this account of the end of the march from the Bitter Root:

"It was a unique and, to some minds, pathetic spectacle, when Charlot and his band of Indians marched to their future home, the Jocko reservation. Their coming had been heralded and many of the reservation Indians had gathered at the agency to give them welcome. When within a mile of the agency church, the advancing Indians spread out into a broad column. The young men kept constantly discharging their firearms, while a few of the number mounted on fleet ponies, arrayed in fantastic Indian paraphernalia, with long blankets partially draping the forms of the warriors and steeds, rode back and forth in front of the advancing caravan, shouting and firing their guns until they neared the church, where a large banner of the Sacred Hearts of Mary and Jesus was erected on a tall pole. Near the sacred emblem stood a valiant soldier of Jesus Christ, Rev. Canistrelli, S.J. With outstretched hands the good priest blessed and welcomed the forlorn-looking pilgrims. Chief Charlot's countenance retained his habitual expression of stubborn pride and gloom as he advanced on foot, shaking hands with all who had come to greet him. After the handshaking was over, all assembled in the agency chapel to the benediction of the most Holy Sacrament. The *O Salutaris* and *Tantum Ergo*, chanted by those untutored children of the forest, told better than any other words could of the patient teachings of the Jesuit fathers. Every word of the beautiful Latin verses sounded as distinct as if coming from cultivated voices. If the poor creatures reflected on the meaning of these words:

> *'Bella premunt hostilia,*
> *Da robur, fer auxilium,*

they must have felt that the touching sentiment truly expressed the feelings of their hearts. After the benediction, the good and learned Father Canistrelli, who has spent many years laboring among the Indians, striving to enlighten their hearts, addressed them in their own language. The good words seemed to console and comfort them, if the peaceful expression of their countenances indexed aright their

856

minds."

Such was the end of Charlot's last march. At its end he did not find immediately the peace that had been promised him. To the last he nursed his grievances and they were many. Genuine wrongs he had and he brooded over them until they magnified and multiplied. He never loved the Jocko. He was never reconciled to this change of homes. Some satisfaction he found in the better condition of his people and that was all. He distrusted all whites. Had it not been for the endorsement I brought him from Mrs. Ronan and the subsequent recommendation that Major Catlin gave me—the major had been one of Charlot's trusted Stevensville friends—I doubt if any of the several visits I made at the Jocko cabin would have been as pleasant and as satisfactory as they were. But I gained an insight into the old man's heart that always gives me sympathy even with his utter stubbornness. If the whites had been as honest with him as he was with them, his last days would have been happier.

As I walked along the route of his last march the other day, I could not help thinking of this thing. The beauty of the valley he loved so much and all of the associations that gathered about its scenes must have been constant visions before his sightless eyes during those last bitter years. And the memory of that last sad march down the valley must have been a painful thought for him. Next Monday his people will march again over the old trail, but it will be a travesty of that march of 20 years ago.

About the author

Charles J. Keim helped sugar refineries and farmers collect buffalo bones from the prairies around Judith Gap, Montana, his 1921 birthplace. At age ten he spent his $1.25 life savings for the Winchester 45-70 rifle of a deceased professional buffalo hunter. Farmers quit bidding when they heard Keim's soprano voice. He was capital city correspondent for United Press before serving in Montana's 163rd Infantry Regiment in New Guinea as a decorated first sergeant. After two years in Army hospitals, he returned to university. After graduate school, he earned a living at writing before joining the University of Alaska faculty. He headed the Department of Journalism and Creative Writing before becoming Dean of the College of Arts and Letters. He was a registered big-game guide for twenty-one of his twenty-six years in Alaska. He served on the fifteen-member National Commission on Arts and Sciences. Keim is Emeritus Professor of Journalism and English at the University of Alaska and a Fellow of The Explorers Club of New York. He and his wife, Bettyjoyce, now live on Fox Island, Washington.

Charlot's last march, October 1891: Crossing Missoula's Higgins Avenue Bridge en route to the reservation at Jocko